Integrating Mathematics and Science for Intermediate and Middle School Students

Integrating Mathematics and Science for Intermediate and Middle School Students

Richard D. Kellough
California State University, Sacramento

James S. Cangelosi
Alfred T. Collette and Eugene L. Chiappetta
Randall J. Souviney
Leslie W. Trowbridge and Rodger W. Bybee

Merrill,
an imprint of Prentice Hall

Englewood Cliffs, New Jersey   Columbus, Ohio

Library of Congress Cataloging-in-Publication Data

Integrating mathematics and science for intermediate and middle school
    students / Richard D. Kellough . . . [et al.].
        p. cm.
    Includes bibliographical references (p. -) and index.
    ISBN 0-02-362591-0
    1. Mathematics—Study and teaching (Secondary) 2. Science—Study
and teaching (Secondary) I. Kellough, Richard D. (Richard Dean)
QA11.I468 1996
507'.1'2—dc20

95-11915

Cover art: © Manuel Morales/The Image Bank
Editor: Bradley J. Potthoff
Photo Editor: Anne Vega
Cover Designer: Proof Positive/Farrowlyne Associates
Production Manager: Deidra M. Schwartz
Project management and text design provided by Elm Street Publishing Services, Inc.

This book was set in Times Roman by Carlisle Communications, Ltd., and was printed and bound
by The Banta Company. The cover was printed by The Banta Company.

© 1996 by Prentice-Hall, Inc.
A Simon & Schuster Company
Englewood Cliffs, New Jersey 07632

Photo credits: Scott Cunningham, Merrill/Prentice Hall.

Printed in the United States of America

10 9 8 7 6 5 4 3 2 1

ISBN: 0-02-362591-0

Prentice-Hall International (UK) Limited, *London*
Prentice-Hall of Australia Pty. Limited, *Sidney*
Prentice-Hall of Canada, Inc., *Toronto*
Prentice-Hall Hispanoamericana, S.A., *Mexico*
Prentice-Hall of India Private Limited, *New Delhi*
Prentice-Hall of Japan, Inc., *Tokyo*
Simon & Schuster Asia Pte. Ltd., *Singapore*
Editora Prentice-Hall do Brasil, Ltda., *Rio de Janeiro*

To many educators, it has become quite clear that to be most effective in teaching the diversity of children in today's classrooms, they must integrate much of the learning in each discipline with the whole curriculum and make it meaningful to the lives of the children, rather than simply teach it as unrelated disciplines at the same time each day.

It is also quite clear that if we define learning as being only the accumulation of bits and pieces of information, then we already know how to teach. The accumulation of pieces of information is at the lowest end of a wide spectrum of types of learning, however. For higher levels of thinking and for learning that is most meaningful and longest lasting, research supports the use of an integrated curriculum and instructional techniques that involve the children in social, interactive learning.

This book is designed to facilitate your understanding of how to teach mathematics and science in the most effective way to children in grades 4–9. Beginning with a review of important historical and recent work of cognitive psychologists, work that has led to a modern view of teaching for meaningful understanding (Chapter 1), we discuss planning and providing an effective and supportive learning environment (Chapter 2), planning and implementing curriculum and lessons appropriate to children of middle-level grades (Chapters 3 and 4), assessment of student learning (Chapter 5), and the selection and use of instructional aids and resources (Chapter 6).

As a classroom teacher, your instructional task is twofold: (1) to plan for and provide developmentally appropriate hands-on experiences, with appropriate materials and the supportive environment necessary for children's meaningful exploration and discovery; and (2) to facilitate the most meaningful and longest lasting learning possible once the child's mind has been activated by the hands-on experience. It is our hope that we have designed a book that will help you learn how better to complete those tasks.

While the six chapters in Part I provide fundamentals important to all teachers of children in grades 4–9, Parts II through IV are specific to instruction in mathematics and science.

In Part II, Chapter 7 discusses the mathematics curriculum, using the curriculum standards developed by the National Council for Teachers of Mathematics. Chapters 8 through 12 address the specific topics relevant to teaching mathematics in grades 4–9: the multiplication and division of whole numbers; patterns and functions; fraction operations; decimals, proportions, and integers; and graphing, statistics, and probability. In addition, in each of those chapters you will find strategies and resources for using calculators and computers in the mathematics curriculum, sample lesson plans, boxed practice exercises and problems, topical lists of children's books, techniques for accommodating special-needs learners, a dialogue between a student teacher and an experienced cooperating teacher about a pertinent issue in mathematics, and a discussion of useful assessment strategies.

Although each of the first two chapters of Part III focuses on the science curriculum, the second (Chapter 14) narrows in on Science-Technology-Society (STS) as the primary theme for an integrated curriculum design for grades 4–9 One of the most promising aspects of the trend to integrate student learning, STS is an approach that engages students in the active exploration of problems and issues that they have identified and encountered.

Student-centered instruction and project-centered methodology are especially empha-sized in Chapter 15, "Projects, Science Fairs, and Field Experiences," followed by a chap-ter on the use of demonstrations and laboratory work. Building on the topics of aids and re-sources that were introduced in Chapter 6, Part III ends with a focus on the use of modern electronic technology (Chapter 17).

Part IV presents classroom-tested instructional activities that encourage interaction and cooperation among students, depend on collaborative learning between students and teach-ers, and in interesting ways integrate the disciplines of mathematics and science and, in some instances, other disciplines as well.

The term *integrated curriculum* (or any of its synonyms) refers to both a way of teach-ing and a way of planning and organizing the instructional program so the discrete disci-plines of subject matter are related to one another in a design that matches the developmental needs of the learners and that helps to connect their learning in ways that are meaningful to their current and past experiences. It is the antithesis of traditional, disparate, subject-matter–oriented teaching and curriculum designations.

Today's interest in the development and implementation of integrated curriculum and in-struction derives from (1) the successful curriculum integration enjoyed by exemplary mid-dle-level schools, (2) the literature-based movement in reading and language arts, and (3) recent research in cognitive science and neuroscience about how children learn.

As is true for traditional curriculum and instruction, an integrated curriculum approach is not without critics, nor is it the best approach for every school, the bast basis for all learn-ing for every child, nor necessarily the manner by which every teacher should or must al-ways plan and teach. Efforts to connect children's learning with their experiences fall at var-ious places on a spectrum or continuum of sophistication and complexity.

The activities presented in this book, especially those in Chapter 18 and in the interdis-ciplinary thematic unit at the end of the book, are designed to encourage interaction and co-operation among students, to encourage collaborative learning between students and their teachers, and to integrate in interesting and meaningful ways the disciplines of mathemat-ics and science, and sometimes other disciplines as well. Where the use of each falls on the spectrum of integrated learning is up to you and your special set of circumstances.

Chapters begin with advance organizers and statements of chapter intent and end with questions and activities for individual and group study and discussion.

We, its editors, authors, and other contributors, hope that you find this book useful. We value your feedback about it.

Richard D. Kellough

BRIEF CONTENTS

CONTENTS

PART III
METHODS AND ACTIVITIES FOR SCIENCE   380

Integrating Mathematics and Science for Intermediate and Middle School Students

Integrating Student Learning: Rationale and Methods

No matter how well prepared your instructional plans, those plans will likely go untaught or only poorly taught if presented to children in a classroom that is nonsupportive and poorly managed.
   —*Richard D. Kellough*

Teaching children and preparing them for the 21st century requires a shift in paradigm from what was previously believed about good instruction.
   —*Randall J. Souviney*

In a well-managed classroom students know what to do, have the materials necessary to do it well, and stay on task while doing it; the classroom atmosphere is supportive, the assignments and procedures for doing those assignments are clear, the materials of instruction current, interesting, and readily available, and the classroom proceedings are businesslike.
   —*Richard D. Kellough*

Middle school students are in a formative stage of mental development, which requires actions on objects for the development of reasoning. What the teacher must supply is a variety of minds-on/hands-on activities in which the students manipulate objects, are guided to see relationships, and draw conclusions.
   —*Arthur A. Carin*

Unless you believe that your students can learn, they will not. Unless you believe that you can teach them, you will not. Unless your students believe that they can learn and until they want to learn, they will not.
   —*Richard D. Kellough*

We have two simple, yet inclusive school rules that are posted in every classroom, and they are enforced. The rules are: respect people, respect property.
   —*Barry S. Raebeck*

Children need models more than they need critics.
   —*Joseph Joubert*

We are establishing a "success breeds success" scenario for all students. We gave one F out of a total of 2,600 grades in the first marking period this past year.
   —*Barry S. Raebeck*

Novelty is no substitute for quality.
   —*Anonymous*

In recent years, to many teachers it has become quite clear that to be most effective in teaching the diversity of children in today's classrooms, much of the learning in each discipline must be integrated with the whole curriculum and made meaningful to the lives of the children, rather simply taught as unrelated disciplines at the same time each day.

It is also quite clear that if learning is defined as being only the accumulation of bits and pieces of information, then we already know how to teach. The accumulation of pieces of information is at the lowest end of a spectrum of types of learning, however. For higher levels of thinking and for learning that is most meaningful, recent research supports the use of an integrated curriculum and instructional techniques that involve the learners in social, interactive learning, such as cooperative learning, peer tutoring, and cross-age teaching.

THE SPECTRUM OF *INTEGRATED CURRICULUM*

When learning about *integrated curriculum,* it is easy to be confused by the plethora of terms that are used, such as *thematic instruction, transdisciplinary instruction, multidisciplinary teaching, integrated studies, interdisciplinary curriculum, interdisciplinary thematic instruction,* and *integrated curriculum.* In essence, today, all of these terms mean the same thing. Further, because it is not always easy to tell where curriculum leaves off and instruction begins, let's assume for now that there is no difference between *curriculum* and *instruction.* We shall use the two terms interchangeably in this text.

Definition of *Integrated Curriculum*

The term *integrated curriculum* (or any of its synonyms) refers to both a way of teaching and a way of planning and organizing the instructional program so the discrete disciplines of subject matter are related to one another in a design that matches the developmental needs of the learners and that helps to connect their learning in ways that are meaningful to their current and past experiences. It is the antithesis of traditional, disparate, subject matter–oriented teaching and curriculum designations.

The concept of integrated curriculum is not new. It has surfaced and gone in and out of fashion throughout most of the history of education in this country. Efforts to integrate student learning have had varying labels, and that accounts for the plethora of terms.

Without reviewing that history in depth, the most recent popularity of the concept stems from the following:

1. Some of the National Science Foundation–supported, discovery-oriented, student-centered projects of the late 1950s, such as *Elementary School Science (ESS),* an integrated science program for grades K-6; *Man: A Course of Study (MACOS),* a hands-on, anthropology-based program for fifth graders; *Interdisciplinary Approaches to Chemistry (IAS),* for high school chemistry; and *Environmental Studies* (name later changed to *ESSENCE*), an interdisciplinary program for use at all grades, K-12, regardless of subject-matter orientation.
2. The "middle school movement," which began in the 1960s.
3. The whole-language movement in language arts, which had its beginning in the 1980s.

The authors of *Teaching and Learning in the Middle Level School* state, "Historically, there has been a need to develop an integrated curriculum that would consider the unique personal needs of middle level learners as well as the serious challenges found in their surrounding world" (Allen et al., 1993, p. 149). The exemplary middle-level schools continue to work at developing a curriculum that integrates personal, social, and academic dimensions into a developmentally appropriate curriculum for young adolescents. "To integrate these dimensions into a balanced curriculum framework requires interdisciplinary topics, themes, or units from the various subject matters" (p. 202).

Today's renewed interest in the development and implementation of integrated curriculum and instruction has arisen from at least three sources: (1) the successful curriculum integration enjoyed by exemplary middle-level schools (discussed in Chapter 3) and by elementary and high schools, too, (2) the literature-based movement in reading and language arts, and (3) recent cognitive science and neuroscience research about how children learn (discussed in Chapter 1).

As is true for traditional curriculum and instruction, an integrated curriculum approach is not without critics. As stated by Jarolimek and Foster, "Parents and teachers who find conventional schools too highly structured, too regimented, and too adult dominated find the child-centered activities of the integrated curriculum mode attractive [but] with its apparent lack of organization, its informality, and the permissiveness allowed [and] at a time when the nation seems to be calling for more fundamental approaches to education [and because school budgets are tighter], the integrated curriculum mode faces an uncertain future" (1993, p. 149).

An integrated curriculum approach may not necessarily be the best approach for every school, nor the best basis for all learning for every child, nor necessarily the manner by which every teacher should or must always plan and teach.

Levels of Curriculum Integration

Efforts to connect children's learning with their experiences fall at various places on a spectrum or continuum, as illustrated in the accompanying table, from the least integrated instruction (level 1) to the most integrated (level 5).

I do not intend for the table to be interpreted as going from "worst case scenario" (far left) to "best case scenario" (far right), although some experts may interpret it in exactly that way. It is meant solely to show how efforts to integrate fall on a continuum of sophistication and complexity. As a generalization, for intermediate and middle school education, and for reasons that should become evident as you proceed through the chapters of this book, my personal preference is for a scenario somewhere at or between levels 3 and 4. Let me now describe each level of the continuum.

Level 1 is the traditional organization of curriculum and classroom instruction, in which teachers plan and arrange the subject-specific scope and sequence using a topic outline format. Any attempts to help students connect their learning and their experiences are up to individual classroom teachers. A fourth-grade student in a school and

LEAST INTEGRATED LEVEL 1	LEVEL 2	LEVEL 3	LEVEL 4	**MOST INTEGRATED** LEVEL 5
Subject-specific topic outline	Subject-specific thematic approach	Multidisciplinary thematic approach	Interdisciplinary thematic approach	Integrated thematic approach
No student collaboration in planning	Minimal student input	Some student input	Considerable student input in selecting themes and in planning	Maximum student and teacher collaboration
Teacher solo	Solo or teams	Solo or teams	Solo or teams	Solo or teams
Student input into decision making low		Student input into decision making high		Student input into decision making very high

classroom that have subject-specific instruction at varying times of the day (reading and language arts at 8:00, mathematics at 9:00, social studies at 10:30, and so on) is likely learning in a level 1 instructional environment, especially when what is being learned in one subject has little or no connection with the content in another. The same is true of the junior high school student who moves during the school day from classroom to classroom, teacher to teacher, subject to subject, and from one topic to another. A topic in science, for example, might be "earthquakes." A related topic in social studies might be "the social consequences of natural disasters." These two topics may or may not be studied by a student at the same time.

If the same students are learning English/language arts, or social studies/history, or mathematics, or science using a thematic approach rather than a topic outline, then they are learning at **level 2** integration. At this level, themes in one discipline are not necessarily planned to correspond with themes in another or to be taught simultaneously. The difference between a topic and a theme is not always clear. But, for example, whereas "earthquakes" and "social consequences of natural disasters" are topics, "natural disasters" could be the theme or umbrella under which these two topics could fall. At this level, the students may have some input into the decision making involved in planning themes and content.

When the same students are learning two or more of their core subjects (English/language arts, social studies/history, mathematics, and science) around a common theme, such as "natural disasters," from one or more teachers, they are learning at **level 3** integration. At this level, teachers agree on a common theme, then they *separately* deal with that theme in their individual subject areas, usually at the same time during the school year. So what the student is learning from a teacher in one class is related to what the student is concurrently learning in another or several others. Students may have some input into the decision making involved in selecting and planning themes and content. This is a commonly used approach and is the minimum level of expected participation for which this book is designed.

When teachers and students collaborate on a common theme and its content, and when discipline boundaries begin to disappear as teachers teach about this common theme, either solo (as in a self-contained fourth-grade classroom) or as an interdisciplinary teaching team (several teachers working with a common group of students, such as in a school-within-a-school configuration), that is **level 4** integration. This is the level of integration at which many exemplary middle schools function (see Chapter 3).

When teachers and their students have collaborated on a common theme and its content and discipline boundaries are truly blurred during instruction, and teachers of several grade levels (e.g., grades 6, 7, and 8) and of various core and exploratory subjects teach toward student understanding of aspects of the common theme, then this is **level 5,** an integrated thematic approach. For detailed accounts of teaching at this level of integration, see Chris Stevenson and Judy F. Carr (Eds.), *Integrated Studies in the Middle Grades* (New York: Teachers College Press, 1993).

Assumptions in an Integrated Curriculum

According to Jarolimek and Foster (1993), theoretically and philosophically, the integrated curriculum mode is tied most closely to the inquiry mode. When using this mode, it is assumed that children have certain natural drives, urges, and interests and that they bring these to school with them. Rather than teaching a predetermined curriculum, the teacher explores the backgrounds and interests of the children, and out of this interaction, significant activities emerge. The activities selected should capitalize on these natural interests and inclinations. A rigid time schedule and the compartmentalizing of curriculum components are rejected because they run counter to the natural exploration of children. A rich and stimulating learning environment is essential so that children may have many opportunities to explore their interests and to learn from direct experience. The teacher serves more as a guide, advisor, and expeditor than as a director of learning. Learning takes place best in settings that encourage social interaction and cooperation—children working with each other. It provides an ideal setting for cooperative learning projects. Cross-age grouping is encouraged because children learn from each other; thus, older children can help younger ones to learn.

Major Purposes

The major purpose of the integrated curriculum mode is to teach children to become self-reliant, independent problem solvers, consistent with what is known about the nature of childhood. Thus, it involves children directly and purposefully in learning. Another of its purposes is to help the children to understand and appreciate the extent to which school learning is interrelated rather than separated into a variety of discrete subjects and skills, as is the case in the traditional curriculum. It is designed to create a high level of interest in learning that will become personalized and individualized. It seeks to construct situations in which children can learn what they want and need to know rather than what the curriculum specifies. As in inquiry, the purpose of the integrated curriculum mode is to stress the process of learning as opposed to specific subject matter and skills. Moreover, it is designed to capitalize on the social values of learning. Children are encouraged to work with others in cooperative learning endeavors.

Role of the Teacher

In the integrated curriculum mode, the teacher's role can be described as setting the stage and providing the environment within which the children can engage in learning activities in terms of their own interests, needs, capabilities, personalities, and motivations. This requires a warm and stress-free atmosphere. The teacher needs to structure and guide the explorations of the children but should do so without stifling their initiative. The teacher must be skillful and resourceful in being able to capitalize on the interests of the children and to convert such leads into appropriate and workable learning activities. Also, the teacher must be imaginative in seeing the possibilities for other school-related learnings in the activities that interest the children. The teacher must provide a carefully selected assortment of learning materials for the children to handle, to use for construction, to manipulate, to experiment with, to explore, and to puzzle over. The teacher should guide and provide. The teacher's role should be that of a catalyst to stimulate children's learning. In this environment, the teacher should also be a learner along with the children.

Role of the Learner

Here, more than in any of the other modes, we find the children centrally involved in the learning process. It is expected that they will initiate activities and that they will assume responsibility for their own learning. The exercise of *initiative* and *responsibility* is basic to the role of the learner in the integrated curriculum mode. Emphasis is on cooperation; therefore, children are expected to work harmoniously with others on cooperative learning activities and projects. They are not expected to be seated at their desks, completing assignments that have been prepared by the teacher. They will, instead, be working on a project or activity in which they are interested and will be searching for answers to questions that they themselves have raised. This necessitates a mind-set of curiosity and wonderment about the environment. Considerable intellectual and physical freedom prevails. The children may move about, ask any questions they choose, and consult whatever data sources would seem to be appropriate.

Use of Instructional Resources

The integrated curriculum mode necessitates a wide variety of assorted learning materials. These should include the conventional ones (books, films, pictures, maps, and so on) and others, such as electric motors, branding irons, a computer, science equipment, carpenters' tools, historical artifacts, construction kits, art supplies, musical instruments, and audiovisual material. Indeed, anything at all that allows children to construct, explore, and manipulate might be a legitimate learning resource. A rich and responsive environment is essential to the success of the integrated curriculum mode. Because much of the learning is self-directed, these resources will be used to satisfy learner needs rather than to respond to requirements established by the teacher.

Method of Evaluation

Evaluation of learning in the integrated curriculum mode is more difficult than in the other modes because it may bear little similarity to traditional evaluative procedures. As in all cases, evaluation must be conducted in accordance with the major purposes of the mode. Therefore, in the integrated curriculum mode, the teacher would look for such things as the extent to which the children are involving themselves in their own learning; how well they are sharing, cooperating, and assuming responsibility; how well they are able to attack and puzzle through problems as they confront them; how well they are able to use the tools of learning (i.e., reading, writing, spelling, and speaking) in solving problems and meeting their needs; the extent to which their work products show evidence of improvement; and the extent to which they are overcoming their learning deficiencies. Because these programs are highly individualized, emphasis is placed on progress in terms of prior status rather than on comparing achievement with that of classmates or with nationally derived norms.

In this first part of the book, you will review important historical and recent work of cognitive psychologists, work that has led to a modern view of teaching for meaningful understanding, and a presentation of the relevant instructional methodology. As a classroom teacher, your instructional task is twofold: (1) to plan for and provide developmentally appropriate hands-on experiences, with useful materials and the supportive environment necessary for children's meaningful exploration and discovery; and (2) to know how to facilitate the most meaningful and longest lasting learning possible once the child's mind has been activated by the hands-on experience. This book is designed to help you complete that task. Although using examples that are mostly from mathematics and science, the six chapters of Part I provide fundamentals that are important to all teachers of children in grades 4–9. ■

REFERENCES

Allen, H. A., et al. (1993). *Teaching and learning in the middle level school.* New York: Macmillan.

Jarolimek, J., & Foster, C. D., Sr. (1993). *Teaching and learning in the elementary school* (5th ed.). New York: Macmillan.

CHAPTER 1

Learning and the Intellectual Development of Children

A n understanding of children—how they develop intellectually, how they think, what they think about, and how they learn and process information—is essential to being an effective classroom teacher. Much of what is known about how children learn and process information derives from cognitive research of recent years.

This chapter focuses your attention on how children learn and process information. Specifically, this chapter is designed to help you understand the following:

1. What is meant by *meaningful learning*.
2. The characteristics and developmental needs of young adolescents, children in grades 4–9.
3. How learning is constructed.
4. The contributions of learning theorists Jean Piaget, Lev Vygotsky, Robert Gagné, Jerome Bruner, and David Ausubel.
5. The importance of learning as a cyclic process.
6. The importance of using multilevel instruction.
7. The rate of cognitive development and factors that affect it.
8. The importance of learning as a cooperative and collaborative effort.
9. How conceptual understanding develops.
10. The process and benefits of learning by discovery.
11. The value of concept mapping as a cognitive tool.
12. The significance of decision making and the thought-process phases of instruction.
13. The value and variety of styles in teaching and learning.
14. The significance of the concept of learning modalities.

A. MEANINGFUL LEARNING: THE CONSTRUCTION OF UNDERSTANDING

If we define learning as being only the accumulation of bits and pieces of information, then we already know how to teach. However, the accumulation of pieces of information is at the lowest end of a spectrum of types of learning. We are still learning about learning and teaching for higher forms of learning, that is, for meaningful understanding and the reflective use of that understanding. Meanwhile, for higher levels of thinking and for learning that is most meaningful, recent research supports the use of instructional strategies that help students to make connections to what is being learned, strategies such as the whole-language approach to reading and interdisciplinary thematic teaching, with a curriculum that is integrated and connected to children's life experiences.

Let's begin with a review of important historical and recent work of cognitive psychologists, work that has led to a modern view of teaching for meaningful understanding. In opposition to the traditional view that sees teaching as covering the prescribed material, this modern view stresses the importance of learning being a personal process, by which each learner builds on the personal knowledge and experiences that he or she brings to the learning experience. *Meaningful learning is learning that results when the learner makes connections between a new experience and prior knowledge and experiences that were stored in long-term memory.* For meaningful learning to occur, the concept of correct instruction, then, is to begin where the children are, with what they have experienced and know, or think they know, and correct their misconceptions while building upon and connecting their understandings and experiences.

Like the construction of a skyscraper, meaningful learning is a gradual and sometimes painstakingly slow process. As emphasized by Watson and Konicek (1990, p. 685), when compared with traditional instruction, teaching in this constructivist mode is slower, involving more discussion, debate, and re-creation of ideas. Rather than following clearly defined and previously established steps, the curriculum evolves, it depends heavily on materials, and to a great extent it is determined by the children's interests and questions. Less content is covered, fewer facts are memorized and tested for, and progress is sometimes very slow.

The methodology uses what is referred to as a *hands-on doing* (the learner is learning by doing) and *minds-on learning* (the learner is thinking about what she or he is learning and doing) approach to constructing, and often reconstructing, the child's perceptions. Hands-on learning engages the learner's mind, causing questioning. Hands-on and minds-on learning encourages students to question and then to devise ways of investigating tentative but temporarily satisfactory answers to their questions. As a classroom teacher, your instructional task, then, is essentially twofold: (1) to plan for and provide the hands-on experiences, providing the materials and the supportive environment necessary for children's meaningful exploration and discovery; and (2) to know how to facilitate the most meaningful and longest lasting learning possible once the child's mind has been activated by the hands-on experience.

B. YOUNG ADOLESCENTS

Young adolescents have been given several epithets, including "transescent," "preadolescent," "preteen," "prepubescent," "in-betweenager," and "tweenager." These are youngsters as young as 10 (those enrolled in the fifth grade), or as old as 14 (the students you will find in an eighth-grade class). Although the cognomen is, perhaps, inconsequential, some understanding of the various developmental stages associated with such a group of children is essential to tailoring an educational program and instruction to address their needs.

To be most effective at facilitating meaningful and long-lasting learning in young adolescents, you must be aware of and use what is known about children of that age. Knowing and understanding their characteristics will do much to make teaching and learning an enjoyable and rewarding experience for both you and your students. Some characteristics are common to all young adolescents regardless of their individual genetic or cultural differences. A condensation of these facts about the intellectual, physical, psychological, social, and moral and ethical development of middle school students is presented later in this section. First, let's review the research about youngsters in this fascinating phase of their development.

Transescence

Donald Eichhorn (1966) called this developmental phase *transescence* and defined it summarily as follows:

[Transescence is] the stage of development which begins before the onset of puberty and extends through the early stages of adolescence. Since puberty does not occur for all precisely at the same chronological age in human development, the transescent designation is based on the many physical, social, emotional, and intellectual changes in body chemistry that appear before the time which the body gains a practical degree of stabilization over these complex pubescent changes (p. 3).

In 1962, Tanner reported that people are biologically maturing at an accelerated rate. For example, he notes that the "age of menarche has been getting earlier by some four months per decade in Western Europe over the period of 1830–1960" (p. 43). Eichhorn believes that students should be grouped according to developmental stages rather than the traditional chronological method. Robert J. Havighurst's developmental tasks suggest that transescence encompasses a broader range of skills and abilities than those experienced at any other maturational period before or after. Havighurst (1972) separates those tasks clearly associated with what he labels "middle childhood" from those associated with what he labels "adolescence"; however, he makes no clear distinction of the developmental tasks between middle childhood and adolescence.

Although child development studies confirm that the time near age 10 through age 14 fairly well defines the transescent in chronological terms, the issue of what these children can achieve academically is less clear. The physical and biological changes occurring in transescence may be even less a factor than their lack of sophistication in adjusting to the mental changes affecting their cognitive and affective development.

Theoretically, according to Piaget's intellectual characteristics at different stages of cognitive development, youngsters in their middle teens are developing from concrete thinkers (thinking that relies on concrete objects) to formal operational thinkers (thinking that incorporates more deductions and abstractions). Epstein (1980) argues that transescent youth have not yet reached a high enough level of "formal operational reasoning" to benefit from two or three years of curriculum that require children to perform at this level. Curricula requiring formal operational reasoning would be ineffective because of the young adolescent's inability to adjust. On the other hand, it can be argued that middle schoolers are otherwise too often faced with repetition and drill and become bored and disinterested in school (Flanders, 1987; Muther, 1987).

What do diverse developmental stages suggest about middle-level schooling, and how does diverse development relate to academic performance? First, the differences may be more a matter of degree than of kind. That is, young adolescents undergo and face the same physiological, psychological, social, and emotional development challenges common to all humans; however, these encounters are greatly magnified during the transescent years. The changes are so magnified and so diverse that giant gaps emerge between expected maturation and the child's actual ability to cope. Second, academic success may be more directly related to the affective domain (the learning domain that involves attitudes, beliefs, values, and interests) than conventional science has yet been able to show fully. Mager (1968) and Rosenshine (1980), for example, provide data that show that student attitude is directly related to learning, and that school climates directly affect student attitudes. A given environment may not directly correlate with either higher or lower achievement, but it will directly correlate with attitude. Likewise, peer acceptance has been shown to be related to academic achievement (Johnston et al., 1982). Research on learning styles and classroom climates most often concentrates on within-class groupings, not on grade-spanning organizational structures (Dunn, Beaudry, & Klavas, 1989).

From experience and research, experts have come to accept certain precepts about young adolescents. These are characteristics of young adolescents regardless of their individual genetic or cultural differences.

Characteristics of Young Adolescents

Young adolescents are egocentric. Most young people are egocentric to some degree. To egocentric youth, things are important insofar as they relate to themselves. In young children, this egocentricity is quite natural, because children find themselves in a strange yet wonderful world, filled with phenomena that are constantly affecting them. They tend to interpret the phenomena based on how they affect them personally and to use everything they learn for the express purpose of adjusting to the world in which they live, whether for better or for worse. As a teacher you can help students understand this world and adjust to it in positive ways. As children develop psychologically, emotionally, and intellectually, they overcome this egocentricity.

An important skill needed to overcome egocentricity is that of listening to others, with understanding and empathy; however, many young people, and even many adults, are not very good at listening. Teachers must help students to develop that skill. One way is to ask a student to paraphrase what another has said and then ask the first student if, in fact, that is what he or she said. If it isn't, then have the student repeat what he or she said and again ask another student to paraphrase that statement. Keep doing that until the original student's statement is correctly understood.

Young adolescents are interpretive. Young people are constantly interpreting their environment. Very often these interpretations are incomplete or even incorrect (referred to variously in the literature as *naive theories* or misconceptions, conceptual misunderstandings, or incongruent schemata, discussed shortly). However, children will continue to arrive at interpretations that satisfy them and allow them to function adequately in their daily lives.

Learners try to attach meaning to their experiences by referring to a body of related information from past experiences and knowledge stored in long-term memory. These experiences and this knowledge are called networks or *schemata*. A schema (plural, schemata) is a mental construct by which the learner organizes his or her perceptions of the environment. Learning continues by assimilating new information into a schema and modifying or forming a new schema (a process known as *accommodation*), thus allowing the learner to function adequately.

Young people's interpretations of phenomena change with their increasing maturity. Consequently, students are engaged in a constant process of revising interpretations as they grow in ability to understand and to think abstractly. A technique called concept mapping, discussed later in this chapter, is a learning strategy useful in helping students integrate their knowledge and understandings in useful schemata (Novak, 1993).

Students come to your classroom with existing schemata about almost everything, which from an adult's point of view may not always be congruent with accepted views but, nevertheless, are valid. As a teacher, one of your more important tasks is to correct students' misconceptions. Like many adults, young people are naturally resistant to change, so changing their misconceptions and promoting correct understandings is no easy task. Even after they have had corrective instruction, students will often persist in their misconceptions. Bear in mind, however, that "whenever students are asked to think about an idea in a way that questions common sense or a widely accepted assumption, that relates new ideas to ones previously learned, or that applies an idea to the problems of living, then there is a chance that good teaching is going on" (Haberman, 1991, p. 294).

Regardless of the subject and grade level, children come to your classroom with misconceptions, and correcting their misconceptions is often a long and arduous task that demands your understanding, patience, and creative instruction. Students are much more likely to modify data from their experiences to accommodate their schemata than they are to change their beliefs as a result of new experiences (Watson & Konicek, 1990, p. 683). Perhaps this shouldn't be so difficult to understand. There are stories of reputable scientists, politicians, and attorneys who were tempted to modify data to support their beliefs. Stubborn persistence and remaining open to change are virtuous, although conflicting, human attributes. In the words of Brooks and Brooks (1993, p. 113):

> Students of all ages develop and refine ideas about phenomena and then tenaciously hold onto these ideas as eternal truths. Even in the face of "authoritative" intervention and "hard" data that challenge their views, students typically adhere staunchly to their original notions. Through experiences that might engender contradictions, the frameworks for these notions weaken, causing students to rethink their perspectives and form new understandings.

Young adolescents are persistent. As implied in the preceding discussion, children are tenacious. They like to achieve their objectives and will spend remarkable time and effort at activities that are important and interesting to them. With those efforts comes a feeling of personal satisfaction and a sense of accomplishment. You must take advantage of this persistence and desire to achieve by helping children to acquire ownership of what is to be learned and by providing instruction in the form of interesting and meaningful learning activities.

Young adolescents are curious. Children are naturally curious. While a young child's world is filled with wonder and excitement, an older child's curiosity will vary, depending upon what catches his or her interest. Generally speaking, students are more interested in things that move than things that don't. They are more interested in objects that make things happen than those to which things are happening. Things that appear mysterious and magical peak their curiosity. Good instruction takes advantage of this natural curiosity. That is why, for example, the use of "magic" and discrepant events (events that cause cognitive dissonance) is so popular and successful in motivating student learning in science. In the words of Brooks and Brooks, "The line between cognitive dissonance, which can provoke a student's desire to persevere, and intrapersonal frustration, which interferes with the student's desire to resolve dissonance, is a fine one that is often difficult to recognize. To foster the development of students' abilities to organize and understand their individual worlds, teachers need to encourage students to find their own problems" (p. 29).

Young adolescents are adventurous. Young people love to explore. When given an object with which to play, younger children try to take it apart and then put it together again. They love to touch and feel objects. Children are always wondering "what will happen if . . . ?" and suggesting ideas for finding out. Children are natural questioners. The words *what, why,* and *how* are common in their vocabulary. While investigating, young people work and learn best when they experience firsthand. Therefore, you should provide a wide variety of experiences that involve hands-on learning. Hands-on learning engages the learner's mind, causing questioning. You should encourage rather than discourage students' questions.

Young adolescents are energetic. Students of middle school age would rather not sit for a long time; for some, it is nearly impossible. They would rather do than listen, and even while listening, may move their bodies restlessly. This difficulty sitting quietly has a direct bearing on the student's attention span. As a result, teaching should promote kinesthetic learning by providing many activities that give students the opportunity to be physically active.

Young adolescents are social. Children of the middle school years are social beings. They like to be with and to be accepted by their peers. They like to work together in planning and carrying out their activities. They work very well together when given proper encouragement, when they understand the procedures, and when they are given clear direction and a worthwhile task. Each student forms a self-concept through these social interactions in school. The student will develop satisfactory self-esteem when given an opportunity to work with others, to offer ideas, and to work out peer relationships. Your teaching can help foster not only learning but also the development of each student's self-esteem by incorporating social-interaction teaching strategies, such as cooperative learning, peer tutoring, and cross-age teaching.

Young adolescents have a variety of psychological needs. Abraham Maslow (1970) presented a continuum of psychological needs ranging from the most basic—*physiological needs* (for food, clothing, and shelter) and *security needs* (for a feeling of safety)—to *social needs* (for a sense of love and belonging) and *self-esteem needs* to the highest, *self-actualization needs* (for full use of talents, capacities, and abilities and acceptance of self and others). When children are frustrated because of lack of satisfaction of one or more of these needs, their classroom behavior is affected, and their learning is stifled (Reed & Sautter, 1990). Some students become aggressive and disrupt normal classroom procedures, hoping in this way to satisfy a basic need for recognition. Others become antisocial, apathetic, and fail to participate in class activities. Perhaps psychological needs are best explained by D. S. Eitzen (1992):

> Everyone needs a dream. Without a dream, we become apathetic. Without a dream, we become fatalistic. Without a dream and the hope of attaining it, society becomes our enemy. We educators must realize that some young people act in antisocial ways because they have lost their dreams.

And we must realize that we as a society are partly responsible for that loss. Teaching is a noble profession whose goal is to increase the success rate for *all* children. We must do everything we can to achieve this goal. If not, we—society, schools, teachers, and students—will all fail (p. 590).

The wise teacher is alert to any student whose basic psychological needs are not being satisfied. Perhaps it is the one who comes to school hungry. Perhaps it is the one who comes to school feeling insecure because of problems at home. Maybe it is the one who comes to school tired from having to spend each night sleeping in an automobile or from being abused by a parent, friend, or relative. Although the classroom teacher cannot solve all the ailments of society, you do have an opportunity and responsibility to make all students feel welcome, respected, and wanted, at least while in your classroom.

Historically, many teachers have found children of ages 10 to 14 particularly troublesome to teach. To further your understanding of children and your ability to work with them, let's now review the general characteristics of children of that age span.

Working with Young Adolescents

Through experience and research, experts have come to accept certain precepts about young adolescents' intellectual, physical, psychological, social, and moral and ethical development. The following list is taken from the California State Department of Education's *Caught in the Middle: Educational Reform for Young Adolescents in California Public Schools* (1987, pp. 144–148).

Intellectual development
Young adolescents tend to

1. Be egocentric; argue to convince others; exhibit independent, critical thought.
2. Be intellectually at risk; that is, they face decisions that have the potential to affect major academic values and have lifelong consequences.
3. Be intensely curious.
4. Consider academic goals a secondary priority, whereas personal-social concerns dominate their thoughts and activities.
5. Display a wide range of individual intellectual development as their minds change from the concrete-manipulatory stage to the capacity for abstract thought. This change makes possible:
   - The ability to project thought into the future, to expect, and to formulate goals.
   - Analysis of the power of a political ideology.
   - Appreciation for the elegance of mathematical logic expressed in symbols.
   - Consideration of ideas contrary to fact.
   - Insight into the nuances of poetic metaphor and musical notation.
   - Insight into the sources of previously unquestioned attitudes, behaviors, and values.
   - Interpretation of larger concepts and generalizations of traditional wisdom expressed through sayings, axioms, and aphorisms.
   - Propositional thought.
   - Reasoning with hypotheses involving two or more variables.
6. Experience the phenomenon of metacognition—that is, the ability to think about one's thinking, and to know what one knows and does not know.
7. Exhibit strong willingness to learn what they consider to be useful, and enjoy using skills to solve real-life problems.
8. Prefer active over passive learning experiences; favor interaction with peers during learning activities.

Physical development
Young adolescents tend to

1. Be concerned about their physical appearance.
2. Be physically at risk; major causes of death are homicide, suicide, accident, and leukemia.
3. Experience accelerated physical development marked by increases in weight, height, heart size, lung capacity, and muscular strength.

4. Experience biological development five years sooner than adolescents of the nine-teenth century; since then, the average age of menarche has dropped from 17 to 12 years of age.
5. Experience bone growth faster than muscle development; uneven muscle/bone devel-opment results in lack of coordination and awkwardness; bones may lack protection of covering muscles and supporting tendons.
6. Experience fluctuations in basal metabolism, which at times can cause either extreme restlessness or listlessness.
7. Face responsibility for sexual behavior before full emotional and social maturity has occurred.
8. Have ravenous appetites and peculiar tastes; they may overtax their digestive system with large quantities of improper foods.
9. Lack physical health; have poor levels of endurance, strength, and flexibility; be fatter and less healthy as a group.
10. Mature at varying rates of speed. Girls are often taller than boys for the first two years of early adolescence and are ordinarily more physically developed than boys.
11. Reflect a wide range of individual differences that begin to appear in prepubertal and pubertal stages of development. Boys tend to lag behind girls at this stage, and there are marked individual differences in physical development for both boys and girls. The greatest variation in physiological development and size occurs at about age 13.
12. Show changes in body contour, including temporarily large noses, protruding ears, long arms; have posture problems.

Psychological development
Young adolescents tend to

1. Be easily offended and sensitive to criticism of personal shortcomings.
2. Be erratic and inconsistent in their behavior; anxiety and fear contrast with periods of bravado; feelings shift between superiority and inferiority.
3. Be moody, restless; often feel self-conscious and alienated; lack self-esteem; be intro-spective.
4. Be optimistic, hopeful.
5. Be psychologically at risk; at no other point in human development is an individual likely to meet so much diversity in relation to self and others.
6. Be searching for adult identity and acceptance even in the midst of intense peer group relationships.
7. Be searching to form a conscious sense of individual uniqueness—"Who am I?"
8. Be vulnerable to naive opinions, one-sided arguments.
9. Exaggerate simple occurrences and believe that personal problems, experiences, and feelings are unique to themselves.
10. Have an emerging sense of humor based on increased intellectual ability to see abstract relationships; appreciate the double entendre.
11. Have chemical and hormonal imbalances that often trigger emotions that are frighten-ing and poorly understood; they may regress to more childish behavior patterns at this point.

Social development
Young adolescents tend to

1. Act out unusual or drastic behavior at times; they may be aggressive, daring, boister-ous, argumentative.
2. Be confused and frightened by new school settings that are large and impersonal.
3. Be fiercely loyal to peer group values and sometimes cruel or insensitive to those out-side the peer group.
4. Be impacted by the high level of mobility in society; they may become anxious and disoriented when peer group ties are broken because of family relocation.
5. Be rebellious toward parents but still strongly dependent on parental values; want to make their own choices, but the authority of the family is a critical factor in final decisions.

6. Be socially at risk; adult values are largely shaped during adolescence; negative interactions with peers, parents, and teachers may compromise ideals and commitments.
7. Challenge authority figures; test limits of acceptable behavior.
8. Experience often-traumatic conflicts because of conflicting loyalties to peer group and family.
9. Refer to peers as sources for standards and models of behavior; media heroes and heroines are also singularly important in shaping both behavior and fashion.
10. Sense the negative impact of adolescent behaviors on parents and teachers; realize the thin edge between tolerance and rejection; feelings of adult rejection can drive the adolescent into the relatively secure social environment of the peer group.
11. Strive to define sex role characteristics; search to set up positive social relationships with members of the same and opposite sex.
12. Want to know and feel that significant adults, including parents and teachers, love and accept them; need frequent affirmation.

Moral and ethical development
Young adolescents tend to

1. Ask broad, unanswerable questions about the meaning of life; they do not expect absolute answers but are turned off by trivial adult responses.
2. Be morally and ethically at risk; depend on the influences of home and church for moral and ethical development; explore the moral and ethical issues that are met in the curriculum, the media, and daily interactions with their families and peer groups.
3. Be idealistic; have a strong sense of fairness in human relationships.
4. Be reflective, introspective, and analytical about their thoughts and feelings.
5. Experience thoughts and feelings of awe and wonder related to their expanding intellectual and emotional awareness.
6. Face hard moral and ethical questions with which they are unprepared to cope.

Understanding the characteristics of young adolescents and their basic needs is the foundation for studying how they learn and think and how you can use that knowledge in your teaching.

C. INTELLECTUAL DEVELOPMENT AND HOW CHILDREN LEARN

Jean Piaget, Lev Vygotsky, Robert Gagné, Jerome Bruner, and David Ausubel are five learning theorists who have played major roles in the development of today's theory of effective instruction. Of the several psychologists whose theories of learning had an impact during the last half of the twentieth century, perhaps no other had such a wide-ranging influence on education than did Swiss psychologist Jean Piaget (1896–1980). Although Piaget began to publish his insights in the 1920s, his work was not popularized in this country until the 1960s.

Piaget's Theory of Cognitive Development

Regarding the intellectual development of the child, we now know of the importance of the richness of a child's learning experiences, especially from birth to about age 11. Maintaining that knowledge is created as children interact with their social and physical environment, Piaget postulated four stages (or periods) of cognitive development that occur in a continuing process from birth to post-adolescence (see Figure 1.1). Mental development begins with the first stage and, without skipping a stage, progresses developmentally through each succeeding stage.

Age ranges in Piaget's stages of cognitive development. Although the ages listed in Figure 1.1 indicate when the *majority* of children are likely to attain each stage of development, actually children can reach these stages at *widely* varying ages, depending on a number of factors, including the assessment procedures used. You must be cautious about placing much reliance on the age ranges assigned to Piaget's periods of cognitive development. For example, about 5 percent of middle school children, that is, children ages 10–14, operate at the preoperational level. Furthermore, when confronted with perplexing situations, evidence indicates that many learners, including adults, tend to revert to an earlier developmental stage.

Multilevel Instruction

As a teacher of grades 4–9, you will likely find students in your classroom to be at different stages (and substages) of mental development. It is important to try to attend to where each child is developmentally. To do that, many teachers use multilevel instruction (known also as multitasking). Multilevel instruction occurs when different students are working at different tasks to accomplish the same objective or are working at different tasks to accomplish different objectives. As discussed in Part IV, when integrating disciplines, multitasking is an important and useful, perhaps even necessary, strategy.

Rate of Cognitive Development and Factors That Affect It

Piaget's four stages are general descriptions of the psychological processes in cognitive development, but the rate of development varies widely among children. The rate of cognitive development is affected by the individual's maturation, which is controlled by inherited biological factors, and by the child's health, the richness of the child's experiences and social interactions, and the child's equilibration. (Equilibration, discussed shortly, is the process of mentally neutralizing the effect of cognitive disequilibrium, that is, moving from disequilibrium to equilibrium, merging new and discrepant information with established knowledge.)

Lev Vygotsky: Cooperative Learning in a Supportive Environment

A contemporary of Piaget, the Soviet psychologist Lev Vygotsky (1896–1934) studied and agreed with Piaget on most points but differed with Piaget on the importance of a child's social interactions. Vygotsky argued that learning is most effective when students cooperate with one another in a supportive learning environment under the careful guidance of a teacher. Cooperative learning, group problem solving, and cross-age tutoring are instructional strategies used today that have grown in popularity as a result of research evolving from the work of Vygotsky. (For an example of how one sixth-grade teacher has found success using cross-age tutoring, see Smith & Burrichter, 1993.)

Concept Development

Equilibration is the regulator of the relation between *assimilation* (input of new information into existing schemata) and *accommodation* (development of new or modification of old schemata). *Equilibrium* is the balance between assimilation and accommodation, and the brain is always internally striving for this balance. Disequilibrium is the state of imbalance. When disequilibrium occurs, the brain is motivated to assimilate and to accommodate. With or without a teacher's guidance a learner *will* assimilate information. The task of the teacher is to facilitate the learner's continuing, accurate construction of old and new schemata. Concept mapping (discussed later) has been shown to be an excellent tool for facilitating the learner's assimilation and accommodation.

To understand conceptual development and change, Piaget developed a theory of learning that involves children in a three-phase learning cycle. The three phases are (1) an exploratory hands-on phase, (2) a concept development phase, and (3) a concept application phase. A similar learning cycle approach to science teaching was developed by Robert Karplus for the Science Curriculum Improvement Study (SCIS) program. In that approach the three stages are *exploratory,* in which students explore materials freely, leading to their own questions and tentative answers; *invention,* in which, under the guidance of the teacher, the children invent concepts and principles that help them answer their questions and reorganize their ideas; and *application,* in which the children try out their new ideas by applying them to new situations that are relevant and meaningful to them. (For a further discussion of use of the learning cycle model in a constructivist classroom, see Brooks & Brooks, 1993.)

When a learner is applying a concept (the third phase), the learner is involved in a hands-on activity. During application of a concept the learner may discover new information that

FIGURE 1.1
Piaget's Stages of Cognitive Development

Sensorimotor Stage (Birth to Age 2)

This is the stage from birth until about age 2. At this stage, children are bound to the moment and to their immediate environment. Learning and behaviors at this stage derive from direct interaction with stimuli that the child can see or feel. Objects that are not seen are found only by random searching. Through direct interaction the child begins to build mental concepts, associating actions and reactions, and later in the stage will begin to label people and objects and to show imagining. For example, seeing a parent preparing the child's food tells the child that he or she will soon be eating. The child, then, is developing a practical base of knowledge that forms the foundation for learning in the next stage.

Preoperational Stage (Ages 2–7)

Lasting from about 2 to 7, the preoperational stage is characterized by the ability to imagine and think before acting, rather than only to respond to external stimuli. This stage is called "preoperational" because the child does not use logical operations in thinking. In this stage the child is egocentric. The child's world view is subjective rather than objective. Because of egocentrism, it is difficult for the child to consider and accept another person's point of view. The child is perceptually oriented, that is, makes judgments based on how things look to him or her. The child does not think logically, and therefore does not reason by implication. Instead, an intuitive approach is used and judgments are made according to how things look to the child. At this stage, when confronted with new and discrepant information about a phenomenon, the child adjusts the new information to accommodate his or her existing beliefs about it.

Children at this stage can observe and describe variables (properties of an object or aspects of a phenomenon) but concentrate on just one variable at a time, usually a variable that stands out visually. The child cannot coordinate variables, so has difficulty realizing that an object has several properties. Consequently, it is difficult for the child to combine parts into a whole. The child can make simple classifications according to one or two properties but finds it difficult to realize that multiple classifications are possible. Also, the child can arrange objects in simple series but has trouble arranging them in a long series or inserting a new object in its proper place within a series. To the child, space is restricted to the child's neighborhood, and time is restricted to hours, days, and seasons.

The child in this stage has not yet developed the concept of conservation. This means the child does not understand that several objects can be rearranged and that the size or shape or volume of a solid or liquid can be changed, yet the number of objects and the amount of solid or liquid will be unchanged or conserved. For example, if two rows of ten objects are arranged so they take up the same area, the child will state that the two rows are the same and there are the same number of objects in each row. If the objects in one row are spread out so the row is longer, the child is likely to maintain that the longer row now has more objects in it. Similarly, if the child is shown two identical balls of clay, the child will agree that both balls contain the same amount of material. When, in full view of the child, one of the balls is stretched out into the shape of a sausage, the child is likely to say the sausage has more clay because it is larger or less clay because it is thinner. Either way, the child at this stage is centering his or her attention on just one particular property (here, length or thickness) to the neglect of the other properties.

In both of the preceding examples the reason for the child's thinking is that the child does not yet understand reversibility. The child's thinking cannot yet reverse itself back to the point of origin. As a

---

causes a change in his or her understanding of the concept being applied. Thus, the process of learning is cyclic.

Concept Attainment: A Continuing Cyclic Process

We can think of the learner's developing understanding of concepts (concept attainment) as being a cyclical (continuing) three-stage process. The first stage is an increasing awareness that is stimulated by the quality and richness of the child's learning environment; the second stage is disequilibrium; the third stage is reformulation of the concept, which is brought on by the learner's process of equilibration.

From neuroscience, new principles are emerging that may have profound effects on teaching and on how schools are organized. For example, as stated by Caine and Caine (1990, p. 66), "Because there can be a five-year difference in maturation between any two 'average' children, gauging achievement on the basis of chronological age is inappropriate." Research indicates brain-growth spurts for students in grades 1, 2, 5, 6, 9, and 10. If schools were organized solely on this criterion, they would be configured in grade clusters

FIGURE 1.1   cont'd

result, the child does not understand that since nothing has been removed or added, the extended row of objects can be rearranged to its original length, and the clay sausage can be made back into the original ball. The child does not yet comprehend that actions and thought processes are reversible.

Not yet able to use abstract reasoning and only beginning to think conceptually, students at this stage of development learn best by manipulating objects in concrete situations rather than by abstract, verbal learning alone. For children at this stage of development, conceptual change comes very gradually.

Concrete Operations Stage (Ages 7–11)

In this stage the learner can now perform logical operations. The child can observe, judge, and evaluate in less egocentric terms than in the preoperational stage and can formulate more objective explanations. As a result, the learner knows how to solve physical problems. Because the child's thinking is still concrete and not abstract, the student is limited to problems dealing with actual concrete situations. Early in this stage the learner cannot generalize, deal with hypothetical situations, or weigh possibilities.

The child can make multiple classifications and can arrange objects in long series and place new objects in their proper place in the series. The child can begin to comprehend geographical space and historical time. The child develops the concepts of conservation according to their ease of learning: first, number of objects (age 6 or 7), then matter, length, area (age 7), weight (ages 9–12), and volume (age 11 or more), in that order. The child also develops the concept of reversibility and can now reverse the physical and mental processes when numbers of objects are rearranged or when the size and shape of matter are changed.

Later in this stage children can hypothesize and do higher-level thinking. Not yet able to use abstract reasoning and only beginning to be able to think conceptually, students at this stage of development still learn best by manipulating objects in concrete situations rather than by verbal learning alone. At this stage hands-on, active learning is most effective.

Formal Operations Stage (Age 11 and Up)

Piaget initially believed that by age 15 most adolescents reach formal operational thinking, but now it is quite clear that many high school students—and even some adults—do not yet function at this level. Essentially, students who are quick to understand abstract ideas are formal thinkers. Most middle-grade-level students are not at this stage, however. For them, *metacognition* (planning, monitoring, and evaluating one's own thinking) may be very difficult. In essence, metacognition is today's term for what Piaget referred to as *reflective abstraction,* or reflection upon one's own thinking, without which continued development cannot occur. (For further clarification of the concept of metacognition, see Braten, 1991.)

In this stage the individual's method of thinking shifts from the concrete to the more formal and abstract. The learner can now relate one abstraction to another and grows in ability to think conceptually. It is in this stage that the learner can develop hypotheses, deduce possible consequences from them, then test these hypotheses with controlled experiments in which all the variables are identical except the one being tested. When approaching a new problem, the learner begins by formulating all the possibilities and then determining which ones are substantiated through experimentation and logical analysis. After solving the problem, the learner can reflect upon or rethink the thought processes that were used.

K, 1–4, 5–8, and 9–12 (Sylvester, Chall, Wittrock, & Hart, 1991). With an increasing use of the 5–8 grade span, the middle school may be an indicator of an advance in that direction. (From 1981 to 1992, the number of middle-level schools using a 5–8 grade span tripled; only about one-third of middle-level schools in 1992 used the 7–9 grade span. See Valentine, et al., 1993, p. 19.)

Robert Gagné and the General Learning Hierarchy

Robert Gagné is well known for his hierarchy of learning levels. According to Gagné, learning is the establishing of a capability to do something that the learner was not capable of doing previously. Notice the emphasis on the learner "doing."

Gagné postulates a hierarchy of learning capabilities. Learning one particular capability usually depends upon having previously learned one or more simpler capabilities.

For Gagné, observable changes in behavior comprise the *only* criteria for inferring that learning has occurred. It follows, then, that the beginning, or lowest, level of a learning hierarchy would include very simple behaviors. These behaviors would form the basis for

TABLE 1.1
Gagné's Learning Hierarchy

Level 8: Problem Solving
Level 7: Principle Learning
Level 6: Concept Learning
Level 5: Multiple
          Discrimination
Level 4: Verbal
          Association
Level 3: Chaining
Level 2: Stimulus-Response
          Learning
Level 1: Signal Learning

learning more complex behaviors in the next level of the hierarchy. At each higher level, learning requires that the appropriate simpler, or less complex, behaviors have been acquired in the lower learning levels.

Gagné identifies eight levels of learning in this hierarchy. Beginning with the simplest and progressing to the most complex, these levels, shown in Table 1.1, are described briefly as follows.

Signal learning. The individual learns to make a general, conditioned response to a given signal. Examples are a child's pleasure at the sight of a pet animal or the child's expression of fright at the sound of a loud noise.

Stimulus-response learning. The individual acquires a precise physical or vocal response to a discriminated stimulus. Examples include a child's initial learning of words by repeating sounds and words of adults and the training of a dog to sit.

Chaining. Sometimes called skill learning, chaining involves the linking together of two or more units of simple stimulus-response learning. Chaining is limited to physical, nonverbal sequences. Examples include winding up a toy, writing, running, and opening a door. The accuracy of the learning at this level depends on practice, prior experience, and reinforcement.

Verbal association. This is a form of chaining, but the links are verbal units. Naming an object is the simplest verbal association. In this case, the first stimulus-response link is involved in observing the object, and the second is involved in enabling the child to name the object. A more complex example of verbal chaining would be the rote memorization of a sequence of numbers, a formula, or the letters of the alphabet in sequence. Considered alone, these learned behaviors are not usually seen as important goals of teaching. However, viewed as a level in a hierarchy, they may be important first steps to certain higher levels of learning.

Multiple discrimination. Individual learned chains are linked to form multiple discriminations. Examples of learning at this level include the identification of the names of students in a classroom, in which the learner associates each student with his or her distinctive appearance and correct name; and, in science, learning the distinction between solids, liquids, and gases.

Concept learning. Learning a concept means learning to respond to stimuli by their abstract characteristics (such as position, shape, color, and number), as opposed to concrete physical properties. A child may learn to call a two-inch cube a "block" and to apply this name to other objects that differ from it in size and shape. Later, the child learns the concept "cube," and by so doing can identify a class of objects that differ physically in many ways (say, by material, color, texture, and size). Rather than learning concepts in a trial-and-error, accidental fashion, under the careful guidance of the teacher a child's learning is sequenced in such a way as to lead to the child's improved conceptual understanding.

Principle learning. In simplest terms, a principle is a chain of two or more concepts. In principle learning the individual must relate two or more concepts. An example is the relation of a circle's circumference to its diameter. Three separate concepts (circumference, pi, and diameter) are linked or chained together.

Problem solving. According to Gagné, and as most learning theorists will agree, problem solving is the most sophisticated type of learning. In problem solving, the individual applies learned principles in order to achieve a goal. While achieving this goal, however, the learner becomes capable of new performances by using the new knowledge. When a problem is solved, new knowledge has been acquired, and the individual's capacity advances. The individual is now able to handle a wide class of problems similar to the one solved. What has been learned, according to Gagné, is a higher-order principle, which is the combined product of two or more lower-order principles.

Thus, when a child has acquired the capabilities and behaviors of a certain level of learning, we assume that the child has also acquired the capabilities and behaviors of all the learning levels below this level. Furthermore, if the child were having difficulty in demonstrating the capabilities and behaviors for a certain level, the teacher could simply test the child on the capabilities and behaviors of the lower levels to determine which one or ones were causing the difficulty.

Jerome Bruner and Discovery Learning

While a leading interpreter and promoter of Piaget's ideas, Bruner also made his own significant contributions on how children learn. Some of his thinking was influenced by the work of Vygotsky (Bruner, 1985). Like Piaget, Bruner maintains that each child passes through stages that are age related and biologically determined and that learning will depend primarily on the developmental level that the child has attained.

Bruner's theory also encompasses three major sequential stages that he refers to as representations. They can be thought of as ways of knowing. These are *enactive representation* (knowing that is related to movement, such as through direct experiencing or concrete activities); *ikonic representation* (knowing that is related to visual and spatial, or graphic, representations, such as films and still visuals); and *symbolic representation* (knowing that is related to reason and logic, or that depends on the use of words and abstract symbolization). They correspond to the sensorimotor, concrete operations, and formal operations stages of Piaget. While Bruner's description of what happens during these three representations corresponds to that of Piaget's stages, he differs from Piaget in his interpretation of the role language plays in intellectual development.

Piaget believes that although thought and language are related, they are different systems. He posits that the child's thinking is based on a system of inner logic that evolves as the child organizes and adapts to experiences. Bruner, however, maintains that thought is internalized language. The child translates experience into language, and then uses language as an instrument of thinking.

Bruner and Piaget differ also in their attitude toward the child's readiness for learning. Piaget concluded that the child's readiness for learning depends upon maturation and intellectual development. Bruner and some other researchers, however, believe that a child is always ready to learn a concept at some level of sophistication. Bruner states that any subject can be taught effectively in some intellectually honest form to any child in any stage of development. He supports this concept, for example, by noting that the basic ideas of science and mathematics are simple, and only when these ideas are out of context with the child's life experiences and formalized by equations and complex verbal statements do they become incomprehensible to children (and to adults).

According to Bruner, a child can learn concepts only within the framework of whichever stage of intellectual development the child is in at the time. In teaching children, it is essential then that each child be helped to pass progressively from one stage of intellectual development to the next. Schools can do this by providing challenging but developmentally appropriate problems and opportunities for children that tempt them to forge ahead into the next stages of development. As a result, the children will acquire a higher level of understanding.

Bruner and the Act of Learning

Bruner describes the act of learning as involving three almost simultaneous processes. The first is the process of acquiring new knowledge. The second is the process of manipulating this knowledge to make it fit new tasks or situations. The third is the process of evaluating the acquisition and manipulation of this knowledge. A major objective of learning is to introduce the child at an early age to the ideas and styles that will help the child become literate. Consequently, the school curriculum should be built around major conceptual schemes, skills, and values that society considers to be important. These should be taught as early as possible in a manner that is consistent with the child's stages of development and forms of thought, then revisited many times throughout the school years to increase and deepen the learner's understanding.

Bruner has been an articulate spokesperson for discovery learning. He advocates that, whenever possible, teaching and learning should be conducted in such a manner that children are given the opportunity to discover concepts for themselves.

Benefits of Discovery Learning

Bruner cites four major benefits derived from learning by discovery. First, there is an increase in intellectual potency. By this he means that discovery learning helps students learn how to learn. It helps the learner develop skills in problem solving, enabling the learner to arrange and apply what has been learned to new situations, and thus learn new concepts.

Second, there is a shift from extrinsic to intrinsic rewards. Discovery learning shifts the motive for learning away from that of satisfying others to that of satisfying oneself—the source of motivation is intrinsic rather than extrinsic.

Third, there is an opportunity to learn the working heuristics of discovery. By heuristics Bruner means the methods in which a person is educated to find out things independently. Only through the exercise of problem solving and by the effort of discovery can the learner find out things independently. The more adept the learner becomes in the working heuristics of discovery, the more effective the decisions the learner will make in problem solving and the quicker they will be made.

Fourth, there is an aid to memory processing. Knowledge resulting from discovery learning is more easily remembered, and it is more readily recalled when needed. Bruner's work, strongly supported by recent brain research, provides a rationale for using discovery and hands-on learning activities.

Gagné and Bruner differ in their emphasis upon learning. While Gagné emphasizes primarily the product of learning (the knowledge), Bruner's emphasis is on the process of learning (the skills). While for Gagné the key question is, "*What* do you want the child to know?" for Bruner it is, "*How* do you want the child to know?" For Gagné the emphasis is on learning itself, whether by discovery, review, or practice. For Bruner the emphasis is on learning by discovery; it is the method of learning that is important.

Gagné emphasizes problem solving as the highest level of learning, with the lower learning levels prerequisite to this highest level. For Gagné, the appropriate sequence in learning (and teaching) is from these lower levels toward problem solving. The teacher begins with simple ideas, relates all of them, builds on them, and works toward the more complex levels of learning. On the other hand, Bruner *begins* with problem solving, which in turn leads to the development of necessary skills. The teacher poses a question to be solved and then uses it as a catalyst to motivate children to develop the necessary skills.

Piaget, Bruner, and Gagné also differ in their attitude toward the child's readiness for learning. As has been stated earlier, Piaget believes that readiness depends upon the child's maturation and intellectual development. Bruner believes that the child is always ready to learn a concept at some level of sophistication. Gagné, however, feels that readiness is dependent on the successful development of lower level skills and prior understandings.

David Ausubel and Meaningful Verbal Learning

David Ausubel (1963) advocates reception learning, the receipt of ideas through transmission. He agrees with other psychologists that the development of problem-solving skills is a primary objective in teaching. As does Gagné, however, he feels that effective problem solving and discovery are more likely to take place after children have learned key and supporting concepts, primarily through reception learning, that is, through direct instruction (expository teaching).

Ausubel strongly urges teachers to use learning situations and examples that are familiar to the students. This helps students to assimilate what is being learned with what they already know, making their learning more meaningful. Unlike Bruner, Ausubel believes that discovery learning is too time consuming to enable students to learn all they should know within the short time allotted to learning. Like Bruner and Gagné, he suggests that children in the primary grades should work on as many hands-on learning activities as possible, but for children beyond the primary grades, he recommends the increased use of learning by transmission using teacher explanations, concept mapping, demonstrations, diagrams, and illustrations. Ausubel cautions against learning by rote memorization, however.

An example of learning by rote is when you memorize your social security number. One must learn by rote memorization information that is not connected to any prior knowledge. Learning by rote is easier if one can connect that which is to be memorized to some prior knowledge. Often used to bridge the gap between rote learning and meaningful learning is the strategy known as *mnemonics,* which is any strategy that will assist memory. Examples of common mnemonics include:

1. The periods of the Paleozoic Era are *C*avemen *O*bject *S*trenuously *D*uring *M*ost *P*olite *P*arties (*C*ambrian, *O*rdovician, *S*ilurian, *D*evonian, *M*ississippian, *P*ennsylvanian, and *P*ermian).
2. The order of the planets from the Sun are *M*y *V*ery *E*ducated *M*other *J*ust *S*erved *U*s *N*ine *P*izzas (*M*ercury, *V*enus, *E*arth, *M*ars, *J*upiter, *S*aturn, *U*ranus, *N*eptune, and *P*luto).
3. The hierarchy of the biological classification system is *K*indly *P*rofessors—or *D*octors—*C*an *O*nly *F*ail *G*reedy *S*tudents (*K*ingdom, *P*hylum—or *D*ivision—*C*lass, *O*rder, *F*amily, *G*enus, and *S*pecies).
4. The order of colors in the color spectrum is *ROY G. BIV,* for *r*ed, *o*range, *y*ellow, *g*reen, *b*lue, *i*ndigo, and *v*iolet.

To avoid rote memorization, Ausubel encourages teachers to make the learning meaningful and longer lasting by using *advance organizers,* ideas that are presented to the students before the new material and that mentally prepare students to integrate the new material into previously built cognitive structures. Most mathematics and science textbook programs today are designed in this way.

There is no doubt that the most effective teaching occurs when students see meaning in what is being taught. A danger in expository teaching (in which the student listens to the teacher, reads, and memorizes) is the tendency to rely too heavily on spoken communication, which for many learners is highly abstract and thus unlikely to be effective. This is especially so in classrooms with students who are diverse in their language proficiency, cultural backgrounds, and skill levels.

Concept Mapping

Based on Ausubel's theory of meaningful learning, a technique called concept mapping has been found useful for helping students change their misconceptions. Simply put, concepts can be thought of as classifications that attempt to organize the world of objects and events into a smaller number of categories. Or, stated in another way, concepts are "regularities in events or objects designated by some arbitrary label" (Novak, 1984, p. 607). And, as stated by Carin, "scientific concepts are mental organizations about the world that are based on similarities among objects or events" (1993, p. 7). Concepts embody a meaning that develops in complexity with experience and learning over time. Examples of science concepts are *water, electricity,* and *animal.* And, in mathematics, a concept is "the underlying pattern that relates sets of objects or actions to one another. For example, an underlying pattern that defines the geometric concept of *triangle* is: all closed figures that have exactly three straight sides" (Souviney, 1994, p. 34).

A concept map typically refers to a visual or graphic representation of concepts with connections (bridges) to show their relationships. See Figure 1.2, a concept map in integrated science and social studies showing middle school students' connections of relationships while studying concepts in fruit farming and marketing.

The general procedure for concept mapping is to have students (1) identify important concepts in materials being studied, often by circling those concepts, (2) rank order the concepts from the most general to the most specific, and then (3) arrange the concepts on a sheet of paper, connect related ideas with lines, and define the connections between the related ideas. Concept mapping has been found to help students in their ability to organize and represent their thoughts and to connect new knowledge to their past experiences and schemata. (For further information about concept mapping, see Novak, 1990; Wolff-Michael & Bowen, 1993.)

FIGURE 1.2
Sample Concept Map
SOURCE: Reprinted with the permission of Simon & Schuster, Inc. from the Macmillan College text A RESOURCE GUIDE FOR TEACHING: K–12 by Richard D. Kellough. Copyright ©1994 by Macmillan College Publishing Company, Inc.

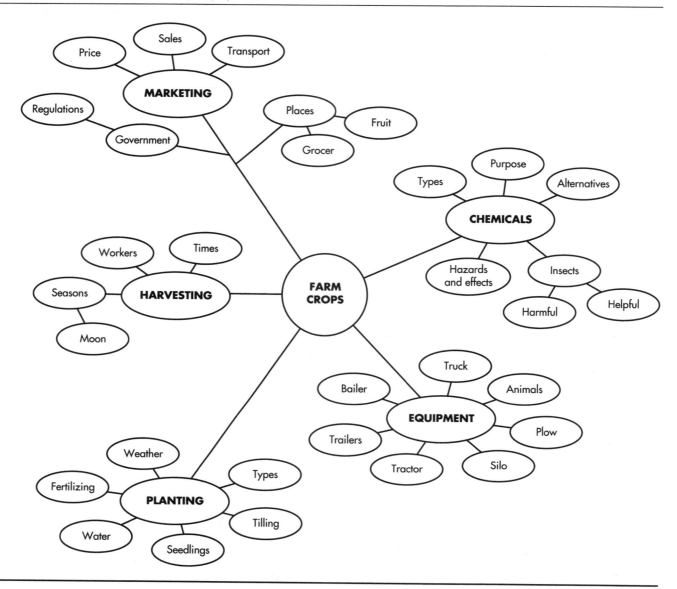

D. THE TEACHER AS DECISION MAKER

As you undoubtedly are aware, during any school day you will make hundreds of decisions, many of which must be made instantaneously. In addition, to prepare for the teaching day you will have already made many decisions about it. During one school year a teacher makes literally thousands of decisions, many of which can and will affect the lives of children for years to come. For you this should seem an awesome responsibility, and it is.

To be an effective teacher, you must become adept at decision making and make decisions that are carefully reasoned over time as well as those that are made on the spot. To be adept in making decisions that affect the students in the most positive ways you need (1) common sense, (2) intelligence, (3) a background of theory in curriculum and instruction with extended practical experience in working with young people, and (4) the willingness to think about and to reflect upon your teaching and to continue learning all that is necessary to become an exemplary teacher.

Initially, of course, you will make errors in judgment, but you will also learn that young people are fairly resilient and that there are experts who will guide you, aid you, and help you ensure that the students are not damaged severely by your errors in judgment. You can learn from your errors. Keep in mind that the sheer number of decisions you make each day will mean that not all of them will be the best ones that could have been made had you had more time to think and better resources for planning.

Although effective teaching is based on scientific principles, good classroom teaching is as much an art as it is a science, and few rules apply to every teaching situation. In fact, decisions about the selection of content, of instructional objectives, of materials for instruction, of teaching strategies, of a teacher's response to a student's inappropriate behavior, and of techniques for the assessment of achievement in student learning are all the result of subjective judgments. Although many decisions are made at a somewhat unhurried pace when you are planning for your instruction, many others will be made intuitively on the spur of the moment. Once the school day has begun, you may lack the time for making carefully thought-out judgments. At your best, you will base decisions on your knowledge of school policies, your teaching style, pedagogical research, the curriculum, and the nature of the children in your classroom. You will also base your decisions on instinct, common sense, and reflective judgment. The better your understanding of and experience with schools, the content of the curriculum, and the students and how they develop intellectually, and the more time you devote to thinking and careful reflection, the more likely it will be that your decisions will result in the student learning that you had planned. You will reflect upon, conceptualize, and apply understandings from one teaching experience to the next. As your understandings about your classroom experiences accumulate, your teaching will become more routinized, predictable, and refined.

Decision Making and the Thought-Processing Phases of Instruction

Teaching has been defined as "the process of making and implementing decisions before, during, and after instruction—decisions that, when implemented, increase the probability of learning" (Hunter, 1994, p. 6). Instruction can be divided into four decision-making and thought-processing phases. These are the *preactive* (planning) phase, the *interactive* (teaching) phase, the *reflective* (analyzing and evaluating) phase, and the *projective* phase (in which your reflections upon your teaching are applied) (Costa, 1991). The preactive phase consists of all those intellectual functions and decisions you will make prior to actual instruction. The interactive phase includes all the decisions made during the immediacy and spontaneity of the teaching act. As said earlier, decisions made during this phase are likely to be more intuitive, unconscious, and routine than are those made during the planning phase. The reflective phase is the time you will make to reflect on, analyze, and judge the decisions and behaviors that occurred during the interactive phase. As a result of this reflection, you will decide to use what was learned in subsequent teaching actions. At this point, you are in the projective phase, abstracting from your reflection and projecting your analysis into subsequent teaching actions.

Reflection and the Locus of Control

It is during the reflective phase that you have a choice as to whether to assume full responsibility for all instructional outcomes or for only the positive outcomes of the planned instruction while placing the blame for the negative outcomes on outside forces (parents and guardians, student peer pressure, other teachers, administrators, textbooks). Where you place responsibility for outcomes is referred to as your locus of control. It seems axiomatic that teachers who are professional and competent tend to assume full responsibility for instructional outcomes, regardless of whether those outcomes were as intended in the planning phase.

Personal Style of Teaching

Every teacher develops a personal style of teaching with which she or he feels most comfortable. This style develops from a combination of personal traits and the expertise the teacher has in methodology, subject matter, and instructional theory. The most effective teachers can vary their styles—that is, their styles are flexible enough to encompass a variety of strategies and are therefore readily adaptable to the different sorts of situations that may develop. *Teaching style is the way teachers teach, their distinctive mannerisms complemented by their choices of teaching behaviors and strategies.*

Effective teachers can modify their styles by selecting and using the strategy that is most appropriate, thus securing active student involvement and the greatest amount of student achievement. Highly effective teaching of this sort requires both expertise in a wide variety of methods and a feeling for the appropriate situation in which to use each method, as well as a command of the subject matter and an understanding of the children being taught. This may sound like a large order, but many beginning teachers become adept at this surprisingly quickly.

Thus, to be an effective teacher you should (1) develop a large repertoire of instructional strategies; (2) learn as much as you can about your students and their individual styles of learning; and (3) develop an eclectic style of teaching, one that is flexible and adaptable, that can function at many locations along the spectrum of integrated learning as introduced at the opening of Part I.

E. STYLES OF LEARNING

The most effective teachers are those who adapt their teaching styles and methods to their students, using approaches that interest the students, that are neither too easy nor too difficult, that match the students' learning styles, and that are relevant to their lives. This adaptation process is further complicated because each student is different from every other. All do not have the same interests, abilities, backgrounds, or learning styles. As a matter of fact, students not only differ from one another, but each student can change to some extent from day to day. What appeals to a student today may not have the same appeal tomorrow. Therefore, you need to consider the nature of both students in general (for example, methods appropriate for a particular fifth-grade class are unlikely to work best for most ninth graders) and each student in particular. What follows is a synopsis of what has been learned about aspects of student learning styles.

Brain Laterality

Research has shown that how a person learns is related to differences in the left and right hemispheres of the brain. This theory is sometimes referred to as brain laterality or brain hemisphericity. Verbal learning, logical and convergent thinking, and the academic cognitive processes are dominated by the left cerebral hemisphere, while affective, intuitive, spatial, emotional, divergent thinking and visual elements are dominated by the right cerebral hemisphere. Some students are oriented toward right cerebral hemisphere learning and others toward the left. This means that some students learn better through verbal interactions while others learn through visual, kinesthetic, and tactile involvement. However, "in a healthy person the two hemispheres are inextricably interactive, irrespective of whether a person is dealing with words, mathematics, music, or art" (Caine & Caine, 1990, p. 67).

Brain laterality and its implications for teaching. When integrating the disciplines and helping students connect what is being learned with real-life situations, the teacher is more likely to be teaching to both hemispheres.

Learning Modalities

Learning modality refers to the sensory portal means by which a student prefers to receive sensory reception (modality preference), or the actual way a student learns best (modality adeptness). Some students prefer learning by seeing, a visual modality; others prefer learning through instruction from others (through talk), an auditory modality; while still others prefer learning by doing and being physically involved, referred to as kinesthetic modality, and by touching objects, the tactile modality. Sometimes a student's modality preference is not that student's modality strength. While primary modality strength can be determined by observing students, it can also be mixed, and it can change as the result of experience and intellectual maturity. As one might suspect, modality integration (using several modalities at once) has been found to contribute to better achievement in student learning.

Learning modality and its implications for teaching. Because most students have neither a preference for nor a strength in auditory reception, teachers should limit their use of the lecture method of instruction, that is, of talk. Instruction that uses a singular approach, such as auditory instruction (lecturing), cheats students who learn better another way. This difference can affect student achievement. Finally, if a teacher's verbal communication conflicts with his or her nonverbal messages, students can become confused, and this too can affect their learning. (When there is a discrepancy between what the teacher says and what that teacher does, the teacher's nonverbal signal will be believed every time.)

As a general rule, students of intermediate and middle grade levels prefer to learn by touching objects, by feeling shapes and textures, by interacting with each other, and by moving things around. In contrast, sitting and listening are difficult for many of these students. Dependence on the tactile and kinesthetic modalities decreases with maturity. Some students are visual learners who can read easily and rapidly and can visualize what they are reading about.

You are advised to use strategies that integrate the modalities. Combining reception learning and cognitive mapping is an example of modality integration. When well designed, thematic units incorporate modality integration, too. In conclusion, then, when teaching a group of students of mixed learning abilities, mixed modality strengths, mixed language proficiency, and mixed cultural backgrounds, the integration of learning modalities is a must for the most successful teaching.

Learning Styles

Related to learning modality is learning style, which can be defined as independent forms of knowing and processing information. While some students are comfortable beginning their learning of a new idea in the abstract (say, through visual or verbal symbolization), others feel the need to begin with the concrete (to learn by actually doing). Some prosper while working in groups, while others prefer to work alone. Some are quick in their studies, whereas others are slow and methodical, cautious and meticulous. Some can focus their attention on a single topic for a long time, becoming more absorbed in their study as time passes. Others are slower starters and more casual in their pursuits but are capable of shifting with ease from subject to subject. Some can study in the midst of music, noise, or movement, whereas others need quiet, solitude, and a desk or table. The point is that students vary not only in their skills at and preferences for receiving knowledge, but also in how they mentally process that information once it has been received. This latter is a person's style of learning, "a gestalt combining internal and external operations derived from the individual's neurobiology, personality, and development and reflected in learner behavior" (Keefe & Ferrell, 1990, p. 59).

Classification of Learning Styles

Although there are probably as many types of learning styles as there are individuals, most learning style classifications center around the recognition of four general types, based on the earlier work of Carl Jung (see Jung, 1923; Gregorc, 1985; Dunn & Dunn, 1978).

Anthony Gregorc (1979) classifies learning styles according to whether students prefer to begin with the concrete or the abstract and whether they prefer random or sequential ordering of information. As a result, his learning style classification has four categories:

- The *concrete sequential learner* prefers direct, hands-on experiences presented in a logical sequence.
- The *concrete random learner* prefers a more wide-open, exploratory kind of activity, such as games, role-playing, simulations, and independent study.
- The *abstract sequential learner* is skilled in decoding verbal and symbolic messages, especially when presented in logical sequence.
- The *abstract random learner* can interpret meaning from nonverbal communications and consequently does well in discussions, debates, and media presentations.

Most students are better at one of the two categories of concrete learning than at either category of abstract learning.

David Kolb (1985) described two major differences in how people learn: how they perceive situations and how they process information. In their perception of the same new situation, some people are watchers and others are doers. It is important to note that learning style is not an indicator of intelligence, but rather an indicator of how a person learns.

More recently, Bernice McCarthy (1990, p. 32) has described the following four major learning styles:

- The *imaginative learner* perceives information concretely and processes it reflectively. Imaginative learners learn well by listening and sharing with others, integrating the ideas of others with their own experiences. Imaginative learners often have difficulty adjusting to traditional teaching, which depends less on classroom interactions and students' sharing and connecting of their prior experiences. In a traditional classroom, the imaginative learner is likely to be an at-risk student.
- The *analytic learner* perceives information abstractly and processes it reflectively. The analytic learner prefers sequential thinking, needs details, and values what experts have to offer. Analytic learners do well in traditional classrooms.
- The *common sense learner* perceives information abstractly and processes it actively. The common sense learner is pragmatic and enjoys hands-on learning. Common sense learners sometimes find school frustrating unless they can see an immediate use for what is being learned. In the traditional classroom, the common sense learner is likely to be a learner who is at risk of not completing school.
- The *dynamic learner* perceives information concretely and processes it actively. The dynamic learner also prefers hands-on learning and is excited by anything new. Dynamic learners are risk takers and are frustrated by learning if they see it as being tedious and sequential. In a traditional classroom, the dynamic learner also is likely to be an at-risk student.

With a system developed by McCarthy (called the 4MAT System), teachers employ a learning cycle of instructional strategies that reach each student's learning style. As stated by McCarthy, in the cycle, learners "sense and feel, they experience, then they watch, they reflect, then they think, they develop theories, then they try out theories, they experiment. Finally, they evaluate and synthesize what they have learned in order to apply it to their next similar experience. They get smarter. They apply experience to experiences" (1990, p. 33). And, with this process, they are likely to be using all four learning modalities. (Compare the learning cycle described here with the learning cycle concepts of Piaget and Karplus discussed earlier in this chapter; see Figure 1.1.)

Finally, in contrast to Jung's four learning styles, Howard Gardner and others have introduced seven learning styles or types of intelligences: *verbal-linguistic, logical-mathematical, intrapersonal, visual-spatial, musical-rhythmic, body-kinesthetic,* and *interpersonal* (Blythe & Gardner, 1990; Gardner, 1987; Gardner & Hatch, 1989). As implied previously, many educators believe that students who are at risk of not completing school are those who may be dominant in a cognitive learning style that is not in synch with traditional teaching methods (see, for example, Armstrong, 1988). Traditional methods are largely of McCarthy's analytic style, where information is presented in a logical, linear, sequential fashion, and of the first three Gardner types: verbal-linguistic, logical-mathematical, and intrapersonal. Consequently, to better synchronize methods of instruction with learning styles, some teachers (see Ellison, 1992) and schools (see Hoerr, 1992) have restructured the curriculum and instruction around Gardner's seven ways of knowing.

Learning style and its implications for teaching. The importance of the preceding information about learning styles is twofold:

1. Intelligence is not a fixed or static reality but can be learned, taught, and developed (Lazear, 1992; Bracey, 1992). This concept is important for your students to understand, too. When students understand that intelligence is incremental, something that is developed through use over time, they tend to be more motivated to work at learning than when they believe intelligence is a fixed entity (Resnick & Klopfer, 1989, p. 8).

2. Not all students learn and respond to learning situations in the same way. A student may learn differently according to the situation or according to the student's ethnicity, cultural background, or socioeconomic status. (For relevant discussions about students' cultural differences and learning styles, see Willis, 1993, p. 7; Gallegos, 1993.) A teacher who uses only one style of teaching for all students or who teaches to only one or a few styles of learning, day after day, is shortchanging those students who learn better another way.

A trap the teacher must avoid is to regard all students who have difficulty or who have a history of doing poorly in school as being alike. In a culture such as ours that values quantity, speed, and measurement, it is easy to make the mistake that being a slow learner is the same as being a poor learner. The perceptive teacher understands that slowness may be simply another style of learning, with potential strengths of its own. Slowness can reflect many things—caution, a desire to be thorough or a meticulous style, a great interest in the matter being studied. To ignore the slow student or to treat all students who seem slow as though they were victims of some deficiency is to risk discouraging those who have deliberately opted for slowness, thus limiting their learning opportunities.

SUMMARY

As a teacher you must acknowledge that children have different ways of receiving information and different ways of processing that information—different ways of knowing and of constructing their knowledge. These differences are unique and important, and they are what you should address in your teaching. You should try to learn as much as you can about how each student learns and processes information. But because you can never know everything about each student, the more you vary your teaching strategies and assist students in integrating their learning, the more likely you are to reach more of the students more of the time.

To be an effective teacher, you should (1) learn as much about your students and their preferred styles of learning as you can; (2) develop an eclectic style of teaching, one that is flexible and adaptable; and (3) integrate the disciplines, thereby assisting students in their conceptual understandings by helping them to make bridges or connections between what is being learned.

QUESTIONS AND ACTIVITIES FOR DISCUSSION

1. Give an example of how you would use multilevel teaching. Of what benefit is the use of multilevel teaching?

2. Explain why knowledge of teaching styles and student learning styles is important for a teacher.

3. Describe the relationship between awareness, disequilibrium, and reformulation in learning.

4. Explain why integration of the curriculum is important for learning at the intermediate and middle grade levels.

5. Explain the concept of spectrum of curriculum integration. What relevance does this concept have for you?

6. For a concept usually taught in science or mathematics at a 4–9 grade level, demonstrate specifically how you might help students bridge their learning of that concept with what is going on in their lives and with other disciplines.

7. Could the technique of concept mapping be used as an advance organizer? Explain your answer.

8. Colleen, a science teacher, has a class of 33 eighth graders who, during her lectures, teacher-led discussions, and recitation lessons, are restless and inattentive and creating a major problem in classroom management. At Colleen's invitation, the school psychologist tests the children for learning modality and finds that of the 33 children, 29 are predominantly kinesthetic learners. Of what use is this information to Colleen? Describe what, if anything, she should try as a result of having this information.

9. Identify a topic of a science or mathematics lesson for a grade level of your choice, grade 4 through 9. Describe how you would teach that lesson from a behaviorist viewpoint; then describe how you would teach the same lesson from a constructivist viewpoint. Explain the differences.

10. Could you accept the view that learning is the product of creative inquiry through social interaction, with the students as active participants in that inquiry? Explain why you would or would not agree.

11. Assume that you are a junior high school teacher and that your teaching schedule includes three sections of general science. Furthermore, assume that students at your school are tracked (as they are in many junior high schools) and that one of your classes is a so-called "academic" class with 30 students, another is a regular education class with 35 students, 2 of whom have special needs because of physical handicaps, and the third is a sheltered English class with 13 students, 9 of whom are Hispanics with limited proficiency in English (the other 4 are Southeast Asians, 2 of whom have no proficiency yet in the use of English). Will one lesson plan using lecture and discussion as the primary instructional strategies work for all three sections? If so, explain why. If not, explain what you will have to do and why.

12. Can you recall or invent mnemonics that would be useful in your teaching? Compare them with those of your classmates.

13. Describe any prior concepts you held that changed as a result of your experiences reading this chapter. Describe the changes.

REFERENCES

Armstrong, T. (1988). Learning differences–Not disabilities. *Principal, 68*(1), 34–36.

Ausubel, D. P. (1963). *The psychology of meaningful verbal learning.* New York: Grune & Stratton.

Blythe, T., & Gardner, H. (1990). A school for all intelligences. *Educational Leadership, 47*(7), 33–37.

Bracey, G. W. (1992). Getting smart(er) in school. *Phi Delta Kappan, 73*(5), 414–416.

Braten, I. (1991). Vygotsky as precursor to metacognitive theory: I. The concept of metacognition and its roots. *Scandinavian Journal of Educational Research, 35*(3), 179–192.

Brooks, J. G., & Brooks, M. G. (1993). *In search of understanding: The case for constructivist classrooms.* Alexandria, VA: Association for Supervision and Curriculum Development.

Bruner, J. (1985). Vygotsky: A historical and conceptual perspective. In J. Wertsch (Ed.), *Culture, communication and cognition: Vygotskian perspectives.* Cambridge, England: Cambridge University Press.

Caine, R. N., & Caine, G. (1990). Understanding a brain-based approach to learning and teaching. *Educational Leadership, 48*(2), 66–70.

California State Department of Education. (1987). *Caught in the middle: Educational reform for young adolescents in California public schools.* Sacramento, CA: Author.

Carin, A. A. (1993). *Teaching science through discovery* (7th ed.). New York: Merrill.

Costa, A. L. (1991). *The school as a home for the mind.* Palatine, IL: Skylight Publishing.

Dunn, R., Beaudry, J. S., & Klavas, A. (1989). Survey of research on learning styles. *Educational Leadership, 47*(6), 50–58.

Dunn, R., & Dunn, K. (1978). *Teaching students through their individual learning styles.* Reston, VA: Reston Publications.

Eichhorn, D. H. (1966). *The middle school.* New York: Center for Applied Research.

Eitzen, D. S. (1992). Problem students: The sociocultural roots. *Phi Delta Kappan, 73*(8), 584–590.

Ellison, L. (1992). Using multiple intelligences to set goals. *Educational Leadership, 50*(2), 69–72.

Epstein, H. T. (1980). Brain growth and cognitive functions. In D. Steer (Ed.), *Emerging adolescent, characteristics and educational implications.* Columbus, OH: National Middle School Association.

Flanders, J. R. (1987). How much of the content in mathematics textbooks is new? *Arithmetic Teacher, 35*(1), 18–23.

Gallegos, G. (1993, Fall). Learning styles in culturally diverse classrooms. *California Catalyst,* pp. 36–41.

Gardner, H. (1987). The theory of multiple intelligences. *Annals of Dyslexia, 37,* 19–35.

Gardner, H., & Hatch, T. (1989). Multiple intelligences go to school: Educational implications of the theory of multiple intelligence. *Educational Researcher, 18*(8), 4–9.

Gregorc, A. (1979, January). Learning and teaching styles—Potent forces behind them. *Educational Leadership,* 234–236.

Gregorc, A. (1985). *Gregorc style delineator.* Maynard, MA: Gabriel Systems.

Haberman, M. (1991). The pedagogy of poverty versus good teaching. *Phi Delta Kappan, 73*(4), 290–294.

Havighurst, R. J. (1972). *Developmental tasks and education.* New York: David McKay.

Hoerr, T. R. (1992). How our school applied multiple intelligences theory. *Educational Leadership, 50*(2), 67–68.

Hunter, M. (1994). *Enhancing teaching.* New York: Macmillan.

Johnston, H. J., et al. (1982). What research says to the practitioner about peer relations in the classroom. *Middle School Journal, 13*(3), 22–26.

Jung, C. G. (1923). *Psychological types.* New York: Harcourt Brace.

Keefe, J. W., & Ferrell, B. G. (1990). Developing a defensible learning style paradigm. *Educational Leadership, 48*(2), 57–61.

Kolb, D. (1985). *The learning style inventory.* Boston: McBer & Co.

Lazear, D. G. (1992). *Teaching for multiple intelligences.* Fastback 342. Bloomington, IN: Phi Delta Kappa Educational Foundation.

Mager, R. F. (1968). *Developing attitudes toward learning.* Belmont: Fearson.

Maslow, A. H. (1970). *Motivation and personality.* New York: Harper and Row.

McCarthy, B. (1990). Using the 4MAT system to bring learning styles to schools. *Educational Leadership, 48*(2), 31–37.

Muther, C. (1987). What do we teach, and when do we teach it? *Educational Leadership, 45*(1), 77–80.

Novak, J. D. (1984). Application of advances in learning theory and philosophy of science to the improvement of chemistry teaching. *Journal of Chemistry Education, 61*(7), 607–612.

Novak, J. D. (1990). Concept maps and vee diagrams: Two metacognitive tools to facilitate meaningful learning. *Instructional Science, 19*(1), 29–52.

Novak, J. D. (1993). How do we learn our lesson? *The Science Teacher, 60*(3), 50–55.

Reed, S., & Sautter, R. C. (1990). Children of poverty: The status of 12 million young Americans. *Phi Delta Kappan, 71*(10), K1–K12.

Resnick, L. B., & Klopfer, L. E. (1989). *Toward the thinking curriculum: Current cognitive research. 1989 ASCD Yearbook.* Alexandria, VA: Association for Supervision and Curriculum Development.

Rosenshine, B. (1980). How time is spent in elementary classrooms. In C. Denham & A. Lieberman, *Time to learn.* Washington, DC: Department of Health, Education and Welfare, National Institute of Education.

Smith, W. S., & Burrichter, C. (1993). Look who's teaching science today!: Cross-age tutoring makes the grade. *Science and Children 30*(7), 20–23.

Souviney, R. J. (1994). *Learning to teach mathematics* (2nd ed.). New York: Merrill.

Tanner, J. M. (1962). *Growth at adolescence* (2nd ed.). London: University of London Press.

Valentine, J. W., et al. (1993). *Leadership in middle level education.* Reston, VA: National Association of Secondary School Principals.

Watson, B., & Konicek, R. (1990). Teaching for conceptual change: Confronting students' experience. *Phi Delta Kappan, 71*(9), 680–685.

Willis, S. (1993, September). Multicultural teaching strategies. *ASCD Curriculum Update.* Alexandria, VA: Association for Supervision and Curriculum Development.

Wolff-Michael, M., & Bowen, W. (1993). The unfolding vee. *Science Scope 16*(5), 28–32.

SUGGESTED READINGS

Allen-Sommerville, L. (1994). Middle level science in a multicultural society. *Science Scope, 17*(6), 16–18.

Anderson, O. R. (1992). Some interrelationships between constructivist models of learning and current neurobiological theory, with implications for science education. *Journal of Research in Science Education, 29*(10), 1037–1058.

Aron, B. H., et al. (1994). Atmospheric misconceptions. *The Science Teacher, 61*(1), 31–33.

Banks, C. B. (1991). Harmonizing student-teacher interactions: A case for learning styles. *Synthesis, 2*(2), 1–5.

Beeler, R. (1994). An inner-city science and cultural experience. *Science Scope, 17*(6), 20–24.

Beilin, H. (1992). Piaget's enduring contribution to developmental psychology. *Developmental Psychology, 28*(2), 191–204.

Bracey, G. W. (1991). Why can't they be like we were? *Phi Delta Kappan, 73*(2), 105–117.

Bruner, J. S. (1960). *The process of education.* Cambridge: Harvard University Press.

Bruner, J. S. (1966). *Toward a theory of instruction.* Cambridge, MA: Harvard University Press.

Bruner, J. S. (1990). *Acts of meaning.* Cambridge, MA: Harvard University Press.

Caine, R. N., & Caine, G. (1991). *Making connections: Teaching and the human brain.* Alexandria, VA: Association for Supervision and Curriculum Development.

Carns, A. W., & Carns, M. R. (1991). Teaching study skills, cognitive strategies, and metacognitive skills through self-diagnosed learning styles. *School Counselor, 38*(5), 341–346.

Clough, M. P., & Clark, R. (1994). Cookbooks and constructivism. *The Science Teacher 61*(2), 34–37.

Cooper, J. D. (1993). *Literacy: Helping children construct meaning* (2nd ed.). Burlington, MA: Houghton Mifflin.

Cronin, J. F. (1993). Four misconceptions about authentic learning. *Educational Leadership, 50*(7), 78–80.

Cuevas, G. J. (1991). Developing communication skills in mathematics for students with limited English proficiency. *Mathematics Teacher, 84*(3), 186–189.

Curry, L. A critique of the research on learning styles. *Educational Leadership, 48*(2), 50–56.

Darling-Hammond, L. (1993). Reframing the school reform agenda. *Phi Delta Kappan, 74*(10), 753–761.

Dreyfus, A., et al. (1990). Applying the "cognitive conflict" strategy for conceptual change—Some implications, difficulties, and problems. *Science Education, 74*(5), 555–569.

Ernest, P. (1993). Constructivism, the psychology of learning, and the nature of mathematics: Some critical issues. *Science and Education, 2*(1), 87–93.

Fourgurean, J. M., et al. (1990). The link between learning style and Jungian psychological type: A finding of two bipolar preference dimensions. *Journal of Experimental Education, 58*(3), 225–237.

Fowler, C. (1990). Recognizing the role of artistic intelligence. *Music Educators Journal, 77*(1), 24–27.

Gardner, H. (1982). *Art, mind and brain.* New York: Basic Books.

Gardner, H. (1985). *Frames of mind.* New York: Basic Books.

Gardner, H. (1991). *The unschooled mind: How students think and how schools should teach.* New York: Basic Books.

Gardner, H. (1993). *Creating minds.* New York: Basic Books.

Gardner, H., & Boix-Mansilla, V. (1994). Teaching for understanding—Within and across the disciplines. *Educational Leadership, 51*(5), 14–18.

Glasson, G. E., & Lalik, R. V. (1993). Reinterpreting the learning cycle from a social constructivist perspective: A qualitative study of teachers' beliefs and practices. *Journal of Research in Science Teaching, 30*(2), 187–207.

Grady, M. P. (1990). *Whole brain education.* Fastback 301. Bloomington, IN: Phi Delta Kappa Educational Foundation.

Hampton, E., & Gallegos, C. (1994). Science for all students. *Science Scope, 17*(6), 5–8.

Jaworski, B. (1992). Mathematics teaching: What is it? *For the Learning of Mathematics, 12*(1), 8–14.

Jenkins, J. M. (1991). Learning styles: Recognizing individuality. *Schools in the Middle, 1*(12), 3–6.

Jones, B. F., & Fennimore, T. (1990). *The new definition of learning.* Oakbrook, IL: North Central Regional Educational Laboratory.

Keefe, J. W. (1990). Learning style: Where are we going? *Momentum, 21*(1), 44–48.

Lockhead, J. (1992). Knocking down the building blocks of learning: Constructivism and the ventures program. *Educational Studies in Mathematics*, 23(5), 543–552.

Lombardi, T. P. (1992). *Learning strategies for problem learners.* Fastback 345. Bloomington, IN: Phi Delta Kappa Educational Foundation.

Martens, M. L. (1992). Inhibitors to implementing a problem-solving approach to teaching elementary science: Case study of a teacher in change. *School Science and Mathematics, 92*(3), 150–156.

Okebukola, P. A., & Olugbemiro, J. J. (1988). Cognitive preference and learning mode as determinants of meaningful learning through concept mapping. *Science Education, 72*(4), 489–500.

Perkins, D., & Blythe, T. (1994). Putting understanding up front. *Educational Leadership, 51*(5), 4–7.

Peterson, P. L., & Knapp, N. F. (1993). Inventing and reinventing ideas: Constructivist teaching and learning in mathematics. In G. Cawelti (Ed.), *Challenges and Achievement of American Education.* 1993 ASCD Yearbook. Alexandria, VA: Association for Supervision and Curriculum Development.

Phillips, D. R., et al. (1994). Beans, blocks, and buttons: Developing thinking. *Educational Leadership, 51*(5), 50–53.

Piaget, J. (1977). *The development of thought: Elaboration of cognitive structures.* New York: Viking.

Samples, B. (1992). Using learning modalities to celebrate intelligence. *Educational Leadership, 50*(2), 62–66.

Samples, B. (1994). Instructional diversity. *The Science Teacher 61*(2), 14–17.

Saunders, W. L. (1992a). The constructivist perspective: Implications and teaching strategies for science. *School Science and Mathematics, 92*(3), 136–141.

Saunders, W. L. (1992b). The constructivist perspective: Implications and teaching strategies for science. *School Science and Mathematics, 92*(3), 136–141.

Shaughnessy, M. F. (1990). Cognitive structures of the gifted: Theoretical perspectives, factor analysis, triarchic theories of intelligence, and insight issues. *Gifted Education International, 6*(3), 149–151.

Sigel, I. E., & Cocking, R. R. (1977). *Cognitive development from childhood to adolescence: A constructivist perspective.* New York: Holt, Rinehart and Winston.

Soled, S. W. (1994). What affects student performance? *The Science Teacher, 61*(1), 34–37.

Stepans, J., & Veath, M. L. (1994). How do students really explain changes in matter? *Science Scope 17*(8), 31–35.

Stevenson, C., & Carr,. J. F. (Eds.). (1993). *Integrated studies in the middle grades.* New York: Teachers College Press.

Sylwester, R. (December 1993/January 1994). What the biology of the brain tells us about learning. *Educational Leadership, 51*(4), 46–51.

Titus, T. G., et al. (1990). Adolescent learning styles. *Journal of Research and Development in Education, 23*(3), 165–171.

Vygotsky, L. (1926). *Thought and language.* Cambridge, MA: The M. I. T. Press.

Wang, M. C., Haertel, G. D., & Walberg, H. J. (December 1993/January 1994). What helps students learn? *Educational Leadership, 51*(4), 74–79.

Wertsch, J. (1985). *Vygotsky and the social formation of mind.* Cambridge, MA: Harvard University Press.

Woods, R. K. (1994). A close-up look at how children learn science. *Educational Leadership, 51*(5), 33–35.

Yager, R. (1991). The constructivist learning model: Toward real reform in science education. *The Science Teacher, 58*(6), 52–57.

Yager, R., et al. (1993). Applying science across the curriculum. *Educational Leadership, 50*(8), 79–80.

Yarusso, L. (1992). Constructivism vs. objectivism. *Performance and Instruction, 31*(4), 7–9.

CHAPTER 2

Planning and Implementing
a Supportive Environment
for Learning

No matter how well prepared your instructional plans (the topic of Chapter 4), those lessons will likely go untaught or only poorly taught if presented to children in a classroom that is nonsupportive and poorly managed. Thoughtful and thorough planning of your procedures for managing the classroom is as important a part of your preactive phase decision making as is the preparation of units and daily lessons, and that is the reason it is included here, preceding the chapter on instructional planning. And, as is true for unit and lesson planning, your management system should be planned and written by you long before you first meet your students. In this chapter you will learn how to do that. You will learn what is meant by a "supportive classroom environment," how to provide it, and how to effectively manage it for the most efficient instruction resulting in the best student achievement.

Specifically, this chapter is designed to help you understand:

1. The role of the teachers' and student's perceptions in effective teaching and successful learning.
2. How to provide a supportive environment for learning.
3. How to most effectively manage the classroom.
4. The importance of getting the school year off to a good start and how to do it.
5. How to establish classroom procedures and rules of acceptable behavior.
6. How to avoid mistakes commonly made by beginning teachers.
7. How to provide a safe learning environment.

A. PERCEPTIONS

Unless you believe that your students can learn, they will not. Unless you believe that you can teach them, you will not. Unless your students believe that they can learn and until they want to learn, they will not. We all know of teachers who get the very best from their students, even from those students that many teachers find the most difficult to teach. Regardless of individual circumstances and individual teaching styles, successful teachers (1) know that all students can learn; (2) expect the very best from each student; (3) establish a classroom climate that is conducive to student learning, that motivates students to do their very best; and (4) effectively manage their classrooms so class time is most efficiently used, with the least amount of disturbance to the learning process.

It has long been known that the effort a student is willing to spend on a learning task is a product of two factors: (1) the degree to which the student believes he or she can successfully complete the task and achieve the rewards of that completion, and (2) the degree of value the student places on that reward. This is sometimes referred to as the expectancy × value theory (Feather, 1982). For student learning to occur, both aspects must be present—that is, the student must see meaning or value in the experience and perceive that he or she can achieve the intended outcome of the experience. A student is less likely to try to learn when he or she perceives no meaning or value in the material or feels incapable of learning it. In other words, before students *do,* they must feel they *can do,* and they must perceive the importance of doing.

Therefore, regardless of how well planned you are for the instruction, the students must have certain perceptions to support the successful implementation of those plans:

- Students must feel that the classroom environment is supportive of their efforts.
- Students must feel welcome in your classroom.
- Students must perceive the expected learning as being challenging but not impossible.
- Students must perceive the expected learning outcomes as being worth the time and effort to achieve.

This chapter provides you with strategies for setting up and managing your classroom in a way that demonstrates to students that they can learn.

B. PROVIDING A SUPPORTIVE LEARNING ENVIRONMENT

It is probably no surprise to you that teachers whose classrooms are pleasant, positive, and stimulating places to be find that their students learn and behave better than do the children of teachers whose classroom atmospheres are harsh, negative, and unchallenging. What follows now are specific suggestions for making your classroom atmosphere a pleasant, positive, and stimulating place, that is, ways of providing a supportive environment for the development of meaningful understandings.

Get to Know Your Students

For classes to move forward smoothly and efficiently, they should fit the students' abilities, needs, interests, and goals. To make the children's learning most meaningful and longest lasting, you must build your instruction around their interests, perceptions, and perspectives. Therefore, you need to know your students well enough to be able to provide learning activities that they will find interesting, valuable, motivating, challenging, and rewarding. Here are a number of things you can do to get to know your students as people:

- *Classroom sharing during the first week of school.* During the first week of school, many teachers take time to have each student present information about himself or herself. For instance, each child answers questions such as: "What name would you like to be called by?" "Where did you attend school last year?" "Tell us about your hobbies and other interests." You might have children share information of this sort with each other in groups of three or four while you visit each group in turn. Yet another approach is to include everyone in a game, having children answer the question on paper and then, as you read their answers, asking them to guess which student wrote each.
- *Observations of children in the classroom.* During classroom learning activities the effective teacher is constantly alert to the individual behavior (nonverbal as well as verbal) of each child in the class, noting whether the student is on task or gazing off and perhaps thinking about other things. Be cautious, however; gazing out the window does not necessarily mean that the student is not thinking about the learning task. During small-group work is a particularly good time to observe students and get to know more about each one's skills and interests.
- *Observations of students outside the classroom.* Another way to learn more about children is to observe them outside class, for example, at lunchtime, during intramural activities, on the playground, and during other school functions.

- *Conversation with students.* To learn more about your students you can spend time casually talking with individual or small groups of students during lunchtime, on the playground, and during other out-of-class activities.

- *Conferences and interviews with students.* Conferences with students, and sometimes with their parents or guardians as well, afford yet another opportunity to show that you are genuinely interested in each child as a person as well as a student. Some teachers plan a series of conferences during the first few weeks in which they interview small groups of three or four students, talking with each. Such conferences and interviews are managed by the use of open-ended questions. The teacher indicates by the questions, and by nonjudgmental and empathic responses, a genuine interest in the students.

- *Student writing.* Much can be learned about students by what they write. It is important to encourage writing in your classroom, and you will want to read everything that students write for you and to ask for clarification when needed. Journals and portfolios, discussed in Chapters 4 and 8, are useful for this.

- *Open-ended questionnaires.* Many teachers of students in grade 4 and up use open-ended questionnaires to learn more about them. Being careful to avoid asking questions that might infringe upon a student's right to privacy, teachers ask students to write answers to questions such as:

  When at lunch with your friends, what do you usually talk about?

  When you read for fun or pleasure, what do you usually read?

  What are your favorite movies, videos, or TV shows?

  Who are your favorite music video performers?

  What do you like to do when you just hang around?

  With whom do you like to hang around, and where?

  What do you plan to do after you graduate from high school?

  Describe your favorite hobby or non-school-related activity.

- *Cumulative record.* Held in the school office is the cumulative record for each child, containing information recorded from year to year by teachers and other school professionals. Although you must use discretion before arriving at any conclusion about information in the file, the file may afford information for getting to know a particular student better.

- *Discussions with other professionals.* To better understand a child, it is often helpful to talk with that child's other teachers or counselor to learn of their perceptions and experiences with the student. One of the advantages of schools that are divided into "villages" (discussed in Chapter 3) is that teachers with a village get to know their students better, sometimes over a period of two or three years. Talking with other teachers of the village can be enlightening when you want to better know and understand a particular child.

Learning styles. A topic discussed in Chapter 1, learning style is included here as another important way of getting to know your students so that your instruction can be made most effective. Students who are exceptional and/or culturally different from you, in particular, may prefer to learn in ways that differ from your own preferred way of learning. As stated by Grant and Sleeter (1989), "Learning styles overlap somewhat with cultural background and gender. Although not all members of a cultural or gender group learn in the same way, patterns exist in how members of different groups tend to approach tasks. . . . [However,] rather than generalizing about your own students based on the research on group differences, it is much more useful to investigate directly your own students' learning style preferences" (pp. 12–13). For doing that, you can use the Learning Styles Record Sheet for recording five categories of data (see Figure 2.1).

After analyzing data collected on your students you may notice certain learning style patterns based on gender and ethnic background, but Grant and Sleeter emphasize that you should avoid stereotyping certain groups as learning a certain way. Instead, use the patterns you discover in your students' learning style preferences as guides for planning the lessons and selecting teaching strategies.

FIGURE 2.1

Learning Styles Record Sheet

SOURCE: Reprinted with the permission of Simon & Schuster, Inc. from the Macmillan College text TURNING ON LEARNING by Carl A. Grant and Christine E. Sleeter. Copyright ©1989 by Merrill, an imprint of Macmillan College Publishing Company, Inc.

Directions: For each student, record data you collect about the following items related to the student's preferred style of learning.

Student's name _____

		Method of Data Collection	Findings
1. Style of working:	Alone With others		
2. Learning modality:	Watching Reading Listening Discussing Touching Moving Writing		
3. Content:	People Things		
4. Need for structure:	High Low		
5. Details versus generalities			

Students' experiential background. Another way of getting to know your students is to spend time in the neighborhoods in which they live. Observe and listen, finding things that you can use as examples or as lessons to help teach concepts. Record your observations in a table (see Table 2.1).

C. CLASSROOM MANAGEMENT

Effective teaching requires a well-organized, businesslike classroom in which motivated students work diligently at their learning tasks, free from distractions and disruptions caused by inappropriate behavior. Providing such a setting for learning is called effective classroom management.

Essential for effective classroom management is the maintenance of classroom control, that is, the process of controlling student behavior in the classroom. Classroom control involves both steps for preventing inappropriate student behavior and ideas for responding to students whose behavior is inappropriate.

The control aspect of teaching is frequently the most worrisome to beginning teachers—and they have good cause to be concerned. Even experienced teachers sometimes find control difficult, particularly at the middle school and junior high school level, where students are going through rapid physiological changes, and where so many come to school with psychological baggage and have already been alienated by bad experiences in their lives.

Another part of effective classroom management is a good organization and administration of activities and materials. In a well-managed classroom students know what to do, have the materials necessary to do it well, and stay on task while doing it. The classroom atmosphere is supportive; the assignments and procedures for doing those assignments are clear; the materials of instruction are current, interesting, and readily available; and the classroom proceedings are businesslike. At all times, the teacher is in control, seeing that

TABLE 2.1
Sample Observation Table

Observations	Related Academic Concepts	Ideas for Using Observations
1.		
2.		
3.		
4.		
5.		
6.		
7.		

SOURCE: Reprinted with the permission of Simon & Schuster, Inc. from the Macmillan College text TURNING ON LEARNING by Carl A. Grant and Christine E. Sleeter. Copyright ©1989 by Merrill, an imprint of Macmillan College Publishing Company, Inc.

students are spending their time on appropriate tasks. For your teaching to be effective you must be skilled in managing the classroom.

Effective classroom management is the process of organizing and conducting a classroom so that it results in maximum student learning. To manage your classroom successfully, you need to plan your lessons thoughtfully and thoroughly; provide students with a pleasant, supportive atmosphere; instill a desire and the confidence to learn and to achieve; establish control procedures; prevent distractions and disturbances; deal quickly and quietly with distractions and disturbances that are unavoidable; and, in general, promote effective student learning. If this sounds like a tall order, don't fret: if you adhere to the guidelines set forth in this chapter, you will be successful.

What is a well-managed, effectively controlled classroom? A well-managed classroom is one where the teacher is clearly in charge and the students learn. Let's now look at how that is done.

D. PREPARATION PROVIDES CONFIDENCE AND SUCCESS

For successful classroom management, beginning the school year well may make all the difference in the world. Therefore, you should appear at your first class meeting, and every meeting thereafter, as well prepared and as confident as possible. Perhaps you will feel nervous and apprehensive, but being ready and well prepared will probably help you at least appear to be confident. Then, if you proceed in a businesslike, matter-of-fact way, the impetus of your well-prepared beginning will cause the day to proceed as desired.

E. CLASSROOM PROCEDURES AND RULES OF ACCEPTABLE BEHAVIOR

You undoubtedly have heard it before, and now you are going to hear it again: it is impossible to overemphasize the importance of getting the school year off to a good start, so let's begin this section by discussing how to do that.

FIGURE 2.2
Establishing Classroom Behavior Rules and Procedures

When establishing classroom behavior procedures and rules, remember this point: the learning time needs to run efficiently (with no "dead" spots), smoothly (with routine procedures and smooth transitions between activities) , and with minimum disruption. Try to state your expectations for student classroom behavior in a positive manner, emphasizing procedures and desired behaviors, stressing what students *should* do rather than what they should *not* do.

As you prepare your procedures and rules for classroom behavior, you need to consider what information students need to know from the start. This should then be reviewed and rehearsed with the students several times during the first week of school, then followed consistently throughout the school year. Things that students need to know from the start include:

- *How to obtain your attention and help.* Most middle school teachers who are effective classroom managers expect students to raise their hands until the teacher acknowledges (usually by a nod) that the student's hand has been seen. With that acknowledgment, the student should lower his or her hand. To prevent the student from becoming bored and restless while waiting, you should attend to the student as quickly as possible. Expecting students to raise their hands before speaking allows you to control the noise and confusion level and to be proactive in deciding who speaks. The latter is important if you are to manage a classroom with equality—that is, with equal attention to individuals regardless of their gender, ethnicity, proximity to the teacher, or any other personal characteristic.
- *How to enter and leave the classroom.* From the time that the class is scheduled to begin until it officially ends, teachers who are effective classroom managers expect students to be in their assigned seats or at their assigned learning stations and to be attentive to the teacher or to the learning activity.
- *How to maintain, obtain, and use materials for learning and items of personal use.* Students need to know where, when, and how to store, retrieve, and care for items such as their coats, backpacks, books, pencils, and medicines; how to get papers and materials, laboratory or shop items; and when they may use the pencil sharpener and wastebasket. Classroom control is easiest to maintain when (1) items that students need for class activities and for their personal use are neatly arranged in places that require minimum foot traffic, (2) there are established procedures that students clearly expect and understand, (3) there is the least amount of student off-task time, and (4) students do not have to line up for anything. Therefore, you will want to plan the room arrangement, equipment and materials storage, preparation of equipment, materials, and transitions between activities so as to avoid needless delays and confusion. At this age level in particular, problems in classroom control will most certainly occur whenever some or all students have nothing to do, even for a brief time.
- *When they can go to the drinking fountain and the bathroom.* Normally, at this age, students should be able to take care of these matters between classes; however, sometimes they do not or, for medical reasons, can not. Reinforce the notion that they should do those things before coming into your classroom, but be flexible enough for the occasional student who has an immediate need.
- *How to behave during a class interruption.* Unfortunately, class interruptions do occur, and in some schools they occur far too often. For an important reason, the principal or some other person from the school's office may need to interrupt the class to see the teacher or a student or to make an announcement to the entire class. Students need to know what behavior is expected of them during those interruptions.
- *What to do when they are late to your class or will be leaving early.* You need to understand and reinforce school policies on early dismissals and tardiness. Routinize your own procedures so students clearly understand what they are to do if they must leave your class early (say, for a medical appointment) or when they arrive late. The procedures should be such that late-arriving and early dismissal students do not have to disturb you or the lesson in process.
- *What the consequences are for inappropriate behavior.* Most teachers who are effective classroom managers routinize their procedures for handling inappropriate behavior, ensuring that the students understand its consequences. The consequences are posted in the classroom and, when not counter to school policy, may be similar to the following five-step model (see Baron, 1992; Blendinger et al., 1993):
  1. *First offense* results in a warning to the student.
  2. *Second offense* results in the student being given a 10-minute time out in an isolation area.
  3. *Third offense* results in a 15-minute time out (in isolation).
  4. *Fourth offense* results in a phone call to the student's parents or guardian.
  5. *Fifth offense* results in the student being sent to the vice-principal's or principal's office.
- *Rules for behavior and procedures to follow during emergency drills, real or practice.* Students need to know what to do, where to go, and how to behave in emergency conditions, such as might occur because of a fire, storm, earthquake, or because of a disruptive campus intruder.

Getting the School Year Off to a Good Beginning

Part of your preparation before the first day of school should be the determination of your classroom procedures and expectations for the behavior of the children while they are in your classroom. These procedures and rules must seem reasonable to your students, and in enforcing them you must be consistent. Sometimes procedures and rules can cause trouble, especially if there are too many. To avoid difficulty, it is best at first to present only the minimum number of procedures and rules necessary to get off to an orderly beginning. Too many procedures and rules at the beginning will only confuse students and make the classroom atmosphere seem repressive. By establishing, explaining, and sticking to only a few, you can leave yourself some room for judgments and maneuvering. The procedures and rules should be quite specific so that students know exactly what is expected and the consequences for breaking the rules and not following procedures. (To encourage a constructive and supportive classroom environment, when responding to inappropriate behavior, we encourage you and your students to practice thinking in terms of "consequences" rather than "punishment.")

Once you have decided on your initial procedures and rules, you are ready to explain them to your students and to begin rehearsing some of the procedures on the very first day of class. You will want to do this in a positive way (see Figure 2.2). Students work best when teacher expectations are clear to them and when procedures are clearly understood and have become routine.

F. FIFTY COMMON TEACHER MISTAKES THAT CAUSE STUDENT MISBEHAVIOR*

Oftentimes the inappropriate behavior of students is a direct result of something that the teacher did or did not do. Following are mistakes commonly made by beginning teachers. Read and understand the relevancy of each to your teaching.

1. *Lack of or inadequate long-range planning.* Long-range, detailed planning is important for reasons discussed in the next chapter. A beginning teacher who inadequately plans ahead is heading for trouble.
2. *Sketchy daily planning.* Sketchy, inadequate daily planning is a precursor to ineffective teaching, classroom management problems, and eventual teaching failure. Sometimes, after finding a few strategies that seem to work well for them, beginning teachers' lesson planning becomes increasingly sketchy, they fall into a rut of doing pretty much the same thing day after day (too much lecture and discussion, too many videos and worksheets), and they fail to consider and plan for individual student differences. By mid-semester, they have stopped growing professionally and are experiencing an increasing number of problems with students and with parents.
3. *Emphasizing the negative.* Too many verbal warnings to students for their inappropriate behavior and too little recognition for their positive behavior do not help to establish the positive climate needed for the most effective learning to take place. Reminding students of procedures is more positive, and less repressive, than is reprimanding them when they do not follow procedures.
4. *Letting students' hands be raised too long.* Allowing students to have their hands raised too long before recognizing them and attending to their questions or responses provides them with time to fool around. Although you don't have to call on students as soon as they raise a hand, you should acknowledge them quickly, such as with a nod or a wave of your hand, so they can lower their hand and return to their work. Then get to the student as quickly as possible. These procedures should be clearly understood by the students and consistently implemented by you.
5. *Spending too much time with one student or one group while failing to monitor the entire class.* Spending too much time with any one student or a small group of students

---

*Adapted from J. F. Callahan, L. H. Clark, and R. D. Kellough, *Teaching in the Middle and Secondary Schools*, 5th ed. (Englewood Cliffs, NJ: Prentice-Hall, 1995), p. 237–241. Copyright 1994 by Richard D. Kellough.

is, in effect, ignoring the rest of the class. For the best classroom management, you must continually monitor the entire classroom of students. How much time is too much? As a general rule, more than 30 seconds with any one student or small group is probably approaching too much time.

6. *Beginning a new activity before gaining student attention.* A teacher who fails to consistently insist that students follow procedures and who does not wait until all students are in compliance before starting a new activity is destined for major problems in classroom control. You must establish and maintain classroom procedures. Starting an activity before all students are in compliance is, in effect, telling the students that it is not necessary for them to follow expected procedures. You cannot afford to tell students one thing and then do another. That is poor modeling behavior. Remember, what you do has greater impact on student behavior than what you say (Williams, 1993).

7. *Too-fast pacing.* Students need time to mentally engage and understand words a teacher uses. They need time to mentally and physically disengage from one activity and engage in the next. You must remember that this always will take more time for a classroom of 30 students than it does for just one person.

8. *Voice level that is always either too loud or too soft.* A teacher's voice that is too loud day after day can become irritating to some students, as can one that cannot be heard or understood. Students will tune out a teacher they cannot understand or whose voice is too soft or too loud.

9. *Assigning a journal entry without first giving the topic careful thought.* Many teachers often begin each class meeting by assigning students the task of writing an entry in their journals. If the question or topic students are supposed to write about is ambiguous and was hurriedly prepared, without thought to how students would interpret and respond to it, students will perceive it as busywork (for example, something to do while the teacher takes attendance) and not important. Then, if they do it at all, it will be only with a great deal of disruptive commotion and much less enthusiasm than if they were writing on a topic that had meaning for them.

10. *Standing too long in one place.* When in the classroom, you must be mobile, as often said by experienced teachers, "to work the crowd."

11. *Sitting while teaching.* There is rarely time to sit while teaching. You cannot monitor the class while seated, nor can you afford to appear casual and uninterested in what students are doing.

12. *Being too serious, no fun.* No one would argue with the statement that good teaching is serious business. Students respond best, however, to teachers who obviously enjoy and have fun working with them and helping them learn.

13. *Using the same teaching strategy or combination of strategies day after day (being in a rut).* After a while, such a teacher's classroom becomes boring to students. Because of their differences, students respond best to a variety of well-planned and meaningful classroom activities.

14. *Inadequate use of silence (wait time) after asking a subject content question.* When expected to think deeply about a question, students need time to do it. (This is discussed further in Chapter 4.)

15. *Poor or inefficient use of the overhead projector and the writing board.* A poorly prepared transparency and the ineffective use of the overhead projector and writing board say to students that you are not a competent teacher. Like a competent surgeon or automobile mechanic, a competent teacher selects and effectively uses the best professional tools available for the jobs to be done.

16. *Ineffective use of facial expressions and body language.* Your gestures and body language say more to students than do your words. For example, a teacher didn't understand why his class of seventh-grade math students would not respond to his repeated expression, "I need your attention." In one instance he used that verbal expression eight times in less than 15 minutes. Viewing his teaching that day on video helped him to understand the problem. He had been dressing very casually and standing most of the time with one hand in his pocket. At five foot eight, with a slight build and rather deadpan facial expression and nonexpressive voice, he did not have a commanding presence in the classroom. He returned to his classroom wearing a tie and using his hands, face,

and voice more expressively. Rather than saying, "I need your attention," he waited in silence for the students to become attentive. It worked.

17. *Too much reliance on teacher talk for instruction and for classroom control.* Beginning teachers have a tendency to rely too much on teacher talk. Too much teacher talk is deadly. Unable to discern between the important and the unimportant verbiage, students will quickly tune the teacher out. In addition, useless verbalism, such as global praise and verbal fill-ins like "okay," causes students to pay less attention when the teacher has something to say that is truly important.

18. *Inefficient use of teacher time.* Think carefully about what you are going to be doing every minute, planning for the most efficient and therefore effective use of your time in the classroom. Consider the following example. During a lesson, Angelica, a middle school teacher, is recording student contributions on a large sheet of butcher paper taped to the writing board. The tasks of soliciting student responses, acknowledging those responses, holding and manipulating a writing pen, and writing on the paper require decisions and actions that consume valuable time and can distract Angelica from her students. An effective alternative is to have a reliable student helper do the writing while Angelica handles the solicitation and acknowledgment of student responses. That way Angelica has fewer decisions and fewer actions to distract her and maintains eye contact and proximity with the children in the classroom.

19. *Talking to and interacting with only a portion of students.* When leading a class discussion, too many beginning teachers favor (by their eye contact, proximity, and verbal interaction) only 40 to 65 percent of the students, sometimes completely ignoring the others for an entire class period. Feeling ignored, those students will, in time, become disinterested and unruly. Remember to spread your interactions and to try to establish eye contact with every student at least once each minute.

20. *Not requiring students to raise their hands and to be acknowledged before responding.* You cannot be proactive and in control of your interactions with students if you allow them to shout out responses and questions whenever they feel like it. In addition, fueling their natural impulsivity is not helping them to mature intellectually.

21. *Collecting and returning homework papers before assigning students something to do.* Students will become restless and inattentive if they have nothing to do while waiting to turn in or receive papers. It is best to avoid any kind of "dead" time—time where students have nothing to do.

22. *Verbally or nonverbally interrupting students once they are on task.* Avoid doing or saying anything once students are working on a learning task or taking a test. If there is an important point you must make, write it on the board. If you want to return some papers while they are working, do it in a way and at a time when they are least likely to be distracted from their learning task.

23. *Using "Shh—" to obtain student attention or to quiet them.* When doing this, you will sound like a balloon with a slow leak. "Shh—" and the overuse of verbal fill-ins such as "okay" should be eliminated from a teacher's professional vocabulary.

24. *Overuse of verbal efforts to halt inappropriate student behavior.* Beginning teachers seem to have a tendency to rely too much on verbal interaction and not enough on nonverbal intervention techniques. To verbally reprimand a student for interrupting class activities is a use and therefore a reinforcement of that very behavior you are trying to discourage. Instead, develop indirect, silent intervention techniques.

25. *Poor body positioning in the classroom.* Always position your body so you can visually monitor the entire class.

26. *Settling for less when you should be trying for more; not getting the most from student responses to content discussion.* Don't hurry a discussion; squeeze student responses for all you can, especially when discussing a topic they are obviously interested in. Ask students for clarification or reasons for a response, ask for verification or data, have another student paraphrase what one student said, and pump students for deeper thought and meaning. Too often, a teacher will ask a question, get an abbreviated (often one-word) response from a student, and then move on to new content. Instead, follow a student response to your question with a sequence of questions to prompt and try to push student thinking to higher levels.

27. *Using threats.* One middle school teacher told her class of students that if they continued their inappropriate and disruptive talking, they would lose their break time. Have that consequence as part of the understood procedures, then don't threaten to take away their break time, do it. Follow through with procedures, but avoid threats of any kind. (It is useful, however, to remind students of procedures. Reminding students of procedures is different and more positive than is threatening them with punishment.) In addition, be very cautious about punishing the entire class for the misbehavior of only some students. Although we understand the rationale behind this tactic—to get group pressure working for you—oftentimes it backfires, and students who have been behaving well become alienated from the teacher because they feel they have been punished unfairly for the misbehavior of others. Those students (and their parents) expect the teacher to be able to handle the misbehaving students without punishing those whose behavior is appropriate; they are right.

28. *Global praise.* "Your rough drafts were really wonderful" says nothing and is simply another instance of useless verbalism. Instead, be specific, explaining what it was about their drafts that made them so wonderful.

29. *Using color but without meaning.* Use of color, such as colored pens for overhead transparencies or colored chalk for chalkboard writing, is nice but will lose its effectiveness in a very short time unless the colors have meaning. Color code everything in the classroom so students understand the meaning of the colors and their learning is facilitated.

30. *Verbally reprimanding a student from the opposite side of the classroom.* This is needless distraction of all students, plus, because of peer pressure, it simply perpetuates the "you versus them" syndrome. Reprimand when necessary, but do it quietly and privately.

31. *Interacting with only a "chosen few," rather than spreading the interactions among all students.* It is easy to fall into the habit of interacting with only a few students, especially those who are vocal and have "intelligent" contributions. However, your job is to teach all students, and to do that you must be proactive in your interactions, not reactive.

32. *Being too slow to intervene during inappropriate student behavior.* Unless you nip it in the bud, inappropriate student behavior usually gets worse, not better. It won't go away by itself. It's best to stop it quickly and resolutely. A teacher who ignores inappropriate behavior is, in effect, approving it. That approval reinforces its continuation.

33. *Not learning and using student names.* A teacher who does not know or use student names when addressing students is seen by the students as impersonal and uncaring. You will want to quickly learn student names and then use them when calling on students.

34. *Reading student papers only for correct answers and not for process and student thinking.* Reading student papers only for "correct" responses reinforces the misconception that the process of arriving at answers or solutions (thinking) and alternative solutions or answers are unimportant.

35. *Not putting time plans on the board.* Rather than yelling out how much time is left for an activity, such as a quiz or a writing or cooperative learning activity (and thereby interrupting student thinking), before the activity begins you should write on the board how much time is allowed for it. Write the time the activity is to end. If during the activity a decision is made to change that, then write the changed time on the board. Avoid distracting students once they are on task.

36. *Asking global questions that nobody will likely answer or rhetorical questions for which you do not expect a response.* Example: "Does everyone understand how that was done?" or "Are there any questions?" or "How do you all feel about . . . " If you want to check for student understanding or opinions, do a spot check by asking specific questions, allowing some time to think, then calling on students. With children of this age, it is advisable to avoid rhetorical questions. Otherwise students will not be able to tell when you expect them to think and respond.

37. *Failure to do frequent comprehension checks to see if students are understanding.* Too often, teachers simply plow through their lesson without checking for student comprehension, assuming that students are understanding everything. As a general rule, dur-

ing direct instruction, do a comprehension check about once every ten minutes. Comprehension checks may be verbal, as when you ask a question, or nonverbal, as when you observe student body language and facial expressions.

38. *Use of poorly worded, ambiguous questions.* Plan your questions, write them out, answer them yourself, and try to predict whether students will understand and how they will respond to a particular question.

39. *Failure to balance interactions with students according to student gender.* Many teachers (experienced as well as beginning and female as well as male) interact more often with male than with female students. Avoid that inequity.

40. *Trying to talk over student noise.* This simply tells students that their being noisy while you are talking is okay. All that you will accomplish when trying to talk over a high student noise level is a sore throat by the end of the school day, and you will be reinforcing the unwanted behavior.

41. *Wanting to be liked by the students.* Of course, every teacher wants to be liked by the children, but for now don't worry about their liking you. Just teach. Respect will be earned as a result of your good teaching and your caring about the learning of the children. Their like for you will develop over time. Otherwise, in the beginning they may "like" you, but they will lose respect (and affection) for you later.

42. *Failure to keep students attentive to an educationally useful video or movie.* This usually happens because the teacher failed to give the students a written handout about what they are to learn from watching the audiovisual. Sometimes students need an additional focus. Furthermore, an audiovisual is exactly that—audio and visual. To reinforce the learning, add a kinesthetic aspect—in this instance, the writing. This helps to organize student learning and encourages the hands-on and minds-on learning that you want.

43. *False or stutter-start instruction.* A false or stutter start is when the teacher begins an activity, is distracted, begins again, is again distracted, tries again to start, and so on. During stutter starts, students become increasingly restless and inattentive, making the final start almost impossible for the teacher to achieve. Avoid false starts. Begin each activity clearly and decisively.

44. *Failure to give students a pleasant greeting on Monday or following a holiday or to remind them to have a pleasant weekend or holiday.* Students are likely to perceive such a teacher as uncaring or impersonal.

45. *Sounding egocentric.* Whether you are or are not egocentric, you want to avoid sounding egocentric. Sometimes egocentrism is subtle, such as when a teacher says, "What *I* am going to do now is . . . " rather than, "What *we* are going to do now is . . . " If you want to strive for group cohesiveness, that is, a sense of we-ness, then teach not as if you are the leader and your students are the followers, but rather in a manner that empowers your students in their learning.

46. *Taking too much time to give verbal directions for a new activity.* Students get impatient and restless during long verbal instructions from the teacher. It is better to give brief instructions (no more than 60 seconds should do it) and get your students started on the task. For more complicated activities, you can teach three or four students the instructions and then have them lead "workshops" with five or six students in each workshop group, thereby freeing you to monitor the progress of each group.

47. *Taking too much time for an activity.* Whether lecturing or doing group work, think carefully about how much time students can effectively pay attention. A general rule of thumb is that for most intermediate and middle school classes, when only one or two learning modalities (for example, auditory and visual) are involved, the activity should not extend beyond about 15 minutes; when more than two senses are involved (if tactile and/or kinesthetic are added), then the activity might extend for 20 or 30 minutes.

48. *Being uptight and anxious.* Consciously or subconsciously, children are quick at detecting a teacher who is uptight and anxious, and for that teacher, events in the classroom will probably not go well. It's like a highly contagious disease. If you are uptight and anxious, your students will sense it and become the same. To prevent being uptight and anxious to the extent that it is a hindrance to good teaching and student learning, you must prepare lessons carefully, thoughtfully, and thoroughly, and then focus on

their implementation. Unless there is something personal going on in your life making you anxious and uptight, you are more likely to be in control and confident in the classroom when you have lessons that are well prepared. If you have a personal problem, you will need to concentrate on ensuring that your anger, hostility, fear, or other negative emotions do not negatively affect your teaching and your interactions with the children. Regardless of what is going on in your personal life, your students will face you each day expecting to be taught.

49. *Resorting too quickly to punishment for classroom misbehavior.* Too many beginning teachers mistakenly either try to ignore inappropriate student behavior or skip steps, resorting too quickly to such punishment as taking away PATs (preferred activity time) or break time or assigning detention. In-between steps include the use of alternative activities in the classroom. Too many teachers unrealistically expect to successfully have all 30 students doing the same thing at the same time rather than having several alternative activities simultaneously occurring in the classroom (multilevel teaching). For example, a student who is being disruptive during a class discussion (perhaps the student is an immature kinesthetic learner) might behave better when given the choice of moving to a quiet reading center in the classroom or to a learning activity center to work alone or with one other student. If, after trying an alternate activity, a student continues to be disruptive, then you may have to try another alternate activity or send the student to another supervised out-of-the-classroom location arranged by you prior to the incident until you have time (after class or after school) to talk with the student about the problem.

50. *Use of negative language.* Too many beginning teachers try to control their students with negative language, such as "There should be *no* talking" or "*No* gum or candy in class or else you will get detention" (double mistake—negative language and threat) or "*No* getting out of your seats without my permission." Negative language is repressive and does not help instill a positive classroom environment. Students need to know what is expected of them, to understand classroom procedures. Therefore, to encourage a positive classroom atmosphere you should use concise, positive language reminding students exactly what they are expected to do rather than what they are not to do.

G. PRACTICING SAFETY IN THE CLASSROOM

While all teachers must be constantly alert to potential safety hazards for their students while in the classroom and on school-sponsored excursions outside the classroom, this can be even more important when children are doing science-related activities. An unavoidable result of increased student involvement in active learning is the increased risk of injury due to the exposure to potentially harmful apparatus and materials. This fact should not deter you, however, from planning and implementing the most meaningful lessons for your children, including lessons that involve the students in meaningful science investigations. Just be as aware as possible of potential hazardous situations, and then prepare yourself, your classroom, and your students well to prevent accidents from happening and to handle an emergency situation.

"Safety First" should be the dictum for all learning activities. Many teachers have developed and use special lessons on safety instructions in the classroom. Regardless of whether you use such a special lesson, you should remind students of the rules and procedures before beginning any lesson with a potential safety hazard.

Guidelines for Classroom Safety

Although your school district or state department of education may be able to provide specific guidelines on safety in your school, and professional journals such as *Science Scope* and *Science and Children* frequently have articles dealing with safety in the classroom, here are general guidelines for your consideration. (Additional guidelines for science safety are in Chapter 16.)

1. Post safety rules and classroom procedures in the classroom. Be sure you model them yourself at all times. Review and rehearse the rules and procedures with students until they become routine.

2. Animal pets should not be handled by students. It is probably best they not even be brought into the classroom.

3. Avoid using flammable materials and alcohol burners. Rather than alcohol burners, use lighted candles or hot plates, and do so with caution.

4. Be alert to any child who has the potential for an allergic reaction to plants, animal fur, dust, and so on.

5. Students should wear laboratory safety goggles when appropriate and should not wear contact lenses when working with chemicals.

6. Periodically inspect all electrical equipment for frayed cords. If frayed, do not use them.

7. Because of potential diseases, dead animals and decaying plant material should never be handled by children nor brought to the classroom.

8. For absolutely no reason should blood or any other body fluid be extracted from students in the classroom.

9. No child should ever be left unattended or unsupervised in the classroom or while on an outing. Every child should be within sight of the teacher or another supervising adult. All activities must be carefully monitored by the teacher or other supervising adult. Students must be prohibited from doing any unauthorized activity.

10. Every classroom should be equipped with a fully charged ABC-type fire extinguisher, and you must know how to use it.

11. If your classroom is equipped with natural gas, the master control for the gas outlets should be kept turned off.

12. Heavy or otherwise dangerous items (such as glass items) should never be stored above the heads of students.

13. Maintain a neat and orderly classroom, with aisles kept clear and books, backpacks, and other personal belongings kept in designated storage areas.

14. Maintain accurate labels on all drawers, cupboards, and containers.

15. Never allow students to climb or to be in potentially dangerous body positions.

16. Avoid using extension cords; never overload an electrical circuit.

17. Plants, animals, chemicals, and apparatus that are poisonous or otherwise dangerous should never be allowed in the classroom for any reason, even if brought and intended to be used for a demonstration by the teacher or a guest speaker.

18. Sharp objects and items that could shatter when broken should not be in the classroom without teacher approval and proper supervision.

19. Students should never be permitted to taste unknown substances.

20. Students should not be permitted to overheat or to overexert themselves in the name of scientific or mathematics experimentation.

21. You and your students should know what to do in case of emergencies. Emergency procedures should be posted conspicuously in the classroom.

22. Use caution whenever using mechanical equipment with moving parts.

23. When working with molds, mushrooms, or bacteria, students should be provided with face masks and disposable gloves.

24. Before taking students on a field trip, solicit reliable adult help, even if only going a short distance from the school. A reasonable ratio—a rule in many schools—is one adult for every ten children.

25. Use proper methods for the disposal of waste materials. Contact your school district to learn the local regulations for the disposal of various kinds of waste.

26. A useful rule of thumb is that if you have doubts about the appropriateness of an activity for a particular group of children, then it probably is not appropriate. In any case, when in doubt discuss it with other teachers and the school principal or the principal's designee.

SUMMARY

Students are more likely to learn when they feel that the learning is important, interesting, and worth the time. In this chapter we described factors important for learning to occur. As significant as specific attempts to motivate your students is how you manage your classroom, strategies that you select, and how those strategies are implemented.

As a classroom teacher you should not be expected to solve all the societal woes that can spill over into the classroom. But, on the other hand, as a professional you have certain responsibilities, including to thoughtfully and thoroughly prepare for your classes; to professionally manage and control your classes; to maintain a safe learning environment; and to be able to diagnose and remedy those learning difficulties, disturbances, and minor misbehaviors that are the norm for classrooms and for the age group with which you are working. If you follow the guidelines that are provided in this book, you will be well on your way to developing a teaching style and management system that, for the most part, should allow your teaching to run smoothly and effectively, without serious problems.

It is important to select the most appropriate strategies to accompany your teaching plans and complement your management system. Chapters that follow present guidelines for doing that.

QUESTIONS AND ACTIVITIES FOR DISCUSSION

1. Identify at least four guidelines for your use of praise for a student's appropriate behavior.

2. Explain why it is important to prevent behavior problems before they occur. Describe at least five preventive steps you will take to reduce the number of management problems that you will have.

3. Too many teachers attempt to resolve problems with individual students within the regular class period. Describe two recommendations for what you can do if you have a problem with the classroom behavior of a specific student.

4. Explain the rationale for the phrase, "Catch them being good."

5. Explain why many learning psychologists (e.g., Montessori and Piaget) oppose the teacher's use of extrinsic reinforcement for managing student behavior.

6. Explain how and why your classroom management procedures and expectations might differ depending upon the nature of the students, the grade level you are teaching, and the activities in your classroom.

7. Explain why supervisors of student teachers may expect student teachers to prepare written classroom management plans.

8. Explain the difference between reprimanding a student for his or her inappropriate classroom behavior and reminding that student of classroom procedures.

9. Explain why interrupting the discussion of a topic of study to verbally reprimand a student for his or her inappropriate behavior is inappropriate teacher behavior.

10. It has been said that 90 percent of control problems in the intermediate or middle school classroom are teacher caused. Do you agree or disagree? Why or why not?

11. Some supervisors of student teachers prefer that the student teacher never conduct a class while seated. Is it ever appropriate for a teacher to sit down while teaching? Can a teacher effectively monitor a classroom while seated?

12. In groups of four, outline a safety program that you would institute if you were members of a teaching team in a middle-level school. Ask a science chairperson or team leader in a local middle-level school to critique the program. Share the results with others in groups in your class.

13. Select a recent journal article for teachers about safety in the classroom, and after critically reviewing the article, share your review with your classmates. For example, several articles are in the November/December 1989 theme issue of *Science Scope, 13*(3).

14. From your current observations and fieldwork related to this teacher preparation program, clearly identify one specific example of educational practice that seems contradictory to exemplary practice or theory as presented in this chapter. Present your explanation for the discrepancy.

15. Describe any prior concepts you held that changed as a result of your experiences with this chapter. Describe the changes.

REFERENCES

Baron, E. B. (1992). *Discipline strategies for teachers.* Fastback 344. Bloomington, IN: Phi Delta Kappa Educational Foundation.

Blendinger, J., et al. (1993). *Win-win discipline.* Fastback 353. Bloomington, IN: Phi Delta Kappa Educational Foundation.

Feather, N. T. (Ed.). (1982). *Expectations and actions.* Hillsdale, NJ: Erlbaum.

Grant, C. A., & Sleeter, C. E. (1989). *Turning on Learning.* New York: Merrill.

Williams, M. M. (1993). Actions speak louder than words: What students think. *Educational Leadership, 51* (3), 22–23.

SUGGESTED READINGS

Black, S. (1992). In praise of judicious praise. *Executive Editor, 14*(10), 24–27.

Chance, P. (1992). The rewards of learning. *Phi Delta Kappan, 74*(3), 200–207.

Chance, P. (1993). Sticking up for rewards. *Phi Delta Kappan, 74*(10), 787–790.

Collette, A. T., & Chiappetta, E. L. (1994). *Science instruction in the middle and secondary schools* (3rd ed.). Chapter 9. New York: Merrill.

Froyen, L. A. (1993). *Classroom management: The reflective teacher-leader* (2nd ed.). New York: Macmillan.

Hunter, M. (1994). *Enhancing teaching.* New York: Macmillan.

Jones, F. (1987). *Positive classroom discipline.* New York: McGraw-Hill.

Kounin, J. (1977). *Discipline and group management in classrooms.* New York: Holt, Rinehart and Winston.

Merrett, R., & Wheldall, K. (1992). Teachers' use of praise and reprimands to boys and girls. *Educational Review, 44*(1), 73–79.

O'Brien, S. J. (1990). For parents particularly: Praising children—Five myths. *Childhood Education, 66*(4), 248–249.

Phillips, D. R., et al. (1994). Beans, blocks, and buttons: Developing thinking. *Educational Leadership, 51*(5), 50–53.

Sanders, P. (1991). Helpful hints for teaching mathematics for children. *Rural Educator, 13*(1), 13–15.

Soled, S. W. (1994). What affects student performance? Creating an atmosphere for achievement. *The Science Teacher, 61*(1), 34–37.

Tauber, R. T. (1990). Criticism and deception: The pitfalls of praise. *NASSP Bulletin, 74*(528), 95–99.

Thomas, J. (1991). You're the greatest! *Principal, 71*(1), 32–33.

Tingley, S. (1992). Negative rewards. *Educational Leadership, 50*(1), 80.

Wiske, M. S. (1994). How teaching for understanding changes the rules in the classroom. *Educational Leadership, 51*(5), 19–21.

Woods, R. K. (1994). A close-up look at how children learn science. *Educational Leadership, 51*(5), 33–35.

CHAPTER 3

Planning the Curriculum

For teachers of grades 4–9, the curriculum can present a unique challenge. Unlike the curriculum in lower grades, which is usually developed for a single-grade-level teacher in a self-contained classroom, and unlike the high school curricula developed for teachers of various subjects in departmentalized classrooms, the curricula of many middle schools are developed by a common group of teachers. They collectively plan special programs for specific cohorts of children.

The backbone of an effective instructional program is the curriculum. To learn how it is developed, you must first understand how the middle school is organized—that is, how teachers are assigned to subject matter and how students are grouped for instruction.

Planning for instruction is a very large and important part of a classroom teacher's job. Responsible for planning at three levels, you will participate in long-range planning (the planning of courses for a semester or academic year and planning of units of instruction) and short-range planning (the preparation of daily lessons). Throughout your career you will be engaged almost continually in planning at each of these three levels; planning for instruction is a steady and cyclic process that involves the preactive and reflective thought-processing phases discussed in Chapter 1. The importance of mastering the process at the very beginning of your career cannot be overemphasized.

Long-range curriculum planning for grades 4–9 is the focus of this chapter. The chapter that follows prepares you for daily planning. Additional mathematics- and science-specific discussions of curriculum are presented in Chapters 7 and 13, respectively.

Specifically, this chapter is designed to help you understand:

1. How middle schools are organized for curriculum development.
2. The components of the middle school curriculum.
3. A model for curriculum development specific to middle school education.
4. The nature and role of core curriculum.
5. The nature and role of exploratory programs.
6. The nature and role of co-curricular activities.
7. The meaning of *thematic*.
8. The meaning of *teaching unit*.
9. Procedures for preparing any type of instructional unit.
10. Procedures for developing an interdisciplinary thematic unit.

Let us begin by clarifying a few terms. A *course* is sequence of instruction that presents to students a major division of subject matter or a discipline or integrates a couple of disciplines, such as language arts and literature, language arts and social studies, or science and mathematics. Courses are laid out for a year, a semester, a quarter, or even a few weeks, as is the case with the minicourses common to the exploratory programs found in some middle schools. A course is broken up into teaching units. A *teaching* (or *instructional*) *unit* is a major subdivision of a course, comprising a series of lessons of planned instruction about some central theme, topic, issue, or problem for a period of several days to several weeks. (In contrast, a *resource unit* is a general plan for a unit or a particular topic, and is designed to be used as a basis for building a teaching unit. Resource units, often found in curriculum centers and curriculum libraries, although often rich in resources, are not comprised of sequentially planned lessons, as are teaching units.) Unless they are interdisciplinary thematic units, teaching units that take much longer than three weeks tend to lose their effectiveness as recognizable units of instruction. Units are divided into lessons. A *lesson* is a subdivision of a unit, usually taught in a single class period or, on occasion, over two or three successive periods.

A. CURRICULUM DEVELOPMENT AND IMPLEMENTATION

Grade-span configurations at the school where you will be teaching might be K–8, 5–8, 6–8, 7 and 8, 7–9, 7–12, or some other. For middle-level education, the trend is toward a 5–8 grade-level configuration, with a continuing decline in the traditional 7–9 junior high grade configuration (used with permission from Valentine et al., 1993, p. 19). Regardless of the grade-span configuration you encounter, the middle school grades are usually organized into some type of scheduling (block, modular, or flexible) that is an alternative to the traditional method of assigning students to six or seven different classes for 45 to 50 minutes each, five days a week, for the entire school year (p. 62).

Interdisciplinary Teaching and Teaching Teams

Middle-grades teachers are members of a professional team, especially those teachers of grades 5–8. Usually, two to five teachers from different subject areas work together to plan the curriculum for a common group of students each has in a classroom. Commonly, these teaching teams are made up of one teacher each from English/language arts, mathematics, science, and history/social studies. These four subject areas comprise what is called the *core curriculum*. In addition, specialty teachers may be part of the teaching team. These may include teachers of physical education, art, and music, as well as learning disabilities and at-risk specialty personnel. Because a growing number of students in grades 4–9 are identified as being at risk of not completing school, some teams may ask a school counselor or a community resource person to be a member. Because the core and specialty subjects cross different disciplines of study, these teams are commonly called *interdisciplinary teaching teams* or simply interdisciplinary teams. Valentine has identified the following advantages of interdisciplinary teaming:

1. Teachers experience real collaboration within the workplace and become more satisfied professionally.
2. Students feel less isolation and, therefore, more social bonding with peers and individual teachers.
3. Teachers and students develop a strong sense of community and share a common rationale and mission for education.
4. The instructional program becomes highly coordinated across content areas in a way that encourages student creativity and critical thinking.

Many at-risk youth disengage from school during the middle grade years before physically dropping out sometime during their high school years. A Massachusetts Advocacy Center study (1986) found that as many as 50 percent of Boston's school dropouts left after grade eight, and almost 17 percent of middle school students were not promoted. These numbers become staggering when added to the number of students who drop out during high school but mentally disengage during the middle grade years, deciding not to try any more. (Other terms used for students who have mentally disengaged but who still attend school are *on-campus dropouts, disconnected youth,* and *students at risk.*)

In California, the State Department of Education (1986) has recommended that an increased emphasis be placed on dropout prevention at the middle and junior high school levels. Making learning more meaningful for these students at school, at home, and in life is an imperative responsibility of middle grades teachers who, for many students, are the last hope.

One method shown to be successful in making the learning meaningful for students is the use of *interdisciplinary thematic units (ITU).* Although the specifics of this approach will be presented later (and a complete ITU is presented in Chapter 18), for now, understand that the purpose of the thematic unit approach is to integrate the content of various subject areas by finding a common thread or theme, thereby connecting the students' learning. Students need to know that the information being learned will be practical not only in school, but in the workplace and throughout life. The essence of today's middle school concept is based on connecting *life with learning* through interdisciplinary thematic units. As explained at the opening of this part, integrated instruction, the theme of this book, is one step in that direction.

School-within-a-School

An interdisciplinary team can be thought of as a "house" or "school-within-a-school" (also called "village" or "pod"), in which each team of teachers is assigned each day to the same group of about 125 students for a common block of time. Within this block of time, teachers on the team are responsible for the many professional decisions necessary, such as how to make school meaningful to students' lives, what specific responsibilities each teacher has to fulfill each day, which guidance activities are to be implemented, what sort of special attention is needed by individual students, and how students will be grouped for instruction.

The school-within-a-school concept (used not only in many middle schools but also in some elementary schools, junior high schools, and high schools) helps students make important and meaningful connections among disciplines and provides them with peer and adult group identification that offers a significant sense of belonging. Classes for a village's teachers and students are often clustered in rooms that are close to one another, thereby increasing teacher-teacher and student-teacher communication. "Proximity of team members' classrooms can facilitate coordination of instruction, allow more flexibility in scheduling, and promote collaboration between colleagues. Classrooms scattered about the school are less likely to facilitate a cohesive learning environment" (Valentine, p. 53).

Common Planning Time and Lead Teachers

For an interdisciplinary team to plan a common curriculum, members must meet frequently. This is best accomplished by scheduling a shared preparation period to plan the curriculum and to discuss the progress and needs of individual students. Experts agree that having a common planning time is critical to the success of interdisciplinary teaming.

Each teaching team assigns a member to be a lead teacher or teacher leader. The lead teacher organizes the planning meetings, facilitates discussions during these sessions, and acts as a liaison to other school groups and to administrators to make sure the team has the necessary resources to put its plans into action. Being a lead teacher may be a responsibility rotated among team members throughout the school year, or lead teachers may be appointed by the administration or selected by team members.

Block Scheduling

To accommodate common planning time for teachers and to allow for more instructional flexibility, most middle schools use some form of block scheduling to assign students to teachers for instruction. Blocks of time ranging from 70 to 90 minutes replace the traditional class length of 45 to 60 minutes. The sample block schedule in Figure 3.1 illustrates the assignment of teachers to different classes. The sample student schedule in Figure 3.2 shows how a seventh grader might be assigned to different classes on different days.

FIGURE 3.1
Block Schedule
SOURCE: Reprinted with the permission of Macmillan Publishing Company from Richard D. Kellough, Noreen C. Kellough, and David L. Hough, *Middle School Teaching: Methods and Resources*, p. 77. Copyright © 1993 by Macmillan Publishing Company.

TEACHER	ADVISOR-ADVISEE	BLOCK 1 M W F	BLOCK 1 T TH	BLOCK 2 M W F	BLOCK 2 T TH	BLOCK 3 M W F	BLOCK 3 T TH	BLOCK 4 M W F	BLOCK 4 T TH
A	yes	Sci-6	Sci-6	Plan time	Plan time	Sci-6	Sci-6	Reading-6	Exploratory-6
B	yes	Eng-6	Eng-6	Plan time	Plan time	Eng-6	Eng-6	Reading-6	Exploratory-6
C	yes	SS-6	SS-6	Plan time	Plan time	SS-6	SS-6	Reading-6	Exploratory-6
D	yes	Mth-6	Mth-6	Plan time	Plan time	Mth-6	Mth-6	Reading-6	Exploratory-6
E	yes	Eng-7	Eng-7	Eng-7	Eng-7	Plan time	Plan time	Speech	Exploratory-6
F	yes	Sci-7	Sci-7	Sci-7	Sci-7	Plan time	Plan time	Reading-7	Exploratory-6
G	yes	SS-7	SS-7	SS-7	SS-7	Plan time	Plan time	Reading-7	Exploratory-6
H	yes	Pre Alg-7	Mth-7	Mth-7	Mth-7	Plan time	Plan time	Reading-7	Exploratory-6
I	yes	Plan time	Plan time	SS-8	SS-8	SS-8	SS-8	Reading-7	Exploratory-7
J	yes	Plan time	Plan time	Alg I-8	Pre Alg-7	Pre Alg-8	Mth-8	Mth-8	PreAlg-8
K	yes	Plan time	Plan time	Sci-8	Sci-8	Sci-8	Sci-8	Intramurals	Sci-8
L	yes	Plan time	Plan time	Eng-8	Eng-8	Eng-8	Speech	Eng-8	Eng-8
M	yes	Computer	Computer	Home Ec-8	Home Ec-8	Plan time	Plan time	Home Ec-8	Exploratory-7
N	yes					Shop-8	Shop-8	Shop-8	Exploratory-7
O	yes							Spanish-8	Exploratory-7
P	yes	Plan time	Plan time	Art-6	Art-6	Art-7	Art-7	Art-8	Exploratory-7
Q	no						Art-8		
R	no	LD	LD	LD	LD	LD	LD	Plan time	Plan time

Often, no bells are rung to signal movement from one block to the next. Instead, teachers verbally dismiss their classes. When the school building is so designed, or if the blocks are planned appropriately, students move only a short distance between classes, perhaps just across the hall or next door. Such arrangements often produce serendipitous results. For example, students may not have to carry as many books and may need to go to their lockers only twice a day between blocks. In many schools, student lockers are not used at all. Teachers can more easily supervise unstructured time and thereby have better control over the "hidden" or unplanned curriculum, as students are not roaming the halls for several minutes five or six times a day. And the reduction of bell ringing from as often as eight times a day to perhaps only two or three times a day creates less disturbance. As reported by one administrator, when village classrooms are in close proximity, there is less travel, noise, and congestion throughout a school building than there is in a traditional school setting (Raebeck, 1990).

B. MIDDLE SCHOOL CURRICULUM COMPONENTS

Within the framework of middle school organization lie several components that form a comprehensive program. Two terms, *curriculum* and *instruction,* combine to form the program that students experience.

FIGURE 3.2
A Seventh-Grade Student Schedule
SOURCE: Richard D. Kellough, Noreen C. Kellough, and David L. Hough, *Middle School Teaching: Methods and Resources* (New York: Macmillan, 1993), p. 75.

Student Schedule

Name: Gibbons, Sarah   Gender: Female   Grade: 7 Counselor: Jones
Date of Birth: 5/19/79   Home Phone: 765-2098   Emergency Phone: 765-6781
Address: 1373 E. Main, Wilmington, Ohio 45177

A Week Schedule

		Mon Wed Fri	Tue Thur
7:45–8:10		Advisor-advisee	Advisor-advisee
8:10–9:35	1st Block	Social studies	Mathematics
9:35–11:35	2nd Block	English	Science
11:35–1:00	3rd Block	General music (1/2)	Art (1/2)
		P.E./Health (1/2)	P.E./Health (1/2)
1:00–2:25	4th Block	Reading	Exploratory

B Week Schedule

		Mon Wed Fri	Tue Thur
7:45–8:10		Advisor-advisee	Advisor-advisee
8:10–9:35	1st Block	Mathematics	Social studies
9:35–11:35	2nd Block	Science	English
11:35–1:00	3rd Block	Art (1/2)	General music (1/2)
		P.E./Health (1/2)	P.E./Health (1/2)
1:00–2:25	4th Block	Exploratory	Reading

Note that there are two schedules, one for "A Week" and one for "B Week." With this plan, the student's schedule alternates each week.

Curriculum is defined in various ways. Some define it as the planned learning that is presented to students. Others say that the curriculum is only that which students actually learn. Still others hold that the curriculum is all experiences students encounter, whether planned or unplanned, learned or unlearned. William Alexander, the "father of middle school education" defines curriculum as "the sum of experiences of learners which take place under the auspices of the school" (1988, p. 33).

Alexander's definition implies that many different educational experiences collectively comprise the curriculum. Four programs are identified that contribute in different ways to student learning: (1) the program of *studies* (courses offered), (2) the program of *activities* (sports, clubs, and organizations), (3) the program of *services* (transportation, lunch, nurse), and (4) the *hidden curriculum* (school climate and informal student interactions that take place before and after school, at social events, and in the halls, bathrooms, and other areas of the school that are not monitored as closely as individual classrooms).

A working definition that adheres to the middle school philosophy is one that considers curriculum as the *entire school program,* including academic course content, planned and unplanned activities, and structured and semistructured nonacademic components of schooling.

Instruction, likewise, has several definitions, some of which are not clearly distinguishable from curriculum. Where curriculum is more narrowly associated with *content,* instruction is associated with *methods*—that is, ways of conveying information or presenting content. Curriculum and instruction must go hand in hand to affect learning.

Looking at the total school program and analyzing its various component parts, or domains, you can readily see the importance of studying curriculum and instruction. In a study of middle school curricula and instruction, Hough (1989) found that student learning experiences are affected by six domains. The six domains with their components are illustrated in Figure 3.3.

FIGURE 3.3
Six Domains Affecting Middle School Curricula
SOURCE: Dr. David Hough, Associate Dean, College of Education, Southwest Missouri State University.

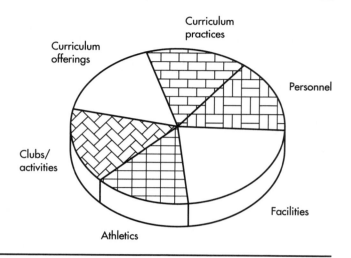

1. Domain of curriculum offerings (*content*)
   - Core subjects—usually English, science, mathematics, history/social studies
   - Specialty classes—reading, art, music, band, orchestra, typing, drama, journalism, industrial arts, home economics, foreign languages, speech, media, leadership, study skills, health, physical education, computer, and others
   - Exploratory classes—nonacademic and nongraded classes taught for a shorter time by teachers, parents, and community members and designed to provide special opportunities for students to discover learning outside the traditional classroom format
2. Domain of curriculum practices (*instruction*)
   - Cooperative learning
   - Electives
   - Learning how to learn
   - Mastery learning
   - Mini-classes and experimental projects
   - Parental involvement
   - Personal development
   - Philosophy (mission)
3. Domain of specialized personnel (*faculty and staff*)
   - Administrators
   - Art teachers
   - Coaches
   - Counselors
   - Hall monitors and security staff
   - Music teachers
   - Physical education teachers
4. Domain of *clubs and activities*
   - Assemblies
   - Cheerleading
   - Clubs (academic honors, art, audiovisual, chess, computer, drama, foreign language, Future Farmers of America, Future Teachers of America, glee, math, pep, photography, science, and others)
   - Formal dances
   - Newspaper
   - Parties
   - Student government
   - Yearbook

5. Domain of athletics
   - Interscholastic sports (baseball, basketball, cross country, football, golf, handball, track and field, soccer, softball, tennis, volleyball, wrestling)
   - Intramural sports (any of the preceding sports and others in which students participate for fun and experience—not competition against another school—for both girls and boys)
6. Domain of *facilities*
   - Auditorium
   - Concession stand
   - Football field
   - Gymnasium
   - Natrium
   - Nature center or trail
   - Outdoor classroom
   - Track

Although Hough's six domains do not address the so-called hidden curriculum, it is implied that various amounts and degrees of informal (unplanned) learning take place within each of the domains listed. In addition, whereas some schools include certain specialty classes as part of the core curriculum, others do not. In other words, any school's philosophy (often articulated via a mission statement) forms the underpinnings for the development of its curriculum. The middle school philosophy asserts that the needs of young adolescent youth are different from those in other stages of human development and therefore require a curriculum that attends to these needs.

Based on this principle, the various parts of the middle school curricula are grouped into three areas that combine all programs, components, and domains into a comprehensive middle school educational program. The three areas are the core curriculum, exploratories, and co-curricular activities. Following is a review of each of those three areas.

Core Curriculum

The core subjects are English, mathematics, science, and history/social studies—also referred to as the academic classes. It is in these classes that most interdisciplinary thematic units are taught. The purpose of teaching subject matter on a central theme is to avoid a departmentalized mentality that all too often communicates the wrong message to students—that learning is piecemeal and separate from one experience to another. On the contrary, the core curriculum facilitates the integration of subjects of the thematic units taught in tandem by the core teaching team. Specialty subject teachers (such as those for art, home economics, industrial arts, music, and physical education), although not part of the core, often will cooperate with the core team in developing and implementing thematic units.

Exploratory Programs

The purpose of exploratory classes is to provide a variety of experiences to help students discover areas of interest for future pursuit that perhaps will develop into a lifelong passion. Allowing middle school students opportunities to discover and explore unusual and novel topics can spawn or rekindle interests in life and school.

Exploratory classes differ from core and specialty classes in several respects. Exploratories are classes that students take to gain experience and appreciation even though they are not assigned a grade. Usually, exploratory classes are of shorter duration than the core classes, say, 30 to 45 minutes instead of 70 to 90 minutes, and might be taken only two days a week. Some exploratory programs last an entire term, but most last for two to six weeks. Sometimes students can choose 6 to 15 exploratory classes from a list of 20 or more. More common, however, is establishing an exploratory wheel, in which several classes are offered (usually 12, but ranging from 9 to 15) and each student must take each exploratory in turn.

Sometimes teachers are asked to develop exploratory classes by choosing topics of personal interest and sharing these with the students. Sometimes students are asked to list their interests and the topics they would like to study. The school then assigns a task force to find qualified personnel to design and staff the classes. Parents and community members provide a wealth of input by actually teaching exploratories, in partnership with or under the guidance of a credentialed teacher.

All students are encouraged to participate in exploratory activities, but none are penalized for not becoming proficient at a given skill or in a base of knowledge. Subject content of exploratory classes relates to areas of work and life not usually covered in core and specialty classes. These nontraditional learning experiences are therefore not associated with a specific "discipline."

Figure 3.4 lists a sampling of exploratory classes that are being implemented by middle schools throughout the United States.

Co-Curricular Activities

In traditional junior highs and comprehensive high schools, athletics, clubs, and activities are commonly labeled "extracurricular" activities. That is because they are considered separate from the academic learning of the regular school day. However, in middle schools many activities are significant components of the total educational program and are "co-curricular," rather than extracurricular. *Co-curricular* means that the activities go *with* the regular school program whether they are conducted before, during, or after school, or in some combination. The idea is to integrate these activities into the regular school program, including them as part of the total school experience, not as "add-ons" or "extras."

The co-curricular program includes student clubs, school and class activities, service organizations, and sports. Clubs can be for academic purposes, such as a math club, or they can be for fun, as a chess club. Activities can range from spirit squads and drill teams to fund-raisers, pizza parties, and student government. Service organizations are often sponsored, in part, by the local business community, represented by such organizations as the Better Business Bureau, Farm Bureau, and the Kiwanis, Rotary, and Soroptomist clubs.

The following is a review of three critical co-curricular components of the middle school.

Intramural versus Interscholastic Sports

The co-curricular sports program in the middle school is achieved through *intramural* rather than *interscholastic* sports. Some middle schools try to offer both, but most experts about middle school curriculum agree that intramural programs are better suited for the needs of young adolescents.

In exemplary middle schools, intramural sports programs are developed to promote participation by *all* students. Emphasis is on fun, teamwork, socialization, and peer relation-

FIGURE 3.4

Examples of Middle School Exploratory Courses

Building a house
Calligraphy
Careers and career opportunities
Conservation (including wildlife, water, plant, soil)
Cultural cooking
Fashion and design
Folk and modern dance
Home decor
Keyboarding
Library science
Map and compass
Nature study
Outdoor life (including hiking, camping, hunting, fishing, bird watching)
Photography
Politics
Recycling
Songwriting
Stars and planets (usually emphasizing our relationship with the universe)
The black hole
The tools of research
Travel (most popular title: "Planes, Trains, and Automobiles")
Water sports (including scuba diving, boating safety, and games)

ships in an unthreatening and relaxed environment. Evaluation is based on a student's willingness to cooperate with others and to participate, not on the student's skill or performance. A variety of intramural activities are scheduled for times before, during, or after school and may, where appropriate, be incorporated into the physical education, advisor-advisee, and exploratory classes. Through intramurals, all students can recognize and feel that they are part of a cohesive group, that they are of value as individuals, and that physical exercise is more important than skilled performance.

In many exemplary middle schools, interscholastic sports programs make every effort to include any student who chooses to participate. The focus is on participation rather than on winning. A middle school interscholastic sports committee is sometimes appointed with the responsibility to regulate all competitive sports and to design innovative ways to nurture the "athletic elite" without excluding students who are less skilled.

Study Skills

Study skills are an integral part of the learning process. The middle school student needs practical application of study skills in all content areas, but can also benefit from an intensive two- to three-week exploratory class. The optimal way to address study skills at the middle school level is to (1) provide each student with an exploratory study skills course, (2) emphasize learning techniques in each core subject content area, and (3) maintain continuous direction and adherence to study skills components throughout the school year. Study skills are also addressed in the homebase (advisor-advisee) class, demonstrating to students that the homebase teacher is interested in their personal and academic development.

In any event, study skills should not be a one-time discussion or a single unit of study in a particular class with no follow-up or integration with other classes, nor should it be the sole responsibility of each student. Middle school teachers share the responsibility for helping children learn how to learn. Giving homework assignments is *not* the same as teaching study skills.

Advisor–Advisee Program

The advisor-advisee (also called "homebase" or "homeroom") program is usually a separate class, no less than 20 minutes in length, without interruptions. All teachers are expected to participate, and it should serve as an avenue for individual and group guidance and counseling. The advisor-advisee program is intended to ensure that each student is known well by at least one adult who can give positive and constructive individual attention to that student. In fact, in many exemplary middle schools, the homebase teachers remain with the same students throughout the students' middle school years.

The homebase program should promote a student's feeling of belonging to a group and is not intended to be used for mechanical tasks. Before implementation, careful preparation of homebase teachers and parents needs to be done. The homebase program is for purposeful group activities that deal with students' social relationships and emotional development. The program should be a vehicle for dealing with affective needs and for teaching study skills, thinking skills, and decision making.

C. A MODEL FOR CURRICULUM DEVELOPMENT

Have you ever wondered how schools and teachers determine what types of learning students are to experience at school? Have you wondered why so many schools across the country have similar classes at given grade levels? Why certain subjects are always a part of the school program? How, from one school to the next, content presented to students is often quite similar? Or why some schools do not fit the norm as they experiment with kinds of learning and structure? Answers to these questions are found by looking at a prototypical model for curriculum building that combines ideals and principles of education.

Curriculum development begins with a model. Emerging from that model is content, both general and specific, that is planned to meet the needs of the learners. From that content, a set of instructional techniques is developed to implement the content. Those techniques are then set in the form of units with daily lessons.

Although many different models of curriculum development have been devised, the most widely noted and probably most frequently applied is that of Ralph W. Tyler (1949).

Tyler's model of curriculum development focuses on three areas: the needs of the students, the needs of society, and the demands of the subject. From careful consideration of each of these areas, broad educational goals are derived. Those goals are then run through screens to derive specific educational programs and precise instructional objectives. The screens are recognition of an educational philosophy; consideration of the effects of groups outside of the classroom; procedures for assessment; and a mechanism for revision. Once these screens are in place, we have a prototypical model of curriculum development, composed of five components. Figure 3.5 depicts this model. Combining the curriculum-building components (or steps) with these principles allows curriculum builders to fashion a middle-level curriculum.

Notice that the model begins with the student, society, and subject needs, and then spirals outward with no sign of closure, even after the assessment and revision phase (component 5). This illustrates the unending, cyclical nature of middle school curriculum development. Continuing to expand as new ideas emerge and as needs change, the process has no outer bounds.

Basic Principles of Middle School Education Theory as Applied to the Curriculum Development Model

The following are descriptions of the basic principles of middle level education as they are applied to the five components of curriculum development shown in Figure 3.5.

1. The *needs component.* As we all are changing individuals in an ever-changing world, middle school educators strive to educate the total child—the social, emotional, intellectual, and physical "self" that also is ever-changing. To do this, curriculum developers consider the needs of students by responding to the question, "What do we want middle school students to feel and do?" Considering the needs of society they ask, "What do we want middle school students to be and to become?" And, considering the

FIGURE 3.5
Curriculum Development Model

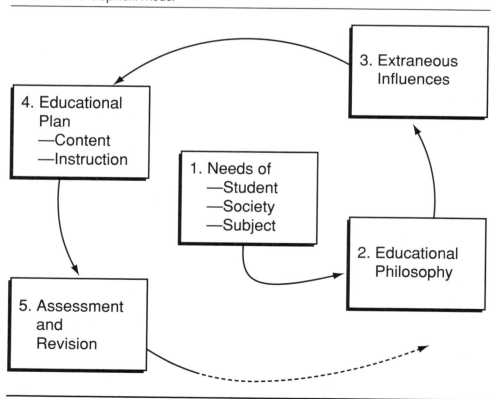

needs of the disciplines, they respond to the question, "What should middle school students know?"

2. The *educational philosophy component*. Transescence is a developmental stage quite distinct from childhood (elementary school age) and from adolescence (high school age). Consequently, exemplary middle schools are those designed to *celebrate* this stage, not to provide a "holding ground" or transitional "waiting room" until the students' hormones have more closely reached equilibrium. To celebrate young adolescence, middle school programs and services must fit the specific needs of this developmental stage.

3. The *extraneous influences component*. Curriculum development is affected by international, national, state, and local interests, actions, and mandates. Federal legislative acts, state curriculum frameworks, district-wide and local guidelines, national reports such as "Turning Points," "A Nation At Risk," "Caught in the Middle," and publications such as *Middle School Journal, Crossroads, NASSP Bulletin, Research in Middle Level Education*, and special interest groups all affect the development of middle school development.

4. The *educational plan component*. Included in the educational plan are the following elements:

   • *Content.* Middle schools provide opportunities for students to learn a common core of information, participate in co-curricular activities, and explore a variety of new areas.

   • *Instruction.* Middle school educators recognize the value and importance of student social interaction as a dynamic learning tool. This recognition is practiced by using interactive teaching strategies such as cooperative learning, peer tutoring, cross-age teaching, and guided practice. Structured and semistructured social activities are woven into the fabric of academic content, thereby positively influencing the "hidden" curriculum.

   • *Scope.* The depth and breadth of the educational experiences are planned so that middle school children understand the value of knowledge and how that knowledge is applied in life.

   • *Sequence.* The order in which these learning experiences take place is smoothly articulated and extends beyond the level of skill acquisition. Exemplary middle schools provide children with new learning experiences that are organized logically and that avoid redundancy, especially with the prior year's experiences.

5. The *assessment and revision component*. All curricula must be continually monitored and evaluated to find ways to improve the educational program. Evaluation of curriculum is both formative (ongoing) and summative (conclusive). Recommendations drawn from the assessment are used to make revisions to the curriculum. The spiral nature of middle school curriculum development is designed to remain responsive to modern issues; middle school curriculum development is a process without end.

D. UNIT PLANNING

Organizing the entire year's content into units makes the teaching process more manageable than when no plan or only random choices are made by a teacher. Whether or not you are teaching in a self-contained classroom, the content you intend to present to children must be organized and carefully planned well in advance. The teaching unit is a major subdivision of a course (for one course or self-contained classroom there are several or many units of instruction), and is comprised of instruction planned around a central theme, topic, issue, or problem.

The teaching unit, whether an interdisciplinary thematic unit (known also as an integrated unit), or a stand-alone, standard, subject unit, is not unlike a chapter in a book, an act or scene in a play, or a phase of work when undertaking a project such as building a house. Breaking down information or actions into component parts and then grouping the related parts makes sense out of learning and doing. The unit brings a sense of cohesiveness and structure to student learning and avoids the piecemeal approach that might otherwise unfold. You can learn to articulate lessons within, between, and among unit plans and focus on important elements while not ignoring tangential information of importance. Students remember "chunks" of information, especially when those chunks are related to specific units.

Types of Units

Although the steps for developing any type of unit are essentially the same, units can be organized in a number of ways, differentiated and described as follows.

Conventional unit. A conventional unit (known also as a standard unit) consists of a series of lessons centered on a topic, theme, major concept, or block of subject matter. In a standard unit, each lesson builds on the previous lesson by contributing additional subject matter, providing further illustrations, and supplying more practice or other added instruction, all of which are aimed at bringing about mastery of the knowledge and skills on which the unit is centered.

Integrated unit. When a conventional unit is centered on a theme, such as "railroads," then the unit may be referred to as a thematic unit. When, by design, the thematic unit integrates disciplines, such as one that combines the learning of science and mathematics (see Figure 4.8 in Chapter 4), or social studies and language arts, or all four of these core disciplines, then it is called an integrated (or interdisciplinary) thematic unit. It is this type of unit that is the emphasis of this book.

Self-instructional unit. A self-instructional unit (known also as a modular unit) is a unit of instruction that is designed for individualized or modularized self-instruction. Such a unit is designed for independent, individual study and, because it covers much less content than the units previously described, can generally be completed in a much shorter time period, frequently in one class period. The unit consists of instruction, references, exercises, problems, self-correcting materials, and all other information and materials that a student needs to independently carry out the unit of work. Consequently, students can work on the units individually at their own speed, and different students can be working on different units at the same time. Students who successfully finish a modular unit can move on to another unit of work without waiting for the other students to catch up. Such units are essential ingredients of continuous-progress courses. Whether for purposes of remediation, enrichment, or make-up, self-instructional units work especially well when done at and in conjunction with a learning activity center.

Contract unit. A contract unit is an individualized unit of instruction for which a student agrees (contracts) to carry out certain activities. Some contract units have a variable-letter-grade agreement built into them. For example, specified on the contract may be information such as the following:

> To pass with a D grade, you must complete activities 1–5 and pass the posttest.
>
> For a grade of C, you must complete activities 1–5, receive at least a C on the posttest, and satisfactorily complete two optional related activities.
>
> For a grade of B, you must complete activities 1–5, plus satisfactorily complete four of the optional related activities and receive a grade of no less than B on the posttest.
>
> For a grade of A, you must complete activities 1–5, plus satisfactorily complete six of the optional activities and receive no less than a B on the posttest.

Planning and Developing Any Unit of Instruction

The steps in planning and developing a conventional unit, a contract unit, a self-instructional unit, and an interdisciplinary thematic unit are the same and are as follows:

1. *Select a suitable topic or theme.* Often these already may be laid out in your course of study or textbook or have been agreed to by members of the teaching team.
2. *Select the goals of the unit.* The goals are written as an overview or rationale, covering what the unit is about and what the students are to learn. In planning the goals, you should do the following:

   a. Become as familiar as possible with the topic and materials used.
   b. Consult curriculum documents, such as courses of study, state frameworks, and re-
      source units, for ideas.
   c. Decide the content and procedures—what the students should learn about the topic
      and how.
   d. Write the rationale or overview, summarizing what you hope the students will learn
      about the topic.
   e. Be sure your goals are congruent with those of the course.
3. *Select suitable specific learning objectives.*
   a. Include understandings, skills, attitudes, appreciations, and ideals.
   b. Be specific, avoiding vagueness and generalizations.
   c. Write the objectives in behavioral terms.
   d. Be as certain as possible that the objectives will contribute to the major learning de-
      scribed in the overview.
4. *Detail the instructional procedures.* These procedures include the subject content and
   the learning activities, established as a series of lessons. Proceed with the following
   steps in your initial planning of the instructional procedures:
   a. Gather ideas for learning activities that might be suitable for the unit. Refer to cur-
      riculum documents, resource units, and other teachers as resources.
   b. Check the learning activities to make sure that they will actually contribute to the
      learning designated in your objectives, discarding ideas that do not.
   c. Make sure that the learning activities are feasible. Can you afford the time, effort, or
      expense? Do you have the necessary materials and equipment? If not, can they be ob-
      tained? Are the activities suited to the intellectual and maturity levels of your stu-
      dents?
   d. Check resources available to be certain that they support the content and learning ac-
      tivities.
   e. Decide how to introduce the unit. Provide introductory activities that
      (1) arouse student interest.
      (2) inform students what the unit is about.
      (3) help you learn about your students—their interests, abilities, and experiences and
          present knowledge of the topic.
      (4) provide transitions that bridge this topic with that which students have already
          learned.
      (5) involve the students in the planning.
   f. Plan developmental activities that
      (1) sustain student interest.
      (2) provide for individual student differences.
      (3) promote the learning as cited in the specific objectives.
   g. Plan culminating activities that
      (1) summarize what has been learned.
      (2) bring together loose ends.
      (3) apply what has been learned to new and meaningful situations.
      (4) provide transfer to the unit that follows.
5. *Plan for preassessment and assessment of student learning.* Preassess what students already know, or think they know. Assessment of student progress in achievement of the
   learning objectives (formative evaluation) should permeate the entire unit. Plan to gather
   information in several ways, including informal observations, observation of student
   performance, portfolio assessment, and paper-and-pencil assessments. Evaluation must
   be consistent with the specific learning objectives.
6. *Provide for the materials of instruction.* The unit cannot function without materials.
   Therefore, you must plan long before the unit begins for media equipment and materials, references, reading materials, reproduced materials, and community resources.
   Material that is not available to the students is of no help to them.

Those are six steps to follow for developing any type of unit. In addition to those six
steps, there are two general points that should be made:

1. *There is no single format for a teaching unit* that always works best. Particular formats may be best for specific disciplines or topics. During your student teaching, your college or university program for teacher preparation will probably have a form that you will be expected to follow.

2. *There is no set time duration for a unit plan,* although, for specific units, curriculum guides will indicate a suggested time duration. Units may extend for a minimum of several days or, as in the case of interdisciplinary thematic units, for several weeks. However, be aware that when conventional units last more than two or three weeks, they tend to lose their identity as clearly identifiable units. The exact time duration will be dictated by several factors, including the topic or theme, the grade level, and the interests and the abilities of the students.

E. INTERDISCIPLINARY THEMATIC UNITS

Whereas curriculum is the backbone of the middle school, interdisciplinary thematic units are its heart and soul. The following syllogistic formula explains why.

- *Proposition One.* To be successful, middle school programs must fit the specific needs of young adolescents.
- *Proposition Two.* Transescence is a developmental stage that embodies characteristics that are quite different from those of children of elementary age and of high school age.
- *Proposition Three.* To address the distinct needs of young adolescents, consideration must be given to the whole individual (physically, psychologically and emotionally, socially, and intellectually) and to the total educational experience, or curriculum (core, co-curricular, and exploratory).
- *Conclusion.* By recognizing the individual child and integrating the whole individual with the total curriculum, the learning experiences become meaningful to the student. Learning that is meaningful engages the student, connecting him or her with the world, thereby compelling the student to want to learn. To the student, learning is then viewed as important, meaningful, and useful.

It is probably fair to say that this syllogistic style of reasoning places more emphasis on merging student needs with specific subject-related content than do other grade-specific philosophies. This means that the primary emphasis for elementary education is on individual child development and basic skills acquisition, and the major emphasis for high school education is subject-oriented specialization. The middle school philosophy views education as a *social enterprise* in which students are challenged to discover underlying structures and meaning within interrelated subject content. This cannot be achieved through the dichotomy of "student versus subject," but rather by merging the two.

The *interdisciplinary thematic unit* is the tool used to link the learning experiences of middle school children in ways to engage them fully in the learning process. *Interdisciplinary* means that the core subjects as well as the co-curricular activities and exploratories are involved. *Thematic* means that the same topic is used to develop the teaching plan (content and instruction) for each of the different subjects in which students are enrolled. *Unit* refers to an extended teaching plan (several days to several weeks), in which a variety of goals and objectives are established that are centered around a common concept, topic, or theme.

The Meaning of *Interdisciplinary*

To comprehend how an interdisciplinary (or integrated) curriculum is fashioned and how it works, you must understand the relationships among core, co-curricular, and exploratory programs. To help in this understanding, we now review each of these middle school programs, followed by a discussion of the makings of an interdisciplinary thematic unit.

The Role of Core Curriculum

You learned that the most common core classes are English/language arts, mathematics, science, and history/social studies. However, in many middle schools, classes in art, music, physical education, and reading are also required of each student. Often, other classes are required as well—home economics, foreign languages, and industrial arts, for example. Whether "academic," "liberal," or "applied arts," all *required* courses taken by middle school children are core subjects.

The philosophical foundation of core education is that a given body of knowledge is considered essential enough for all students to share in the experience afforded by that core of knowledge. Integrating the content of core subjects by coordinating instruction around a central theme creates interdisciplinary content and methods. In many instances the choice of an interdisciplinary theme is first identified in one of the core subjects' master plans. Table 3.1 illustrates a common core of subjects articulated among grades 6, 7, and 8. In Figure 3.6, three different orientations are presented.

The Role of Exploratory Programs

Exploratories should be integrated into the interdisciplinary thematic unit. This can be done by choosing a single area of interest within the unit and either developing a special exploratory class or giving special attention to it within the framework of an existing exploratory.

For example, suppose a teaching team decides to develop a thematic unit centered around the topic of westward expansion. Let's say that the middle school had already developed an exploratory wheel of classes consisting of 12 areas of study that all students will have experienced by the end of the school year. Let's further assume that one of those classes is called "transportation," in which students learn about the history and development of various modes of travel. The team, in cooperation with the exploratory teacher (who may or may not be a member of the team), might decide to structure the westward expansion thematic unit so that it coincides with the exploratory class on transportation. The exploratory teacher then plans the class accordingly. Here is a list of options he or she might consider:

- Ask a community volunteer from a local Department of Transportation office to make a presentation or even help design the course.
- Plan intensive study of one form of transportation, for example, the wagon, stagecoach, prairie schooner, rail, automobile, horse and buggy, water, motorcycle, airplane, subway, walking, bicycling, or horseback riding; or, in a jig-saw format, have student teams study different modes.
- Study cultural or ethnic conflicts that were caused by westward expansion and resultant changes in different types of transportation.
- Retrace the Oregon Trail by examining how horse-, mule-, and ox-drawn wagons dealt with changes in weather and terrain.
- Compare different routes and modes of transportation to determine advantages and disadvantages of each.

TABLE 3.1
Sample Middle School Curriculum by Grade Level

	SIXTH GRADE	SEVENTH GRADE	EIGHTH GRADE
CORE	Language arts Social studies Mathematics Science	Language arts Social studies Mathematics Science	Language arts Social studies Mathematics Science
REQUIRED[a]	Physical education Reading Art	Physical education Reading	Physical education Computer
ELECTIVES	Band, orchestra, or vocal music	Foreign language, speech, art, band, orchestra, or vocal music	Foreign language, speech, art, band, orchestra, or vocal music
REQUIRED[b]	Exploratory Advisor-advisee	Exploratory Advisor-advisee	Exploratory Advisor-advisee
RECOMMENDED[c]	Co-curricular	Co-curricular	Co-curricular

[a]These required classes may or may not be considered part of the core.
[b]Exploratory and advisor-advisee classes are required of all students, but participation is not graded on the traditional A–F scale.
[c]Co-curricular activities are recommended as voluntary activities.

FIGURE 3.6
Comparing and Contrasting Middle School Curriculum Models

Instructions: With this figure you can compare and contrast the curriculum model (Figure 3.5) with that of three middle schools: A, B, and C. Compare the curricula of schools A, B, and C with that of Figure 3.5 by answering the following questions. Upon completion, share and discuss your results with those of your classmates.

1. Explain how schools A, B, and C differ from Figure 3.5 in terms of *core classes*.

2. Explain how schools A, B, and C differ from Figure 3.5 in *exploratories*.

3. Explain how schools A, B, and C differ from Figure 3.5 in *co-curricular programs and activities*.

4. Explain how schools A, B, and C differ from Figure 3.5 in *electives*.

5. Explain how schools A, B, and C differ from Figure 3.5 in *grade levels (vertical articulation)*.

6. Do you see any other differences between the three schools and the model curriculum of Figure 3.5? If so, explain.

School A's Curriculum

Sixth Grade	*Seventh Grade*	*Eighth Grade*
Advisor–advisee	Advisor–advisee	Advisor–advisee
Basic skills	*Basic skills*	*Basic skills*
Language arts	Language arts	Language arts
Mathematics	Math or pre-algebra	Math or pre-algebra
Science	Science	Science
Social studies	Social studies	Social studies
Reading	Study skills (daily or alternates with gifted)	P.E./extended basic skills or gifted
Exploratory wheel	*Exploratory wheel*	
Art	Art	
Speech/drama	Speech/drama	
Health	Health	
Journalism	Industrial arts	
General music	Home economics	

Now, using the same example, let's suppose the school had not determined the specific exploratory classes that it would be providing students, choosing, instead, to let them evolve out of specific needs that present themselves throughout the school year. In this case, the exploratory teacher has an opportunity to develop a number of different activities. For the sake of this example, let's say that the teacher chooses to develop content that focuses on cultural integration caused by the westward movement. Specific and intensive study could evolve around Native Americans and European settlers, or it could focus on the study of a single culture, incident, or individual. In this way, the exploratory teacher can augment core content and provide more in-depth study of important facets of history, art, music, literature, science, and so on than the core subject teacher may have time to provide.

FIGURE 3.6 cont'd

Exploratory electives	*Exploratory electives*	*Exploratory electives*
P.E./yearbook	Instrumental music	Instrumental music
Keyboarding	Journalism	Journalism
French	French	French
German	German	Art
Spanish	Spanish	Spanish
Study skills		Vocal music
		Speech/drama
		Health
		Industrial arts
Academic elective		
Reading plus	Reading plus	Reading plus

School B's Curriculum

Sixth Grade	*Seventh Grade*	*Eighth Grade*
Team	*Team*	*Team*
Reading	Reading	Reading
English	English	English
Mathematics	Social studies	Social studies
Social studies		
Science/health		
Enrichment	Coed/science	Mathematics
Physical education	Physical education	Physical education
	Electives	Science/skills
		Electives

School C's Curriculum

Sixth Grade	*Seventh Grade*	*Eighth Grade*
English	English	English
Science	Science	Science
Mathematics	Mathematics (pre-algebra)	Algebra
Social studies	American studies	American studies
Reading	Reading	Reading
Physical education	Physical education	Enrichment (Spanish
Band, chorus, or project Earth	Band, chorus, or project Earth	or French)
		Physical education
		Band, chorus, or project Earth
Exploratories	*Exploratories*	*Exploratories*
French	Spanish	Sewing
Keyboarding	Speech/drama	Business studies
Shop	Arts/crafts	Great books
Stress management	Foods	Shop

The Role of Co-Curricular Activities

All too often co-curricular activities are less a part of the interdisciplinary thematic unit than are the core and exploratories, but they are nonetheless integral components of the curriculum and must not be ignored. Again, using the theme of westward expansion, the following are examples of clubs with theme-related activities:

- Glee club: plan for students to study, sing, and play songs unique to the time. If the concept of westward expansion is not constricted by time, students could trace the underlying movement by following strands in music of that period that depict the expansion

- Social committee or student council: plan and sponsor a westward expansion party, an "old west day," or a special assembly
- Intramural sports: include games of the period
- School newspaper: print a special edition representative of the westward movement.

The co-curricular options available are limited only by the creativity of the students, teacher, and staff who plan them. Even study skills and technology classes can be included, perhaps by comparing different approaches to problem solving from one time, culture, or mode of transportation to another. Multicultural components should be an integral part of every facet of the curriculum, and the hidden curriculum is less enigmatic when teachers are aware of how students spend their free or leisure time, and plan activities (sometimes homework) that bring an air of structure into an otherwise unstructured and unsupervised situation. Such an approach is favored by John Holt in his book, *Learning All the Time* (1989).

The Meaning of *Thematic*

The underlying concept that allows for the structure and organization of specific content across disciplines is called a *theme*. Hence, a thematic unit is an instructional unit based on a common learning denominator that lends itself to integrated study—sharing a common idea within various frameworks for content, instruction, materials, and evaluation. Units of instruction can last for several days to several weeks. However, caution must be followed because teaching units that last much longer than three weeks may lose their effectiveness as recognizable units of learning. *Lessons* are subdivisions of units, usually taught in a single period or in one day.

Themes are commonly discussed in the language arts. For instance, literature might be studied thematically by grouping together stories about heroes undertaking journeys or quests; the suffering servant; people's inhumanity to other human beings, nature, or self; alienation; lost innocence; love or nature regained; and so on. In social studies the following themes might emerge: the workplace; people and the urge to create; their urge to move, explore, discover, or rule or be ruled; the search for the unknown. In science examples might include the nurturing earth, quenching thirst, environmental disasters, the body's ecosystem, atoms and anatomies, and the forces within you. Mathematics classes might study the geometry of building a house; equations for all time; numbers with special meanings; statistical tools; or gambling odds.

Themes such as those just listed can be developed for virtually any academic or nonacademic class in the middle school, whether it is reading, physical education, art, or music, or whether it involves co-curricular, exploratory, or advisor-advisee programs. Again, the creativity of the teacher is important, and the dynamics of interactive teaching teams can produce any number of themes that are meaningful, interesting, and cohesive.

F. DEVELOPING AN INTERDISCIPLINARY THEMATIC UNIT

Of special interest to many teachers are units built around interdisciplinary themes, rather than content topics that are single-subject specific. Interdisciplinary thematic teaching helps students bridge the disciplines and connect school learning with real-life experiences. The six steps outlined earlier are essential steps for planning any type of teaching unit, including the interdisciplinary thematic (or integrated) unit. The interdisciplinary thematic unit is made of smaller subject-specific units, developed according to the preceding guidelines.

For example, in 1991, four teachers at a school in Yorktown, VA, decided to make connections for their ninth-grade students in their disciplines—science, algebra, geography, and English.

> Using a common planning period to collaborate, the teachers began modestly with an assignment to summarize earth science articles that strengthened students' knowledge of science as well as their writing skills. Later in the year, the teachers launched an interdisciplinary project focused on the winter Olympics in Albertville, France. In small groups, students were presented with a problem related to one aspect of hosting the Olympics—providing transportation, food, lodging, entertainment, or security. The groups wrote proposals setting forth their solutions, drawing on what they had learned about the geography of the region and applying science knowledge and math skills (Willis, 1992b, p. 1).

In the York School project, the English teacher taught vocabulary that students would encounter in their algebra and earth science classes. Primary responsibility for the development of interdisciplinary thematic units often depends upon the cooperation of several teachers, who, as in this example, usually represent two or more disciplines. This interdisciplinary team of teachers may meet daily during a common planning time. Careful planning of the scheduling allows for instructional blocks of time so team members have common planning time and unit lessons can, likewise, be more flexible and less constrained by time.

Some teaching teams develop one interdisciplinary thematic unit each year, semester, trimester, or quarter; that is, from one to four a year. Over time, then, the team will have developed several units for implementation. The most effective units, however, are often the most current or most meaningful to students. This means that ever-changing global, national, and local topics provide a veritable smorgasbord from which to choose, and teaching teams must constantly be aware of the changes in the world and society and the interests of students in order to update old units and develop new and exciting ones.

One teaching team's unit should not conflict with another's at the same or another grade level. If a school has two or more seventh-grade teams, for example, the teams may want to develop units on different themes and share their products. As another example, a junior high school team may want to share its units with high school teams, and, perhaps, with feeder elementary schools. Open lines of communication within, between, and among teams and schools are critical to the success of thematic teaching.

Because developing interdisciplinary thematic units is increasingly becoming an essential task for many teachers, it behooves you to learn now the process that you may be practicing later as an employed teacher (or even when student teaching). One other point needs to be made: an interdisciplinary thematic unit can be prepared and taught by one teacher, but more often these units are prepared and taught by a team of teachers. The latter instructional strategy is referred to as *interdisciplinary thematic team teaching*. Most often the team is composed of teachers from at least four areas: social studies or history, language arts or English, mathematics, and science. A thematic unit and teaching team might also consist of fewer than four areas—math and science, history and English, or social studies and language arts, for example.

Following are steps for developing an interdisciplinary thematic unit:

1. *Agree on the nature or source of origin for the interdisciplinary thematic unit.* Team members should view the interdisciplinary approach as a collective effort in which all team members (and other faculty) participate nearly equally. Discuss how the team wants students to profit from interdisciplinary instruction. Troubleshoot possible stumbling blocks.
2. *Discuss subject-specific frameworks, goals and objectives, curriculum guidelines, textbooks and supplemental materials, and units already in place for the school year.* This discussion should focus on what each teacher must teach, and it should explain the scope and sequence so all team members share an understanding of perceived constraints and limitations.
3. *Choose a topic and develop a time line.* From the information provided by each subject-specialist teacher in step 2, start listing possible topics within existing course outlines that can be drawn from. Give-and-take is essential at this step, as some topics will fit certain subjects better than others. The chief goal here is to find a workable topic, that is, one that can be adapted to each subject without detracting from the educational plan already in place. This may require choosing and merging content from two or more other previously planned units. The theme is then drawn from the topic. When a team is considering a theme, it should consider these questions (Willis, 1992a):
   - Can this theme lead to a unit that is of proper duration, not too short and not too long?
   - Is it worth the time needed to create and implement it? Do we have sufficient materials and resources to supply information we might need?
   - Is the theme within the realm of understanding and experience of the teachers involved? Is the theme topic one with which teachers are not already too familiar so they can share in the excitement of the learning? Will the theme be of interest to all members of the teaching team? Does it apply broadly to a wide range of subject areas?

- What is so important about this theme that it will promote future learning? Does the theme have substance and application to the real world? Does it lend itself to active learning? Will it be of interest to students; will it motivate them to do their best? Will it fascinate students once they are into it?

4. *Set two time lines.* The first time line is for the team only and is to ensure that given dates for specific work required in developing the unit will be met by each member. The second time line is for students and teachers and shows how long the unit will be, when it will start, and in which classes.

5. *Develop the scope and sequence for content and instruction.* Follow the six steps for "Planning and Developing Any Unit of Instruction" (page 58), to develop the interdisciplinary thematic unit. This should be done by each team member and also as a group during common planning time so the team members can coordinate dates and activities in logical sequence and depth. This organic process will generate ideas but also produce some anxiety. Members of the team, under the guidance of the team leader, should strive to maintain anxiety at a level conducive to learning, experimenting, and arriving at group consensus.

6. *Share goals and objectives.* Each team member should have a copy of the goals and objectives of every other member. This helps refine the unit and lesson plans and prevent unnecessary overlap and confusion.

7. *Give the unit its name.* The unit has been fashioned based on a common topic and is being held together by the theme you have chosen. Giving the theme a name and using that name lets the students know that this unit of study is integrated, important, and meaningful to school and to life.

8. *Share subject-specific units, lesson plans, print and nonprint materials.* After teachers have finalized their units, exchange them for review comments and suggestions. Keep a copy of each teacher's unit(s), and see if you could present a lesson from it for your own subject area. If you can, the plans are probably workable. If you can't, some modification may be necessary.

9. *Field-test the thematic unit.* Beginning at the time, on the date, and in the class(es) agreed upon, present the lessons. Team members may trade classes from time to time. Team teaching may take place when two or more classes can be combined for instruction, as can be done with flexible and block scheduling. After field testing, there is, of course, one final step: assessing the thematic unit and perhaps adjusting and revising it. Team members discuss successes and failures during their common planning time and determine what needs to be changed, how, and when, to make the unit successful. Adjustments to the unit can be made along the way (by collecting data during formative assessments) and revisions made after the unit has been completed (from data collected during summative assessment).

The preceding steps are not absolutes and should be viewed only as guides. Differing compositions of teaching teams and levels of teacher experience and knowledge make strict adherence to any procedural steps less productive than group-generated plans. For instance, many teachers have found that the topic for an interdisciplinary thematic unit should be one that the team already knows well. In practice, the process that works for the team—that results in meaningful student learning and in students feeling good about themselves, about learning, and about school—is the appropriate process.

SUMMARY

In this chapter you learned about the essence of the middle school concept and the organization of the middle school curriculum—its domains and major components. You have learned how teachers' and students' schedules are organized to meet the demands of the middle school curriculum. These components are organized to include team teaching, common planning time, interdisciplinary thematic units, co-curricular activities, exploratory classes, advisor-advisee programs, intramurals, and study skills.

The middle school curriculum is predicated on the notion that children aged 10 to 14 are in a developmental stage quite distinguishable and separate from that of students of elementary school and high school age. Therefore, neither elementary nor high school curricula are appropriate for middle school children. Curriculum development should focus on the needs of the total young adolescent.

This is accomplished by providing a core curriculum, co-curricular activities and programs, and exploratory classes. Developing units of instruction that integrate learning and provide a sense of meaning for the students requires coordination throughout the total curriculum, which has been defined as all the experiences students encounter while at school. Hence, learning for middle school children is a process of discovering how information, knowledge, and ideas are interrelated and making sense out of self, school, and life.

The chapter that follows will guide you through the process of developing lessons that fit the needs of the middle school student.

QUESTIONS AND ACTIVITIES FOR DISCUSSION

1. Explain why the curriculum development model is presented as a spiral shape as opposed, for example, to a line, and begins with needs.

2. Describe the five phases of curriculum development.

3. Explain why integrated units fit the middle school syllogism articulated earlier in this chapter.

4. Explain the importance of organizing instruction into units.

5. Assuming that a middle-grades teaching team is made up of four teachers, list three possible combinations of classes that might constitute the core curriculum. Discuss your lists with your classmates.

6. Describe the purpose of an interdisciplinary thematic unit.

7. Suppose that you are a key decision maker in charge of designing a three-year core curriculum for a grades 6–8 middle school. Assume that the sixth graders are to have a five-course core, seventh graders a four-course core, and eighth graders a three-course core. Which courses would you place together for each student cohort? Share and discuss your lists with your classmates.

8. Explain the difference between activities that are co-curricular and those that are extracurricular. Provide examples of each.

9. Describe the chief difference between intramural and interscholastic sports programs. Why do you suppose experts place greater importance on intramural sports programs for the middle school?

10. Examine the interdisciplinary thematic unit displayed in Chapter 18. At what level of integration (as discussed at the opening of this part) do you suppose it is designed to be implemented? Why? Could it be used at another level? If so, what changes would have to be made?

11. What questions do you have about the content of this chapter? How might you find answers?

REFERENCES

Alexander, W. M. (1988). Schools in the middle: Rhetoric and reality. *Social Education, 52*(2),107–109.

California Department of Education. (1986). *California dropouts: A status report.* Sacramento, CA: Author.

Holt, J. (1989). *Learning all the time.* Reading, MA: Addison-Wesley.

Hough, D. L. (1989). *Middle level education in California: A survey of programs and organization.* Riverside, CA: University of California, Educational Research Cooperative.

Massachusetts Advocacy Center. (1986). *The way out: Student exclusion practices in Boston middle schools.* Boston: Author.

Raebeck, B. S. (1990). Transformation of a middle school. *Educational Leadership, 47*(7),18–21.

Tyler, R. W. (1949). *Basic principles of curriculum and instruction.* Chicago: University of Chicago Press.

Valentine, J. W., et al. (1993). *Leadership in middle level education, volume 1.* Reston, VA: National Association of Secondary School Principals.

Willis, S. (1992a, November). Choosing a theme. *ASCD Curriculum Update,* pp. 4–5.

Willis, S. (1992b, November). Interdisciplinary learning: Movement to link disciplines gains momentum. *ASCD Curriculum Update,* p. 1.

SUGGESTED READINGS

Arnold, J. (1990). *Visions of teaching and learning: 80 exemplary middle level projects.* Columbus, OH: National Middle School Association.

Ayres, L. R. (1994). Middle school advisory programs: Findings from the field. *Middle School Journal 25*(3),8–14.

Beane, J. A. (1990). *A middle school curriculum: From rhetoric to reality.* Columbus, OH: National Middle School Association.

Beane, J. A. (1992). Creating an integrative curriculum: Making the connections. *NASSP Bulletin, 76*(547),46–54.

Beane, J. A. (1993). The search for a middle school curriculum. *School Administrator, 50*(3),8–14.

Boling, A. N. (1991). They don't like math? Well, let's do something. *Arithmetic Teacher, 38,*(7),17–19.

Boyer, M. R. (1993). The challenge of an integrated curriculum: Avoid the isolated road. *School Administrator, 50*(3),20–21.

Brandt, R. S. (Ed.). (1988). *Content of the curriculum.* 1988 ASCD Yearbook. Alexandria, VA: Association for Supervision and Curriculum Development.

Caine, G., & Caine, R. N. (1993, Fall). The critical need for a mental model of meaningful learning. *California Catalyst,* 18–21.

Cuban, L. (1993). The lure of curricular reform and its pitiful history. *Phi Delta Kappan, 75*(2),182–185.

Darling-Hammond, L. (1993). Reframing the school reform agenda. *Phi Delta Kappan, 74*(10),753–761.

Dempster, F. N. (1993). Exposing our students to less should help them learn more. *Phi Delta Kappan, 74*(6),433–437.

Elias, M. J. & Branden-Muller, L. R. (1994). Social and life skills development during the middle school years: An emerging perspective. *Middle School Journal 25*(3),8–14.

Erb, T. O., & Doda, N. M. (1989). *Team organization: Promise—Practices & possibilities.* Washington, DC: National Education Association.

Fogarty, R. (1991). *How to integrate the curricula.* Palatine, IL: Skylight Publishing.

Gehrke, N. J. (1991). Explorations of teachers' development of integrative curriculum. *Journal of Curriculum and Supervision, 6*(2),107–117.

Jacobs, H. H. (1989). *Interdisciplinary curriculum: Design and implementation.* Alexandria, VA: Association for Supervision and Curriculum Development.

Jordan, C., & Smith, L. J. (1992). Planning for whole language across the curriculum (in the classroom). *Reading Teacher, 45*(6),476–477.

Kenta, B. (1993). The challenge of an integrated curriculum: Moving with cautious velocity. *School Administrator, 50*(3),17, 19.

Messick, R. G., & Reynolds, K. E. (1992). *Middle level curriculum.* White Plains, NY: Longman.

Resnick, L. B., & Klopfer, L. E. (Eds.). *Toward the thinking curriculum: Current cognitive research.* 1989 ASCD Yearbook. Alexandria, VA: Association for Supervision and Curriculum Development.

Seif, E. (1993). Integrating skill development across the curriculum. *Schools in the Middle, 2*(4),15–19.

Stevenson, C., & Carr, J. F. (Eds.)(1993). *Integrated studies in the middle grades.* New York: Teachers College Press.

Tobias, R. (1992). Math and science education for African-American youth: A curriculum challenge. *NASSP Bulletin, 76*(546),42–48.

Vars, G. F. (1987). *Interdisciplinary teaching in the middle grades: How and why.* Columbus, OH: National Middle School Association.

Wood, K. D., & Jones, J. P. (1994). Integrating collaborative learning across the curriculum. *Middle School Journal 25*(3),35–39.

CHAPTER 4

Daily Lesson Planning

The emphasis in this chapter is on the importance and the details of planning for your daily instruction. You will be guided through the process, from selecting content for a course to preparing the specific learning outcomes expected as students learn that content. Then, from a content outline and the related and specific learning outcomes, you will learn how to prepare units and daily lessons.

Specifically, this chapter will help you understand:

1. Reasons for and components of careful instructional planning
2. How to plan a course of instruction
3. The meaning of *diagnostic assessment, formative assessment,* and *summative assessment*
4. The variety of documents that provide guidance for course content selection
5. The status of the development of national curriculum standards for mathematics and science
6. How student textbooks can be useful
7. Using cooperation and collaboration in instructional planning
8. Aims, goals, and objectives
9. Learning objectives and how to prepare them
10. Using a response journal to assess for meaningful learning
11. Today's interest in *character education*
12. Preparing and using questions for instruction
13. Ensuring equity in the classroom
14. Processes in instructional planning
15. Preparing and using a course syllabus
16. Preparing daily lessons.

Although careful planning is a critical skill for a teacher, a well-developed plan for teaching will not guarantee the success of a lesson or unit or even the overall effectiveness of a course. The lack of a well-developed plan will, however, almost certainly result in poor teaching. Like a good map, a good plan facilitates reaching the planned destination with more confidence and with fewer wrong turns.

The heart of good planning is good decision making. For every plan, you must decide what your goals and objectives are, what specific subject matter should be taught, what materials of instruction are available and appropriate, and what methods and techniques should be employed to accomplish the objectives. Making these decisions is complicated because there are so many choices. Therefore, you must be knowledgeable about the principles that provide the foundation for effective course, unit, and lesson planning. That the principles of all levels of educational planning are much the same makes mastering the necessary skills easier than you might now think.

A. REASONS FOR PLANNING

Thoughtful and thorough planning is vital if effective teaching is to occur. It helps produce well-organized classes and a purposeful classroom atmosphere, and it reduces the likelihood of problems in classroom control. A teacher who has not planned or who has not planned well will have more problems than are imaginable. During planning it is useful to keep in mind these two important teacher goals: (1) to not waste anyone's time and (2) to select strategies that keep students physically and mentally engaged on task and that ensure student learning.

Also, planning well helps guarantee that you know the subject, for in planning carefully you will more likely become an expert on the subject matter content and the methods of teaching it. You cannot know all there is to know about the subject matter, but careful planning is likely to prevent you from fumbling through half-digested, poorly understood content, making too many errors along the way. Thoughtful and thorough planning is likely to make your classes more lively, more interesting, more accurate, and more relevant and your teaching more successful. Although good planning ensures that you know the material well, have thought through the methods of instruction, and are less likely to have problems in classroom control, there are other reasons for planning carefully.

Careful planning helps to ensure program coherence. Daily plans are an integral part of a larger plan represented by course goals and objectives. Students' learning experiences are thoughtfully planned in sequence, then orchestrated by a teacher who understands the rationale for their respective positions in the curriculum—not precluding, of course, an occasional diversion from planned activities.

Unless the subject matter you are teaching stands alone, follows nothing, and leads to nothing (which is unlikely), there are prerequisites to what you want your students to learn, and there are learning objectives that follow and build on this learning. Good planning provides a mechanism for *scope* (the content that is studied) and *sequence* (the order in which content is studied) articulation.

The diversity of students in today's classrooms demands that you give planning considerations to individual differences—whether they be cultural experiences, different learning styles, various levels of proficiency in the use of the English language, special needs, or any other concerns.

Another reason for careful planning is to ensure program continuation. In your absence, a substitute teacher or other members of the teaching team can fill in, continuing your program.

Thorough and thoughtful planning is important for a teacher's self-assessment. After an activity, a lesson, a unit, and at the end of a semester and the school year, you will assess what was done and the effect it had on student achievement. As discussed in Chapter 1, this is the reflective phase of the thought-processing phases of instruction.

Finally, administrators expect you to plan thoroughly and thoughtfully. Your plans represent a criterion recognized and evaluated by administrators, because for those experienced in such matters, it is aphoristic that poor planning is a precursor to incompetent teaching.

B. COMPONENTS OF PLANNING

These eight components should be considered in instructional planning:

1. *Statement of Philosophy.* This is a general statement about why the plan is important and about how students will learn its content.
2. *Needs Assessment.* By its wording, the statement of philosophy should reflect an appreciation for the cultural plurality of the nation and of the school, with a corresponding perception of the needs of society and its children and of the functions served by the

school. The statement of philosophy and needs of the students should be consistent with the school's mission or philosophy statement. (Every school or school district has such a statement, which usually can be found posted in the office and in classrooms and written in the student and parent handbook.)

3. *Aims, Goals, and Objectives.* The plan's stated aims, goals, and objectives should be consistent with the school's mission or philosophy statement. (The differences between these terms are discussed later in this chapter.)

4. *Sequence.* Sometimes referred to as *vertical articulation, sequence* refers to the plan's relationship to the content learning that preceded and that follows, in the kindergarten through twelfth-grade curriculum.

5. *Integration.* Sometimes referred to as *horizontal articulation, integration* refers to the plan's connection with other curriculum and co-curriculum activities across the grade level. For example, the mathematics program may be articulated with the science program. In many schools, the improvement of student writing is an aim in all disciplines, thus "writing across the curriculum" is an example of integration across grade level (see for example Artzt, 1994).

6. *Sequentially Planned Learning Activities.* This is the presentation of organized and sequential units and lessons appropriate for the subject, grade level, and age and diversity of the students.

7. *Resources Needed.* This is a listing of resources, such as books, speakers, field trips, and media materials.

8. *Assessment Strategies.* Consistent with the objectives, assessment strategies include procedures for diagnosing what students know or think they know (their misconceptions) *prior* to the instruction (diagnostic assessment or preassessment) and evaluating student achievement *during* instruction to find out what students are learning (formative assessment) and *after* the instruction to find out what they have learned (summative assessment).

C. PLANNING A COURSE

When planning a course, you need to decide what is to be accomplished in that time period for which students are assigned to your classroom, whether for an academic year, a semester, or some lesser time period. To help in deciding what is to be accomplished, you will

- Probe, analyze, and translate your own convictions, knowledge, and skills into behaviors that foster the intellectual development of your students
- Review school and other public resource documents for mandates and guidelines
- Talk with colleagues and learn of common expectations.

In addition, and as discussed later in this chapter, to determine what exactly is to be accomplished and how, many teachers collaboratively plan with their students.

Documents That Provide Guidance for Content Selection

Documents produced at the national level, state department of education curriculum publications, district courses of study, and school-adopted printed and nonprinted materials are the sources you will examine. Your college or university library may be a source of such documents. Others may be reviewed at local schools.

To receive accreditation (which normally occurs every three to six years), high schools are reviewed by an accreditation team. Prior to its visit, the schools prepare self-study reports in which each department reviews and updates the curriculum guides that provide descriptive information about the objectives and content of each course and program offered. In about half of the states, middle schools and junior high schools also are accredited by state or regional agencies. In other states, those schools can volunteer to be reviewed for improvement. Elementary schools are not involved in formal accreditation.

National Curriculum Standards

The National Council on Education Standards and Testing has recommended that national standards for subject matter content in education be developed for all core subjects—the arts, civics/social studies, English/language arts/reading, geography, history, mathematics, and science. Standards are a definition of what students should know and be able to do. For the subjects and grade level of interest to you, you will want to follow the development of national curriculum standards.

In 1989, the National Council of Teachers of Mathematics (NCTM) issued standards for mathematics for grades K–12 (see Chapters 7–12). By 1992, more than 40 states, usually through state curriculum frameworks, were following those standards to guide what and how mathematics is taught and how student progress is assessed. (For an account of a K–12 mathematics program that does *not* follow NCTM guidelines, see Hill, 1993.) National standards for mathematics and arts education were completed in March 1994, and standards for science education are still in the process of being developed. Addresses for information or ordering follow:

> *Mathematics.* To order *Curriculum and Evaluation Standards for School Mathematics,* write to The National Council of Teachers of Mathematics (NCTM), Order Processing, 1906 Association Drive, Reston, VA 22091. Item number 398E1, ISBN 0-87353-273-2. Cost is $25.

> *Science.* With a grant from the U.S. Department of Education, the National Research Council's National Committee on Science Education Standards and Assessment, with input from the American Association for the Advancement of Science and the National Science Teachers Association, is developing standards for science education, expected to be completed in 1995. For information, contact National Academy of Sciences, National Research Council, 2101 Constitution Avenue, NW, Washington, DC 20418.

Once the science standards have been completed, they will also be used by state and local school districts to revise their curriculum documents (for example see Willis, 1994.) Guided by these standards and the content of state frameworks, especially those of the larger states such as California, Florida, and Texas, publishers of student textbooks and other instructional materials will develop their new or revised printed and nonprinted instructional materials. By the year 2000, all new standards will likely be in place and be having a positive effect upon student achievement in classroom learning.

Student Textbooks

Traditionally, at the intermediate and middle school level, much class time learning science and mathematics is devoted to use of the textbook and other printed materials. There has often been a gap between what is needed in textbooks and what is available for student use. In recent years, considerable national attention has been given to finding ways of improving the quality of student textbooks, with particular attention given to the need to develop student skills in critical thinking and higher-order problem solving.

For several reasons—the recognition of different individual learning styles of students, the increasing costs of textbooks and decreasing availability of funds, and the availability of nonprint learning materials—textbook appearance, content, and use have changed considerably in recent years. Still, "ninety percent of all classroom activity is regulated by textbooks" (Starr, 1989, p. 106).

School districts have textbook adoption cycles (usually every five or so years), meaning books are used for several years, until the next adoption cycle. If you are a student teacher or a first-year teacher, most likely someone will tell you, "Here are the books you will be using." Starting now, you should become familiar with textbooks you may be using and how you may be using them.

How a textbook can be helpful to students. How can textbooks be of help? Textbooks can help students in their learning by providing

- A base for building higher-order thinking activities (inquiry discussions, problem recognition, and problem solving) that help develop critical thinking skills
- A basis for selecting subject matter that can be used for deciding content
- An organization of basic or important content with models and examples

- Information about other readings and resources to enhance the learning experiences of students
- Previously tested practice activities and suggestions for learning experiences.

Problems with reliance on a single textbook. The student textbook, however, should not be the be-all and end-all of the instructional experience. (For specific information on use of the textbook in mathematics and science, see Chapters 7 and 13, respectively.) The textbook is only one of many teaching tools and should not be cherished as the ultimate word. Of the many methods from which you may select how you use student textbooks, the least acceptable is to show a complete dependence on a single book and require students to simply memorize content from it. That is the lowest level of learning; furthermore, it implies that you are unaware of other sources of instructional materials and have nothing more to contribute to student learning.

Another potential problem brought about by reliance upon a single textbook is that because textbook publishers prepare books for use in a larger market, that is, for national or statewide use, your state- and district-adopted textbook may not, in the view of some members of the school community, adequately address issues of special interest and importance to your community of children and their parents or guardians. That is another reason why some teachers and schools, as well as many textbook publishers, provide supplementary printed and nonprint materials. (At least 24 states use statewide textbook adoption review committees to review books and to provide public school districts with lists of recommended books from which they may select books purchased with funds provided by the state.)

Another very important reason to provide supplementary reading materials is to ensure multicultural balance. A single textbook may not provide the balance needed to ensure the noncontinuance of the traditional cultural and ethnic biases that need to be corrected in our schools and in our teaching, such as linguistic bias (the use of masculine terms and pronouns); stereotyping; invisibility of women, minorities, and disabled persons on printed pages; and imbalance (the glossing over of controversial topics or complete avoidance of the discussion of reality, discrimination, and prejudice) (Sadker, Sadker, & Long, 1989). See Banks and Banks, 1989, for excellent ideas and resources on bringing multicultural balance to your curriculum.

Still another problem brought about by reliance upon a single source is that for many students the adopted textbook may just not be at the appropriate reading level. In today's heterogeneous (mixed-ability-grouping) classrooms, the reading range can vary by as much as two-thirds of the chronological age of the students in the classroom. That means that if the chronological age is 12 years (as is typical for seventh-grade students), then the reading-level range would be 8 years; that is to say, the class may have some children reading only at a preschool level while others may be reading at a level beyond high school. All teachers, not only those responsible for teaching language arts, need to know about the kinds of problem readers and share in the responsibility of seeing that those students get help in developing their skills in reading.

General guidelines for textbook use. Your attention is directed now to the following general guidelines about the use of the textbook as a learning tool.

For science and mathematics in grades 4 through 9, students can benefit from having their own textbooks, especially when the textbooks are current. Due to school budget constraints, the textbooks may *not* be the latest editions, however, and in some schools there may be only classroom sets—textbooks that students are allowed to use only while in the classroom. When that is the case, students either may not be allowed to take the books home or may only occasionally be allowed to check them out. In other classrooms there may be no textbooks at all. Maintain supplementary reading materials for student use in the classroom. School and community librarians usually are delighted to cooperate with teachers in the selection and provision of such materials.

Some students benefit from drill, practice, and reinforcement afforded by accompanying workbooks, but not all necessarily do. As a matter of fact, the traditional workbook, now nearly extinct, is being replaced by the modern technology afforded by computer software, videodiscs, and compact discs. As the costs of hardware and software programs decline, the use of programs by individual students is also becoming more common. Computers provide students with a psychologically safer learning environment. With computer programs and interactive media, the student has greater control over the pace of the instruction and can repeat instruction if necessary or ask for further clarification without fear of having to publicly ask for help.

Provide vocabulary lists to help students learn meanings of important words and phrases. Teach students how to study from their textbook, perhaps by using the SQ4R method: *survey* the chapter, ask *questions* about what was read, *read* to answer the questions, *recite* the answers, *record* important items from the chapter in a notebook, then *review* it all. Or, use the SQ3R method—*survey* the chapter, ask *questions* about what was read, *read, recite,* and *review.*

Encourage students to search other sources for content that will update that found in their textbook, especially the science book and any books that are several years old. (See, for example, Chiappetta, Sethna, & Fillman, 1993.) This is especially important in disciplines such as science, where there is such a tremendous growth in the amount of new information, and, as discussed in the preceding section, it is important whenever a multicultural balance is needed.

Encourage students to be alert for errors in their books—content errors, printing errors, and discrepancies or imbalance in the treatment of minorities, women, and persons with special needs—and perhaps give students some sort of reward, such as points, when they bring an error to your attention. Encouraging students to be alert for errors in the textbook encourages critical reading, critical thinking, and healthy skepticism.

Progressing from one cover of the textbook to the other in one school year is not necessarily an indicator of good teaching. The emphasis in instruction should be on *mastery* of content rather than simply on *coverage* of content. The textbook is one resource; to enhance their learning, children should be encouraged to use a variety of resources.

Individualize the learning for students according to their reading and learning abilities. Consider differentiated assignments in the textbook and supplementary materials. When using supplementary materials, consider using several rather than just one. Except to make life a bit simpler for the teacher, it makes no sense in the typical classroom today, with its diversity of students, to have all students doing the same assignments. When students use materials not designed to accompany their text, however, edit the materials so they relate well to your instructional objectives.

Within the span of your teaching career it is likely that you will witness and be a part of a revolution in the design of school textbooks. Already some school districts and states allow teachers in certain disciplines (where the technology is available) to choose between student textbooks as we have known them and interactive videodisc programs. For example, for elementary school science, the state of Texas allows its schools to adopt Optical Data's *Windows on Science* videodisc-based program. The program comes with a Curriculum Publishing Kit that allows teachers to design their own curriculum from the *Windows on Science* program, and users periodically receive updated data discs. Texas, followed by Utah and West Virginia, were the first states to allow schools to choose between a textbook-centered program and one that is videodisc centered for specific curriculum areas.

With the revolution in computer chip technology, it has been predicted that student textbooks may soon take on a whole new appearance. With that will come dramatic changes in the importance and use of student texts, as well as new problems for the teacher, some of which are predictable. Student "texts" may become credit-card size, increasing the chance of students losing their books. On the positive side, the classroom teacher will probably have available a variety of "textbooks" to better address the reading levels, interests, learning styles, and abilities of individual students. Distribution and maintenance of reading materials could create an even greater demand on the teacher's time. Regardless, dramatic and exciting changes have begun to transform a teaching tool that has not changed much throughout the history of education in this country. As an electronic, multimedia tool, the textbook of the twenty-first century may be "an interactive device that offers text, sound, and video" (Gifford, 1991, pp. 15–16).

D. COLLABORATIVE AND COOPERATIVE TEAM PLANNING

As you have learned, you need not do all your planning from scratch, and neither do you need to do all your planning alone. Planning for teaching can be thought of as rehearsing what will be done in the classroom, both mentally and on paper (Murray, 1980). In classrooms today, which tend to be more project oriented and student and group centered than traditional classrooms, where the teacher was the primary provider of information, students more actively participate in their learning. The teacher provides some structure and assistance, but the collaborative approach requires students to inquire and interact, to generate ideas, to seriously listen to and talk with one another, and to recognize that their thoughts and experiences are valuable and essential to meaningful learning.

Team Planning

As discussed in the previous chapter, many teachers plan together in teams. Planning procedures are the same as discussed earlier in this chapter, except that team members plan together or split the responsibilities and then share their individual planning, cooperatively working up a final plan. As we learned earlier, team planning works best when members of the teaching team share a common planning time.

Collaborative Teacher-Student Planning

Many teachers encourage students to participate in the planning of some phase of their learning, from planning an entire course of study or units within that course of study to planning specific learning activities within a unit of study. Such participation tends to give students a proprietary interest in the activities, thereby increasing their motivation for learning. That which students have contributed to the plan often seems more meaningful to them than what others have planned for them. And they like to see their own plans succeed. Thus, teacher-student collaboration in planning can be an effective motivational tool. (For a report on how one seventh-grade class of students designed their own course of study for an integrated unit, see Smith & Johnson, 1993.)

Preparing for the Year

While some authors believe that the first step in preparing to teach is to write the objectives, others believe that a more logical first step is to prepare a sequential topic outline, and that is the procedure followed here. The sequential outline might be prepared by one teacher, by a teaching team, or collaboratively with the children. Whatever the case, from that outline, you can then prepare some of the important expected learning outcomes. Once you have decided the content and anticipated outcomes, you are ready to divide that into subdivisions or units of instruction and then prepare those units with the daily lessons.

Most beginning teachers are presented with the topic outlines and the instructional objectives (in the course of study or in the teacher's edition of the student textbook) with the often unspoken expectation that they will teach from them. And, for you, this may be the case, but someone had to have written those, and that someone was one or several teachers. So, as a beginning teacher, you should know how it is done, for someday you will be concentrating on it in earnest.

A Caution about Selection and Sequencing of Content

Please be cautioned that beginning teachers sometimes have unrealistic expectations about the amount of content that a heterogeneous group of children can study, comprehend, and learn over a given period of time, especially as learning by those students is influenced by special needs and diverse cultural and language backgrounds. Reviewing school and other public documents and talking with experienced teachers in your school are very helpful in arriving at a realistic selection and sequencing of content and later developing a time frame for teaching that content. Citing the work of Duckworth (1986), Eisner (1985), and Katz (1985), Brooks and Brooks (1993) conclude,

> Constructivist teachers have discovered that the prescribed scope, sequence, and timeline often interferes with their ability to help students understand complex concepts. Rigid timelines are also at odds with research on how human beings form meaningful theories about the ways the

world works, how students and teachers develop an appreciation of knowledge and understanding, and how one creates the disposition to inquire about phenomena not fully understood. Most curriculums simply pack too much information into too little time—at a significant cost to the learner. (p. 29)

Once you have analyzed various curriculum documents and prepared a content outline, you are ready to prepare the anticipated learning outcomes and write the specific instructional objectives, known also as behavioral (or performance) objectives—statements that describe what the student will be able to do upon completion of the instructional experience.

E. THE ROLE OF AIMS, GOALS, AND OBJECTIVES

You will encounter the compound structure that reads "goals and objectives." A distinction needs to be understood. The easiest way to understand the difference between the two words *goals* and *objectives* is to look at your intent.

Goals are ideal states that you intend to reach, that is, ideals that you would like to have accomplished. Goals may be stated as teacher goals, as student goals, or, collaboratively, as course goals. Ideally, in all three, the goal should be the same. If, for example, the goal is to improve students' ability to solve simple equations, it could be stated as follows:

> "To help students improve their ability to   *Teacher or course goal*
> identify and to solve problems"
> or
> "To improve my ability to identify and   *Student goal*
> solve problems"

Goals are general statements of intent, prepared early in course planning. Goals are useful when planned cooperatively with students and/or shared with students as advance mental organizers. The students then know what to expect and will begin to prepare mentally to learn that material. Whereas goals are general, the objectives based on them are specific. The value of stating learning objectives in behavioral terms and in providing advance organizers is well documented by research (Good & Brophy, 1994, p. 244). Objectives are *not* intentions. They are the actual behaviors teachers intend to cause students to display. In short, objectives are what students *do*.

The terminology used for designating the various types of objectives is not standardized. In the literature, the most general educational objectives are often called *aims;* the general objectives of schools, curricula, and courses are called *goals;* the objectives of units and lessons are called *instructional objectives.* Whereas some authors distinguish between "instructional objectives" (objectives that are *not* behavior specific) and "behavioral" or "performance objectives" (objectives that *are* behavior specific), the terms are used here interchangeably to stress the importance of writing objectives for instruction in terms that are measurable. Aims are more general than goals, goals are more general than objectives. Instructional (behavioral) objectives are quite specific.

As implied in the preceding paragraphs, goals guide the instructional methods; objectives drive student performance. Assessment of student achievement in learning should be an assessment of that performance. Assessment procedures that match the instructional objectives are sometimes referred to as aligned or authentic assessment (discussed in the next chapter).

Goals are general statements, usually not even complete sentences, often beginning with the infinitive "to," which identify what the teacher intends the students to learn. Objectives, stated in performance (behavioral) terms, are specific actions and should be written as complete sentences that include the verb "will" to indicate what each student is expected to be able to do as a result of the instructional experience.

While instructional goals may not always be quantifiable, that is, readily measurable, instructional objectives should be measurable. Furthermore, those objectives are, in essence, what is measured by instruments designed to authentically assess student learning.

Consider the following examples of goals and objectives.

Goals	1. To provide reading opportunities for students.
	2. To demonstrate the relationship between mathematics and the natural environment.
Objectives	1. The student will read two books, three short stories, and five newspaper articles at home, within a two-month period. The student will maintain a daily written log of these activities.
	2. Using a sheet of graph paper, the student will plot the diagonals formed by Fibonacci numbers, forming an Archimedian spiral. The student will list at least three different forms in nature that resemble the Archimedian spiral formed by the drawing on the graph paper.

F. INSTRUCTIONAL OBJECTIVES AND THEIR RELATIONSHIP TO INSTRUCTION AND ASSESSMENT

One purpose for writing objectives in specific (i.e., behavioral) terms is to be able to assess with precision whether the instruction has resulted in the desired behavior. In many school districts the educational goals are established as competencies that the students are expected to achieve. This is known variously as *competency-based, performance-based,* or *outcome-based education.* (For informative articles about outcome-based education, see the March 1994 issue of *Educational Leadership.*) These goals are then divided into specific performance objectives, sometimes referred to as *goal indicators.* When students perform the competencies called for by these objectives, their education is considered successful. Expecting students to achieve one set of competencies before moving on to the next set is called *mastery learning.* The success of school curricula, teacher performance, and student achievement may each be assessed according to these criteria.

Assessment is not difficult when the desired performance is overt, that is, when it can be observed directly. Each of the two sample objectives of the preceding section is an example of an overt objective.

Assessment is more difficult when the desired behavior is covert, that is, when it is not directly observable. Although certainly no less important, behaviors that call for "appreciation," "discovery," or "understanding," for example, are not directly observable because they occur within a person and so are covert. Since covert behavior cannot be observed directly, the only way to tell whether the objective has been achieved is to observe behavior that may be indicative of that achievement. The objective, then, must be written in overt language, and evaluators can only assume or trust that the observed behavior is, in fact, indicative of the expected learning outcome.

Behaviorism and Constructivism: Are They Compatible?

While behaviorists (and behaviorism) assume a definition of learning that deals only with changes in observable (overt) behavior, constructivists (and cognitivism), as discussed in Chapter 1, hold that learning entails the construction or reshaping of mental schemata and that mental processes mediate learning, and so are concerned with both overt and covert behaviors (Perkins & Blythe, 1994).

Furthermore, when assessing whether an objective has been achieved, the assessment device must be consistent with the desired learning outcome; otherwise the assessment is invalid. When the measuring device and the learning objective are compatible, the assessment is referred to as being authentic. For example, a person's competency to teach mathematics to fifth-grade children is most reliably measured by directly observing that person *doing* that very thing—teaching mathematics to fifth-grade students. That is assessment that is referred to as being authentic. Using a standardized paper-and-pencil test to determine a person's ability to teach mathematics to fifth graders is not. (Assessment is the topic of the next chapter.)

Does this mean that you must be one or the other, a behaviorist or a constructivist? Probably not. For now, the point is that when writing instructional objectives, you should write most or all of your minimal competency expectations in overt terms (the topic of the next section). On the other hand, you cannot be expected to foresee all learning that will occur or to translate all that is learned into behavioral terms. We agree with those who argue that any effort to write all learning objectives in behavioral terms, in effect, neglects the individual learner; such an approach does not give the greatest consideration to the diversity among learners. Learning that is most meaningful to children is not so neatly and easily predicted and isolated. Rather than teaching one objective at a time, much of the time your teaching will be directed toward the simultaneous learning of multiple objectives, understandings, and appreciations. When you assess for learning, however, assessment is cleaner, and certainly easier, when objectives are assessed one at a time.

G. PREPARING INSTRUCTIONAL OBJECTIVES

When preparing instructional objectives you must ask yourself: "How will the student demonstrate that the objective has been reached?" The objective must include an action that demonstrates that the objective has been achieved. That portion of the objective is sometimes referred to as the *terminal behavior,* or the *anticipated measurable performance,* and is important in an outcome-based educational (OBE) program (Kudlas, 1994).

Four Key Components to Writing Objectives

When completely written, an instructional objective has four key components. To aid in your understanding and remembering, you can refer to them as the ABCDs of writing objectives.

One of these components is the *audience*—that is, the student for whom the objective is intended. To address this audience, sometimes teachers begin their objectives with the phrase "The student will be able to . . ." or personalize the objective as "You will be able to . . . ."

The second key component of an objective is the expected *behavior.* The expected behavior (or performance) should be written with action verbs that are measurable so it is directly observable that an objective has been reached. As discussed in the previous section, some verbs describe covert behaviors that are vague, ambiguous, and not clearly measurable, such as appreciate, believe, comprehend, enjoy, know, learn, like, and understand (see Figure 4.1). These are to be avoided.

The third ingredient is the *conditions*—the setting in which the behavior will be demonstrated by the student and observed by the teacher. In our earlier sample objective beginning, "The student will read . . . ," the conditions are "at home, within a two-month period." For the second sample objective, the conditions are, "Using a sheet of graph paper, ..."

The fourth ingredient, not always included in objectives written by teachers, is the *degree of expected performance.* This is the ingredient that allows for the assessment of student learning. When mastery learning is expected (achievement of 85 to 100 percent), the level of expected performance is usually omitted because it is understood. (In teaching for mastery learning, the performance-level expectation is 100 percent. In reality, however, the performance level will most likely be between 85 and 95 percent, particularly when working with a group of students rather than an individual student. The 5 to 15 percent difference allows for human error, as can occur with written and oral communication.)

Performance level is used to evaluate student achievement and, sometimes, the effectiveness of the teaching. Student grades might be based on performance levels; evaluation of teacher effectiveness might be based on the level of student performance. Now, using Figure 4.2, try your skill at recognizing objectives that are measurable.

H. CLASSIFICATION OF INSTRUCTIONAL OBJECTIVES

Three domains for classifying instructional objectives are useful for planning and assessing student learning. These are

- *Cognitive domain.* This is the domain of learning that involves mental operations, from the lowest level of simple recall of information to high-level and complex evaluative processes.

- *Affective domain.* This domain of learning involves feelings, attitudes, and values, from lower levels of acquisition to the highest level of internalization and action.
- *Psychomotor domain.* The is the domain of learning that involves simple manipulation of materials on up to the higher level of communication of ideas, and finally, the highest level of creative performance.

Schools attempt to provide learning experiences designed to meet the needs of the total child. Specifically, five areas of developmental needs are identified: (1) intellectual, (2) physical, (3) psychological, (4) social, and (5) moral and ethical. You should include learning objectives that address each of these developmental needs. While intellectual needs fall primarily within the cognitive domain and physical needs within the psychomotor domain, the others are mostly affective. Too many teachers direct their attention to the cognitive, assuming that psychomotor and affective needs will take care of themselves.

To better organize instruction to help students become scientifically and technologically literate, Alan J. McCormack and Robert E. Yager (1989) propose five domains in a taxonomy for science teaching: knowing and understanding scientific information; exploring and discovering scientific processes; imagining and creating; feeling and valuing; and using applications and making connections.

FIGURE 4.1
Verbs to Avoid When Writing Objectives

appreciate	enjoy	indicate	like
believe	familiarize	know	realize
comprehend	grasp	learn	understand

FIGURE 4.2
Recognizing Objectives That Are Measurable

Assess your skill in recognizing objectives that are measurable, that is, that are stated in behavioral terms. Place an X before each of the following that is a student-centered behavioral objective that is clearly measurable. Although "audience," "conditions," and "performance levels" may be absent, ask yourself, "As stated, is it a student-centered objective that is measurable?" If it is, then place the X in the blank. An answer key follows. After checking your answers, discuss any problems with your classmates and instructor.

_____ 1. To develop an appreciation for logic.

_____ 2. To identify numbers that are whole numbers.

_____ 3. To provide meaningful experiences for the children.

_____ 4. To recognize lowest common denominators.

_____ 5. To boot up the program on the computer.

_____ 6. To correctly solve a series of equations when there is one unknown.

_____ 7. To develop skills in inquiry.

_____ 8. To prepare an argument for or against the use of clear cutting.

_____ 9. To illustrate an awareness of the importance of the hole in the ozone layer by supplying relevant newspaper articles.

_____ 10. To know the times tables.

Answer key: 2, 4, 5, 6, 8, 9.
Items 1, 3, 7, and 10 are inadequate because of their ambiguity. Item 3 is not even a student learning objective; it is a teacher goal. "To develop" and "to know" can have too many interpretations.
Although the conditions are not given, items 2, 4, 5, 6, and 8 are clearly measurable. The teacher would have no difficulty recognizing when a learner had reached those objectives. For item 9, however, which is in the affective domain, the teacher can only trust (and assume) that student awareness is demonstrated when the student brings in the newspaper articles.

Regardless of taxonomy chosen, the important point is that effective teachers direct their planning and sequence their instruction so students are guided from the lowest to highest levels of operation within and across each of the domains of learning.

Returning to the widely accepted taxonomy, the following discussion of the three developmental hierarchies will guide your understanding of how to address each of the five areas of needs. Notice the illustrative verbs within each hierarchy of each domain. These verbs help you to fashion objectives for your lesson plans.

Cognitive Domain Hierarchies

In the taxonomy of objectives that is most widely accepted, Benjamin Bloom and his associates (1984) arranged cognitive objectives into classifications according to the complexity of the skills and abilities embodied in them. The resulting taxonomy portrays a ladder ranging from the simplest to the most complex intellectual processes. Rather than an orderly progression from simple to complex mental operations as illustrated by Bloom's taxonomy, other researchers prefer an identification of cognitive abilities that ranges from simple information storage and retrieval, through a higher level of discrimination and concept attainment, to the highest cognitive ability to recognize and solve problems (Gagné, Briggs, & Wager, 1988).

It is important to understand that regardless of the domain and within each, prerequisite to a student's ability to function at one level of the hierarchy is the student's ability to function at the preceding level or levels. In other words, when a student is functioning at the third level of the cognitive domain, then that student is automatically and simultaneously functioning also at the first and second levels. For example, we cannot apply knowledge that we do not have or cannot recall or understand.

The six major categories (or levels) in Bloom's taxonomy of cognitive objectives are

1. *Knowledge*—recognizing and recalling information
2. *Comprehension*—basic understanding of the meaning of information
3. *Application*—using information in new situations
4. *Analysis*—ability to dissect information into component parts and see relationships
5. *Synthesis*—putting components together to form new ideas
6. *Evaluation*—judging the worth of an idea, notion, theory, thesis, proposition, information, or opinion.

The last three—analysis, synthesis, and evaluation—are generally thought of and referred to as *higher-order thinking skills.*

Although space here does not allow elaboration, Bloom's taxonomy includes various subcategories within each of these six major categories. It is less important that an objective be absolutely classified than that you are cognizant of hierarchies of levels of thinking and doing and understand the importance of attending to student cognitive development and intellectual behavior from lower to higher levels of operation in all three domains.

A discussion of each of Bloom's six categories follows.

Knowledge. The basic element in Bloom's taxonomy concerns the acquisition of knowledge—that is, the ability to recognize and recall information. Although this is the lowest level of the six categories, the information to be learned may not itself be of a low level. In fact, the information may be extremely complex. Bloom includes at this level knowledge of principles, generalizations, theories, structures, and methodology, as well as knowledge of facts and ways of dealing with facts.

Action verbs appropriate for this category include *choose, complete, define, describe, identify, indicate, list, locate, match, name, outline, recall, recognize, select,* and *state.* (Note that because of imperfections in the English language some verbs may be appropriately used at more than one cognitive level. For example, a student may be asked to *describe* what he or she recalls—knowledge—about mixing an acid and a base, or a student might be asked to *describe* his or her understanding—comprehension—of the procedure for mixing an acid and a base.)

The following are examples of objectives at this cognitive level. Note especially the verb used in each example.

- The student *will state* how many angles there are inside a triangle.
- Beginning with prophase, the student *will list* in order the stages of mitosis.

The remaining five categories of Bloom's taxonomy of the cognitive domain deal with the *use* of knowledge.

Comprehension. Comprehension includes the ability to translate or explain knowledge, to interpret that knowledge, and to extrapolate from it to address new situations.

Action verbs appropriate for this category include *change, classify, convert, defend, derive, describe, estimate, expand, explain, generalize, infer, interpret, paraphrase, predict, recognize, summarize,* and *translate.*

Examples of objectives in this category are

- The student *will explain* the characteristics that are true for all triangles.
- The student *will summarize* each stage of mitosis.

Application. Once students understand information, they should be apply to apply it. This is the category of operation above comprehension.

Action verbs include *apply, compute, demonstrate, develop, discover, discuss, modify, operate, participate, perform, plan, predict, relate, show, solve,* and *use.*

Examples of objectives in this category are

- The student *will compute* the measure of

- The student *will discuss* each stage of mitosis, demonstrating her or his comprehension of how, even though cells duplicate themselves, the cell's chromosome number remains constant.

Analysis. This category includes objectives that require students to use the skills of analysis.

Action verbs appropriate for this category include *analyze, break down, categorize, classify, compare, contrast, debate, deduce, diagram, differentiate, discriminate, identify, illustrate, infer, outline, relate, separate,* and *subdivide.*

Examples of objectives in this category include

- The student *will contrast* how all triangles differ from all rectangles.
- The student *will diagram* each stage of mitosis to *illustrate* what is happening to the nuclear material of the original parent cell.

Synthesis. This category includes objectives that involve such skills as designing a plan, proposing a set of operations, and deriving a series of abstract relations.

Action verbs appropriate for this category include *arrange, categorize, classify, combine, compile, constitute, create, design, develop, devise, document, explain, formulate, generate, modify, organize, originate, plan, produce, rearrange, reconstruct, revise, rewrite, summarize, synthesize, tell, transmit,* and *write.*

Examples of objectives in this category are

- Using what is known about triangles, the student *will explain* how to find the sum of interior angles of any parallelogram.
- The student *will devise* an experiment suitable for testing a hypothesis related to the concept of mitosis.

FIGURE 4.3
Classifying Cognitive Objectives

Assess your ability to recognize the level of cognitive objectives. For each of the following cognitive objectives, identify by appropriate letter the *highest* level of operation that is called for: (K) knowledge; (C) comprehension; (AP) application; (AN) analysis; (S) synthesis; (E) evaluation. Check your answers with the answer key, and discuss the results with your classmates and instructor. Your understanding of the concepts involved is more important than whether you score 100 percent against the answer key.

_____ 1. In a few sentences, the student will summarize the difference between the two processes, photosynthesis and cellular respiration.

_____ 2. The student will name the number of legs that arachnids have.

_____ 3. The student will explain how to get a tightly fitted metal lid off of an empty jar without breaking the jar or the lid.

_____ 4. The student will collect data and make a graph to determine the average life of a pencil used in school.

_____ 5. If you were to repeat the experiment, explain how you might do it better.

_____ 6. The student will solve the problem, $7 \times 8 = $ _____.

_____ 7. In 45, the student will tell which digit represents the largest value, the 4 or the 5, and will justify her or his answer.

_____ 8. The student will find the next value in the number pattern: 1, 1, 2, 3, 5, 8, 13, _____

_____ 9. The student will devise a method to prove a ray to be the bisector of an angle.

_____ 10. Given a list of five solids, five liquids, and five gases, the student will describe the physical and chemical properties of each list.

Answer Key: 1 = C; 2 = K; 3 = AP; 4 = S; 5 = E; 6 = K; 7 = E; 8 = AN; 9 = S; 10 = K.

Evaluation. The highest cognitive category of Bloom's taxonomy is evaluation. This includes offering opinions and making value judgments.

Action verbs appropriate for this category include *appraise, argue, assess, compare, conclude, consider, contrast, criticize, decide, discriminate, evaluate, explain, interpret, judge, justify, rank, rate, relate, standardize, support,* and *validate.*

Examples of objectives in this category are

- The student *will validate* that the sum of interior angles of a triangle is equal to a straight line.
- While observing living plant cells, the student *will justify* his or her interpretation that specified nuclei are in certain stages of mitosis.

Now, by referring to Figure 4.3, check your understanding.

Affective Domain Hierarchies

Krathwohl, Bloom, and Masia (1964) developed a taxonomy for the affective domain. The following are their major levels (or categories), from least internalized to most internalized:

1. *Receiving.* Being aware of the affective stimulus and beginning to have favorable feelings toward it.
2. *Responding.* Taking an interest in the stimulus and viewing it favorably.
3. *Valuing.* Showing a tentative belief in the value of the affective stimulus and becoming committed to it.
4. *Organizing.* Organizing values into a system of dominant and supporting values.
5. *Internalizing values.* Making beliefs and behavior consistent—a way of life.

The following paragraphs provide an understanding of the types of objectives that fit the categories of the affective domain. Although there is considerable overlap from one category to another, the categories do provide a basis by which to judge the quality of objectives and the level of learning within this domain.

Receiving. At this level, the least internalized, the student exhibits willingness to give attention to particular phenomena or stimuli, and the teacher is able to arouse, sustain, and direct that attention.

Action verbs appropriate for this category include *ask, choose, describe, differentiate, distinguish, hold, identify, locate, name, point to, recall, recognize, reply, select,* and *use.*

Examples of objectives in this category are

- The student pays close attention to the directions for the laboratory activities.
- During class discussions, the student listens attentively to the ideas being expressed by others.
- During instructional activities, the student demonstrates sensitivity to the property of others.

Responding. Students respond to the stimulus they have received. They may do so because of some external pressure (an extrinsic source of motivation) or voluntarily because they find it interesting or because responding gives them satisfaction (because of intrinsic motivation).

Action verbs appropriate for this category include *answer, applaud, approve, assist, comply, command, discuss, greet, help, label, perform, play, practice, present, read, recite, report, select, spend (leisure time in), tell,* and *write.*

Examples of objectives at this level are

- The student voluntarily selects books on science from the library for pleasurable reading.
- The student discusses what others have said.
- The student willingly cooperates with others during laboratory and mathematics cooperative group learning activities.

Valuing. Objectives at the valuing level have to do with students' beliefs, attitudes, and appreciations. The simplest objectives concern a student's acceptance of beliefs and values. Higher objectives concern a student's learning to prefer certain values and finally becoming committed to them.

Action verbs appropriate for this level include *argue, assist, complete, describe, differentiate, explain, follow, form, initiate, invite, join, justify, propose, protest, read, report, select, share, study, support,* and *work.*

Examples of objectives in this category include

- The student initiates a movement against an action that could have a negative impact on the school campus environment.
- The student supports actions against gender, racial, and ethnic discrimination.
- The student argues in favor of or against women's right to have an abortion.

Organizing. This fourth level in the affective domain concerns the building of a personal value system. At this level the student is conceptualizing values and arranging them in a value system that recognizes priorities and the relative importance of various values faced in life.

Action verbs appropriate for this level include *adhere, alter, arrange, balance, combine, compare, defend, define, discuss, explain, form, generalize, identify, integrate, modify, order, organize, prepare, relate,* and *synthesize.*

Examples of objectives at this level are

- The student modifies his or her own behavior in order to conform with acceptable social behavior in the classroom, school, and community.
- The student forms and adheres to a personal standard of social ethic.
- The student defines and integrates with the larger culture the important values of his or her own culture.

Personal value system. This is the last and highest level within the affective domain. At this level the student's behaviors are consistent with his or her beliefs.

Action verbs appropriate for this level include *act, complete, display, influence, listen, modify, perform, practice, propose, qualify, question, revise, serve, solve,* and *verify.*

Examples of objectives appropriate for this level are

- The student behaves according to a well-defined and ethical code of behavior.
- The student practices accuracy in his or her verbal communication.
- The student works independently and diligently.

Psychomotor Domain Hierarchies

Whereas classification within the cognitive and affective domains is generally agreed upon, there has been less agreement on classification within the psychomotor domain. Originally of interest primarily to physical education teachers and teachers of young children, this domain's goal was simply developing and categorizing proficiency in skills, particularly those dealing with gross and fine muscle control. Today's classification of that domain, however, as presented here, also includes higher creative and inventive behaviors, thus coordinating skills and knowledge from all three domains. Consequently, the objectives are arranged in a hierarchy from simple gross locomotor control to the most creative and complex, requiring originality and fine locomotor control—for example, from simply threading a needle to designing and making a piece of clothing.

Harrow (1977) developed the following taxonomy of the psychomotor domain. Included are sample objectives as well as a list of possible action verbs for each level of the psychomotor domain. The levels are

1. *Movement.* This involves gross motor coordination.
   Action verbs appropriate for this level include *adjust, carry, clean, locate, obtain,* and *walk.*
   Sample objectives for this level are
   - The student correctly manipulates a hand-held calculator.
   - The student correctly grasps and carries the microscope to the workstation.
2. *Manipulating.* This level involves fine motor coordination.
   Action verbs appropriate for this level include *assemble, build, calibrate, connect,* and *thread.*
   Sample objectives for this level are
   - The student will do specified calculations using the hand-held calculator.
   - The student will focus the microscope correctly.
3. *Communicating.* This level involves the communication of ideas and feelings.
   Action verbs appropriate for this level include *analyze, ask, describe, draw, explain,* and *write.*
   Sample objectives for this level are
   - The student will develop a technique to calculate and analyze for time efficiency and learning effectiveness the ways that people move from one place to another on the school campus.
   - The student draws accurate details of what is depicted while observing a prepared slide through the microscope.
4. *Creating.* This is the highest level of this and all domains and represents the student's coordination of thinking, learning, and behaving in all three domains.
   Action verbs appropriate for this level include *create, design,* and *invent.*
   Sample objectives for this level are
   - From his or her own data collecting and calculations, the student will design a more time-efficient and learning-effective way of moving people from one place to another on the school campus.
   - From materials that have been discarded in the environment, the student will design an environment for an imaginary animal that he or she has mentally created.

I. USING THE TAXONOMIES

Theoretically, as noted earlier, the taxonomies are so constructed that students achieve each lower level before being ready to move to the next higher level. But because categories overlap, this theory does not always hold in practice. The taxonomies are important in that they emphasize the various levels to which instruction must aspire. For learning to be worthwhile, you must formulate and teach to objectives from the higher levels of the taxonomies (the higher-order thinking skills) as well as from the lower ones. Student thinking and behaving must be moved from the lowest to the highest levels.

In using the taxonomies, remember that the point is to formulate the best objectives for the job to be done. The taxonomies provide the mechanism for ensuring that you do not spend a disproportionate amount of time on simple recall of facts and low-order learning, that is, learning that is relatively trivial. Writing objectives is essential to the preparation of good items for the assessment of student learning. Clearly communicating your behavioral expectations to students and then specifically assessing student learning against those expectations makes the teaching most efficient and effective, and it makes the assessment of the learning closer to authentic. This does not mean that you will *always* write behavioral objectives for everything taught, nor will you always be highly accurate in measuring what students have learned. Learning that is meaningful to students is not as easily compartmentalized as the taxonomies of educational objectives would imply.

Using a Response Journal to Assess for Meaningful Learning

In learning that is most important and that has the most meaning to students, the domains are inextricably interconnected, that is, "we 'think' with our feelings and 'feel' with our thoughts" (Caine & Caine, 1993, p. 19). Consequently, when assessing for student learning, you must look for those connections. One way of doing that is to have students maintain a journal in which they reflect on and respond to their learning using the following categories, adapted with permission from Fersh (1993, pp. 23–24):

1. *"I never knew that."* In this category, student responses are primarily to factual information, new knowledge, and bits and pieces of raw information, often expected to be memorized, regardless of how meaningful to students it might be. Because this is only fragmented knowledge and merely scratches the surface of meaningful learning, it must not be the end-all of student learning. Learning that is meaningful goes beyond the "I never knew that" category, expands upon the bits and pieces, and connects them, allowing the learner to make sense out of what he or she is learning. Learning that does not extend beyond the "I never knew that" category is dysfunctional.
2. *"I never thought of that."* Here, student responses reveal an additional way of perceiving. Their responses may include elements of "I never knew that" but also contain higher-level thinking as a result of their reflection on that knowledge.
3. *"I never felt that."* In this category, student responses are connected to the affective, eliciting more of an emotional response than a cognitive one. Meaningful learning is much more than intellectual understanding; it includes a "felt" meaning (Caine & Caine, 1993).
4. *"I never appreciated that."* Responses in this category reflect a sense of recognition that one's own life can be enriched by what others have created or done, or that something already known can be valued from an additional perspective.
5. *"I never realized that."* In this fifth category, student responses indicate an awareness of overall patterns and dynamic ways in which behavior is holistic, establishing meaningful and potentially useful connections among knowledge, values, and purposes.

Character Education

Related especially to the affective domain, although not exclusive of the cognitive and psychomotor domains, is a resurgence in national interest in the development of students' values (Massey, 1993), especially honesty, kindness, respect, and responsibility—what is called character education. For example, Wynne and Ryan (1993) state that "transmitting character, academics, and discipline—essentially, 'traditional' moral values—to pupils is a vital educational responsibility" (p. 3). Thus, if one agrees with that interpretation, then the teaching of moral values is the transmission of character, academics, and discipline and clearly implies learning that transcends the three domains of learning presented in this chapter.

Whether defined as ethics, citizenship, moral values, or personal development, character education has long been part of public education in this country (Burrett & Rusnak, 1993, p. 10). Today, stimulated by a perceived need to reduce student antisocial behaviors (such as drug abuse and violence) and to produce more respectful and responsible citizens, with a primary focus on the affective domain, many schools and districts are developing curricula in character education and instruction in conflict resolution, with the ultimate goal of "developing mature adults capable of responsible citizenship and moral action (p. 15). Some specific techniques are to sensitize students to value issues through role-playing and creative drama, have students take the opposite point of view in discussions, promote higher-order thinking about value issues through appropriate questioning techniques, arrange action-oriented projects, use parents and community members to assist in projects, highlight examples of class and individual cooperation in serving the school and community, and make student service projects visible in the school and community (p. 29).

J. QUESTIONING TECHNIQUES

Properly following the discussion of instructional objectives and character education is this discussion of an instructional strategy fundamental to teaching—the use of questioning. You will use questioning for so many purposes that you must be highly skilled in its use to teach most effectively.

Purposes for Using Questioning

You will adapt the type and form of each question that you ask to the purpose for which it is asked. The purposes that questions can serve can be separated into five categories. These are

1. *To politely give instructions.* For example, "Lucy, would you please turn out the lights so we can show the slides?" Teachers sometimes use rhetorical questions to regain student attention and maintain classroom control—for example, "Donald, would you please attend to your work?"
2. *To review and remind students of classroom procedures.* For example, if students continue to talk without first raising their hands and being recognized by you, you can stop the lesson and ask, "Class, I think we need to review the procedure for answering my questions. For talking, what is the procedure that we agreed upon?"
3. *To gather information.* For example, "How many of you have finished the exercise?" Or, to find out whether a student knows something, "Carol, can you please tell us how to convert from Fahrenheit to Celsius temperatures?"
4. *To discover student interests or experiences.* For example, "How many of you have already been to the marine aquarium?"
5. *To guide student thinking and learning.* It is this category of questioning that is the focus of our attention now. Questions in this category are used to
   - Clarify a student response
   - Develop appreciation
   - Develop student thinking
   - Diagnose learning difficulty
   - Emphasize major points
   - Encourage students
   - Establish rapport
   - Evaluate learning
   - Give practice in expression
   - Help students in their own metacognition
   - Help students interpret materials
   - Help students organize materials
   - Probe deeper into a student's thinking
   - Provide drill and practice
   - Provide review
   - Show agreement or disagreement
   - Show relationships, such as cause and effect.

Types of Cognitive Questioning

Before going further let us define, describe, and provide examples for each of the types of cognitive questions that you will use in teaching. Then, in the section that follows, we will focus your attention on the levels of cognitive questions.

Clarifying question. The clarifying question is used to gain more information from a student to help the teacher better understand a student's ideas, feelings, and thought processes. Oftentimes, asking the child to elaborate on an initial response will cause the student to think deeper, restructure his or her thinking, and while doing so, discover a fallacy in the original response. One example of a clarifying question is "What I hear you saying is that you would rather work alone than in your group. Is that correct?" Research has shown a strong positive correlation between student learning and development of metacognitive skills and the teacher's use of questions that ask students for clarification (Costa, 1991). In addition, by seeking clarification, the teacher is likely to be demonstrating an interest in the student and her or his thinking.

Convergent thinking question. Convergent thinking questions (also called "narrow" questions) are low-order thinking questions that have a singular answer (such as recall questions discussed and exemplified in the next section). Examples of convergent questions are "If the radius of a circle is 20 feet, what is the circle's circumference?" "What is the name of the plant cell organelle that contains the chloroplast?"

Cueing question. If you ask a question to which, after sufficient wait time (2 to 9 seconds), no students respond, or if their inadequate responses indicate they need more information, then you can ask a question that cues the answer or response you are seeking. In essence, you are going backward in your questioning sequence to cue the students. For example, if a teacher asks her students, "How many legs do crayfish, lobsters, and shrimp have?" and there is no accurate response, then she might cue the answer with the following information and question: "The class to which those animals belong is class Decapoda. Does that give you a clue about the number of legs they have?"

Divergent thinking question. Divergent thinking questions (also known as "broad," "reflective," or "thought" questions) are open ended, high-order thinking questions requiring analysis, synthesis, or evaluation that force students to think creatively, to leave the comfortable confines of the known and reach out into the unknown. An example of a question that requires divergent thinking is "What measures could be taken to improve the effectiveness of mathematics teaching and learning at Jefferson Middle School?"

Evaluative question. Some types of questions, whether convergent or divergent, require students to place a value on something. These are referred to as evaluative questions. If the teacher and the students all agree on certain premises, then the evaluative question would also be a convergent question. If original assumptions differ, then the response to the evaluative question would be more subjective, and therefore that evaluative question would be divergent. An example of an evaluative question is "Should the United States allow clear cutting in its national forests?"

Focus question. This is any question designed to focus student thinking. For example, the question of the preceding paragraph is a focus question when the teacher is attempting to focus student attention on the social and scientific issues involved.

Probing question. Similar to a clarifying question, the probing question requires student thinking to go beyond superficial "first-answer" or single-word responses. Examples of probing questions are "Why, Sean, do you think that every citizen has the right to say what he or she believes?" or "Could you give us an example?"

Levels of Cognitive Questions and Student Thinking

Questions posed by you are cues to your students to the level of thinking expected of them, ranging from the lowest level of mental operation, requiring simple recall of knowledge (convergent thinking), to the highest, requiring divergent thought and application of that thought. It is important that you (1) are aware of the levels of thinking, (2) understand the importance of attending to student thinking from low to higher levels of operation, and (3) understand that what may be a matter of simple recall of information for one student may require a higher-order mental activity for another.

You should structure and sequence your questions in a way that is designed to guide students to higher levels of thinking. Three levels of questioning and thinking have been identified by various authors (see, for example, Costa, 1989, 1991; Eisner, 1979). You should recognize the similarity between these three levels of questions and the six levels of thinking from Bloom's taxonomy of cognitive objectives. For your daily use of questioning it is just as useful but more practical to think and behave in terms of these three levels, rather than of six.

1. *Lowest level (the data input phase): gathering and recalling information.* At this level questions are designed to solicit from students concepts, information, feelings, or experiences that were gained in the past and stored in memory. Sample key words and desired behaviors are *complete, count, define, describe, identify, list, match, name, observe, recall, recite, select.*
2. *Intermediate level (the data processing phase): processing information.* At this level questions are designed to draw relationships of cause and effect, to synthesize, analyze, summarize, compare, contrast, or to classify data. Sample key words and desired behaviors are *analyze, classify, compare, contrast, distinguish, explain, group, infer, make an analogy, organize, plan, synthesize.*
3. *Highest level (the data output phase): applying and evaluating in new situations.* Questions at this level encourage students to think intuitively, creatively, and hypothetically; to use their imaginations; to expose a value system; or to make a judgment. Sample key words and desired behaviors are *apply a principle, build a model, evaluate, extrapolate, forecast, generalize, hypothesize, imagine, judge, predict, speculate.*

You should use the type of question that is best suited for the purpose, use a variety of different levels of questions, and structure questions to move student thinking to higher levels. When their teachers use higher-level questions, students tend to score higher on tests of critical thinking and on standardized tests of achievement (Newton, 1978; Redfield & Rousseau, 1981).

Developing your skill in the use of questioning needs your attention to detail and practice. The following guidelines will provide that detail.

Guidelines for Using Questioning

As is emphasized many times in several ways throughout this book, your goals are to help your students learn how to solve problems, to make decisions and value judgments, to think creatively and critically, and to feel good about themselves and their learning rather than to simply fill their minds with bits and pieces of information. How you construe your questions and how you carry out your questioning strategy is important to the realization of these goals.

Preparing questions. When preparing questions, consider the following:

1. Cognitive questions should be planned, thoughtfully worded, and written into your lesson plan. Thoughtful preparation of questions helps to ensure that they are clear, specific, and not ambiguous, that the vocabulary is appropriate, and that each question matches its purpose. Incorporate questions into your lessons as instructional devices, welcomed pauses, attention grabbers, and as checks for student comprehension. Thoughtful teachers even plan questions that they intend to ask specific students.
2. Match questions with their purposes. Carefully planning questions allows them to be sequenced and worded to match the levels of cognitive thinking expected of students.

Demonstrate to students how to develop their thinking skills. To demonstrate, you must use terminology that is specific and that provides students with examples of experiences consonant with the meanings of the cognitive words. You should demonstrate this every day so students learn the cognitive terminology (Costa, 1991). As stated by Brooks and Brooks (1993), "framing tasks around cognitive activities such as analysis, interpretation, and prediction—and explicitly using those terms with students—fosters the construction of new understandings" (p. 105). Here are three examples:

Instead of	*Say*
"How else might it be done?"	"How could you *apply . . . ?*"
"Are you going to get quiet?	"If we are going to hear what Joan has to say, what do you need to do?"
"How do you know that is so?"	"What evidence do you have?"

Implementing questions. Careful preparation of questions is one part of skill in questioning; implementation is the other part. Here are guidelines for effective implementation:

1. Avoid bombarding students with too much teacher talk. Sometimes teachers talk too much. This could be especially true for teachers who are nervous, as are many during initial weeks of their student teaching. Knowledge of the guidelines presented here will help you avoid that syndrome. Remind yourself to be quiet after you ask a question that you have carefully formulated. Sometimes, due to lack of confidence or preparation, the teacher asks a question, then, with a slight change in wording, asks it again, or asks several questions, one after another. That is too much verbiage, and "shotgun" questioning only confuses students while allowing too little time for them to think.

2. After asking a question, provide students with adequate time to think. Knowing the subject better than the students know it and having given prior thought to it, too many teachers fail to allow students sufficient time to think after asking a question. Plus, by the time they have reached middle school (or sooner), students have learned how to play the "game"—that is, they know that if they remain silent long enough, the teacher will probably answer his or her own question. After asking a well-worded question, you should remain quiet for awhile, allowing students time to think and to respond. And, if you wait long enough, they usually will.

   After asking a question, how long should you wait before you do something? You should wait at least 2 seconds, and as long as 9. Stop reading now, and look at your watch or a clock to get a feeling for how long 2 seconds is. Then, observe how long 9 seconds is. Did 9 seconds seem a long time? Because most of us are not used to silence in the classroom, 2 seconds of silence can seem quite long, while 9 seconds may seem an eternity. If for some reason students have not responded after a period of 2 to 9 seconds of wait time, then you can ask the same question again using the same words, pause for several seconds, then, if you still haven't received a response, call on a student, then another, if necessary, after sufficient wait time. Soon you will get a response that can be built upon. Never answer your own question! For a further discussion of the importance of wait time in a constructivist classroom, see Brooks and Brooks (1993, pp. 114–115).

3. Practice calling on all students, not just the bright or the slow, not just the boys or the girls, not only those in the front of the room, but all of them. To do these things takes concentrated effort on your part, but it is important, especially in teaching mathematics and science. For useful tips, see Feder-Feitel (1994, pp. 56–60, 64–66) and Leach (1994, pp. 54–59).

4. Give the same amount of wait time (think time) to all students. This, too, will require concentrated effort on your part but is also important. A teacher who waits for less time when calling on a slow student or students of one gender is showing prejudice or a lack of confidence in certain students, both of which are detrimental to striving to establish for all students a positive, equal, and safe environment for classroom learning. Show confidence in all students, and never discriminate by expecting less or more from some than from others.

5. When you ask questions, don't let students randomly shout out their answers; instead, require them to raise their hands and be called on before they respond. Establish that procedure and stick with it. This helps ensure that you equally distribute your interactions with the students and that girls are not interacted with less because boys tend to be more obstreperous. Even at the college level, male students tend to be more vociferous than female students and, when allowed by the instructor, tend to outtalk and to interrupt their female peers. Every teacher has the responsibility to guarantee a nonbiased and equal distribution of interaction time in the classroom.

6. Use strong praise sparingly. Use of strong praise is sometimes appropriate, especially when working with students who are different or asking questions of simple, low-level

recall. But when you want students to think divergently and creatively, you should be stingy with your use of strong praise of student responses. Strong praise from a teacher tends to terminate divergent and creative thinking.

One of your goals is to help students find intrinsic sources of motivation, that is, an inner drive that causes them to want to learn. Use of strong praise tends to build conformity, causing students to depend on outside forces (the giver of praise) for their worth, rather than on themselves. An example of strong praise is when a teacher responds to a student answer with, "That's right! Very good." On the other hand, passive acceptance responses, such as "Okay, that seems to be one possibility," keep the door open for further thinking, particularly for higher level, divergent thinking.

Another example of a passive acceptance response is one used in brainstorming sessions: "After asking the question and giving you time to think about it, I will hear your ideas and record them on the board." Only after all student responses have been heard and recorded does the class begin its consideration of each. In the classroom, that kind of nonjudgmental acceptance of all ideas will generate a great deal of expression of high-level thought. (For further discussion of research findings about the use of praise and rewards in teaching, see Joyce & Showers, 1988; Lepper & Green, 1978.)

7. Encourage students to ask questions about content and process. There is no such thing as a "dumb" question. Sometimes students, like everyone else, ask questions that could just as easily have been looked up. Those questions can consume precious class time. For a teacher, this can be frustrating. A teacher's initial reaction might be to quickly and mistakenly assume that the student is too lazy to look up an answer and respond with sarcasm. In such instances, you are advised to think before responding and to respond kindly and professionally, although in the busy life of a classroom teacher, that may not always be easy. Be assured that there is a reason for a student's question. Perhaps the student is signaling a need for recognition.

   In large schools, it is easy for a student to feel alone and insignificant sometimes (although this seems less the case in schools that use a school-within-a-school plan), and a student's making an effort to interact with you can be a positive sign. So carefully gauge your responses to those efforts. If a student question is really off track, off the wall, out of order, and out of context with the content of the lesson, consider this possible response: "That is an interesting question (or comment) and I would like to talk more with you about it. Could we meet at lunchtime, or before or after school?"

   Student questions can and should be used as springboards for further questions, discussion, and investigations. Students should be encouraged to ask questions that challenge the textbook, the process, or another person's statements, and they should be encouraged to seek the facts or evidence behind a statement.

8. Being able to ask questions may be more important than having right answers. Knowledge is derived from asking questions. Being able to recognize problems and to formulate questions is a skill and the key to problem-solving and critical thinking skill development. While teaching mathematics or science, you have a responsibility to encourage students to formulate questions and to help them word their questions in such a way that tentative answers can be sought. That is the process necessary to build a base of knowledge that can be called upon over and over to link, interpret, and explain new information in new situations (Resnick & Klopfer, 1989).

9. Questioning is the cornerstone of critical thinking and real-world problem solving. In real-world problem solving, there are usually no absolute right answers. Rather than being "correct," some answers are merely better than others. The person with a problem recognizes the problem, formulates a question about that problem (Should I buy a house or rent? Should I date this person or not? Should I take this job or not?), collects data, and arrives at a temporarily acceptable answer to the problem, while realizing that later data may dictate a review of the conclusion. For example, if an astronomer believes she has discovered a new galaxy, there is no textbook (or teacher) to which she may refer to find out if she is right. Rather, on the basis of her self-confidence in identifying problems, asking questions, collecting enough data, and arriving at a tentative conclusion based on those data, she assumes that for now her conclusion is safe.

FIGURE 4.4
Examining Course Materials for Level of Questioning

Examine course materials for the levels of questions presented to students. Examine a student textbook (or other instructional material) for a subject and grade level you intend to teach; specifically, the questions posed for the students, probably at the ends of chapters. Also examine workbooks, examinations, instructional packages, and any other printed or electronic (i.e., computer software programs) materials used by students in the course. Share your findings with other members of your class. Include the following:

1. Materials examined (include date of publication and target students)
2. Examples of level-one (input-recall-level) questions found
3. Examples of level-two (processing-level) questions found
4. Examples of level-three (application-level) questions found
5. Approximate percentages of questions at each level:
      Level 1 = _____%   Level 2 = _____%   Level 3 = _____%
6. Did you find evidence of question-level sequencing? If so, describe it.
7. From your analysis, what can you conclude about the level of student thinking expected of students using the materials analyzed?

10. Avoid bluffing when asked a question for which you do not have an answer. Nothing will cause you to lose credibility with students quicker than faking an answer. There is nothing wrong with admitting that you do not know. It helps students realize that you are human. It also helps them maintain adequate self-esteem, realizing that it's okay not to always know all the answers. What *is* important is that you know where and how to find possible answers and help students develop that same knowledge and those same skills.

Examination of the level of questions in course materials. It is reported that of more than 61,000 questions found in materials for teaching history, more than 95 percent were devoted to factual recall (California State Department of Education, 1987, p. 13). In a recent analysis of end-of-chapter questions in eight middle-grade science textbooks, 87.5 percent were at the input level, and 78.8 percent of all textbook questions were at the input level (Pizzini et al., 1992). Using the questions in Figure 4.4, examine course materials used by a school where you might soon be teaching, and compare the results of your analysis with those data.

K. PROCESSES IN INSTRUCTIONAL PLANNING

Complete planning for instruction is an eight-step process. Some of the steps that follow have previously been addressed and are included here so you will understand where they fit in the planning process. Here are the steps and guidelines for what is referred to as the "eight-step planning process":

1. *Course and school goals.* Consider and understand your course goals and their relationship to the goals and mission of the school. Your course is not isolated but is an integral part of the total school curriculum, both vertically (in grades K-12) and horizontally (across grade levels).
2. *Expectations.* Consider topics and skills that you are "expected" to teach, such as ones that may be found in the course of study.
3. *Academic year-long calendar plan.* You must consider where you want the class of students to be months from now. So, working from your tentative topic outline and with the school calendar in hand, begin by deciding approximately how much class time should be devoted to each topic, penciling those times onto the subject outline.
4. *Course or class schedule.* This schedule becomes a part of the course syllabus that is presented to students during the first week of school. The schedule must remain flexible to allow for the unexpected, such as cancellation or interruption of a class meeting or an unpredictable extended study of a particular topic.

5. *Class meeting lessons.* Working from the course schedule, you are now ready to prepare lessons for each class meeting, keeping in mind the abilities and interests of your students while making decisions about appropriate strategies and learning experiences. Preparation of daily lessons takes considerable time and continues throughout the year and throughout your career. You will arrange and prepare instructional notes, demonstrations, discussion topics and questions, classroom exercises, appearances of guest speakers, use of audiovisual equipment and materials, field trips, and tools for assessment of student learning.

   Because what is covered in one class meeting is often determined by the accomplishments of the preceding meeting (especially if you are teaching toward mastery and/or using a constructivist approach), your lessons are never "set in stone" and, regardless of your approach, will need continual revision and evaluation.

6. *Instructional objectives.* With the finalized course or subject schedule, and as you prepare the daily lessons, you will complete your preparation of the instructional objectives. These instructional objectives are critical for accomplishment of step 7.

7. *Assessment.* This important step deals with how you will preassess student understandings and assess student achievement. Included in this component are your decisions about assignments, diagnostic tools such as tests, and the procedure by which grades will be determined. Assessment is the topic of the next chapter.

8. *Classroom management.* This final and important step in planning involves your decisions and planning for a safe and effective classroom environment so that the most efficient learning of your units and lessons will occur, and was the topic of Chapter 2.

Those are the steps in planning. They may seem overwhelming, but we will proceed step by step toward the development of your first instructional plan. First, let's consider the nature of the course syllabus.

The Course Syllabus

You probably know that a course syllabus is a written statement of information about the workings of a particular class. As a college or university student, you have seen a variety of syllabi written by professors, containing their own ideas about what general and specific logistical information is most important for students to know about a course. Even some instructors don't realize, however, that a course outline is not a course syllabus. A course outline is just one component of a syllabus.

Related to the development and use of a course syllabus are three issues: (1) *Why?* What value is a syllabus? What use can be made of it? What purpose does it fulfill? (2) *How?* How do I develop a course syllabus? When do I begin? Where do I start? (3) *What?* What information should be included? When should it be distributed to students? How rigidly should it be followed? Let's now consider each of those three questions.

Reasons for a course syllabus. The course syllabus is printed information about the course that is presented to students (grades 4 and up), usually on the first day or during the first week of school. It should be designed so that it

- Helps establish rapport between students, parents (or guardians), and the teacher
- Helps students feel at ease by providing an understanding of what is expected of them
- Helps students organize, conceptualize, and synthesize their learning experiences
- Provides a reference, helping to eliminate misunderstandings and misconceptions about the nature of the class—its rules, expectations, procedures, requirements, and other policies
- Provides students with a sense of connectedness (often by allowing students to work in cooperative groups and actually participate in fashioning the syllabus)
- Serves as a plan to be followed by the teacher and the students
- Serves as a resource for members of a teaching team. Each team member should have a copy of every other member's syllabus.
- Documents what takes place in the classroom for those outside the classroom (parents or guardians, administrators, other teachers, and students).

Development of a course syllabus. Usually the course syllabus is prepared by the classroom teacher long before the first class meeting. If you maintain a syllabus template on your computer, then it is rather simple to customize it for each class of students that you teach. You may find that it is more useful if students participate in the development of the syllabus, thereby gaining a feeling of ownership of and commitment to it.

The steps shown in Figure 4.5 are suggested as a cooperative learning experience in which students spend approximately 30 minutes during an early class meeting brainstorming the content of their syllabus.

Content of a course syllabus. The course syllabus should be concise, matter-of-fact, uncomplicated, and brief—perhaps no more than two pages—and should include the following information:

1. *Descriptive information about the course.* Include the teacher's name, course title and grade level, class period, beginning and ending times, and room number.
2. *Explanation of the importance of the course.* Describe the course, cite how students will profit from it, and tell whether it is a required course, a core curriculum course, a co-curriculum course, an exploratory or elective, or some other type.
3. *Materials required.* Explain what materials—textbook, notebook, portfolio, supplementary readings, safety goggles—are needed. Include which are supplied by the school, which must be supplied by each student, and what materials must be brought to class each day.
4. *Statement of goals and objectives.* Include a few general goals and some specific objectives.
5. *Types of assignments that will be given.* These should be clearly explained in as much detail as possible this early in the course. State where daily assignments will be posted in the classroom (a regular place each day) and procedures for completing and turning in assignments. (Assignments are statements of *what* students will do; procedures are statements of *how* they will do it.) Parents or guardians will want to know your expectations regarding their helping their child with assignments.

FIGURE 4.5
Steps for Involving Students in the Development of Their Course Syllabus
SOURCE: Richard D. Kellough, Noreen G. Kellough, and David L. Hough, *Middle School Teaching: Methods and Resources* (New York: Macmillan, 1993), p. 110. By permission of Macmillan Publishing Company.

1. Sometime during the first few days of the course, arrange students in small groups of mixed abilities to brainstorm the development of their course syllabus.
2. Instruct each group to spend five minutes listing everything they can think of that they would like to know about the course. Tell the class that a group *recorder* must be chosen to write their ideas on paper and then, when directed to do so, transfer them to the writing board or to sheets of butcher paper hung in the classroom for all to see. (You can also make a transparency sheet and pen available to each group and use an overhead transparency.) Tell them to select a group *spokesperson* who will address the class, explaining the group's list. Each group could also appoint a *materials manager*, whose job is to see that the group has the necessary materials (pen, paper, transparency, chalk), and a *task master*, whose job is to keep the group on task and to report to the teacher when each task is completed.
3. After five minutes, have the recorders prepare their lists. When using a transparency or butcher paper, the lists can be prepared simultaneously while recorders remain with their groups. If using the writing board, have recorders, one at a time, write their lists on areas of the board that you have designated for each group's list.
4. Have the spokesperson of each group explain the group's list. As this is being done, you should make a master list. If transparencies or butcher paper are being used, you can ask for them as backup to the master list you have made.
5. After all spokespersons have explained their lists, ask the class collectively for additional input: "Can anyone think of anything else that should be added?"
6. Use the master list to design a course syllabus, being careful to address each question and to include items of importance that students may have omitted. However, your guidance during the preceding five steps should ensure that all bases have been covered.
7. At the next class meeting, give each student a copy of the final syllabus. Discuss its content. (Duplicate copies to distribute to colleagues, especially those on your teaching team, interested administrators, and parents and guardians at Back-to-School Night.)

6. *Assessment criteria.* Explain the assessment procedures. Will there be quizzes, tests, homework, projects, and group work? What will be their formats, coverage, and weights in the grading procedure? For group work, how will the contributions and learning of individual children be evaluated?
7. *Special information specific to the course.* Field trips? Special privileges? Class projects? Classroom procedures and rules for expected behavior should be included here.

L. THE DAILY LESSON PLAN

Effective teachers are always planning for their classes. For the long range, they plan the scope and sequence of courses and develop content for courses. Within courses they develop units, and within units they design the activities to be used and the assessments of learning to be done. They familiarize themselves with textbooks, materials, media, and innovations in their fields of interest. Yet—despite all this planning—the daily lesson plan remains pivotal to the planning process.

Assumptions about Lesson Planning

Not all teachers need elaborate written plans for every lesson. Some effective and skilled teachers need only a sketchy outline. Sometimes they may not need written plans at all. Experienced teachers who have taught the topic many times in the past may need only the presence of a class of students to stimulate a pattern of presentation that has often been successful. Beware, however, of the frequent use of old patterns that may lead to the rut of unimaginative teaching. You probably do not need to be reminded that the obsolescence of many past classroom practices has been substantiated repeatedly by researchers.

Considering the diversity among teachers, their instructional styles, their students, and what research has shown, certain assumptions can be made about lesson planning:

1. Not all teachers need elaborate written plans for all lessons.
2. Beginning teachers need to prepare detailed written lesson plans.
3. Some subject matter fields and topics require more detailed planning than do others.
4. Some experienced teachers have clearly defined goals and objectives in mind even though they have not written them into lesson plans.
5. The depth of knowledge a teacher has about a subject or topic influences the amount of planning necessary for the lessons.
6. The skill a teacher has in following a train of thought in the presence of distraction will influence the amount of detail necessary when planning activities.
7. A plan is more likely to be carefully plotted when it is written out.
8. The diversity of students within today's classroom necessitates careful and thoughtful consideration about individualizing the instruction; these considerations are best implemented when they have been thoughtfully written into lesson plans.
9. There is no particular pattern or format that all teachers need to follow when writing out plans. (Some teacher-preparation programs have agreed on certain lesson-plan formats for their student teachers; you need to know if this is the case for your program.)
10. All effective teachers have a planned pattern of instruction for every lesson, whether that plan is written out or not.

Written Lesson Plans

Well-written lesson plans have many uses. They give a teacher an agenda or outline to follow in teaching a lesson. They give a substitute teacher a basis for presenting appropriate lessons to a class. They are certainly very useful when a teacher is planning to use the same lesson again in the future. They provide the teacher with something to fall back on in case of a memory lapse, an interruption, or some other distraction, such as a call from the office or a fire drill. Above all, they provide beginners with security, because with a carefully prepared plan a beginning teacher can walk into a classroom with the confidence gained from having developed a sensible framework for that day's instruction.

Thus, as a beginning teacher, you should make considerably detailed lesson plans. Naturally, this will require a great deal of work for at least the first year or two, but the reward of knowing that you have prepared and presented effective lessons will compensate for that effort. Since most teachers plan their daily lessons only a day or two ahead, you can expect a busy first year of teaching.

Some prospective teachers are concerned about being seen using a written plan in class, thinking it may suggest that they have not mastered the subject. On the contrary, a lesson plan is a visible sign of preparation on the part of the teacher. A written lesson plan shows that thinking and planning have taken place and that the teacher has a road map to work through the lesson no matter what the distractions. Most experienced teachers agree that there is no excuse for appearing before a class without evidence of careful preparation.

A Continual Process

Experienced teachers may not require plans as detailed as those necessary for beginning teachers—after all, experienced teachers often can develop shortcuts to lesson planning without sacrificing effectiveness. Yet lesson planning is a continual process even for them, for there is always a need to keep materials and plans current and relevant. Because no two classes of students are ever exactly the same, today's lesson plan will probably need to be tailored to the peculiar needs of each classroom of students. Also, because the content of a course will change as new developments occur or new theories are introduced, your objectives and the objectives of the students, school, and teaching faculty will change.

For these reasons, lesson plans should be in a constant state of revision. Once the basic framework has been developed, however, the task of updating and modifying becomes minimal. If you maintain your plans on a computer, making necessary changes from time to time is even easier.

The daily lesson plan should provide a tentative outline of the class period but should always remain flexible. A carefully worked-out plan may have to be set aside because of the unpredictable, serendipitous effect of a "teachable moment" or because of unforeseen circumstances, such as a delayed school bus, an impromptu school assembly program, or a fire drill. A daily lesson planned to cover six aspects of a given topic may end with only three of the points having been considered. These occurrences are natural in a school setting, and the teacher and the plans must be flexible enough to accommodate this reality.

The Problem of Time

A lesson plan should provide enough materials and activities to consume the entire class period. Since planning is a skill that takes years of experience to master, a beginning teacher should overplan rather than run the risk of having too few activities to occupy the time the children are in the classroom. One way of ensuring that you overplan is to include alternate activities in your lesson plan, as shown in the sample lesson plan in Figure 4.6. (Sample lesson plans for mathematics are shown at the ends of Chapters 8 through 12.)

When a lesson plan does not provide enough activity to occupy the entire class period, a beginning teacher often loses control of the class, and behavior problems develop. Thus, it is best to prepare more than you likely can accomplish in a given class period. Students are very perceptive; they will know if you have finished the plan for the period and are attempting to bluff through the remaining minutes. If you ever do get caught short—as most teachers do at one time or another—ways to avoid embarrassment are to spend the remaining time in a review of material that has been covered that day or in the past several days, or to allow students time to begin work on a homework assignment or project.

The Daily Plan Book

At this point, a distinction needs to be made between actual lesson plans and the book of daily plans that many schools require teachers to maintain and even submit to their supervisors a week in advance. A daily plan book is most assuredly not a daily lesson plan. Rather, it is a layout sheet on which the teacher shows what lessons will be taught during the week, month, or term. Usually the book provides only a small lined box for each class period for each day of the week. These books are useful for outlining the topics, activities, and assignments projected for the week or term, and supervisors sometimes use them to check the adequacy of teachers' course plans. They can also be useful for substitute teachers, who must try to fill in for you when you are absent. But they are not daily plans. Teachers who believe that the notations in the daily plan book are lesson plans are fooling themselves. Student teachers should be wary of using these in place of authentic lesson plans.

FIGURE 4.6
Sample Lesson Plan with Alternate Activities
SOURCE: Unpublished lesson plan, courtesy of Michelle Yendrey, 1994.

LESSON PLAN

1. **Descriptive Course Data**
   Instructor: Michelle Yendrey   Course: Western Civilizations   Period: 1
   Grade level: 9   Unit: The History of Religion   Topic: Persecution of Christians
2. **Objectives**
   Upon completion of this lesson, students will be able to:
   a. Make connections between persecutions today and persecutions that occurred approximately 2,000 years ago.
   b. Describe the main teachings of Christianity and how the position of Christianity within the Roman Empire changed over time.
   c. Share ideas in a positive and productive manner.
3. **Instructional Components**
   Activity 1 (Anticipatory Set)—10 minutes
   Write on overhead: "You have until 8:40 (5 minutes) to write a defense to one of the following statements (Remember, there are no right or wrong answers. Support your position to the best of your ability):"
   a. The recent hate crimes in our city can be related to our current unit on the history of religion.
   b. The recent hate crimes in our city cannot be related to our current unit on the history of religion.
   Activity 2—3–5 minutes
   Students will be asked, by a show of hands, how many chose statement A and how many chose statement B. Some reasons for each will be shared orally and then all papers collected.
   Activity 3—3–5 minutes
   Return papers from previous assignment. Give students new seat assignments for the activity that follows and have them assume their new seats.
   Activity 4—15 minutes
   The students are now arranged into seven groups. Each group will write a paragraph using the concepts from certain assigned words (for their definition sheets of Section 3 of Chapter 7, "Christianity spread through the empire") to answer the essay question(s) at the end of the definition sheet.
   Each group will select a
   ● *Task master* to keep members of the group on task.
   ● *Recorder* to write things down.
   ● *Spokesperson* to present the results.
   ● *Time keeper* to keep group alert so task is completed on time.
      In addition, some groups will have a
   ● *Source master* to look up or ask about any questions that arise.
   Activity 5—15–20 minutes
   Each group's spokesperson will come to the front of the classroom and present the group's result of activity 4.
   Alternate Activity (Plan B)—5–10 minutes
   Should the activities run more quickly than anticipated, the students will take out their "Religion Comparison Sheets." Using the Chapter 2, Section 2 "Jews worshipped a single God" and Chapter 7, Section 3 definition sheets, with the teacher's direction, the students will fill in the boxes for "similar" and "different" with regard to Christianity and Judaism.
   Second Alternate Activity (Plan C)—25–30 minutes
   In the unlikely event that timing is really off, each student will be given a blank grid and assigned 10 vocabulary words from the definition sheets. Students will be directed to create a crossword puzzle using the definitions as clues and the words as answers. After 15 to 20 minutes, the crosswords will be collected and distributed to different students to solve. If not completed in class, students will finish and hand them in later along with their essays, for a few points of extra credit. Students will be required to write their names in the appropriate spaces marked, "Created By" and "Solved By."
   Activity 6—7–10 minutes
   Collect the overhead sheets and pens. Hand out the take-home essay test. Explain and take questions about exactly what is expected from the essay (this is their first take-home test).
4. **Materials and Equipment Needed**
   Overhead projector and transparency sheets (7) and transparency markers (7); 36 copies of the essay question plus directions; 36 copies of the blank grid sheets.

FIGURE 4.7
Sample Lesson Plan Format with Six Components
SOURCE: Reprinted with the permission of Simon & Schuster, Inc. from the Macmillan College text MIDDLE SCHOOL
TEACHING: METHODS AND RESOURCES by Richard D. Kellough, Noreen G. Kellough, and David L. Hough. Copyright
©1993 by Macmillan College Publishing Company, Inc.

---

1. **Descriptive Course Data**
   Teacher _____ Class _____ Date _____

   Grade level _____ Room number _____ Period _____

   Unit _____ Lesson topic _____

2. **Lesson Goals and Objectives**
   Instructional goals (general objectives):

   Specific (performance) objectives:
      Cognitive:

      Affective:

      Psychomotor:

3. **Rationale**

4. **Plan**
   Content:

   Procedure with time plan:
      Set (introduction):

      Modeling:

      Guided (coached) practice:

      Assignments:

      Closure:

5. **Materials Needed**
   Audiovisual:

   Other:

6. **Assessment and Revision**
   Assessment of learning:

   Plan for revision:

M. CONSTRUCTING A DAILY LESSON PLAN

Each teacher should develop a personal system of lesson planning—the system that works best for that teacher. But a beginning teacher probably needs a more substantial framework from which to work. For that reason, this section provides a "preferred" lesson plan format. In addition, you will find alternative formats in this and later chapters. Nothing is sacred about any of these formats, however. Each has worked for some teachers in the past, as have the formats illustrated in Figures 4.6 and 4.7. As you review the preferred format and the others throughout the book, determine which appeals to your style of presentation and use it with your own modifications until you find or develop a better model.

Whatever the format, however, all plans should be written out in an intelligible style. There is good reason to question teachers who say they have no need for a written plan because they have their lessons planned "in their heads." The periods in a school day are many, as are the numbers of students in each class. When multiplied by the number of school days in a week, a semester, or a year, the task of keeping so many things in one's head becomes mind-boggling. Until you have considerable experience behind you, you will need to write and keep detailed daily plans for guidance and reference.

Components of a Daily Lesson Plan

As a rule, your written lesson plan should contain the following basic elements: (1) descriptive course data, (2) materials, (3) goals and objectives, (4) rationale, (5) body of the lesson plan, and (6) assessment and revision plans. These components need not be present in every written lesson plan, nor must they be presented in any particular format, nor are they inclusive or exclusive. You might choose to include additional components or subsections. You may not want to spend time developing a formal rationale, although you probably should. Figure 4.7 illustrates a format that includes the six components and sample subsections of those components.

Following are descriptions of the six major components, with explanations of why each is essential and examples.

Descriptive course data. This is the demographic and logistical information that identifies details about the class. Anyone reading this information should be able to identify when and where the class meets, who is teaching it, and what is being taught. Although as the teacher you know this information, someone else may not. Administrators, members of the teaching team, and substitute teachers—and, if you are the student teacher, your university supervisor and cooperating teacher—appreciate this information, especially when asked to fill in for you, even if only for a few minutes. Most middle school teachers find out which items of descriptive data are most beneficial in their situation and then develop their own identifiers.

Remember: *The mark of a well-prepared, clearly written lesson plan is the ease with which someone else (such as another member of your teaching team or a substitute teacher) could implement it.*

As shown in Figures 4.6 and 4.8, the descriptive data include

1. *Name of course and grade level.* These serve as headings for the plan and facilitate orderly filing of plans. As shown in Figures 4.6 and 4.8, the examples are

Western Civilizations	Grade 9
Science	Grade 7

2. *Name of the unit.* Inclusion of this facilitates the orderly control of the hundreds of lesson plans a teacher constructs. For example:

Western Civilizations	Grade 9 Unit: The History of Religion
Science	Grade 7 Unit: What's the Matter?

3. *Topic to be considered within the unit.* This is also useful for control and identification. For example:

Western Civilizations	Grade 9 Unit: The History of Religion	Topic: Persecution of Christians
Science	Grade 7 Unit: What's the Matter?	Topic: Density of Solids

Goals and objectives. In a lesson plan, the instructional goals are general statements of what students will learn from that lesson. Teachers and students need to know what the lesson is designed to accomplish. In clear, understandable language, the general goal statement provides that information. Examples of goals are

- To make connections between persecutions today and persecutions that occurred approximately 2,000 years ago
- To develop students' understanding of the concept of matter
- To develop students' understanding of the concepts of length, area, volume, mass, and time
- To appreciate the effect that the life-style of Edgar Allan Poe had on his writing.

The objectives of the lesson are included as specific statements detailing precisely what students will be able to do as a result of the learning of the lesson. Teachers and students need to know that. Behavioral objectives provide clear statements of what learning is to occur. In addition, from clearly written behavioral objectives, assessment items can be written to measure whether students have accomplished the objectives. The type of assessment item used (discussed in the next chapter) should not only *measure for* the instructional objective but should also *be compatible with* the objective being assessed. As discussed earlier, your specific objectives might be covert, overt, or a combination of both. Examples include

- The student will be able to list the four states of matter and give an example of each. (overt, cognitive)
- The student will be able to describe the main teachings of Christianity and how the position of Christianity within the Roman Empire changed over time. (overt, cognitive)
- The student will be able to add, subtract, multiply, and divide two-digit numbers using a hand calculator. (overt, cognitive and psychomotor)
- The student will demonstrate appreciation for the symbolism in *Lord of the Flies*. (covert, affective)

Setting specific objectives is a crucial step in the development of any lesson plan. It is at this point that many lessons go wrong. In writing specific objectives, teachers sometimes mistakenly list what they intend to do—such as "cover the next five pages" or "do the next ten problems"—and fail to focus on just what their objective in these activities truly is. When you approach this step in your lesson planning, ask yourself, "What do I want my students to learn from these lessons?" Your answer to that question is your objective!

Rationale. The rationale is an explanation of why the lesson is important and why the instructional methods chosen will achieve the objectives. Parents, students, teachers, administrators, and others have the right to know why specific content is being taught and why the methods employed are being used. Teachers become reflective decision makers when they challenge themselves to think about what they are teaching, how they are teaching it, and why it must be taught. Sometimes teachers include the rationale statement in the beginning of the unit plan, but not in each daily lesson. See Figure 4.8 for a sample rationale statement.

Body of the lesson. The plan is what the lesson consists of. For reasons discussed earlier, teachers must plan their lessons carefully. The body of the lesson plan consists of the following elements:

Content. The substance of the lesson; the information to be presented, obtained, and learned. Appropriate information is selected to meet the learning objectives, the level of competence of the students, and the requirements of the course.

To make sure your lesson actually covers what it should, you should write down exactly what content you intend to cover. This material may be placed in a separate section or combined with the procedure section. The important thing is to be sure that your information is written down so you can refer to it quickly and easily when you need to. If, for instance, you are going to introduce new material using a 10- to 15-minute lecture, you will want to outline the content of that lecture. You need not have pages of notes to sift through, nor should you ever read declarative statements to your students. You should be familiar enough with the content so that an outline (in detail, if necessary) will be sufficient to carry on the lesson, as is the following content outline:

FIGURE 4.8
Sample Integrated Unit Plan with a Daily Lesson
SOURCE: Adapted by permission from unpublished material by William Hightower.

Course _Science (adaptable to students of grades 4–9)_

Teacher _____ **Duration of Unit** _Ten days_

Unit Title _What's the Matter?_

Purpose of the Unit

This unit is designed to develop students' understanding of the concept of matter. At the completion of the unit, students should have a clearer understanding of matter and its properties, of the basic units of matter, and of the source of matter.

Rationale of the Unit

This unit topic is important for building a foundation of knowledge for subsequent courses in science. This can increase students' chances of success in those courses, and thereby improve their self-confidence and self-esteem. A basic understanding of matter and its properties is important because of daily decisions that affect the manipulation of matter. It is more likely that students will make correct and safe decisions when they understand what matter is, how it changes form, and how its properties determine its use.

Goals of the Unit

The goals of this unit are for students to:

1. Understand that all matter is made of atoms.
2. Understand that matter stays constant and that it is neither created nor destroyed.
3. Develop certain basic physical science laboratory skills.
4. Develop a positive attitude about physical science.
5. Look forward to taking other science courses.
6. Understand how science is relevant to their daily lives.

Instructional Objectives of the Unit

Upon completion of this unit of study, students should be able to:

1. List at least ten examples of matter.
2. List the four states of matter, with one example of each.
3. Calculate the density of an object when given its mass and volume.
4. Describe the properties of solids, liquids, and gases.
5. Demonstrate an understanding that matter is made of elements and that elements are made of atoms.
6. Identify and explain one way that knowledge of matter is important to their daily lives.
7. Demonstrate increased self-confidence in pursuing laboratory investigations in physical science.
8. Demonstrate skill in communicating within the cooperative learning group.
9. Demonstrate skill in working with the triple-beam balance.

Unit Overview

Throughout this unit, students will be developing a concept map of matter. Information for the map will be derived from laboratory work, class discussions, lectures, student readings, and research. The overall instructional model is that of concept attainment. Important to this is an assessment of students' concepts about matter at the beginning of the unit. The preassessment and the continuing assessment of their concepts will center on the following:

1. What is matter and what are its properties? Students will develop the concept of matter by discovering the properties that all matter contains (that is, it has mass and takes up space).
2. Students will continue to build upon their understanding of the concept of matter by organizing matter into its four major states (that is, solid, liquid, gas, plasma). The concept development will be used to define the attributes of each state of matter, and students will gather information by participating in laboratory activities and class discussions.
3. What are some of the physical properties of matter that make certain kinds of matter unique? Students will experiment with properties of matter such as elasticity, brittleness, and density. Laboratory activities will allow students to contribute their observations and information to the further development of their concept of matter. Density activities enable students to practice their lab and math skills.
4. What are the basic units of matter, and where did matter come from? Students will continue to develop their concept of matter by working on this understanding of mixtures, compounds, elements, and atoms.

FIGURE 4.8 cont'd

Assessment of Student Achievement

For this unit, assessment of student achievement will be both formative and summative. Formative evaluation will be done daily by checklists of student behavior, knowledge, and skills. Summative evaluation will be based on the following criteria:

1. Student participation as evidenced by completion of daily homework, class work, laboratory activities, and class discussions, and by the information on the student behavior checklists.
2. Weekly quizzes on content.
3. Unit test.

Lesson Number _____ **Duration of Lesson** *1–2 hours* _____

Unit Title *What's the Matter?* _____ **Teacher** _____

Lesson Title *Mission Impossible* _____ **Lesson Topic** *Density of Solids* _____

Objectives of the Lesson

Upon completion of this lesson, students should be able to:

1. Determine the density of a solid cube.
2. Based on data gathered in class, develop their own definition of density.
3. Prepare and interpret graphs of data.
4. Communicate the results of their experiments to others in the class.

Materials Needed

1. Two large boxes of cereal and two snack-size boxes of the same cereal.
2. Four brownies (two whole and two cut in halves).
3. Four sandboxes (two large plastic boxes and two small boxes, each filled with sand).
4. Two triple-beam balances.
5. Several rulers.
6. Six hand-held calculators.
7. 18 colored pencils (six sets with three different colors per set).
8. Copies of lab instructions (one copy for each student).

Instructional Procedure with Approximate Time Line

ANTICIPATORY SET (10–15 MINUTES)
Begin class by brainstorming to find what students already know about density. Place the word on the board or overhead, and ask students if they have heard of it. Write down their definitions and examples. Hold up a large box of cereal in one hand and the snack-size box in the other. Ask students which is more dense. Allow them time to explain their responses. Then tell them that by the end of this lesson they will know the answer to the question and that they will develop their own definition of density.

LABORATORY INVESTIGATION (30–60 MINUTES)
Students are divided into teams of four students of mixed abilities. Each member has a role:

1. *Measure master:* In charge of the group's ruler and ruler measurements.
2. *Mass master:* In charge of the group's weighings.
3. *Engineer:* In charge of the group's calculator and calculations.
4. *Graph master:* In charge of plotting the group's data on the graph paper.

Each team has eight minutes before switching stations. Each team completes three stations, and then meets to make its graphs and to discuss results.

***Station 1:* Cereal Box Density.** Students calculate the density of a large and a small box of cereal to determine if a larger and heavier object is more dense. The masses versus the volumes of the two boxes are plotted on graph paper using one of the pencil colors.

INSTRUCTIONS

1. The density of any object is determined by dividing its mass by its volume. Density in grams is divided by volume in cubic centimeters. Example: $20 \text{ g}/10 \text{ cm}^3 = 2\text{g}/\text{cm}^3$.
2. Measure the volume of the small cereal box (length $\times$ width $\times$ height), and use the balance to determine its mass in grams. The engineer can do the calculations on the calculator. The graph master should graph the results of each trial and connect two points with a straight line.
3. Repeat the procedure using the large box of cereal.

FIGURE 4.8   cont'd

4. The engineer computes the density of both cereal boxes with the calculator, and records the results on the proper blank below the graph.

Mass (g)

Volume (cm³)

1. Density of large box of cereal _____
2. Density of small box of cereal _____
3. Density of large brownie _____
4. Density of small brownie _____
5. Density of large sandbox _____
6. Density of small sandbox _____

FIGURE 4.8 cont'd

Station 2: **Brownie Density.** Students calculate the density of a full-size brownie and a half-size brownie. Results are plotted on the same graph as in Station 1, but with the second color.

INSTRUCTIONS

1. The density of any object is determined by dividing its mass by its volume. Density in grams is divided by volume in cubic centimeters. Example: 20 g/10 cm^3 = 2g/cm^3.
2. Measure the volume of a small brownie (length × width × height), and use the balance to determine its mass in grams. The engineer can do the calculations on the calculator. The graph master should graph the results of each trial and connect two points with a straight line.
3. Repeat the procedure using the large brownie.
4. The engineer computes the density of both brownies and records the result on the proper blank.

Station 3: **Sandbox Density.** Students calculate the density of a large and a small box filled with sand. Results are plotted on the graph, but with the third color.

INSTRUCTIONS

1. The density of any object is determined by dividing its mass by its volume. Density in grams is divided by volume in cubic centimeters. Example: 20 g/10 cm^3 = 2g/cm^3.
2. Measure the volume of the small sandbox (length × width × height), and use the balance to determine its mass in grams. The engineer can do the calculations on the calculator. The graph master should graph the results of each trial and connect two points with a straight line.
3. Repeat the procedure using the large sandbox.
4. The engineer computes the density of both boxes, and records the results on the proper blank.

Lab Worksheet. Teams return to their seats to do the graphing, analyze the results, and answer the following questions from their lab sheets:

1. Is a larger, heavier object more dense than its smaller counterpart? Explain your evidence.
2. What is your definition of density?
3. Which is more dense, a pound of feathers or a pound of gold? Explain your answer.

Lesson Closure (10 minutes or more). When all teams are finished, teams should display their graphs, and share and discuss the results.

Concepts

1. Density is one of the properties of matter.
2. Mass and volume are related.
3. Density is determined by dividing mass by volume.

Extension Activities

1. Use a density graph to calculate the mass and volume of a smaller brownie.
2. Explore the story of Archimedes and the king's crown.

Evaluation and Revision of Lesson

Upon completion of this lesson and of the unit, revision in this lesson may be made on the basis of teacher observations and student achievement.

Causes of Civil War

A. Primary causes
    1. Economics
    2. Abolitionist pressure
    3. Slavery
    4. _____
B. Secondary causes
    1. North-South friction
    2. Southern economic dependence
    3. _____

If you intend to conduct the lesson using discussion, you should write out the key discussion questions. For example:

What do you think Golding had in mind when he wrote *Lord of the Flies?*

What did the conch shell represent? Why did the other boys resent Piggy?

Instruction. The procedure or procedures to be used, sometimes referred to as the *instructional components.* Appropriate instructional methods are chosen to meet the objectives, to match the students' learning styles, and to ensure that all students have an equal opportunity to learn.

This is the section in which you establish what you and your students will do during the lesson. Ordinarily, you should plan this section of your lesson as an organized entity having a beginning (an introduction or set), a middle, and an end (called the closure). This structure is not always needed, because some lessons are simply parts of units or long-term plans and merely carry on activities spelled out in those long-term plans. Still, most daily lessons need to include in their procedure

1. an *introduction,* the process used to prepare the students mentally for the lesson
2. *lesson development,* the detailing of activities that occur between the beginning and the end of the lesson
3. plans for *guided (or coached) practice,* ways that you intend to have students interacting in the classroom, receiving guidance or coaching from each other and from you
4. the *lesson conclusion (or closure),* the planned process of bringing the lesson to an end, thereby providing students with a sense of completeness and (through effective teaching) accomplishment and comprehension by helping them synthesize the information learned from the lesson
5. a *timetable* that serves simply as a planning and implementation guide, and
6. *assignments,* that is, what students are instructed to do as follow-up to the lesson, either as homework or as in-class work, providing students an opportunity to learn further and to practice what is being learned.

Let's now consider lesson plan elements in further detail.

Introduction to the lesson. Like any good performance, a lesson needs an effective beginning. In many respects the introduction sets the tone for the rest of the lesson by alerting the students that the business of learning is to begin. The introduction should be an attention-getter. If it is exciting, interesting, or innovative, it can create a favorable mood for the lesson. In any case, a thoughtful introduction serves as a solid indicator that you are well prepared.

Although it is difficult to develop an exciting introduction to every lesson taught each day, there are always various options to spice up the launching of a lesson. You might, for instance, begin the lesson by briefly reviewing the previous lesson, thereby helping students connect the learning. Another possibility is to review vocabulary words from previous lessons and to introduce new ones. Still another possibility is to use the key point of the day's lesson as an introduction and then again as the conclusion. Sometimes teachers begin a lesson by demonstrating a discrepant event—an event that is contrary to what one might expect. Yet another possibility is to begin the lesson with a writing activity on some controversial aspect of the ensuing lesson. Brief examples of introductions (taken from the lessons shown in Figures 4.6 and 4.8) are

- "You have 5 minutes to write an argument in support of or against the following statement: The recent hate crimes in our city can be related to what we are learning about the history of religion."
- Using the technique called *think-pair share,* students are asked to brainstorm what they already know about the concept of density. (In this metacognitive strategy, students are given a concept or idea and asked to think about it and share their thoughts in pairs. Each pair then shares their ideas about the concept with the entire class while the teacher records these thoughts on the chalkboard, a useful technique to discover what students already know or think they know—misunderstandings—about a topic about to be studied.)

In short, you can use the introduction of the lesson to review past learning, tie the new lesson to the previous lesson, introduce new material, point out the objectives of the new lesson, help students connect their learning with other disciplines or with real life, or—by showing what will be learned and why the learning is important—induce in students a mind-set favorable to the new lesson.

Lesson development. The developmental activities, which make up the bulk of the sample lesson plan, are the specifics by which you intend to achieve your lesson objectives. They include activities that present information, demonstrate skills, provide reinforcement of previously learned material, and provide other opportunities to develop understanding and skill. In addition, by actions and words, during lesson development the teacher models the behaviors expected of the students. Middle grade students need such modeling. By effective modeling, the teacher can exemplify the anticipated learning outcomes. Activities of this section of the lesson plan should be described in some detail so you will know exactly what it is you plan to do and, during the stress of the class, not forget details of your plan and the subject content. For this reason, you should note the answers to the questions you intend to ask and the solutions to problems you intend to have your students solve.

Lesson conclusion. Having a clear-cut closure to the lesson is as important as having a strong introduction. The closure complements the introduction. The concluding activity should summarize and bind together what has ensued in the developmental stage and should reinforce the principal points of the lesson. One way to accomplish these ends is to restate the key points of the lesson. Another is to briefly outline the major points. Still another is to repeat the major concept. No matter what the chosen way, the concluding activity is usually brief and to the point.

Timetable. To estimate the time factors in any lesson can be very difficult. A good procedure is to gauge the amount of time needed for each learning activity and note that alongside the activity and strategy in your plan, as shown in the sample lesson plans. Placing too much faith in your time estimate may be foolish—an estimate is more for your guidance in planning than for anything else. Beginning teachers frequently find that their discussions and presentations do not last as long as expected. To avoid being embarrassed by running out of material, try to make sure you have planned enough work to consume the entire class period. Another important reason for including a time plan in your lesson is to give information to students about how much time they have for a particular activity, such as a laboratory activity or cooperative learning group activity.

Materials and equipment. Materials of instruction include the textbook, supplementary readings, media, and other supplies necessary to accomplish the lesson objectives. Teachers must be sure that the proper and necessary materials are available for the lesson, which takes planning. Students cannot use what they do not have available.

Assignments. When an assignment is to be given, it should be noted in your lesson plan. When to present it to the students is optional, except that it should never be yelled as an afterthought as the students are exiting the classroom at the end of the period. Whether begun and completed during class time or done out of school, assignments are best written on the writing board or in a special place on the bulletin board, on a handout, or in the course syllabus. Take extra care to be sure that assignment specifications are clear to the students. It is also important to remember that assignments and procedures are not the same thing. An assignment tells students *what* is to be done, while procedures explain *how* to do it. Although an assignment may include specific procedures, merely spelling out procedures is not the same thing as making an academic assignment. When students are given an assignment, they need to understand the reasons for doing it as well as have some notion as to ways the assignment might be done.

Many middle-level teachers give assignments to their students on a weekly basis, requiring that the students maintain an assignment schedule in their portfolios. When given on a periodic rather than daily basis, assignments should still appear in your daily lesson plans so you can remind students of them. Once assignment specifications have been given it is a good idea not to make major modifications to them, and it is especially important not to change assignment specifications several days after an assignment has been given. Last-minute changes in assignment specifications can be very frustrating to students who have already begun or completed the assignment and show little respect for those students.

Benefits of coached practice. Allowing time in class for students to begin work on homework assignments and long-term projects is highly recommended; it provides an opportunity for the teacher to give individual attention (guided or coached practice) to students. Being able to coach students is the reason for in-class time to begin assignments. Many middle-level schools have extended class periods to allow more in-class time for teachers to guide students in their homework. The benefits of coached practice include being able to (1) monitor student work so a student doesn't go too far in the wrong direction, (2) help students to reflect on their thinking, (3) assess the progress of individual students, and (4) discover or create a "teachable moment." For example, while observing and monitoring student practice, the teacher might discover a shared student misconception. The teacher could then talk about and attempt to clarify that misconception or, collaboratively with students, plan a subsequent lesson centered around exploring the misconception.

Special notes and reminders. Many teachers provide a place in their lesson plan format for special notes and reminders. Most of the time you will not need such reminders, but when you do, it helps to have them in a regular location in your lesson plan so you can refer to them quickly. In this special section you can place reminders concerning announcements to be made, school programs, makeup work for certain students, and so on. These things may not always be important, but they do need to be remembered.

Assessment and revision. You must include in your lesson plan details of how you will assess how well students are learning (formative assessment) and how well they have learned (summative assessment). Comprehension checks for formative assessment can be in the form of questions you and the students ask during the lesson. Questions you intend to ask (and possible answers) should be built into the developmental section.

For summative assessment, teachers typically use review questions at the end of a lesson (as a closure) or the beginning of the next lesson (as a review or transfer introduction), independent practice at the completion of a lesson, and tests. Again, questions for checking for comprehension should be detailed in your lesson plan.

In most lesson plan formats there is also a section reserved for the teacher to make notes or comments about the lesson. It can be particularly useful if you plan to use the lesson again at some later date.

SUMMARY

When you reviewed curriculum documents and student textbooks, you probably found most of them well organized and useful. When comparing and analyzing courses of study and the teachers' editions of student textbooks, you probably will discover that some are accompanied by sequentially designed resource units from which the teacher can select and build specific teaching units. A resource unit usually consists of an extensive list of objectives, a large number and variety of kinds of activities, suggested materials, and extensive bibliographies for teachers and students, from which the teacher will select those that best suit his or her needs to build an actual teaching unit.

As you also may have discovered, some courses of study contain actual teaching units that have been prepared by teachers of that particular school district. An important question often asked by beginning teachers and by student teachers is How closely must I follow the school's curriculum guide or course of study? That is a question that you need to have the answer to before you begin teaching. To obtain the answer, talk with teachers and administrators of your particular school.

In conclusion, your final decisions about what content to teach are guided by all of the following:

- Articles in professional journals
- Discussions with other teachers
- Local courses of study
- State curriculum documents
- The differences, interests, and abilities of your students
- Your own personal convictions, knowledge, and skills.

After discovering what you will teach comes the process of preparing the plans. Although teachers' textbook editions and other curriculum documents make the process easier, they should never substitute for your own specific planning.

Attempting to blend the best of the behaviorism and constructivism theories of learning, many teachers do not bother to try to write specific objectives for all the learning activities that are in their teaching plans. Yet it is clear that when teachers do prepare specific objectives (by writing them themselves or borrowing them from other sources) and teach toward those objectives, student learning is better. Most school districts require teachers to use objectives that are specifically stated. There is no question that clearly written instructional objectives are worth the time, especially when the teacher teaches toward those objectives and evaluates students' progress and learning against them (performance-based teaching or outcome-based or criterion-referenced assessment). It is not imperative that you write all the instructional objectives that you will need. As a matter of fact, many are usually already available in textbooks and other curriculum documents.

As a teacher, you are expected to plan well and specifically that which you intend your students to learn; to convey your expectations to your students; and to assess their learning against that specificity. The danger inherent in such performance-based or criterion-referenced teaching, however, is that, because it tends toward high objectivity, it could become too objective and have negative consequences. If students are treated as objects, then the relationship between teacher and student is impersonal and counterproductive to real learning. Highly specific and impersonal teaching can discourage serendipity, creativity, and the excitement of real discovery and meaningful learning, to say nothing of its possible negative impact on the development of students' self-esteem.

Performance-based instruction works well when teaching toward mastery of basic skills, but the concept of mastery learning tends to imply that there is some foreseeable end point to learning—an obviously erroneous assumption. With performance-based instruction, the source of student motivation tends to be mostly extrinsic. Teacher expectations, grades, and social and peer pressures are examples of extrinsic sources that drive student performance. To be an effective teacher, the challenge to you is to use performance-based criteria, but with a teaching style that encourages the development of intrinsic sources of student motivation and allows for, provides for, and encourages coincidental learning—learning that goes beyond what might be considered predictable, immediately measurable, minimal results.

Developing units of instruction that integrate student learning and provide a sense of meaning for the students requires coordination throughout the curriculum—defined in this book as consisting of all the planned experiences students encounter while at school. Hence, for students, learning is a process of discovering how information, knowledge, and ideas are interrelated and learning to make sense out of self, school, and life. Combining chunks of information into units and units into daily lessons helps students process and make sense out of knowledge.

There is no single best way to organize a daily lesson plan, no foolproof formula that will guarantee a teacher an effective lesson. With experience and the increased competence that comes from reflecting on that experience, you will develop your own style, your own methods of implementing that style, and your own formula for preparing a lesson plan. Like a map, your lesson plan charts the course, places markers along the trails, pinpoints danger areas, highlights areas of interest and importance along the way, and ultimately brings the traveler to the objective.

QUESTIONS AND ACTIVITIES FOR DISCUSSION

1. Explain the rationale for organizing instruction into units.

2. Identify and describe criteria for selecting a topic for a unit of study.

3. Explain three reasons why a student teacher and a first-year teacher need to prepare detailed lesson and unit plans.

4. Explain why you should know how to prepare detailed plans even when the textbook program you are using provides them.

5. When, if ever, during instruction, can or should you divert from the written plan?

6. Explain the importance of preassessment of student learning. When do you do a preassessment? How can it be done?

7. Explain why lesson planning should be a continual process.

8. Explain some differences between ordinary unit planning and interdisciplinary thematic unit planning.

9. Explain the concept of "student-negotiated curriculum." Is it used today? Why or why not?

10. Explain the relationship of planning to the preactive and reflective thought-processing phases of instruction.

11. Explain the intent of having national standards for each subject discipline taught in public schools. Who prepares these standards? Who decides how the standards are to be implemented and student learning assessed?

12. Explain how a textbook can be helpful to a student's learning in science and mathematics. How might reliance on a single textbook for each subject be a hindrance to student learning?

13. Using the format presented in Figure 4.7, prepare one integrated mathematics and science daily lesson plan for a specific grade level, and then share your lesson plan with your colleagues for their feedback.

14. From your current observations and fieldwork related to this teacher preparation program, clearly identify one specific example of educational practice that seems contradictory to exemplary practice or theory as presented in this chapter. Present your explanation for the discrepancy.

15. Describe any prior concepts you held that changed as a result of your experiences with this chapter. Describe the changes.

REFERENCES

Artzt, A. F. (1994) Integrating writing and cooperative learning in the mathematics class. *Mathematics Teacher 87* (2), 80–85.

Bloom, B. S. (Ed.) (1984). *Taxonomy of educational objectives, Book I: Cognitive domain.* White Plains, NY: Longman.

Brooks, J. G., & Brooks, M. G. (1993). *In search for understanding: The case for constructivist classrooms.* Chapter 9. Alexandria, VA: Association for Supervision and Curriculum Development.

Burrett, K., & Rusnak, T. (1993). *Integrated character education.* Fastback 351. Bloomington, IN: Phi Delta Kappa Educational Foundation.

Caine, G., & Caine, R. N. (1993, Fall). The critical need for a mental model of meaningful learning. *California Catalyst,* pp. 18–21.

California State Department of Education. (1987). *Caught in the middle.* Sacramento, CA: Author.

Chiappetta, E. L., Sethna, G. H., & Fillman, D. A. (1993). Do middle school life science textbooks provide a balance of scientific literacy themes? *Journal of Research in Science Teaching, 30*(7), 787–797.

Costa, A. L. (1989). *The enabling behaviors.* Orangeville, CA: Search Models Unlimited.

Costa, A. L. (1991). *The school as a home for the mind.* Palatine, IL: Skylight Publishing.

Duckworth, E. (1986). Teaching as research. *Harvard Educational Review, 56*(4), 481–495.

Eisner, E. (1979). *The educational imagination.* New York: Macmillan.

Eisner, E. (Ed.). (1985). Aesthetic modes of knowing. In *Learning and teaching the ways of knowing* (pp. 23–36). Chicago: University of Chicago Press.

Feder-Feitel, L. (1994). How to avoid gender bias: Part II. *Creative Classroom, 8*(5), 56–60, 64–66.

Gagné, R. M., Briggs, L., & Wager, W. (1988). *Principles of instructional design* (3rd ed.). New York: Holt, Rinehart and Winston.

Gifford, B. R. (1991). The textbook of the 21st century. *Syllabus, 19,* 15–16.

Good, T. L., & Brophy, J. E. (1994). *Looking in classrooms* (6th ed.). New York: HarperCollins.

Harrow, A. J. (1977). *Taxonomy of the psychomotor domain.* White Plains, NY: Longman.

Hill, D. (1993). Math's angry man. *Teacher Magazine, 5*(1), 24–28.

Joyce, B., & Showers, B. (1988). *Student achievement through staff development.* New York: Longman.

Katz, L. G. (1985). Dispositions in early childhood education. *ERIC/EECE Bulletin, 18*(2).

Krathwohl, D. R., Bloom, B. S., & Masia, B. B. (1964). *Taxonomy of educational goals, Handbook II: Affective domain.* New York: David McKay.

Kudlas, J. M. (1994). Implications of OBE: What you should know about outcome-based education. *The Science Teacher, 61*(5), 32–35.

Leach, L. S. (1994). Sexism in the classroom: A self-quiz for teachers. *Science Scope, 17* (6), 54–59.

Lepper, M., & Green, D. (Eds.). (1978). *The hidden cost of rewards: New perspectives on the psychology of human motivation.* New York: Erlbaum.

Massey, M. (1993). Interest in character education seen growing. *ASCD Update, 35*(4), 4–5.

McCormack, A. J., & Yager, R. E. (1989). A new taxonomy of science education. *The Science Teacher, 56*(2), 47–48.

Murray, D. M. (1980). Writing as process: How writing finds its own meaning. In T. R. Donovan & B. W. McClelland (Eds.), *Eight approaches to teaching composition* (p. 62). Urbana, IL: National Council for Teachers of English.

Newton, B. (1978). Theoretical basis for higher cognitive questioning—An avenue to critical thinking. *Education, 98*(3), 286–290.

Perkins, D., & Blythe, T. (1994). Putting understanding up front. *Educational Leadership, 51*(5), 4–7.

Pizzini, E. L., Shepardson, D. P., Abell, S. K., (1992). The questioning level of select middle school science textbooks. *School Science and Mathematics, 92*(2), 74–78.

Redfield, D., & Rousseau, E. (1981). A meta-analysis of experimental research on teacher questioning behavior. *Review of Educational Research, 51*(2), 237–245.

Resnick, L. B., & Klopfer, L. E. (Eds.) (1989). *Toward the thinking curriculum: Current cognitive research.* 1989 ASCD Yearbook. Alexandria, VA: Association for Supervision and Curriculum Development.

Smith, J. L., & Johnson, H. A. (1993). Control in the classroom: Listening to adolescent voices. *Language Arts, 70*(1), 18–30.

Starr, J. (1989). The great textbook war. In H. Holtz, I. Marcus, J. Dougherty, J. Michaels, & R. Peduzzi (Eds.), *Education and the American dream: Conservatives, liberals and radicals debate the future of education.* Grandy, MA: Bergin and Garvey.

Willis, S. (1994). Making use of national standards. *ASCD Update 36* (9), 1, 6.

Wynne, E. A., & Ryan, K. (1993). *Reclaiming our schools: A handbook on teaching character, academics, and discipline.* New York: Macmillan.

SUGGESTED READINGS

Ahlgren, A., & Rutherford, F. J. (1993). Where is Project 2061 today? *Educational Leadership, 50*(8), 19–22.

Aldridge, B. G. Project on scope, sequence, and coordination: A new synthesis for improving science education. *Journal of Science Education and Technology, 1*(1), 13–21.

Alvino, J., et al. (1990). Building better thinkers. *Learning 90, 18*(6), 40–55.

Barba, R. H., et al. (1993). User-friendly text: Keys to readability and comprehension. *The Science Teacher, 60*(5), 15–17.

Bellamy, N. (1994). Bias in the classroom: Are we guilty? *Science Scope, 17*(6), 60–63.

Berlin, D. F., & White, A. L. (1992). Report from the NSF/SSMA Wingspread conference: A network for integrating science and mathematics teaching and learning. *School Science and Mathematics, 92*(6), 340–342.

Boling, A. N. (1991). They don't like math? Well, let's do something. *Arithmetic Teacher, 38*(7), 17–19.

Bomeli, C. L. (1991). Mathematics and meteorology: Perfect partners. *School Science and Mathematics, 91*(1), 31–33.

Brandt, R. S. (Ed.). (1988). *Content of the curriculum.* 1988 ASCD Yearbook. Alexandria, VA: Association for Supervision and Curriculum Development.

Brandt, R. S. (December-January 1992–1993). On outcome-based education: A conversation with Bill Spady. *Educational Leadership, 50*(4), 66–70.

Brutlag, D., & Maples, C. (1992). Making connections: Beyond the surface. *Mathematics Teacher, 85*(3), 230–235.

Dempster, F. N. (1993). Exposing our students to less should help them learn more. *Phi Delta Kappan,74*(6), 433–437.

Dolan, D. (1991). Implementing the standards: Making connections in mathematics. *Arithmetic Teacher, 38*(6), 57–60.

Easterday, K. E., & Bass, D. T. (1993). Using environmental issues to integrate science and mathematics. *School Science and Mathematics, 93*(5), 234–236.

Eisner, E. (1993). Why standards may not improve schools. *Educational Leadership, 50*(5), 22–23.

Erb, T. O., & Doda, N. M. (1989). *Team organization: Promise—Practices & possibilities.* Washington, DC: National Education Association.

Evans, K. M., & King, J. A. (1994). Research on OBE: What we know and don't know. *Educational Leadership, 51*(6), 12–17.

Feder-Feitel, L. (1993). How to avoid gender bias. *Creative Classroom, 7*(5), 56–63.

Gollnick, D. M., & Chinn, P. C. (1994). *Multicultural education in a pluralistic society* (4th ed.). New York: Macmillan.

Gray, I. L., & Hymel, G. M. (Eds.). (1992). *Successful schooling for all: A primer on outcome-based education and mastery learning.* Johnson City, NY: Network for Outcome-Based Schools.

Heckman, P. E., et al. (1994). Planting seeds: Understanding through investigation. *Educational Leadership, 51*(5), 36–39.

Hilke, E. V., & Conway-Gerhardt, C. (1994). *Gender equity in education.* Fastback 372. Bloomington: IN. Phi Delta Kappa Educational foundation.

Hinton, N. K. (1944). The pyramid approach to reading, writing, and asking questions. *Science Scope, 17*(5), 44–49.

Hoffman, K. M., & Stage, E. (1993). Science for all: Getting it right for the 21st century. *Educational Leadership, 50*(5), 27–31.

Horgan, K. (1992). Making waves about our oceans. *PTA-Today, 17*(5), 29.

Klein, M. F. (1993). Mathematics as current events. *Mathematics Teacher, 86*(2), 114–116.

LaPorte, J., & Sanders, M. (1993). The T/S/M Integration Project: Integrating technology, science, and mathematics in the middle school. *Technology Teacher, 52*(6), 17–21.

Lewis, B., et al. (1993). Fostering communication in mathematics using children's literature. *Arithmetic Teacher, 40*(8), 470–473.

Marcincin, L. W. (1992). Getting involved: An interdisciplinary project on homelessness. *Schools in the Middle, 1*(3), 6–10.

Martin, B. L., & Briggs, L. J. (1986). *The affective and cognitive domains.* Englewood Cliffs, NJ: Educational Technology Publications.

Nelson, J. R., & Frederick, L. (1994). Can children design curriculum? *Educational Leadership, 51*(5), 71–74.

O'Neil, J. (1993). Can national standards make a difference? *Educational Leadership, 50*(5), 4–8.

Passarello, L. M., & Fennell, F. (1992). Ideas. *Arithmetic Teacher, 39*(6), 32–39.

Ravitch, D. (1993). Launching a revolution in standards and assessments. *Phi Delta Kappan, 70*(10), 767–772.

Romberg, T. A. (1993). NCTM's standards: A rallying flag for mathematics teachers. *Educational Leadership, 50*(5), 36–41.

Roth, W. M. (1992). Bridging the gap between school and real life: Toward an integration of science, mathematics and technology in the context of authentic practice. *School Science and Mathematics, 92*(6), 307–317.

Siegel, M., & Borasi, R. (1992). Toward a new integration of reading in mathematics instruction. *Focus on Learning Problems in Mathematics, 14*(2), 18–36.

Singer, H., & Donlan, D. (1990). *Reading and learning from text.* Hillsdale, NJ: Lawrence Erlbaum.

Smith, M. S., et al. (1994). National curriculum standards: Are they desirable and feasible? In R. F. Elmore and S. H. Fuhrman (Eds.), *The governance of curriculum* (Chapter 2). Alexandria, VA: Association for Supervision and Curriculum Development.

Sosniak, L. A., & Stodolsky, S. S. (1993). Teachers and textbooks: Materials use in four fourth-grade classrooms. *Elementary School Journal, 93*(3), 249–275.

Swinson, K. (1992). Writing activities as strategies for knowledge construction and the identification of misconceptions in mathematics. *Journal of Science and Mathematics Education in Southeast Asia, 15*(2), 7–14.

Tchudi, S. (Ed.). (1993). *The astonishing curriculum: Integrating science and humanities through language.* Urbana, IL: National Council of Teachers of English.

Towers, J. M. (1992). Outcome-based education: Another educational bandwagon? *Educational Forum, 56*(3), 291–305.

Welchman-Tischler, R. (1992). Making mathematical connections. *Arithmetic Teacher, 39*(9), 12–17.

Willoughby, S. S. (1990). *Mathematics education for a changing world.* Alexandria, VA: Association for Curriculum and Supervision Development.

Wiske, M. S., & Levinson, C. Y. (1993). How teachers are implementing the NCTM standards. *Educational Leadership, 50*(8), 8–12.

Wood, K. D. & Jones, J. P. (1994) Integrating collaborative learning across the curriculum. *Middle School Journal, 25*(3), 19–23.

CHAPTER 5

Assessment of Learning

Assessment is an integral, ongoing process within the educational scene. Curricula, buildings, materials, specific courses, teachers, supervisors, administrators, equipment—all must be periodically assessed in relation to student learning, the purpose of any school. When gaps between anticipated results and student achievement exist, efforts are made to eliminate those factors that seem to be limiting the educational output or to in some other way improve the situation. Thus, educational progress occurs.

To learn effectively, students need to know how they are doing. Similarly, to be an effective teacher, you must be informed about what each student knows, feels, and can do so that you can help the student build on her or his skills, knowledge, and attitudes. Therefore, you and your students need continuous feedback on their progress and problems in order to plan appropriate learning activities and to make adjustments to those already planned. If this feedback says that progress is slow, you can provide alternative activities; if it indicates that some or all of the students have already mastered the desired learning, you can eliminate unnecessary activities and practice for some or all of the children. In short, assessment is the key to both effective teaching and effective learning.

The importance of continuous assessment mandates that you know the principles and techniques of assessment. This chapter explains some of those and shows you how to construct and use assessment instruments and make sense from the data obtained. We define the terms related to assessment, consider what makes a good assessment instrument, relate the criteria to both standardized and nonstandardized instruments, suggest procedures to use in the construction of assessment items, point out the advantages and disadvantages of different assessment items and procedures, and explain the construction and use of alternative assessment devices (see also Chapters 8 through 12 for examples of alternative assessment in mathematics).

In addition, this chapter discusses grading and reporting of student achievement, two responsibilities that can consume much of a teacher's valuable time. Grading is time consuming and frustrating for many teachers. What should be graded? Should marks represent student growth, level of achievement in a group, effort, attitude, general behavior, or a combination? What should determine grades—homework, tests, projects, class participation and group work, or all of these? And what should be their relative weights? These are just a few of the questions that plague teachers and parents when decisions about summative assessment and grades must be made.

In too many schools, the grade progress report and final report card are about the only communication between the school and the student's home. Yet, unless the teacher and the school have clearly determined what grades represent and periodically reviewed that information with each new set of parents or guardians, these reports may create unrest and dissatisfaction on the part of parents, guardians, and students and prove to be alienating devices. The grading system and reporting scheme, then, instead of informing parents and guardians, may separate even further the home and the school, which do have a common concern—the intellectual, physical, social, and emotional development of the student.

The development of the student encompasses growth in the cognitive, affective, and psychomotor domains. Traditional, objective paper-and-pencil tests provide only a portion of the data needed to indicate student progress in those domains. Many experts today question the traditional sources of data and encourage the search for, development of, and use of alternative means to more authentically assess the students' development of thinking and higher-level learning. Although many things are not yet clear, one thing is certain: various techniques of assessment must be used to determine how the student works, what the student is learning, and what the student can produce as a result of that learning. As a teacher, you must develop a repertoire of means of assessing learner behavior and academic progress.

Grades have been a part of school for about 100 years. Although some schools are experimenting with other ways of reporting student achievement in learning, (see for example the October 1994 issue of *Educational Leadership*) grades still seem firmly entrenched—parents, students, colleges, and employers have come to expect grades as evaluations. Some critics suggest that the emphasis in schools is on getting a high grade rather than on learning, arguing that, as traditionally measured, the two do not necessarily go hand in hand. Today's emphasis is more on what the student can do as a result of learning (performance testing) than merely on what the student can recall from the experience (memory testing).

In addition, there have been complaints about subjectivity and unfair practices. As a result of these concerns, various systems of assessment and reporting have evolved and will likely continue to evolve throughout your professional career.

When teachers are aware of alternative systems, they may be able to develop assessment and reporting processes that are fair and effective for particular situations. So, after beginning with assessment, this chapter's final focus is on today's principles and practices in grading and reporting student achievement.

Specifically, this chapter will assist your understanding of

1. Various roles of the assessment component of teaching and learning
2. Using the assessment component
3. Terms used in assessment
4. The meaning of *authentic assessment*
5. The role of assessment in cooperative learning
6. Involving students in self-assessment
7. Using portfolios for assessment
8. Using checklists for assessment
9. Maintaining records of student achievement
10. Grading, marking, and reporting student achievement
11. The difference between criterion-referenced and norm-referenced measurement
12. Determining grades
13. Testing for student learning
14. Preventing and dealing with cheating
15. The meaning of *performance* and *alternative assessment*
16. Preparation of 12 different types of assessment items
17. Meeting and collaborating with parents and guardians.

A. PURPOSES OF ASSESSMENT

Assessment of achievement in student learning is designed to serve several purposes. These are

1. *To assess and improve student learning.* To assess and improve student learning is the function usually first thought of when speaking of assessment and is the topic of this chapter.
2. *To identify children's strengths and weaknesses.* Identification and assessment of children's strengths and weaknesses are necessary for two purposes: to structure and restructure the learning activities and to restructure the curriculum. Concerning the first purpose, data on student strengths and weaknesses regarding content and process skills are important in planning activities appropriate for both skill development and intellectual development. This is diagnostic assessment (also known as preassessment). For the second purpose, data on student strengths and weaknesses in content and skills are useful for making appropriate modifications to the curriculum.
3. *To assess the effectiveness of a particular instructional strategy.* It is important for you to know how well a particular strategy helped accomplish a particular goal or objective. Competent teachers continually evaluate their strategy choices, using a number of sources: student achievement as measured by assessment instruments, their own intuition, informal feedback given by the children, and informal feedback given by colleagues, such as by members of a teaching team.
4. *To assess and improve the effectiveness of curriculum programs.* Components of the curriculum are continually assessed by committees of teachers and administrators. The assessment is done while students are learning (formative assessment) and after (summative assessment).
5. *To assess and improve teaching effectiveness.* Today's exemplary middle-level teachers are education specialists and are as unique as the clientele they serve. To improve student learning, teachers are periodically evaluated on the basis of their commitment to working with students at this level, their ability to cope with children at a particular age or grade level, and their ability to show mastery of appropriate instructional techniques—techniques that are articulated throughout this text.
6. *To communicate to and involve parents and guardians in their children's learning.* Parents, communities, and school boards all share in accountability for the effectiveness of the learning of their children. Today's schools are reaching out and engaging parents, guardians, and the community in their children's education. All teachers play an important role in the process of communicating with, reaching out to, and involving parents.

B. GUIDELINES FOR ASSESSING LEARNING

Because the welfare and, indeed, the future of so many people depend on the outcomes of assessment, it is impossible to overemphasize its importance. For a learning endeavor to be successful, the learner must have answers to basic questions: Where am I going? Where am I now? How do I get where I am going? How will I know when I get there? Am I on the right track? These questions are integral to a good program of assessment. Of course, in the process of teaching and learning, the answers may be ever-changing, and the teacher must continue to assess and adjust plans as appropriate and necessary.

Principles That Guide the Assessment Program

Based on the preceding questions, the following principles guide the assessment program:

- Teachers need to know how well they are doing.
- Students need to know how well they are doing.
- Evidence and data regarding how well the teacher and students are doing should come from a variety of sources.

- Assessment is an ongoing process. The selection and implementation of plans and activities require continuous monitoring and assessment to check on progress and to change or adopt strategies to promote desired behavior.
- Self-assessment is an important component of any successful assessment program. It also involves helping children develop the skills necessary for them to assume increasingly greater ownership of their own learning.
- The program of assessment should promote teaching effectiveness and contribute to the intellectual and psychological growth of children.
- Assessment is a reciprocal process that includes assessment of teacher performance as well as student achievement.
- A teacher's responsibility is to facilitate student learning and to assess student progress, and for that, the teacher should be held accountable.

C. CLARIFICATION OF TERMS USED IN ASSESSMENT

When discussing the assessment component of teaching and learning, it is easy to be confused by the terminology. To help in your reading and understanding, we offer the following clarification.

Assessment and Evaluation

Although some authors distinguish between the terms *assessment* (the process of finding out what children are learning, a relatively neutral process) and *evaluation* (making sense of what was found out, a subjective process), in this text I do not. I consider the difference to be slight and the terms essentially synonymous.

Measurement and Assessment

Measurement refers to quantifiable data about specific behaviors. Tests and the statistical procedures used to analyze the results are examples. Measurement is a descriptive and objective process, that is, it is relatively free from human value judgments.

Assessment includes objective data from measurement but also other information, some of which is more subjective, such as information from anecdotal records and teacher observations and ratings of student performance. In addition to the use of objective data (data from measurement), assessment also includes arriving at value judgments made on the basis of subjective information.

An example of the use of these terms is as follows. A teacher may share the information that Sarah Jones received a score in the 90th percentile on the eighth-grade statewide achievement test in science (a statement of measurement) but may add that "according to my assessment of her work in my science class, she has not been an outstanding student" (a statement of assessment).

Validity and Reliability

The degree to which a measuring instrument actually measures that which it is intended to measure is called the instrument's validity. When we ask if an instrument (such as a performance assessment instrument) has validity, key questions concerning that instrument are

- Does the instrument adequately sample the intended content?
- Does it measure the cognitive, affective, and psychomotor skills that are important to the unit of content being tested?
- Does it sample all the instructional objectives of that unit?

As a specific example, if a science teacher wants to find out if the students have learned how the position of the fulcrum in a first-class lever will make a difference in the amount of effort exerted, the teacher should carefully select a test question (or performance situation) that will clearly indicate what is being measured. One way would be to make a line drawing of a first-class lever, showing a weight at one end of the lever, an effort at the other end, and a fulcrum at a certain position between them. Or, for a performance situation (a more authentic assessment procedure), the teacher would set up an actual working first-class lever, with weights and the application of force. (In this example, the force could be one of the students and that student's known body weight.) The students would then be asked to predict the effect of the fulcrum's position on the effort exerted.

The accuracy with which a technique consistently measures that which it does measure is called its reliability. If, for example, you know that you weigh 114 pounds and a scale consistently records 114 pounds when you stand on it, then that scale has reliability. However, if the same scale consistently records 100 pounds when you stand on it, we can still say the scale has reliability. This example demonstrates that an instrument can be reliable (it produces similar results when used again and again) yet not necessarily valid (in this second instance, the scale is not measuring what it is supposed to measure, so although it is reliable, it is not valid). Although a technique can be reliable but not valid, it must have reliability before it can have validity.

The need for reliability can be shown clearly through the previous example, that of the effect of the fulcrum's position on the effort exerted on a first-class lever. If the teacher asks the students to predict this effect on the basis of just one position of the fulcrum, the answer will give the teacher no assurance that the students know what will happen. It is necessary to have the students predict what will happen using several positions of the fulcrum to be confident that the students know how the fulcrum's position affects the effort exerted. Thus, the greater the number of test items or situations in this problem, the higher the reliability. The higher the reliability, the more consistency there will be in students' scores measuring their understanding of this particular concept.

D. ASSESSING STUDENT LEARNING

There are three general approaches for assessing a student's achievement: you can assess (1) what the student *says*—for example, a student's contributions to class discussions; (2) what the student *does*—for example, a student's performance, as in the preceding example involving setting up a first-class lever; and (3) what the student *writes*—for example, homework assignments, checklists, written tests, and the student's journal entries. Although your own situation and personal philosophy will dictate the weight you give to each avenue of assessment, you should have a strong rationale if you value and weigh the three categories differently than one-third each.

Authentic Assessment

When assessing for student achievement, it is important that you use procedures that are compatible with the instructional objectives. This is referred to as "authentic assessment." Other terms used for "authentic" assessment are "accurate," "active," "aligned," "alternative," and "direct" assessment. Although "performance" assessment is sometimes used, performance assessment refers to the type of student response being assessed, whereas "authentic" assessment refers to the assessment situation. Although not all performance assessments are authentic, assessments that are authentic are most assuredly performance assessments (Meyer, 1992).

In science, for example, "if students have been actively involved in classifying objects using multiple characteristics, it sends them a confusing message if they are then required to take a paper-and-pencil test that asks them to 'define classification' or recite a memorized list of characteristics of good classifications schemes (Rakow, 1992, p. 3). An authentic assessment technique would be a performance test that actually involves the students in classifying objects. For an authentic assessment of the student's understanding, you would use a performance-based assessment procedure.

Assessment: A Three-Step Process

Assessing a student's achievement is a three-step process. It involves (1) diagnostic assessment, which is an assessment (sometimes called a preassessment) of the student's knowledge and skills *before* the new instruction; (2) formative assessment, the assessment of learning *during* the instruction; and (3) summative assessment, the assessment of learning *after* the instruction, ultimately represented by the student's term, semester, or year's achievement grade. Grades shown on unit tests, progress reports, deficiency notices, and six-week or quarter grades (in a semester-based program) are examples of formative evaluation reports. An end-of-the-chapter test or a unit test is summative, however, when the test represents the absolute end of the student's learning of material of that instructional unit.

Assessing what a student says and does. When evaluating what a student says, you should (1) listen to the student's questions, responses, and interactions with others and (2) observe the student's attentiveness, involvement in class activities, and responses to challenges.

Notice that we say you should listen and observe. While listening to what the student is saying, you should also be observing the student's nonverbal behaviors. For this you can use checklists and rating scales, behavioral growth record forms, observations of the student's performance in classroom activities, and periodic conferences with the student. Figure 5.1 illustrates a sample form for recording and evaluating teacher observations of a student's verbal and nonverbal behaviors.

Please remember that, with each technique used, you must proceed from your awareness of anticipated learning outcomes (the instructional objectives), and you must evaluate a student's progress toward meeting those objectives. That is referred to as criterion-referenced assessment.

To evaluate what a student says and does, follow these guidelines:

1. Maintain an anecdotal record book or folder, with a separate section in it for your records of each student.
2. For a specific activity, list the desirable behaviors.
3. Check the list against the specific instructional objectives.
4. Record your observations as quickly as possible following your observation. Audio or video recordings and, of course, computer software programs can help you check the accuracy of your memory, but if this is inconvenient, you should spend time during school, immediately after, or later that evening recording your observations while still fresh in your memory.
5. Record your professional judgment about the student's progress toward the desired behavior, but think it through before transferring it to a permanent record.
6. Write comments that are reminders to yourself, such as:

    "Check validity of observation by further testing."
    "Discuss observations with student's parent."
    "Discuss observations with school counselor."
    "Discuss observations with other teachers on the teaching team."

Assessing what a student writes. When assessing what a student writes, you can use worksheets, written homework, student journal entries, student portfolios, and tests. In many schools, portfolios, worksheets, and homework assignments are the tools usually

FIGURE 5.1
Evaluating and Recording Student Behaviors: Sample Form

Student _____	Course _____	School _____
Observer _____	Date _____	Period _____
Objective for Time Period	Desired Behavior	What Student Did, Said, or Wrote
Teacher's (observer's) comments:		

used for the formative evaluation of each student's achievement. Tests, too, should be a part of this assessment process, but tests are also used for summative evaluation at the end of a unit, and for diagnostic assessment as well.

Your summative assessment of a student's achievement, and any other final judgment made by you about a student, can have an impact on the emotional and intellectual development of that student. Special attention is given to this later, in the section titled, "Recording Teacher Observations and Judgments."

When assessing what a student writes, use the following guidelines:

1. Worksheets, homework, portfolio assessment criteria, and test items should correlate with and be compatible with specific instructional objectives.
2. Read everything a student writes. If it is important enough for the student to do, it is equally important that you give your professional attention to it.
3. Provide positive written or verbal comments about the student's work. Rather than just writing "good" on a student's paper, briefly state what it was about it that made it "good." Try to avoid negative comments. Rather than simply pointing out that the student didn't do it right, tell or show the student acceptable ways to complete the work and how to do so. For reinforcement, use positive rewards as frequently as possible.
4. Think before writing a comment on a student's paper, asking yourself how you think the student (or a parent or guardian) will interpret the comment and if that is the interpretation you intend.
5. Avoid writing negative comments or grades in student journals. Student journals are for encouraging students to write, to think about their thinking, and to record their creative thoughts. In journal writing, students should be encouraged to write about their experiences in and out of school, especially about their experiences related to what is being learned. They should be encouraged to write about their feelings about what is being learned and how they are learning it. Writing in journals gives them practice in expressing themselves in written form and in connecting their learning, and you should provide the nonthreatening freedom to do it. Comments and evaluations from teachers might discourage creative and spontaneous expression.
6. When reading student journals, talk individually with students to seek clarification of their expressions. Student journals are useful to the teacher (of any subject field) in understanding the student's thought processes and writing skills (diagnostic assessment), and journals should *not* be graded. For grading purposes, teachers may simply record whether the student is maintaining a journal and, perhaps, make a judgment about the quantity of writing in it, but not the quality.
7. When reviewing student portfolios, discuss with students individually the progress in their learning shown by the materials in their portfolio. As with student journals, the portfolio itself should *not* be graded or compared in any way with those of other students. Its purpose is for student self-assessment and to show progress in learning. For this to happen, students should keep in their portfolio all papers related to the course.

Regardless of avenues chosen and their relative weights given by you, you must evaluate against the instructional objectives. Any given objective may be checked by using more than one method and more than one instrument. Subjectivity, inherent in the evaluation process, may be reduced as you check for validity, comparing results of one measuring technique against those of another.

While evaluation of cognitive objectives lends itself to traditional written tests of achievement, the evaluation of affective and psychomotor domains requires the use of performance checklists based on observing student behaviors in action. As indicated in the earlier discussion, however, for cognitive learning as well, educators today are encouraging the use of assessment alternatives to traditional paper-and-pencil written testing. Alternative assessment strategies include the use of projects, portfolios, skits, papers, oral presentations, and performance tests. Advantages claimed for the use of authentic assessment include their direct (performance-based, criterion-referenced, outcome-based) measurement of what students should know and can do and their emphasis on higher-order thinking. On the other hand, disadvantages of authentic assessment include a higher cost, difficulty in making results consistent and usable, and problems with validity, reliability, and comparability.

Unfortunately, the teacher who may never see a student again after a given school year is over may never observe the effects that teacher has had on a student's values and attitudes. On the other hand, in schools where groups or teams of teachers remain with the same cohort of students throughout several years of school (often called "houses," or "villages"), those teachers often do have the opportunity to observe the positive changes in their students' values and attitudes.

E. COOPERATIVE LEARNING AND ASSESSMENT

The purpose of a cooperative learning group is for the group to learn, which means that individuals within the group must learn. Group achievement in learning, then, depends on the learning of individuals within the group. Rather than competing for rewards for achievement, members of the group cooperate with each other by helping each other to learn so the group will earn a reward. Theoretically, when small groups of students of mixed backgrounds, skills, and capabilities work together toward a common goal, their liking and respect for one another increase. As a result, there is an increase in each student's self-esteem *and* academic achievement.

When recognizing the achievement of a cooperative learning group, group as well as individual achievement is rewarded. Remembering that the emphasis must be on peer support rather than peer pressure, you must be cautious about ever giving group grades. Some teachers give bonus points to all members of the group to add to their individual scores when everyone in the group has reached preset criteria. These preset standards can be different for individuals within a group, depending on each member's ability and past performance. It is important that each member of a group feel rewarded and successful. Some teachers also give subjective grades to individual students on their role performances within the group.

For determination of students' report card grades, individual student achievement is measured later through individual results on tests and other sources of data, and the final grade is based on those as well as on the student's performance in the group.

F. INVOLVING STUDENTS IN SELF-ASSESSMENT

In exemplary school programs, students' continuous self-assessment is an important component of the evaluation process. If students are to progress in their understanding of their own thinking (metacognition) and in their intellectual development, they must receive instruction and guidance in how to become more responsible for their own learning (empowered). During that process they learn to think better of themselves and of their individual capabilities. To achieve this self-understanding and improved self-esteem requires the experiences afforded by successes, along with guidance in self-understanding.

Using Portfolios

To meet these goals, teachers should provide opportunities for students to think about what they are learning, how they are learning it, and how far they have progressed. One procedure is for students to maintain portfolios of their work, periodically using rating scales or checklists to assess their own progress. The student portfolio should be well organized and contain assignment sheets, class worksheets, the results of homework, forms for student self-evaluation and reflection on their work, and other class materials thought important by the students and teacher.

Although portfolio assessment as an alternative to traditional methods of evaluating student progress has gained momentum in recent years, setting standards is very difficult. Thus far, research on the use of portfolios for assessment indicates that validity and reliability of teacher evaluation are quite low (O'Neil, 1993). Before using portfolios as an alternative to traditional testing, teachers must consider and clearly understand the reasons for doing it, carefully decide on portfolio content, consider parent and guardian reactions, and anticipate grading problems (Black, 1993). For specific information about mathematics portfolios, see Chapter 8. General information on portfolio assessment for educators is included in two publications: *Portfolio News,* Portfolio Assessment Clearinghouse, San Dieguito High School District, 710 Encinitas Blvd., Encinitas, CA 92024; and *Portfolio Assessment*

Newsletter, Northwest Evaluation Association, 5 Centerpointe Drive, Suite 100, Lake Oswego, OR 97035.

While emphasizing the criteria for evaluation, rating scales and checklists provide students with means of expressing their feelings and give the teacher still another source of input data for use in evaluation. To provide students with reinforcement and guidance to improve their learning and development, teachers meet with individual students to discuss their self-evaluations. Such conferences should provide students with understandable and achievable short-term goals, as well as help them develop and maintain adequate self-esteem.

Although most any of the instruments used for evaluating student work can be used for student self-evaluation, in some cases it might be better to use those constructed with the student's understanding of the instrument in mind. Student self-evaluation and reflection should be done on a regular and continuing basis, so comparisons can be made by the student from one time to the next. You will need to help students learn how to analyze these comparisons. Comparisons should provide a student with information previously not recognized about his or her own progress and growth.

One of the items maintained by students in their portfolios is a series of self-evaluation checklists.

Using Checklists

Items on the student's self-evaluation checklist will vary depending on your grade level. Generic items similar to those in Figure 5.2 can be used. Checklist items can be used easily by a student to compare present with previous self-evaluations, while open-ended questions allow the student to provide additional information as well as an opportunity to do some expressive writing.

Here are general guidelines for using student portfolios in your assessment of student learning:

- Contents of the portfolio should reflect your instructional aims and course objectives.
- Date everything that goes into the portfolio.
- Determine what materials should be kept in the portfolio and announce when, how, and by what criteria portfolios will be reviewed by you; announce these things clearly, preferably in your course syllabus.
- Give all responsibility for maintenance of the portfolio to the students.
- Portfolios should be kept in the classroom.

G. MAINTAINING RECORDS OF STUDENT ACHIEVEMENT

You must maintain well-organized and complete records of student achievement. You may do this in a written record book or on an electronic record book (that is, a commercially developed computer software program or one you develop yourself, perhaps by using a computer software program spreadsheet as the base). The record book should include tardies and absences as well as all records of scores on tests, homework, projects, and other assignments.

Anecdotal records can be maintained in alphabetical order in a separate binder with a separate section for each student. Daily interactions and events occur in the classroom that may provide informative data about a student's intellectual, emotional, and physical development. Maintaining a dated record of your observations of these interactions and events can provide important information that might otherwise be forgotten if you do not write it down. At the end of a unit and again at the conclusion of a grading term, you will want to review your records. During the course of the school year your anecdotal records (and those of other members of your teaching team) will provide important information about the intellectual, psychological, and physical development of each student and reveal whether extra attention needs to be given to individual students.

Recording Teacher Observations and Judgments

As said before, you must carefully think through any written comments that you intend to make about a student. Students can be quite sensitive to what others say about them, particularly to negative comments about them made by a teacher.

FIGURE 5.2

Student Self-Evaluation: Sample Generic Form

Student Self-Evaluation Form
(to be kept in student's portfolio)

Student: Date:

Teacher: Number:

Circle one response for each of the first six items.

1. Since my last self-evaluation my assignments have been turned in
   a. always on time.
   b. always late.
   c. sometimes late; sometimes on time.
   d.
2. Most of my classmates
   a. like me.
   b. don't like me.
   c. ignore me.
   d.
3. I think I am
   a. smart.
   b. the smartest in the class.
   c. the slowest in the class.
   d.
4. Since my last self-evaluation, I think I am
   a. doing better.
   b. doing worse.
   c. doing about the same.
   d.
5. In this course
   a. I am learning a lot.
   b. I am not learning very much.
   c. I am not learning anything.
   d.
6. In this course
   a. I am doing the best work I can.
   b. I am not doing as well as I can.
   c.
7. Describe what you have learned in this class since your last self-evaluation that you have used outside of school. Tell how you used it. (You can refer to your previous self-evaluation.)
8. Describe anything that you have learned about yourself since you completed your last self-evaluation. (You can refer to your previous self-evaluation.)

Additionally, we have seen anecdotal comments in students' permanent records that said more about the teachers who made the comments than the students. Comments that have been carelessly, hurriedly, and thoughtlessly made can be detrimental to a student's welfare and progress in school. Teacher comments must be professional, that is, they must be diagnostically useful to the continued intellectual and psychological development of the child. This is true for any comment you make or write, whether on a student's paper, on the student's permanent school record, or on a note sent home to a parent or guardian.

As an example, consider the following unprofessional comment observed in one student's permanent record. A teacher wrote, "John is lazy." Anyone could describe John as "lazy"; it is nonproductive, and it is certainly not a professional diagnosis. How many times do you suppose John needs to receive such negative descriptions of his behavior before he begins to believe that he is just that—lazy—and, as a result, act that way even more often? Written comments like that can also be damaging because they may be read by John's next teacher, who will simply perpetuate the same expectation of John. To say that John is lazy merely describes behavior as judged by the teacher who wrote the comment. More important, and more professional, would be for the teacher to try to analyze *why* John is behaving that way, then prescribe activities likely to motivate John to assume a more constructive attitude and take charge of his own learning behavior.

For students' continued intellectual and emotional development, your comments should be useful, productive, analytical, diagnostic, and prescriptive. The professional teacher makes diagnoses and prepares descriptions; a professional teacher does *not* label students as "lazy," "vulgar," "slow," "stupid," "difficult," or "dumb." The professional teacher sees the behavior of a student as being goal directed. Perhaps "lazy" John found that particular behavioral pattern won him attention. John's goal, then, was attention (don't we all need attention?), and John assumed negative, even self-destructive, behavioral patterns to reach that goal. The professional task of any teacher is to facilitate the learner's understanding (perception) of a goal and to identify positive behaviors designed to reach that goal.

That which separates the professional teacher from anyone off the street is the teacher's ability to go beyond mere description of behavior. Keep that in mind always when you write comments that will be read by students, by their parents or guardians, and by other teachers.

H. GRADING AND MARKING STUDENT ACHIEVEMENT

If conditions were ideal (which they are not), and if teachers did their job perfectly well (which many of us do not), then all students would receive top marks (the ultimate in mastery learning), and there would be less of a need to talk here about grading. Mastery learning implies that some end point of learning is attainable, but there probably isn't an end point. In any case, because conditions for teaching are never ideal and we teachers are mere humans, let us continue with the topic of grading, which is undoubtedly of special interest to you, your students, their parents or guardians, school counselors, administrators, school boards, and college admissions offices.

In this chapter we have frequently used the term *achievement*. What is meant by this term? Achievement means accomplishment, but is it accomplishment of the instructional objectives as measured against preset standards, or is it simply accomplishment? Most teachers would probably choose the former, in which the teacher subjectively establishes a standard that must be met in order for a student to receive a certain grade for an assignment, a test, a quarter, a semester, or a course. Achievement, then, is decided by degrees of accomplishment.

Preset standards are usually expressed in percentages (degrees of accomplishment) needed for marks or ABC grades. If no student achieves the standard required for an A grade, for example, then no student receives an A. On the other hand, if all students meet the preset standard for the A grade, then all receive A's. Determining student grades on the basis of preset standards is referred to as criterion-referenced grading.

Criterion-Referenced versus Norm-Referenced Grading

As stated in the preceding paragraph, criterion-referenced grading is grading that is based on preset standards. Norm-referenced grading, on the other hand, is based on the relative accomplishment of individuals in the group (say, one classroom of ninth-grade English students or a larger group, perhaps all students enrolled in ninth-grade English). It compares and ranks students and is commonly known as "grading on a curve." Because it encourages competition and discourages cooperative learning, norm-referenced grading is not recommended. Norm-referenced grading is educationally dysfunctional. After all, each student is an individual and should not be converted to a statistic on a frequency-distribution curve. For your own information, after several years of teaching, you can produce frequency-distribution studies of grades you have given in a course you have been teaching, but do *not* grade students on a curve. Grades for student achievement should be tied to performance levels and determined on the basis of each student's achievement toward preset standards.

In criterion-referenced grading, the aim is to communicate information about an individual student's progress in knowledge and work skills in comparison to that student's previous attainment or in the pursuit of an absolute, such as content mastery. Criterion-referenced grading is featured in continuous-progress curricula, competency-based (outcome-based) curricula, and other programs that focus on individualized education.

Criterion-referenced or competency-based grading is based on the level at which each student meets the specified objectives (standards) for the course. The objectives must be clearly stated to represent important student learning outcomes. This approach implies that effective teaching and learning result in high grades (A's) for most students. In fact, when a mastery concept is used, the student must accomplish the objectives before being allowed to proceed to the next learning task. The philosophy of teachers who favor criterion-referenced procedures recognizes individual potential. Such teachers accept the challenge of finding teaching strategies to help students progress from where they are to the next designated level. Instead of wondering how Sally compares with Juanita, the comparison is between what Juanita could do yesterday and what she can do today, and how well these performances compare to the preset standard.

Most school systems use some combination of both norm-referenced and criterion-referenced data. In beginning keyboarding, for example, a certain basic speed and accuracy are established as criteria. Perhaps only the upper third of the advanced keyboarding class is to be recommended for the advanced class in computer programming. The grading for the beginning class might appropriately be criterion based, but grading for the advanced class might be norm referenced. Sometimes both kinds of information are needed. For example, a report card for a student in the eighth grade might indicate how that student is meeting certain criteria, such as an A grade for addition of fractions. Another entry might show that this mastery is expected, however, at the sixth grade. Both criterion- and norm-referenced data may be communicated to the parents or guardians and students. Appropriate procedures should be used: a criterion-referenced approach to show whether the student can accomplish the task and a norm-referenced approach to show how well that student performs compared to the larger group to which the student belongs. Sometimes, one or the other is needed; other times, both are required.

Determining Grades

Once entered onto school transcripts, grades have a significant impact on the futures of students. Determining achievement grades for student performance is serious business, for which several important and professional decisions must be made by you. Although in a few schools, and for certain classes or assignments, only marks such as "E, S, and I" or "pass/no pass" are used, for most courses taught in middle-level schools, percentages of accomplishment and ABC grades are used. To arrive at grades, consider the following guidelines:

1. At the start of the school term, explain your marking and grading policies *first to yourself,* then to your students and to their parents or guardians at "Back-to-School Night," by a written explanation that is sent home, or both.
2. When converting your interpretation of a student's accomplishments to a letter grade, be as objective as possible.
3. Build your grading policy around accomplishment rather than failure, where students proceed from one accomplishment to the next. This is continuous promotion, not necessarily from one grade to the next, but within the classroom. (Some schools have done away with grade-level designation and, in its place, use the concept of continuous promotion from the time of student entry into the school through graduation or exit.)
4. For the selection of criteria for ABC grades, select a percentage standard, such as 92 percent for an A, 85 percent for a B, 75 percent for a C, and 65 percent for a D. Cutoff percentages used are your decision, although the district, school, or program area may have established guidelines to which you are expected to adhere.
5. "Evaluation" and "grading" are *not* synonymous. As you learned earlier, evaluation implies the collection of information from a variety of sources, including measurement techniques and subjective observations. These data, then, become the basis for arriving at a final grade, which in effect is a final value judgment. Grades are one aspect of evaluation and are intended to communicate educational progress to students and to their parents or guardians. For final grades to be valid indicators of that progress, you *must* use a variety of sources of data for their determination.
6. For the determination of students' final grades, we recommend using a point system, in which things that students write, say, and do are given points (except journals or portfolios, unless simply based on whether the student has completed one); then the possible point total is the factor for grade determination. For example, if 92 percent is the cutoff for an A, and 500 points are possible, then any student with 460 points or more (500 × .92) has achieved an A. Likewise, for a test or any other assignment, if the value is 100 points, the cutoff for an A is 92 (100 × .92). With a point system and preset stan-

dards, the teacher and students, at any time during the year, always know the current points possible and can easily calculate a student's current grade standing. That way, students always know where they stand in the course.

7. Students will be absent and will miss assignments and tests, and it is best that you decide beforehand your policy about makeup work. Your policies about late assignments and missed tests must be clearly communicated to students and to their parents or guardians. For makeup work, please consider the following.

Homework assignments. For homework assignments, my recommendation is that, after due dates have been negotiated or set, you adhere to them, giving no credit or reduced credit for work that is turned in late. Generally, experience has shown this to be a good policy to which children can and should adjust. It prepares them for the workplace (as well as for high school and college) and is a policy that is sensible for a teacher who deals with many papers each week.

For this policy to work well, however, assignment deadlines must be given to students well in advance, and not at the last minute. You must be sympathetic and understanding to individual children and their problems. There will be times when you will accept a late paper without penalty, such as when a student has been ill or has had a serious problem at home. Many children come to school with considerable excess psychological baggage, and your acceptance of a student's late paper could mean the difference between that student continuing to perform at school and to grow intellectually, or the acceleration of that student's eventual dropping out of school entirely.

Teachers must be sympathetic and understanding to children and what is happening in their world outside of school. Establishing and following classroom rules, procedures, and assignment deadlines is important. However, as a classroom teacher, you are a professional and that means when it comes to individual children you must make intelligent and professional judgments or decisions. As someone once said, there is nothing democratic about treating unequals as equals. As a professional classroom teacher, alone or collaboratively with your students, rules, procedures, and deadlines will be set, but there will be occasional individual adjustments as good sense dictates.

Tests. Sometimes students are absent when tests are given. In such cases, you have several options. Some teachers allow students to miss or discount one test per grading period. Another technique is to allow each student to substitute a written homework assignment or project for one missed test. Still another option is to give the absent student the choice of either taking a makeup test or having the next test count double. When a makeup test is given, it should be taken within a week of the regular test unless there is a compelling reason (such as a medical problem or family problem) why this cannot happen.

Some students miss a testing period because of their involvement in other school activities. In those instances, the student may be able to arrange to come to another of your class periods, on that day or the next, to take the test.

If a student is absent during performance testing, the logistics and possible diminished reliability of having to readminister the test for one student may necessitate giving the student an alternate written test.

I. TESTING FOR ACHIEVEMENT

One source of information used for determining grades are data obtained from testing for student achievement. Competent planning, preparing, administering, and scoring of tests are important professional skills, for which you will gain valuable practical experience during your student teaching. Here are helpful guidelines that you will want to refer to while you are student teaching and again, occasionally, during your first few years as a credentialed teacher.

Purposes for Testing

Although textbook publishers' tests, test item pools, and standardized tests are available from a variety of sources, because schools are different, teachers are different, and children are different, most of the time you will be designing and preparing your tests for your purposes for your distinct group of children.

Tests can be designed for several purposes, and a variety of kinds of tests and alternate test items will keep your testing program interesting, useful, and reliable. As a university student, you are probably most experienced with testing for measuring achievement, but, when teaching in grades 4 through 9, you will use tests for other reasons as well. Other purposes for which tests are used include

- To assess and aid in curriculum development
- To help determine teaching effectiveness
- To help students develop positive attitudes, appreciations, and values
- To help students increase their understanding and retention of facts, principles, skills, and concepts
- To motivate students
- To provide diagnostic information for planning for individualization of the instruction
- To provide review and drill to enhance teaching and learning
- To serve as a source of information for students and parents.

When and How Often to Test for Achievement

It is difficult to generalize about how often to test for student achievement, but we believe that testing should be cumulative and frequent—that is, each assessment should measure the student's understanding of previously learned material as well as of the current unit of study, and testing should occur as often as once a week. Advantages of assessment that is cumulative include the review, reinforcement, and articulation of old material with the recent. The advantages of frequent assessment include a reduction in student anxiety over tests and an increase in the validity of final grades.

Test Construction

After determining the reasons for which you are designing and administering a test, you need to identify the specific instructional objectives the test is being designed to measure. (As you learned in the previous chapter, your written instructional objectives are specific so that you can write test items to measure against those objectives.) So, the first step in test construction is identification of the purpose(s) of the test. The second step is to identify the objectives to be measured, and the third step is to prepare the test items. The best time to prepare draft items is after you have prepared your instructional objectives; that is, while the objectives are fresh in your mind, which means before the lessons are taught. After a lesson has been taught, you will want to rework your first draft of the test items for that lesson to make any modifications as a result of what was taught and learned.

Administering Tests

For many students, test taking can be a time of high anxiety. To more accurately measure student achievement, you will want to take steps to reduce that anxiety. Students demonstrate test anxiety in various ways. Just before and during testing some are quiet and thoughtful, while others are noisy and disruptive. To control or reduce student anxieties, consider the following guidelines when administering tests.

Since students respond best to familiar routines, plan your program so tests are given at regular intervals (perhaps the same day each week) and administered at the same time and in the same way. In some junior high schools, days of the week for administering major tests are assigned to departments. For example, Tuesdays might be assigned for mathematics department testing, while Wednesdays are for science testing.

Avoid writing tests that are too long and that will take too much time. Sometimes beginning teachers have unreasonable expectations of students' attention spans during testing. Frequent testing with frequent sampling of student knowledge is preferred over infrequent and long tests that attempt to cover everything.

When giving paper-and-pencil tests, try to arrange the classroom so it is well ventilated, the temperature is comfortable, and the seats are well spaced. If spacing is a problem, consider using alternate forms of the test—giving students seated adjacent to one another different forms of the same test, for example, with multiple-choice answer alternatives arranged in different order.

Before test time be certain that you have a sufficient number of copies of the test. Although this may sound trite, we have known too many instances of teachers' starting testing with an insufficient number of test copies. Perhaps the test was duplicated for the teacher by someone else and a mistake was made in the number run off. However it is done, to avoid a serious problem, be sure you have sufficient copies of the test.

Before distributing the test, explain to students what they are to do when finished, such as begin a homework assignment, because not all of the students will finish at the same time. Rather than expecting students to sit quietly after finishing a test, give them something to do.

When ready to test, don't drag it out. Distribute tests quickly and efficiently. Once testing has begun, avoid interrupting the students. Important information can be written on the board or saved until all are finished with the test. During testing, remain in the room and visually monitor the students. If the test is not going to take an entire class period (and most shouldn't) and it's a major test, give it at the beginning of the period if possible, unless you are planning a test review just prior to it. Both just prior to and immediately after a major test, it's improbable that any teacher can create a high degree of student interest in a lesson.

Cheating

Cheating on tests does occur, but you can take steps to discourage it or to reduce the opportunity and pressure to cheat. Consider the following:

1. Space students or, as mentioned before, use alternate forms of the test.
2. Frequent testing and not allowing a single test to count too much reduce test anxiety and the pressure that can cause cheating and increase student learning by "stimulating greater effort and providing intermittent feedback" to the student (Walberg, 1990, p. 472).
3. Prepare test questions that are clear and not ambiguous, thereby reducing the frustration caused by a question or instructions that students do not understand.
4. As said before, avoid tests that are too long and that will take too much time. During long tests, some students get discouraged and restless, and that is when classroom management problems can occur.
5. Performance tests, by their sheer nature, can cause even greater pressure on students and also provide more opportunity for cheating. When administering performance tests to an entire class, it is best to have several monitors or, if that isn't possible, to test groups of students, such as cooperative learning groups, rather than individuals. Evaluation of test performance, then, would be based on group rather than individual achievement.
6. Consider using open-text and open-notebook tests. When students can use their books and pages of notes, it not only reduces anxiety but helps them with the organization and retention of what has been learned.

If you suspect cheating *is* occurring, move to the area of the suspected student. Usually that will stop it. When you suspect cheating *has* occurred, you are faced with a dilemma. Unless your suspicion is backed by solid proof, you are advised to forget it, but keep a close watch on the student the next time to prevent cheating from happening. Your job is not to catch students being dishonest, but to prevent it. If you have absolute proof that a student has cheated, then you are obligated to proceed with school policy on student cheating, and that may call for a session with the counselor or the student and the student's parent or guardian, and perhaps an automatic F grade on the test, or even suspension.

Time Needed to Take a Test

Again, avoid giving tests that are too long and that will take too much time. Preparing and administering good tests is a skill that you will develop over time. In the meantime, it is best to test frequently and to use tests that sample student achievement rather than try for a comprehensive measure of that achievement.

Some students take more time on the same test than do others. You want to avoid giving too much time, or classroom management problems will result. On the other hand, you don't want to cut short the time needed by students who can do well but need more time to think and to write. As a guide for determining the approximate amount of time to allow students to complete a test, see Table 5.1. For example, a test made up of ten multiple-choice items, five arrangement items, and two short-explanation items should require about 30 minutes for a group of students to complete.

J. PREPARING ASSESSMENT ITEMS

Writing good assessment items is yet another professional skill, and to become proficient at it takes study, time, and practice. Because of the recognized importance of an assessment program, please approach this professional charge seriously and responsibly. Although poorly prepared items take no time at all to prepare, they will cause you more trouble than you can ever imagine. As a professional, you should take the time to study different types of assessment items that can be used and how best to write them, then practice writing them. When preparing assessment items, you should ensure that they match and sufficiently cover the instructional objectives. In addition, you should prepare each item carefully enough to be reasonably confident that it will be understood by the student in the manner that you anticipate its being understood.

Classification of Assessment Items

Assessment items can be classified as verbal (oral or written words), visual (pictures and diagrams), and manipulative or performance based (handling of materials and equipment). Written verbal items have traditionally been most frequently used in testing. However, visual tests are useful, for example, when working with students who lack fluency in the written word or testing for the knowledge of students who have limited proficiency in English.

Performance and Alternative Assessment

Performance items and tests are useful when measuring psychomotor skill development, as is common in performance testing of locomotor skills, such as a student's ability to manipulate a compass or to carry a microscope (gross motor skill) or to focus a microscope (fine motor skill). Performance testing can also be a part of a wider testing program that includes testing for higher-level skills and knowledge, as when a student or small group of children are given the task (objective) of creating from discarded materials a habitat for an imaginary animal, and then displaying and describing their product to the rest of the class.

As mentioned earlier, educators today have a rekindled interest in performance testing as a more authentic means of assessing learning. In a program for teacher preparation, the student teaching experience is an example of performance assessment, that is, it is used to assess the teacher candidate's ability to teach. Most of us would probably agree that student teaching is a more authentic assessment of a candidate's ability to teach than is a written (paper-and-pencil test) or verbal (oral test) assessment.

TABLE 5.1
Time to Allow for Testing as Determined by the Types of Assessment Items

TYPE OF TEST ITEM	TIME NEEDED PER ITEM
matching	1 minute per matching item
multiple choice	1 minute per item
completion and correction	1 minute per item
completion drawing	2–3 minutes
arrangement and grouping	2–3 minutes
identification	2–3 minutes
short explanation	2–3 minutes
essay and performance	10 or more minutes

Performance testing is usually more expensive than is verbal, and verbal testing is more time consuming and expensive than is written testing. Regardless, a good program of assessment will use alternate forms of assessment and not rely solely on one form (such as written) or only on one type of that form (such as multiple choice).

The type of test and items you use depend on your purpose and objectives. Carefully consider the alternatives within that framework. As noted, a good assessment program will likely include all three types of items to provide validity checks and to account for the individual differences of students. That is what writers of articles in professional journals are referring to when they talk about alternative assessment. They are encouraging the use of multiple assessment items, as opposed to the traditional heavy reliance on objective items such as multiple-choice questions.

General Guidelines for Preparing Assessment Items

In preparing assessment items, you should

1. Include several kinds of items.
2. Ensure that content coverage is complete, that is, that all objectives are being measured.
3. Ensure that each item of the test is reliable, that it measures the intended objective. One way to check item reliability is to have more than one test item measuring for the same objective.
4. Ensure that each item is clear and unambiguous.
5. Plan the item to be difficult enough for the poorly prepared student but easy enough for the student who is well prepared.
6. Maintain a bank of your assessment items, with each item coded according to its matching instructional objective and domain (cognitive, affective, or psychomotor); perhaps according to its level within the hierarchy of that particular domain; and according to whether it requires low-level recall, processing, or application. Computer software programs are available for this purpose. Ready-made test item banks are available on computer disks and accompany many programs or textbooks. If you use them, be certain that the items match your course objectives and that they are well written. Some state departments of education have made efforts to develop test banks for teachers. For example, see Willis (1990). When preparing items for your own test bank, use your best creative writing skills—prepare items that match your objectives, put them aside, think about them, then rework them. Because writing good assessment items is so time consuming, maintaining a test bank will save you valuable time.

The test you administer to your students should represent your best professional effort and so be free of spelling and grammar errors. A quickly and poorly prepared test can cause you more grief than you can imagine. One that is obviously hurriedly prepared and fraught with spelling errors will quickly be frowned upon by discerning parents or guardians and, if you are a student teacher, will certainly bring about a strong admonishment from your university supervisor. If the sloppiness continues, expect your speedy dismissal from the program.

Attaining Content Validity

To ensure that your test measures what is supposed to be measured, you can construct a table of specifications. This two-way grid indicates behavior in one dimension and content in the other (Figures 5.3a and 5.3b).

In this grid, behavior relates to the three domains: cognitive, affective, and psychomotor. In Figure 5.3a, the cognitive domain, involving mental processes, is divided according to Bloom's taxonomy (Chapter 4) into six categories: (1) knowledge or simple recall, (2) comprehension, (3) application, (4) analysis, (5) synthesis (often involving an original product in oral or written form), and (6) evaluation. The specifications table of Figure 5.3a does not specify levels within the affective and psychomotor domains.

To use a table of specifications, the teacher examining objectives for the unit decides what emphasis should be given to the behavior and to the content. For instance, if vocabu-

FIGURE 5.3A
Table of Specifications I

CONTENT	BEHAVIORS								TOTAL
Science Grades 5–6	Cognitive						Affective	Psychomotor	
Electromagnetism	Knowledge	Comprehension	Application	Analysis	Synthesis	Evaluation			
I. Vocabulary Development		2 (1, 2)	3 (2)						
II. Concepts		2 (3, 4)	1 (4)						
III. Applications	1 (5)	1				1 (5)			
IV. Problem solving		1 (6)							
TOTAL	1	6	4			1			12

FIGURE 5.3B
Table of Specifications II

CONTENT	BEHAVIORS							TOTAL
	Cognitive			Affective		Psychomotor		
	Input	Processing	Application	Low	High	Low	High	
I.								
II.								
III.								
IV.								
TOTAL								

lary development is a concern for this class, then probably having 20 percent of the test be on vocabulary is appropriate, but 50 percent would be unsuitable. This planning enables the teacher to design a test to fit the situation, rather than a haphazard test that does not correspond to the content or behavior objectives.

Since knowledge questions are easy to write, tests often fail to go beyond that level even though the objectives state that the student will analyze and evaluate. The sample table of specifications for a science unit on electromagnetism indicates a distribution of questions on a test. Since this test is to be an objective test and it is so difficult to write objective items to test analysis, synthesis and affective and psychomotor behavior, this table of specifications calls for no test items in these areas. If these categories are included in the unit objectives, some other additional assessment devices must be used to test learning in these categories. The teacher could also show the objectives tested, as indicated within parentheses in Figure 5.3a. Then, a later check on inclusion of all objectives will be easy.

The alternative table shown in Figure 5.3b is preferred by some teachers. Rather than differentiating among all six of Bloom's cognitive levels, this table separates cognitive objectives into just three levels—those that require simple low-level recall of knowledge, those that require information processing, and those that require application of the new knowledge (refer to "Levels of Cognitive Questions and Student Thinking" in Chapter 4). In addition, in this table the affective and psychomotor domains are each divided into low- and high-level behaviors. A third alternative, not illustrated here, is a table of specifications that shows all levels of each of the three domains or uses another classification system, such as that of McCormack and Yager (see Chapter 4).

K. SPECIFIC GUIDELINES FOR PREPARING ITEMS FOR USE IN ASSESSMENT

The section that follows presents the advantages, disadvantages, and guidelines for use of 12 types of items in what is referred to as alternative assessment. When reading the advantages and disadvantages of each type, you will notice that some types are appropriate for use in direct or performance assessment, while others are not.

Arrangement Type

Description: Terms or real objects (realia) are to be arranged in a specified order.

Example 1: Arrange the following list of planets in our solar system in order, beginning with the one closest to the sun.

Example 2: The assortment of balls on the table represents the planets in our solar system. (Note: The balls are of various sizes, such as marbles, golf balls, tennis balls, and basketballs, and are labeled with their appropriate planetary names, with a large sphere in the center representing the sun.) Arrange the balls in their proper order around the sun.

Advantages: This type of item tests for knowledge of sequence and order and is good for review, for starting discussions, and for performance assessment. Example 2 is a manipulative (performance) test item. Recommended for observing and assessing the skill and intellectual development of students.

Disadvantages: Scoring may be difficult, so be cautious and meticulous when using this type for grading purposes.

Guideline for use: When it is a paper-and-pencil arrangement, as in example one, instruct students to include the rationale for their arrangement, making it a combined arrangement and short-explanation type and enhancing reliability. Allow space for explanations on an answer sheet.

Completion-Drawing Type

Description: An incomplete drawing is presented, and the student is to complete it.

Example 1: Connect the following items with arrow lines to show the stages from planting of cotton to the distribution of wearing apparel to consumers.

Example 2: In the following food web, draw arrow lines showing which organisms are consumers and which are producers.

Advantages: This type requires less time than is required for a complete drawing, as may be required in an essay item. Scoring is relatively easy.

Disadvantages: Care needs to be exercised in the instructions so students do not misinterpret the expectation.

Guidelines for use: Use occasionally for diversion, but take care in preparing. Example 1 is typical of this type when used in integrated thematic teaching. This type can be instructive when assessing for student thinking. Consider making the item a combined completion-drawing, short-explanation type by having students include their rationales for their drawings. Be sure to allow space for their explanations.

Completion-Statement Type

Description: An incomplete sentence is presented, and the student is to complete it by filling in the blank space(s).

Example 1: The product of 2x and x is _____.

Example 2: To test their hypotheses, scientists conduct _____.

Advantages: This type is easy to devise, to take, and to score.

Disadvantages: Although the first example is a performance type, when using completion-statement items, there is a tendency to emphasize rote memory. It is difficult to write this type of item to measure for higher levels of cognition. You must be alert for a correct response different from the expected. For example, although the teacher's key has "experiments" as the correct answer for Example 2, a student might answer the question with "investigations," which is equally correct.

Guideline for use: Use occasionally for review. Except when it is a performance item, as in the first example, and unless you can write quality items that extend student thinking beyond that of mere recall, you are advised to avoid using the type for grading. In all instances, avoid copying items verbatim from the student book. As with all types, be sure to provide adequate space for students' answers.

Correction Type

Description: Similar to the completion type, except that sentences or paragraphs are complete but with italicized or underlined words that can be changed to make the sentence correct.

Example: Photosynthesis in *Alabama* is the breakdown of *kids* into hydrogen and oxygen, the release of *isotopes,* and then the combining of the *arms* with carbon dioxide to make *dinosaurs.*

Advantages: Writing this type for the purpose of review can be fun for the teacher. Students may enjoy this type for the tension relief afforded by the incorrect absurdities.

Disadvantages: Like the completion type, the correction type tends to measure for low-level recall and rote memory. The underlined incorrect items could be so whimsical that they might cause more classroom disturbance than you want.

Guidelines for use: Use occasionally for diversion. Try to write items that measure for higher-level cognition. Consider making it a combined-correction, short-explanation type. Be sure to allow space for student explanations.

Essay Type

Description: A question or problem is presented, and the student is to compose a response in the form of sustained prose, using the student's own words, phrases, and ideas, within the limits of the question or problem.

Example 1: Explain the procedure you would use to determine and verify the exact square footage we have available to establish a soccer field on our school campus.

Example 2: Discuss the relationship and the difference between these two plant flower processes—pollination, fertilization.

Advantages: Measures higher mental processes, such as ability to synthesize material and to express ideas in clear and precise written language. Especially useful in integrated thematic teaching. Provides practice in written expression.

Disadvantages: Essay items require a good deal of time to read and to score. They tend to provide an unreliable sampling of achievement and are vulnerable to teacher subjectivity and unreliable scoring. Furthermore, they tend to punish the student who writes slowly and laboriously, who has limited proficiency in the written language, but who may have achieved as well as a student who writes faster and is more proficient in the language. Essay items tend to favor students who have fluency with words but whose achievement may not necessarily be better. In addition, unless the students have been given instruction in their meaning and in how to respond to them, the teacher should not assume that students understand key directive verbs such as *explain* and *discuss*.

Guidelines for use:

1. When preparing an essay-only test, many questions, each requiring a relatively short prose response (see short explanation type) are preferable to a smaller number of questions requiring long prose responses. Briefer answers tend to be more precise, and many items provide a more reliable sampling of student achievement. When preparing short prose response-type questions, be sure to avoid using words verbatim from the student textbook.
2. Allow students adequate test time for a full response.
3. Different qualities of achievement are more likely comparable when all students must answer the same questions, as opposed to selecting those they answer from a list.
4. After preparing essay items, make a tentative scoring key, deciding the key ideas you expect students to identify and how many points will be allotted to each.
5. Students should be informed about the relative test value of each essay item. Point values, if different for each item, can be listed in the margin next to each item.
6. When reading student essay responses, read all student answers one item at a time. While doing that, make notes to yourself, then read all the answers again, scoring each student's paper for that item. Repeat the process for the next item. While scoring essay responses, keep in mind the nature of the objective being measured, which may or may not include handwriting, grammar, spelling, and neatness.
7. To nullify the "halo effect," some teachers have students write a number code rather than their names on essay papers. That way, the teacher is unaware of whose paper is being read. If you do this, use caution not to misplace or confuse the identification codes.
8. While they have some understanding of a concept, many students are not yet facile with written expression, so you must remember to be patient, tolerant, positive, and helpful. Mark papers with positive and constructive comments, showing students how they could have explained or responded better.
9. Prior to using this type of test item, give your students instruction and practice in responding to key directive verbs that will be used (see Jenkinson, 1988, for example):

   Compare asks for an analysis of similarity and difference, but with a greater emphasis on similarities or likenesses.

   Contrast asks more for differences than for similarities.

   Criticize asks for the good and bad aspects of an idea or situation.

Define asks the student to express clearly and concisely the meaning of a term, as in the dictionary or in the student's own words.

Diagram asks the student to put quantities or numerical values into the form of a chart, graph, or drawing.

Discuss asks the student to explain or argue, presenting various sides of events, ideas, or situations.

Enumerate means to count or list one after another, which is different than "explain briefly" or "tell in a few words."

Evaluate means to express worth, value, and judgment.

Explain means to describe, with emphasis on cause and effect.

Illustrate means to describe by means of examples, figures, pictures, or diagrams.

Interpret means to describe or explain a given fact, theory, principle, or doctrine in a specific context.

Justify asks the student to show reasons, with an emphasis on correct, positive, and advantageous aspects.

List means just that, to simply name items in a category or to include them in a list, without much description.

Outline means to give a short summary with headings and subheadings.

Prove means to present materials as witnesses, proof, and evidence.

Relate means to tell how specified things are connected or brought into some kind of relationship.

Summarize asks the student to recapitulate the main points without examples or illustrations.

Trace asks the student to follow a history or series of events step by step by going backward over the evidence.

Grouping Type

Description: Several items are presented, and the student is to select and group those that are related in some way.

Example 1: Separate the following numbered triangles into two groups; place those that are equilateral in group A and those that are not in group B.

Example 2: Circle the one figure that is least like the others (wrench, screwdriver, saw, and swing).

Advantages: This type of item tests knowledge of grouping and can be used to measure for higher levels of cognition and to stimulate discussion. If students manipulate actual items, then it is closer to an authentic assessment type as well. As in Example 2, it can be similar to a multiple-choice type item.

Disadvantage: Remain alert for the student who has a valid alternative rationale for grouping.

Guideline for use: To allow for an alternative correct response, consider making the item a combination grouping and short-explanation type, being certain to allow adequate space for student explanations.

Identification Type

Description: Unknown specimens are to be identified by name or some other criterion.

Example 1: Identify each of the flowers on the table by its common name.

Example 2: Identify by name and use each of the math tools on the table.

Advantages: Verbalization (the use of abstract symbolization) is less significant, as the student is working with real objects. This item should measure higher-level learning than simple recall. It can also be written to measure procedural understanding (as in the second example), such as by asking for identification of steps in booting up a computer program. This is another useful type for authentic assessment.

Disadvantages: To be fair, specimens used should be equally familiar or unfamiliar to all students. Adequate materials must be provided.

Guidelines for use: If photographs, drawings, photocopies, and recordings are used, they must be clear and not confusing to students.

Matching Type

Description: Match related items from a list of numbered items to a list of lettered choices, or in some way connect those items that are the same or are related. Or, to eliminate the paper-and-pencil aspect and make the item more direct, use instructions such as, "Using the items from the table, pair up those that are most alike."

Example 1: In the blank space next to each equation in Column A put the letter of the best answer from Column B.

Stem Column	*Answer Column*
_____ 1. $2x + 3 = 7$	A. $x = 9$
_____ 2. $4x = x + 9$	B. $x = 7$
_____ 3. (etc.)	C. $x = 5$
	D. (etc.)

Example 2: Match items in Column A (stem column) to those of Column B (answer column) by drawing lines between the matched pairs.

Column A	*Column B*
snake	worm
eagle	mammal
whale	reptile
praying mantis	insect
	bird

Advantages: Can measure ability to judge relationships and to differentiate between similar ideas, facts, definitions, and concepts. Easy to score. Can test a broad range of content. Reduces guessing, especially if one group contains more items than the other. Interesting to students. Adaptable for performance assessment.

Disadvantages: Not easily adapted to measuring for higher cognition. Because all parts must be homogeneous, it is possible that clues will be given, thus reducing item validity. A student might have a legitimate rationale for an "incorrect" response.

Guidelines for use: The number of items in the answer column should exceed the number in the stem column. The number of items to be matched should not exceed 12. Matching sets should have high homogeneity, that is, items in both columns (or groups) should be of the same general category. If answers can be used more than once, the directions should so state. Be prepared for the student who can legitimately defend an "incorrect" response.

Multiple-Choice Type

Description: Similar to the completion item in that statements are presented, sometimes in incomplete form, along with several options. Requires recognition or even higher cognitive processes, rather than mere recall.

Example 1: Of the following four cylinders, the one that would cause the lowest-pitched sound would be _____.

a. short and thick

b. short and thin

c. long and thick

d. long and thin

Example 2: From the following list of planets, the planet in our solar system that is farthest from our sun is _____.

a. Earth

b. Mercury

c. Pluto

d. Saturn

Advantages: Items can be answered and scored quickly. A wide range of content and higher levels of cognition can be tested in a relatively short time. Excellent for all testing purposes—motivation, review, and assessment of learning.

Disadvantages: Unfortunately, because multiple-choice items are relatively easy to write, there is a tendency to write items measuring only for low levels of cognition. Multiple-choice items are excellent for major testing, but it takes time to write quality questions that measure higher levels of learning.

Guidelines for use:

1. If the item is in the form of an incomplete statement, it should be meaningful in itself and imply a direct question rather than merely lead into a collection of unrelated true and false statements.
2. Use a level of language that is easy enough for even the poorest readers to understand, and avoid unnecessary wordiness.
3. If there is much variation in the length of alternatives, arrange the alternatives in order from shortest to longest.
4. Consistent alphabetical arrangement of single-word alternatives is recommended (as in Example 2).
5. Incorrect responses (called distracters) should be plausible and related to the same concept as the correct alternative. Although an occasional humorous distracter helps to relieve test anxiety, they should be avoided. They offer no measuring value.
6. Alternatives should be uniformly arranged throughout the test and listed in vertical (column) form rather than in horizontal (paragraph) form.
7. Every item should be grammatically consistent; for example, if the stem is in the form of an incomplete sentence, it should be possible to complete the sentence by attaching any of the alternatives to it.
8. It is not necessary to maintain a fixed number of alternatives for every item, but the use of less than three is not recommended. The use of four or five reduces chance responses and guessing, thereby increasing reliability for the item.
9. The item should be expressed in positive form. A negative form presents a psychological disadvantage to students. Negative items are those that ask what is *not* characteristic of something or what is the *least* useful. Discard the item if you cannot express it in positive terminology.
10. Responses such as "all of these" or "none of these" should be used only when they will contribute more than another plausible distracter. Care must be taken that such responses answer or complete the item. "All of the above" is a poorer alternative than "none of the above" because items that use it as a correct response need to have four or five correct answers; also, if it is the right answer, knowledge of any two of the distracters will cue it.
11. There must be only one correct or best response. This is easier said than done (refer to guideline 19).
12. The stem must mean the same thing to every student.
13. Measuring for understanding of definitions is better tested by furnishing the name or word and requiring choice between alternative definitions than by presenting the definition and requiring choice between alternative words.
14. The stem should state a single and specific point.
15. The stem must not clue the correct alternative. Consider, for example, "A four-sided figure whose opposite sides are parallel is called _____. a. an octagon. b. a parallelogram. c. a trapezoid. d. a triangle." The use of the word "parallel" clues the answer.
16. Avoid using alternatives that include absolute terms such as *never* and *always*.
17. Multiple-choice items need not be entirely verbal. Consider the use of realia, charts, diagrams, and other visuals. They will make the test more interesting, especially to students with low verbal abilities or limited proficiency in English and, consequently, make the assessment more authentic.
18. Once you have composed a multiple-choice test, tally the position of answers to be sure they are evenly distributed to avoid the common psychological mistake (when there are four alternatives) of having the correct alternative in the third position.

19. Consider providing space between test items for students to include their rationales for their response selections, thus making the test a combination multiple-choice and short-explanation item type. This provides for the student who can rationalize an alternative that you had not considered plausible. It also provides for the measurement of higher levels of cognition and encourages student writing.

20. While scoring, on a blank copy of the test, tally the incorrect responses for each item. Analyze these to discover potential errors in your scoring key. If, for example, many students select "b" for an item and your key says "a" is the correct answer, you may have made a mistake in your scoring key or in teaching the lesson.

Performance Type

Description: Provided with certain conditions or materials, the student solves a problem or accomplishes some other action.

Example 1: According to a particular hospital's records, the number of people treated in the emergency room for drug-induced traumas were as follows for the year 1991 (adapted with permission from Cangelosi, 1992, p. 255):

Jan: 31	Apr: 40	Jul: NA	Oct: 37
Feb: 33	May: 39	Aug: 48	Nov: 35
Mar: NA	Jun: 45	Sep: NA	Dec: 34

("NA" indicates records not available for that month)

Does the given data suggest any possible pattern relative to the relation between frequency of drug-induced traumas and time of year? Explain your answer:

_____

_____

Based on the data, what would you guess the records for March, July, and September would show if they were available? Explain your answer.

_____

_____

Estimate the total number of drug-induced traumas treated at that hospital's emergency room during 1991. Explain how you arrived at your estimate.

_____

Example 2: Show your understanding of diffusion by designing and completing a laboratory experiment using only the chemicals and equipment located at the learning-activity station.

Advantages: Performance test item types come closer to direct measurement (authentic assessment) of certain expected outcomes than do most other types, although other types of questions can be prepared as performance-type items. Learning that is difficult to verbalize can be assessed since little or no verbalization may be necessary. Students who do poorly on verbal tests may do well on performance tests. This is often true, for example, for students who have learning disabilities.

Disadvantages: As with the second example, the item can be difficult and time consuming to administer to a group of students. Scoring may tend to be subjective. It could be difficult to give make-up tests to students who were absent.

Guidelines for use: Use your creativity to design and use performance tests, as they tend to measure the most important objectives. To reduce subjectivity in scoring, prepare distinct scoring guidelines (rubrics), as was discussed in the section on scoring essay-type questions. To set up a performance test situation you should:

1. Specify the performance objective.
2. Specify the test situation or conditions.
3. Establish the criteria (scoring rubric) for judging the excellence of the process and/or product.
4. Make a checklist by which to score the performance or product. (This checklist is simply a listing of the criteria you established in step 3. It would be impossible to use a rating scale; ordinarily, a rating scale makes scoring too complicated.)

5. Prepare directions in writing, outlining the situation, with instructions for the students to follow.

For example, this is a checklist for map work:

Check each item if the map comes up to standard in this particular category.

_____   1. Accuracy.
_____   2. Neatness.
_____   3. Attention to details.

And here is a sample scoring rubric for assessing a student's skill in listening.

A. Strong listener: characteristics
    Responds immediately to oral directions
    Focuses on speaker
    Maintains appropriate attention span
    Listens to what others are saying

B. Capable listener: characteristics
    Follows oral directions
    Usually attentive to speaker and to discussions
    Listens to others without interrupting

C. Developing listener: characteristics
    Has difficulty following oral directions
    Often inattentive
    Short attention span
    Often interrupts the speaker

Short-Explanation Type

Description: The short-explanation question is an essay type but requires a shorter answer.
  Example 1: (See Example 1 of preceding type.)
  Example 2: Explain what is incorrect or misleading about the following drawing.

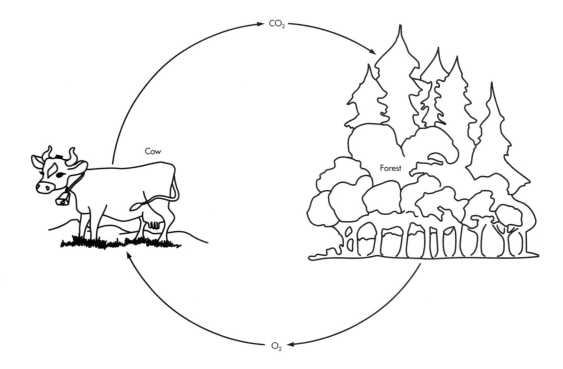

Advantages: As in the essay type, the student's understanding is assessed, but this type takes less time for the teacher to read and to score. In Example 2, for instance, the diagram of the cow and the forest is similar to drawings seen in some science books and represents a misconception about our own place in nature. The intent of the makers of such a diagram is to illustrate the interdependence of animals and plants; the lesson frequently learned is that plants use carbon dioxide produced by animals and that animals use oxygen produced by plants. Following such a study, we asked teachers and their students, "Do plants use oxygen?" The majority said "no." A misconception was learned: the teachers and their students did not understand that all living organisms need oxygen. The focus was too much on what humans gain from "interdependence," rather than on the nature of "interdependence." *Artificialism* is the term used by Piaget to represent the tendency to believe that everything here on Earth is for the benefit of humans. Although natural for children in early grades, it does represent a selfish, prejudiced, nonobjective misconception that should be corrected and avoided by teachers. As discussed in Chapter 1, teachers have an obligation to correct student misconceptions, providing they themselves have a correct understanding of the concept. This type of test item can be useful in assessing conceptual understanding and critical thinking.

Several questions of this type can cover a greater amount of content than fewer essay questions. This type of question is good practice for students to learn to express themselves succinctly in writing.

Disadvantages: Some students will have difficulty expressing themselves in a limited fashion, or in writing. They need practice in doing so.

Guidelines for use: Useful for occasional reviews and quizzes and as an alternative to other types of questions. For scoring, follow the same guidelines as for the essay-type item.

True-False Type

Description: Students judge whether a statement is accurate or not.

Example 1: Photosynthesis goes on only in green plants. T or F?

Example 2: $2 + 4 = 6$. T or F?

Advantages: Many items can be answered in a relatively short time, making broad content coverage possible. Scoring is quick and simple. True-false items are good for starting discussions, for review, and for diagnostic evaluation (preassessment).

Disadvantages: As illustrated by the examples, it is difficult to write true-false items that are purely true or false, or without qualifying them in such a way that clues the answer. Much of the content that most easily lends itself to this type of test item is trivial. Students have a 50 percent chance of guessing the correct answer, thus giving this item type poor validity and poor reliability. Scoring and grading give no clue as to why the student missed an item. For example, for the second example, what if the student was thinking of 2 apples plus 4 oranges? The disadvantages of true-false items far outweigh the advantages; pure true-false items should *never* be used for arriving at grades. For grading purposes, you may use modified true-false items, where space is provided between items for students to write in explanations, thus making the item a combined true-false, short-explanation type.

Guidelines for preparing true-false items:
1. First write the statement as a true statement, then make it false by changing a word or phrase.
2. Avoid using negative statements since they tend to confuse students.
3. A true-false statement should include only one idea. For more than one reason, Example 1 is a poor item. One reason is that it measures two ideas: that photosynthesis goes on in plants (which is true) and that it does so only in plants that are green in color (which is false). To avoid "wrong" answers caused by variations in thinking, as could occur with Example 2, the question could be written as follows: 2 apples + 4 apples = 6 apples. T or F?
4. Use close to an equal number of true and false items.
5. Avoid specific determiners, which may clue that the statement is false—for example, "always," "all," or "none."

6. Avoid words that may clue that the statement is true, such as "often," "probably," and "sometimes."
7. Avoid words that may have different meanings for different students.
8. Avoid using verbatim language from the student textbook.
9. Avoid trick items.
10. As stated earlier, for grading purposes, you may use modified true-false items that allow students to write in their explanations, thus making the item a combined true-false, short-explanation type. Another form of modified true-false item is the use of "sometimes-always-never," where a third alternative, "sometimes," is introduced to reduce the chance of guessing a correct answer.

L. REPORTING STUDENT ACHIEVEMENT

One of your major responsibilities as a classroom teacher is to report student progress in achievement to parents or guardians. In some schools the reporting is of student progress and effort as well as achievement. Reporting is done in at least two and sometimes three ways, described as follows.

The Grade Report

Every six to nine weeks a grade report (report card) is issued (from four to six times a year, depending on the school district). This grade report represents an achievement grade (formative evaluation), and the second or third one of the semester is also the semester grade. For courses that are only one semester long, it is also the final grade (summative evaluation). In essence, the first and sometimes second reports are progress notices, with the semester grade being the one that is transferred to the student's transcript of records. In some schools the traditional report card is marked and sent home either with the student or by mail. In many schools, reporting is done by computer printouts, often sent by mail directly to the student's home address. (In some schools, as an effort to involve them, parents or guardians are expected to come to the school on a given day and pick up the grade report.) Computer printouts might list all the subjects or courses taken by the student while enrolled at the school.

Whichever reporting form is used, you must separate your assessment of a student's social behaviors (classroom conduct) from that of the student's academic achievement. Academic achievement (or accomplishment) is represented by a letter (sometimes a number) grade (A through E or F; or E, S, and U; or 1 to 5; and sometimes with minuses and pluses), and social behavior by a "satisfactory" or an "unsatisfactory" or by more specific items, sometimes supplemented by the teacher's written or computer-generated comments. In some instances there is a location on the reporting form for the teacher to check whether basic grade-level standards have been met in language arts, mathematics, science, and social studies. See Figure 5.4.

Direct Contact with Parents

Although not always obligatory, some teachers contact parents or guardians by telephone, especially when a student has shown a sudden turn either for the worse or for the better in academic achievement or in classroom behavior. That initiative by the teacher is usually welcomed by parents and can lead to private and productive conferences with the teacher. A telephone conversation saves valuable time for both the teacher and the parent.

Another way of contacting parents is by letter. Contacting a parent by letter gives you time to think, to make clear your thoughts and concerns to that parent, and to invite the parent to respond at the parent's convenience by letter, by phone, or by arranging to have a conference with you.

Conferences and Meetings with Parents

You will meet many parents or guardians early in the school year during Back-to-School Night and throughout the year in individual parent conferences. For the beginning teacher, these meetings with parents can be anxious times. Here are guidelines to help you with those experiences.

FIGURE 5.4
Sample Progress Report

Progress Report Form

STUDENT'S NAME: _____ GRADE: _____ YEAR: _____

TEACHER: _____ SCHOOL: _____

SYMBOLS: ACHIEVEMENT AND EFFORT

A = Outstanding
B = Good
C = Satisfactory
D = Unsatisfactory
F = Failing

HONORS STUDENT:	1st Qtr.	2nd Qtr.	3rd Qtr.	4th Qtr.
	☐	☐	☐	☐

SUBJECTS	1st Quarter	2nd Quarter	3rd Quarter	4th Quarter
Reading				
Mathematics				
Language				
Social Studies				
Spelling				
Science				

Citizenship				
Physical Education				
Handwriting				
Art				
Music				

O = Outstanding
G = Good
S = Satisfactory
N = Needs Improvement
U = Unsatisfactory

The Basic Grade Level Standards have been satisfactorily passed in:

Reading ☐   Mathematics ☐   Language ☐

FIRST QUARTER PROGRESS REPORT COMMENTS: _____
_____
_____
_____

SECOND QUARTER PROGRESS REPORT COMMENTS: _____
_____
_____
_____

THIRD QUARTER PROGRESS REPORT COMMENTS: _____
_____
_____
_____

FOURTH QUARTER PROGRESS REPORT COMMENTS: _____
_____
_____
_____

ASSIGNMENT FOR NEXT YEAR: _____
_____
_____

Back-to-School Night is the evening early in the school year when parents can come to the school and meet their child's teachers. The parents arrive at the child's homebase and then proceed through a simulation of their son's or daughter's school day, and as a group meet each class and each teacher for a few minutes. Later, there is an "Open House," where parents may have more time to talk individually with teachers, but Open House is usually a time for the school and teachers to show off the work and progress of the students for that year. Throughout the school year there will be opportunities for you and parents to meet and to talk about the children.

At back-to-school night. On this evening parents are anxious to learn as much as they can about their child's new teachers. You will meet each group of parents for about ten minutes. During that brief meeting you will provide them with a copy of the course syllabus, make some straightforward remarks about yourself, then briefly discuss your expectations of the students.

Although there will be precious little time for questions from the parents, during your introduction the parents will be delighted to learn that you have your program well planned, are a taskmaster, and will communicate with them. The parents and guardians will be pleased to know that you are from the school of the three F's—firm, friendly, and fair.

Specifically, parents will expect to learn about your curriculum—goals and objectives, any long-term projects, and testing *and* grading procedures. They will need to know what you expect of them: will there be homework, and if so, should they help their children with it? How can they contact you? Try to anticipate other questions. Your principal, department chair, or colleagues can be of aid in helping you anticipate and prepare for these questions. Of course, you can never prepare for the question that comes from left field. Just stay calm and don't get flustered. Ten minutes will fly by quickly, and parents will be reassured to know you are an in-control person.

As parents who have attended many back-to-school nights at the schools our children have attended, we continue to be both surprised and dismayed that so few teachers seem well prepared for the few minutes they have with the parents. Considering how often we hear about teachers wanting more involvement of parents, so few seem delighted that parents have indeed come, and so few take full advantage of this time with parents to truly celebrate their programs.

Parent–teacher conference. When meeting parents for conferences, you should be as specific as possible when explaining the progress of their child in your class. Help them understand, but don't saturate them with more information than they need. Resist any tendency to talk too much. Allow time for the parent to ask questions. Keep your answers succinct. Never compare one student with another or with the rest of the class. If the parent asks a question for which you do not have an answer, say you will try to find an answer and will phone the parent as quickly as you can. And do it. Have the student's portfolio and other work with you during parent conferences so you can show the parent examples of what is being discussed. Also have your grade book or a computer printout of it on hand, but be prepared to conceal from the parent the names and records of the other students.

Sometimes it is helpful to have a three-way conference, a conference with the parent, the student, and you, or a conference with the parent, the principal or counselor, and several or all of the student's teachers.

Ideas for Teacher–Parent Collaboration

When a parent asks how she or he may help in the child's learning, here are suggestions for your consideration:

- As needed, plan short family meetings after dinner, but while you are still seated at the table. Ask for a "tableside report" on what's happening in the school. Ask, "How can I help?" When your child expresses a concern, emphasize ways to solve problems that occur. Help the child develop his or her problem-solving skills.
- Ask your child to share with you each day one specific thing learned that day.

- Consider having students take their portfolios home each Friday to share with their parents, having a place in the portfolio where parents or guardians sign to show they have reviewed their child's work, and then having the student return the portfolio on Monday. The form for a parent's signature could also have a column for teacher and parent comments or notes to each other, to maintain this important line of communication between parent and teacher.
- Helping students become critical thinkers is one of the aims of education and one that parents can reinforce by asking "what if" questions, thinking aloud as a model for your child's thinking development, and encouraging the child's own metacognition by asking questions such as, "How did you arrive at that conclusion?" or "How do you feel about your conclusion now?" Ask these questions about the child's everyday social interactions and topics that are important to the child; ask your child to elaborate on his or her ideas, allowing him or her to make mistakes and learn from them.
- Limit and control the child's pleasure viewing of television.
- Set up a regular schedule of reviewing with the child his or her portfolio.
- Set up a regular time each evening for a family discussion about school.
- Several books are available for parents to use at home. For example, the United States government has a variety of free or low-cost booklets available. For information, contact the Consumer Information Center, Department TH, Pueblo, CO 81109. Other useful resources are *Helping Your Child Use the Library* (item 465V); *Becoming a Nation of Readers: What Parents Can Do* (item 459V); *Help Your Child Do Better at School* (item 412V). You also can encourage the parent to go to the neighborhood public library and ask for a librarian's help in locating helpful resources. If you and parents are interested in strategies for increasing home-school collaboration, read *Beyond the Bake Sale: An Educator's Guide to Working with Parents* (Columbia, MD: National Committee for Citizens in Education, 1985) by Anne T. Henderson, Carl Marburger, and Theodora Ooms; the special section, "Parent Involvement," in *Phi Delta Kappan* (volume 72, no. 5, January 1991); *Communicating with Parents* by Janet Chrispeels, Marcia Boruta, and Mary Daugherty (San Diego: San Diego County Office of Education, 1988); *The Evidence Continues to Grow: Parent Involvement Improves Student Achievement* (Columbia, MD: National Committee for Citizens in Education, 1987); and *Parenting for Education* by Paula Lowe and Carl Trendler (Seattle: U.S. West Education Foundation, 1989).

Dealing with an Angry Parent

If a parent or guardian is angry or hostile towards you and the school, here are guidelines for dealing with that hostility:

- Remain calm in your discussion with the parent, allowing the parent to talk out his or her hostility while you say very little. Usually, the less you say, the better off you will be. What you do say must be objective and to the point concerning the child's work in your classroom. The parent may just need to vent frustrations that have very little to do with you, the school, or even the child.
- Do *not* allow yourself to be intimidated or backed into a corner. If the parent tries to do so by attacking you personally, do not press your defense at this point. Perhaps the parent has made a point that you should take time to consider, and now is a good time to arrange for another conference with the parent for about a week later. In a follow-up conference, if agreed to by the parent, you may want to bring in a mediator, such as another member of your teaching team, an administrator, or a school counselor.
- You must *not* talk about other students; keep the conversation focused on this parent's child's progress. The parent is *not* your rival. You both share a concern for the academic and emotional well-being of the child. Use your best skills in critical thinking and problem solving, trying to focus the discussion by identifying the problem(s), defining it, and then arriving at some decision about how mutually to go about solving it. To this end you may need to ask for help from a third party, such as the child's school counselor. If agreed to by the parent, please take that step.

- Parents do *not* need to hear about how busy you are, or about your personal problems, or about how many other students you are dealing with on a daily basis, unless, of course, they ask. Parents expect you to be a capable professional who knows what to do and to be doing it.

SUMMARY

Since assessment is an integral factor in the teaching-learning process, you must aim to include the following in your teaching performance:

1. Use a variety of instruments to assess the learning of students that focus on their individual development. Keep students informed of their progress. Return tests promptly, review answers to all questions, and respond to inquiries about marks given.

2. Use assessment procedures continuously so as to contribute to the positive development of the individual student. Such an emphasis requires that the assessment be important to the student and related to what the student considers important. Effective assessment is helping the student know her or his competencies and achievements. It encourages further learning and the selection of appropriate tasks. The goals of assessment instruments should serve as a challenge, but they should be attainable. Goals set too high or tests that are too hard discourage students and so diminish the motivational factor. Goals set too low and questions that are too easy encourage disregard of the subject content taught and a lackadaisical approach to study.

3. Adapt the grading system of the school to your situation. Establish your own standard and grade each student in relation to it.

4. Avoid using grades as a threat or overstressing them for motivational purposes. It is legitimate to consider as tentative the grade you arrive at after consideration of the objective data that have been accumulated. Consideration of extenuating circumstances, such as sudden illness, prolonged absence for a serious matter, and so on, should then take place before marking permanent grades. Raising a borderline mark to the higher alternative in the light of classroom performance is indeed a professionally defensible decision. Almost never, though, is it prudent to award a lower grade to a student than that student has already earned on the basis of the objective data.

5. Consider your grading procedures carefully, plan them, and explain your policies to the students. The various factors to be considered in arriving at a grade and the weight accorded to such things as homework, written assignments, and oral contributions should all be explained before study is begun.

6. Involve the students, whenever feasible, in setting up criteria and establishing the relative importance of activities. Such cooperative planning is a learning experience for students and encourages self-assessment.

7. Make sure that students understand the directions on any assessments that you give. Before permitting students to begin, make sure to explain any ambiguities that result from the terminology used. Base your assessments on the material that has been taught. Your purpose in giving assessments, of course, is not to trap or confuse students but to evaluate how well they have assimilated the important aspects of learning.

8. Strive for objective and impartial assessment as you put your assessment plan into operation. Do not allow personal feelings to enter into a grade. Whether you like or dislike a student, the grade earned should reflect the student's level of achievement based on the same objective standard used for all.

9. Try to minimize arguments about grades, cheating, and teacher subjectivity by involving students in the planning, reinforcing individual student development, and providing an accepting, stimulating learning environment. Remain alert while students are taking a test. Do not occupy yourself with other tasks at your desk. Circulate, observe, and present at least a psychological deterrent to cheating by your demeanor and presence, but be sure not to distract.

10. Maintain accurate and clear records of assessment results so that you will have an adequate supply of data on which to base your judgmental decisions about achievement. Sufficient data of this sort are especially helpful when final grades are called into question or when students or parents require in-depth information.

Additional discussions of assessment specific to mathematics and science teaching are presented in Parts II and III.

QUESTIONS AND ACTIVITIES FOR DISCUSSION

1. Other than a paper-and-pencil test, identify three alternative assessment techniques for assessing student learning during or at completion of an integrated science and mathematics unit.

2. Investigate various ways that intermediate and middle schools are experimenting today with assessing and reporting student achievement. Share with your colleagues what you find. Analyze the pros and cons of various systems of assessing and reporting.

3. When using a point system for determining student grades for a class of students, is it educationally defensible to give a student a higher grade than that student's points call for? A lower grade? Give your rationale for your answers.

4. Explain the dangers in using true-false and completion-type items in assessing student learning in mathematics and science and using the results for grade determination.

5. Explain the concept of "authentic assessment." Is it the same as "performance assessment"? Explain why or why not.

6. Describe any student learning activities or situations in math and science that should *not* be graded but could be used for assessment of student learning.

7. For a specified grade level that you intend to teach, describe the items that you would use for determining grades for science and mathematics and their relative weights. Explain your rationale for the percentage weight distribution.

8. Explain the value of and give a specific example of a performance test item that you would use in teaching mathematics.

9. Explain the value of and give a specific example of a performance test item that you would use in teaching science.

10. From your current observations and fieldwork related to this teacher preparation program, clearly identify one specific example of educational practice that seems contradictory to exemplary practice or theory as presented in this chapter. Present your explanation for the discrepancy.

11. Describe any prior concepts you held that changed as a result of your experiences with this chapter. Describe the changes.

REFERENCES

Black, S. (1993). Portfolio assessment. *Executive Educator, 15*(1), 28–31.

Cangelosi, J. S. (1992). *Teaching mathematics in secondary and middle school.* New York: Macmillan.

Jenkinson, E. B. (1988). Practice helps with essay exams. *Phi Delta Kappan, 69*(10), 726.

Meyer, C. A. (1992). What's the difference between "authentic" and "performance" assessment? *Educational Leadership, 49*(8), 39–40.

O'Neil, J. (1993). Portfolio assessment bears the burden of popularity. *ASCD Update, 35*(8), 3, 8.

Rakow, S. J. (1992). Assessment: A driving force. *Science Scope, 15*(6), 3.

Walberg, H. J. (1990). Productive teaching and instruction: Assessing the knowledge base. *Phi Delta Kappan, 71*(6), 470–478.

Willis, J. A. (1990). Learning outcome testing program: Standardized classroom testing in West Virginia through item banking, test generation, and curricular management software. *Educational Measurement: Issues and Practices, 9*(2), 11–14.

SUGGESTED READINGS

Abruscato, J. (1993). Early results and tentative implications from the Vermont portfolio project. *Phi Delta Kappan, 74*(6), 474–477.

Bracey, G. W. (1993). Assessing the new assessments. *Principal, 72*(3), 34–36.

Chambers, D. L. (1993). Standardized testing impedes reform. *Educational Leadership, 50*(5), 80–81.

Davis, S. J. (1994). Teaching practices that encourage or eliminate student plagiarism. *Middle School Journal 25*(3), 55–58.

Doran, R. L., et al. (1993). Authentic assessment: An instrument for consistency. *The Science Teacher, 60*(6), 37–41.

Feuer, M. J., & Fulton, K. (1993). The many faces of performance assessment. *Phi Delta Kappan, 74*(6), 478.

Grady, E. (1992). *The portfolio approach to assessment.* Fastback 341. Bloomington, IN: Phi Delta Kappa Educational Foundation.

Haas, N. M., & LoPresto, S. (1994). Panel assessments: Unlocking math exams. *Educational Leadership, 51*(5), 69–70.

Hamm, M., & Adams, D. (1991). Portfolio assessment. *The Science Teacher, 58*(5), 18–21.

Hansen, J. (1992). Evaluation: My portfolio shows who I am. *Quarterly of the National Writing Project and the Center for the Study of Writing and Literacy, 14*(1), 5–6, 9.

Harmon, J. L., Aschbacher, P., & Winters, L. (1992). *A practical guide to alternative assessment.* Alexandria, VA: Association for Supervision and Curriculum Development.

Kohn, A. (1991). Group grade grubbing versus cooperative learning. *Educational Leadership, 48*(5), 83–87.

LeBuffe, J. R. (1993). Performance assessment. *The Science Teacher, 60*(6), 46–48.

Madaus, G. F., & Tan, A. G. A. (1993). The growth of assessment. In G. Cawelti (Ed.), *Challenges and achievements of American education.* 1993 ASCD Yearbook. Alexandria, VA: Association for Supervision and Curriculum Development.

Pallrand, G. J. (1993). Multi-media assessment: Evaluating your students' thinking skills. *The Science Teacher, 60*(6), 42–45.

Schulz, E. (1993). Putting portfolios to the test. *Teacher Magazine, 5*(1), 36–41.

Simmons, R. (1994). The horse before the cart: Assessing for understanding. *Educational Leadership, 51*(5), 22–23.

Walbert, H. J., Haertel, G. D., & Gerlach-Downie, S. (1994). Fastback 377. Bloomington, IN: Phi Delta Kappa Educational Foundation.

Wiggins, G. (1993). Assessment: Authenticity, context, and validity. *Phi Delta Kappan, 75*(3), 200–214.

Wiggins, G. (1994). Toward better report cards. *Educational Leadership 52*(2), 28–37.

Willis, S. (1994). The well-rounded classroom: Applying the theory of multiple intelligences. *ASCD Curriculum Update 36*(8), 1, 5, 6, 8.

Worthen, B. R. (1993). Critical issues that will determine the future of alternative assessment. *Phi Delta Kappan, 74*(6), 444–454.

CHAPTER 6

The Selection and Use of Aids and Resources

Cognitive tools are important in helping students construct their understandings. You will be delighted to know that there is a large variety of useful and effective educational materials, aids, and resources from which to draw as you plan your instructional experiences for science and mathematics learning. On the other hand, you could also become overwhelmed by the sheer quantity of different materials available for classroom use—textbooks, pamphlets, anthologies, encyclopedias, tests, supplementary texts, paperbacks, programmed instructional systems, dictionaries, reference books, classroom periodicals, newspapers, films, records and cassettes, computer software, transparencies, realia, games, filmstrips, audio- and videotapes, slides, globes, manipulatives, CD-ROMs and videodiscs, and graphics. You could spend a lot of time reviewing, sorting, selecting, and practicing with the materials and tools for your use. Although nobody can make the job easier for you, this chapter will expedite the process by providing guidelines for the use of nonprojected and projected aids and materials and information about where to obtain additional resources. Additional information that is more specific to science instruction is provided in Chapter 17.

Specifically, this chapter will help you in

1. Using printed instructional materials.
2. Finding sources of free and inexpensive printed and audiovisual materials.
3. Discovering the variety of professional journals and periodicals relevant to teaching mathematics and science in grades 4–9.
4. Locating sources for additional information relevant to teaching mathematics and science in intermediate and middle schools.
5. Understanding copyright laws for copying printed materials, video, and software programs.
6. Using the classroom writing board.
7. Using the classroom bulletin board.
8. Using charts, posters, and graphs.
9. Using the community as a rich instructional resource.
10. Using audiovisual aids.
11. Knowing what to do when equipment malfunctions.
12. Using the overhead projector.
13. Finding sources of overhead transparencies.
14. Using slides, filmstrips, and 16-mm films.

15. Using instructional television.
16. Using videos, videodiscs, and CD-ROMs.
17. Locating sample titles and sources of videodiscs for mathematics and science.
18. Using computers and multimedia programs.
19. Locating sample titles and sources of software programs for mathematics and science.

A. NONPROJECTED INSTRUCTIONAL TOOLS

Whereas projected aids are those that require electricity to project images onto screens, we begin this chapter with a discussion about nonprojected materials—printed materials, three-dimensional objects, and flat materials on which to write or display—and about the community as a rich resource.

Printed Materials

Historically, of all the nonprojected materials for instruction, the printed textbook has had the greatest influence on teaching. When selecting textbooks and other printed materials, one item of concern to teachers should be the reading level, or readability, of the material. (Additional guidelines for mathematics and science textbook selection, respectively, are found in Chapters 7 and 13.) Sometimes the reading level is supplied by the textbook publisher. If not, you can apply selections to a readability formula or use a simpler method of merely having students read selections from the book aloud. If they can read the selections without stumbling over many of the words and can tell you the gist of what has been written, you can feel confident that the textbook is not too difficult.

Readability Formulas

To estimate the reading-grade level of a student textbook, you can use a readability formula such as the Fry technique. The procedure for the Fry technique is to

1. Determine the average number of syllables in three 100-word selections taken one from the beginning, one from the middle, and one from the ending parts of the book.
2. Determine the average number of sentences in the three 100-word selections.
3. Plot the two values on the readability graph (Figure 6.1). Their intersection will give you an approximation of the text's reading level at 50 percent to 75 percent comprehension.

Since readability formulas give only the technical reading level of a book, you will have to interpret the results by subjectively estimating the conceptual reading level of the work. To do so, consider your students' experience with the subject, the number of new ideas introduced, the abstraction of the ideas, and the author's external and internal cues. Then raise or lower the estimated level of difficulty.

To tell how well your students can read the text, use the Cloze technique or an informal reading inventory. The Cloze technique that was first described by Bormuth (1968) has since appeared in a number of versions. The procedure is as follows. From the textbook, select several typical passages so that you will have a total of 400 to 415 words. Delete every eighth word in the passage except for the words in the first and last sentences, proper names, numbers, and initialed words in sentences. It will be helpful if you eliminate 50 words. Duplicate the passages with 10 to 15 blank spaces replacing the eliminated words. Pass out these "mutilated" readings to the students. Ask them to fill in the blanks with the most appropriate words they can think of. Collect the papers. Score them by counting all the words that are the exact words in the original text and by dividing the number of actual correct responses by the number possible. McKenna suggests that you not count synonyms or verbs of different tense (1976). (Having 50 blanks makes this division easy.)

FIGURE 6.1
Fry Readability Graph
SOURCE: Fry Readability Chart from Edward Fry, "A Readability Formula That Saves TIME."*Journal of Reading, 11* (April 1968): p. 587.

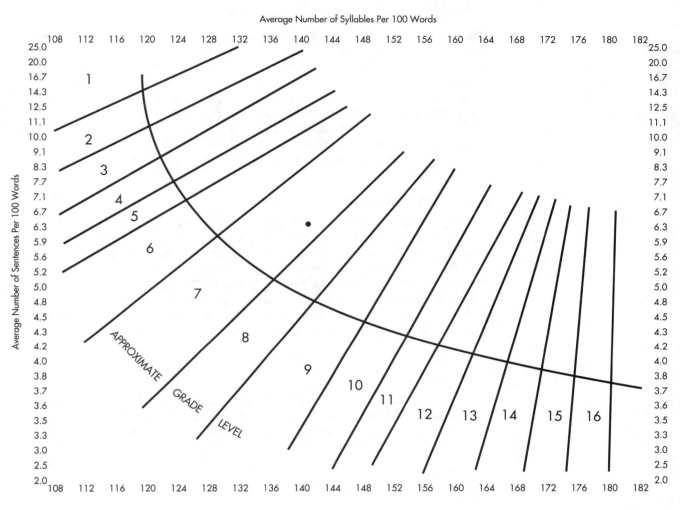

Average Number of Syllables Per 100 Words

Directions:
Randomly select three 100-word passages from a book or an article. Plot average number of syllables and average number of sentences per 100 words on graph to determine the grade level of the material. Choose more passages per book if great variability is observed and conclude that the book has uneven readability. Few books will fall in gray area but when they do grade level scores are invalid.

Count proper nouns, numerals, and initializations as words. Count a syllable for each symbol. For example, "1945" is 1 word and 4 syllables and "IRA" is 1 word and 3 syllables.

Example:	**Syllables**	**Sentences**	
1st Hundred Words	124	6.6	
2nd Hundred Words	141	5.5	
3rd Hundred Words	158	6.8	
Average	141	6.3	**Readability 7th Grade** (see dot plotted on graph)

You can assume that students who score better than 50 percent can read the book quite well, students who score between 40 and 50 percent can read the book at the instructional level, and students who score below 40 percent will probably find the book difficult.

To conduct an informal silent reading inventory, ask your students to read four or five pages of the book, then give them a ten-item quiz on what they read. You can consider the text too difficult for any student who scores less than 70 percent on the quiz. Similarly, to conduct an informal oral reading inventory, have a student read a 100-word passage. The text is too difficult if the student stumbles over and misses more than 5 percent of the words (Johnson & Kress, 1965).

Multitext and Multireading Approaches

Expressing dissatisfaction with the single-textbook approach to teaching, some teachers have substituted a multitext strategy, in which they use one set of books for one topic and another set for another topic. This strategy provides some flexibility, though it really is only a series of single texts.

Other teachers, especially those using an integrated thematic approach, use a strategy that incorporates many readings for a topic during the same unit. This multireading strategy gives students a certain amount of choice in what they read. The various readings allow for differences in reading ability and interest level. By using a study guide, all the students can be directed toward specific information and concepts, but they do not all have to read the same selections.

Beginning a Resources File

Besides the student textbook and perhaps an accompanying workbook, there is a vast array of other printed materials available for use in teaching science and mathematics, many of which are available without cost. (See sources of free and inexpensive materials that follow.) It is a good idea to immediately begin a file of printed materials and other resources that you can use in your teaching. Figure 6.2 is offered to help you begin that process.

Printed materials include books, workbooks, pamphlets, magazines, brochures, newspapers, professional journals, periodicals, and duplicated materials. When reviewing these materials, factors to be alert for are the following:

FIGURE 6.2
Beginning a Professional Materials Resource File

You should start now building your own personal file of aids and resources for teaching, a file that will continue throughout your professional career. Begin your file either on a computer data base program or on 3 × 5 file cards that are color coded by listing:

a. Name of resource
b. How to get it and when available
c. How to use it
d. Evaluative comments including grade level best suited for.

Organize the file in whatever way makes most sense to you. Cross-reference or color code your system to accommodate the following categories of aids and resources:

1. Articles from magazines, newspapers, journals, and periodicals
2. Assessment items
3. Compact disk sources
4. Computer software sources
5. Games and game sources
6. Guest speakers and other community resources
7. Mathematics manipulatives
8. Media catalogs
9. Motivational ideas
10. Multimedia program sources
11. Pictures, posters, and other stills
12. Sources of free and inexpensive items
13. Student worksheets
14. Supply catalogs
15. Thematic unit ideas
16. Unit and lesson plan ideas
17. Unit and lesson plans completed
18. Videocassette titles and sources
19. Videodisc titles and sources
20. Other or Miscellaneous.

- Appropriateness of the material in both content and reading level.
- Articles in newspapers, magazines, and periodicals related to the content that your students will be studying or the skills they will be learning.
- Assorted materials that emphasize thinking and problem solving rather than rote memorization. With an assortment of materials, you can have students working on similar but different assignments depending on their interests and abilities—an example of multilevel teaching.
- Pamphlets, brochures, and other duplicated materials that students can read for specific information and viewpoints about particular topics.
- Relatively inexpensive paperback books that would provide multiple book readings for your class and make it possible for students to read primary sources.

Sources of Free and Inexpensive Printed Materials

For free and inexpensive printed materials, look in your college or university or public library or in the resource center at a local school district (see Figure 6.3).

Professional Journals and Periodicals for Mathematics and Science Teachers of Grades 4–9

Shown in Figure 6.4 is a sample listing of the many professional periodicals and journals that can provide useful teaching ideas for teaching science and mathematics and information about instructional materials and how to get them. Most of these periodicals are likely

FIGURE 6.3

Resources for Free and Inexpensive Printed Materials

A Guide to Print and Nonprint Materials Available from Organizations, Industry, Governmental Agencies and Specialized Publishers. New York: Neal Schuman.

Civil Aeronautics Administration, *Sources of Free and Low-Cost Materials.* Washington, DC: U.S. Department of Commerce.

Educator's Guide to Free Health, Physical Education, and Recreation Materials. Randolph, WI: Educators Progress Service.

Educator's Guide to Free Materials. Randolph, WI: Educators Progress Service.

Educator's Guide to Free Science Materials. Randolph, WI: Educators Progress Service.

Educator's Guide to Free Teaching Aids. Randolph, WI: Educators Progress Service.

Ewing, S. *A Guide to Over One Thousand Things You Can Get for Free.* Lynn, MA: Sunnyside Publishing Company, 1984.

Free and Inexpensive Learning Materials. Nashville, TN: Division of Surveys and Field Services, George Peabody College for Teachers.

Index to Multi-Ethnic Teaching Materials and Teaching Resources. Washington, DC: National Education Association.

NSTA Reports! Published six times each year by the National Science Teachers Association and distributed to its membership, *Reports!* includes a section titled "Science Teacher's Grab Bag," which provides a current listing of resources for free and inexpensive materials for science teachers. Arlington, VA: National Science Teachers Association.

FIGURE 6.4

Professional Periodicals for Teachers of Intermediate and Middle School Mathematics and Science

American Biology Teacher, The	*Learning*
American Teacher	*Mathematics Teacher, The*
Arithmetic Teacher, The	*Mathematics Teaching in the Middle School*
Computing Teacher, The	*Middle School Journal*
Educational Horizons	*Phi Delta Kappan*
Educational Leadership	*Quantum*
Educational Researcher	*School Science and Mathematics*
Instructor	*Science*
Journal for Research in Mathematics Education	*Science Scope*
Journal of Computers in Mathematics and	*Science Teacher, The*
Science Teaching	*Teacher Magazine*
Journal of Learning Disabilities	

to be in your university or college library. Check there for these and other titles of interest to you.

The ERIC Information Network

The Educational Resources Information Center (ERIC) system, established by the United States Office of Education, is a widely used network providing access to information and research in education. While there are 16 clearinghouses providing information on specific subjects, addresses for those of particular interest for teaching science and mathematics follow:

> *Handicapped and Gifted Children.* Council for Exceptional Children, 1920 Association Drive, Reston, VA 22091.
>
> *Reading and Communication Skills.* Indiana University, 2606 East 10th St., Smith Research Center, Suite 150, Bloomington, IN 47408.
>
> *Science, Mathematics, and Environmental Education.* Ohio State University, 1200 Chambers Road, 3rd Floor, Columbus, OH 43212-1792.
>
> *Tests, Measurements, and Evaluation.* American Institutes for Research, Washington Research Center, 1055 Thomas Jefferson St., NW, Washington, DC 20007-3893.

Copying Printed Materials

You must know the laws about the use of copyrighted materials, printed and nonprinted. Although space here prohibits full inclusion of U.S. legal guidelines, your local school district should be able to provide a copy of current district policies for compliance with copyright laws.

When preparing to make a copy, you must find out whether the copying is permitted by law under the category of "permitted use." If not allowed under "permitted use," then you must get written permission to reproduce the material from the holder of the copyright. When using printed materials, adhere to the guidelines shown in Figure 6.5.

B. THE WRITING BOARD

Can you imagine a classroom without a writing board? They used to be slate blackboards. Today, your classroom may have a board that is painted plywood (chalkboard), a magnetic chalkboard (plywood with a magnetic backing), or a white or colored multipurpose board

FIGURE 6.5
Guidelines for Copying Copyrighted Printed Materials
SOURCE: Section 107 of the 1976 Federal Omnibus Copyright Revision Act.

Permitted uses—You may make
1. Single copies of:
   - A chapter of a book
   - An article from a periodical, magazine, or newspaper
   - A short story, short essay, or short poem whether or not from a collected work
   - A chart, graph, diagram, drawing, cartoon
   - An illustration from a book, magazine, or newspaper.
2. Multiple copies for classroom use (not to exceed one copy per student in a course) of:
   - A complete poem if less than 250 words
   - An excerpt from a longer poem, but not to exceed 250 words
   - A complete article, story, or essay of less than 2,500 words
   - An excerpt from a larger printed work not to exceed ten percent of the whole or 1,000 words
   - One chart, graph, diagram, cartoon, or picture per book or magazine issue.

Prohibited uses—You may not
1. Copy more than one work or two excerpts from a single author during one class term (semester or year).
2. Copy more than three works from a collective work or periodical volume during one class term.
3. Reproduce more than nine sets of multiple copies for distribution to students in one class term.
4. Copy to create or replace or substitute for anthologies or collective works.
5. Copy "consumable" works, e.g., workbooks, standardized tests, or answer sheets.
6. Copy the same work year after year.

on which you write with special marking pens. Multipurpose boards are important for classrooms where chalk dust would create problems—where it would aggravate allergies or interfere with computer maintenance. In addition to providing a surface upon which you can write and draw, the multipurpose board can be used as a projection screen and as a surface to which figures cut from colored transparency film will stick. It may also have a magnetic backing.

Extending the purposes of the multipurpose board is an electronic whiteboard that can transfer whatever information is written on it to a connected PC or Mac computer monitor, which in turn can save the material as a computer file. The board uses special dry-erase markers and erasers that have optically encoded sleeves that enable the device to track their position on the board. The data are then converted into a display for the computer monitor, which may then be printed, cut and pasted into other applications, sent as e-mail or a fax message, or networked to other sites. (For information, contact Microfield Graphics, Inc., 9825 SW Sunshine Court, Beaverton, OR 97005 503-626-9393.)

Except for announcements that you place on the board, each day, each class, and even each new idea should begin with a clean board., At the end of each class, clean the board, especially if another teacher follows you in that room.

Use colored chalk (or marking pens) to highlight your "board talk." This is especially helpful for students with learning difficulties. Beginning at the top left of the board, print or write neatly and clearly, with the writing intentionally positioned to indicate content relationships—"causal, oppositional, numerical, comparative, categorical, and so on" (Hunter, 1994, p. 135).

Use the writing board to acknowledge acceptance and to record student contributions. Print instructions for an activity on the board, rather than giving them orally. At the top of the board frame you may find clips that are handy for hanging posters, maps, and charts.

Learn to write on the board without having to entirely turn your back to students or blocking their view of the board. When you have a lot of material to put on the board, do it before class, and then cover it, or better yet, put the material on transparencies and use the overhead projector rather than the board, or use both. Be careful not to write too much information. When using the writing board to complement your teacher talk, Hunter suggests that you write only key words and simple diagrams, thereby making it possible for the student's right brain hemisphere to process what is seen, while the left hemisphere processes the elaboration provided by your words (p. 133).

C. VISUAL DISPLAYS

Visual displays include bulletin boards, charts, graphs, flip charts, magnetic boards, realia (real objects), pictures, and posters. As a new or visiting member of a faculty, one of your first tasks is to find out what visual materials are available for your use and where they are kept. Here are guidelines for their use.

The Classroom Bulletin Board

Bulletin boards are found in nearly every classroom; although sometimes poorly used or not used at all, they can be relatively inexpensively transformed into attractive and valuable instructional tools. When preparing a bulletin board, it is important to be sure that the board display reflects gender and ethnic equity. Read the following suggestions for ideas for the effective use of the classroom bulletin board.

Making a CASE for bulletin boards. How can you effectively use a classroom bulletin board? Your classroom bulletin board will be most effective if you consider your "CASE" (adapted with permission from Kellough & Roberts, 1994, pp. 394–396):

   C: for colorful constructions and captions

   A: for attractive arrangement

   S: for simple and student prepared

   E: for enrichment and extensions of learning.

C: colorful constructions and captions. Take time to plan the colors you select for your board and, whenever possible, include different materials for the letters and for the background of the board. For letter variety, consider patterns on bright cloth such as denim, felt, and corduroy. Search for special letters: they might be magnetic or ceramic, or precut letters of different sizes. Or make unique letters by cutting them from magazines, newspapers, posters, or stencils or by printing the letters with rubber stamps, sponges, or vegetable prints. You may print out the shapes of letters by dabbing colors on ABC shapes with sponges, rubber stamps, or vegetable slices that leave an imprint.

For the background of your board and the borders, consider gift-wrapping paper, wallpaper samples, shelf paper, remnants of fabric—flowers, polka dots, plaids, solids, or checks. Corrugated cardboard makes sturdy borders: cut out scallops for the shape of a picket fence, or make jagged points for an icicle effect. Other colorful borders can be made with wide braid, wide rickrack, or a contrasting fabric or paper. Constructions for the board may be simple ones made of yarn, ribbon, braid, cardboard pointers, maps, scrolls, banners, pennants, wheels that turn, cardboard doors that open, shuttered windows to peek through, or flaps that pull down or up and can be peered under or over.

If you need more bulletin board space, prepare large, lightweight screens from the cardboard sides of a tall refrigerator carton, available from an appliance store. One creative teacher asked for, and received without charge, several empty gallon ice-cream containers from a local ice-cream shop. The teacher then stacked five of the containers on top of one another, fastened them together with wide masking tape, painted them, and prepared her own bulletin board "totem pole" for display in the corner of the classroom. On that circular display space, the students placed their items about a current unit of study.

A: attractive arrangement. Use your imagination to make the board attractive. Is your arrangement interesting? Did you use texture? Did you consider the shapes of the items selected? Are the colors attractive? Does your caption draw student attention?

S: simple and student prepared. The bulletin board should be simple, emphasizing one main idea, concept, topic, or theme, and captions should be short and concise.

Are your students interested in preparing the bulletin board for your classroom? Plan class meeting time to discuss this with them. They have great ideas.

- They can help plan. Why not let them diagram their ideas and share them with each other?
- They can discuss. Is there a more meaningful way to begin to discuss their perceptions, the internal criteria that each student brings to class, or the different values that each student may have?
- They can arrange materials. Why not let them discover the concepts of balance and symmetry?
- They can construct and contribute. Will they feel they are more actively involved and are really participating if it is *their* bulletin board?
- When the bulletin board is finished, your students can get further involved by (1) reviewing the board during a class meeting, (2) discussing the materials used, and (3) discussing the information their bulletin board is emphasizing.

Additional class projects may be planned during this meeting. For instance, do the students want a bulletin board group or committee for their class? Do they want a permanent committee or one in which the membership changes from month to month? Or do they prefer that existing cooperative learning groups assume bulletin board responsibility, with periodic rotation of that responsibility? Do they want to meet on a regular basis? Can they work quietly and not disturb other students who may still be completing their other learning tasks? Should they prepare the board, or should the committee ask everyone to contribute ideas and items for the weekly or monthly bulletin board? Does the committee want to keep a register, guest book, or guest file of students who contribute to the board? Should there be an honorary list of bulletin board illustrators? Should the authors of selected captions sign their names beneath each caption? Do they want to keep a file binder of all of the different diagrams of proposed bulletin boards? At each class meeting, should they discuss the proposed diagrams with the entire class? Should they ask the class to evaluate which idea would be an appropriate one for a particular study topic? What other records do they want to keep? Should there be a bulletin board medal or a classroom award?

E. enrichment and extensions of learning. Illustrations on the bulletin board can accent learning topics; verbs can vitalize the captions; phrases can punctuate a student's thoughts; and alliteration can announce anything you wish on the board. Following are some examples.

Animals can accent! Pandas, panthers, and parrots can help present punctuation symbols; a giant octopus can show students eight rules to remember, eight things to remember when preparing a book report, or eight activities to complete when academic work is finished early; a student can fish for anything—math facts, correctly spelled words, or the meanings of science words; a bear character helps students to "bear down" on errors of any kind; a large pair of shoes helps "stamp out" errors, incomplete work, forgotten school materials, or student misbehavior. Dinosaurs can begin a search for any topic, and pack rats can lead readers into phrases, prose, or poetry.

Verbs can vitalize! Someone or something (your choice) can "swing into" any curriculum area. Some of the verbs used often are *soar, win, buzz, rake, scurry,* and *race.*

Phrases point out! Some of the short, concise phrases used as captions may include

Roll into _____	All aboard for _____	Race into _____
Hop into _____	Peer into _____	Grow up with _____
Bone up on _____	Tune into _____	Monkey with _____
Looking good with _____	Fly high with _____	Get on track with _____

Alliteration announces! Some classroom bulletin boards show Viking ships or Voyages that guide a student to vocabulary words; Monsters monitor Math Madness; other boards present Surprises of Spring, Fantasies of Fall, Wonders of Winter, and Safety in Summer; still other boards send messages about Library Lingo, Dictionary Dynamite, and Thesaurus Treats.

Charts, Posters, and Graphs

Charts, posters, and graphs can be used for displays just as bulletin boards are, but, as a rule, they are better suited for explaining, illustrating, clarifying, and reinforcing specific points in lessons. Charts, posters, and graphs might also be included in a bulletin board display. The previous guidelines for use of the writing board and bulletin board also apply to the use of charts, posters, and graphs. Clarity, simplicity, and attractiveness are essential considerations. Here are additional suggestions for their preparation and use.

Most students enjoy making charts, posters, and graphs. Involve them in doing so, in finding information, planning how to represent it, and making the chart or poster. Have the author(s) of the chart or poster sign it, and then display it in the classroom. Students should credit their sources on the graphs and charts.

Students may need help in keeping graphs proportional, and that provides an opportunity to help students develop mathematics and thinking skills.

Students can also enjoy designing flip charts, a series of charts or posters (that may include graphs) to illustrate certain points or a series of related points. To make a large flip chart, they can use the large pads used by artists for sketching; to make mini–flip charts to use in dyads, they can use small notepads.

D. THE COMMUNITY AS A RESOURCE

One of the richest resources is the local community and the people and places in it. You will want to build your own file of community resources—speakers, sources of free materials, and field trip locations. Your school may already have a community resource file available for your use. It may need updating, however.

A community resource file should contain information about possible field trip locations (see Figure 6.6), community resource people who could serve as guest speakers or mentors, and local agencies that can provide information and instructional materials.

FIGURE 6.6
Community Resources for Speakers and Field Trips

Airports	Nature preserves
Apiaries	Newspaper plants
Aquariums	Observatories
Automobile service stations	Orchards
Backyards	Parks
Bird and wildlife sanctuaries	Photography establishments
Botanical gardens	Planetariums
Buildings under construction	Power plants
Chemical plants	Quarries
Dairies	Radio stations
Farms	Recycling centers
Fire departments	Research laboratories
Flower shows	Sanitation departments
Forests and forest preserves	Sawmills
Gardens	Scientific supply companies
Gas companies	Shorelines (streams, lakes, oceans)
Geological sites	Telecommunications centers
Gravel pits	Telephone companies
Greenhouses	Television stations
Health departments and hospitals	Universities and colleges
Highway construction sites	Water reservoir and treatment plants
Industrial plants	Weather bureau and storm centers
Mines	Wildlife parks and preserves
Museums	Zoos

E. PROJECTED AND RECORDED INSTRUCTIONAL TOOLS

Continuing with our discussion of instructional tools that are available for use in teaching, we next focus on equipment that depends upon electricity to project light and sound and to focus images on screens. Included are projectors of various sorts, computers, CD-ROMs, sound recorders, video recorders, and laser videodisc players. The aim is *not* to teach you how to operate modern equipment, but to help you develop a philosophy for using it and to provide strategies for using these instructional tools in your teaching.

Media Equipment

Certain teaching tools that rely upon sight and sound fall into the category of media known as audiovisual aids. Included in this general category are such teaching tools as charts, models, pictures, graphs, maps, mock-ups, globes, flannel boards, writing boards, and all of the other tools previously discussed. Also included in the general category of audiovisual aids are those devices that require electricity for their operation—projectors of various sorts, computers, sound recorders, video recorders, videodisc and compact disc players, and so forth. This section is about the selection and use of tools of this second group, the ones that require electricity to project sight and sound and that focus images onto screens.

These instructional tools are aids to your teaching. It is important to remember that their role is to aid you, not to teach for you. You must still select the objectives, orchestrate the instructional plan, assess the results, and follow up the lessons. If you use audiovisual aids prudently, your teaching and students' learning will benefit.

Uses of Audiovisual Aids

The main effort of any teacher in instruction is to make the learning clear—communicate the idea, capture the content, clarify the obscure for the students. Hence, teachers almost universally rely on the spoken word as their primary medium of communication. Most of the day is filled with explanation and discourse, to the point that the teaching profession has been accused of making words more important than reality—perpetuating a culture of verbalism in the schools. Teachers use definitions, recitations, and—perhaps too often—rote memorization in quest of the goals for the day.

The learning experiences ladder. To rely on verbalism is to rely on communication through abstract symbolization. Symbols (in this case, letters and words) may not always communicate what is intended. Audiovisual aids can serve to facilitate communication and understanding by adding dimensions to the learning, thus making the learning less abstract. To better understand this concept, which to this point has been presented entirely in one dimension (by words), let's add a dimension (a visual representation); see the Learning Experiences Ladder of Figure 6.7.

The Learning Experiences Ladder represents the range of learning experiences from most direct (bottom of ladder) to most abstract (top of ladder). When selecting learning experiences, it is important to select activities that are as direct as possible. *When students are involved in direct experiences, they are using more of their sensory input modalities (auditory, visual, tactile, kinesthetic), which leads to the most effective and longest-lasting learning.* As discussed in Chapter 1, this is hands-on/minds-on learning. This is learning at the bottom of the ladder. At the other end are abstract experiences, in which the learner is exposed only to symbolization (that is, words and numbers) requiring only one or two senses (auditory or visual). The teacher talks while the students watch and listen. Visual and verbal symbolic experiences, although impossible to avoid when teaching, are less effective in ensuring that planned learning occurs. This is especially true with younger children, children with special needs, slower learners, learners with limited proficiency in using the English language, and intellectually immature learners. It is even true for many adult learners.

As seen from the Learning Experiences Ladder, when teaching about tide pools, the most effective mode is to take the students to a tide pool (bottom of the ladder; the most direct experience) where students can see, hear, touch, smell, and perhaps even taste (if not toxic) the tide pool. The least effective mode is for the teacher merely to talk about a tide pool (top of the ladder; the most abstract symbolic experience), which engages only one sense—the auditory sense.

Of course, for various reasons—safety, lack of resources for a field trip, location of your school—you may not be able to take the students to a tide pool. Because you cannot (and should not) always use the most direct experience, at times you must select an experience higher on the ladder, and audiovisual aids can provide the avenue for doing that. Self-discovery teaching is not always appropriate. Sometimes it is better to build upon what others have discovered and learned. Although learners do not need to "reinvent the wheel," the most effective learning engages most or all of their senses. On the Learning Experiences Ladder, these are the experiences within the bottom three rungs—the direct, simulated, and vicarious categories. Simulated and vicarious learning experiences, such as can be provided with videos and computers, can be nearly as useful as direct experiences.

Another value of direct, simulated, and vicarious experiences is that they tend to be interdisciplinary, that is, they cross subject boundaries. This makes those experiences especially useful for teachers who want to help students connect the learning of one discipline with that of others and with their own life experiences. Direct, simulated, and vicarious experiences are more like real life.

General Guidelines for Using Audiovisual Aids

Like any other boon to progress, audiovisual aids must be worked with if they are to yield what is expected. The mediocre teacher who is content to get by without expending additional effort will in all likelihood remain just that, a mediocre teacher, despite the excellent quality of whatever aids he or she chances to use. Because the mediocre teacher fails to rise to the occasion and hence presents poorly, that teacher's lesson will be less effective and less impressive than it could have been. The effective teacher makes the inquiry about available audiovisual aids and expends the effort needed to implement them well for the benefit of the students. The effective teacher will capitalize on the drama made possible by the shift in interaction strategy and enhance the quest for knowledge by using vivid material. Such teaching involves four steps:

1. Selecting the proper audiovisual material
2. Preparing for using the material

FIGURE 6.7

The Learning Experiences Ladder

SOURCE: Reprinted with the permission of Simon & Schuster, Inc. from the Macmillan College text A RESOURCE GUIDE FOR TEACHING: K–12 by Richard D. Kellough. Copyright ©1994 by Macmillan College Publishing Company, Inc. For earlier versions of this concept, see Charles F. Hoban, Sr., et al., *Visualizing the Curriculum* (New York: Dryden, 1937), p. 39; Jerome S. Bruner, *Toward a Theory of Instruction* (Cambridge: Harvard University Press, 1966), p. 49; Edgar Dale, *Audio-Visual Methods in Teaching* (New York: Holt, Rinehart & Winston, 1969), p. 108; and Eugene C. Kim and Richard D. Kellough, *A Resource Guide for Secondary School Teaching: Planning for Competence,* 2nd ed. (New York: Macmillan, 1978), p. 136.

Verbal Experiences

Teacher talk, written words; engaging one sense; the most abstract symbolization; students are physically inactive.

Examples

1. Listening to the teacher talk about tide pools.
2. Listening to a student report on the Grand Canyon.
3. Listening to a guest speaker talk about how the state legislature functions.

Visual Experiences

Still pictures, diagrams, charts; engaging one sense; typically symbolic; students are physically inactive.

Examples

1. Viewing slides of tide pools.
2. Viewing drawings and photographs of the Grand Canyon.
3. Listening to a guest speaker talk about the state legislature as he or she shows slides of it in action.

Vicarious Experiences

Laser video-disc programs, computer programs, video programs; engaging more than one sense; students are indirectly "doing," possibly some limited physical activity.

Examples

1. Interacting with a computer program about wave action and life in tide pools.
2. Viewing and listening to a video program on the Grand Canyon.
3. Taking a field trip to observe the state legislature.

Simulated Experiences

Role-playing, experiments, simulations, mock-ups, working models; all or nearly all senses are engaged; activity often integrates disciplines and is closest to the real thing.

Examples

1. Building a working model of a tide pool.
2. Building a working model of the Grand Canyon.
3. Role-playing a session of the state legislature.

Direct Experiences

Students are actually doing what is being learned; true inquiry; all senses are engaged; activity usually integrates disciplines.

Examples

1. Visiting a tide pool.
2. Visiting the Grand Canyon.
3. Designing an elected representative body, patterned after the state legislature, to oversee the operation of the school-within-the-school program.

Abstract

Concrete

3. Guiding the audiovisual activity
4. Following up the audiovisual activity.

Selecting the proper audiovisual material. Care must be exercised in the selection of an audiovisual aid for use in the classroom. A poor selection of inappropriate material can turn an excellent lesson plan into a disappointing fiasco. An audiovisual aid that projects garbled sound, outdated pictures, or obscure or shaky images will not be met with a delighted response from the students. Material that is too difficult or boring, takes too long to set up, or is not suitable for students at the intermediate or middle school age level will dampen their enthusiasm.

In your selection of audiovisual materials, you should follow an inquiry routine similar to this:

1. Is the contemplated material suitable? Will it help to achieve the objective of the intended lesson? Will it present an accurate understanding of the facts in the case? Will it highlight the important points? Will it work with the equipment available at the school?
2. Is the material within the level of understanding of the students? Is it too mature? Too embarrassing? Too dated?
3. Is the material lucid in its presentation? Is it clear in its images and sounds?
4. Is the material readily available? Will it be available when needed?

The best response for most of these questions can come after a careful previewing of the material. Sometimes, because of existing conditions, this dry run is not possible. However, the best way to discover the inadequacies of catalog descriptions of films, filmstrips, videotapes, videodiscs, computer software, and compact discs—or of the condition in which they have been left by previous users—is to try them out yourself under practice conditions.

Preparing for using the audiovisual material. To use audiovisual aids with maximum effectiveness usually will require preparation of two types: psychological and physical. From the psychological standpoint, students have to be prepped for the utilization of the material and coached on how best to profit from its presentation. You will need to set the scene, make clear the purpose of the activity, suggest points to look for, present problems to solve, and, in general, clue your students about potential dangers that may mislead them.

From the physical standpoint, preparation pertaining to the machine to be used, the equipment involved, and the arrangement of the classroom furniture will have to be attended to. Sometimes, as with the writing board, preparation is minimal. All that may be necessary may be a sufficient supply of chalk and erasers, the identification of the aid, and a brief recitation concerning the use you intend to make of it. At other times, however, as when the morning or afternoon sun affects classroom visibility, you will have to check the view from each section of the classroom, as well as check the focusing dials of the apparatus for appropriate sharpness of images and the amplitude dials for clarity of sound. In the absence of preparation, bedlam can ensue. The missing chalk, the borrowing and lending of board erasers among the students, or the absence of an extension cord can spell defeat for even the best audiovisual aid. Double-checking the action readiness of the equipment to be used is vital to success.

Guiding the audiovisual activity. The purpose of audiovisual materials is not to replace teaching but to make teaching more effective. Therefore, you cannot always expect the tool to do all the work. You should, however, make it work for your purposes. You will have to highlight in advance the things that you want to be remembered most completely. You may have to enumerate the concepts that are developed or to illustrate relationships or conclusions that you wish to be drawn. You may have to prepare and distribute a study guide or a list of questions for students to respond to, to stop the presentation periodically for hints or questions, or maybe even to repeat the entire performance to ensure a more thorough grasp of particulars. Student learning via the use of audiovisual materials can be enhanced by your coached guidance before, during, and after viewing or use of the materials.

Following up the audiovisual activity. Audiovisual presentations that are allowed to stand alone squander valuable learning opportunities. Some activity and/or discussion should ensue that is pointed and directed toward closure. Such postmortems should have been a vital part of your lesson plan and preparation for the use of the material. Upon completion of the use of the aid, students should be expected to respond to the sets of questions proposed in the preview activity. Points that were fuzzily made should be clarified. Questions that were not answered should be pursued in depth. Deeper responses that go beyond the present scope of the inquiry should be noted and earmarked for further probing at some later date. Quizzes, reviews, practice, and discussions all can be used to tie loose ends together, to highlight the major concepts, to connect and clinch the essential learnings. The planned, efficient use of the aid helps create the atmosphere that audiovisual presentations are learning opportunities rather than recreational time outs.

When Equipment Malfunctions

When using audiovisual equipment, it is nearly always best to set up the equipment and have it ready to go before children arrive in the classroom. That helps avoid problems in classroom management that can occur when there is a delay because the equipment was not ready. Of course, delays may be unavoidable when equipment breaks down, or if a videotape breaks.

Remember the "law" that says if anything can go wrong it will? It is particularly relevant when using equipment discussed in this section. The professional teacher is prepared for such emergencies. Effectively planning for and responding to this eventuality is a part of your system of movement management. That preparation includes consideration of the following.

When equipment malfunctions, three principles should be kept in mind: (1) You want to avoid dead time in the classroom; (2) You want to avoid causing permanent damage to equipment; (3) You want to avoid losing content continuity of a lesson. So what do you do when equipment breaks down? The answer is, *be prepared.*

If a projector bulb goes out, quickly insert another. That means that you should have an extra bulb on hand. If a tape breaks, you can temporarily splice it with cellophane tape. That means that tape should be readily available. And, if you must do a temporary splice, do it on the film or videotape that has already run through the machine, rather than on the end yet to go through, so as not to mess up the machine or the film. Then, after class or after school, be sure to notify the person in charge of the tape that a temporary splice was made, so the tape can be permanently repaired before use again.

If a fuse blows, or for some other reason you lose power, or you can see that there is going to be too much dead time before the equipment is working again, that is the time to go to an alternate lesson plan. You have probably heard the expression, "go to Plan B." It is a useful phrase and means that, without missing a beat in the lesson, you immediately and smoothly switch to an alternate learning activity. For you, the beginning teacher, it doesn't mean that you must plan *two* lessons for every one, but, when planning a lesson that utilizes audiovisual equipment, plan an alternative activity, just in case. Then you can move your students into the planned alternative activity quickly and smoothly.

F. PROJECTORS

Projection machines today are lighter, more energy efficient, and easier to operate than they were a few years ago; they have been almost "defanged." Among the most common and useful to the classroom teacher are the overhead projector, the slide projector, the filmstrip projector, and, of course, the 16-mm film projector. Because limited space in this book disallows the luxury of presenting the operating procedures for every model of projector that you may come across in classrooms, this presentation is limited to guidelines for their use. Since operations from one projector to the next are quite similar, learning to use them should be no major problem for you. At any school there are teachers who will gladly answer questions you may have about a specific projector.

The Overhead Projector

The overhead projector is a versatile, effective, and reliable teaching tool. Except for the bulb burning out, not much else can go wrong with an overhead projector. There is no film to break nor program to crash. And, along with a bulletin board and a writing board, nearly every classroom has one.

The overhead projector consists of a glass-topped box that contains a light source and a vertical post mounting a head that contains a lens. It projects light through objects that are transparent (see Figure 6.8). An overhead projector usually works quite well in a fully lit room. Truly portable overhead projectors are available that can be carried easily from place to place in their compact cases.

Other types of overhead projectors include rear-projection systems that allow the teacher to stand off to the side rather than between students and the screen, and overhead video projectors that use video cameras to send images that are projected by television monitors. Some schools use overhead video camera technology that focuses on an object, pages of a book, or a demonstration, while sending a clear image to a video monitor with a screen large enough for an entire class to clearly see.

In some respects, the overhead projector is more practical than the writing board, particularly for a beginning teacher who is nervous. Use of the overhead projector rather than the writing board can help avoid tension by decreasing the need to pace back and forth to the board. And, by using an overhead projector rather than a writing board, you can maintain both eye contact and physical proximity with students, both of which are important for maintaining classroom control.

Consider the following specific guidelines when using the overhead projector:

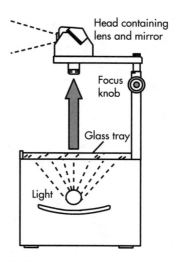

FIGURE 6.8
The Overhead Projector
SOURCE: Joseph F. Callahan, Leonard H. Clark, and Richard D. Kellough, *Teaching in the Middle and Secondary Schools*, 4th ed. (New York: Macmillan Publishing Company, 1992), p. 435. Copyright © 1991 by Macmillan Publishing Company.

1. For writing using an overhead projector, ordinary felt-tip pens are not satisfactory. Select a transparency marking pen available at an office supply store. The ink of these pens is water soluble, so keep the palm of your hand from resting on the transparency or you will have ink smudges on your transparency and on your hand. Non-water-soluble pens—permanent markers—can be used, but to reuse the transparency it must be cleaned with a plastic eraser or an alcohol solvent (ditto fluid works, but, for safety, be sure there is proper ventilation). With a cleaning solvent, you can clean and dry with paper toweling or a soft rag. To highlight the writing on a transparency and to organize student learning, use pens in a variety of colors. Transparency pens tend to dry out quickly, and they are relatively expensive, so the caps must be taken on and off frequently, which is something of a nuisance when working with several colors. Practice writing on a transparency, and also practice making overlays.

2. You can use an acetate transparency roll or single sheets of flat transparencies. Flat sheets of transparency come in different colors—clear, red, blue, yellow, and green— which can be useful in making overlays.

3. Some teachers prefer to prepare an outline of a lesson in advance, on transparencies, which allows more careful preparation of the transparencies and their reuse at another time. Some teachers prefer to use an opaque material, such as 3 × 5 note cards, to block out prewritten material and then uncover it at the moment it is being discussed. For preparation of permanent transparencies, you will probably want to use "permanent marker" pens rather than those that are water soluble and easily smudged. Heavy paper frames are available for permanent transparencies; marginal notes can be written on the frames.

4. An overhead projector can show other transparent materials, such as transparent rulers, protractors, Petri dishes, and even objects that are opaque if you want to simply show a silhouette.

5. Find the best place in your classroom to place the projector. If there is no classroom projection screen, you can hang white paper or a sheet or use a white multipurpose board or a white or near-white wall.

6. Have you ever attended a presentation by someone using an overhead projector improperly? It can be frustrating to members of an audience when the image is too small, out of focus, partially off the screen, or partially blocked from view by the presenter. To use this teaching tool in a professional manner: Turn on the projector (the switch is probably on the front), place the projector so that the projected white light covers the entire screen and hits the screen at a 90-degree angle, then focus the image to be projected. Face the students while using the projector. The fact that you do not lose eye contact with your students is a major advantage of using the overhead projector rather

than a writing board. What you write, as you face your students, will show up perfectly (unless out of focus or off the screen). Rather than using your finger to point to detail or pointing to the screen (thereby turning away from your students), lay a pencil directly on the transparency, with the tip of the pencil pointing to the detail being emphasized.

7. To lessen distraction, you may want to turn the overhead projector off when you want student attention to be shifted back to you or when changing transparencies.

8. Personal computers with laser printers and thermal processing (copy) machines, probably located in the teachers' workroom or in the school's main office, can be used to make permanent transparencies.

9. Calculators specifically for use on the overhead projector are available, as is a screen that fits onto the platform and is circuited to computers, so whatever is displayed on the computer monitor is also projected onto the classroom screen.

10. Tracing enlarged versions of transparent charts or drawings onto paper or onto the writing board is easily done with use of the overhead projector. The image projected onto the screen can be made smaller or larger by moving the projector closer or farther away, respectively, and then traced when you have the size you want.

11. An overhead projector or a filmstrip projector can be used as a light source (spotlight) to highlight demonstrations by you or by your students.

12. Commercial transparencies are available from a variety of school supply houses. For sources, check the catalogs available in your school office or at the audiovisual and resources centers in your school district. See Figure 6.9 for sample sources.

Slides and Filmstrips

Slides and filmstrips are variations of the same medium, and most of what can be said about the use of one is true for the other. In fact, one projector may sometimes serve both functions. Filmstrips are, in effect, a series of slides connected on a roll of film. Slides can be made into filmstrips. Relatively inexpensive technology is now available that allows you to convert slides or home movies into videocassettes. Because of their low cost and greater instructional flexibility and visual impact, videocassettes have literally replaced films and filmstrips for school use.

For teaching purposes, 35-mm slides are still quite useful and are available from school supply houses and, of course, from your own collection and from students and friends. Some schools have the equipment for making slides from computer programs.

16-Mm Films

Because they are less expensive to make and because they offer more instructional flexibility, videocassettes and videodiscs have largely replaced 16-mm films. In fact, laser videodiscs may eventually replace traditional textbooks as well. For example, in 1991, Texas became the first state to allow its schools to use state textbook funds to purchase videodisc programs as an alternative to traditional textbooks in science, and, in 1992, Utah adopted a multimedia system for teaching English as a second language. Other states will most certainly follow these precedents. Although there are still some effective and new 16-mm films available for instruction, many others are old and include dated or incorrect information. As with filmstrips, you need to view films carefully and critically before showing them to your class. Many classic films are now available on videocassette or on videodisc.

FIGURE 6.9
Sources of Overhead Transparencies

BJ's School Supplies, 1807 19th Street, Bakersfield, CA 93301.
Carolina Biological Supply Company, 2700 York Road, Burlington, NC 27215.
Cuisenaire Co. of America, Inc., P.O. Box 5026, White Plains, NY 10602-5026.
Denoyer-Geppert Audiovisuals, 5235 Ravenswood Ave., Chicago, IL 60640.
MMI Corporation, 2950 Wyman Parkway, P.O. Box 19907, Baltimore, MD 21211.
Stasiuk Enterprises, 3150 NE 30th Ave., P.O. Box 12484, Portland, OR 97212.
3M Audio Visual, Building 225-3NE, 3M Center, St. Paul, MN 55144.
United Transparencies, P.O. Box 688, Binghamton, NY 13902.
Ward's Natural Science, 5100 West Henrietta Rd., P.O. Box 92912, Rochester, NY 14692-9012.

G. TELEVISION, VIDEOS, AND VIDEODISCS

Everyone knows that television, videos, and videodiscs represent a powerful medium. Their use as teaching aids, however, may present scheduling, curriculum, and physical problems that some school systems cannot adequately handle.

Television

For purposes of professional discussion, television programming can be divided into three categories: instructional television, educational television, and general commercial television. Instructional television refers to programs specifically designed as classroom instruction; educational television, to programs of cable television and of public broadcasting designed to educate in general, but not aimed at classroom instruction; general commercial television programs, to the entertainment and public service programs of the television networks and local stations.

Instructional television. As just noted, television is not always used well in schools. Ideally, television should not be used for classroom instruction, but rather reserved for supplementing ordinary curricula and instruction. Nevertheless, sometimes instructional television that takes on the role of classroom instruction is necessary. Perhaps courses could not otherwise be successfully mounted, because they are beyond the capabilities of the local resources, staff, and facilities. By using television well, schools can offer students courses that otherwise would be impossible. In other school systems, to save money or bring the students in touch with master teachers, instructional television courses have been introduced as substitutes for regular courses.

The fact that a television class is taught by a master television teacher does not relieve the classroom teacher of any teaching responsibilities. He or she must plan, select, introduce, guide, and follow up, as in any other course. Otherwise, the television teaching will leave the students with learning gaps and misunderstandings. In spite of the marvels of television, students still need the personal guidance of teachers. To use instructional television properly, you should follow a procedure similar to the following (Callahan, et al. 1995):.

1. Prepare for the telecast.
   a. Study the advance material. If possible, preview the telecast.
   b. Arrange the classroom.
   c. Prepare and distribute materials and supplies as needed.
   d. Discuss the lesson to be viewed. Fill in any necessary background. Teach any vocabulary necessary.
2. Guide the learning.
   a. Circulate to help students, if necessary.
   b. Observe student response. Note signs of lack of understanding or misunderstanding.
3. Follow up.
   a. Question and discuss.
   b. Reteach and clarify as necessary.
   c. Use the telecast as a springboard to new experiences involving student participation, creativity, problem solving, and critical thinking.
   d. Tie learning to past and future lessons and experiences.

General and educational television programs. Both public broadcasting stations and commercial stations offer a multitude of programs that can be used to supplement and enrich your teaching. Such programs can be excellent sources of material for use in all sorts of courses. For example, every day the weather map and the radar patterns shown on the weather report portion of the local news give you ammunition for the study of highs, lows, air currents, and the reading of weather maps. Science editors report on new developments in science almost every day and bring attention to important science knowledge in their science news specials.

Educational television courses, such as those given by public broadcasting stations or by colleges and universities on commercial stations, often include lectures, demonstrations, and background information usable for public school courses. Although these courses may be aimed at adults pursuing college credit, they are usually not too difficult for many advanced middle school students.

Television studios do not ordinarily adapt their schedules to those of the schools. This problem may be met in several ways. One solution is to tape programs for replay during the class period. Attention should be paid, however, to copyright laws (discussed later in this chapter). Another solution is to ask students to watch the telecast at home. This solution is fraught with problems because not everyone will be able to watch that television program. Some may not have television sets available (the family may not own one), some may have an adult in the house who wants to watch another show at that time, and some may not have the time available to watch that show. Consequently, you should make such assignments selectively to certain individuals or committees who will report what they have seen and heard. Sometimes, when a major event is to be telecast on several networks, you might do well to ask different students to watch different channels so that they can compare the coverage. For instance, the difference in opinions of various commentators on a presidential message might be quite revealing.

Finally, television program listings can be obtained from your local commercial, educational, or cable companies or by writing directly to network stations. Addresses for the major national networks are listed below:

- American Broadcasting Company, Inc. (ABC), 77 West 66th St., New York, NY 10019. (212) 458–7777.
- Arts & Entertainment Network (A&E), 235 E. Forty Fifth Street, New York, NY 10017. (212) 661–4500.
- Black Entertainment Television, 1899 Ninth Street, NE, Washington, DC 20018. (202) 636–2400.
- Cable News Network—WTBS, 1050 Techwood Drive, NW, Atlanta, GA 30318. (404) 827–1896.
- Columbia Broadcasting System, Inc. (CBS-TV), 51 West 52nd Street, New York, NY 10019. (212) 975–3166.
- C-Span, 400 North Capitol Street, NW, Washington, DC 20001. (202) 737–3220.
- Discovery Channel, The, 7700 Wisconsin Ave., Bethesda, MD 20814-3522. (301) 986–1999.
- Disney Channel, The, 4111 West Alameda Ave., Burbank, CA 91505. (818) 569–7500.
- ESPN, ESPN Plaza, 935 Middle Street, Bristol, CN 06010. (203) 585–2000.
- Fox Broadcasting, 10201 W. Pico Blvd., Los Angeles, CA 90035. (310) 203–3553.
- Learning Channel, The, 7700 Wisconsin Ave., Bethesda, MD 20815-3579. (301) 986–0444.
- Lifetime, 36-12 35th Avenue, Astoria, NY 11106. (718) 482–4000.
- National Broadcasting Company (NBC-TV), RCA Building, 30 Rockefeller Plaza, New York, NY 10112. (212) 664–4444.
- Public Broadcasting Service (PBS), 1320 Braddock Place, Alexandria, VA. (703) 739–5068.
- Turner Broadcasting, One C&N Center, Atlanta, GA 30348-5366. (404) 827–1647.
- United Paramount Network, 5555 Melrose Ave., MOB 1200, Los Angeles, CA 90038. (213) 956–5000.
- USA Network, 1230 Avenue of the Americas, New York, NY 10020. (212) 408–9166.
- Warner Brothers Television Network, 4000 Warner Blvd., Bldg. 34R, Burbank, CA 91522. (818) 954–6000.

Videos and Videodiscs

Combined with a television monitor, the VCR (videocassette recorder) is one of the most popular and frequently used pieces of audiovisual equipment in today's classroom. In a teacher survey conducted by *Instructor* ("Teachers Speak Out on Technology in the Classroom," April 1991), the videocassette recorder was reported as the most popular technology device used by teachers. Videotaped programs can do nearly everything that 16-mm films can do. In addition, combined with a video camera, the VCR makes it possible to record student activities, practice, projects, demonstrations, and your own teaching. It gives students a marvelous opportunity to self-assess as they see and hear themselves in action.

Entire course packages, as well as supplements, are now available on videocassettes or on computer programs. The schools where you student teach and where you eventually are employed may have a collection of such programs. Some teachers make their own.

Laser videodiscs and players for classroom use are reasonably priced, with an ever-increasing variety of disc topics for classroom use. There are two formats of laser videodisc: (1) freeze-frame format (CAV—constant angular velocity, or standard play) and (2) non-freeze-frame format (CLV—constant linear velocity, or extended play). Both will play on all laser disc players. Laser videodisc players are quite similar to VCRs and just as easy to operate. The discs are visual archives or data bases containing large amounts of information that can be easily retrieved, reorganized, filed, and controlled by the user with the remote control that accompanies the player. Each side of a double-sided disc stores 54,000 separate still frames of information—pictures, printed text, diagrams, films, or any combination of these. Both still and moving visuals can be stored and then selected for showing on a television monitor or programmed onto a computer disc for a special presentation. More than 2,000 videodisc titles are now available for educational use. By the time you read these words, there may be more than 3,000 titles. (See Figure 6.10 for sample titles.) Your school or district audiovisual or curriculum resource center probably has some titles already. For additional titles, refer to the latest annual edition of *Videodisc*

FIGURE 6.10

Sample Videodisc Titles and Sources for Mathematics and Science

SUBJECT	TITLE	SAMPLE SOURCE
EARTH SCIENCE	Earth Science	Systems Impact Inc.
	Explore Antarctica!	Emerging Technology Consultants
	Gems and Minerals	Smithsonian
	Planet Earth: The Force Within	Coronet/MTI
	Restless Earth	National Geographic
ENVIRONMENTAL EDUCATION	Global Warming: Hot Times Ahead?	Churchill Media
	Garbage: The Movie—An Environmental Crisis	Churchill Media
	Picture Atlas of Our World	National Geographic
	Planet Earth: The Blue Planet	Coronet/MTI Film & Video
GEOGRAPHY	The Explorers: A Century of Discovery	National Geographic
	Great Cities of Europe	Ztek
	Our Environment	Optilearn
	Regard for the Planet	Voyager
HEALTH	AIDS/HIV: Answers for Young People	Churchill Media
	AIDS—What Everyone Needs to Know	Churchill Media
	A Million Teenagers	Churchill Media
	When Your Unborn Child is on Drugs, Alcohol or Tobacco	Churchill Media
	Have a Healthy Baby: Pregnancy	Churchill Media
LIFE SCIENCE	African Wildlife	National Geographic
	Atoms to Anatomy: A Multimedia View of Human Systems	Videodiscovery
	Dinosaurs	Smithsonian
	Encyclopedia of Animals	Pioneer
	Insects	Smithsonian
	Living Cell, The	Coronet/MTI
	National Zoo, The	Smithsonian
	Rain Forest	National Geographic
MATHEMATICS	Adventures in Mathland	Mindscape, Inc.
	Interactions	D. C. Heath
	Math Sleuths	Videodiscovery
	Mastering Fractions	Systems Impact, Inc.
PHYSICAL SCIENCE	Flying Machines	Smithsonian
	Physical Science Sides 1-4	Optical Data Corp.
SCIENCE/TECHNOLOGY/SOCIETY	Science Sleuths	Videodiscovery
	STS Science Forums	Videodiscovery

Compendium, published and sold by Emerging Technology Consultants Inc., 2819 Hamline Avenue North, St. Paul, MN 55113. Phone (612) 639-3973, Fax (612) 639-0110.

Resources for Videodisc Titles

Check school supply catalogs for additional titles and sources for videodiscs. Here are addresses to which you can write for information:

Addison-Wesley Publishing Co., 2725 Sand Hill Rd., Menlo Park, CA 94025.

AIMS Media, 9710 De Soto Ave., Chatsworth, CA 91311.

Beacon Films, 1560 Sherman Ave., Ste. 100, Evanston, IL 60201.

Central Scientific Co., 3300 CENCO Pkwy., Franklin Park, IL 60131.

Churchill Media, 12210 Nebraska Ave., Los Angeles, CA 90025-3600.

CLEARVUE/eav, Inc., 6465 N. Avondale Ave., Chicago, IL 60631.

Coronet/MTI Film & Video, 108 Wilmot Rd., Deerfield, IL 60015.

DEMCO, Inc., 4810 Forest Run Rd., P.O. Box 7488, Madison, WI 53707.

Educational Activities, Inc., P.O. Box 392, Freeport, NY 11520.

Edunetics Corporation, 1600 Wilson Blvd., Ste. 710, Arlington, VA 22209.

Emerging Technology Consultants, Inc., 2819 Hamline Ave., North, St. Paul, MN 55112.

Encyclopaedia Britannica Educational Corp., 310 S. Michigan Ave., 6th floor, Chicago, IL 60604-9839.

Films Incorporated, 5547 N. Ravenswood, Chicago, IL 60640.

Frey Scientific, 905 Hickory Lane, Mansfield, OH 44905.

GPN, P.O. Box 80669, Lincoln, NE 68501.

Hubbard Scientific, Inc., 3101 Iris Ave., Ste. 215, Boulder, CO 80301.

Information Access Company, 362 Lakeside Dr., Foster City, CA 94404.

Instructional Video, P.O. Box 21, Maumee, OH 43537.

Macmillan/McGraw-Hill School Division, 4635 Hilton Corporate Dr., Columbus, OH 43232-4163.

MECC, 6160 Summit Drive North, Minneapolis, MN 55430-4003.

Miramar Productions, 200 Second Ave., West Seattle, WA 98119-4203.

MMI Corporation, 2950 Wyman Pkwy., P.O. Box 19907, Baltimore, MD 21211.

Nasco, P.O. Box 901, Fort Atkinson, WI 53538-0901.

National Geographic Society Education Services Division, 1145 17th St., NW, Washington, DC 20036.

National Science Programs, Inc., P.O. Box 41, W. Wilson St., Batavia, IL 60510.

Nystrom, 3333 N. Elston Ave., Chicago, IL 60618.

Optical Data Corporation, 30 Technology Dr., Warren, NJ 07059.

Optilearn, Inc., Park Ridge Dr., Ste. 200, Stevens Point, WI 54481.

Phoenix Learning Group, 2349 Chaffee Dr., St. Louis, MO 63146.

Prentice Hall School Group, 113 Sylvan Ave., Englewood Cliffs, NJ 07632.

Queue, Inc., 338 Commerce Dr., Fairfield, CT 06430.

Sargent-Welch Scientific Co., P.O. Box 1026, Skokie, IL 60076-8026.

Satellite Data Systems, Inc., P.O. Box 219, Cleveland, MN 56017.

Scholastic Software, 730 Broadway, New York, NY 10003.

Science for Kids, 9950 Concord Church Rd., Lewisville, NC 27023.

Science Kit and Boreal Laboratories, 777 E. Park Dr., Tonawanda, NY 14150.

Tom Snyder Productions, 80 Coolidge Hill Rd., Watertown, MA 02172.

Sunburst/Wings for Learning, 101 Castleton St., Pleasantville, NY 10570-0100.

SVE, 1345 W. Diversey Pkwy., Chicago, IL 60614.

Tandy Corp./Radio Shack, 1600 One Tandy Center, Ft. Worth, TX 76102.

Videodiscovery, Inc., 1700 Westlake Ave., N, Ste. 600, Seattle, WA 98109-3012.

Ztek Co., P.O. Box 1055, Louisville, KY 40201-1055.

H. COMPUTERS

As a teacher in the twenty-first century, you must understand and be able to use computers as well as you can read and write. To complete your teaching credential, your teacher education program and state teacher licensing commission probably require some level of computer competency, or will soon.

The computer can be valuable to you in several ways:

- The computer can be useful in managing instruction by obtaining information, storing and preparing test materials, maintaining attendance and grade records, and preparing programs to aid in the academic development of individual students. This category of uses of the computer is referred to as computer-managed instruction, or CMI.
- The computer can be used directly for instruction, thanks to various instructional software programs. In their analysis of research studies, Hancock and Betts (1994) report that "in some schools, computer-assisted instruction (CAI) using integrated learning systems (individualized academic tutorials) has shown impressive gains, especially in the early years and among under-achieving urban populations" (p. 25). At Benjamin Banneker Computers Elementary School (Kansas City, MO), where students are expected to spend 50 percent of their daily learning time on a computer (and where there is one classroom computer for every two students), fourth and fifth graders now test out on the Iowa Test of Basic Skills (ITBS) at grades 5.4 and 5.8, respectively. When these same fifth graders entered the program as third graders, many were more than a year behind. Today, some of those fifth graders work at a tenth-grade level (Richey, 1994).
- The computer can be used to teach about computers and to help students develop their skills in computer use.
- And, with the help of software programs about thinking, the computer can be used to help students develop their thinking skills.

Benefits of Computers

For a student, the computer is motivating, exciting, and effective as an instructional tool. Consider the following examples.

Computer programs can motivate. One teacher motivated his students to write by sending their writing work to another class electronically. That was the beginning of the *kids2kids Writing Circle,* a national electronic writing project. (For information on necessary equipment, how to participate, and how to register with the network, see Pinney, 1991.)

Computer programs can activate. In Maine, a group of students prepares maps of local land and water resources from computer analyses of satellite images of the coastline, analyzes the maps, and then advises local authorities on development. Mixing technology and environmental awareness, the students have learned that they can exercise some control over their environment and their future (Wolcott, 1991).

Computer programs can excite. Especially exciting to students are computers with telecommunications systems that connect with other students from around the world, providing an exciting format for comparing data, sharing ideas, and encouraging students to challenge each other toward better understandings of global environmental problems. As an example, many middle school classrooms have joined the World School for Adventure Learning, one goal of which is to establish and sustain a global telecommunications network of schools for ongoing, interactive environmental studies. For more information about World School, contact University of St. Thomas World School for Adventure Learning, 2115 Summit Avenue, St. Paul, MN 55105. Similarly, the National Association of Secondary School Principals has joined the Global Learning Corporation to produce World Classroom, a telecommunications network involving K–12 students and teachers in global educational activities. For further information, contact NASSP Partnerships International at 800-253-7746.

The Placement and Use of Computers in Schools

The way that you use the computer for instruction is determined by your knowledge of and skills in its use, the number of computers available, where computers are placed in the school, and the software available. Despite tight budgets, schools continue to purchase computers. Approximately 50 percent of the computers in schools are found in classrooms, and about 40 percent are in computer labs. The days of a computer in every classroom are far from having yet arrived (National School Boards Association, 1993). Here are some possible scenarios of computer placement and how classroom teachers work within each.

Scenario 1. Many schools have one or more *computer labs* to which a teacher may take an entire class or send a small group of students for computer work. For example, at Skowhegan Area Middle School (Maine), computers have been integrated into the whole curriculum. In collaboration with members of the interdisciplinary teaching teams, the manager of the school's computer lab assists students in using computers as a tool to build their knowledge—to write stories with word processors, to illustrate science diagrams with paint utilities, to create interactive reports with hypermedia, and to graph data they have gathered using spreadsheets (Muir, 1994). In many school computer labs, student computers are networked to the teacher's computer so that the teacher can control and monitor the work of each student. (For a discussion on how to use cooperative learning groups on computers and a recommended list of science software that works in a cooperative learning environment, see Neal, 1994.)

Scenario 2. In some schools, students can take "Computers" as an elective course. Students in your classes who are simultaneously enrolled in the computer course may be given special computer assignments that they can then share with the rest of the class.

Scenario 3. Some classrooms have one computer that is connected to a large-screen video monitor. The teacher or student works the computer, and the monitor screen can be seen by the entire class. As they view the screen, students can verbally respond to and interact with what is happening on the computer.

Scenario 4. In your classroom, you may be fortunate enough to have one or more computers, a videodisc player, an overhead projector, and an LCD (liquid crystal display) projection system. Coupled with the overhead projector, the LCD projection system allows you to project onto your large wall screen (and TV monitor at the same time) any image from computer software or a videodisc. With this system, all students can see and verbally interact with the multimedia instruction.

Scenario 5. Many classrooms have one or more computers. If this is the case in your classroom, you most likely will have one or two students working at the computer while others are doing other learning activities (an example of multilevel teaching).

Computers can be an integral part of a learning activity center and an important aid in your overall effort to individualize the instruction within your classroom.

Computer and Multimedia Programs

When selecting software programs, you and your colleagues need, of course, to choose those that are compatible with your brand of computer(s) and with your instructional objectives. According to a recent study of computers in U.S. schools (National Science Teachers Association, 1994, p. 3), about half are old computers for which software is no

FIGURE 6.11
Sample Computer Software Programs
ªKey to computer brands: AP = Apple; AT = Atari; C64 = Commodore 64 or 128; Comp = Compaq; FR = Franklin; IBM = International Business Machines; TRS = Radio Shack.

TOPIC	TITLE	Computerª	COMPANY
MATH	Bumble Plot	AP/C64/IBM/TRS	The Learning Co.
	Fractions	AP/FR	Encyclopaedia Britannica
	Power Drill	AP/IBM	WINGS for Learning/Sunburst
	The Quarter Mile Series	AP	Barnum Software
PROBLEM SOLVING	Botanical Gardens	AP/IBM	WINGS for Learning/Sunburst
	Creative Play	AP/IBM	Math and Computer Education Project, (Lawrence Hall of Science, Berkeley, CA)
	Gertrude's Puzzles	AP/C64/Comp/IBM	The Learning Co.
	The Factory	AP/AT/C64/Comp/IBM/TRS	Sunburst Communications
SCIENCE	Middle School Science Series	AP/IBM/Comp/Tandy	SCICON: Science Consultants, Inc.
	Project Zoo	AP	National Geographic
	The Weather Machine Courseware Kit	AP	National Geographic

longer made and multimedia software and computer networks are not available. As budgets permit, schools will need to replace their old computers.

Like laser videodiscs and compact discs, computer software programs are continually being developed and are too many and varied to list here. For a brief sampling, see Figure 6.11. For additional listings of computer programs for teaching mathematics, refer to Heddens and Speer (1992) , and to Souviney (1994). See also Chapters 8–12 of this book.

The Online Classroom*

Teachers looking to make their classrooms more student-centered, collaborative, and interactive, are turning to telecommunications networks. Ranging in scale from local bulletin board systems (BBS) to the Internet, these webs of connected computers allow teachers and students from around the world to reach each other directly and gain access to quantities of information previously unimaginable.

Students using networks learn new inquiry and analytical skills in a stimulating environment and, as many people believe, they also gain an increased awareness of their role as world citizens. For example, Leisa Winrich, a teacher at North Middle School in Menomonee Falls, Wisconsin, connected her mathematics students to KidLink network to share local weather data with distant classes. The Menomonee students compile the international data and send it back out over the network. Winrich says, "We discovered that math does help us communicate; we can grow to better understand our global neighbors and their environments by exchanging and studying numbers." (Cohen, p. 6).

Many network service providers exist. Directories are available in most bookstores. Here are a few samples:

- K12Net. A network of bulletin board systems for teachers, students, and parents. For information, contact (503) 280–5280, ext. 450.
- I*EARN. The International Education Resource Network, connecting students and teachers internationally with electronic mail, conferences, and travel exchanges. For information, contact (914) 962–5864.
- PBS Online's Learning Link. A network of BBS based at locally public TV stations. For information, contact (703) 739–8464.
- Global SchoolNet. Develops collaborative electronic mail projects. For information, contact (619) 475–4852.

*Adapted from Philip Cohen, (December 1994) The online classroom, *Association for Supervision and Curriculum Development Update* 36(10),1, 5–6. Reprinted with permission of the Association for Supervision and Curriculum Development. Copyright © 1994 by ASCD. All rights reserved.

- International Society for Technology and Education. Promotes use of technology in schools. For information, contact (503) 346–4414.
- TERC. Devoted to math and science, network programs include Global Laboratory and LabNet. For information, contact (617) 547–0430.
- Classroom Connect. A monthly teacher's guide to Internet and commercial online services. For information, contact (800) 638–1639.

Selecting Computer Software

In addition to selecting software programs that are compatible with your brand of computer(s) and with your instructional objectives, you must evaluate and test them for their compatibility with your science or mathematics objectives. Evaluation forms are usually available from the local school district or from the state department of education and from professional associations, such as the National Science Teachers Association.

When reviewing computer software, you should reject any software that

- Gives an audible response to student errors. No student should be forced to advertise mistakes to the whole class.
- Rewards failure. Some programs make it more fun to fail than to succeed.
- Has sound that cannot be controlled. The teacher should be able to easily turn sound on and off.
- Has technical problems. Is the software written so that it will not crash if the user accidentally types the wrong key? Incorrect responses should lead to software-initiated help comments.
- Has uncontrolled screen advance. Advancing to the next page should be under user control, not automatically timed.
- Gives inadequate on-screen instructions. All necessary instructions to run the program must be interactively displayed on the screen (in a continuously displayed instruction window, if possible).
- Has factual errors. Information displayed must be accurate in content, spelling, and grammar.
- Contains insults, sarcasm, and derogatory remarks. Students' character should not be compromised.
- Has poor documentation. Demand a teacher's guide that compares in quality to a textbook teacher's guide or other teaching aid.
- Does not come with a backup copy. Publishers should recognize the unique vulnerability of magnetic disks and offer low-cost replacement. (Information from Souviney, 1994, p. 135; used with permission of Macmillan Publishing Company.)

The CD-ROM

Computers have three types of storage disks—the floppy disk, the hard disk, and the CD-ROM, which is an abbreviation for "compact disc—read only memory." Use of a CD-ROM disc requires a CD-ROM drive. Newer computers may have built-in CD-ROM drives, while older ones must be connected to one. As with floppy and hard disks, CD-ROMs are used for storing characters in a digital format, while images on a videodisc are stored in an analog format. The CD-ROM is capable of storing approximately 250,000 pages of text, or the equivalent of 1,520 360K floppy disks or eight 70M hard disks, and therefore is ideal for storing large amounts of information such as dictionaries, encyclopedias, and general reference works full of graphic images that you can copy and modify. Some CD-ROM discs contain information that cannot be erased, transferred to a computer, or modified in any way.

The same material is used for both CD-ROM discs and laserdiscs, but the laserdisc platter is 12 inches across, while the CD-ROM disc is just 4.5 inches across. All CD-ROM discs require the use of a computer that is connected to a CD-ROM player or has one built in. Newer CD-ROM discs include video segments, just like those of videodiscs.

Any information stored on a CD-ROM disc or a videodisc can be found and retrieved within a few seconds. CD-ROMs are available from the distributors of videodiscs. Sample CD-ROM multimedia programs appropriate for students in grades 4-9 include *Cell"ebra-*

tion, Forces & Motion, and *Simple Machines,* available from Science for Kids, 9950 Concord Church Rd., Lewisville, NC 27023; *A Field Trip to the Rainforest* available from Sunburst, 101 Castleton Street, P. O. Box 100, Pleasantville, NY 10570; and *Space Shuttle,* from The Follette Software Company, 800 N. Front St., McHenry, IL 60050. Resources for teachers include *MathFinder* and *Science Helper K-8,* from The Learning Team, Armonk, NY. Two publications that focus on CD-ROM products are CD-ROM Professional, available at newsstands, and the newsletter *Children's Software Revue,* available from 520 N. Adams St., Ypsilanti, MI 48197. A comprehensive listing of multimedia educational software (i.e., titles that have either a CD-ROM or a laser videodisc component) is available from the Educational Software Institute, 4213 South 94th Street, Omaha, NE 68127 (toll free phone 1–800–955–5570).

Use of copyrighted CD-ROMs. Usually, when purchasing CD-ROMs and other multimedia software packages intended for use by schools, you pay for a license to modify and use its contents for instructional purposes. However, not all CD-ROMs include copyright permission, so always check the copyright notice on any disk you purchase and use. Whenever in doubt, don't use it until you have asked your district media specialist about copyrights, or have obtained necessary permission from the original source.

Sources of Free and Inexpensive Audiovisual Materials

Check your college or university library for sources of free and inexpensive audiovisual materials, listed in Figure 6.12.

Using Copyrighted Video and Computer Programs

You must be knowledgeable about the laws on the use of videos and computer software materials that are copyrighted. Although space here prohibits full inclusion of U.S. legal guidelines, your local school district undoubtedly can provide a copy of current district policies to ensure compliance with all copyright laws. As said earlier in the discussion about the use of printed materials that are copyrighted, when preparing to make any copy you must find out whether the copying is permitted by law under the category of "permitted use." If not, then you must get written permission to reproduce the material from the holder of the copyright. Figures 6.13 and 6.14 present guidelines for the copying of videotapes and of computer software. As of this writing, there are no guidelines for fair use of films, filmstrips, and slides.

I. CALCULATORS

The National Council of Teachers of Mathematics (NCTM) recommends that mathematics programs at all levels take full advantage of calculators and computers in mathematics instruction. The value of the use of calculators in the integration of instruction in both mathematics and science is well documented by numerous research studies (see Souviney, 1994, p. 113). For example, research has shown a positive relationship between calculator use and higher scores on basic skills tests (Hancock & Betts, 1994). With calculators, students can

---

FIGURE 6.12
Resources for Free and Inexpensive Audiovisual Materials

1. Professional periodicals and journals for teachers.
2. *An Annotated Bibliography of Audiovisual Materials Related to Understanding and Teaching the Culturally Disadvantaged.* Washington, DC: National Education Association.
3. *Catalog of Audiovisual Materials: A Guide to Government Sources* (ED 198 822). Arlington, VA: ERIC Documents Reproduction Service.
4. *Catalog of Free-Loan Educational Films/Video.* St. Petersburg, FL: Modern Talking Picture Service.
5. From Educator's Progress Service, Randolph, WI:
   Educator's Guide to Free Audio and Video Materials
   Educator's Guide to Free Films
   Educator's Guide to Free Filmstrips
   Guide to Free Computer Materials

FIGURE 6.13

Copyright Law for Off-Air Videotaping

SOURCE: Reprinted with the permission of Simon & Schuster, Inc. from the Macmillan College text INSTRUCTIONAL MEDIA 4/E by Robert Heinch, Michael Molenda, and James D. Russell. Copyright ©1993 by Macmillan College Publishing Company, Inc.

Permitted uses
You may
1. Request your media center or audiovisual coordinator to record a program for you if you cannot or if you lack the equipment.
2. Keep a videotaped copy of a broadcast (including cable transmission) for 45 calendar days, after which the program must be erased.
3. Use the program in class once during the first 10 school days of the 45 calendar days, and a second time if instruction needs to be reinforced.
4. Have professional staff view the program several times for evaluation purposes during the full 45-day period.
5. Make a few copies to meet legitimate needs, but these copies must be erased when the original videotape is erased.
6. Use only a part of the program if instructional needs warrant (but see the next list).
7. Enter into a licensing agreement with the copyright holder to continue use of the program.

Prohibited uses
You may *not*
1. Videotape premium cable services such as HBO without express permission.
2. Alter the original content of the program.
3. Exclude the copyright notice on the program.
4. Videorecord before a request for use—the request to record must come from an instructor.
5. Keep the program, and any copies, after 45 days.

FIGURE 6.14

Copyright Law for Use of Computer Software

SOURCE: From the December, 1980, Congressional amendment to the 1976 Copyright Act.

Permitted uses
You may
1. Make a single back-up or archival copy of the computer program.
2. Adapt the computer program to another language if the program is unavailable in the target language.
3. Add features to make better use of the computer program.

Prohibited uses
You may *not*
1. Make multiple copies.
2. Make replacement copies from an archival or back-up copy.
3. Make copies of copyrighted programs to be sold, leased, loaned, transmitted, or given away.

concentrate on the problem-solving process rather than on the calculations associated with problems. The problem-solving performance of students, particularly girls, improves significantly with ready access to calculators because students are freed to concentrate on higher-level aspects of the problem instead of routine calculations (Souviney, p. 13). Specific advantages and techniques for using the calculator in instruction are demonstrated in Chapters 8–12.

SUMMARY

You have learned of the variety of tools available to supplement your instruction. When used widely, these tools will help you to reach more of your students more of the time. As you know, teachers must meet the needs of a diversity of students, many of whom are linguistically and culturally different. The material presented in this chapter should be of help in doing that. The future will undoubtedly bring technological innovations that will be even more helpful—compact discs, computers, and telecommunications equipment mark only the beginning of a teaching revolution. Within the next decade, new instructional delivery systems made possible by microcomputers and multimedia workstations will likely fundamentally alter the role of the classroom teacher.

You should remain alert to developing technologies for your teaching. Laser videodiscs and CD-ROMs interfaced with computers (that is, multimedia) and telecommunications offer exciting technologies for teachers. New instructional technologies are advancing at an increasingly rapid rate. For example, in 1993, the states of California, Florida, and Texas jointly awarded a contract to a software developer and textbook publishing company to cooperate in the development of a multimedia history and social science curriculum targeted for LPE students. Called Vital Links, the program will consist of an interrelated series of videodiscs, CD-ROMs, and print materials and is planned for availability in 1995.

You and your colleagues must maintain vigilance over new developments, constantly looking for those that will not only help make student learning meaningful and interesting and your teaching effective, but be cost effective as well.

QUESTIONS AND ACTIVITIES FOR DISCUSSION

1. Explain how your effective use of the writing board can help students see relationships among verbal concepts or information.

2. In selecting student reading materials, what should you look for?

3. Where could you turn to find out more about instructional materials that might be suitable for use in your teaching?

4. Describe what you should look for when deciding whether material that you have obtained free is suitable for use in your teaching.

5. Describe ways that you could use your school neighborhood and community as a rich resource for learning.

6. Describe how the use of specific cognitive tools helps to reinforce student learning.

7. It has been said that the overhead projector can be one of the teacher's best friends. Why?

8. Describe two ways that the laser videodisc or the CD-ROM can be used in teaching integrated science and mathematics.

9. Share with others in your class your knowledge, observations, and feelings about the use of multimedia and telecommunications for teaching. From your discussion, what more would you like to know about the use of multimedia and telecommunications for teaching integrated mathematics and science? How might you learn more about these things?

10. Describe any prior concepts you held that changed as a result of your experiences with this chapter. Describe the changes.

REFERENCES

Bormuth, J. (1968). The Cloze readability procedure. *Elementary English, 45,* 429–436.

Hancock, V., & Betts, F. (1994). From the lagging to the leading edge. *Educational Leadership, 51* (7), 24–29.

Heddens, J. W., & Speer, W. R. (1992). *Today's mathematics* (7th ed.). New York: Macmillan.

Hunter, M. (1994). *Enhancing teaching.* New York: Macmillan.

Johnson, M. S., & Kress, R. A. (1965). *Informal reading inventories.* Newark, DE: International Reading Association.

McKenna, N. (1976). Synonymic versus verbatim scoring of the Cloze procedure. *Journal of Reading, 20,* 141–143.

Muir, M. (1994). Putting computer projects at the heart of the curriculum. *Educational Leadership, 51*(7),30–32.

National School Boards Association. (1993). Education vital signs. *The American School Board Journal, 180* (12), A22.

National Science Teachers Association. (1994, February/March). *NSTA Reports!,* 3.

Neal, J. S. (1994). The interpersonal computer. *Science Scope, 17* (4), 24–27.

Pinney, S. (1991). Long distance writing. *Instructor, 100* (8), 69–70.

Richey, E. (1994). Urban success stories. *Educational Leadership, 51* (7), 55–57.

Souviney, R. J. (1994). *Learning to teach mathematics* (2nd ed.). New York: Merrill.

Wolcott, L. (1991). The new cartographers. In Maine, students are helping map the future. *Teacher Magazine, 2* (6), 30–31.

SUGGESTED READINGS

Allen, D. (1994). Computing your way through science. *Teaching PreK-8 24*(5),18–23.

Beardslee, E. C., & Davis, G. L. (1989). *Interactive videodisc and the teaching-learning process.* Fastback 294. Bloomington, IN: Phi Delta Kappa Educational Foundation.

Bosch, K. A. (1993). Is there a computer crisis in the classroom? *Schools in the Middle, 2*(4),7–9.

Chiappetta, E. L., et al. (1993). Do middle school life science textbooks provide a balance of scientific literacy themes? *Journal of Research in Science Teaching, 30*(7),787–797.

Dalton, D. W. (1990). The effects of cooperative learning strategies on achievement and attitudes during interactive video. *Journal of Computer Based Instruction, 17*(1),8–16.

Dockterman, D. A. (1991). A teacher's tools. *Instructor, 100*(5),58–61.

Driscoll, M. P. (1994). How does the textbook contribute to learning in a middle school science class? *Contemporary Educational Psychology 19*(1),79–100.

Dyer, D. C., et al. (1991). Changes in teachers' beliefs and practices in technology-rich classrooms. *Educational Leadership, 48*(8),45–52.

Elliot, I. (1994). Using technology to teach science. *Teaching PreK-8, 24*(5), 38–41.

Green, L. (1982). *501 ways to use the overhead projector.* Littleton, CO: Libraries Unlimited.

Hancock, M. K., & Baugh, I. W. (1991). The new kid graduates. *Computing Teacher, 18*(7),17–19, 21.

Heinich, R., Molenda, M., & Russell, J. D. (1993). *Instructional media* (4th ed.). New York: Macmillan.

Huang, S. D., & Aloi, J. (1991). The impact of using interactive video in teaching general biology. *American Biology Teacher, 53*(5),281–284.

Hunter, B., et al. (1993). Technology in the classroom: Preparing students for the information age. *Schools in the Middle, 2*(4),3–6.

Is It Okay for Schools to Copy Software? (1991). Washington, DC: Software Publishers Association.

Johnson, L. N., & Tulley, S. (1989). *Interactive television: Progress and potential.* Fastback 289. Bloomington, IN: Phi Delta Kappa Educational Foundation.

Kanning, R. G. (1994). What multimedia can do in our classrooms. *Educational Leadership, 51*(7),40–44.

Kaplan, N., et al. (1992). The classroom manager. Hands-on multimedia. *Instructor, 101*(8),105.

Kemeny, J. G. (1991). Software for the classroom. *Mathematics and Computer Education, 25*(1),33–37.

Kernan, M., et al. (1991). Making and using audiovisuals. *Book Report, 10*(2),16–17, 19–21, 23, 25–35.

Malouf, D. B., et al. (1991). Integrating computer software into effective instruction. *Teaching Exceptional Children, 23*(3),54–56.

McDermott, C., & Trimble, K. (1993, Fall). Neighborhoods as learning laboratories. *California Catalyst, 28*–34.

Mead, J., et al. (1991). Teaching with technology. *Teacher Magazine, 2*(4),29–57.

Murray, K. T. (1994). Copyright and the educator. *Phi Delta Kappan, 75*(7),4552–4555.

Oaks, M., & Pedras, M. J. (1992). Technology education: A catalyst for curriculum integration. *Technology Teacher, 51*(5),11–14.

O'Neil, J. (1993). Using technology to support 'authentic learning'. *ASCD Update, 35*(8),1, 4–5.

Rakow, S. J., & Brandhorst, T. R. (1989). *Using microcomputers for teaching science.* Fastback 297. Bloomington, IN: Phi Delta Kappa Educational Foundation.

Reich, C. F., et al. (1991). Teaching earth science through a computer network. *Perspectives in Education and Deafness, 9*(5),4–7.

Roberts, N., et al. (1990). *Integrating telecommunications into education.* Englewood Cliffs, NJ: Prentice Hall.

Rock, H. M., & Cummings, A. (1994). Can videodiscs improve student outcomes? *Educational Leadership, 51*(7),46–50.

Snider, R. C. (1992). The machine in the classroom. *Phi Delta Kappan, 74*(4),316–323.

Strauss, R. T., & Kinzie, M. B. (1991). Hi-tech alternatives to dissection. *American Biology Teacher, 53*(3),154–158.

Talab, R. S. (1989). *Copyright and instructional technologies: A guide to fair use and permissions* (2nd ed.). Washington, DC: Association for Educational Communications and Technology.

ten Brink, B. (1993). New frontiers with science videodiscs. *Educational Leadership, 50*(8),42–43.

Wilburg, K. (1994). Teaching science with technology: Telecommunications and multimedia. *Computing Teacher, 21*(7),6–8.

Wishnietsky, D. H. (1993). *Using computer technology to create a global classroom.* Fastback 356. Bloomington, IN: Phi Delta Kappa Educational Foundation.

Methods and Activities for Mathematics

To many educators, it is clear that to be most effective in teaching the diversity of children in today's classrooms, learning in each discipline must be integrated with the learning in other disciplines, and thus made more meaningful to the lives of the children.

For higher levels of thinking and for learning that is most meaningful, recent research supports the use of an integrated curriculum and instructional techniques for social interaction. As a classroom teacher, your instructional task is twofold: (1) to plan for and provide developmentally appropriate hands-on experiences, with useful materials and the supportive environment necessary for children's meaningful exploration and discovery; and (2) to know how to facilitate the most meaningful and longest lasting learning possible once the child's mind has been activated by the hands-on experience. In Parts II through IV, we present techniques designed to help you complete those tasks, beginning in Part II with a discussion of the teaching of mathematics.

Chapter 7 discusses the mathematics curriculum relevant to teachers of grades 4–9. Chapters 8–12 are consistent with the approach recommended by the National Council of Teachers of Mathematics (NCTM) in its 1989 publication, *Curriculum and Evaluation Standards for School Mathematics.* Addressing the specific strands relevant to the grades 4–9 mathematics curriculum, the topics of Chapters 8–12, respectively, are the multiplication and division of whole numbers; patterns and functions; fraction operations; decimals, proportions, and integers; and graphing, statistics, and probability. In addition, in each of those chapters you will find strategies and resources for using calculators and computers in the mathematics curriculum, sample lesson plans, boxed practice exercises and problems called "Figure It Out," topical lists of children's books, techniques for accommodating special-needs learners, a dialogue between a student teacher and an experienced cooperating teacher about a pertinent issue raised in each chapter, and a discussion of useful assessment strategies.

The NCTM presents mathematics curriculum standards for three divisions of grade levels: K–4, 5–8, and 9–12. The standards are introduced at the beginning of Chapters 8–12 for only grades K–4 and 5–8. Because the proposed standards for grades 5–8 are intended to enable students to enter the ninth grade "with substantial gains in their conceptual and procedural understandings of algebra, in their knowledge of geometric concepts and relationships, and in their familiarity with informal, but conceptually based, methods for dealing with data and situations involving uncertainty" (NCTM, 1989, p. 125), instruction in mathematics for students in grade 9 is a continuation of the development of the concepts and skills of the K–8 standards curriculum.

The NCTM recommends that, in addition to unique standards that address each level, four common standards address *all* students. These common standards focus on mathematics as problem solving, as communication, and as reasoning, and on making connections among topics within mathematics and other disciplines. These four common standards and their application to grade levels K–4, 5–8, and 9–12 are as shown in the accompanying table.

CHAPTER 7
The Mathematics Curriculum
This chapter is adapted from James S. Cangelosi, Teaching Mathematics in Secondary and Middle School: Research-Based Approaches *(New York: Macmillan, 1992), pp. 21–56. By permission of James S. Cangelosi and the Macmillan Publishing Company.*

CHAPTER 8
The Multiplication and Division of Whole Numbers
This chapter is adapted from Randall J. Souviney, Learning to Teach Mathematics, *2nd ed. (New York: Macmillan, 1994), pp. 316–364. By permission of Randall J. Souviney and the Macmillan Publishing Company.*

CHAPTER 9
Patterns and Functions
This chapter is adapted from Randall J. Souviney, Learning to Teach Mathematics, *2nd ed. (New York: Macmillan, 1994), pp. 367–400. By permission of Randall J. Souviney and the Macmillan Publishing Company.*

STANDARD	GRADES K–4
Standard 1: *Mathematics as* *Problem Solving*	Use problem-solving approaches to investigate and understand mathematics content. Formulate problems from everyday and mathematical situations. Develop and apply strategies to solve a wide variety of problems. Verify and interpret results in the context of the original problem. Acquire confidence in using mathematics meaningfully.
Standard 2: *Mathematics as* *Communication*	Relate physical materials, pictures, and diagrams to mathematical ideas. Reflect on and clarify thinking about mathematical ideas and situations. Relate everyday language to mathematical language and symbols. Realize that representing, discussing, reading, writing, and listening to mathematics are a vital part of learning and using mathematics.
Standard 3: *Mathematics as* *Reasoning*	Draw logical conclusions about mathematics. Use models, known facts, properties, and relationships to explain thinking. Justify answers and solution processes. Use patterns and relationships to analyze mathematical situations. Believe that mathematics makes sense.
Standard 4: *Mathematical* *Connections*	Link conceptual and procedural knowledge. Relate various representations of concepts or procedures to one another. Recognize relationships among different topics in mathematics. Use mathematics in other curriculum areas. Use mathematics in daily life.

SOURCE: Adapted from *Curriculum and Evaluation Standards for School Mathematics,* (pp. 23, 26, 29, 62, 75, 78, 81, 84, 137, 140, 143, 148). Reston, VA: National Council of Teachers of Mathematics. Copyright 1989 by the National Council of Teachers of Mathematics. Reprinted by permission.

Use problem-solving approaches to investigate and understand mathematical content.

Formulate problems from situations within and outside mathematics.

Develop and apply a variety of strategies to solve problems, with emphasis on multistep and non-routine problems.

Verify and interpret results in the context of the original problem.

Generalize solutions and strategies to new problem situations.

Acquire confidence in using mathematics meaningfully.

Model situations using oral, written, concrete, pictorial, graphic, and algebraic methods.

Reflect on and clarify thinking about mathematical ideas and situations.

Develop common understandings of mathematical ideas, including the role of definitions.

Use the skills of reading, listening, and viewing to interpret and evaluate mathematical ideas.

Discuss mathematical ideas and make conjectures and convincing arguments.

Appreciate the value of mathematical notation and its role in the development of mathematical ideas.

Recognize and apply deductive and inductive reasoning.

Understand and apply reasoning processes, with special attention to spatial reasoning and reasoning with proportions and graphs.

Make and evaluate mathematical conjectures and arguments.

Validate one's own thinking.

Appreciate the pervasive use and power of reasoning as a part of mathematics.

See mathematics as an integrated whole.

Explore problems and describe results using graphic, numerical, physical, algebraic, and verbal mathematical models or representations.

Use a mathematical idea to further understanding of other mathematical ideas.

Apply mathematical thinking and modeling to solve problems that arise in other disciplines, such as art, music, psychology, science, and business.

Value the role of mathematics in our culture and society.

Use, with increasing confidence, problem-solving approaches to investigate and understand mathematical content.

Apply integrated mathematical problem-solving strategies to solve problems from within and outside mathematics.

Recognize and formulate problems from situations within and outside mathematics.

Apply the process of mathematical modeling to real-world problem situations.

Reflect upon and clarify their thinking about mathematical ideas and relationships.

Formulate mathematical definitions and express generalizations discovered through investigations.

Express mathematical ideas orally and in writing.

Read written presentations of mathematics with understanding.

Ask clarifying and extending questions related to mathematics they have read or heard about.

Appreciate the economy, power, and elegance of mathematical notation and its role in the development of mathematical ideas.

Make and test conjectures.

Formulate counterexamples.

Follow logical arguments.

Judge the validity of arguments.

Construct simple, valid arguments.

In addition, college-intending students can—
Construct proofs for mathematical assertions, including indirect proofs and proofs by mathematical induction.

Recognize equivalent representations of the same concept.

Relate procedures in one representation to procedures in an equivalent representation.

Use and value the connections among mathematical topics.

Use and value the connections between mathematics and other disciplines.

Specifically, for mathematics instruction in grades 9–12, it is recommended that there be

Increased attention to—
- The active involvement of students in constructing and applying mathematical ideas
- Problem solving as a means as well as a goal of instruction
- Effective questioning techniques that promote student interaction
- The use of a variety of instructional formats (small groups, individual explorations, peer instruction, whole-class discussions, project work)
- The use of calculators and computers as tools for learning and doing mathematics
- Student communication of mathematical ideas orally and in writing
- The establishment and application of the interrelatedness of mathematical topics
- The systematic maintenance of student learnings and embedding review in the context of new topics and problem situations
- The assessment of learning as an integral part of instruction.

Decreased attention to—
- Teacher and text as exclusive sources of knowledge
- Rote memorization of facts and procedures
- Extended periods of individual seatwork practicing routine tasks
- Instruction by teacher exposition
- Paper-and-pencil manipulative skill work
- The relegation of testing to an adjunct role with the sole purpose of assigning grades. ■

CHAPTER 7

The Mathematics Curriculum

In this chapter, your attention is focused on the teacher's impact on curricula, the discrepancy between typical and research-based mathematics curricula, and thoughts on how you might go about developing curricula. Specifically, this chapter is designed to help you:

1. Define *curriculum* and *curriculum guidelines* and explain the relationship among school, course, mathematics, school-district, and state-level curricula.
2. Describe how teachers develop and control curricula as they design and conduct lessons.
3. Explain the differences between (a) a curriculum based on the view that students should learn mathematics for the purpose of being able to learn more mathematics and (b) a curriculum based on the view that students learn mathematics for the purpose of solving real-life problems.
4. Describe a mathematics curriculum based on the NCTM standards and contrast it with a more traditionally based mathematics curriculum.
5. Define a mathematics *teaching unit* and describe how a mathematics course is composed of a sequence of teaching units.
6. Explain how courses differ according to whether they are designed by (a) the following-a-textbook approach, (b) the contrived problem–solving approach, (c) the real-world problem–solving approach, or (d) a combination of these three approaches.
7. List types of learning materials, resources, equipment, and facilities needed to conduct a mathematics course and explain factors influencing their selection for your classroom.

A. A CURRICULUM

As discussed in section B of Chapter 3, *curriculum* is defined in various ways. Many teachers, instructional supervisors, and school administrators perceive it as "the textbook series adopted, mandated state or local curriculum guides, and/or content and skills appearing on mandated tests" (Zumwalt, 1989, p. 174). Definitions range from that very narrow view to the broad, all-encompassing views forwarded by Alexander (see Chapter 3) and by Brubaker: ". . . curriculum is defined as *what persons experience in a setting.* This includes all the interactions among persons as well as the interactions between persons and their physical environment" (1982, p. 2).

Herein, the meaning of *curriculum* falls between the two extremes:

A *school curriculum* is a system of the planned experiences (e.g., coursework, school-sponsored social functions, and contacts with school-supported services [such as the library]) designed to educate students.

A *course curriculum* is a sequence of teaching units designed to provide students with experiences that help them achieve specified learning goals. A *teaching unit* consists of (a) a learning goal defined by a set of specific objectives, (b) a planned sequence of lessons, each consisting of learning activities designed to help students achieve specific objectives, (c) mechanisms for monitoring student progress and utilizing feedback on that progress to guide lessons, and (d) a summative evaluation of student achievement of the learning goal.

A *mathematics curriculum* is a sequence of mathematics courses, as well as any other school-sponsored functions for the purpose of furthering students' achievements with and attitudes about mathematics.

A *school-district curriculum* is the set of all the school curricula within that school district.

A *state-level curriculum* is the set of all school-district curricula within a state (from Cangelosi, Copyright © 1991 by Longman Publishers. Reprinted with permission).

State-level, district-level, school-level, and mathematics *curricula guidelines* are articulated in documents stored in the files of virtually every school. The consistency between official curricula guidelines and actual school curricula varies considerably. Obviously, a school's curriculum can be no more in line with official guidelines than the composite of the course curricula developed by its teachers.

Because mathematics is widely misunderstood to be a linear sequence of skills to be mastered one at a time in a fixed order, some people think teaching mathematics is a matter of following a prescribed curriculum guideline or mathematics textbook. In reality, there are three reasons you must creatively develop curricula to succeed as a mathematics teacher. First of all, state-level and district-level curriculum guidelines typically list objectives for mathematics courses but leave the responsibility of designing lessons for achieving those objectives up to individual teachers. Textbooks present information and exercises on mathematical topics. However, each teacher needs to select, supplement, and organize text content so the objectives listed in curriculum guidelines are addressed and tailor lessons to the unique characteristics of that teacher's students.

Second, although understanding of one mathematical topic (e.g., solving first-degree equations) is requisite to the understanding of another topic (e.g., solving quadratic equations), there is no fixed linear sequence that is optimal for all groups of students. Effective teaching requires teachers who arrange topics in response to feedback on their students' progress, diagnoses of students' needs, and students' interests at any one time.

Third, the way you design and conduct lessons usually influences what your students learn about mathematics more than which mathematical topics are addressed in the lessons. Compare the following four examples.

VIGNETTE 7.1 Mr. Jackson's algebra students have learned to solve quadratic equations by factoring, providing the left side of the equation in standard form can be factored easily (e.g., $x^2 - 6x - 16 = 0$). To teach them how to solve any quadratic equation (e.g., $3x^2 + 5x + 1 = 0$), he introduces the quadratic formula by displaying it on an overhead transparency and saying, "Here is a formula for finding the solutions of any quadratic equation. For example, suppose we want to solve for $3x^2 + 2x = 7$. Watch how much easier it is to use the formula than to try and factor the polynomial. First, we rewrite the equation in standard form, and then . . . ."

He continues, working through several examples and then assigning some exercises in which the students practice using the formula.

VIGNETTE 7.2 Ms. Youklic's algebra students have learned to solve quadratic equations by factoring, providing the left side of the equation in standard form can be factored easily (e.g., $x^2 - 12x + 32 = 0$). She wants to teach them to solve any quadratic equation (e.g., $x^2 + 6x + 4 = 0$) using the quadratic formula. But instead of simply stating the quadratic formula, she introduces a real-world problem whose solution requires finding roots to quadratic equations. Because of some of her students' interest in baseball, she takes an idea from a *Mathematics Teacher* article (Eisner, 1986) and uses baseball-related situations to establish a need for solving quadratic equations. Most of the equations are not easily factored, so she leads them through the process by which they solve them by completing the square.

Using inductive questioning strategies, she has them generalize from their experiences completing the square and ultimately leads the students to discover the quadratic formula.

After agreeing to and articulating the formula, Ms. Youklic uses direct teaching strategies to improve their algorithmic skills with the quadratic formula.

VIGNETTE 7.3 Ms. Estrada tells her students, as she lists the rules for multiplying signed numbers on the chalkboard, "A positive times a positive is positive. A positive times a negative is negative. A negative times a positive is negative. A negative times a negative is positive. Zero times any number or any number times zero is zero. Do you understand?"

She directs them to complete a worksheet at their places and she circulates among them looking at their work, correcting errors, and individually responding to questions. She notices that Bonita's paper includes the following:

$$(17)(10) = \underline{\textbf{170}} \qquad (.3347)(0) = \underline{\textbf{0}} \qquad (-4.1)(3) = \underline{\textbf{--12.3}}$$

$$(1/4)(-2/3) = \underline{\hspace{1cm}} \qquad (-20)(9) = \underline{\textbf{--180}} \qquad (-5)(-10) = \underline{\textbf{--50}}$$

$$(0)(-19) = \underline{\textbf{0}} \qquad (-11)(-1/17) = \underline{\hspace{1cm}} \qquad 4\pi(8) = \underline{\textbf{32}\,\pi}$$

Ms. Estrada:	Bonita, what is -5 times -10?
Bonita:	Minus 50, it's right here.
Ms. Estrada:	But a negative times a negative is positive.
Bonita:	Why?
Ms. Estrada:	Because that's the rule. See, I have it listed on the board and it's right here on page 23 of the text.

VIGNETTE 7.4 With an overhead projector, Mr. Cocora displays Figure 7.1 to his class and says, "A friend of mine works for the city's Traffic Control Department. She asked if I could help her solve a problem. I said yes, with your help. Here's the situation. The department wants to estimate when and where city traffic is likely to be congested. Part of the data they're collecting is at this observation post marked here on the screen. The post is located at Highway 30 right at the west edge of the city. She tells me most of the traffic entering from west of the city passes this observation point.

"Here's the deal. Using a radar gun, the observer measures the direction and rate in miles per hour of vehicles traveling on Highway 30. They want some rules for using this one observation to determine where the vehicle will be or was at any point in time. Do you think we can help?"

FIGURE 7.1
Mr. Cocora's Overhead Transparency for His Conceptual-Level Lesson on the Rules for Multiplying Signed Numbers

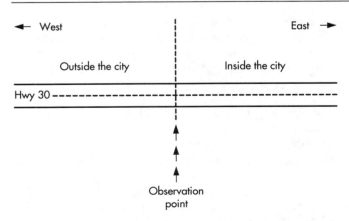

A discussion ensues in which the problem is clarified and Mr. Cocora explains that at traffic control, (1) travel into the city is coded as a *positive* (+) number of miles per hour, (2) travel out of the city is coded as a *negative* (−) number of miles per hour, (3) locations to the city-side of the observation point (i.e., east) are coded *positive* (+), (4) locations to the west, outside of the city are coded *negative* (−), (5) time in the future is coded *positive* (+), and time in the past is coded *negative* (−).

Moving a toy car over the highway on the transparency, Mr. Cocora confronts the students with each of the following questions:

1. Where will a red Chevrolet that is headed into the city at 60 miles per hour be located 6 minutes from now?
2. Where will a dump truck that is headed out of the city at 60 miles per hour be located 6 minutes from now?
3. Where was the red Chevrolet 6 minutes ago?
4. Where was the dump truck 6 minutes ago?
5. Where is a green Toyota that is passing the observation point right now?
6. Where will a yellow van that is broken down and not moving in front of the observation point be in 5 minutes?

Mr. Cocora directs his class into small task groups that are to answer the six questions and then generalize rules for the Traffic Department to use. All the groups answer the questions by applying the relation *rate* × *time* = *distance* as follows:

1. $(+60)(+0.1) = +6$ (i.e., 6 miles east of the observation point)
2. $(-60)(+0.1) = -6$ (i.e., 6 miles west of the observation point)
3. $(+60)(-0.1) = -6$ (i.e., 6 miles west of the observation point)
4. $(-60)(-0.1) = +6$ (i.e., 6 miles east of the observation point)
5. $(?)(0) = 0$ (i.e., in front of the observation point)
6. $(0)(+5) = 0$ (i.e., in front of the observation point)

After further discussions led by Mr. Cocora, the students settle on the rules for the Traffic Department that are tantamount to the usual rules for multiplying signed numbers.

The next day, Mr. Cocora restates the rules they devised in the more conventional textbook form. He then uses direct instructional techniques to help them remember the rules.

Both Mr. Jackson and Ms. Youklic taught lessons on the quadratic formula, so their students learned about a different mathematics topic than Ms. Estrada's and Mr. Cocora's students. However, Mr. Jackson's and Ms. Estrada's lessons were similar in that both their classes of students learned to think of mathematics as a set of rules to be memorized and used but not necessarily understood. Both Ms. Youklic's and Mr. Cocora's students experienced discovering and inventing mathematics. Thus, although according to a curriculum guideline or textbook section, Mr. Jackson and Ms. Youklic were "covering" the same topic, student outcomes were vastly different.

Two Views

Learn mathematics to learn more mathematics. Over the past 20 years, I have asked hundreds of mathematics teachers and others who have been instrumental in the development of state-level and district-level mathematics curricula guidelines why students should learn mathematics. Virtually all the answers were given without hesitation and could hardly be contested. For example,

- "Mathematical literacy is a necessity in today's world. It's needed for everything from budgeting, to being a wise consumer, to holding down many jobs. The mathematically able have more options available to them. If we didn't teach mathematics, we would deny opportunities to individuals and fail to produce the brainpower society needs for scientific, sociological, and technological advancement."
- "Obviously, fundamental mathematical skills are needed as basic survival tools for life. Furthermore, the world is changing so rapidly, we don't know what kinds of problems today's children will be facing tomorrow. So above all, they need to be able to be

systematic, logical problem solvers. Appropriate experiences with mathematics enhance that ability."

However, most of those I queried were much slower to respond to questions about why selected topics are included in mathematics curricula. For example,

- *"Why do you teach sixth graders about primes?"* "Well, it's in all the textbooks I've ever seen. And, prime factorization is critical to finding least common multiples and greatest common divisors."
- *"Why is there so much emphasis on associativity and commutativity of operations in the seventh-grade curriculum?"*
  "That's a good question. I guess students are expected to know that before they get into algebra."
- *"I see volume formulas are included in the prealgebra section of your curriculum guidebook. Why is that?"*
  "It's always been a part of our junior high math. I think it's because volume problems provide a lot of nice applications of solving open sentences. We want to get these kids ready to learn how to solve equations."
- *"Why do you spend so much time on factoring polynomials in algebra?"*
  "Well, the book really emphasizes it. And then, the students need it when they get into solving second-degree and higher equations and inequalities."

After listening to hundreds of such comments, it is obvious that many teachers and other curriculum developers recognize intrinsic value in mathematics; thus, mathematics courses (except for consumer, business, and general mathematics courses) are viewed as preparation for subsequent courses. To many, the most honorable goal of precollege school mathematics is preparing students to pass calculus.

Mathematics curricula based on the goal of preparing students to learn more mathematics are justifiable in light of the following:

1. Generally speaking, the further individuals advance in school mathematics, the greater the variety of occupational opportunities available to them (Steen, 1987, 1988).
2. Society needs a mathematically literate citizenry and an increasing number of mathematicians, scientists, engineers, and other mathematically expert professionals (NCTM, 1989, pp. 3–5).

Learn mathematics to solve real-life problems. Although the inclusion of mathematics in school curricula can be justified solely on the intrinsic merit of mathematics, research findings suggest that such a curriculum fails for three reasons:

1. Most students seem unable to transfer mathematical processes learned in isolation from situations they perceive as real life to solve problems dissimilar from example problems directly presented in lessons (Dossey et al., 1988, pp. 8–13; Schoenfeld, 1985).
2. Students are likely to retain algorithmic skills and knowledge of rules only as long as they continue to use them. Unless they've learned to apply them to solve problems from their own real world, they're hardly motivated to continue to use them once the skill has been tested and they have moved on to other lessons (Schoenfeld, 1989). Hence, it is typical for a mathematical topic to be repeatedly cycled through curricula, being taught initially and then reviewed each time it is a prerequisite to another topic.
3. Most adolescents are simply not highly motivated to work toward goals whose benefits appear only to be long range (Santrock, 1984, pp. 553–563). "Learn this now so you'll be able to pass calculus next year," seems reasonable to most 16-year-olds but pales as a motivator in comparison to immediate concerns.

These research-based findings have implications for mathematics curricula: As new topics are introduced, students need to be provided with experiences that lead them to be able to apply their understanding of that topic to solve problems they consider to be real life and relate that topic to previously learned mathematical topics.

Adherence to this curriculum-design principle does not preclude teaching mathematics for the purpose of learning more mathematics, but it does rule out completely divorcing topics from students' real-life problems.

Real-Life Problems

According to Merriam-Webster (1986, p. 1807), a *problem* is "an unsettled matter demanding solution or decision and requiring usually considerable thought or skill for its proper solution or decision: an issue marked by usually considerable difficulty, uncertainty, or doubt with regard to its proper settlement: a perplexing or puzzling question . . . a source usually of considerable difficulty, perplexity, or worry."

Because problems are associated with difficulty and perplexity, some people consider them distasteful. However, the existence of problems serves as a strong motivator for human endeavor. A perfectly satisfied person, one who feels no need to solve a problem, lacks the motivation to change and, thus, to learn (Cangelosi, 1988, p. 136).

Do not confuse *problems* with mathematical textbook exercises. Schoenfeld (1989, pp. 87–88) states

> For any student, a mathematical *problem* is a task (a) in which the student is interested and engaged and for which he wishes to obtain a resolution, and (b) for which the student does not have a readily accessible mathematical means by which to achieve the resolution.
>
> As simple as this definition may seem, it has some significant consequences. First, it presumes that engagement is important in problem solving; a task isn't a problem for you until you've made it *your* problem. Second, it implies that tasks are not "problems" in and of themselves; whether or not a task is a problem for you depends on what you know. Third, most of the textbook and homework "problems" assigned to students are not problems according to this definition, but exercises. In most textbooks, the majority of practice tasks can be solved by direct application of procedures illustrated in the chapter—e.g., solving quadratic equations after you have been taught the quadratic formula, or a "moving trains" problem when the text has illustrated the specific procedures for solving "distance-rate-time" problems. In contrast, real problem solving confronts individuals with a difficulty. They know where they are, and where they want to get—but they have no ready means of getting there. Fourth, the majority of what has been called "problem solving" in the past decade—introducing "word problems" into the curriculum—is only a small part of problem solving. (Reprinted with permission of the Association for Supervision and Curriculum Development. Copyright 1989 by ASCD. All rights reserved.)

Who outside of school is ever moved to engage in mathematics unless she or he has a problem to solve? People have problems to solve whenever they have questions they want to answer. Before you are in a position to design mathematics lessons around problems students are interested in solving, you need to identify problems they perceive from their real worlds. Figure 7.2 contains a list of problems adolescent students identified as important to them. These problems were successfully incorporated into lessons relevant to mathematical topics included in middle, junior high, and high school curricula.

The National Council of Teachers of Mathematics (NCTM) Standards

The gap between research-based curricula and typical practice.
In the early 1900s, experimental studies of teaching and learning (e.g., James, 1890; Thorndike & Woodworth, 1901) undermined the faculty psychology and formal discipline principles upon which the prevailing mathematics curricula of the day were based (Strom, 1969). Unfortunately, a gap still exists between how mathematics is typically taught and how research-based principles indicate it should be taught (Brophy, 1986). Even in today's schools, the most commonly practiced method of teaching mathematics follows a tiresome pattern (Jesunathadas, 1990):

> The teacher introduces a topic by stating a rule or definition and then demonstrating it on the chalkboard or on overhead transparencies with textbook examples. Students work on exercises at their seats as the teacher provides individual help to those experiencing difficulties with exercises. Similar exercises are completed for homework and checked as "right" or "wrong" in the beginning of the next class period. Homework exercises that were particularly troublesome are worked out for the class either by the teacher or student volunteers.

Emphasis is almost entirely on algorithmic skills. Neither understanding of why rules and algorithms work nor applications to real-life problems are stressed. The teacher's expectations for all but a few students are very low. The pace of lessons is slow with plodding, repetitive exercises.

Research-based principles do not suggest that these expository, drill, and review lessons should be eliminated, but they should not continue to be the dominant form of instruction. Acquiring algorithmic skills should not be the primary goal of school mathematics curricula.

Numerous curricula-reform efforts have attempted to bring the teaching of mathematics more in line with the research-based principles that indicate students need experiences discovering and inventing mathematics and utilizing mathematics to solve real-life problems. Among them are The 1908 Committee of Fifteen on the Geometry Syllabus (Kinney & Purdy, 1952, pp. 22–23), The Joint Commission to Study the Place of Mathematics in Secondary Education (NCTM, 1940), The School Mathematics Study Group (Begle, 1958), *An Agenda for Action: Recommendations for School Mathematics of the 1980s* (NCTM, 1980), *Educating Americans for the 21st Century* (National Science Board Commission on Precollege Education in Mathematics, Science, and Technology, 1983), *The Mathematical Sciences Curriculum K–12: What is Fundamental and What Is Not* (Conference Board of the Mathematical Sciences, 1983a), *New Goals for Mathematical Sciences Education* (Conference Board of the Mathematical Sciences, 1983b).

One of the more promising and expansive curricula reform projects produced the *Curriculum and Evaluation Standards for School Mathematics* (NCTM, 1989). This NCTM-sponsored document was developed with broad input from mathematics teachers, mathematics education specialists, cognitive scientists, mathematicians, and instructional supervisors and has been endorsed by scores of relevant professional associations (e.g., Mathematical Association of America, American Mathematical Society, School Science and Mathematics Association, and Association for Women in Mathematics). It has the potential of serving as a national-level mathematics curriculum guideline. It states (NCTM, 1989, pp. v, 1):

> The *Standards* is a document designed to establish a broad framework to guide reform in school mathematics in the next decade. In it a vision is given of what the mathematics curriculum should include in terms of content priority and emphasis. The challenge we issue to all interested in the quality of school mathematics is to work collaboratively to use these curriculum and evaluation standards as the basis for change so that the teaching and learning of mathematics in our schools is improved. . . .
>
> These standards are one facet of the mathematics education community's response to the call for reform in the teaching and learning of mathematics. They reflect and are an extension of the community's responses to those demands for change. Inherent in this document is a consensus that all students need to learn more, and often different, mathematics and that instruction in mathematics must be significantly revised.
>
> As a function of NCTM's leadership in current efforts to reform school mathematics, the Commission on Standards in School Mathematics was established by the Board of Directors and charged with two tasks:

1. Create a coherent vision of what it means to be mathematically literate both in a world that relies on calculators and computers to carry out mathematical procedures and in a world where mathematics is rapidly growing and is extensively being applied to diverse fields.
2. Create a set of standards to guide the revision of the school mathematics curriculum and its associated evaluation toward this vision.

Curriculum and evaluation standards for school mathematics. The 265-page document lists, explains, and illustrates

- Thirteen curriculum standards for grades K–4
- Thirteen curriculum standards for grades 5–8
- Fourteen curriculum standards for grades 9–12
- Fourteen evaluation standards.

FIGURE 7.2

Problems Identified as Important by Adolescents That Have Been Incorporated into Mathematics Lessons
SOURCE: J. S. Cangelosi, (1990) *Using Mathematics to Solve Real-Life Problems* (A Videotape Program), Logan, UT, Utah State University. Sponsored by the National Science Foundation.

Art and aesthetics
- While thinking about how to sketch a picture: At what angles should I make these lines intersect to give the illusion I'm trying to create?
- In deciding how to decorate a room: What color combinations do people tend to associate with being happy?

Cooking
- While planning a mean: How should I expand this recipe so all my guests get enough to eat, but I don't have a lot of food left over?
- What, if any, functions can I formulate (and then write a computer program for) for relating recipe ingredients to output variables such as calories, fat content, nutrients, sweetness, and sourness?

Earning money
- In considering a fund-raising class project: Would we net more money with a car wash, a bake sale, a "run for donations," used book sale, or "rent-a-teenager" offer?
- Is this offer to sell greeting cards I just received in the mail a good deal for me?

Electronics
- How can I efficiently interlink this cable television, videotape recorder, and computer?
- What, if any, functions can I formulate for maximizing amplification of this sound system while minimizing reverberations?

Employment
- Considering time on the job, travel, expenses, opportunity for advancement, security, and benefit from experiences, which of these three jobs should I take?

- Is my paycheck accurate, considering my hours and overtime?

Environmental concerns
- What's the most efficient way for us to get our message across to the most influential people?
- In preparing for a field trip: How can we minimize our impact on the flora and fauna of the forest?

Family
- In response to her father's claim that she spends too much time listening to music and watching television and not enough time working on school work and doing chores: How much time do I usually spend a day on each of those four things?
- How can I help my brother manage his time better?

Friends
- Do people really care how their friends dress?
- What factors create friendships?

Gardening and growing plants
- What, if any, rules can I formulate (and then write a computer program for) to maximize the growth of beans as a function of soil composition, space, exposure to sun, moisture, etc.?
- What effects do varying the amount and frequency of watering these types of plants have on their health?

Health
- What's the best exercise program for me?
- How should I change my diet?

Managing money
- How should I go about saving enough money to buy a car when I'm 16?
- How should I budget my money?

The following two types of standards are described:

Curriculum Standards. When a set of curricular standards is specified for school mathematics, it should be understood that the standards are value judgments based on a broad, coherent vision of schooling derived from several factors: societal goals, research on teaching and learning, and professional experience. Each standard starts with a statement of what mathematics the curriculum should include. This is followed by a description of the student activities associated with that mathematics and a discussion that includes instructional examples. (NCTM, 1989, p. 7)

The Evaluation Standards. The evaluation standards are presented separately, not because evaluation should be separated from the curriculum but because planning for the gathering of evidence about student and program outcomes is different. The difference is most clearly illustrated in comparing the curriculum standards titled Connections and the evaluations standards titled Mathematical Power. Both deal with connections among concepts, procedures, and intellectual methods, but the curriculum standards are related to the instructional plan whereas the evaluation standards address the ways in which students integrate these connections intellectually so that they develop mathematical power. (NCTM, 1989, p. 11)

Although many of the standards for grades 4–9 are listed in the remaining chapters of this part, without the explanations of student activities and the examples, the ideas behind each standard are lost. Thus, you should obtain your own personal copy of *Curriculum and Evaluation Standards for School Mathematics* from NCTM as a guide for developing curricula and designing lessons (for the address, see Chapter 3).

FIGURE 7.2 cont'd

Music
- Who is the hottest music group right now?
- Since I eventually want to work in a rock group, would I be better starting off learning to play the piano, guitar, or drums?

Parties
- How many people should we invite?
- What kind of food should we serve?

Personal appearance
- What's the best way to treat pimples?
- How do different people respond to "muscular" women?

Personal planning
- How should I budget my time?
- Would I be better off taking more college-prep or business courses in high school?

Pets and raising animals
- What kinds and numbers of fish can this aquarium support?
- Is the behavior modification I've started with my cat working?

Politics
- What strategies should we employ to get Allison elected to the student council?
- What can we do to sway people's thinking on this gun-control issue?

School grades
- What's the relation between the amount of time I study and the grades I get?
- Is it best to "cram" the night before a test or spread test preparation out over a longer period of time?

School subjects other than mathematics
- In response to a problem assigned in science class: How much does it cost to burn a light bulb?
- In response to a health and physical education assignment: How many push-ups would I need to do to burn 100 calories?

Social issues
- Considering the composition of our school body with respect to ethnicity and gender, did ethnic or sex bias influence the outcome of the last school election?
- What can we do to discourage drug abuse in our school?

Sports and games
- What kind of tennis racquet should I buy?
- What strategy (e.g., regarding lap times) should I use to minimize my time in the 1500-meter run?

Television, movies, and videos
- How does gun use in movies compare to gun use in real life?
- In what ways are people influenced by television commercials?

Travel
- What is the most efficient way for me to get from here to Tucson?
- In planning a class trip: Where should we plan to stop along the way?

Vehicles
- Which of these two skateboards is better for speed, control, and durability?
- Regarding a remote-control model car: How are speed, acceleration, maneuverability, and response time affected by battery power and distance between controller and car?

A curriculum developed with the *Standards* as a guide emphasizes the following far more than traditional mathematics curricula:

- Real-life problem solving
- Conceptualization of why rules and algorithms work
- Experiences with mathematical discovery and invention
- Integration across mathematical topics
- Use of calculators and computers
- Comprehension of the language of mathematics
- Writing and speaking about mathematics
- Testing for guiding instruction
- Testing for comprehension, conceptual, and application levels of learning

Furthermore, compared to traditional curricula, a *Standards*-based curriculum places somewhat less emphasis on the following:

- Word problems that do not reflect real-world situations
- Paper-and-pencil calculations
- Segregation of topics and subdisciplines of mathematics
- Memorization of formulas
- Verification by appeal to authority

- Mindless exercises
- Problems with one exact solution
- Testing at the knowledge cognitive level
- Testing solely for grades

The ideas, suggestions, and illustrations in this textbook will help you develop curricula and design and conduct lessons that are consistent with the *Standards*. This is important because lessons consistent with the *Standards* are consistent with research-based principles, and the *Standards* is the guide for state-of-the-art mathematics curricula of the 1990s and the twenty-first century ("Emphasize Application of Math Skills," 1989; Holden, 1989; Dossey, 1987; "Use New Standards to Upgrade Math," 1989).

Mathematics Curricula Outcomes

Elementary school–level outcomes. We turn now to an examination of the differences between the outcomes of using the traditional curriculum and the outcomes of using the NCTM *Standards*–based curriculum at the elementary school level.

Traditional curriculum. As a mathematics teacher of grades 4–9, you need to understand what your students experienced and achieved while in prior grades. After all, you are responsible for building upon those experiences and advancing those achievements. Of course, there are considerable differences among students on these two variables. Besides the differences among students in how they respond to similar experiences, the differences among teachers are also great. Some students will have enjoyed the benefits of effective teachers who provided them with enriching experiences discovering and inventing mathematics. But research suggests that most are not so fortunate.

Typically, students engage in activities with hands-on manipulatives counting, sorting, measuring, and naming objects in kindergarten and the beginning of first grade. But by second grade, such concrete activities are usually replaced almost entirely by skill-level drills for memorizing addition and subtraction facts. Some conceptual work in identifying geometric figures and fractions is included, but fluency with facts and algorithms involving the four fundamental operations are paramount through the fifth grade.

On the average—but with wide variation about this average—the impact of this traditional elementary school mathematics curricula on students is as follows:

- Most students exit fifth grade with an arsenal of memorized algorithms for adding, subtracting, multiplying, and dividing whole numbers and rational numbers expressed in decimal form. Their facility for manipulating numbers expressed as fractions is typically limited to one- and two-digit numerators and denominators whose prime factors are obvious to them. Computational skills with numbers expressed as percentages are emphasized by many teachers and ignored by many others. However, having topics accurately presented in textbooks and by teachers does not imply that most students learn them accurately. What is "covered" is not necessarily what is learned. Many students' arsenals of algorithms include memorized error patterns (Ashlock, 1990; Ginsburg, 1977, pp. 79–149) that produce incorrect computational results. Analyze, for example, the following sample of Phil's work on a "review exercise" administered by his teacher on the first day of sixth grade:

$$
\begin{array}{r}
230 \\
\times\ 23 \\
\hline
690 \\
460 \\
\hline
5{,}290
\end{array}
\qquad
\begin{array}{r}
{}^{3\,2\,5}197 \\
\times\ 18 \\
\hline
40426 \\
197 \\
\hline
42{,}396
\end{array}
\qquad
\begin{array}{r}
{}^{3}14 \\
+\ 8 \\
\hline
{}^{}322 \\
{}^{2}33 \\
+\ 8 \\
\hline
404
\end{array}
\qquad
\begin{array}{r}
{}^{2}1\ {}^{2}1 \\
435 \\
\times\ 43 \\
\hline
1525 \\
2400 \\
\hline
25{,}525
\end{array}
$$

Phil faithfully follows the algorithm he remembers, not even bothered by the fact that the product he got for 197 and 18 is considerably larger than the one he got for 230 and 23. He is likely to continue this error pattern until a teacher diagnoses that he is adding carried digits one step too soon. (For instance, in the second exercise, he begins by thinking, "Eight times 7 is 56. Put down the 6 and carry 5. Five plus 9 is 14. Fourteen times 8 is. . . .") Although most of Phil's products are not even approximately correct, he correctly executes the vast majority of the steps in the algorithm; he simply executes one repeated step out of order. Typically, students' computational errors are not random.

- Students fail to detect their own error patterns because they have learned to execute algorithms faithfully with a myopic step-by-step view, never conceptualizing the whole process or bothering to predict a reasonable outcome (Schoenfeld, 1989). The following example illustrates the phenomenon.

VIGNETTE 7.5 For the purpose of stimulating discussion and giving him some insights about his students as they begin sixth grade, Mr. Stokes displays the following on the overhead screen and directs the class, "Simplify this":

$$\frac{8.47 + 8.47 + 8.47 + 8.47}{4}$$

Without hesitation, 23 of the 26 students begin the process of adding 8.47 to itself four times and dividing the sum by four. One asks, "Can we use a calculator?" Another inquires about the number of decimal places Mr. Stokes wants in the answer.

Mr. Stokes asks, "Why did you go to all that trouble, when you could see that four of any number divided by four is the number?" Brad: "That's not the way we learned to do it." Molina: "Yeah, the rule is to simplify the numerator first and then. . . ."

- Students are generally proficient in completing one-step skill-level tasks (e.g., recalling facts, associating names with figures, and executing the first step of an algorithm) alluded to in curriculum guidelines. However, there is a dramatic drop in proficiency for multistep tasks (e.g., working two-step word problems) ("U.S. Teens Lag Behind in Math, Science," 1989).
- Considering traditional curricula's distinctions among topics (e.g., percents and fractions, expanded notation and counting, graphs and word problems, and sets and ratios) and mathematical specialties (e.g., arithmetic, algebra, geometry, probability, statistics, and measurement), it is not surprising that most students fail to interrelate what they learn in one lesson to what they learn in other lessons.
- Most students have access to calculators at home but not in school (Dossey et al., 1988, p. 79). In general, students are able to use calculators for trivial tasks (e.g., checking answers to computational exercises) but use them neither to save time spent in computation nor in ways that take advantage of special functions (e.g., Σ) or features such as memory storage (Kansky, 1986).
- Only a small proportion of students appear to possess the conceptual understanding necessary to explain why (1) the algorithms they know work (e.g., why, when multiplying 84 by 3, one should first multiply 3 by 4 and then carry the 1 from the 12) or (2) relations they've memorized (e.g., area of rectangle = length $\times$ width) are facts ("U.S. Students Again Rank Near Bottom in Math and Science," 1989).
- Only a small proportion of students appear to possess the application-level understanding necessary to distinguish among appropriate and inappropriate mathematical procedures when confronted with a problem-solving task (Carpenter et al., 1988).
- By the time students enter sixth grade, they tend to believe mathematics has little or nothing to do with real-life problem solving, mathematical tasks are completed either quickly or not at all, and only geniuses can be creative with mathematics (Schoenfeld, 1985, p. 43).
- Although most students perceive mathematics to be composed mainly of rule memorization and do not expect to use mathematics outside the classroom, those with more favorable attitudes tend to be more skillful with mathematics and also learn mathematics at more sophisticated cognitive levels (e.g., conceptual and application levels) (Dossey et al., 1988, p. 11).

NCTM Standards–based curriculum. In response to the question, "What in the *Standards* is new compared with current practice?" NCTM's 1988–1990 president, Shirley Frye (1989a, p. 7; 1989b, p. 316), states

These new major themes are woven throughout all levels: communications, reasoning, and connections. New topics include data analysis and discrete mathematics, and the usual content topics are either expanded or modified. The *Standards* makes specific recommendations about the increased and decreased emphasis that should be placed on certain topics, skills, and procedures at all levels.

The evaluation standards focus on assessment of students' performance and curricular programs, with an emphasis on the role of evaluative measures in gathering information on which teachers can base subsequent instruction. A key factor in the general assessment section is alignment, the agreement of the assessment with the curriculum.

For all students to be mathematically literate, the instructional strategies must include collaborative experiences, the use of calculators and computers, exploration activities that enable students to hypothesize and test, applications of mathematics, and experience in problem posing and writing.

Finally, the challenges to teach mathematics as an integrated whole and to link mathematics to the physical world are the relatively new focal points of the standards.

Some teachers—but not most—have been adhering to the principles forwarded by the *Standards* for years. One hopes NCTM's efforts to infuse mathematics curricula with those principles (Frye, 1989a, 1989b) will increase the number of elementary school classrooms in which the items in Figure 7.3 are emphasized and the ones in Figure 7.4 are deemphasized.

Middle school– and junior high school–level outcomes. We now examine the differences between the outcomes of using the traditional curriculum and the outcomes of using the NCTM *Standards*–based curriculum at the middle school and junior high school levels.

Traditional curriculum. As discussed in Part I, in most school systems, middle school includes grades six, seven, and eight; junior high includes grades seven, eight, and nine. Traditional middle or junior high school mathematics curricula impact students in ways very similar to those previously listed for traditional elementary school curricula. There are, however, these differences:

- There is a much more formal treatment of algebra (often labeled prealgebra) and geometry.
- More emphasis is placed on percents, ratios, proportions, and formulas (e.g., for rate of speed, interest, area, volume, perimeter, and averages).

FIGURE 7.3
Points for Increased Emphasis in the Elementary Grades According to the *Standards*
SOURCE: Adapted from *Curriculum and Evaluation Standards for School Mathematics* (NCTM 1989).

EMPHASIZE

Conceptual understanding of numbers and relationships between numbers (e.g., between numbers expressed as fractions and numbers expressed as decimals)
Estimation of quantities
Work with approximate figures
Conceptual understanding of fundamental operations
Conceptual understanding of why algorithms work
Mental computations
Application-level understanding of how to select appropriate algorithms
Prediction of computational results
Arithmetic work with numbers resulting from empirical measurements (as opposed to textbook numerals)
Integration of geometry, arithmetic, probability, and data gathering (i.e., measurement),
Exploration of patterns
Use of variables to express relationships
Word problems with a variety of structures
Applications to real-life problems
Problem-solving strategies
Concrete activities with manipulatives
Cooperative work among students
High cognitive-level question/discussion sessions (i.e., thought-provoking as opposed to recitation)
Writing, speaking, and reading about mathematics
Use of calculators and computers to reduce time spent in complex algorithms
Use of calculators and computers as learning tools

- There is even more separation among topics and mathematical specialty areas (e.g., between algebra and geometry).
- There is even less emphasis on manipulatives and concrete experiences.
- Perceptions of students about mathematics deteriorate even further (Dossey et al., 1988, p. 11).

Students' myopic view and lack of inclination to make sense out of mathematical tasks are illustrated by the beginning ninth graders in the following example.

VIGNETTE 7.6 For the purpose of stimulating discussion and giving her some insights about her students on the first day of algebra I class, Ms. Koa asks one student, Barbara, to multiply 307 and 4/5 at the board. Barbara computes:

$$307 \times \frac{4}{5}$$

$$\frac{307}{1} \times \frac{4}{5} = \frac{1228}{5}$$

$$= 245 \frac{3}{5}$$

$$\begin{array}{r} 245 \\ 5\overline{)1228} \\ \underline{10} \\ 22 \\ \underline{20} \\ 28 \\ \underline{25} \\ 3 \end{array}$$

Ms. Koa: "Thank you, Barbara." Barbara starts to erase her work, but Ms. Koa intervenes, "No, please leave it there and work one more next to it. This time find 80% of 307." Barbara writes:

$$80 \% \ of \ 307$$

$$\begin{array}{r} 307 \\ \times .80 \\ \hline 24.56 \end{array}$$

Ms. Koa:	So, you found 4/5 of 307 to be 245 3/5, but 80% of 307 is 24.56. Does that seem okay to you?
Barbara:	I think I did it right. You want me to rework it?
Dudley:	The second one's not right because you didn't put the decimal in the right place.
Barbara:	But you're supposed to have as many decimal places in the answer as there are in the problem. See two here, so I put two here.
Dudley:	But that's because you didn't bring the zero down.
Barbara:	I thought you were supposed to . . .

FIGURE 7.4
Points for Decreased Emphasis in the Elementary Grades according to the *Standards*
SOURCE: Adapted from *Curriculum and Evaluation Standards for School Mathematics* (NCTM 1989).

DEEMPHASIZE

Early attention to reading, writing, and ordering numbers symbolically
Complex paper-and-pencil computations
Treatment of algorithms in isolation from their applications
Use of rounding or other memorized processes for estimating numbers
Addition and subtraction without renaming
Long division without remainders
Paper-and-pencil computations with fractions
Naming geometric figures
Memorization of equivalence between units of measurements
Use of clue words to determine which operations to use in solving word problems
Rote memorization
One-answer-only, one-method-only problems to solve
Teaching by telling

> **Ms. Koa:** Wait a minute. Doesn't anyone care whether or not the answer makes sense? About what would 50% of 300 be?
>
> **Lucy:** One hundred fifty.
>
> **Ms. Koa:** Then should 80% of 307 be more or less than 150?

The discussion continues, with most of the students focusing on steps in algorithms and Ms. Koa striving to get them to make sense out of the task.

The failure of Ms. Koa's algebra students to recognize that 4/5 of 307 is the same as 80% of 307 is not surprising, considering how traditional mathematics curricula isolate topics. Students tend to disassociate fractions from percents, arithmetic from algebra, geometry from numbers, and measurements from numerals that appear in textbooks.

NCTM Standards–*based curriculum*. In middle and junior high school classrooms where the *Standards'* principles are put into practice, the items in Figure 7.5 are emphasized, whereas those in Figure 7.6 are deemphasized.

High school–level outcomes. It is important also for you to understand what your students will likely experience and achieve when they are in high school.

***Traditional curriculum*.** Traditional high school curricula impact students in much the same ways enumerated for elementary, middle, and junior high grades. But the following also occur at the high school level:

- Differences among students' mathematical competence and attitudes are further exaggerated as students are separated into 3- or 4-year course sequences for the "mathematically inclined" college bound; 1- or 2-year course sequences for the "less mathematically inclined" college bound; a 1- or 2-year sequence of business and consumer mathematics courses; or "remedial" mathematics courses.

FIGURE 7.5
Points for Increased Emphasis in the Middle and Junior High Grades According to the *Standards*
SOURCE: Adapted from *Curriculum and Evaluation Standards for School Mathematics* (NCTM 1989).

EMPHASIZE

Investigation of open-ended problems
Problem-solving projects that extend for weeks
Representations of a problem and possible solutions verbally, numerically, graphically, geometrically, and symbolically
Speaking, writing, listening, and reading about mathematical ideas
Higher-order cognitive processes (e.g., inductive, deductive, analytical, and divergent thinking)
Interrelating mathematics with other school subjects and to the real world outside of the school
Interrelating topics within mathematics and across mathematical specialties
Real-life problem solving
Conceptual understanding of rational numbers and their relations among themselves and other variables
Inventing algorithms and procedures
Predicting problem solutions and results of algorithms
Discovering concepts and relationships
Distinguishing between *representations of numbers and concepts* and the *numbers and concepts themselves*
Identifying functional relationships and associating mathematical functions with real-world situations
Using a variety of methods to solve linear equations and inequalities
Informal investigation of nonlinear relationships
Exploration and application of experimental and theoretical probability models
Application of descriptive statistical methods to real-life decision making
Problem-solving applications of geometric relationships
Acquisition of numbers through measurement and measurement approximations
Using technology (e.g., computers, calculators, and video) for exploration
Using computers and calculators to reduce time spent executing algorithms
Cooperative and group learning activities
Using concrete models and manipulatives

- The separation among traditional mathematics specialties (e.g., algebra, geometry, trigonometry, statistics, "computer mathematics," "business mathematics," arithmetic, analytical geometry, and calculus) becomes even more distinct in the minds of students.
- The treatment of mathematics, except in the consumer and business mathematics courses, becomes even more formalized, abstract, and removed from real-life situations.
- Perceptions of the less mathematically inclined students deteriorate even further.

Students' tendencies to adhere faithfully and mindlessly to the execution of algorithms continue in high school, even in courses that are considered advanced.

NCTM Standards–based curriculum. As you and other teachers develop curriculum and teach in harmony with the *Standards,* high school mathematics courses will tend to emphasize the items in Figure 7.7 and deemphasize those in Figure 7.8.

B. COURSES

Traditionally, the mathematics curriculum in most schools has consisted primarily of a sequence of courses. Although course titles have varied from school district to school district, the following listing is representative of many:

- In *fourth-* and *fifth-grade mathematics,* arithmetic operations with nonnegative rational numbers has been the primary concern.
- In *sixth-grade mathematics,* although arithmetic operations with nonnegative rational numbers has been the primary concern, geometric and measurement topics are also emphasized.

FIGURE 7.6
Points for Decreased Emphasis in the Middle and Junior High Grades According to the *Standards*
SOURCE: Adapted from *Curriculum and Evaluation Standards for School Mathematics* (NCTM 1989).

DEEMPHASIZE

Practicing routine, one-step tasks
Practicing solving problems categorized by type (e.g., coin, age, and reversed-digit problems)
Recitations and worksheets requiring only rote, one-step memory
Relying on appeal to authority (e.g., the teacher or textbook answer key) for solutions
Learning about topics in isolation from other topics
Developing skills out of context
Memorizing rules, formulas (e.g., in statistics) and algorithms (e.g., cross multiplication or for manipulating algebraic symbols) without understanding why or how they work
Tedious paper-and-pencil computations

FIGURE 7.7
Points for Increased Emphasis in High School According to the *Standards*
SOURCE: Adapted from *Curriculum and Evaluation Standards for School Mathematics* (NCTM 1989).

EMPHASIZE

The use of real-world problems to motivate the exploration and application of traditional topics from algebra, geometry, trigonometry, and analysis as well as topics recently introduced into the curriculum from probability, statistics, and discrete mathematics
The use of computers to facilitate conceptual understanding of relations (e.g., with computer-based methods of successive approximations and multidimensional geometric representations)
Integration of both geometry and discrete mathematics within other specialty areas and across grade levels
Integration of functions in all specialty areas
Use of calculators and computers to facilitate the execution of algorithms
Deductive arguments expressed in natural rather than artificially rigid forms of communication
Interrelations among topics and specialties
Construction of functions as models for real-world problems

FIGURE 7.8
Points for Decreased Emphasis in High School According to the *Standards*
SOURCE: Adapted from *Curriculum and Evaluation Standards for School Mathematics* (NCTM 1989).

DEEMPHASIZE

Word problems by type, such as coin, digit, and work
The simplification of radical expressions
The use of factoring to solve equations and to simplify rational expressions
Logarithmic and trigonometric calculations using tables
Solving systems of equations using determinants
Conic sections
Euclidean geometry as a complete axiomatic system
Algorithmic-like approaches to proving theorems (e.g., with two-column format)
Distinction between analytic and Euclidean geometries
Inscribed and circumscribed polygons
Paper-and-pencil calculations
Memorization of formulas and identities
Graphing of functions by hand using table values
Unexplained formulas given as models of real-world problems

- In *seventh-grade mathematics,* the emphasis on the arithmetic of rational numbers has continued. Applications of arithmetic are extended into such areas as probability and statistics. Negative integers are introduced, as is a more formal treatment of Euclidean geometry.

- In *eighth-grade general mathematics,* the focus is still on the arithmetic of rational numbers. Some elements of number theory are introduced, as are linear algebraic equations and the Cartesian coordinate systems. The study of geometry has emphasized constructions, areas, and volumes.

- *Prealgebra* has been intended to provide more advanced work for seventh and eighth graders or basic work for ninth graders, as preparation for elementary algebra, and its content has overlapped that of general eighth-grade mathematics and the first half of elementary algebra.

- In *elementary algebra,* or *algebra I,* the real-number system is developed. Variable expressions, linear equations, linear inequalities, and operations with polynomials (including those with exponents) are emphasized. Work with quadratic relations may or may not be included, depending on the pace of the course.

- *Basic mathematics* is designed to provide students with a review of mathematic work.

C. APPROACHES TO DESIGNING COURSES
The Follow-a-Textbook Approach

Some teachers "design" courses by religiously following prescribed textbooks page by page; teaching units are equated to textbook chapters. Here, for example, is a glimpse into Ms. McCuller's thoughts as she begins planning a two-semester elementary algebra course.

VIGNETTE 7.7 Ms. McCuller thinks to herself: "Let's see, where's the table of contents? Okay, it looks like I've got 16 chapters to cover, from 'The Language of Algebra' to Chapter 16, 'Trigonometry.' I don't remember anything about trigonometry in the district curriculum guide for elementary algebra. I wonder if it's okay to skip that. Probably so, since it's the last chapter, so nothing else would be depending on it. . . . Oh well, I'll cover it unless we run out of time.

"Let's see just how many instructional weeks are available per semester. Where's that district calendar? All right, we've got a total of 36 weeks. But there's 1 week each semester for finals, so that leaves only 34. And then there's standardized test week in the spring, so we've got 17 weeks for the first semester and 16 for the second to cover 16 chapters. So, we should average about 2 weeks per chapter.

"Chapter 1, 'The Language of Algebra' . . . it won't take us but a week to get through this. Same with Chapters 2 and 3; it's all review. So we get through the first three chapters the first

3 weeks. Now, Chapter 4 on inequalities—this'll take us longer. Let's see, pages 114 to 140. That's 26 pages, not too many for 2 weeks. Let's see how involved this gets. . . . This is mostly new for these students. I thought with the NCTM *Standards,* we were supposed to start emphasizing applications! There's not much application in here. How are we supposed to follow the *Standards* if the textbooks don't? Of course, by the time the textbooks catch up, they'll be telling us to do something else! Anyway, two weeks for Chapter 4. . . ."

When Ms. McCuller gets to Chapter 9, "Factoring and Rational Expressions," she exclaims to herself, "This is just the kind of stuff the *Standards* suggests we deemphasize and yet I've got to cover a whole chapter on it. It'll probably take us 4 weeks to get through all these algorithms!"

During the school year, Ms. McCuller manages to cover the book page by page, skipping only the brief "Extending Your Knowledge" and "Computer Excursion" inserts near the end of each chapter. Faithfully, she assigns the even-numbered exercises for every section covered. Student learning is limited mostly to memory-level skills with virtually no conceptual- or application-level achievement. However, most students take comfort in being able to appeal to a single source, the textbook, for all they need to know about mathematics.

The Contrived Problem–Solving Approach

To provide students with heuristic experiences discovering and inventing mathematics, some teachers incorporate concrete mathematical models or problem-solving tasks into every teaching unit (Posamentier & Stepelman, 1990, pp. 109–136). The same mathematical topics enumerated in curriculum guides and textbook tables of contents may well be included, but each topic relating to a concept or relation is introduced through a problem-solving or model-analysis experience. For example, consider Vignette 7.8.

VIGNETTE 7.8 Mr. Theron is just beginning a teaching unit intended to help his algebra students extend their abilities to (1) apply arithmetic and geometric sequence formulas they discovered in a previous unit, (2) discover new relations among integers, and (3) invent new algorithms with integers. He introduces the unit by confronting the students with the following problem, which he first read in a book by Posamentier and Stepelman (1990, pp. 252–253):

Form a 3×3 matrix with the whole numbers 1, 2, . . . , 9 so that the sum of the elements in each row, column, and diagonal is the same.

He indicates to them that any $n \times n$ matrix of real numbers in which the sum of the numbers in each row, column, and diagonal is the same is called a *magic square* (Sobel & Maletsky, 1988, pp. 123–129). For example:

7	2	16	9
12	13	3	6
1	8	10	15
14	11	5	4

Working in small task groups, the students' trial-and-error method succeeds in producing magic squares with the desired attributes; the following is one:

2	7	6
9	5	1
4	3	8

Mr. Theron then leads an inductive questioning/discussion session in which students determine that they can utilize the sum of an arithmetic series formula (i.e., $\sum_{i=1}^{n} a_i = (n/2)(a_1 + a_n)$) that they discovered in a previous unit in formulating a general algorithm, or function, for producing magic squares.

Lessons such as Mr. Theron's, in which students analyze and attempt to solve problems or puzzles that have been contrived because of their mathematical features, provide experiences needed for conceptual-level learning. However, if these are the only types of lessons in which students engage, then they will fail to polish their algorithmic skills and apply what they conceptualized in the contrived situations to real-world situations. Thus, teachers also need to include direct instruction for knowledge-level skills and application lessons in which students work on solutions to real-life problems.

Teachers who adhere to the contrived problem–solving approach to designing courses are hardly able to sequence teaching units in the same order they appear in textbooks. The vast majority of textbooks arrange content so that there is a building of algorithmic skills from easier to more difficult tasks. But teachers (e.g., Mr. Theron) who focus on concept attainment through analysis of contrived problems and models typically design units so that students (1) first attempt the more difficult tasks (e.g., creating a magic square by trial and error), (2) next, discover easier methods from that struggle, and then (3) complete the unit applying the easier method (e.g., creating a magic square via the algorithm).

The Real-World Problem–Solving Approach

Ms. Asgil uses an approach quite similar to Mr. Theron's; however, she uses real-life instead of contrived problems for her students to analyze. Share her thoughts as she begins designing an algebra course.

> **VIGNETTE 7.9** Ms. Asgil: "In order for these students to appreciate the utility of mathematics they have to discover its power to help them solve their own real-life problems. I ought to have a year-long project that they all work on and to which they'd apply the algebra as they learn it. I once heard about a whole high school curriculum that revolved around a year-long project to build and sell a house. That would be great! Virtually everything I want to teach them about algebra could be applied. There would be functions to formulate and equations to solve to assess costs, work time, construction questions, carpentry decisions, purchasing questions, and on and on. That's a way to really teach math at the application level! But I've got to be realistic. This school won't be ready for that for another 300 years. Then maybe I'll try it!
>
> "Okay, so we can't build a house, but maybe we could try something a little more realistic—like running a school store. That would involve work time, wages, buying, interest, and so on. But, now that I think about it, students would only learn to apply the algebra to store-related problems. What they need is a variety of real-life situations for analysis. . . .
>
> "I've got it! I'll begin the year by conducting a survey to find out what interests them and come up with a list of problems from their real worlds to which we can apply the algebra. Then, I'll introduce each unit with three or four problems built from that list. I could, for example, have those interested in motor vehicles discover functional relations from working on things like effects of tire size on acceleration. Those concerned with body fitness could examine diet and exercise variables against body-fat variables. They might work on those in separate groups and report to the large group; then we could abstract what's common to the solution of all problems. They'd be doing real mathematics that was motivated from their own concerns! Oh, another brilliant idea! If I could get some of their other teachers in on this, we could coordinate some of the problems we're working on with what they're doing in social studies, science, physical education, and so on. Maybe I could. . . ."

The real-life problem-solving approach tends to develop students' appreciation for mathematics and provides experiences necessary for them to learn to apply it creatively in real-life situations. However, the realities of today's schools make it impractical to design courses so that *every* lesson focuses on real-life problems. Although Ms. Asgil's approach is needed and possible, practicality dictates that some learning activities utilize contrived models and problems and others include textbook-type drills. Otherwise, some conceptual and skill-level gaps will go unfilled in most students' mathematical preparation.

Combining Approaches

Students need structured experiences (1) systematically confronting real-life problems, (2) inducting mathematical principles and processes from analyses of those confrontations, (3) working with mathematical models and on contrived problems to refine and validate those principles and processes, (4) engaging in direct-instruction lessons to develop memory and comprehension skills, (5) engaging in textbook-type drill and practice exercises to polish those skills, and (6) engaging in deductive lessons for application-level achievement of mathematics.

D. SELECTION OF LEARNING MATERIALS, RESOURCES, EQUIPMENT, AND FACILITIES

In Vignette 7.7, Ms. McCuller, like many other mathematics teachers, allows textbooks to dictate curricula. Although such blind faith in any textbook is inadvisable, textbook selections as well as other learning materials and resources cannot help but profoundly affect curriculum design and implementation (Usiskin, 1985). For his contrived problem–solving lesson with magic squares, Mr. Theron took advantage of an idea he gained from a resource book for teachers. Even how you arrange and equip your classroom influences what and how you teach (Cangelosi, 1988, pp. 165–177; 1990a, pp. 13–20). As Winston Churchill said, "We shape our buildings; thereafter, they shape us."

Your judgment regarding the selection of learning materials, resources, equipment, and facilities should be a function of just what you hope to accomplish with your students (i.e., learning goals) and practical considerations (e.g., cost and convenience). You will, of course, be constrained by budget and administrative considerations. Typically, school mathematics departments are provided with only paltry resources for obtaining anything more than textbooks. As one school superintendent told me, "Textbooks and a classroom with desks, chalk, and chalkboard are all mathematics teachers ever need. Math isn't like science, where they need lab equipment, nor like English, in which they need different books to read." The hope is that one impact of the NCTM *Standards* will be to publicize the need for a variety of learning materials, equipment, and mathematics laboratory facilities for every mathematics teacher.

Textbooks

The degree of control you can exercise regarding the selection of textbooks for your courses varies considerably, depending on your school situation. Typically, panels of teachers and school administrators select textbooks available from state-adopted or district-adopted lists of approved textbooks (see Chapter 4). In some schools, teachers have virtual control over which textbooks or textbook series are adopted. Of course, options for new texts are hardly open until existing texts are worn or clearly out of date. In other schools, teachers are required to "live with" whatever textbooks have been adopted for them. Subsequent chapters of this book are intended to help you work with whatever text you have.

In addition to the guidelines presented in Chapters 4 and 6, when selecting a textbook, the following questions should be raised:

- *How well do the book's topics match those specified by relevant curriculum guides (e.g., the one you're supposed to follow at your school) and the ones you have listed for your teaching units?* It is not a drawback for the book to include topics you do not plan to include in any of your teaching units as long as the book's treatment of topics you include is not dependent on book topics you delete. However, it is inconvenient to include more than a few topics that are not treated in the book.
- *Does the book provide high-quality exercises relevant to the learning objectives you want your students to achieve?* More than anything else, textbooks provide teachers with an abundance of exercises for students to practice. Traditionally, the preponderance of textbook exercises are of the skill-level variety. Even most textbook word problems require only algorithmic skills once the wording is deciphered. However, some of the more recently published textbooks also include some concept-building exercises, such as the "Explore and Discover" inserts in Elich and Cannon (1989) and a few word problems that at least border on situations interesting to adolescents (Keedy et al., 1986, p. 371).
- *How accurate is the mathematics presented in the textbook?* Virtually all books contain a few misprints and report a few incorrect computational results. Sometimes such mistakes provoke healthy discussions that enhance rather than detract from learning. However, conceptual errors or mathematical treatises that conflict with what you want

your students to learn can hinder your lessons. For example, many algebra books define a variable as "a *letter* that stands for a number" (e.g., Brumfiel, Golden, & Heins, 1986, p. 22; Coxford & Payne, 1987, p. 9; Keedy et al., 1986, p. 562). If you take that definition literally, and I assume you want your students to take mathematical definitions literally, then interest rates, age, speed, time, shape, set, location, length, number of, angle, and all the other variables we deal with in problem solving are not "variables." These books' definitions say a variable is a *letter*—not what the letter stands for, but the letter itself. Such a restrictive definition precludes associations of mathematics with real-life situations. Furthermore, rigorous mathematics defines operations such as addition on numbers, not letters. Operations such as intersection ($\cap$) are defined for sets, not letters. Consequently, you need to consider the conceptual treatment of key topics (e.g., variables, functions, and measurement) in textbooks before adopting one.

- *How consistent are the book's organization and presentations with research-based teaching and learning principles?* Few if any mathematics textbooks are written in accordance with research-based teaching and learning principles (principles such as those explained in Chapter 1). Thus, you can expect to have to organize your lessons somewhat differently from your textbook's presentations. However, it would be convenient to use a text that is somewhat in harmony with teaching strategies you employ.
- *How readable is the textbook for your students? Will the explanations be intelligible to them?* Typically, students do not read explanations in mathematics textbooks. Generally, they read only examples and exercises (Cangelosi, 1985). However, the need for students to read about mathematics is now well publicized (NCTM, 1989).
- *What practical supplements for the teacher are available?* You may find the annotated teachers' editions, organizational plans for translating the book into teaching units, and test items provided with some books to be helpful. Be particularly cautious regarding validity of tests and test items (as explained in Chapter 6).
- *How much does the textbook cost?* Cost factors may or may not be critical, depending on the particular textbook-acquisition arrangement under which your school administrators work.
- *How attractively packaged is the book?* The book's aesthetic appeal (e.g., colorful pictures and clever use of white space) may influence the amount of time your students spend with the book.

Sources of Ideas on Teaching Mathematics

The complexities and dynamics of classrooms dictate that (1) teachers either continue to develop their instructional talents throughout their careers or be incompetent and (2) teachers should not attempt to deal with all their classroom problems without the help of colleagues and instructional supervisors. The traditional model, in which preservice teacher-preparation programs provide their graduates with "teaching tools" and the wish "Good luck in learning how to use these tools on the job!" simply doesn't work for most (Cangelosi, 1991, p. 209). Quality professional support is essential for every teacher (Stallion, 1988).

Colleagues.   Other teachers, especially mathematics teachers, in your school district and geographical area are probably the most immediate and sympathetic resource for suggestions, information, and thoughts on designing lessons, managing your classroom, dealing with student behavior problems, motivating students, acquiring materials, and evaluating student achievement. Visiting one another's classrooms (Allen et al., 1984), peer coaching (Chase & Wolfe, 1989; Chrisco, 1989; Raney & Robbins, 1989), colleague mentoring (Duke, Cangelosi, & Knight, 1988), sharing responsibilities for students (Cangelosi, 1988, pp. 120–124, 198–199), and think sessions are invaluable means for you to learn from other teachers as they learn from you.

Professional organizations.   Besides supporting teachers' causes, professional organizations such as NCTM, National Education Association (NEA), Mathematical Association of America (MAA), and American Federation of Teachers (AFT) provide forums for idea sharing and resource materials in the form of journals, books, pamphlets, and video programs. If you are not already a member, you should join NCTM. Membership benefits include the following:

- A subscription to either *Mathematics Teacher* or *Arithmetic Teacher*. *Mathematics Teacher* contains articles specifically for the purpose of providing middle, junior high, and high school mathematics teachers with practical ideas they can implement in their classrooms. *Arithmetic Teacher* is a similar journal, but it is directed at elementary and middle school teachers.
- A subscription to *NCTM News Bulletin,* which reports on current events relevant to the mathematics teaching profession.
- A discount on subscriptions to *Journal for Research in Mathematics Education* and to *Arithmetic Teacher* (assuming you selected *Mathematics Teacher* as part of your membership fee). The *Journal for Research in Mathematics Education* includes reports of scholarly studies relevant to questions about teaching and learning of mathematics.
- Opportunities to participate in national and regional NCTM conferences consisting of lectures, workshops, seminars, displays, business meetings, and exchanges of ideas among an international group of colleagues.
- Ready access to and discounts for acquiring books, monographs, display materials, videotape programs, tests, manipulatives, and computer software relevant to professional improvement and your work with students.

If there isn't a local (district-, county-, or city-wide) NCTM affiliate for you to join in your area, then organize one. To do so contact your statewide affiliate or the NCTM headquarters in Reston, Virginia.

Other professional organizations (e.g., NEA and MAA) coordinate many of their activities with NCTM's and can also provide you with invaluable services.

School-district-sponsored resource centers and workshops. Most school districts maintain a resource center from which their teachers can borrow professional enrichment materials, including publications, computer software, and videotapes. In-service assistance is also provided in the form of periodic workshops and arrangements with universities and colleges for credit courses for enhancing classroom effectiveness.

Colleges, universities, foundations, and research and development centers. Besides offering coursework for in-service teachers, colleges and universities, like educational research and development centers (e.g., the National Center for Research on Teacher Education in East Lansing, Michigan, and Far West Laboratory in San Francisco), are a source of professional enrichment materials. Foundations (such as the National Science Foundation in Washington, D.C.) distribute reports on funded projects for both in-service education for teachers (e.g., Math COUNTS at the University of Arizona in Tucson) and professional enhancement materials (e.g., Mathematics Teacher Inservice Project at Utah State University in Logan).

Publishing houses. As a school faculty member, you can expect to be on the mailing lists of publishing houses, from which you will receive advertisements, catalogs, and sample products of books and other materials. You will find some of these products helpful. The following entries from the reference list for this chapter have helped many teachers design more effective lessons: Artino, Gaglione, and Shell (1983); Ashlock (1990); Brissenden (1980); Bushaw et al. (1980); Easterday, Henry, and Simpson (1981); Hirsch (1986); Hirsch and Zweng (1985); Hunkins (1989); Johnson (1982, 1986); Krulik and Reys (1980); Nelson and Reys (1976); Posamentier and Stepelman (1990); Salkind and Earl (1973); Saunders (1981); Schoenfeld (1985); Sharron and Reys (1979); Skemp (1973); Sobel and Maletsky (1988); and Souviney (1981).

Sources for Mathematical Topics

Not only are you likely to make use of resources on how to teach mathematics, but you will also use resources on mathematics per se. Besides the usual myriad of mathematics textbooks, there are books about mathematics for both you and your students. From the reference list, for example, are Beskin (1986), Bowers (1988), Collins (1987), Court (1961), Devaney (1990), Dudeney (1958), Gardner (1986), Gnanadesikan et al. (1986), Hoffman (1988), Honsberger (1973, 1976, 1979), Karush (1989), Kasner and Newman (1989), Kogleman and Heller (1986), Nielsen (1962), Niven (1961, 1965, 1981), Packel (1981), Péter (1961), Peterson (1988), Pòlya (1977, 1985), Shapiro (1977), Yaglom (1978), and Zippin (1975).

Given the emphasis in the NCTM *Standards* on students reading about mathematics, engaging students in reading about mathematics from nontextbooks appears particularly important.

Sources for Mathematics History

Cajori (1985) quotes J. W. L. Glaisher: "I am sure that no subject loses more than mathematics by any attempt to disassociate it from its history." The following books from the reference list are but a few of the many historical treatises of mathematics: Aaboe (1964), Cajori (1985), Eves (1983a, 1983b), NCTM (1969), and Schiffer and Bowden (1984).

Manipulatives and Concrete Models

Learning activities in which students work with hands-on, concrete objects and models are common in mathematics lessons in the primary grades but are relatively rare at the middle and secondary levels. However, older students (even in high school and college) need experiences working with manipulatives and concrete models to gain conceptual-level understanding of mathematical concepts (e.g., conic sections) and relationships (e.g., the Pythagorean theorem) (Brissenden, 1980, pp. 5–32, 131–164). Once teachers begin involving their students in hands-on activities with concrete objects, they tend to continue doing so because students prefer them to more passive paper-and-pencil exercises and, consequently, are more cooperative, appreciative, and easier to manage. However, manipulatives should not be selected only for the purpose of keeping students busy and entertained, as in the following vignette.

> **VIGNETTE 7.10** In the faculty lounge at the end of the school day, mathematics teachers Lottie Walker and Fred King have the following exchange:
>
> | | |
> |---|---|
> | **Fred:** | How'd your day go? |
> | **Lottie:** | Fantastic! We worked with Möbius strips (Sobel & Maletsky, 1988, pp. 92–93) in all my classes today. They had a ball, got some great discussions going! They were fascinated. |
> | **Fred:** | What's a Möbius strip? |
> | **Lottie:** | Here, I'll show you. See this strip of paper? I'll mark it *A* and *B*, like this. Now, I'll twist it and attach *A* to *B* with tape. Now, use your pencil to draw a line from *A* to *B*. |

Möbius strip.

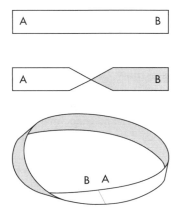

Fred: There, but I never crossed an edge.
Lottie: Use these scissors to cut down the middle on the line.
Fred: Oh, wow! How can that be? It's still only one large band! Why did that happen?
Lottie: That's what the lively discussions in my classes were all about today. I told them if they cooperate during the next unit on polynomial operations, we could do more of these fun sorts of things afterwards.

Ms. Walker seems to think of her Möbius strip activity as an aside from her regular lessons, solely for the purpose of entertaining and fascinating students. Such fascinations can lead some students to appreciate mathematical relationships and motivate them to pursue other mathematical ideas. But more is gained from experiences with concrete objects when those experiences are integrated with other types of activities and are relevant to the learning goal of the unit.

Materials collected from students' everyday environments usually make manipulatives and mathematical models that are more meaningful to students than prepared instructional materials available from commercial outlets. Such "natural" materials help associate mathematics with real life. However, the commercial products (such as algebra tiles, create-a-cube puzzles, root blocks, and fraction tiles (Activity Resources Company, 1989)) are valuable supplements for contrived problem–solving lessons leading to conceptual-level learning.

Computers, Printers, and Computer Software

Uses. In selecting or organizing materials, equipment, and facilities for a course, you should plan for your own use of computers and how you want your students to use them. You need ready access to your own computer to teach mathematics effectively today as much as you need access to paper, pencil, and textbooks. Teaching responsibilities for which you need a computer include the following.

Producing documents. Word-processing capabilities allow you efficiently to produce worksheets, exercises, memos and letters (e.g., to students, parents, and other faculty members), tests, outlines, and lesson plans.

Illustrations. Combining word processing with art and desktop publishing programs provides a ready means for producing professional-style displays and instructional materials. It took a teacher with a pen 6 minutes to produce the transparency slide illustration depicted in Figure 7.9. A teacher generated the one in Figure 7.10 in 4 minutes with a computer and printer. The illustration in Figure 7.10 is stored in a file the teacher can recall and easily modify for subsequent use.

Simulations, generating mathematical models, and executing functions for classroom demonstrations. You can use your computer in conjunction with a classroom display screen for conceptual-level and application-level lessons in which you demonstrate fitting data to curves, manipulating matrices, transforming graphs, rotating solids, plotting graphs, searching for patterns, and other executions of functions.

As a tool for exploring mathematics. You can hardly teach students to discover and invent mathematics unless you remain an active student of mathematics yourself. You need your own computer as a tool for advancing your own mathematical abilities and to gain insights into ideas, which you can share with your students.

Calculations. By preprogramming your computer to execute multistep, repetitive algorithms, you save time checking students' answers and working out examples for use in class.

Identifying patterns in students' work. Consider the following scenario.

VIGNETTE 7.11 Twelve of the 61 students in Mr. Heidingsfelder's two algebra I sections consistently obtain incorrect answers on exercises that involve simplifying rational polynomial expressions such as $(6a^2 - 15ab + 9b^2)/(3b^2 - 4ab + a^2)$. Mr. Heidingsfelder has a computer program that searches out student error patterns from the answers students give on selected exercises. Thus, he administers the selected exercises to the 12 students and has them save their final answers on a computer disk. He feeds the data into this "error-pattern search" program and attempts to diagnose each student's difficulty.

FIGURE 7.9
Example of a Typical Hand-Produced Transparency

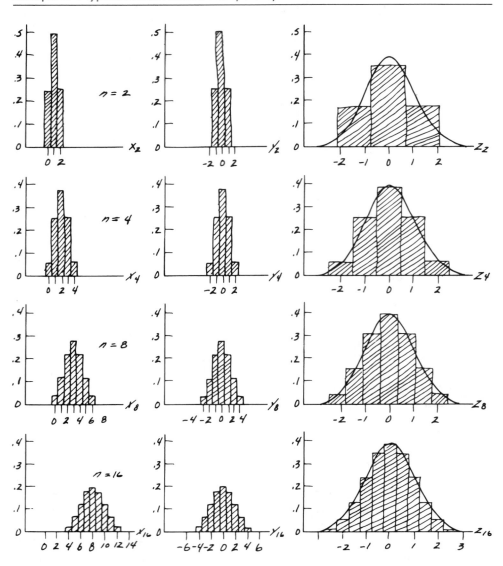

Maintaining item pool files and generating tests. As explained in Chapter 6, having computerized item pool files for generating tests is not only a convenience, it also enhances the likelihood that your tests will provide you with valid data on how well students achieve learning goals.

Record keeping. Maintaining data on 125 students (an average four- or five-section load for mathematics teachers) requires a computer.

As recommended by the NCTM *Standards,* your students also need access to computers in school for many activities.

Simulating mathematical models and manipulatives. Mathematics students can engage in contrived problem–solving learning activities with computer-simulated manipulatives and models in much the same way that biology students use computers to simulate animal dissections.

Explorations of mathematical relationships. Just as language arts students are far more likely to engage in creative writing and editing when they have access to word processing, mathematics students are more likely to experiment with data and test hypotheses creatively when they have a computer to relieve them of mindless work.

FIGURE 7.10
Example of a Computer-Generated Transparency

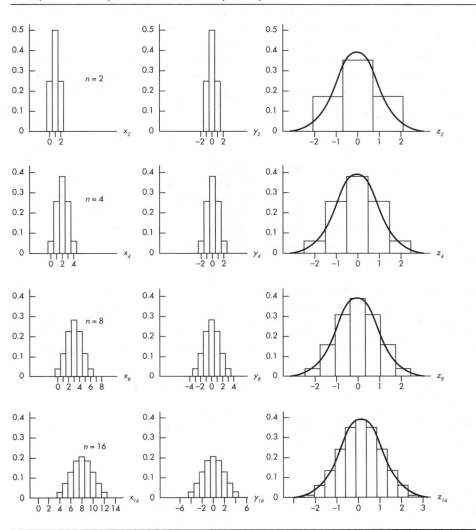

Demonstrating mathematical discoveries and inventions. If students are actu-ally going to engage in the discovery and invention of mathematics, then computers can serve to help them demonstrate and argue their hypotheses and explain their inventions. Consider Vignette 7.12.

Vignette 7.12 Mr. Johnson has Amanda report her conjecture about Pythagorean triples to the class, and although she has no formal proof prepared, she challenges anyone to find a Pythagorean triple that doesn't follow her pattern or to find a non-Pythagorean triple that does. Attempts at counterexamples are quickly dispensed with using a computer program that indi-cates whether or not a given triple is Pythagorean and whether or not it fits Amanda's pattern.

Computer programming. By programming computers to execute algorithms for them, students enhance their understanding of the algorithms themselves. Posamentier and Stepelman (1990, pp. 148–149), for example, suggest that a lesson for learning an algo-rithm for solving systems of linear equations might include activities in which students de-vise a flowchart and write a program for executing that algorithm. To construct the flow-chart and BASIC program shown in Figure 7.11, students must analyze the algorithm, examining it one step at a time.

Calculations and executions of functions. Computers, like calculators, relieve students from the burden of working out algorithms during lessons in which their energies and time should be directed toward more sophisticated cognitive processes (e.g., comprehension, inductive reasoning, deductive reasoning, and creative or divergent thinking). For example, during lessons designed to increase their skill with an algorithm, you may have students execute by hand the algorithm that is programmed in Figure 7.11. However, for application-level lessons, you may choose to have them execute it using computers, allowing them to concentrate their time and energy on how to solve problems rather than repeating algorithmic steps.

Computer-Assisted Instruction (CAI)

Traditionally, the principal use of computers in mathematics classrooms has been in programmed instruction in which students are confronted with exercises (usually computational) and are given feedback on their responses. Programs branch so that a sequence of correct student responses triggers more difficult exercises, whereas incorrect responses trigger easier tasks for students. CAI allows you a degree of flexibility in individualizing lessons according to student achievement levels, especially in accommodating variability in proficiency with algorithms, and affords you more time to conduct conceptual- and application-level learning activities while much of the burden for drill and practice exercises is shouldered by computers. Consider the next vignette.

> **VIGNETTE 7.13** To help him deal with the multiple stages of mathematical achievement levels among his prealgebra students, Mr. Hornacek uses intraclass grouping, so that different subgroups progress at different rates. He often conducts a lecture, discussion, or questioning session with one group of about 10 while a second group is working independently on textbook exercises and a third group polishes algorithmic skills with the help of CAI programs.

FIGURE 7.11
Student-Generated Flowchart and BASIC Program for Solving $\{ax + by = c, dx + ey = f\}$
SOURCE: Excerpted from Posamentier and Stepelman (1990, p. 149). Reprinted by permission of Merrill, an imprint of Macmillan Publishing Company, from *Teaching Secondary School Mathematics*, 3rd ed., by Alfred S. Posamentier and Jay Stepelman. Copyright © 1990 by Merrill Publishing.

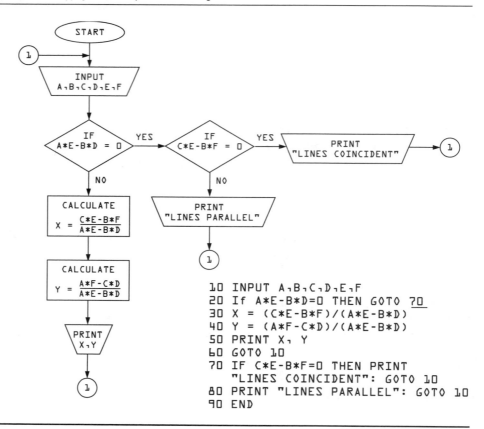

```
10 INPUT A,B,C,D,E,F
20 IF A*E-B*D=0 THEN GOTO 70
30 X = ((C*E-B*F)/(A*E-B*D)
40 Y = (A*F-C*D)/(A*E-B*D)
50 PRINT X, Y
60 GOTO 10
70 IF C*E-B*F=0 THEN PRINT
   "LINES COINCIDENT": GOTO 10
80 PRINT "LINES PARALLEL": GOTO 10
90 END
```

Periodically, the three groups rotate, so Mr. Hornacek spends about the same amount of time with each group while monitoring the other two. He finds this arrangement to be especially important for accommodating the needs of special students (e.g., "learning disabled," "hearing impaired," and "gifted") who are mainstreamed into his classes. Because he depends on CAI for the major share of activities for algorithmic skills, he's able to devote more personally involved time to the more interesting aspects of teaching, namely, inquiry lessons for higher cognitive learning.

Applications. CAI has many useful applications.

Testing. Some types of tests, especially those using multiple-choice items and error-pattern analyses, are more efficiently administered to students via computers than in the more traditional paper-and-pencil format (Cangelosi, 1990b, pp. 131–133).

Students' maintenance of records relative to their own progress. Techniques such as precision teaching have proven to be particularly effective in enhancing students' algorithmic skills when students chart their own progress with the aid of computers (Bowden, 1991).

Accessibility. Some of the aforementioned uses of computers (such as error-pattern searches) might seem a little futuristic and unrealistic for some school districts. But all these uses are quite practical wherever the teacher has exclusive use of a computer and students have at least shared access to a reasonable number of compatible computers. Slightly over 50 percent of the nation's middle and secondary school students have some access to computers at school for use in mathematics classes (Dossey et al., 1988, pp. 82–91).

Availability of microcomputers varies considerably among schools. A relatively small portion of schools enjoy the ideal arrangement of having each desk in mathematics classrooms equipped with a personal computer that is interlinked to one of the teacher's and to several printers clustered in one part of the classroom. A few to a dozen computer stations clustered in one part of the mathematics classroom is a more common arrangement. Students take turns completing assignments, engaging in CAI, taking tests, or working on tasks of their choice at these stations. Many schools have one or more computer labs for students to use in doing individual work outside of class time or use by entire classes, depending on scheduling arrangements and demand.

Selection. At some point in your teaching career, you are likely to have the opportunity of selecting computer hardware for your school. Considering today's rate of technological progress, there is not much advice for you today that will not be obsolete tomorrow. In addition to the information of Chapter 6, here are two suggestions:

- First, identify the software you want (e.g., CAI, mathematical simulations, error-pattern searches, and languages or menus your students can readily use), and then select hardware that can efficiently run that software.
- Without compromising your system, try and acquire equipment that is compatible or can be interfaced with existing equipment.

In addition to titles in Chapter 6 and those that follow in this part, information about available software can be obtained from computer magazines, software catalogs, computer retail outlets, professional journals for mathematics teachers, libraries, professional conferences for mathematics teachers, college and university departments of educational technology, and school district resource and media centers. Such sources provide information relative to technical compatibility, mathematical content, learning levels, targeted student audiences, user friendliness, and practical features. However, it is usually necessary for you actually to try programs yourself before deciding which ones are compatible with your needs and goals.

Calculators

Considering the wealth of research supporting the use of calculators as an integral part of lessons and the relatively low cost of powerful hand-held calculators, it seems mad to teach mathematics unless every student has ready access to a calculator (Kansky, 1986).

FIGURE 7.12
Display on Nate's TI-81 Graphics Calculator with
$Y1 = 2x^2 - 17x + 21$ and $Y2 = (2x - 7)(x - 3)$

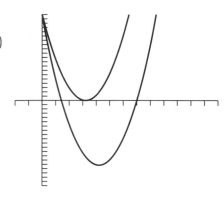

Students' use of calculators has risen since the 1986 National Assessment of Educational Progress reported that approximately 95 percent of secondary students had calculators in their homes but only about 25 percent had access to calculators in school (Dossey et al., 1988, pp. 79–82).

In selecting calculators, keep in mind their value for other things besides straightforward computational tasks. Like computers, calculators are useful in exploration and discovery activities. Consider the next vignette.

VIGNETTE 7.14 Nate works an exercise assigned by his algebra teacher, Ms. Van Dusen, as follows:
Factor $2x^2 - 17x + 21$.

$(2x-7)(x-3)$

He then engages Ms. Van Dusen in the following conversation.

Nate:	Is this right?
Ms. Van Dusen:	I don't know. Check it out on your graphics calculator.
Nate:	How?
Ms. Van Dusen:	Let $Y1 = 2x^2 - 17x + 21$. Good! Now, let $Y2 = (2x - 7)(x - 3)$. Super! Now, graph them both on the same screen.

Nate obtains the results displayed in Figure 7.12.

Ms. Van Dusen:	If $2x^2 - 17x + 21 = (2x - 7)(x - 3)$, what would you expect about the graphs of $Y1$ and $Y2$?
Nate:	I don't know.
Ms. Van Dusen:	Would $Y1 = Y2$?
Nate:	Sure.
Ms. Van Dusen:	Then what would be true about their graphs?
Nate:	They'd be the same.
Ms. Van Dusen:	Look at the two curves on your calculator. Are they the same?
Nate:	No. Oh, then $2x^2 - 17x + 21$ isn't the same as $(2x - 7)(x - 3)$ or else there'd be only one curve!
Ms. Van Dusen:	You've just invented a test of factoring accuracy.

A minute later, Nate enters $2x^2 - 17x + 21$ for $Y1$ and $(2x - 3)(x - 7)$ for $Y2$ in his graphics calculator and obtains the display shown in Figure 7.13.

Measuring Instruments

If you are serious about teaching students real-life applications of mathematics, then your students will need experience working with numbers they obtain from their real-life environments. *Measurement* is the process by which we make empirical observations (i.e., see, hear, feel, taste, smell, or touch) and record what is observed in the form of numbers.

FIGURE 7.13
Display on Nate's TI-81 Graphics Calculator with
$Y1 = 2x^2 - 17x + 21$ and $Y2 = (2x - 3)(x - 7)$

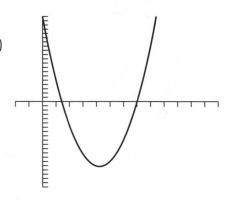

Measuring instruments such as the following provide a conventional means for systematically gathering numbers (or data) during problem solving:

- *Clocks, stopwatches, and timers* (for measuring the variable *time*)
- *Rulers, tape measures, calipers, trundle wheels, and odometers* (for measuring the variable *distance,* or *length*)
- *Thermometers* (for measuring the variable *heat*)
- *Barometers* (for measuring the variable *atmospheric pressure*)
- *Scales and balances* (for measuring the variable *weight*)
- *Protractors* (for measuring the variable *angle size*)
- *Unit cubes and containers* (for measuring the variable *volume*)
- *Counters* (for measuring the variable *cardinality*)

Such instruments should be standard fare in every mathematics classroom. Measuring instruments that are more specific to certain types of problems should be available at least occasionally (e.g., a *sphygmomanometer* for measuring blood pressure and a *docimeter* for measuring sound levels).

Video and Audio

Compare the learning activities described in the following three vignettes with respect to student attention and involvement in the presentations.

VIGNETTE 7.15 Mr. Barkin's students are poised with pencils and notebooks as he announces, "Let's develop a formula for approximating the area of any circular region." He turns toward the chalkboard and draws a circle. Looking over his shoulder, he says, "Does everyone have a circle in their notes? Okay, let's call the radius of the circle *r,*" as he draws on the board. "And circumscribe the circle in a square like this," he continues. Some students, especially those having difficulty seeing his illustrations until he turns around and moves away, entertain themselves with off-task conversations. Mr. Barkin is slightly annoyed with the noise, but because his back is turned he's not sure who is talking, so for now he ignores it.

Facing the class, he asks, "What is the area of the large rectangle?" Some students don't pay attention to the questions because they are now busy copying the figure that they couldn't see while Mr. Barkin was drawing it. Others are cued to stop talking by Mr. Barkin facing the class. Leona answers, "Four *r*-squared." Mr. Barkin: "Why four *r*-squared?" Leona: "Because. . . ."

The lecture/discussion continues, with Mr. Barkin eventually constructing the octagon whose area approximates that of the circle and concluding that the circle's area is approximately $(3.111 \ldots) r^2$. Figure 7.14 illustrates the development of the formula.

Mr. Barkin's presentation was marred by some students' failing to pay attention whenever he turned his back to write on the board. They were restless as he blocked their view of the board, so they entertained themselves in off-task ways. Some of the other students tried to remain on-task but always seemed to be a step behind trying to copy what was on the board as Mr. Barkin went on to the next phase of the explanation.

FIGURE 7.14
Development of a Formula for Approximating the Area of a Circular Region

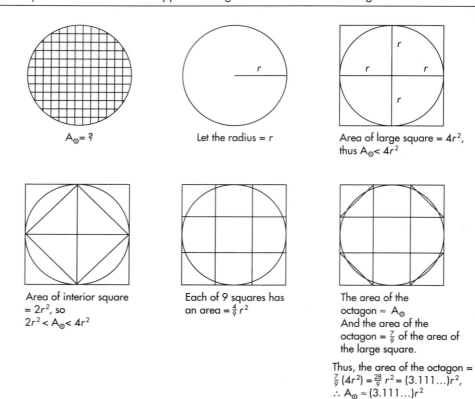

$A_\odot = ?$

Let the radius = r

Area of large square = $4r^2$, thus $A_\odot < 4r^2$

Area of interior square = $2r^2$, so $2r^2 < A_\odot < 4r^2$

Each of 9 squares has an area = $\frac{4}{9}r^2$

The area of the octagon $\approx A_\odot$
And the area of the octagon = $\frac{7}{9}$ of the area of the large square.

Thus, the area of the octagon = $\frac{7}{9}(4r^2) = \frac{28}{9}r^2 = (3.111...)r^2$, $\therefore A_\odot \approx (3.111...)r^2$

VIGNETTE 7.16 Like Mr. Barkin, Ms. Ramos conducts a lecture/discussion session in her class to develop an approximation for area of a circular region, as depicted in Figure 7.14. However, instead of turning her back to the class to illustrate points on the chalkboard, Ms. Ramos uses an overhead projector and transparencies she prepared before class. Thus, she is able to monitor the students' behavior throughout, and all students are able to see and copy the figures and notes on time.

There is much less off-task behavior than there was in Mr. Barkin's class. Ms. Ramos is able to see when students are finished writing before moving on and whose attention is drifting. Students who appear disengaged are immediately asked a question or hear their name used during the presentation. For example, "How many small squares do we have now, Nancy?" or "Okay, everyone quietly count the number of squares there are inside the circle—you too, Scott."

Unlike Mr. Barkin's students, who might be looking at or copying a figure while he talks about something else, Ms. Ramos's see only what she wants them to see, since she controls illustrations with a flip of a switch, placement of a transparency, or exposure of only part of a transparency.

VIGNETTE 7.17 Mr. Pettis also conducts a lecture/discussion session in his class to develop an approximation for the area of a circular region, as depicted in Figure 7.14. However, prior to the session, he videotaped his presentation, along with computer-generated illustrations. He shows the tape on a monitor in front of the room as he walks around with a wireless remote control monitoring students' note taking. At points he judges appropriate, he pauses the tape, raises questions for discussion, and inserts explanations as needed.

More than likely your school will equip your classroom with necessities such as an overhead projector and screen. Videotape players, monitors, and cameras probably need to be checked out of the media center. It is up to you to arrange your classroom to take full advantage of such equipment.

FIGURE 7.15
Mr. Haimowitz's Classroom When He Initially Saw It

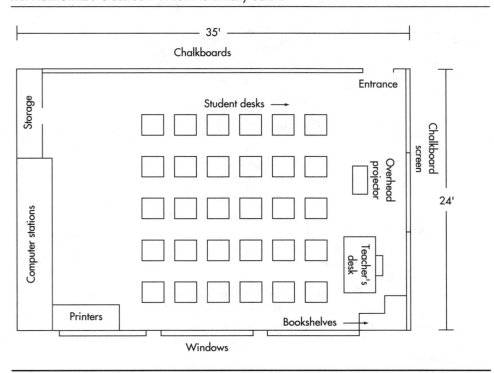

The Classroom Arrangements

Consider Mr. Haimowitz's concerns when he first saw the classroom depicted in Figure 7.15, to which he is assigned to spend a year conducting five mathematics classes each school day.

VIGNETTE 7.18 Surveying the room, Mr. Haimowitz thinks, "This just won't do. First, if I'm at one point in the room, I can't easily get to any one student's desk without negotiating an obstacle course and disturbing other students. If I'm up here explaining something in front of the class and a student in the middle of the fifth row gets off-task, I can't readily walk over to him or her without being a disturbance myself."

Mr. Haimowitz sits down and makes the following "wish list" of classroom features for facilitating his classroom-management style and the type of learning activities he plans to conduct:

1. Quick and easy access between any two points in the room.
2. An area for large-group lecture, discussion, questioning, and desk-work sessions in which students are seated at desks, from which they can view the chalkboard, overhead screen, and video display and listen to whomever has the floor.
3. Areas in which students engage in small-group cooperative learning activities, working on tasks, discussing mathematics, or tutoring one another.
4. Computer stations where students work independently.
5. Work tables for students to work alone, in pairs, or in triples on mathematical laboratory activities.
6. A traffic area for people entering and exiting the room that is easily monitored.
7. A room for Mr. Haimowitz to meet with individuals privately (e.g., to deal with a student's misbehavior away from the rest of the class).
8. A mini-library and quiet reading room for a few students at a time.
9. Cabinets and closets for securely storing equipment and supplies out of sight.
10. A secure teacher's desk at a favorable vantage point.
11. A "for-the-teacher-only" computer station interlinked with a display screen viewed in the large-group areas, students' computers, and printers.

FIGURE 7.16
Mr. Haimowitz's Classroom Set Up for Large-Group Sessions

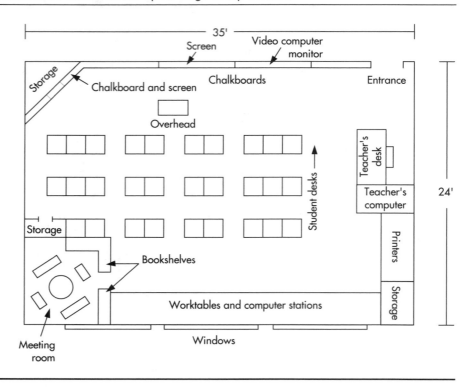

Mr. Haimowitz looks at his room (Figure 7.15) and his list and realizes all 11 features are impossible. But he determines to get the most from what he's been handed, so he takes measurements of the room and its equipment and, after making some scale drawings, designs a workable arrangement. Following a few visits to the school district storehouse, a little trading with a colleague, and some help from a custodian, Mr. Haimowitz begins the school year with the room arranged as indicated in Figure 7.16. To accommodate small-group sessions, students rearrange their desks according to Figure 7.17.

SUMMARY

The formal school curriculum is defined as all the planned experiences designed to educate students. In addition, you have learned of the differences between state-level curriculum, school-district curriculum, mathematics curriculum, and course curriculum. Because mathematics is so often misunderstood to be a linear sequence of skills to be mastered one at a time in a fixed order, many people think that teaching mathematics is a matter of following a prescribed curriculum guideline or adopted mathematics textbook. In this chapter, we have identified reasons why that is not the way it should be and why, to succeed as an effective mathematics teacher, you must be able to tailor your mathematics curriculum to fit the characteristics of your own unique classroom of students. You have learned of four approaches: the textbook approach, the contrived problem–solving approach, a real-world problem-solving approach, and a combination of these.

This chapter surveyed the mathematics curriculum that has evolved in recent years—specifically, the standards or outcomes expected and the content and methods that should be emphasized as well as those that should be deemphasized. In addition, the chapter has provided still more suggestions, sources, and resources for meeting your instructional needs in most effectively teaching mathematics to children in grades 4 through 9.

Chapters that follow in this part provide specific suggestions for teaching particular content.

QUESTIONS AND ACTIVITIES FOR DISCUSSION

1. If you can conveniently do so, examine either a state- or district-level mathematics curriculum guide. Select a list of topics that could conceivably be included in a teaching unit. Describe a unit encom-

FIGURE 7.17
Mr. Haimowitz's Classroom Set Up for Small-Group Sessions

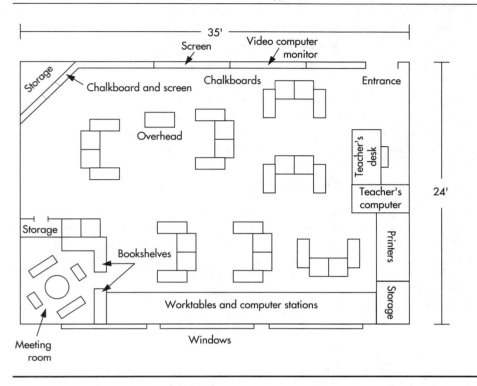

passing those topics as if it were designed solely for the purpose of teaching students mathematics to prepare them to learn more mathematics. Do the same, but this time describe the unit as if it were designed for the purpose of teaching students to apply mathematics to real-life situations. Compare your work on this question with someone else's, and discuss similarities and differences with them.

2. Following is a list of suggestions for mathematics curricula. Which of these suggestions are consistent with the NCTM *Standards?* Which are not?

   a. The distinction between geometry and algebra should be maintained throughout course-work in mathematics.

   b. Calculators may be used as a tool for executing an algorithm but only after students have mastered the algorithm using paper and pencil.

   c. Discrete mathematical problems should be integrated throughout the study of mathematics in grades 4 through 9.

   d. Students' abilities to estimate computational results should be afforded at least as much attention as their abilities to find exact numerical answers.

   e. Students should appeal to authoritative sources (e.g., people with more sophisticated understanding of mathematics than themselves) to validate their own hypotheses.

   f. Graphing should be taught along with other forms of expressing relationships (e.g., algebraic sentences and tables) rather than as a distinct topic.

   g. Euclidean geometry should be taught as a complete rational system separate from applied mathematics, which tends to distort its purity.

   h. Students need to read about, write about, and discuss mathematics as an integral part of everyday life.

   i. Students need to appreciate the rare geniuses who handed down the perfect mathematical systems we study today.

   j. Coordinate geometry should be included in the curriculum only after algebra and before calculus.

   k. Topics from probability and statistics should be emphasized in school mathematics more than they have been in the past.

l. Conceptual-level learning objectives are appropriate for students only after they have reached Piaget's formal-operation stage, somewhere between the ages of 11 and 15.

m. The use of determinants to solve systems of equations should be emphasized less than it has been in traditional curricula.

n. The use of scientific calculators is favored over calculations using tables.

o. Mathematical instruction should proceed in small linear increments to avoid student perplexity.

p. Students' invalid hypotheses should be immediately corrected.

q. Although it may complicate lessons, connections among related topics should be a paramount concern of instruction.

Compare your responses to this: Parts c, d, f, h, k, m, n, and q are consistent with the *Standards.* The others are not.

3. Examine a mathematics textbook for 4th-, 5th-, 6th-, 7th-, 8th-, or 9th-grade students. If the book was to be the primary text for a course you were to teach, to what degree would you follow the sequence of content and presentations in this book? How, if at all, would you deviate from it as you planned your teaching units? Explain the rationale for your decision. How does your response compare with those of others who completed this exercise?

4. Visit a 4th- through 9th-grade mathematics classroom. Which one of Mr. Haimowitz's 11 wish-list features are incorporated in the classroom as it is currently arranged? Make a diagram of the room. In a discussion with colleagues, compare the advantages and disadvantages of the arrangement depicted in your diagram to that in Figure 7.15 and to that in Figure 7.16.

REFERENCES

Aaboe, A. (1964). *Episodes from the early history of mathematics.* Washington, DC: The Mathematical Association of America.

Activity Resources Company: 1989. (1989). Haywood, CA: Activity Resources Co., Inc.

Allen, R. R., Davidson, T., Hering, W., & Jesunathadas, J. (1984). *A study of the conditions of secondary mathematics teacher education.* San Francisco: Far West Laboratory.

Artino, R. A., Gaglione, A. M., & Shell, N. (1983). *The contest problem book IV: Annual high school mathematics examinations 1973–1982.* Washington, DC: Mathematical Association of America.

Ashlock, R. B. (1990). *Error patterns in computation: A semiprogrammed approach* (5th ed.). Columbus, OH: Merrill.

Begle, E. G. (1958). The School Mathematics Study Group. *The Mathematics Teacher, 51,* 616–618.

Beskin, N. M. (1986). *Fascinating fractions.* Moscow, Russia: Mir Publishers.

Bowden, R. (1991). *Precision teaching in algebra.* Unpublished doctoral dissertation, Utah State University, Logan.

Bowers, J. (1988). *Invitation to mathematics.* Oxford, England: Basil Blackwell.

Brissenden, T. H. F. (1980). *Mathematics teaching: Theory in practice.* London, England: Harper & Row.

Brophy, J. (1986). Teaching and learning mathematics: Where research should be going. *Journal of Research in Mathematics Education, 17,* 323–346.

Brubaker, D. L. (1982). *Curriculum planning: The dynamics of theory and practice.* Glenview, IL: Scott, Foresman.

Brumfiel, V., Golden, N., & Heins, M. (1986). *Pre-algebra: Skills, problem solving, applications.* Orlando, FL: Harcourt Brace Jovanovich.

Bushaw, D., Bell, M., Pollack, H. O., Thompson, M., & Usiskin, Z. (1980). *A sourcebook of applications of school mathematics.* Reston, VA: NCTM.

Cajori, F. (1985). *A history of mathematics.* New York: Chelsea Publishing.

Cangelosi, J. S. (1985, October). *Problem-solving and school mathematics textbooks.* Invited paper presented at the annual Conference of the Utah Education Association, Salt Lake City, UT.

Cangelosi, J. S. (1988). *Classroom management strategies: Gaining and maintaining students' cooperation.* New York: Longman.

Cangelosi, J. S. (1990a). *Cooperation in the classroom: Students and teachers together* (2nd ed.). Washington, DC: National Education Association.

Cangelosi, J. S. (1990b). *Designing tests for evaluating student achievement.* New York: Longman.

Cangelosi, J. S. (1991). *Evaluating classroom instruction.* New York: Longman.

Carpenter, T. P., Lindquist, M. M., Brown, C. A., Kouba, V. L., Silver, E. A., & Swafford, J. O. (1988). Results of the fourth NAEP assessment of mathematics: Trends and conclusions. *Arithmetic Teacher, 36,* 38–43.

Chase, A., & Wolfe, P. (1989). Off to a good start in peer coaching. *Educational Leadership, 46,* 37.

Chrisco, I. M. (1989). Peer assistance works. *Educational Leadership, 46,* 31–32.

Collins, A. F. (1987). *Rapid math without a calculator.* Secaucus, NJ: Citadel Press.

Conference Board of the Mathematical Sciences. (1983a). *The mathematical sciences curriculum K–12: What is still fundamental and what is not.* Report to the National Science Board

Commission on Precollege Education in Mathematics, Sciences, and Technology. Washington, DC: Author.

Conference Board of the Mathematical Sciences. (1983b, November). *New goals for mathematical sciences education.* Report. Washington, DC: Author.

Court, N. A. (1961). *Mathematics in fun and earnest.* New York: Mentor Books.

Coxford, A. F., & Payne, J. N. (1987). *HBJ algebra* (rev. ed.). Orlando, FL: Harcourt Brace Jovanovich.

Devaney, R. L. (1990). *Chaos, fractals, and dynamics: Computer experiments in mathematics.* Menlo Park, CA: Addison-Wesley.

Dossey, J. A. (1987). National efforts in curricular reform take shape. *NCTM News Bulletin, 24*(2), 1.

Dossey, J. A., Mullis, I. V. S., Lindquist, M. M., & Chambers, D. L. (1988). *The mathematics report card: Are we measuring up? Trends and achievement based on the 1986 National Assessment.* Princeton, NJ: Educational Testing Service.

Dudeney, H. E. (1958). *Amusements in mathematics.* New York: Dover.

Duke, C. R., Cangelosi, J. S., & Knight, R. S. (1988, February). *The Mellon Project: A collaborative effort.* Colloquium presentation at the annual meeting of the American Association of Colleges for Teacher Education, New Orleans, LA.

Easterday, K. E., Henry, L. L., & Simpson, F. M. (Eds.). (1981). *Activities for junior high school and middle school mathematics: Readings from the Arithmetic Teacher and the Mathematics Teacher.* Reston, VA: NCTM.

Eisner, M. P. (1986). An application of quadratic equations to baseball. *Mathematics Teacher, 79,* 327–30.

Elich, J., & Cannon, L. O. (1989). *Precalculus.* Glenview, IL: Scott, Foresman.

Emphasize application of math skills. (1989). *Education USA, 31,* 218ff.

Eves, H. (1983a). *Great moments in mathematics after 1650.* Washington, DC: Mathematical Association of America.

Eves., H. (1983b). *Great moments in mathematics before 1650.* Washington, DC: Mathematical Association of America.

Frye, S. M. (1989a). The NCTM *Standards*—Challenges for all classrooms. *Arithmetic Teacher, 36,* 4–7.

Frye, S. M. (1989b). The NCTM *Standards*—Challenges for all classrooms. *Mathematics Teacher, 82,* 312–317.

Gardner, M. (1986). *The unexpected hanging and other mathematical diversions.* New York: Simon & Schuster.

Ginsburg, H. (1977). *Children's arithmetic: The learning process.* New York: D. Van Nostrand.

Gnanadesikan, M., Landwehr, J. M., Newman, C. M., Obremski, T. E., Scheaffer, R. L., Swift, J., & Watkins, A. E. (1986). *Quantitative literacy series.* Palo Alto, CA: Seymour.

Hirsch, C. R. (Ed.). (1986). *Activities for implementing curricular themes from the Agenda for Action.* Reston, VA: NCTM.

Hirsch, C. R., & Zweng, M. J. (1985). *The secondary school mathematics curriculum: 1985 yearbook.* Reston, VA: National Council of Teachers of Mathematics.

Hoffman, P. (1988). *Archimedes' revenge: The joys and perils of mathematics.* New York: Fawcett Crest.

Holden, C. (1989). Big changes urged for precollege math. *Science, 243,* 1655.

Honsberger, R. (1973). *Mathematical gems I.* Washington, DC: Mathematical Association of America.

Honsberger, R. (1976). *Mathematical gems II.* Washington, DC: Mathematics Association of America.

Honsberger, R. (Ed.). (1979). *Mathematical plums.* Washington, DC: Mathematical Association of America.

Hunkins, F. P. (1989). *Teaching thinking through effective questioning.* Boston: Christopher-Gordon Publishers.

James, W. (1890). *The principles of psychology,* Vol I and II. New York: Holt, Rinehart and Winston.

Jesunathadas, J. (1990). *Mathematics teachers' instructional activities as a function of academic preparation.* Unpublished doctoral dissertation, Utah State University, Logan.

Johnson, D. R. (1982). *Every minute counts: Making your math class work.* Palo Alto, CA: Seymour.

Johnson, D. R. (1986). *Making every minute count even more: A sequel to every minute counts.* Palo Alto, CA: Seymour.

Kansky, B. (1986). Utilizing appropriate technology in the learning and teaching of mathematics. In R. Lodholz (Ed.), *A change in emphasis: Mathematics for the transition years, grades 7 & 8.* St. Louis, MO: Monsanto Corporation and Parkway School District.

Karush, W. (1989). *Webster's new world dictionary of mathematics.* New York: Simon & Schuster.

Kasner, E., & Newman, J. R. (1989). *Mathematics and the imagination.* Redmond, WA: Tempus Books.

Keedy, M. L., Bittinger, M. L., Smith, S. A., & Orfan, L. J. (1986). *Algebra.* Menlo Park, CA: Addison-Wesley.

Kinney, L. B., & Purdy, C. R. (1952). *Teaching mathematics in the secondary schools.* New York: Holt, Rinehart and Winston.

Kogelman, S., & Heller, B. R. (1986). *The only math book you'll ever need.* New York: Dell Books.

Krulik, S., & Reys, R. E. (Eds.). (1980). *Problem solving in school mathematics: 1980 yearbook.* Reston, VA: NCTM.

Merriam-Webster Inc. (1986). *Webster's Third New International Dictionary.* Chicago: Author.

National Council of Teachers of Mathematics. (1940). *Fifteenth yearbook: The place of mathematics in general education.* New York: Teachers College, Columbia University.

National Council of Teachers of Mathematics (1969). *Historical topics for the mathematics classroom: Thirty-first yearbook.* Reston, VA: Author.

National Council of Teachers of Mathematics. (1980). *An agenda for action: Recommendations for school mathematics of the 1980s.* Reston, VA: Author.

National Council of Teachers of Mathematics. (1989). *Curriculum and evaluation standards for school mathematics.* Reston, VA: Author.

National Science Board Commission on Precollege Education in Mathematics, Science, and Education. (1983). *Educating Americans for the twenty-first century: A plan for action for improving the mathematics, science, and technology education for all American elementary and secondary students so that their achievement is the best in the world by 1995.* Washington, DC: National Science Foundation.

Nelson, D., & Reys, R. E. (Eds.). (1976). *Measurement in school mathematics: 1976 yearbook.* Reston, VA: NCTM.

Nielsen, K. L. (1962). *Mathematics for practical use.* New York: Barnes & Noble.

Niven, I. (1961). *Numbers: Rational and irrational.* Washington, DC: Mathematical Association of America.

Niven, I. (1965). *Mathematics of choice: How to count without counting.* Washington, DC: Mathematical Association of America.

Niven, I. (1981). *Maxima and minima without calculus.* Washington, DC: Mathematical Association of America.

Packel, E. (1981). *The mathematics of games and gambling.* Washington, DC: Mathematical Association of America.

Péter, R. (1961). *Playing with infinity: Mathematical explorations and excursions.* New York: Dover.

Peterson, I. (1988). *The mathematical tourist: Snapshots of modern mathematics.* New York: W. H. Freeman.

Pòlya, G. (1977). *Mathematical methods in science.* Washington, DC: Mathematical Association of America.

Pòlya, G. (1985). *How to solve it: A new aspect of mathematical method* (2nd ed.). Princeton, NJ: Princeton University Press.

Posamentier, A. S., & Stepelman, J. (1990). *Teaching secondary school mathematics: Techniques and enrichment units* (3rd ed.). Columbus, OH: Merrill.

Raney, P., & Robbins, P. (1989). Professional growth and support through peer coaching. *Educational Leadership, 46,* 35–38.

Salkind, C. T., & Earl, J. M. (1973). *The contest problem book III: Annual high school contests 1966–1972.* Washington, DC: Mathematical Association of America.

Santrock, J. W. (1984). *Adolescence* (2nd ed.). Dubuque, IA: W. C. Brown.

Saunders, H. (1981). *When are we ever gonna have to use this?* Palo Alto, CA: Seymour.

Schiffer, N. M., & Bowden, L. (1984). *The role of mathematics in science.* Washington, DC: Mathematical Association of America.

Schoenfeld, A. H. (1985). *Mathematical problem solving.* San Diego, CA: Academic Press.

Schoenfeld, A. H. (1989). Teaching mathematical thinking and problem solving. In L. B. Resnick & L. E. Klopfer (Eds.), *Toward the thinking curriculum: Current cognitive research: 1989 Yearbook of the Association for Supervision and Curriculum Development* (pp. 83–103). Alexandria, VA: ASCD.

Shapiro, M. S. (Ed.). (1977). *Mathematics encyclopedia.* Garden City, NY: Doubleday.

Sharron, S., & Reys, R. E. (Eds.). *Applications in school mathematics: 1979 yearbook.* Reston, VA: NCTM.

Skemp, R. R. (1973). *The psychology of learning mathematics.* Middlesex, England: Penguin Books.

Sobel, M. A., & Maletsky, E. M. (1988). *Teaching mathematics: A sourcebook of aids, activities, and strategies.* (2nd ed.). Englewood Cliffs, NJ: Prentice Hall.

Souviney, R. J. (1981). *Solving problems kids care about.* Santa Monica, CA: Goodyear Publishing.

Stallion, B. K. (1988, April). *Classroom management intervention: The effects of mentoring relationships on the inductee teacher's behavior.* Paper presented at the annual meeting of the American Educational Research Association, New Orleans, LA.

Steen, L. A. (1987). Mathematics education: A predictor of scientific competitiveness. *Science, 237,* 251ff.

Steen, L. A. (1988). Out from underachievement. *Issues in Science and Technology, 10,* 88–93.

Strom, R. D. (1969). *Psychology for the classroom.* Englewood Cliffs, NJ: Prentice Hall.

Thorndike, E. L., & Woodworth, R. S. (1901). The influence of improvement in one mental function upon the efficacy of other functions. *Psychological Review, 8,* 247–256.

U.S. students again rank near bottom in math and science. (1989). *Report on Educational Research, 23*(2), 1–4.

U.S. teens lag behind in math, science. (1989). *Education USA, 31,* 161+.

Use new standards to upgrade math. (1989). *Education USA, 31,* 153+.

Usiskin, Z. (1985). We need another revolution in secondary school mathematics. In C. R. Hirsch & M. J. Zweng (Eds.), *The secondary school mathematics curriculum: 1985 Yearbook.* Reston, VA: National Council of Teachers of Mathematics.

Yaglom, I. M. (1978). *An unusual algebra.* Moscow, Russia: Mir Publishers.

Zippin, L. (1975). *Uses of infinity.* Washington, DC: Mathematical Association of America.

Zumwalt, K. (1989). Beginning professional teachers: The need for a curricular vision of teaching. In M. C. Reynolds (Ed.), *Knowledge base for the beginning teacher* (pp. 173–184). Oxford, England: Pergamon Press.

SUGGESTED READINGS

Artzt, A. F. (February 1994). Integrating writing and cooperative learning in the mathematics class. *Mathematics Teacher 87*(2), 80–85.

Biggerstaff, M. (February 1994). Teacher to teacher: Use color to assess mathematics problem solving. *Arithmetic Teacher 41*(6), 307–308.

Dever, M. T. (March 1994). Dever, M. T. Multiage classrooms: A new way to learn math. *Principal 73*(4), 22, 24, 26.

Farivar, S. H., & Webb, N. M. (January 1994). Are your students prepared for group work? *Middle School Journal 25*(3), 29–30.

Klemp, R. (February 1994). The math museum. *Instructor 103*(6), 49.

McNamara, J. (Winter 1994). Montessori mathematics: A model curriculum for the twenty-first century. *National Arts Trade Association Journal 19*(1), 3–9.

Nattiv, A. (January 1994). Helping behaviors and math achievement gains of students using cooperative learning. *Elementary School Journal 94*(3), 285–297.

Williams, S. E., & Copley, J. V. (April 1994). Promoting classroom dialogue: Using calculators to discover patterns in dividing decimals. *Mathematics Teaching in the Middle Schools 1*(1), 72–75.

Wood, K. D., & Jones, Jeanneine P. (January 1994). Integrating collaborative learning across the curriculum. *Middle School Journal 25*(3), 19–23.

CHAPTER 8

The Multiplication and Division of Whole Numbers

This chapter focuses your attention on how to teach the multiplication and division of whole numbers. Specifically, it is designed to help you understand

1. Developmental concepts associated with the meaningful understanding of multiplication and division.
2. Models and properties of multiplication and division, and classroom activities used to introduce these concepts.
3. Mental arithmetic and techniques to help students memorize the times table.
4. Instructional materials that can be used to introduce the multiplication and division algorithms.
5. Techniques for incorporating technology into multiplication and division lessons.
6. Alternative assessment techniques for mathematics instruction.
7. Techniques for accommodating special-needs students in multiplication and division lessons.

NCTM whole-number operations standards
K–4 level students will

- Develop meaning for the operations by modeling and discussing a rich variety of problem situations
- Relate the mathematical language and symbolism of operations to problem situations and informal language
- Recognize that a wide variety of problem structures can be represented by a single operation
- Develop operation sense
- Apply estimation in working with quantities, measurement, computation, and problem solving
- Model, explain, and develop reasonable proficiency with basic facts and algorithms
- Use a variety of mental computation and estimation techniques
- Use calculators in appropriate computational situations
- Select and use computation techniques appropriate to specific problems and determine whether the results are reasonable.

5–8 level students will

- Compute with whole numbers
- Develop, analyze, and explain procedures for computation and techniques for estimation
- Develop, analyze, and explain methods for solving proportions
- Select and use an appropriate method for computing from among mental arithmetic, paper-and-pencil, calculator, and computer methods
- Use estimation to check the reasonableness of results (NCTM, 1989, pp. 36, 41, 44, 94).

 I WAS JUST THINKING . . .

"Blood is thicker than water." "Climbing mountains was her life's blood." "Blood must be spilled to win a war." Just how much of this vital fluid is available for spilling? Estimate the size of a container needed to hold all the human blood in the world.

Teaching multiplication and division of whole numbers follows an instructional hierarchy that includes early counting experiences, concept development, the memorization of basic facts, and work with algorithms. An example of one possible instructional hierarchy for multiplication and division is shown in Figures 8.1a and b. Reference to an instructional hierarchy can help teachers organize activities into effective lesson sequences.

Children are introduced to informal multiplication and division situations in the early primary grades. Formal work generally begins in grade 2 or 3 for multiplication and grade 3 for division; instruction can extend through grade 6 for more complex exercises.

A. INTRODUCING THE MULTIPLICATION CONCEPT

There are three common models of multiplication. Each represents a different type of multiplication situation found in real-world situations:

1. *repeated addition* multiplication
2. *Cartesian product* multiplication
3. *array* multiplication.

Repeated Addition Multiplication

Children's early experiences with multiplication often begin with skip counting. For example, children learn to skip count by twos when counting shoes, socks, or mittens; by threes when counting the utensils (knives, forks, and spoons) to set the table or the wheels on a group of tricycles; by fours when counting the number of horseshoes in a horse race

---

➥ Answer to   I WAS JUST THINKING . . .

The total population of the world was estimated at 5,333,000,000 in 1990. The average amount of blood per adult is about 4.5 liters, or a little more than a gallon. Thus, about 24,000,000,000 liters of human blood exist in the world. Since there are 1,000 liters in one cubic meter, there are about 24,000,000 cubic meters of blood. The dimension of a cube that would hold this amount of fluid is $\sqrt[3]{24,000,000} \approx 290$ meters on an edge, or the capacity of only about five super tankers. To simplify the solution to this problem, the entire world population was assumed to be adults. Since about one-fourth of the world's population is children under the age of 12, the actual size of the required container would be somewhat smaller. It is surprising how little of this precious fluid there is in the world.

FIGURE 8.1
Instructional
Hierarchies

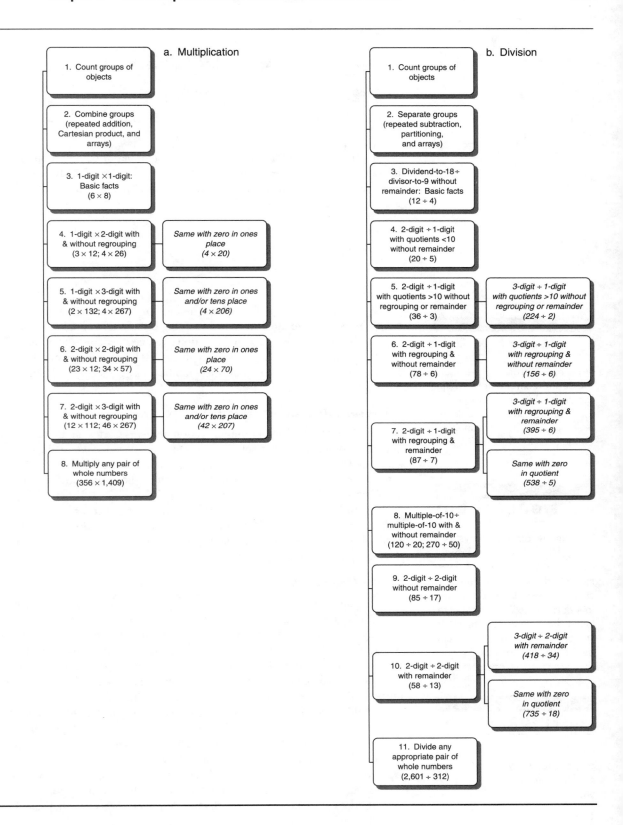

a. Multiplication

1. Count groups of objects

2. Combine groups (repeated addition, Cartesian product, and arrays)

3. 1-digit ×1-digit: Basic facts (6 × 8)

4. 1-digit ×2-digit with & without regrouping (3 × 12; 4 × 26)
— *Same with zero in ones place (4 × 20)*

5. 1-digit ×3-digit with & without regrouping (2 × 132; 4 × 267)
— *Same with zero in ones and/or tens place (4 × 206)*

6. 2-digit × 2-digit with & without regrouping (23 × 12; 34 × 57)
— *Same with zero in ones place (24 × 70)*

7. 2-digit ×3-digit with & without regrouping (12 × 112; 46 × 267)
— *Same with zero in ones and/or tens place (42 × 207)*

8. Multiply any pair of whole numbers (356 × 1,409)

b. Division

1. Count groups of objects

2. Separate groups (repeated subtraction, partitioning, and arrays)

3. Dividend-to-18÷ divisor-to-9 without remainder: Basic facts (12 ÷ 4)

4. 2-digit ÷ 1-digit with quotients <10 without remainder (20 ÷ 5)

5. 2-digit ÷ 1-digit with quotients >10 without regrouping or remainder (36 ÷ 3)
— *3-digit ÷ 1-digit with quotients >10 without regrouping or remainder (224 ÷ 2)*

6. 2-digit ÷ 1-digit with regrouping & without remainder (78 ÷ 6)
— *3-digit ÷ 1-digit with regrouping & without remainder (156 ÷ 6)*

7. 2-digit ÷ 1-digit with regrouping & remainder (87 ÷ 7)
— *3-digit ÷ 1-digit with regrouping & remainder (395 ÷ 6)*
— *Same with zero in quotient (538 ÷ 5)*

8. Multiple-of-10÷ multiple-of-10 with & without remainder (120 ÷ 20; 270 ÷ 50)

9. 2-digit ÷ 2-digit without remainder (85 ÷ 17)

10. 2-digit ÷ 2-digit with remainder (58 ÷ 13)
— *3-digit ÷ 2-digit with remainder (418 ÷ 34)*
— *Same with zero in quotient (735 ÷ 18)*

11. Divide any appropriate pair of whole numbers (2,601 ÷ 312)

or the tires on cars in a parking lot; and by fives when counting fingers and toes in a classroom or the amount of money in a stack of nickels. Skip counting is a handy way to determine the total number of objects in several identical groups (see Figure 8.2).

Adding a column of identical values is called *repeated addition*. Once these special sums are memorized, children no longer need to skip count or calculate to determine the solution.

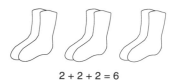

$$2 + 2 + 2 = 6$$

FIGURE 8.2
Skip Counting Pairs of Socks

TABLE 8.1
Cartesian Product

CHILD	WAYS TO WEAR T-SHIRTS					
Sarah	R	R	G	G	B	B
Rebecca	G	B	R	B	R	G

To multiply, then, children need to know the number of equal groupings (e.g., three pairs of socks) and the number in each group (two in each pair). The formal terms for these values—multiplier (first factor), multiplicand (second factor), and product (answer)—are typically introduced in grade 3.

Repeated Addition	*Multiplication*
$2 + 2 = 4$	$\rightarrow 2 \times 2 = 4$
$2 + 2 + 2 = 6$	$\rightarrow 3 \times 2 = 6$
$2 + 2 + 2 + 2 = 8$	$\rightarrow 4 \times 2 = 8$

Simple multiplication, then, can be thought of as the memorized sums of repeated addition exercises. There are 100 sums involving 0 through 9 equal groups, each containing 0 through 9 objects. These repeated addition exercises generate the basic multiplication facts 0×0 through 9×9. Normally, only these 100 basic facts involving single-digit factors are memorized in school. Products for numbers larger than 9 can be calculated using these basic facts.

Cartesian Product Multiplication

A second way to think about multiplication involves Cartesian products. A Cartesian product refers to the number of combinations that can be made using objects from two or more sets. For example, as shown in Table 8.1, if two children (Sarah and Rebecca) each have three T-shirts—one red, one green, and one blue—how many different ways can they wear the three shirts?

If Sarah wears the red shirt, Rebecca can select either a green or blue one. Similarly, Rebecca has two choices if Sarah wears the green or blue shirt. A total of six different combinations are possible. We can find the answer to this combination problem by calculating the multiplication exercise $2 \times 3 = 6$.

Array Multiplication

To show products of larger values efficiently, you can introduce an alternate display of repeated addition. Instead of placing each addend in a separate group, you can place objects into an array—a systematic arrangement of objects with equal rows and columns (see Figure 8.3).

Arrays made from squared paper can be used to display multiplication problems. The factors are the length and width of a rectangle, and the product is the area (see Figure 8.4).

A distinct advantage of array displays becomes apparent when double-digit factors are introduced. Children can take advantage of the structure of base-10 materials to separate large multiplication exercises into more manageable chunks. The manipulations and display correspond directly to the multiplication algorithm. For example, the exercise $6 \times 14 = 84$ is displayed as an array in Figure 8.5a. The factors are positioned outside the vertical and horizontal axes, and the product is displayed as a rectangular array inside. Problems involving two double-digit factors also can be displayed using an array (see Figure 8.5b).

Products larger than 999 are more difficult to display using concrete materials. By the time children are asked to work with larger products, however, they should be proficient in using the symbolic algorithm.

Reversibility

Just as subtraction *undoes* addition, division is the inverse of multiplication. Generally, it is more efficient to introduce an operation and its inverse simultaneously.

8.1

✎ **FIGURE IT OUT**

How many products are there for all the combinations of single-digit and double-digit factors? Do you think it would be useful to memorize the multiplication facts to 99×99? Why?

8.2

✎ **FIGURE IT OUT**

How many different ways can three children wear two T-shirts? Make a table to find out. How many different ways can two children wear three shirts and four hats? Try to find a pattern relating the number of objects in two or more groups with the number of resulting combinations.

8.3

✎ **FIGURE IT OUT**

Using centimeter-squared paper, cut out arrays representing the following multiplication exercises.

1. $4 \times 6 = ?$
2. $3 \times 3 = ?$
3. $5 \times 8 = ?$
4. $8 \times 5 = ?$
5. $7 \times 1 = ?$

FIGURE 8.3
Sock Array

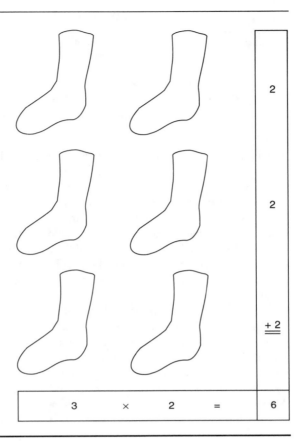

FIGURE 8.4
Squared-Paper Array

$3 \times 2 = 6$

FIGURE 8.5
Base-10 Array

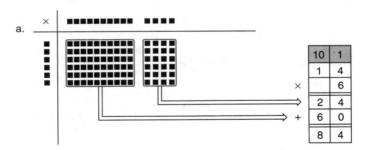

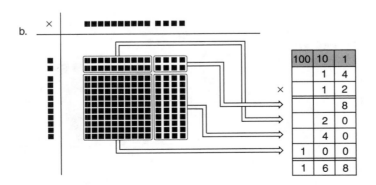

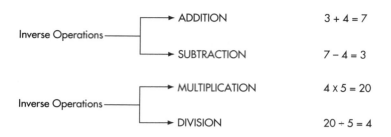

The ability to mentally reverse operations enables children to use their knowledge of addition and multiplication to develop a rational understanding of subtraction and division.

Piaget observed that the transitive relationship, or the concept of multiequivalence, is an important factor in the development of a meaningful understanding of multiplication and division. Transitivity involves the transfer of a relationship from one situation to another. For example, suppose a child is asked to remove all the eggs from a standard carton and place them in a bowl, then refill the carton from another supply, and subsequently put these eggs on a plate. A child who recognizes, without having to recount, that the bowl and plate now contain an equal number of eggs understands the notion of transitivity (see Figure 8.6).

Multiequivalence is an extension of the conservation of number concept. An understanding of multiequivalence requires students to coordinate the transformation of *more* than two equal groups at a time. This concept forms a basis for the rational understanding of multiplication and division. For example, if 80 pennies are systematically counted out into 10 stacks of equal height, a child who understands transitivity can count the pennies in one stack and be confident that the others contain the same amount. Also, the mental ability to reverse the process is an important factor in assuring the child that the total number of distributed objects, plus any remainder, is equal to the initial amount.

Children who have not attained transitivity and reversibility generally find it helpful to use base-10 materials to model multiplication and division concepts and algorithms. In fact, research shows that the premature introduction of symbolic algorithms divorced from manipulative models may be a primary cause in the development of children's systematic arithmetic errors (Ashlock, 1976; Driscoll, 1980).

The Properties of Multiplication

Several properties of multiplication are introduced at the elementary level. The *commutative property* ($3 \times 4 = 4 \times 3$) can be observed in the array display of multiplication. Reversing the factors reorients the display but does not alter the product (see Figure 8.7). In the section on learning the multiplication facts, the commutative property is used to substantially reduce the number of facts that must be memorized.

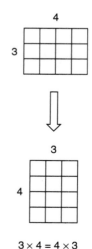

FIGURE 8.7
Commutative Arrays

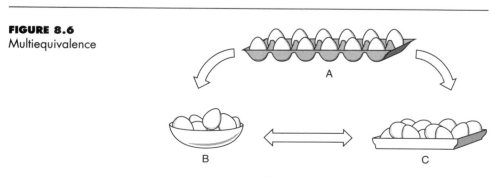

FIGURE 8.6
Multiequivalence

$A = B$ and $A = C$, therefore $B = C$

The *associative property* for multiplication is introduced when more than two factors are multiplied. This property is demonstrated in Figure 8.8, where the rectangular construction has a 3-cube × 3-cube base and is 4 cubes tall. The total number of cubes is $(3 \times 3) \times 4 = 36$. If a rectangular prism is constructed with a 3×4 base and a height of 3 cubes, there would still be a total of 36 cubes: $3 \times (3 \times 4) = 36$. Regardless of the order of the factors, the product remains the same.

The associative property also can be used as a strategy for mentally calculating products of some groups of three or more values. For example, $6 \times 5 \times 5 = 6 \times 25 = 150$; or, $23 \times 2 \times 50 = 23 \times 100 = 2,300$.

The *distributive property of multiplication over addition* means that multiplying a number by the sum of any two values gives the same result as multiplying the number by each of the two values and adding the products: $5 \times (4 + 3) = (5 \times 4) + (5 \times 3)$. The distributive property allows children to use number facts they have already memorized to find the products of larger numbers. For example, the exercise 4×12 can be restated as:

$$4 \times 12 = 4 \times (6 + 6) = (4 \times 6) + (4 \times 6) = 24 + 24 = 48$$

Children can verify the distributive property using arrays. First, they can display the exercise as shown in Figure 8.9a. Next, they can group the second factor as shown in Figure 8.9b and construct the two 4×6 arrays. Other groupings, such as $(4 \times 2) + (4 \times 10)$, also would be possible. The product is written below each array and the sum computed. Children then compare the two arrays side-by-side to verify that the answer remains the same.

The *identity element* for multiplication is 1 ($1 \times n = n$). Have children use arrays to show that any whole number multiplied by one gives a product equal to the original number. Also, arrays can be used to show that any whole number multiplied by zero equals zero. For example, 0×4 gives an array containing no items.

B. INTRODUCING THE DIVISION CONCEPT

There are three common models of division:

1. *repeated subtraction* division
2. *partitive* division
3. *array* division.

Repeated Subtraction Division

Measurement, or *repeated subtraction,* division is the inverse of repeated addition multiplication. For example, suppose a family has 18 ears of corn. If each person can eat 3 ears, how many people will the corn feed? See Figure 8.10. Distributing ears of corn in groups of three and counting the number of groups can be recorded using the following algorithm.

(3 × 3) × 4 = 36

FIGURE 8.8
Associative Property

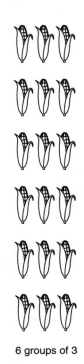

6 groups of 3

FIGURE 8.10
Division Using Repeated Subtraction

FIGURE 8.9
Multiplication Using Distributive Property

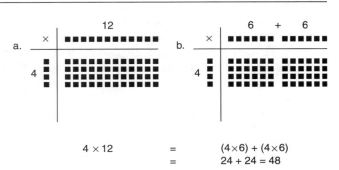

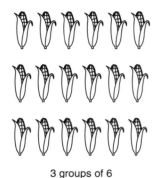

3 groups of 6

FIGURE 8.11
Division Using Partitioning

Division as Repeated Subtraction

Number in each group ⟶

$$
\begin{array}{r}
3\overline{)18} \\
-\ 3 \quad 1 \\
\hline
15 \\
-\ 3 \quad 1 \\
\hline
12 \\
-\ 3 \quad 1 \\
\hline
9 \\
-\ 3 \quad 1 \\
\hline
6 \\
-\ 3 \quad 1 \\
\hline
3 \\
-\ 3 \quad 1 \\
\hline
0 \quad 6 \\
\end{array}
$$

Remainder ⟶   0   6   ⟵ Number of groups

Partitive Division

A second way to think about division involves *partitioning* a set into a given number of equal groups and counting the number of objects in each group. For example, to share 18 ears of corn (3 ears each), children partition the ears into 3 equal piles (each person gets one ear from each pile) and count the number in each group to see how many people can be fed (see Figure 8.11).

The distributing and counting procedure can be recorded using the standard division algorithm.

Partitive Division

⟵Number in each group

Number of groups →

⟵Remainder

Array Division

Introducing the array representation facilitates the coordination of the repeated-subtraction and partitive views of division. Using the organizing mat shown in Figure 8.12a, the division exercise is set up with the divisor (the number of groups or items in each group) along the vertical axis and the dividend (the number of objects to be distributed) inside. The quotient (the number of objects in each group or the number of groups) is displayed above the completed array. These formal terms for the three values in a division exercise are typically introduced in grade 4. The division task is to organize the dividend of 18 into an array with 3 equal rows. Using repeated subtraction, you can systematically count out objects one at a time to each row, making sure all three remain equal in length. When there are not enough objects remaining to distribute and keep the three rows equal, stop. The length of the rows gives the quotient, or number of 3s contained in 18 (see Figure 8.12b,c).

Partitioning offers a more efficient procedure for constructing the division array when large dividends are involved, and facilitates the development of the standard symbolic algorithm. To use partitioning as a division method, children first estimate the number of items that can be distributed equally among the groups, then check to see if enough objects are available in the dividend to distribute. For example, Figure 8.13a shows that for 18 objects, an estimated 5 objects can be equally distributed among the three groups. This first estimate leaves a remainder of 3. As shown in Figure 8.13b, distributing these 3 objects gives the final quotient of 6.

Children can also demonstrate the special role in division of the identity value one. Any number divided by one gives a quotient equal to the original value (see Figure 8.14). Also, any number divided by itself equals one.

8.4

✎ FIGURE IT OUT

Using counters, construct arrays that show the partitioning solution for each of the following division exercises.

1. $2\overline{)8}$ 4. $8\overline{)32}$ 7. $1\overline{)8}$
2. $3\overline{)12}$ 5. $7\overline{)35}$ 8. $1\overline{)12}$
3. $5\overline{)25}$ 6. $6\overline{)36}$ 9. $8\overline{)8}$

FIGURE 8.12
Repeated Subtraction
Division

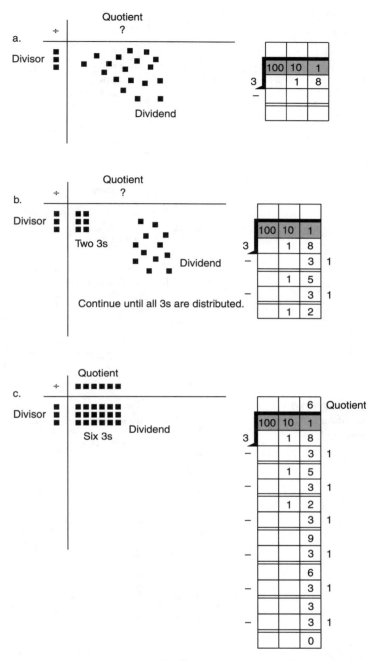

Language

Several English words are commonly used to specify the multiplication and division operations. Most phrases that suggest multiplication can be transcribed symbolically as they are read from left to right. For example:

- I'll take six *of* those cartons of eggs (6 × 12 = 72).
- Take two *of* the six-packs (2 × 6 = 12).
- Find six *times* eight (6 × 8 = 48).
- *Multiply* three and four (3 × 4 = 12).
- Find the *product* of six and seven (6 × 7 = 42).

FIGURE 8.13
Division Using Partitioning

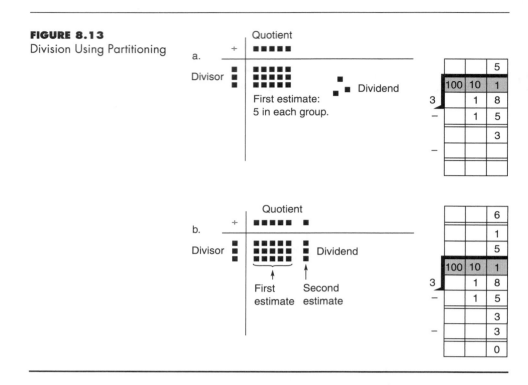

FIGURE 8.14
Dividing by One and
Identity Property

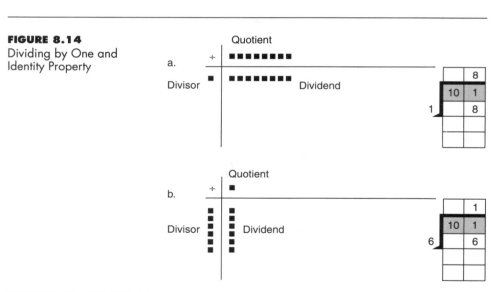

8.5
✎ FIGURE IT OUT

Write a story or draw a picture of a situation representing each of the three models of multiplication: repeated addition, Cartesian products, and arrays. Exchange the problems with a partner and write the type of multiplication model represented next to each problem.

Because multiplication can be thought of as a special kind of addition, phrases that imply summing identical addends can also be interpreted as multiplication. For example:

If three people each have six shells, how many do they have altogether? $(3 \times 6 = 18)$

Because multiplication can be represented by an array, phrases that describe the counting of items displayed in equal rows and columns can refer to multiplication as well. For example:

Find the area of a rectangle four meters by five meters. $(4 \times 5 = 20)$

Finally, Cartesian products introduce additional phrases that signal a multiplication operation:

If a fast-food restaurant offers four kinds of burgers and three drinks, *how many different* meals are possible? ($4 \times 3 = 12$).

When translating story problems involving division, it is important that children have experience identifying examples of the different models of division in real-world situations. For example:

- *Repeated subtraction.* How many *students* will be able to share 40 pencils if each receives 10 pencils?

$$10\overline{)40} \begin{array}{l} 4 \\ \end{array} \quad students$$

- *Partitive.* If there are 10 students, how many *pencils* will each receive if 40 pencils are equally shared?

$$10\overline{)40} \begin{array}{l} 4 \\ \end{array} \quad pencils$$

- *Arrays.* Using a bag of 400 seeds, how many rows of corn can be planted if each row contains 25 seeds?

$$25\overline{)400} \begin{array}{l} 16 \\ \end{array}$$

The first example seeks the number of students, while the second asks for the number of pencils. Both examples imply that division should be used to solve the problem. The third problem shows how arrays also can be used to solve division problems (note that an array could be used to solve the first two problems as well).

Reading division exercises, like subtraction exercises, can be confusing at first because English provides both left-to-right and right-to-left interpretations. For example, if 3 is the divisor and 12 the dividend, the description can read:

- *Left to right.* How many threes are *in* twelve? $3\overline{)12}$
- *Right to left.* Twelve divided *by* three: ($12 \div 3$)

Students often confuse the dividend with the divisor, particularly when the dividend is smaller than the divisor (e.g., $2 \div 4 = 1/2$, or 0.5). When introducing division, teachers may reduce initial confusion by consistently using the left-to-right description. The right-to-left description can be introduced later in the context of rational numbers and ratio.

Depending on the context, some of the words and phrases generally used to specify multiplication or division can also imply another operation. For example, the word *of,* which was used previously to specify multiplication, can also imply subtraction, as in "I want five *of* your ten cookies." Children need practice interpreting a variety of multiplication and division statements to help them learn to translate English story problems into mathematics exercises.

C. RECALLING THE MULTIPLICATION AND DIVISION FACTS
The Multiplication Facts

Before memorizing the 100 basic facts, children need to possess a meaningful understanding of the multiplication operation and be able to recognize the multiplication operation in various real-world situations.

Memorization of the multiplication table generally begins in grade 2 or 3. While many children have mastered the basic facts by the end of grade 4, some may take longer. It is a formidable task for many children, even when the teacher provides alternative drill activities and memory aids.

Despite the teacher's and students' efforts, some children may not memorize the entire table by the end of grade 6. The introduction of important topics in mathematics such as problem solving, geometry, graphing , statistics, and probability should not be delayed if a student lacks perfect mastery of the basic facts. Regular use of a multiplication table or a calculator may be called for with children in grades 6–8 who cannot quickly recall the basic facts. Such tools can help special-needs children participate more effectively in the full range of mathematics instruction during the middle school years and beyond.

Two-Entry Multiplication Table

In general, it is an inefficient use of time for students to approach the task of learning the multiplication facts by sequentially memorizing the entire two-entry multiplication table (see Figure 8.15). Children can employ general rules and patterns to minimize the long-term memory requirements (Brownell & Carper, 1943; Williams, 1971).

For example, since zero times any value equals zero, the nineteen zero facts ($0 \times n$ or $n \times 0$) do not have to be memorized. Children generally work with 0 factors and quickly apply the multiplication-by-zero rule ($0 \times n = 0$). Eliminating the zero facts leaves 81 multiplication facts to memorize.

The *commutative property* allows children to reduce the number of these facts they must commit to memory. Knowing that $6 \times 8 = 48$ obviates the need to also memorize $8 \times 6 = 48$. Eliminating the commuted pairs, only 45 multiplication facts remain.

Finally, using the identity rule that the product of one and any number n is n, children can apply this rule rather than memorizing the 9 remaining "one facts." This leaves only 36 basic facts to commit to memory.

Of these remaining facts, the two facts, five facts, and double facts are easiest for children to recall: the two facts because it is possible to quickly use skip counting or repeated addition to find the product ($2 \times 8 = 8 + 8 = 16$); the five facts because it is easy to skip count by fives (the product always ends in 0 or 5); and the double facts because the identical factors place less demand on the working memory.

Once students demonstrate the ability to recall, or quickly compute, the 21 easy two, five, and double facts, only the 15 hard multiplication facts that are circled in Figure 8.15 must actually be memorized (3×4; 3×6; 3×7; 3×8; 3×9; 4×6; 4×7; 4×8; 4×9; 6×7; 6×8; 6×9; 7×8; 7×9; 8×9). These must be memorized by using a combination of mnemonics, rhymes, patterns, and drills.

FIGURE 8.15
Multiplication Table

×	1	2	3	4	5	6	7	8	9
1	1	2	3	4	5	6	7	8	9
2	2	4	6	8	10	12	14	16	18
3	3	6	9	12	15	18	21	24	27
4	4	8	(12)	16	20	24	28	32	36
5	5	10	15	20	25	30	35	40	45
6	6	12	(18)	(24)	30	36	42	48	54
7	7	14	(21)	(28)	35	(42)	49	56	63
8	8	16	(24)	(32)	40	(48)	(56)	64	72
9	9	18	(27)	(36)	45	(54)	(63)	(72)	81

Children can develop their own rhymes (e.g., "Six times 8 is 48") to help them remember elusive facts. Patterns can be used to help confirm a product. For example, several patterns can be found in the nine facts shown in Table 8.2. An interesting story about one pattern involves a fellow named Gus who always had trouble with his nine facts. He knew that $1 \times 9 = 9$ but could not remember the rest. In desperation on a test, he carefully counted the number of exercises he was sure he would miss. Starting at the bottom, he wrote the digits 1 through 8 as he counted up to his one right answer, $1 \times 9 = 9$. Still frustrated, he counted the wrong items again by writing the digits 1 through 8 from the top down. He was greatly surprised when his test paper came back with a score of 100 percent!

Another nine-fact pattern involves the sum of the digits of the *products*. Notice that adding the digits in the products always gives the answer 9 (e.g., $54 \rightarrow 5 + 4 = 9$). Children can use this pattern as a way to check the nine facts. For example, children often confuse the multiplication facts associated with the products 27 and 28; 32 and 36; 42 and 45; 54 and 56; 63 and 64. When confirming the product of 6×9, an initial guess of 56 can be immediately ruled out since the sum of the digits is not 9. The pattern also helps with the selection of the correct product when the initial guess is in the correct decade. For example, 6×9 must be in the 50s decade because 6×10 is 60, and 63 would be too large. The answer is 54, and not 56, due to the nine pattern.

The six and nine tables also can be quickly found if the five and ten tables are already known. For example, 6×7 is 7 more than 5×7, or $35 + 7 = 42$. Similarly, 6×9 is 6 less than 6×10, or $60 - 6 = 54$.

In the upper grades, children are frequently diagnosed as not knowing their multiplication tables. However, children can generally recall many of the 100 multiplication facts: they may have difficulty remembering about 10 facts that do not follow one of the simplifying rules or patterns that enhance recall. Teachers can test the class to help them identify the precise set of facts that they have difficulty recalling. Children can then concentrate their practice on personalized lists of facts in school and at home. Oral, mental, and written drills, flash cards, calculators, estimation, games, rhymes, mnemonics, patterns, and mental arithmetic can be used by children to help them quickly recall the basic facts. Success at this task is important for social and academic reasons because further mathematics study depends on the quick recall of the basic facts.

Candybar Multiplication

An intriguing way to develop the two-entry multiplication table involves the use of arrays called *candybars* made of centimeter-squared paper. A candybar is a rectangular array with a maximum of nine squares on an edge. There can be no *bites* removed from the candybars (see Figure 8.16).

If we assume pairs of candybars with the same number of pieces but different orientations—2×3 and 3×2, for example—there are 45 candybars in all. Children can work in teams to construct a complete set. They can determine the "name" of each candybar by counting the number of pieces (centimeter squares). The result, of course, is the area of the candybar, or the product of the length and width. Finally, children attach each candybar to a piece of tagboard (12 cm $\times$ 12 cm), write the candybar's name on the back as shown in Figure 8.17, and use the set as flash cards to practice the multiplication facts.

The set of the 45 candybars (without the tagboard packing) also can be used to construct the multiplication table. Have students work in pairs using a blank table made from centimeter-squared paper, as shown in Figure 8.18. Place a candybar so that one corner touches the upper left corner of the table and the edges align with the vertical and horizontal axes. Carefully lift the lower right corner of the candybar and write its name in the square directly under the corner bite. Remove the candybar, rotate it 90°, and repeat the process in its commuted position. Similar placement of all 45 candybars will result in the familiar two-entry multiplication table.

Digit Multiplication

The multiplication facts involving the numbers 6 through 9 can be computed quickly by using the fingers on both hands. To solve the problem 7×8, for example, hold both fists in front with the thumbs on top as shown in Figure 8.19. Store the first factor, seven, on the

TABLE 8.2
Nine Facts

$1 \times 9 =$	9
$2 \times 9 =$	18
$3 \times 9 =$	27
$4 \times 9 =$	36
$5 \times 9 =$	45
$6 \times 9 =$	54
$7 \times 9 =$	63
$8 \times 9 =$	72
$9 \times 9 =$	81

8.6

✎ **FIGURE IT OUT**

Write the 15 hard multiplication facts and write a mnemonic, rhyme, or pattern as an aid for memorizing each.

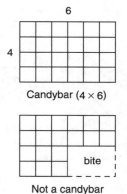

Candybar (4×6)

Not a candybar

FIGURE 8.16
Candybar Multiplication

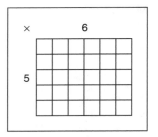

Front

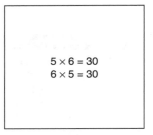

5 × 6 = 30
6 × 5 = 30

Back

FIGURE 8.17
Candybar Flash Card

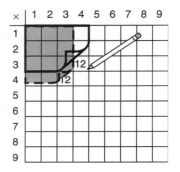

FIGURE 8.18
Constructing the Multiplication Table Using Squared-Paper "Candybars"

FIGURE 8.19
Digit Multiplication

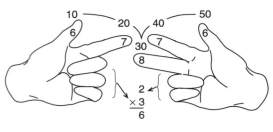

7 × 8 = 50 + 6 = 56

TABLE 8.3
Family of × and ÷ Number Sentences

MULTIPLICATION	DIVISION
7 × 8 = 56	56 ÷ 8 = 7
8 × 7 = 56	56 ÷ 7 = 8

left hand by counting-on from five, extending the thumb and fingers one at a time. Similarly, count up to the second factor, eight, on the right hand.

There are two extended, or *wiggly,* fingers on the left hand and three on the right. Each wiggly is worth ten, giving a total of 50. There are three folded fingers on the left hand and two on the right. Multiply these two values ($3 \times 2 = 6$) and add the result to the wigglies, giving $50 + 6 = 56$. Try other examples to see if the procedure works with all product pairs 6 through 9.

Recalling the Division Facts

Because division is the inverse operation of multiplication, students who know the multiplication tables should find it easy to recall the single-digit quotients for divisors less than 10 and dividends less than 100. Exercises of this type are called the division facts. To recall the quotient for $56 \div 7$, first think of the related multiplication fact

> *Missing-factor division* $7 \times ? = 56$
> *Related multiplication fact* $7 \times 8 = 56$

Just as the difference in a subtraction exercise can be thought of as a missing addend, a quotient can be considered a missing factor. Children who have memorized the multiplication table can practice recalling the second factor, or quotient, given the first factor and the product (e.g., $7 \times ? = 56$). Since multiplication and division are inverse operations, a family of number sentences can be introduced. Knowing any one member of the family shown in Table 8.3 makes it easy to recall the other three number sentences. When students can carry out this process mentally for all number families 1 through 9, they will have memorized the division facts.

Division by Zero

It is important to point out that attempting to divide by zero causes problems. Since the two division models make no sense when zero is used as a divisor, mathematicians say division by zero is *undefined.* For example, $8 \div 0$ does not make sense using any division model.

- *Repeated subtraction.* How many times can zero be subtracted from eight? (Lots!)
- *Partitive.* How many would each person get if eight apples are divided equally among zero people? (The situation makes no sense.)
- *Array.* If you have 100 seeds, how many rows would there be if zero seeds were planted in each row? (Lots again!)

FROM A DIFFERENT ANGLE

ST: Rob and JoAnne are having trouble with division. I think they just don't know their multiplication facts well enough to concentrate on the division skills. What do you think?

CT: I think you're right. They had trouble during our review of multiplication earlier in the year. I had them work hard on memorizing the dozen or so facts they couldn't recall quickly. Maybe they need some review drills.

ST: Should I be teaching them division with the rest of the class? Won't they get frustrated and stop trying?

CT: I think they need to be exposed to the new material or they'll get hopelessly behind. Maybe you can give them some multiplication support while they're learning division.

ST: What do you mean?

CT: Well, they do know some of their multiplication facts. Couldn't you make up problems for them that include only the multiplication facts they know? That way they could focus on the division work and not feel overwhelmed.

ST: But what about the facts they don't know? Won't that just let them off the hook?

CT: No, I don't think so. After all, they're learning to divide like everyone else. It's not a good idea to use a new topic as a way to drill students' shaky skills. New topics should offer opportunities to apply skills they've already mastered.

ST: So, I should get on with division and do the multiplication drill for them as separate activities.

CT: Yes, that's the idea.

Two-Entry Division Table

Initially, it is useful for students to refer to a table of division facts when introduced to more complex division exercises. The multiplication table can serve as such a reference. Interpret the numbers along the vertical axis as the divisors, the numbers in the interior of the table as the dividends, the numbers along the top of the table as the missing factors, or quotients (see Figure 8.20). Teachers should encourage students to practice using this table until they can confidently find quotients for the division facts. Notice the process *undoes* the related multiplication exercise.

Flash Cards

A set of semicircular flash cards like the *six-tables* example shown in Figure 8.21 can be used by pairs of students to practice the multiplication and division facts. One child shows the other either the multiplication or division side of the card and places a pencil in one of the holes to indicate the basic fact the second child is to recall. The partner states the answer and checks the result on a calculator if available. The correct answer is displayed on the leader's side of the card. Have the pairs reverse roles.

Construct one flash card for each of the factors 0 through 9. Use a compass to make circles (about 15 cm in diameter) from tagboard and cut the circles in half along the diameter. Punch 10 holes equally spaced around the arc of the semicircle. Write the first factors for each card (0, 1, 2, . . ., 9) on both sides near the center. Write the second factors (0 through 9) in random order beneath each hole on the multiplication side and the product under the corresponding hole on the division side.

Board Games

To practice the recall of multiplication and division facts, have each child write the facts with which they have difficulty on red cards with the answers on the back and the well-known facts on identical white cards. The multiplication candybars discussed earlier can be used as well, circling the difficult facts with a red marker.

Make a game board similar to the one pictured in Figure 8.22. Students play in groups of two to four. The object is to recall multiplication facts correctly in order to move each rocket along its trajectory. A red card moves the rocket three spaces, a white card one space. Players take turns drawing from their own red or white piles. For each correct answer, the player moves ahead accordingly. For wrong answers, players move back the appropriate number of spaces. If the rocket moves back to earth after it takes off, it crashes. The last move must put the player's rocket exactly into orbit by landing in the orbit insertion window. Players who overshoot and become lost in space can continue playing but are unable to maneuver their rockets. Encourage students to invent other board games to help them practice the basic arithmetic facts.

8.7

✎ **FIGURE IT OUT**

Can you figure out why the digit multiplication procedure works? Referring to patterns in the multiplication table may help with this investigation.

8.8

✎ **FIGURE IT OUT**

Write the family of multiplication and division number sentences for the values 7, 9, and 63.

FIGURE 8.20
Division Table

÷	1	2	3	4	5	6	7	8	9
1	1	2	3	4	5	6	7	8	9
2	2	4	6	8	10	12	14	16	18
3	3	6	9	12	15	18	21	24	27
4	4	8	12	16	20	24	28	32	36
5	5	10	15	20	25	(30)	35	40	45
6	6	12	18	24	30	36	42	48	54
7	7	14	21	28	35	42	49	56	63
8	8	16	24	32	40	48	56	64	72
9	9	18	27	36	45	54	63	72	81

Quotient (column header, with 6 boxed)

Divisor △5 (row label)

Dividend

$$5\overline{)30} \quad 6$$

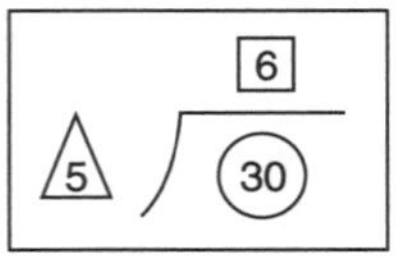

FIGURE 8.21
Multiplication and Division Flash Cards

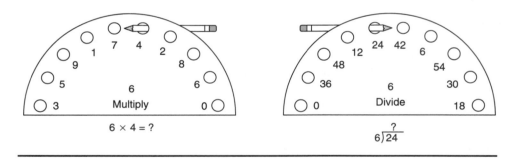

$6 \times 4 = ?$

$$6\overline{)24}\,^{?}$$

FIGURE 8.22
Space Shuttle Orbit Game

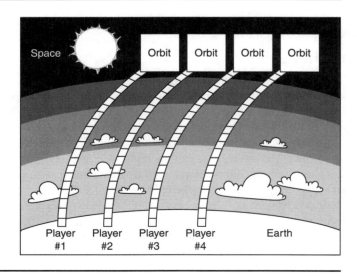

D. THE MULTIPLICATION ALGORITHM
The Transition from Manipulative Models to the Symbolic Algorithm

As with addition and subtraction, proportional base-10 materials (bean sticks or base-10 blocks) can be used to display multiplication exercises as arrays. Intermediary, nonproportional materials like dots, lines, and squares (simplified graphic representations of ones, tens, and hundreds shown in the "F. Classroom Activities" section of this chapter) are introduced when children need a bridging experience or to facilitate work with large numbers. Concrete actions and results are simultaneously recorded in place-value tables to facilitate the transition to the symbolic multiplication algorithm.

Multiplying by 10 and 100

Multiplication by 10 and 100 (and later, larger powers of 10) provides a transition between the basic facts and multidigit exercises. Figure 8.23 shows a multiplication mat with a vertical and horizontal axis. The first factor (5) is placed along the vertical axis and the second factor (10) along the horizontal axis of the multiplication mat. To find the product, construct an array of 5 rows and 10 columns. By using 10-rods instead of rows of 10 separate units, students can construct the array quickly.

Point out that multiplying a number by 10 moves the digit(s) one place value to the left. A zero is entered into the ones column as a placeholder, as shown in Figure 8.23b.

The array procedure for multiplying by 100 is unwieldy because of the large quantity of base-10 blocks needed. After they have had sufficient practice making arrays that show products with 10 as a factor, children find it easier in the exercises involving the factors 100 and 1,000 to extend the pattern of moving the digits of the first factor to the left in the place-value table. The array procedure also can display exercises involving a single-digit value times decade numbers (see Figure 8.24a, b). When products reach 100, the results are regrouped into the hundreds column.

After children have had extensive manipulative experience multiplying decade numbers by single-digit numbers, introduce them to multiples of 100 and 1,000 as factors, using symbols and place-value tables only. Prepare several practice worksheets with examples such as those shown in Figure 8.25.

Single-Digit Times Double-Digit Values

Exercises involving single- and double-digit factors can be displayed using the multiplication mat and base-10 materials. Children construct an appropriately sized array using the largest possible base-10 blocks to simplify the process. The first factor is placed along the vertical axis and the second factor along the top. For example, 4 × 12 is displayed as in Figure 8.26. To find the product, fill in the first row with 1 ten and 2 ones. Then fill in the

FIGURE 8.23
Multiplication Array Using Base-10 Materials (5 × 10)

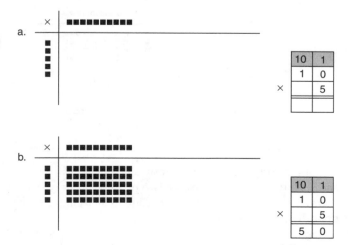

a.

1000	100	10	1
	3	0	0
×			9
2	7	0	0

b.

1000	100	10	1
	4	0	0
×			5
2	0	0	0

c.

1000	100	10	1
2	0	0	0
×			4
8	0	0	0

FIGURE 8.25
Place-Value Table
Multiplication Worksheets

FIGURE 8.24
Multiplication Arrays

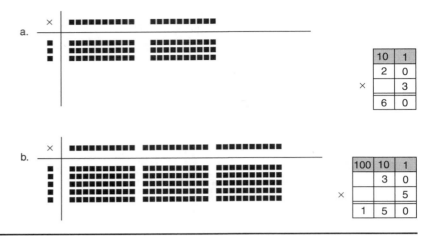

FIGURE 8.26
Partial Products (4 × 12)

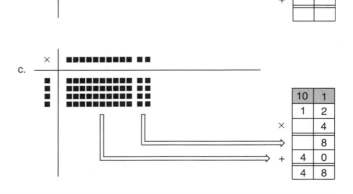

rest of the array and record the results in a place-value table. The two subproducts 4 × 2 and 4 × 10 are displayed by the two parts of the array. The total product is the sum of the two values: 8 + 40 = 48. This procedure is an example of the distributive property of multiplication over addition.

Figure 8.27 shows how exercises with products larger than 99 can be displayed using the same procedure.

FIGURE 8.27
Multiplication Mat
Setup (8 × 13)

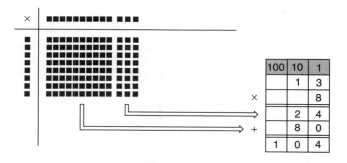

The *display algorithm* presented in a place-value table appears somewhat different from the standard multiplication algorithm. Each subproduct is displayed separately in the display algorithm, whereas the standard procedure is to combine sets of subproducts on one line. For much of the work in elementary school, the display algorithm works as well as the standard algorithm. As the size of the factors increases, however, the number of subproducts grows quickly.

Two-Digit Numbers Times Two-Digit Numbers

The product of two double-digit factors can be displayed in a similar way. When constructing the product array, it is convenient to use the largest possible base-10 blocks to speed the process. For example, using one 100-flat is easier than constructing a 10 × 10 array from unit blocks or 10-rods.

Figure 8.28 shows the steps to compute the product of 12 × 13. The factors are first positioned on the multiplication mat as shown in Figure 8.28a. After the first two rows of 13 are positioned, it is much more efficient to include one 100-flat (10 × 10) and complete each of these 10 rows with three additional unit blocks (see Figure 8.28c). Positioning the required 30 ones would be tedious, however, and as shown in Figure 8.28d, these 30 ones can be replaced by three 10-rods arranged vertically. This arrangement provides the additional 3 ones needed for each of the 10 rows in the 100-flat. The 12 × 13 product array is now complete.

The value of each subproduct can be recorded in a place-value table. In this case there are four subproducts, each represented by a part of the array. The sum of these four values gives the product. Note that subproducts for the display algorithm are calculated in the same order as with the standard algorithm.

Order of subproducts
1. Ones × ones
2. Ones × tens
3. Tens × ones
4. Tens × tens

Because addition is commutative, the order of subproducts makes no difference when using the display algorithm. To ensure a smooth transition to the standard algorithm, however, it is useful to follow the standard sequence.

When the number of subproducts becomes large (i.e., for triple-digit or larger factors), it is more efficient to introduce the standard multiplication algorithm. The relationship between the display and standard algorithms can be made explicit, as shown in Figure 8.29. The groups of subproducts recorded separately in the display algorithm are mentally combined when using the standard algorithm.

Figure 8.30 shows exercises that require regrouping between the first and second subproducts.

The standard algorithm can be further abbreviated by omitting the zero placeholders in each subproduct. Over the course of instruction, children begin with concrete displays of product arrays and record the results using the display algorithm. Once children master the

FIGURE 8.28
Four Partial Products
(12 × 13)

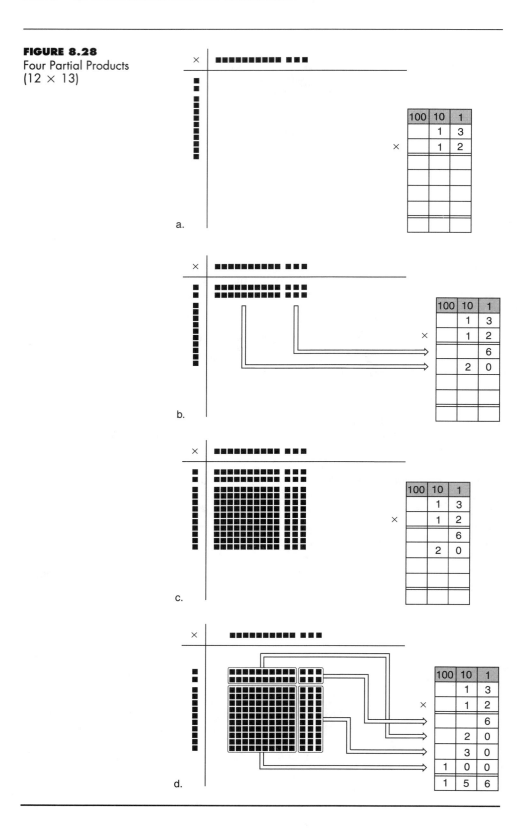

FIGURE 8.29
Standard Multiplication
Algorithm

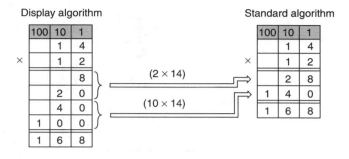

FIGURE 8.30
Standard Multiplication
Algorithm

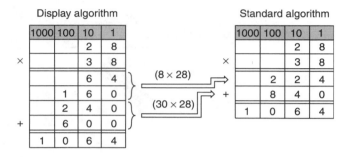

display algorithm double-digit factors, with and without concrete arrays, introduce the standard algorithm. Finally, you can introduce the abbreviated standard algorithm to save time when writing subproducts:

	DISPLAY ALGORITHM		**STANDARD ALGORITHM**		**ABBREVIATED ALGORITHM**
	24		24		24
CONCRETE	36		36		36
PRODUCT →	24	→	144	→	144
ARRAYS	120		720		72
	120		864		864
	600				
	864				

Multiplication of Larger Values

When factors exceed roughly 20, or products 999, the use of arrays becomes unwieldy. By the time such problems are introduced, children should have mastered working smaller exercises, using concrete materials and recording the results in place-value tables. Exercises involving larger numbers can be introduced using squared-paper place-value tables and standard symbols (Figure 8.31).

Teacher-prepared worksheets containing exercises presented in place-value tables are appropriate at this stage of development. Textbooks are a useful source of exercises that are organized according to the level of difficulty. As factors get large, the number of subproducts increases to the extent that the display algorithm may become tedious, encouraging the shift to the standard algorithm.

8.11

✎ **FIGURE IT OUT**

Using proportional base-10 materials, carry out the necessary actions to complete the following multiplication exercises. Record the actions and results in place-value tables.

1. $4 \times 12 = ?$
2. $8 \times 15 = ?$
3. $12 \times 13 = ?$
4. $11 \times 316 = ?$
5. $12 \times 223 = ?$

FIGURE 8.31
Place-Value Table
Multiplication (5 × 324)

Display algorithm

	1000	100	10	1
		3	2	4
×				5
			2	0
		1	0	0
+	1	5	0	0
	1	6	2	0

Standard algorithm

	1000	100	10	1
		2	7	1
×			2	4
	1	0	8	4
+	5	4	2	0
	6	5	0	4

FIGURE 8.32
Division Using Base-10 Materials (30 ÷ 3)

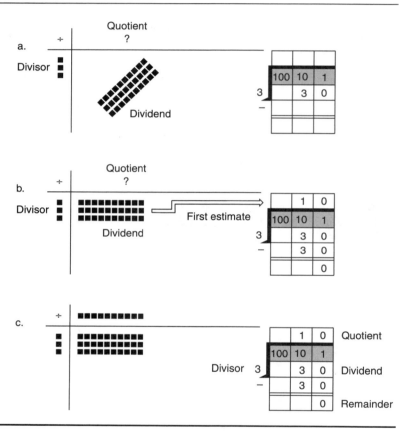

E. THE DIVISION ALGORITHM

After children can readily recall the division facts, teachers can introduce them to selected exercises that have multiples of 10 and 100 for quotients. Figure 8.32 shows how to work the problem 30 ÷ 3 using base-10 materials. The task of constructing an appropriate array from the dividend 30 is simplified when children exploit the structure of the base-10 materials. The 3 tens could be traded for 30 ones and distributed in groups of three by arranging them into 3 rows (i.e., repeated subtraction). A quicker method is to estimate if the dividend is large enough so that each of the three rows can contain at least one 10-rod and check to see if there are enough tens to construct an appropriate array (see Figure 8.32b).

To show the quotient, place a spare 10-rod above the horizontal axis to match the length of the array (see Figure 8.32c). As there are no blocks left undistributed, the *remainder* (the amount left over) is zero. In this case, the first estimate was also the best estimate, because the dividend was completely distributed. This is not always the case, of course. The process

FIGURE 8.33
Partial Quotients (80 ÷ 4)

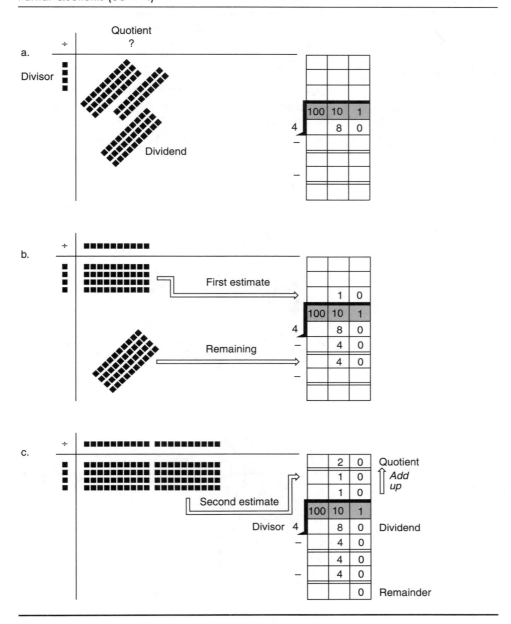

of dividing involves making an initial quotient estimate, checking to see if it is too large, and if not, continuing to distribute the remainder until no more can be equally distributed.

The symbolic record of the division process shown in Figure 8.32c is called the *display algorithm*. This algorithm encourages students to focus on the underlying place-value concept when dividing and facilitates the estimation of partial quotients.

If there are not enough blocks to complete an equal distribution, the estimated quotient is too large. A smaller estimate must then be selected. The sequence of actions involved in making a subsequent estimate when the first was too small is shown in Figure 8.33.

The first estimate of 10 left 4 tens (or 40) undistributed. The second estimate of one additional 10-rod left a remainder of zero. Since all the dividend is distributed, the quotient is the *sum* of the two estimates $10 + 10 = 20$, and the remainder is zero. Of course, as children learn to make better initial estimates, the number of steps needed to complete a division exercise will decrease. A perceptive student might have made an initial guess of 2 tens (or 20) and completed this exercise in one step.

✎ FIGURE IT OUT

Use front-end estimation to mentally compute an initial quotient for each of the following exercises. Use base-10 materials to show the concrete actions involved.

1. 3⟌85
2. 4⟌109
3. 6⟌222
4. 5⟌179
5. 8⟌566

For quotients larger than 40, arrays become tedious to use. Once they are adept at using arrays to solve exercises with small multiple-of-10 quotients, students can tackle exercises involving larger multiples of 10 and 100 using only place-value tables. Place-value tables help children write digits in the proper column. Figure 8.34 shows exercises solved in place-value tables using multiple and best estimates for quotients.

Front-End Estimation of Quotients

Mastery of exercises that have multiples of 10 as quotients can help children make more accurate initial quotient estimates. Students can use front-end estimation to help make these estimates for single-digit divisors. Children round down the dividend to the leading digit, as shown in Figure 8.35. The dividend (368) is thought of as 30 tens. An initial quotient estimate would be $368 \div 4 \approx 300 \div 4 = 30$ tens $\div 4 \approx 7$ tens, or 70.

FIGURE 8.34
Division Using Place-Value
Tables (2,400 ÷ 6)

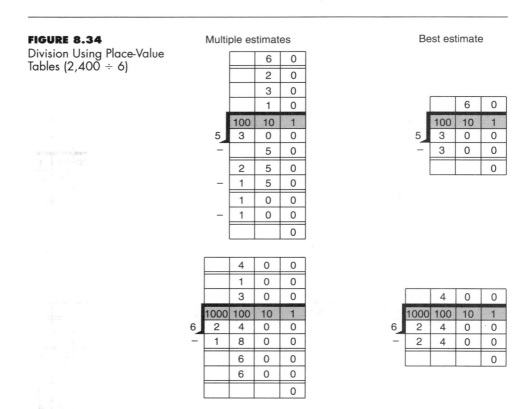

FIGURE 8.35
Rounding Down to
Estimate Quotients

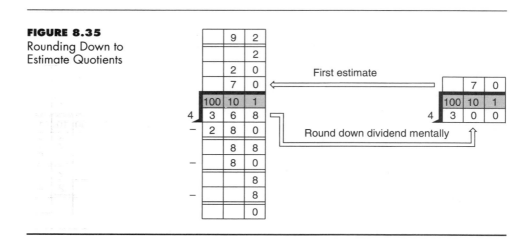

The best quotient estimate shown in Figure 8.35 will be close to this front-end estimate. Students can find more accurate quotient estimates if they round down dividends to the *second* largest place value. For example, $368 \div 4 \approx 360 \div 4 = 36$ tens $\div 4 = 9$ tens, or 90. Encourage children to use a calculator to check the accuracy of initial quotient estimates. Estimating quotients using the front-end estimation method is typically introduced early in the development of the division algorithm.

Single-Digit Divisors

Division involves estimating quotients by exploiting the inherent structure of base-10 materials. The first step is to estimate how much of the dividend can be *equally* distributed to each unit in the divisor. Children can take advantage of the ones, tens, and hundreds blocks in the base-10 materials and the front-end estimation method to select an initial quotient. For example, the front-end quotient estimate for $84 \div 6$ is $80 \div 6 = 8$ tens $\div 6 \approx 1$ ten, or 10 (see Figure 8.36).

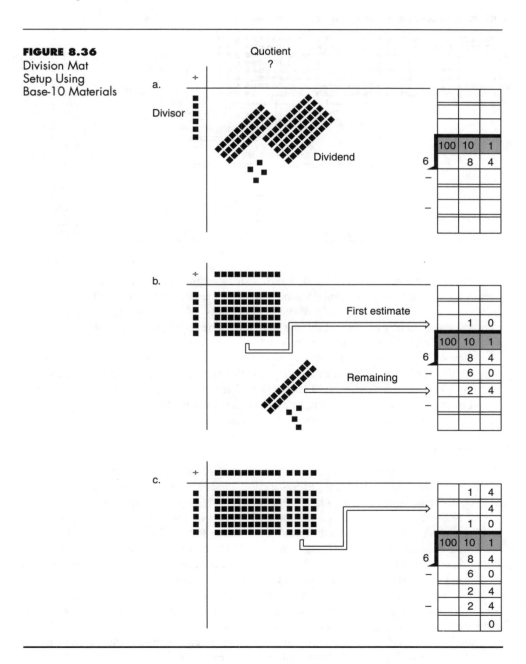

FIGURE 8.36
Division Mat
Setup Using
Base-10 Materials

FIGURE 8.37
Division with
Remainders

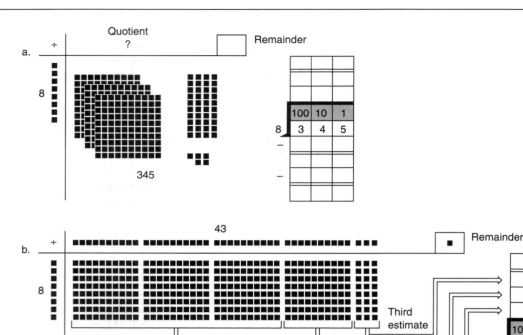

Since there are not enough 10-rods left to distribute among the six rows, the 2 tens and 4 ones remaining must be regrouped into 24 ones for the next distribution. The second distribution can be calculated directly from the basic facts ($24 \div 6 = 4$). Smaller initial quotient values could be used, but additional steps would be required (i.e., first distribute three units to each row, then distribute one more).

Figure 8.37 shows how students can work larger examples if the quotients are reasonably small. For $345 \div 8$, the initial quotient estimate can be found using front-end estimation ($345 \div 8 \approx 300 \div 8 = 30$ tens $\div 8 \approx 3$ tens, or 30). Students can find a better initial quotient estimate by rounding down the dividend to the next to the largest place value ($345 \div 8 \approx 340 \div 8 = 34$ tens $\div 8 \approx 4$ tens, or 40).

Double-Digit Divisors

Determining initial quotient estimates for exercises involving double-digit divisors is somewhat more complicated. For these exercises, it is generally useful to *round off* the divisor and the dividend to the leading place value of each. Figure 8.38 shows the steps for computing $382 \div 18$. First, have children round off the divisor and dividend to their respective leading digits and try to estimate the quotient mentally ($382 \div 18 \approx 400 \div 20 = 20$). Using the initial quotient estimate of 20, arrange part of the dividend into an array as shown in Figure 8.38b. Finally, Figure 8.38c shows how 18 of the remaining undistributed dividend of 22 can be regrouped and positioned in the array. The remainder is 4.

If this method gives a quotient estimate that is too large, as in the example $282 \div 34 \approx 300 \div 30 = 10$, the rounding-off method still makes it easier to specify an accurate *second* estimate (if 10 is too large, the quotient must be 8 or 9).

Exercises involving divisors or quotients less than 40 can be readily displayed using array representation. Figure 8.39 shows examples of worked exercises. Students can improve

8.13
✎ FIGURE IT OUT

Using proportional base-10 materials, carry out the necessary actions to solve each division exercise below. Use front-end estimation and rounding down to the next to the second largest place value to estimate the initial quotient for each exercise. Use place-value tables to record the actions and results.

1. $5\overline{)75}$
2. $6\overline{)108}$
3. $8\overline{)128}$
4. $5\overline{)195}$
5. $9\overline{)216}$

FIGURE 8.38
Rounding Off to
Estimate Quotients
(382 ÷ 18)

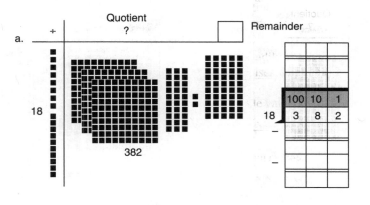

For first quotient estimate,
round off divisor and dividend
and mentally calculate quotient.

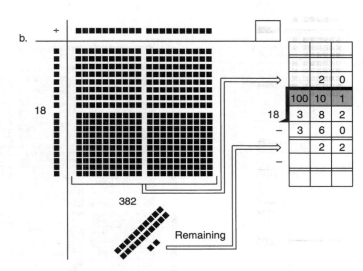

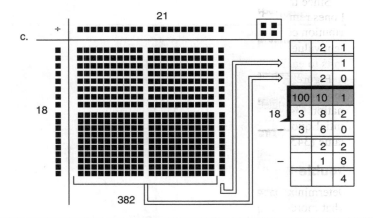

their skill in making accurate initial quotient estimates with sufficient practice using arrays
and the rounding-off method.

Division Involving Larger Values

Exercises involving divisors or quotients larger than 40 can be more readily solved using
place-value tables. After children have mastered working division exercises with quotients
smaller than 40, introduce the standard division algorithm by comparing it with the steps in
the display algorithm. If the initial quotient estimate is the largest possible value, it is called
the *best* estimate. When the best estimate is found for each place value, the display algorithm is similar to the standard algorithm (see Figure 8.40).

✎ **FIGURE IT OUT**

Round off the divisors and dividends in each exercise below to the leading digit and estimate the initial quotient estimates. Use base-10 materials to demonstrate the steps.

1. 13)175
2. 14)224
3. 17)361
4. 25)445
5. 18)272

8.15

✎ **FIGURE IT OUT**

Using place-value tables, carry out the necessary manipulations to solve each division exercise below. Compare the display algorithm to the standard algorithm in each case.

1. 12)75
2. 11)100
3. 13)125
4. 15)194
5. 21)205

8.16

✎ **FIGURE IT OUT**

Solve each division exercise below using the display algorithm in place-value tables. Relate the display algorithm to the standard algorithm in each case.

1. 22)175
2. 63)2105
3. 35)1125
4. 83)4394
5. 121)5205

FIGURE 8.39
Best Quotient Estimates
(715 ÷ 31)

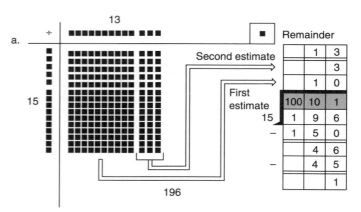

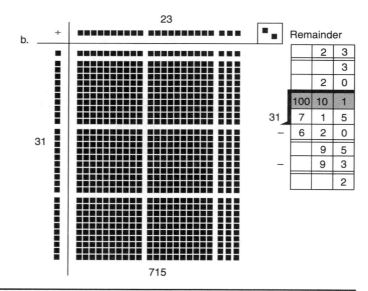

FIGURE 8.40
Place-Value Table
Division (492 ÷ 23)

With the standard division algorithm, children are expected to make accurate best estimates for each partial quotient. The value for each partial quotient is also represented by one digit in its proper column, as opposed to the entire number as in the display algorithm. In Figure 8.40, the best estimates are 2 tens and 1 one. The remainder is the amount left when no further whole-number divisions are possible. This value is commonly displayed along with a capital R (for remainder) next to the quotient.

The Transition from Manipulative Models to the Symbolic Algorithm

The use of proportional base-10 materials and the display algorithm facilitates conceptual understanding of division and provides a flexible algorithm for computing. Skill in making initial quotient estimates improves as children learn to apply their concrete manipulations to symbolic exercises. As with previous number operations, the instructional procedures are intended to serve as a dynamic support system for children learning to divide. As their abilities increase, children take on greater responsibility for coordinating elements within the task.

The recent availability of inexpensive calculators has reduced the importance of accurate, paper-and-pencil long-division computations involving large numbers. However, a thorough understanding of the types of division situations, skill in mentally estimating quotients, and an ability to carry out calculations involving small numbers are still needed to facilitate effective problem solving.

F. CLASSROOM ACTIVITIES
Developmental Activity Sequence

A sequence of activities that provides different levels of perceptual support can help develop the concept of multiplication for a diverse group of children. A direct relationship is established between the concrete actions involved in constructing a product array and the symbolic manipulations of the standard algorithm. Figure 8.41 shows the step-by-step relationship that exists between the same multiplication exercise worked using an array and using the display algorithm. Each subproduct calculated in the sequence (4×3; 2×20; 10×3; and 10×20) is displayed as a part of the array and is recorded in the place-value table.

Many children experience difficulty with the transition from the concrete representation of multiplication exercises to the use of an algorithm. As an intermediate level between concrete base-10 materials and the symbolic algorithm, exercises can be worked using the graphic representation of *dots, lines,* and *squares.* In this scheme, dots represent ones, lines represent tens, and squares represent hundreds (see Figure 8.42).

This graphic representation of base-10 materials allows children to work more efficiently with larger factors. Teachers can prepare worksheets displaying blank array mats and place-value tables like the example in Figure 8.42. Graded exercises can be assigned from a textbook or other source; transferred to the array mats using dots, lines, and squares; and recorded symbolically in place-value tables. While the need for graphic displays will diminish with student experience, these displays remain a useful tool for analyzing and correcting errors.

Division is also introduced using proportional materials. The use of arrays enables students to practice making initial quotient estimates and checking the accuracy of these estimates. Students record the results of their concrete actions using the display algorithm in place-value tables. Later, exercises can be presented symbolically. Students can fix incorrect answers by checking calculations using arrays. If necessary, students experiencing difficulty with symbolic division can solve exercises using a transitional representation like the dots, lines, and squares as shown in Figure 8.43. This representation offers children a simple way to record their work with arrays if they have difficulty using place-value tables. Older students may prefer dots, lines, and squares as a substitute for base-10 materials when working division exercises.

Napier's Bones

John Napier is credited with the invention of a simple calculator that computes products. Children may find constructing and using this device an interesting multiplication extension activity. The tool originally was constructed of nine ivory bars, or *bones,* each respectively inscribed with the first nine multiples of the digits 1 through 9. A simple set of bones can be constructed from tag board or tongue depressors, as shown in Figure 8.44.

To multiply 6×18, select the 1-bone and the 8-bone and place them next to each other as in Figure 8.45a. Next, look at row 6. Add the values along the diagonals, regrouping to the next column to the left as necessary (see Figure 8.45b). This calculation gives the product.

FIGURE 8.41
Multiplication Using Base-10 Materials (14 × 23)

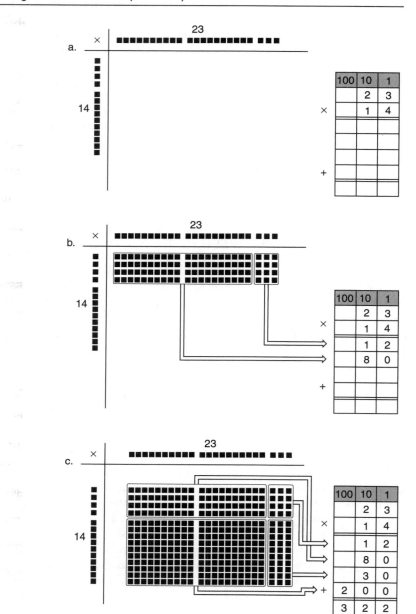

FIGURE 8.42
Multiplication Using
Representational Notation
(22 × 35)

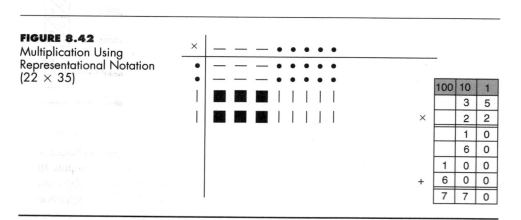

FIGURE 8.43
Division Using
Representational Notation
(565 ÷ 23)

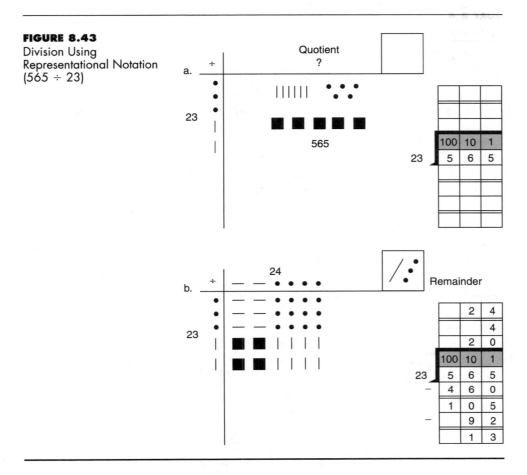

FIGURE 8.44
Napier's Bones

1-bone	2-bone	3-bone	4-bone	5-bone	6-bone	7-bone	8-bone	9-bone
0/1	0/2	0/3	0/4	0/5	0/6	0/7	0/8	0/9
0/2	0/4	0/6	0/8	1/0	1/2	1/4	1/6	1/8
0/3	0/6	0/9	1/2	1/5	1/8	2/1	2/4	2/7
0/4	0/8	1/2	1/6	2/0	2/4	2/8	3/2	3/6
0/5	1/0	1/5	2/0	2/5	3/0	3/5	4/0	4/5
0/6	1/2	1/8	2/4	3/0	3/6	4/2	4/8	5/4
0/7	1/4	2/1	2/8	3/5	4/2	4/9	5/6	6/3
0/8	1/6	2/4	3/2	4/0	4/8	5/6	6/4	7/2
0/9	1/8	2/7	3/6	4/5	5/4	6/3	7/2	8/1

   Products of a 1-digit × 3-digit or larger values can be computed by selecting bones for each digit in a largest factor. When both factors contain more than one digit, compute the subproducts separately and combine them for the final result. Point out that the subproduct must be adjusted one or more place values to the left and zero-placeholder(s) appended when the factor is a multiple of 10, as in Figure 8.46.

FIGURE 8.45
Multiplying Using
Napier's Bones

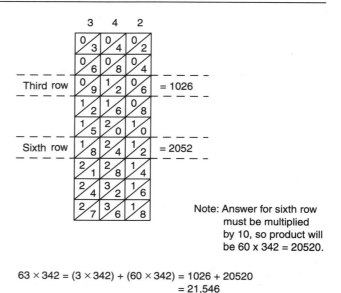

a. 6 × 18

b. Close-up of 6 × 18

FIGURE 8.46
Multiplying Large Values
Using Napier's Bones

Note: Answer for sixth row
must be multiplied
by 10, so product will
be 60 x 342 = 20520.

63 × 342 = (3 × 342) + (60 × 342) = 1026 + 20520
= 21,546

G. PROBLEM-SOLVING EXPERIENCES INVOLVING MULTIPLICATION AND DIVISION

Many problems require the application of repeated addition, finding area, making arrays, or finding combinations. Multiplication and division generally are involved in solving such problems. Experience with concrete problem situations embodying fundamental conceptions of multiplication and division helps children develop skill in selecting the appropriate strategies or operation. Initially, present problems involving only one operation. Later, teachers can introduce situations involving more than one operation (e.g., multiplying, then adding).

Making Tables and Finding Patterns

How many eating utensils are needed for a birthday party? If each place setting includes a knife, fork, and spoon, how many will be required for 22 guests? Children in grades 4–6 may recognize that this is a simple multiplication exercise and calculate the product: $3 \times 22 = 66$.

8.17
✎ **FIGURE IT OUT**

Try to figure out how Napier's Bones multiply. What do the digits on the diagonals stand for? Why do we get the product of two numbers when these digits are summed?

TABLE 8.4
Table Settings

NUMBER OF GUESTS	NUMBER OF UTENSILS
1	3
2	6
3	9
4	12
5	15
6	18
7	21
8	24
9	27
10	30
11	—

TABLE 8.5
Table-Setting Function
(Guests $\times$ 3 = Utensils)

GUESTS	UTENSILS
1	3
2	6
3	9
4	12
5	15
—	—
—	—
87	?

Give each child 22 counters to serve as guests. On the board, draw a two-column table like Table 8.4 with the number of people in the first column and the number of eating utensils in the second. Beginning with the smallest party (one person), have each child draw three utensils, circle them, and place one counter on top of them. Record the number of guests (1) and the number of utensils (3) in the table. Continue drawing sets of utensils, and have the children skip count to find the total. Record the results in the table until reaching 10 guests.

It will take a long time to continue the table all the way to 22 guests, so have the children look for a pattern to help determine the next value without having to count all the utensils. Looking down the second column, notice that the total number of utensils can be found by adding 3 to each current value. For example, to determine the number of utensils required for 11 guests, we add 3 to the number of utensils required for 10 guests. The pattern "add 3" can be extended to include any number of guests. The following list shows this application of repeated addition.

$$3 = 3$$
$$3 + 3 = 6$$
$$3 + 3 + 3 = 9$$
$$3 + 3 + 3 + 3 = 12$$
$$3 + 3 + 3 + 3 + 3 = 15$$

The number of utensils needed for 22 guests could be found, with some effort, using this pattern. Suppose 100 guests showed up, or 1,000 guests. The repeated addition procedure would be tiring indeed. In order to extend patterns to larger values, it is helpful to find a rule that will predict the number of utensils needed based exclusively on the number of guests.

Finding such a rule requires paying careful attention to the relationship between the entries in the first and second columns. The rule in this case for the pairs of values 1 and 3, 2 and 6, 3 and 9, 4 and 12, and 5 and 15 can be summarized as "multiply the number of guests by 3." A rule makes it possible to compute the number of utensils required for any number of guests without knowing the previous step. For example, if you know the function shown in Table 8.5, it is not necessary to know the number of utensils needed for 86 guests in order to determine the number needed for 87 guests.

Formula Gardening

Measuring area often involves multiplication or division. Suppose 16 tomato plants can be grown in each 1 square meter of land. How many plants can be grown in a rectangular garden 25 meters on an edge? Children might first try to draw a sketch of the problem. Since the garden is large, the sketch will have to be scaled quite small, making it difficult to count all the plants. It may be better to sketch a smaller square garden, say 2 meters on an edge, and count the number of plants. Then construct a table that organizes the important information about a whole series of square gardens (edge length, area, number of plants) and try to find a pattern or rule to make the counting easier.

8.18
✎ **FIGURE IT OUT**

For the radish-planting problem, how would the formula $16 \times d^2 = n$ change for rectangular gardens?

TABLE 8.6
Planting Gardens

EDGE LENGTH (d)	AREA (d²)	PLANTS (n)
1	1	16
2	4	64
3	9	144
4	16	256
5	25	400
6	36	576
—	—	—
—	—	—
25	—	—

After students construct Table 8.6, either individually, or for less experienced problem solvers, as a whole class, help them observe that the garden area can be calculated by multiplying edge length by itself (for a garden 6 meters on an edge, the area is 6 m × 6 m = 36 m²). The number of plants can then be found by multiplying the area by 16.

A formula relating edge length d to the number of plants n can be written:

$$16 \times (d \times d) = 16 \times d^2 = n$$

Children can use this formula to find the number of plants for any size garden:

$$16 \times (50)^2 = 40,000 \text{ radish plants}$$

$$16 \times (100)^2 = 160,000 \text{ radish plants}$$

$$16 \times (273)^2 = 1,192,464 \text{ radish plants}$$

Constructing tables, analyzing patterns, and finding formulas are powerful problem-solving strategies. Not only do these strategies help children solve the immediate problem, but they are frequently useful for solving a whole class of similar future problems.

Missing and Superfluous Information

Everyday problems are generally embedded in a complex situation with many unrelated facts and events. For example, when comparison shopping, the ingredients, packaging, date, perceived quality, and brand may be determining factors when choosing a product. However, to identify which of two different sized cans of tuna is the best buy, only the weight and price are used to compute the unit price (price per gram or ounce).

Children need experience separating the pertinent elements needed for the solution from superfluous information included in the problem description. Sometimes, a problem is impossible to solve because important information is missing.

At the outset, students simply identify the values in a problem needed for the solution without attempting a solution. Problem statements with superfluous information and those with missing values can also be introduced. It is more important at this stage that students closely examine problem descriptions than attempt to carry out the solution. Give children examples like the following and ask them to identify the missing and superfluous information in the problem statement.

- *Missing Information.* Darron and Rae wanted to build a ladder for their tree house. They figured it would cost about 50 cents per foot to build the ladder. If they earned $1.00 per hour mowing lawns, how long would it take for them to earn enough to buy the materials for their ladder?
  (What missing information is needed to solve this problem?)
- *Superfluous Information.* Paint is sold in 1-quart and 1-gallon containers at $3.59 and $13.98, respectively. One quart will cover 100 square feet. The quart containers come in 14 colors and the gallons in 11 colors. If Mitch is planning to paint a wall 10 feet by 30 feet, which size container would be the best buy?
  (Circle values needed to solve this problem.)

FIGURE 8.47
Floor Tiles

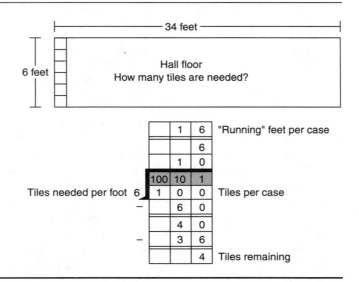

Have children find problems in their textbook and rewrite them to include missing and/or superfluous information. The class can exchange problems to identify the pertinent information needed to solve each problem.

Job Estimates

Suppose a 34-foot-long hall is 6 feet wide and we need to buy enough one-square-foot floor tiles to cover the hall. How many 100-tile cases are needed for the job? Drawing a sketch of this type problem often helps with the solution. The sketch in Figure 8.47 shows that 6 tiles are needed to fit across the hall. Distributing a case of 100 tiles in six equal rows should remind children of a division array. One case would make the rows 16 tiles long with 4 tiles left over. Two cases would cover 33 running feet of hall with two left over. By completing the sketch of the array, or using division, we find that two cases would not quite finish the job.

Measuring Money

How tall is a stack of 1 million dollar bills? Carrying out the actual experiment would be very expensive and time consuming. The problem can be cut down to size by first solving a simpler case of the same problem.

Have children count the number of bills needed to make a stack 1 centimeter high. Substitute play money or pieces of paper if you're a bit short on funds. About 80 bills makes a stack 1 centimeter high. To compute the height of a stack of 1,000 bills, children need to divide, using a calculator or paper and pencil,

$$
\begin{array}{r}
12 \leftarrow \text{centimeters} \\
80\overline{)1{,}000} \leftarrow \text{bills} \\
\underline{800} \\
200 \\
\underline{160} \\
40
\end{array}
$$

The $1,000 stack is about 12 centimeters high. Substitute 1 million for 1,000 and follow the same procedure to find the height.

$$
\begin{array}{r}
12{,}500 \leftarrow \text{centimeters} \\
80\overline{)1{,}000{,}000} \leftarrow \text{bills}
\end{array}
$$

The stack would be 12,500 centimeters, or 125 meters, high, which is taller than a 40-story building! Children should find reducing problems to a simpler case a useful strategy for solving a wide range of problems.

8.19

✎ **FIGURE IT OUT**

A criminal in a recent movie was carrying a briefcase that supposedly contained 2 million dollars in 100-dollar bills. Does this seem possible?

H. CALCULATOR AND COMPUTER APPLICATIONS
Calculator Games and Activities

Twenty-One is a calculator strategy game that encourages children to examine patterns. Pairs of children share one calculator for this activity. Starting with zero, players alternate adding the value 1 or 2 to the current sum shown in the display. The goal is to be the first player to reach *exactly* 21. This game also can be played orally or using pencil and paper. A typical game might proceed as shown in Table 8.7.

Several interesting patterns occur with this game. Have children play it with a partner and keep track of any patterns that may provide clues to a winning strategy. Possible patterns include the odd and even numbers, multiples of 3, and recurrence of key numbers such as 18 and 2. Have children try to devise a strategy that guarantees that player 2 will always win.

Calculator Estimation is an activity that helps children develop increasingly important estimation skills. When solving a problem, the ability to mentally calculate an approximate result can be an invaluable aid in determining whether a solution strategy is reasonable. Students can use calculators to practice estimating quotients when dividing (or for any other operation on the calculator). Have students individually estimate the quotients for division exercises on identical worksheets. After the estimates are completed, have the students pair off and compute the quotients using a calculator. Note that the *Math Explorer*™ (Texas Instruments) gives whole-number answers with remainders while other calculators give decimal solutions. For younger students, select problems that give whole-number quotients. Older students should round off computed quotients to the nearest tenth, or, if you are using the *Math Explorer*™, to, ignore the remainder. Have each student calculate the difference between each actual quotient and its estimate. The student who makes the best estimate (i.e., the difference between the estimate and the computed answer is smallest), circles the estimated quotient. Whoever has the most circled estimates wins. The following are calculator estimation examples:

Grade 4

1. $6\overline{)24}$

   $\overline{\text{Estimate}}$ $\overline{\text{Calculation}}$

2. $9\overline{)36}$

   $\overline{\text{Estimate}}$ $\overline{\text{Calculation}}$

3. $5\overline{)45}$

   $\overline{\text{Estimate}}$ $\overline{\text{Calculation}}$

8.20
✎ FIGURE IT OUT

Play the game *Twenty-One* with a partner. If you discover a winning strategy, change the rules so that 21 is *poison* (if you get to 21 first, you lose); or allow adding 1, 2, or 3; or change the winning number to 25.

TABLE 8.7
Game of *Twenty-One*

MOVE	PLAYER 1	CALCULATOR DISPLAY	PLAYER 2
Start		0	
1	+1 →	1	
2		3	← +2
3	+2 →	5	
4		7	← +2
5	+1 →	8	
6		9	← +1
7	+2 →	11	
8		13	← +2
9	+1 →	14	
10		15	← +1
11	+2 →	17	
12		18	← +1
13	+1 →	19	
14		21	← +2 Player 2 wins

Grades 5–9

1. $18\overline{)48}$

   ‾‾‾‾‾‾‾   ‾‾‾‾‾‾‾‾‾‾‾
   Estimate   Calculation

2. $31\overline{)256}$

   ‾‾‾‾‾‾‾   ‾‾‾‾‾‾‾‾‾‾‾
   Estimate   Calculation

3. $3.25\overline{)12.3}$

   ‾‾‾‾‾‾‾   ‾‾‾‾‾‾‾‾‾‾‾
   Estimate   Calculation

Computer Software

Several computer software products are available to help teach multiplication and division. Concept tutorials, estimation activities, and practice drills provide a range of computer experiences in the classroom or in a laboratory setting.

Multiplying with Balancing Bear (Sunburst) is a simulated balance beam that models multiplication for young children. Balloons are displayed on one side of the balance, each costing, say, 4 cents. What is the total cost of three balloons each costing 4 cents? The child is asked to select balloons for Bear to hold on the other side in order to make the beam balance. This visual model helps children to see the relationship between repeated addition and multiplication. See Figure 8.48.

Power Drill (Sunburst) is an environment for estimation and computation for upper-grade students. Front-end estimation and more sophisticated rounding techniques are explored. For example, the program presents the user with an exercise such as $65{,}278 \div \underline{\hspace{1cm}} = 264$.

Using front-end estimation, the student simplifies the exercise ($60{,}000 \div \underline{\hspace{1cm}} = 200$), mentally calculates the answer, and enters 300. The program displays the result along with the original exercise.

$$65{,}278 \div \underline{\hspace{1cm}} = 264$$

$$65{,}278 \div 300 = 217 \text{ R } 78$$

Since the quotient is too small ($217 < 264$), the estimate must be adjusted to compensate. By refining quotient estimates, children practice using rounding and mental arithmetic skills to solve division problems. The program gives advice if the initial estimate is way off

FIGURE 8.48
Multiplying with Balancing Bear
SOURCE: Sunburst Communications, 1991.

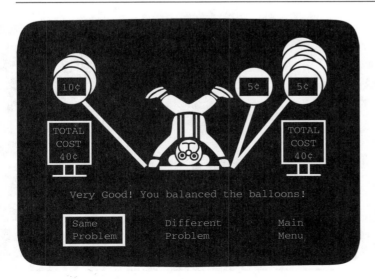

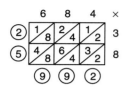

$$38 \times 684 = 25{,}992$$

FIGURE 8.49
Lattice Multiplication

8.21

✎ **FIGURE IT OUT**

Review multiplication using Napier's Bones. What similarities do you see between multiplication with a lattice and Napier's Bones?

---

and displays the number of attempts to find the missing number. There are options for each of the four operations and three levels of difficulty.

I. ADAPTING INSTRUCTION FOR CHILDREN WITH SPECIAL NEEDS
Low-Stress Multiplication and Division Algorithms

Lattice Multiplication is an alternate algorithm that may pique the interest of special-needs children who have failed to learn the standard algorithm. Using squared paper, have children draw a rectangle with the length equal to the number of digits in the multiplier and the width equal to the number of digits in the multiplicand. As shown in Figure 8.49, subproducts are computed for all pairs of digits and written with the tens above the diagonal and ones below the diagonal in the appropriate squares. The subproducts are summed along the diagonals, regrouping to the left as necessary. The product (circled values) is read from left to right around the rectangle.

The *display algorithm* presented in this chapter is a useful transition algorithm for students having difficulty making accurate quotient estimates. In Figure 8.50, two alternate forms of the display algorithm are shown. The first is the algorithm developed previously. The second follows the same procedure, only the quotient estimates are displayed on the right, next to each partial product.

Both of the alternative division algorithms allow students to underestimate the initial quotient and adjust subsequent estimates accordingly without having to start the exercise over. The procedure is often more satisfying because it encourages the students to proceed to the next step without having to erase their work.

To help children who are not confident of their recall of the basic multiplication and division facts, have them first make a list of multiples of the divisor:

$$0 \times 24 = 0$$
$$1 \times 24 = 24$$
$$2 \times 24 = 48$$
$$3 \times 24 = 72$$
$$4 \times 24 = 96$$
$$5 \times 24 = 120$$
$$6 \times 24 = 144$$
$$7 \times 24 = 168$$
$$8 \times 24 = 192$$
$$9 \times 24 = 216$$
$$10 \times 24 = 240$$

FIGURE 8.50
Alternative Division
Algorithms

Students can quickly construct the list by noting that the first multiple is always zero, the second is the divisor, the third is double the divisor, the fourth is the sum of the second and third, and so on. A calculator can also be used to help construct the multiple table. Using this list and an understanding of multiplication by 10, 100, and 1,000, children can estimate initial quotients more accurately. For the example $869 \div 24$, looking at the 24-multiple table, the child can quickly see that 20 is too small and 40 is too large for an initial quotient estimate ($20 \times 24 = 480$, $40 \times 24 = 960$). Therefore, 30 might be about right. Similarly, the table gives the best quotient estimate for $149 \div 24$ (6×24). Children can make a divisor-multiple table for each problem they encounter.

Children who exhibit particular difficulty learning to multiply and divide may need more help with the transition between concept-building activities involving proportional base-10 arrays and the symbolic algorithms. To assist with the transition, teachers can emphasize graphic representations (e.g., dots, lines, and squares) to a greater extent than normal. In such cases, it may be appropriate to allow the continued use of the display algorithm instead of requiring the transition to the standard algorithm.

At some point in each child's education, teachers must make a judgment regarding the benefit of continuing practice of the long division algorithm. For those students who have experienced minimal success by the end of grade 6, it becomes increasingly difficult to justify the time committed to reteaching paper-and-pencil long division when inexpensive calculators compute with ease and accuracy. It is important to think about how often long-division exercises are computed by hand by people outside school. Recent research indicates that nearly all calculations *actually* carried out by individuals in everyday life are approximations based on some estimation procedure (Rogoff & Lave, 1983). Few mathematicians or engineers, who constantly work with numbers, would trust themselves to carry out a vital calculation using only pencil and paper. Virtually everyone who cares about the exact results—accountants, bank clerks, IRS agents—uses calculators to check his or her work.

Peasant multiplication is an alternative multiplication algorithm still used in rural areas of Eastern Europe and Russia. It can be introduced as an extension activity for gifted and talented students. The peasant multiplication algorithm originally was developed by the Hindus and used by Arabs, Greeks, and Romans hundreds of years ago, before place-value systems were invented. Imagine the difficulty a merchant might have had multiplying large numbers using Roman numerals.

This multiplication technique involves doubling and halving, an easy operation even for the Egyptian and Roman numeration systems. To find the product 35×186, systematically halve the first factor (ignoring any remainders) until reaching the quotient 1, as shown in Table 8.8. Next, double the second factor the same number of times. A calculator can be used to halve and double each factor, ignoring the decimal fraction parts of the quotients. In the first column, draw a line through each even number (in this case 8, 4, and 2) and the corresponding values in the second column (744, 1,488, and 2,976). The sum of the remaining values in the second column is the product $35 \times 186 = 6,510$.

Explaining why this procedure works is an interesting problem. One way to explore the procedure is to look at the problem backwards. In Table 8.9, notice that a third column has

TABLE 8.8
Peasant Multiplication

HALVE FIRST FACTOR	DOUBLE SECOND FACTOR
35	186
17	372
~~8~~	~~744~~
~~4~~	~~1,488~~
~~2~~	~~2,976~~
1	5,952
Total	$6,510 = 35 \times 186$

8.22

✎ FIGURE IT OUT

Multiply other values using peasant multiplication and look for patterns to help explain the underlying process.

TABLE 8.9
Peasant Multiplication

HALVE 1st FACTOR	DOUBLE 2nd FACTOR	MULTIPLE OF 2nd FACTOR
35	186	1
17	372	2
~~8~~	~~744~~	~~4~~
~~4~~	~~1,488~~	~~8~~
~~2~~	~~2,976~~	~~16~~
1	5,952	32
Total	6,510 (product)	35 (1st factor)

TABLE 8.10
Multiplication Objectives and Diagnostic Items

OBJECTIVE	DIAGNOSTIC TASK
Given a 1-digit times 2-digit multiplication exercise involving no regrouping, the child will compute the product using paper and pencil.	$\begin{array}{r} 24 \\ \times\ 2 \\ \hline \end{array}$
Given a 1-digit times 2-digit multiplication exercise involving no regrouping, the child will compute the product using base-10 materials and record the results using symbols.	$\begin{array}{r} 25 \\ \times\ 3 \\ \hline \end{array}$
Given a 2-digit times 2-digit multiplication exercise, the child will compute the product using paper and pencil.	$\begin{array}{r} 22 \\ \times 16 \\ \hline \end{array}$
Given a 2-digit times 2-digit multiplication exercise with a zero in the ones place, the child will compute the product using paper and pencil.	$\begin{array}{r} 50 \\ \times 23 \\ \hline \end{array}$

been added that keeps track of the number of times 186 is added to itself to make each value in the second column.

When the *even* lines are extended through column 3, the sum of the remaining values in the third column (1 + 2 + 32) equals the multiplier (35). The sum of the remaining values in the second column, then, must equal 186 added to itself 35 times, or 35 × 186.

J. ASSESSMENT STRATEGY

Teacher-made diagnostic tests are often used to supplement commercial exams that come with textbooks. As discussed in Chapter 6, the teacher is in the best position to design tests specifically aligned with lesson objectives.

Follow these four steps when constructing a diagnostic test:

1. Identify the *concept* or procedure to be assessed.
2. Specify a limited number of *objectives*.
3. Design test *items* for each objective.
4. Evaluate item *validity* for future use.

A diagnostic test assesses a small number of objectives associated with a particular mathematics concept or procedure. For students of grades 4 through 9, paper-and-pencil tests of 10–20 items are more common.

Table 8.10 lists sample objectives and diagnostic items that assess multiplication skills of students in grade 4. It also shows the manipulation of base-10 blocks to solve the sample problems and satisfy the objectives in the table.

It may be impractical to field test an instrument to validate the items prior to using it with your class. Generally, a newly developed test is simply administered to the class. Items that several students found confusing, or those that do not appear to test the appropriate concept or procedure, are discarded. Teachers should design new items to replace the discarded ones, thereby gradually improving the test for future administrations.

For example, a subtraction item designed to assess regrouping might have a zero in the minuend (e.g., $304 - 128 = ?$). While this item does require regrouping, students who *are* able to regroup for subtraction across one place value may still miss this item since it requires regrouping across two place values. Therefore, you might choose to substitute a more appropriate item (e.g., $344 - 128 = ?$). With experience, designing diagnostic tests becomes second nature for most teachers.

K. MULTIPLICATION AND DIVISION SAMPLE LESSON PLAN

An example of a lesson plan that introduces multiplication and division to students in grade 4, written by Loren Lones (UCSD, 1992), follows.

Multiplication and Division Lesson Plan

Grade Level: Grade 4   *Time Allotment:* 1 hour, 20 minutes

NCTM Standard: Develop meaning for the operations by modeling and discussing a rich variety of problem situations.

Essential Understanding: The operations of addition, subtraction, multiplication, and division are related to one another and are used to obtain numerical information.

Goal: Establish a connection between the concrete act of multiplication and the symbolic representation of this act.

Objective: Given the objects necessary to act out story problems, students will act out a story problem and determine the number operations needed to understand a story problem.

Motivation: Tell the class, "We are going to act out a little story. I want you to try to explain what is going on and what questions need to be answered."

Procedure: In a previous lesson, the students made lists of things that come in twos, threes, . . . up to twelves. Present story problems that are connected to these lists. For example: "Maria puts four chairs at the table. There are four legs on each chair. How many chair legs are there at the table?" Have Maria actually put the chairs around the table and ask the students how many chairs there are (four). Write, "4 chairs with" on the board. Then ask how many legs on each chair (four). Add to the sentence on the board "4 legs each." Then ask how many legs there are altogether (16). Complete the sentence on the board: "equals 16."

Other story problems teachers can use are: 1. Juan has four lions (stuffed). Each lion has four legs. How many legs are there altogether? 2. Gabriel puts two boxes on the table. There are six corners on each box. How many corners are there altogether? 3. Barbara has seven dwarfs (she shows picture). Each dwarf has two eyes. How many eyes are there altogether?

Introduce the multiplication symbol after doing five or six of these problems. Change one of the word sentences to numbers and mathematical symbols, and ask students if the sentence still says the same thing. After you talk about the change you just made, ask students if they have any ideas for a story problem. Go through three or four problems that they make up as a class. Then, break them up into groups and have each group write several multiplication story problems.

continued

Multiplication and Division Lesson Plan   cont'd

Closure: At the end of the class, ask one student from each group to read one of its story problems to the class and write it on the board the same way you did. Talk about the process so that they can verbalize the connection between the process of multiplication in the physical world and the abstract representation of that process.

Assessment: Carry out formative assessment by interacting with the children while they are creating their problems. At the end of the class, you will have a sheet of paper from each group of students with a record of their story problems. Evaluate these story problems to make sure that they present a multiplication situation. The only problem with this is that you will be evaluating the work of a group of students, not an individual. This is okay, since the larger unit that this lesson is a part of has activities that you can use to evaluate individual students.

Materials: Lists that the students have made of number groupings, four chairs, table, four stuffed lions, a picture of the seven dwarfs, paper, pencils, chalk, and the board.

Extension: Students can make a book out of their story problems, with one problem on each page. Then they can illustrate each problem to reinforce the idea that the multiplication process is something that occurs in real life.

SOURCE: Loren Lones, University of California, San Diego, 1992.

SUMMARY

- Multiplication and division are fundamental concepts in mathematics education.
- As Piaget observed, a thorough knowledge of transitivity contributes to a meaningful understanding of these operations.
- Repeated addition, Cartesian products, and arrays are three ways children can think about multiplication.
- Division can be modeled using repeated subtraction, partitioning, or arrays.
- Base-10 blocks; bean sticks; chip-trading materials; dots, lines, and squares; and place-value tables can be effectively used to introduce the multiplication and division concepts and develop the symbolic algorithms.
- Multiplication and division are inverse operations that reinforce each other's development when introduced concurrently.
- The commutative property, associative property, and distributive property of multiplication over addition are used by children to help develop the multiplication algorithm and to learn the multiplication facts.
- The special roles of *0* and *1* in multiplication and division are also important concepts teachers should introduce at the elementary level.
- Developmental activity sequences can be used to teach multiplication and division concepts and algorithms to groups of children who are at various levels of development and experience.
- Initially, teachers introduce the class to a new concept or skill using concrete materials, recording their actions and results in place-value tables. Some children may require intermediary work with nonproportional materials such as dots, lines, and squares, while others begin working exercises directly in place-value tables or using the standard algorithm.
- Story and nonroutine problems involving multiplication and division offer opportunities to apply newly developed mathematics and language skills.
- Each multiplication and division model has applications in real-world problem situations. An understanding of the different models helps children identify appropriate operations when they are encountered.
- Introducing alternate low-stress algorithms may be useful when working with special-needs children who have experienced protracted difficulty learning the multiplication or division algorithm. Exploring alternate algorithms is also an interesting extension activity for gifted and talented students.

QUESTIONS AND ACTIVITIES FOR DISCUSSION

1. Working in small groups, compile a list of real-world situations that embody the repeated addition, array, or Cartesian product notions of multiplication. Compile a class list of the situations described, and design story or picture problems based on each situation. Write each problem on a separate card, shuffle the pack, and have individuals try to identify which of the three multiplication types best describes each situation.

2. Survey your friends and members of your class and make a list of the rhymes and mnemonic devices they used to memorize the multiplication facts. Organize these techniques by category (songs, rhymes, etc.) and compile a class list.

3. Construct a set of 81 multiplication candybars using centimeter-squared paper. Make flash cards by attaching each candybar to the front of a file card and writing the corresponding multiplication fact on the back. Write a lesson plan to introduce the multiplication facts to a group of children in grade 4 employing these materials. If possible, implement the lesson and discuss the results.

4. Construct a board game designed to give students practice recalling the multiplication facts. Try it out with your peers or, if possible, a small group of children. Revise the game based on your observations and student responses. Exchange games with other members of your class and compile a set of at least five games for future classroom use.

5. Using a set of proportional base-10 materials, practice setting up multiplication problems, carrying out the necessary manipulations, and recording the actions and results in place-value tables. With your peers, practice demonstrating multiplication exercises with products less than 1,000 until you can confidently verbalize the procedures and evaluate procedural errors. Write a lesson plan to introduce one-digit $\times$ two-digit multiplication to a small group of students in grade 4 and record the interaction on audio- or videotape. Review the session with a peer and look for points where your instructions were confusing or where you misinterpreted a student response.

6. Write story or picture problems that are examples of the repeated subtraction, partitive, and array models of division. Working with a group of peers, mix the cards and try to choose those problems that are examples of each division model. Justify your selection.

7. Using a set of proportional base-10 materials, set up and solve division problems with divisors and quotients less than 40. Practice until you can consistently make accurate initial quotient estimates. Record the concrete actions and results in place-value tables. Write a lesson plan to introduce division using arrays to a small group of peers, and have an observer watch you implement the lesson. Discuss the experience with the observer and other members in your class.

8. Select several word problems from a grade 4–9 textbook or other resource and rewrite them to include superfluous information, or remove one or more of the required values. Write each problem on a separate card. Exchange the cards with a partner and separate problems with missing values from those that have superfluous information.

9. Review a problem-solving resource book or textbook to find problems that can be solved by organizing data in tables, looking for patterns and functions, and working backwards. Solve them and discuss the procedures with your peers. If possible, introduce a problem to a group of students in grades 4–9. Work through the problem with them. Give them a similar problem to solve without your assistance. Discuss the results with your peers.

10. Make a set of Napier's Bones and practice multiplying numbers of various sizes. Write directions that would explain to a novice how the bones can be used to multiply numbers. If possible, introduce the activity to a group of students in grades 5–9. Arrange for an observer to watch the interaction. Review the session immediately afterward with the observer and take note of points of confusion, successful and unsuccessful management techniques, and student responses to the presentation.

11. Discuss the alternative multiplication algorithms described in this chapter and others used by your peers. Solve the problem $27 \times 36 = ?$ on separate index cards using each algorithm and include them in your idea file.

12. Solve $692 \div 24 = ?$ using the two display algorithms shown in this chapter. Coordinate the results of each with the standard algorithm.

13. Include examples of several multiplication and division lessons in your idea file. Organize them according to appropriate grade level.

14. Read one of the *Arithmetic Teacher* articles listed in the "Suggested Readings." Write a brief report summarizing the main ideas of the article, and describe how the recommendations for instruction might apply to your own mathematics teaching.

INSTRUCTIONAL RESOURCES

CHILDREN'S BOOKS

Anno, M. *Anno's mysterious multiplying jar.* Philomel Books. A story that uses multiplication to show how numbers grow using real-world examples.

COMPUTER SOFTWARE

Math Mastery Series. Minnesota Educational Computer Consortium. Set of programs providing practice in number skills and the four operations.

Power Drill. WINGS for Learning/Sunburst. Practice using front-end and other rounding techniques to solve addition, subtraction, multiplication, and division exercises.

Burns, M. *The book of think.* Little, Brown and Company. A delightful collection of thoughtful math problems for children of all ages.

Read and Solve Math Problems. Educational Activities Inc. Tutorial for solving word problems.

REFERENCES

Ashlock, R. (1976). *Error patterns in computation: A semi-programmed approach.* New York: Merrill/Macmillan.

Brownell, W., & Carper, D. (1943). *Learning the multiplication combinations.* Durham, NC: Duke University Press.

Driscoll, M. (1980). *Research within reach: Elementary school mathematics.* St. Louis, MO: CAMREL, Inc.

National Council of Teachers of Mathematics. (1989). *Curriculum and evaluation standards for school mathematics.* Reston, VA: Author.

Rogoff, B., & Lave, J. (1983). *Everyday cognition: Its development in social context.* Cambridge, MA: Harvard University Press.

Williams, J. (1971). *Teaching techniques in primary mathematics.* Slough, Great Britain: Nuffeld Foundation for Educational Research.

SUGGESTED READINGS

Baratta-Lorton, M. (1976). *Mathematics their way.* Menlo Park, CA: Addison-Wesley.

Bates, T., & Rousseau, L. (1986). Will the real division algorithm please stand up? *Arithmetic Teacher, 33*(7), 42–46.

Broadbent, F. (1987). Lattice multiplication and division. *Arithmetic Teacher, 34*(5), 28–31.

Burns, M. (1978). *The book of think.* New York: Little, Brown.

Burns, M. (1991). Introducing division through problem-solving experiences. *Arithmetic Teacher, 38*(8), 14–18.

Cheek, H., & Olson, M. (1986). A den of thieves investigates division. *Arithmetic Teacher, 33*(9), 34–35.

Downie, D., Slesnick, T., & Stenmark, J. (1981). *Math for girls and other problem solvers.* Berkeley, CA: Regents, University of California.

Dubitsky, B. (1988). Making division meaningful with a spreadsheet. *Arithmetic Teacher, 33*(9), 34, 35.

Graeber, A., & Baker, K. (1992). Little into big is the way it will always be. *Arithmetic Teacher, 36*(3), 18–21.

Greenes, C., Immerzeel, G., Ockenga, L., Schulman, J., & Spungin, R. (1980). *Techniques of problem solving.* Palo Alto, CA: Dale Seymour.

Greenes, C., Spungin, R., & Dombrowski, J. (1977). *Problem-mathematics: Mathematical challenge problems with solution strategies.* Palo Alto, CA: Creative Publications.

Haag, V., Kaufman, B., Martin, E., & Rising, G. (1986). *Challenge: A program for the mathematically talented.* Menlo Park , CA: Addison-Wesley.

Hall, W. (1983). Division with base-ten blocks. *Arithmetic Teacher, 31*(3), 21–23.

Hamic, E. (1986). Students' creative computations: My way or your way. *Arithmetic Teacher, 34*(1), 39–41.

Huinker, D. (1989). Multiplication and division word problems: Improving students' understanding. *Arithmetic Teacher, 37*(2), 8–12.

Immerzeel, G., & Ockenga, E. (1977). *Calculator activities: Books 1 & 2.* Palo Alto, CA: Creative Publications.

Lessen, E. & Cumblad, C. (1984). Alternatives for teaching multiplication facts. *Arithmetic Teacher, 31*(5), 46–48.

Pearson, E. (1986). Summing it all up: Pre-1900 algorithms. *Arithmetic Teacher, 33*(7), 38–41.

Quintero, A. (1985). Conceptual understanding of multiplication: Problems involving combination. *Arithmetic Teacher, 33*(3), 36–39.

Remington, J. (1989). Introducing multiplication. *Arithmetic Teacher, 37*(3), 12–14, 60.

Robold, A. (1983). Grid arrays for multiplication. *Arithmetic Teacher, 30*(5), 14–17.

Sharron, S. (Ed.). (1979). *Applications in school mathematics: 1979 yearbook.* Reston, VA: National Council of Teachers of Mathematics.

Silvey, L., & Smart, J. (Eds.). (1982). *Mathematics in the middle grades: 1982 yearbook.* Reston, VA: National Council of Teachers of Mathematics.

Souviney, R., Keyser, T., & Sarver, A. (1978). *Mathmatters: Developing computational skills with developmental activity sequences.* Glenview, IL: Scott, Foresman.

Suydam, M. (Ed.). (1978). *Developing computational skills: 1978 yearbook.* Reston, VA: National Council of Teachers of Mathematics.

CHAPTER 9

Patterns and Functions

T his chapter focuses your attention on how to teach the concepts of patterns and functions. Specifically, it is designed to help you understand

1. The concept of a number pattern, and classroom activities used to introduce this concept.
2. The algebraic concept of a function and its relationship to patterns.
3. The relationship between a function and its coordinate graph, and classroom activities used to introduce these concepts.
4. How to use a finite-difference method to describe the underlying functions expressed in a two-column table.
5. Pattern and function problem-solving activities.
6. Techniques for incorporating technology into pattern and function lessons.

NCTM pattern, function, and algebra standards
K–4 level students will

- Recognize, describe, extend, and create a wide variety of patterns
- Represent and describe mathematical relationships
- Explore the use of variables and open sentences to express relationships.

5–8 level students will

- Describe, extend, analyze, and create a wide variety of patterns
- Describe and represent relationships with tables, graphs, and rules
- Analyze functional relationships to explain how a change in one quantity results in a change in another
- Use patterns and functions to represent and solve problems
- Understand the concepts of variable, expression, and equation
- Represent situations and number patterns with tables, graphs, verbal rules, and equations and explore the interrelationships of these representations
- Analyze tables and graphs to identify properties and relationships
- Investigate inequalities and nonlinear equations informally
- Apply algebraic methods to solve a variety of real-world and mathematical problems. (NCTM, 1989, pp. 80, 98, 102)

Number theory is a branch of mathematics concerned with the characteristics of numbers and groups of numbers. The mathematics curriculum contains many opportunities to study the unique features of numbers. A few number theory examples that are introduced in this chapter include patterns, sequences, primes, divisibility tests, factors, and multiples. A good understanding of patterns and sequences is fundamental to the development of the notion of *function,* or the relationship between two sets of numbers.

A pattern is a systematic configuration of geometric figures, sounds, symbols, or actions. Much of what we learn stems from successfully unraveling the patterns embedded in the events and ideas we encounter in life. Language develops as a consequence of imitating systematic recurrence of speech. In early grades we explore patterns based on attributes such as color, texture, size, and number. These patterns are used to classify objects according to measure and geometric attributes and arrange them into systematic patterns.

A. NUMBER PATTERNS

Number patterns are the outcome of counting and classification activity. In mathematics, the term *pattern* takes on a precise meaning when applied to arithmetic and geometric sequences. The values, or *terms,* in these sequences are related to each other according to a consistent rule. For example, the terms of the odd-number sequences are related to each other according to a consistent rule.

Odd number sequence:	1, 3, 5, 7, 9, . . .
Odd number rule:	$1 + 2 = 3$; $3 + 2 = 5$; . . .
Even number sequence:	0, 2, 4, 6, 8, . . .
Even number rule:	$0 + 2 = 2$; $2 + 2 = 4$; . . .

Give children a supply of small blocks and have them construct the odd and even numbers. Each value in the sequence should be represented by a separate stack. Ask them to describe any patterns they see in their block sequence and draw a sketch of the results.

Arrow diagrams such as those shown in Figure 9.1 can be used to introduce number patterns. Children fill in the circles by carrying out the indicated operation. This activity can be adapted to several grade levels by varying the values and operations involved. Children can make up arrow diagram problems for each other as well.

Other rules relate more than two terms in a sequence. An interesting example was described more than 700 years ago by the Italian mathematician Leonardo Fibonacci. Starting with 0 and 1, subsequent terms in Fibonacci's sequence are computed by adding each previous pair of terms.

Fibonacci sequence:	0, 1, 1, 2, 3, 5, 8, 13, 21, . . .

This sequence appears in a surprising number of contexts, from biology to music. For example, Fibonacci noted that the pattern of reproduction of a pair of rabbits follows this sequence. Rabbits must mature two months before reproducing. Subsequently, each parent-pair produces one new pair of offspring each month. If no rabbits die, the rabbit population (not including the original parents) will multiply as shown in the two-column Table 9.1.

9.1

✎ **FIGURE IT OUT**

Compare the squared Fibonacci sequence to the original Fibonacci sequence. Notice that the sum of consecutive pairs of squares seems to give alternating terms of the original Fibonacci sequence. Carry out the process to a few more terms to see if the pattern continues. What is the property of the Fibonacci sequence that causes this pattern?

TABLE 9.1
Rabbit Reproduction

MONTH	PAIRS OF RABBITS
0	0
1	1
2	1
3	2
4	3
5	5
6	8
—	—
—	—
—	—

FIGURE 9.1
Arrow Diagrams

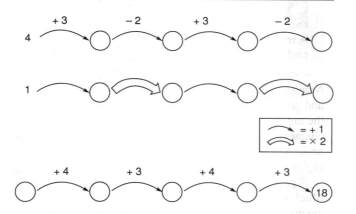

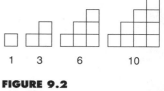

FIGURE 9.2
Triangle Numbers

Other interesting patterns can be generated based on the Fibonacci sequence. For example, each term in the sequence can be squared and these values summed pairwise as in the original sequence:

Fibonacci sequence: 0, 1, 1, 2, 3, 5, 8, 13, . . .
Square each term: 0, 1, 1, 4, 9, 25, 64, 169, . . .
Add pairs: 1, 2, 5, 13, 34, 89, 233, . . .

B. POLYGON AND POLYHEDRON NUMBERS

Historically, number patterns based on the geometric arrangement of objects have taken on special, even mystical significance. The sequence of square numbers (1, 4, 9, 16, and so on) is a familiar example. Other number sequences are also suggested by other geometric shapes.

Triangle Number Sequence

The triangle numbers are constructed by arranging identical counters into a stair-step pattern as shown in Figure 9.2. Beginning with one cube, children continue building larger configurations in the triangle pattern. The triangle numbers grow according to the number of objects in each step. Have children build the triangle numbers using blocks. Ask them to predict the number of blocks in the tenth stack.

The pattern of values can be organized into a table according to the number of steps in each triangular stack of cubes (see Table 9.2).

Several interesting patterns can be found in the triangle number sequence. By examining the figure associated with each triangle number, notice that each subsequent term can be found by adding a new row to the bottom of the preceding value (see Figure 9.3). To compute the next triangle number, simply add to the current term the number equal to the *position value* of the new term. For example, to find the sixth term we add six to the value of the fifth term:

1, 3, 6, 10, 15, 21, . . .
+6

Square Number Sequence

Children can combine adjacent pairs of triangle numbers to show a new sequence called the *square numbers* (see Figure 9.4).

The square numbers derive their name from square arrays that can be constructed using counters of 1, 4, 9, 16, 25, and so on. Several patterns can be explored based on the square number sequence. Using centimeter-squared paper, have children draw the sequence of square numbers with edge lengths of 1 through 10 centimeters. Have them color or cut out

---

9.2

✎ FIGURE IT OUT

Compute 15 terms of the triangle numbers. Record your results in a two-column table.

TABLE 9.2
Triangle Number Pattern

STEPS	TRIANGLE NUMBER
1	1
2	3
3	6
4	10
—	—
—	—
—	—

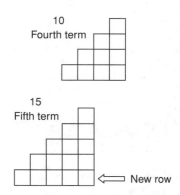

10
Fourth term

15
Fifth term

⇐ New row

FIGURE 9.3
Triangle Numbers

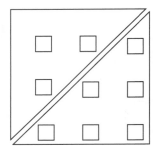

FIGURE 9.4
Relationship between Triangle and Square Numbers

the largest possible square array within each square, leaving an L-shaped figure as shown in Figure 9.5. Using blocks, demonstrate the process on the overhead projector while the children work at their seats. The *L* has equal arms (not including the corner square) that each grow one unit for each step in the sequence. Ask if the arms will always be equal regardless of the size of the original square. If so, then the number of blocks in both arms must be even (two times any whole number *(n)* is even). When the corner object is included, the result must *always* be odd:

$$2 \times n = \text{even number}$$
$$(2 \times n) + 1 = \text{even number} + 1 = \text{odd number}$$

The *L*-shaped figure is the result of subtracting adjacent pairs of square numbers. The *difference sequence* is the odd numbers.

Square numbers: 1, 4, 9, 16, 25, 36, . . .

Differences sequence: 3, 5, 7, 9, 11, . . .

Tetrahedral Numbers

Have children construct piles of marbles with equilateral triangle bases as shown in Figure 9.6. Use a heavy shag carpet scrap to keep the marbles from rolling. These structures are three-dimensional representations of the *tetrahedral number sequence*. The sequence is named for the regular geometric space-figure constructed from four equilateral triangles, the *tetrahedron*.

Cannonballs were commonly stacked according to this pattern. Each stack comprises a triangular arrangement of balls. The largest triangular configuration forms the base. Each subsequent layer is the next smaller term in the triangle number sequence. A tetrahedral number, then, is the sum of all triangle numbers from 1 to the value of its base. Children can use this pattern to find the number of cannonballs in a tetrahedral stack with ten balls along each edge of its base (see Figure 9.7).

Cubic Numbers

Children can construct a model of the *cubic numbers* by stacking blocks to form square cubes (see Figure 9.8). The results can be organized into a table in which the first column indicates the position of the box in the sequence, and the second column lists the corresponding terms of the sequence (see Table 9.3).

FIGURE IT OUT

Using blocks, construct the first ten elements of the square number sequence. Record your results in a table. Subtract adjacent elements in the sequence and record the results in a table. Why must the difference sequence include all the odd numbers larger than 3?

FIGURE IT OUT

Compute the first ten tetrahedral numbers. A calculator may be useful for this exercise. Record your results in a table.

FIGURE 9.5
Difference between Adjacent Square Numbers

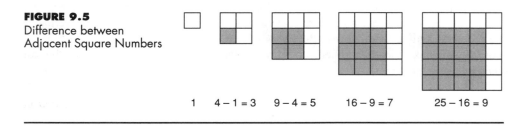

1   4 − 1 = 3   9 − 4 = 5   16 − 9 = 7   25 − 16 = 9

FIGURE 9.6
Tetrahedral Numbers

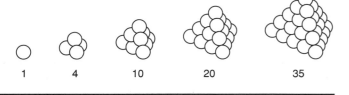

1   4   10   20   35

FIGURE 9.7
Sum of Triangle Numbers = Tetrahedral Number

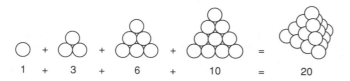

$$1 \;+\; 3 \;+\; 6 \;+\; 10 \;=\; 20$$

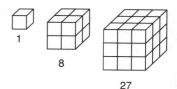

FIGURE 9.8
Cubic Numbers

TABLE 9.3
Cubic Numbers

POSITION	TERM
1	1
2	8
3	27
4	64
5	125
—	—
—	—
—	—

Children should notice that this sequence grows very rapidly compared to previous sequences. Each new cubic term increases the value of the previous term by the total number of the cubes added to all three faces of previous cubes. This increases the value of subsequent terms more quickly than with the triangle, square, and tetrahedral numbers.

C. USING NUMBER PATTERNS
Making Noodles

Noodles are made by hand in some Chinese restaurants. Dough is prepared and stretched using a doubling process. The first doubling gives two very thick noodle strands. The second gives four noodles. Continuing the doubling and stretching process soon produces a large number of very thin noodles. Children can use a long piece of string to demonstrate this doubling process. Then have them try to find a pattern that will allow them to determine how many doublings are required to produce 1,024 noodles by continuing the sequence started in Table 9.4.

Prime and Composite Numbers

A whole number that has exactly two whole-number factors, 1 and itself, is called a *prime number*. All other whole numbers except 1 are called composite numbers. The number 1 is special because it is a factor of all values and, therefore, is considered neither prime nor composite.

Arrays can be used to show the special characteristics of prime numbers. Using squared paper, have children cut rectangular arrays representing the whole numbers 1 through 10 (3 can be represented by a 1×3 array; 4 can be represented by 1×4 and 2×2 arrays). Make a classroom chart to keep track of how many different arrays there are for each value (count commutes as the same array). Primes have *only* one array representation, and composites have more than one (see Figure 9.9).

Larger prime numbers can be identified using the *Sieve of Eratosthenes*. Using a hundred chart, children first circle 1, the identity element that is neither prime nor composite. The next value is 2, so cross out all the multiples of 2 (except 2, of course). The next uncrossed value is 3, so cross out all the multiples of 3 (except 3). Skip 4 because it is already crossed out. Continue this process until all possible multiples are crossed out. The values remaining are primes and the ones crossed out are composite numbers. Ask the children why the Sieve leaves only the prime values (see Figure 9.10). How many multiples need to be checked before no more values will be crossed out? Why? How could this process be extended to identify even larger prime values?

Primes listed from small to large form the sequence of prime numbers. Children with a special interest in this topic can look for prime numbers separated by only 1 whole number, called *twin primes* (3 and 5; 5 and 7; 41 and 43) in the sequence of prime numbers, which is

$$2, 3, 5, 7, 11, 13, 17, 19, 23, 29, 31, 37, 41, 43, 47, \ldots$$

A way to test a value to see if it is prime is to divide it by all smaller whole numbers and check for zero remainders. For large numbers, the procedure becomes tedious even when using a calculator. The amount of work can be reduced by noticing that whole numbers larger than one-half of the value being tested can never give a whole-number quotient (except the

TABLE 9.4
Noodle Numbers

DOUBLINGS	NOODLES
1	2
2	4
3	8
4	16
5	32
6	64
—	—
—	—
—	—

9.5
✎ **FIGURE IT OUT**

Compute ten terms of the cubic number sequence. Record your results in a table.

9.6
✎ **FIGURE IT OUT**

Compute ten terms of the noodle number sequence. Record your results in a table.

FIGURE 9.9
Prime and Composite Number Arrays

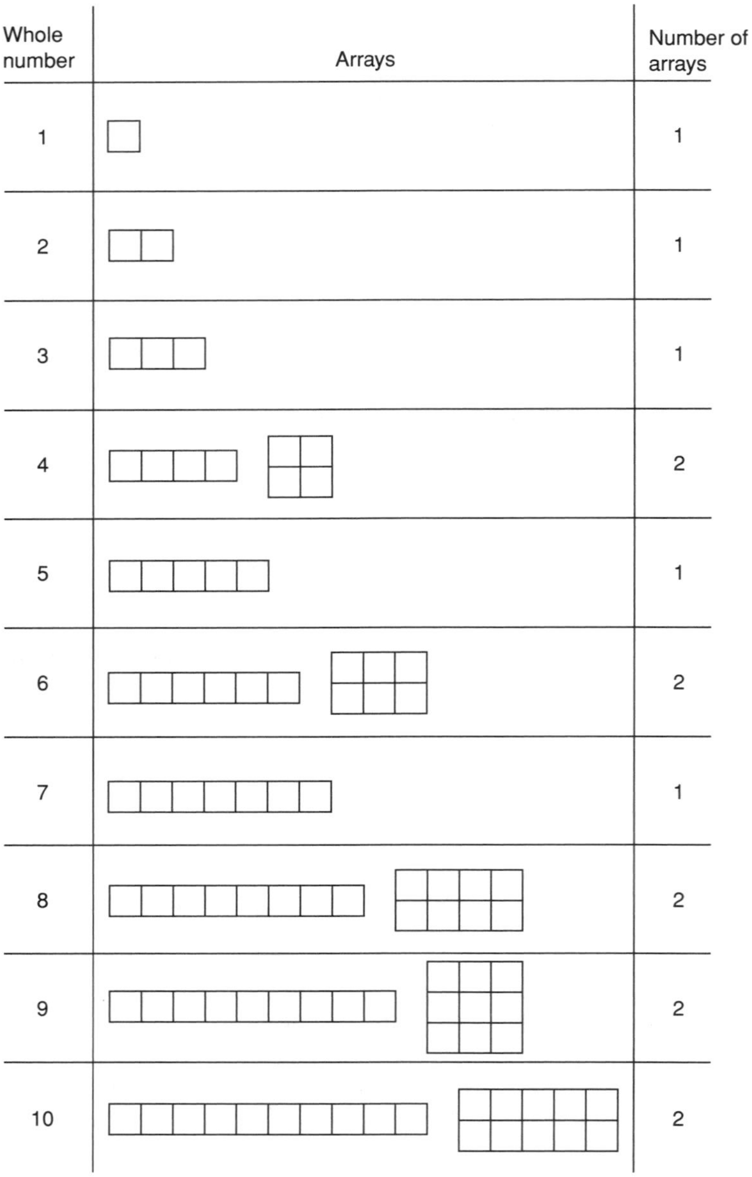

Whole number	Arrays	Number of arrays
1		1
2		1
3		1
4		2
5		1
6		2
7		1
8		2
9		2
10		2

value itself, which gives a quotient of 1). For example, to test if 51 is prime, check each divisor 2 through 25. Except for 51 itself, no divisor 26 through 51 can give a whole-number quotient.

The problem can be further simplified by checking only *prime* divisors less than or equal to one-half of the number being tested. The reason for this is that if a number is divisible by a composite number, it is also divisible by a prime number, so it is necessary only to test prime divisors. To test 51, divide by 2, 3, 5, 7, 11, 13, 17, 19, and 23. Since both 3 and 17 give zero remainders, 51 is not prime. The same test shows that 53 is prime. Though this procedure will determine if a given number is prime, no one has yet discovered a pattern that can be used to determine, say, the 100th or the 167th value in the prime number sequence.

FIGURE 9.10
Sieve of Eratosthenes

①	2	3	X̶4	5	X̶6	7	X̶8	X̶9	X̶10
11	X̶12	13	X̶14	X̶15	X̶16	17	X̶18	19	X̶20
X̶21	X̶22	23	X̶24	X̶25	X̶26	X̶27	X̶28	29	X̶30
31	X̶32	X̶33	X̶34	X̶35	X̶36	37	X̶38	X̶39	X̶40
41	X̶42	43	X̶44	X̶45	X̶46	X̶47	X̶48	X̶49	X̶50
X̶51	X̶52	53	X̶54	X̶55	X̶56	X̶57	X̶58	59	X̶60
61	X̶62	X̶63	X̶64	X̶65	X̶66	67	X̶68	X̶69	X̶70
71	X̶72	73	X̶74	X̶75	X̶76	X̶77	X̶78	79	X̶80
X̶81	X̶82	83	X̶84	X̶85	X̶86	X̶87	X̶88	89	X̶90
X̶91	X̶92	X̶93	X̶94	X̶95	X̶96	97	X̶98	X̶99	X̶100

Casting Out Nines

Interesting number patterns emerge from the process called *casting out nines*. This procedure is based on the observation that for any multiplication fact involving the value 9, the sum of the product's digits is equal to 9 ($2 \times 9 = 18 \rightarrow 1 + 8 = 9$).

The process of adding the digits that comprise any whole number exposes interesting patterns. By adding a value's digits and repeating the process for each result, the sum eventually becomes a single digit that is called the *digital root*. In the example

$$237 \rightarrow 2 + 3 + 7 = 12 \rightarrow 1 + 2 = 3$$

the original number is 237, the *first sum* is $2 + 3 + 7 = 12$, and the *digital root* is 3, the sum of the numbers in the first sum.

Have children find the digital roots of several two- and three-digit numbers. They can try other ways to combine digits. Try adding the digit in the ones column to the remaining digits read as a separate number. Repeat the process until you arrive at a single digit ($371 \rightarrow 37 + 1 = 38 \rightarrow 3 + 8 = 11 \rightarrow 1 + 1 = 2$). Does this process seem to give the same value as the digital root? What if other groupings of digits were allowed? Would the result be the same as the digital root? For example:

$$35,482 \rightarrow 35 + 482 = 517 \rightarrow 5 + 17 = 22 \rightarrow 2 + 2 = 4 \rightarrow \text{digital root?}$$

Children can also verify that the digital root of any whole number is equal to the remainder that results from dividing the value by 9. If the digital root of a number is 9, then the remainder resulting from dividing that number by 9 will be 0 (see Table 9.5).

Children in grades 4–6 often find it challenging to verify that large numbers with the digital root 9 are really divisible by 9. This activity can motivate students to practice long-division and calculator skills.

Casting out nines also can be used as an alternative way to check the accuracy of arithmetic exercises. To check an addition problem, find the digital root of each of the addends and the sum. If the answer is correct, adding of the digital roots of the addends will give a digital root equal to the digital root of the sum.

9.7
 **FIGURE IT OUT**

Look for patterns in the sequence of prime numbers. Show that it is actually necessary to check only for factors up to the *square root* of any value to determine if it is prime.

TABLE 9.5
Casting Out Nines

NUMBER	DIGITAL ROOT	DIVISION BY NINE
27	9	$\begin{array}{r} 3 \text{ R0} \\ 9\overline{)27} \end{array}$
111,111,111	9	$\begin{array}{r} 12\,345\,679 \text{ R0} \\ 9\overline{)111,111,111} \end{array}$

$$\begin{array}{rcl} 254 & \longrightarrow & 2 \quad \text{Digital} \\ \underline{+\,187} & \longrightarrow & \underline{+\,7} \quad \text{Root} \\ 441 & \longrightarrow & 9 \end{array}$$

If the answer is off by exactly a multiple of 9, this checking procedure will, of course, incorrectly *validate* an incorrect answer. For example, if 432 was thought to be the sum for $254 + 187$, the digital roots would *incorrectly* indicate that the answer is right.

More experienced students can use similar checks for multiplication, subtraction, and division. Like addition, multiplication can be checked by carrying out the same operations on the digital roots as with the original values in the exercise.

$$\begin{array}{rcl} 46 & \longrightarrow & 1 \quad \text{Digital} \\ \underline{\times\,23} & \longrightarrow & \underline{\times\,5} \quad \text{Roots} \\ 1{,}058 & \longrightarrow & 5 \end{array}$$

Note that subtraction exercises sometimes give a *negative* difference between the digital roots ($55 - 29$ gives the digital roots $1 - 2 = -1$). If children have not been introduced to work with negative values, use the procedure of adding the difference and the subtrahend to check if it equals the minuend.

$$\begin{array}{rcl} 251 & \longrightarrow & \underline{8} \longleftarrow \text{Digital Root} \\ \underline{-\,67} & \longrightarrow & \underline{+\,4} \\ 184 & & 4 \end{array}$$

or

$$\begin{array}{rcl} 213 & \longrightarrow & \underline{15} \longrightarrow 6 \longleftarrow \text{Digital Root} \\ \underline{-\,89} & \longrightarrow & \underline{+\,8} \\ 124 & & 7 \end{array}$$

For digital root division, it is more convenient to check by using its inverse operation, multiplication.

$$346 \div 26 = 14 \longrightarrow 26 \times 14 = 364 \longrightarrow 4$$
$$\downarrow \qquad \downarrow \qquad \qquad \uparrow$$
$$8 \times 5 = 40 \longrightarrow 4 \quad \text{Digital Root}$$

The casting out nines procedure is a direct result of the base-10 structure of our numeration system. It can be explained by using techniques of modular arithmetic where 0 and 9 are considered equivalent (as 0 and 12 are considered equivalent on the clock). Mathematically mature grade 5–6 students can use this idea to understand why it is possible to add 9 to negative digital-root differences found in some subtraction exercises and continue the checking process (for $213 - 89 = 124$, the digital root difference is $6 - 8 = -2 \rightarrow -2 + 9 = 7$, which equals the digital root for 124).

Divisibility Tests

It is sometimes helpful for children to be able to quickly determine whether a value is evenly divisible by some small number. The use of divisibility rules can facilitate factoring, renaming fractions in simplest terms, and work with ratio and proportion. For example, when renaming fractions in simplest terms, it is necessary to find common factors for

FROM A DIFFERENT ANGLE

ST: I've noticed that several of the students don't seem to get involved in my math activities. They always hold back, waiting for someone else to answer. They seem willing to work hard, but they won't take a risk. What can I do to get them involved?

CT: I think that some children are just shy and need encouragement to speak out in class. If they don't learn to open up, they can feel less and less in control of their own learning, and can develop math anxiety.

ST: What can I do to help them?

CT: One important thing to do is to listen to their ideas and validate their thinking. Even if their answer is wrong, point out where their thinking was valid and what they need to think about some more. It's important for children to feel safe so they'll try out new ideas.

ST: But how can I give validity to their thinking? I think they get tired of my praising them all the time.

CT: That's true—kids see through false praise quickly and start to tune it out if everything they do seems to get your attention. One thing I do that works well is to use the children's ideas in my own speech. I give them credit for thinking of a plan or theory and use it for the next few days whenever it's appropriate.

ST: I remember now—like when we were working on factors and Mary Jane said she just divided by two and three and that gave her all the factors for any number.

CT: That's right. She was only partly right, but that method does work with a lot of numbers. I plan to bring up Mary Jane's theory again when we start talking about greatest common divisor.

the denominators. For the fraction $\frac{21}{51}$, a child can calculate the digital root for 21 (3) and 51 (6) and quickly note that both are divisible by 3 (both numbers are therefore divisible by 3 but not 9). Therefore, $\frac{21}{51}$ can be renamed in simplest terms as $\frac{7}{17}$.

Rules have been invented that allow children to predict whether a number is evenly divisible by the divisors 1–9 without actually carrying out the division. A calculator can serve the same purpose, but divisibility rules provide excellent opportunities for mental arithmetic practice. Verifying why these rules work also can be an interesting mathematical investigation for mathematically able students.

Some of the divisibility rules are easy to verify. For example, all *whole* numbers are evenly divisible by 1. All *even* numbers are divisible by 2. To help children understand the divisibility rule for 4, list all the multiples of 4 up to 100. Notice that every multiple of 4 can be evenly divided by 2 at least two times ($36 \div 2 = 18$ and $18 \div 2 = 9$). Look at larger multiples of 4 such as 112 or 448. To test if 112 is divisible by 4, we first note that its ones digit is even, so it is divisible by 2 ($112 \div 2 = 56$). Since 56 is even, it must also be divisible by 2. To be divisible by 4, then, we are only concerned that the last digit of the quotient be even each of the two times we divide by 2. Regardless of the digits in the larger place values, if the number represented by the ones and tens digits is divisible by 4, then the original number is divisible by 4. Using the same procedure, children can verify that they only need to check the value represented by the final *three* digits of a number to test for divisibility by 8.

In the previous section, we noted that if a digital root is 9, the number is divisible by 9. A number divisible by 9 is also divisible by 3. Further, since the digital root of a number is equal to the remainder after dividing by 9, numbers with digital roots 3, 6, or 9 have remainders divisible by 3 and, therefore, are themselves divisible by 3. Have children test several values using the digital-root method and check the results on a calculator. Have children explain why the divisibility rule for 6 works.

Table 9.6 lists divisibility rules for divisors 1 through 9. Similar tests for larger divisors can be invented as well. Some children may find it challenging to find divisibility tests for divisors 10 through 15 (11 is particularly interesting). When introducing *greatest common factor* and *least common multiple,* encourage children to employ these rules to help them identify factors.

Greatest Common Factor

The ability to identify the largest factor common to two or more numbers is necessary for work with fractions, ratios, proportions, and probability. Cuisenaire™ Rods can be used to introduce the concept of the greatest common factor (GCF). See Figure 9.11. Suppose you

9.10

✎ FIGURE IT OUT

Try to explain why each divisibility rule works. Use divisibility tests to verify the following statements. Check the results with a calculator.

1. The number 111,002,436 is divisible by 3.
2. The number 111,111,112 is divisible by 2.
3. The number 123,456,789 is divisible by 9.
4. The number 6,034 is divisible by 7.
5. The number 999,888,064 is divisible by 8.

TABLE 9.6
Whole-Number Divisibility Rule

DIVISOR	TEST
1	All whole numbers.
2	Units digit is even
3	Digital root is a multiple of 3.
4	Value represented by last two digits is a multiple of 4.
5	Units digit is 0 or 5.
6	Tests for divisors 2 *and* 3 apply.
7	Doubling units digit and subtracting result from remaining digits read as separate number is a multiple of 7 (may need to repeat process).
8	Value represented by last three digits is a multiple of 8.
9	Digital root is 9.

Example 1.   Is 3,472 divisible by 4?
Test:
$$\frac{18}{4)\overline{72}} \qquad \rightarrow \text{Verdict: Yes}$$

Example 2.   Is 62,482 divisible by 6?
Test: Last digit is *even*
but digital root = 4   → Verdict: No

Example 3.   Is 5,761 divisible by 7?
Test: 576
$$\frac{-\ 2}{574} \rightarrow 57$$
$$\frac{-8}{49} \qquad \rightarrow \text{a multiple of 7. Verdict: Yes}$$

FIGURE 9.11
Greatest Common Factor
Using Cuisenaire™ Rods

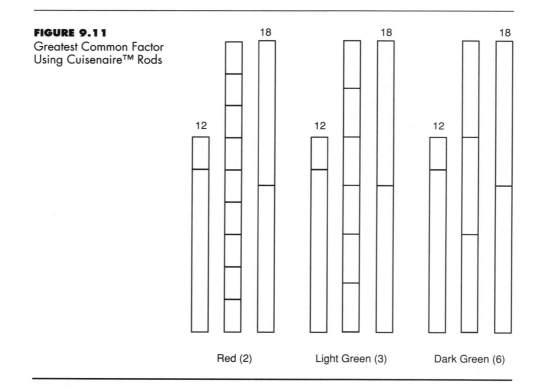

Red (2)   Light Green (3)   Dark Green (6)

want to find the GCF for 12 and 18. One orange and one red rod represent 12 and one orange and one brown rod represent 18. See if both 12 and 18 can be exactly matched using trains of only red (2) rods, then light green (3), then purple (4) rods, and so on up to one-half of the largest number (dark green in this case). Children should discover that there is no need to test rods larger than one-half the largest number since longer rods always require less than two rods to equal the length of the original. In this case, trains of red, light green,

TABLE 9.7
Greatest Common Factor

VALUE	FACTORS
18	1 2 3, 6, 9, 18
24	1 2 3, 4, 6, 8, 12, 24

TABLE 9.8
Prime Factors

VALUE	PRIME FACTORS
18	2, 3, 3
24	2, 2, 2, 3

and dark green rods exactly make up both 12 and 18. These are the common factors for 12 and 18. Since dark green is the longest rod of this set of factors, 6 is the GCF for 12 and 18.

Another method for finding the greatest common factor is to list all the factors of each number and check to see where the two sets of factors intersect (i.e., the values the two sets have in common). The largest of these common factors is called the GCF. For example, give children pairs of values and have them list all the factors for each as shown for the numbers 18 and 24 in Table 9.7. Have them draw a loop around the pairs of common factors (in italics) and circle the largest common factor, the GCF (6).

For large numbers with many factors, a second method for finding the GCF is helpful. Using the previous example, list all the *prime* factors for each number (see Table 9.8). Note that the prime factorization may include repeated values (e.g., 2, 3, 3).

The values 18 and 24 have one 2 and two 3s in common. The product of these common prime factors equals the GCF ($2 \times 3 \times 3 = 18$). This technique is often convenient since only prime factors must be found for each value, making the divisibility checks less tedious.

Factor trees can be used to help children find the prime factorization of a number. To make a factor tree, have children write the value to be factored at the top of a piece of paper. Using divisibility rules, have the class write one pair of factors beneath the value and draw a line to each as shown in Figure 9.12. This process is continued until all the factors are prime numbers. The prime factors of a number are the set of values at the end of each branch of the tree. Have children select different sets of initial factors for a number, complete a factor tree, and compare results. Does everyone eventually get the same set of prime factors? The important observation that every number has a *unique* prime factorization is called the *fundamental theorem of arithmetic*. Although it is too difficult for elementary children to prove this theorem for all whole numbers, the class can verify that any particular whole number has only one set of prime factors (ignoring order, of course).

Once the prime factors for two values are determined, the GCF can be found by multiplying all the prime factors both numbers have in common (2, 3, and 3 for the pair of values, 90 and 252). Have children write the prime factors as in Table 9.9, loop the common factors (shown in italics), and multiply the set of common factors to find the GCF.

Least Common Multiple

When adding fractions, it is sometimes necessary to find a common denominator. This number must be a *common multiple* of all of the denominators. You can always find a common multiple of two or more numbers by simply calculating their product. For example, a common multiple of 6 and 8 is 48. However, 24, which is also a multiple of both 6 and 8, is the smallest and may therefore be easier to work with. The number 24 is the *least common multiple (LCM)* because it is the smallest common multiple of 6 and 8.

Cuisenaire™ Rods also can be used to introduce the LCM, as in Figure 9.13. For example, a dark green rod represents 6 and a brown rod represents 8. By constructing two parallel trains of dark green and brown rods, children can model the multiplication process.

9.11

 **FIGURE IT OUT**

Use Cuisenaire™ Rods or factor trees to find the GCF for each pair of numbers. Use a different pair of initial factors for one exercise and see if you get the same sets of prime factors and GCF.

1. (12, 15)
2. (18, 24)
3. (12, 30)
4. (9, 14)
5. (105, 252)

FIGURE 9.12
Factor Trees

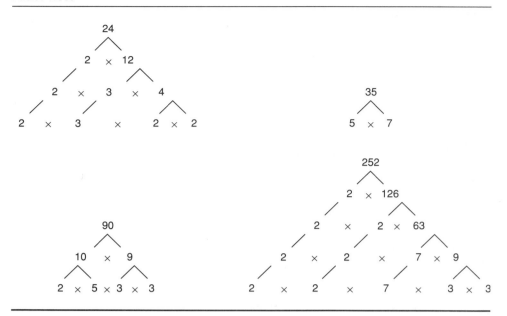

TABLE 9.9
Greatest Common Factor

VALUE	PRIME FACTORS	GCF
90	2, 5, 3, 3	2 × 3 × 3 = 18
252	2, 2, 7, 3, 3	

TABLE 9.10
Least Common Multiple

VALUE	MULTIPLES	LCM
6	6, 12, 18, 24, 30, 36, 42, 48 . . .	
8	8, 16, 24, 32, 40, 48, 56, . . .	24
12	12, 24, 36, 48, 60, . . .	

When the two trains are equal, they show a common multiple, in this case 24. Children can use orange rods and one other rod to determine the base-10 value of the LCM.

Another method for finding the LCM for two or more values is to list several multiples of each number, determine where the sets of multiples intersect, and select the smallest common multiple. For example, have children list the multiples of the three values 6, 8, and 12 as shown in Table 9.10, and loop the common multiples (shown in italics). Both 24 and 48 are common multiples for the 6, 8, and 12. The smallest common multiple, 24, is the LCM.

Children also can use prime factorization as in the previous section to find the LCM of two or more numbers. After finding the prime factors for each number using divisibility rules and factor trees, select the *largest* set of each factor represented. As shown in Table 9.11, for the factors 2 and 3, the 2 appears a maximum of three times (as factors of 8) and the 3 appears at most one time (as a factor of 6 and also 12). Their product gives the LCM = 2 × 2 × 2 × 3 = 24.

Work with the GCF and LCM is often introduced as an application of the divisibility tests and prime numbers. GCF and LCM reappear later in work with fractions and ratios.

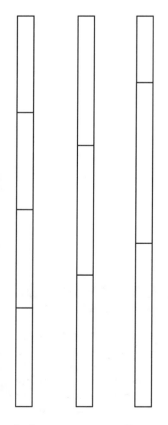

Dark Green (4 × 6)   Brown (3 × 8)   Orange & Purple (20 + 4)

FIGURE 9.13
Least Common Multiple Using Cuisenaire™ Rods

TABLE 9.11
Prime Factors

VALUE	PRIME FACTORS	LCM
6	2, 3	
8	2, 2, 2	$2 \times 2 \times 2 \times 3 = 24$
12	2, 2, 3	

TABLE 9.14
Even Numbers

POSITION Δ	EVEN NUMBER □	
1	2	
2	4	
3	6	$2 \times \Delta = \square$
4	8	
—	—	
—	—	
—	—	

TABLE 9.12
Feet and Sheep Function

FEET	SHEEP
4	1
8	2
12	3
16	4
—	—
—	—
—	—

TABLE 9.13
Even-Number Sequence

POSITION NUMBERS	EVEN NUMBERS
1	2
2	4
3	6
4	8
5	10
6	12
7	—
8	—
9	—
10	—

Using Patterns to Develop Functions

One of the powerful algebra tools available in elementary mathematics is the notion of *function*. A function is a special kind of mathematical relation in which each object in one set is related to *only* one object in a second set. For example, to count sheep the "hard way," count the number of feet and divide by 4. This functional relationship is shown in Table 9.12.

An inequality is one example of a mathematical relation that is *not* a function. For example, suppose everyone in class has a pencil longer than three inches. The relationship of children to pencil lengths is not a function because we cannot predict the exact length of a pencil for any one child. In fact, several children may have the same length pencil.

Functional relations are useful for solving problems. For example, if every truck has 18 tires, the number of tires depends on, or *is a function of,* the number of trucks. Many functions can be written as a number sentence, or *equation*. In the case of tires and trucks, a simple equation that gives the number of trucks for any number of tires is:

$$\text{number of tires} \div 18 = \text{number of trucks}$$

The functional relationship in many arithmetic or geometric sequences also can be written as an equation. An equation relates each term in a number sequence to its position in the sequence. For example, to find the tenth even number, have children list the position numbers in the first column and the corresponding terms of the even-number sequence in the second column (see Table 9.13).

Children can easily extend the pattern to the tenth term. However, to find the hundredth, thousandth, or billionth even number, the process would become tedious indeed. Instead, have students work out a systematic rule relating each position number with its corresponding term in the sequence. Rather than computing each subsequent term in the second column, invent a rule relating each position number to its corresponding even-number term. In Table 9.14, note that doubling the position number always gives the corresponding even-number term. Introduce the placeholder Δ to represent any position number and □ to represent the corresponding term in the number sequence. Later, letters such as *x* and *y* can be substituted for these variable placeholders.

To compute the 100th even term, the 99th even number is no longer required. Applying the equation *2 × position = even number* (or $2 \times \Delta = \square$) gives the 100th even-number term.

$$2 \times 100 = 200$$

9.12
✎ **FIGURE IT OUT**

If the average human head has 50,000 strands of hair, write an equation for counting people the "hard way."

Verify that the equations written next to Table 9.15–9.19 relate each x value to the corresponding y value. To do this, substitute the position numbers for each x value and check to see if the results correspond to the associated y value.

Guess My Rule

Pairs of children can play the game *Guess My Rule,* in which each child makes up a secret rule (e.g., $\Delta + 5 = \square$) and creates a two-column table showing the first six pairs of values based on this rule. They exchange tables and try to discover the rule that was used to create the table. This game also can be used with the whole class by writing a table on the overhead or board and having the group work on the rule. At first limit the rules to simple, linear equations involving small whole-number constants and coefficients.

Function Machines

The concept of *function* can be introduced using function machines. Any number put in the machine will be changed according to some rule. A record of the inputs and corresponding outputs can be maintained in a two-column table. Figure 9.14 shows the function machine ×*3*, where every number entered will be multiplied by 3. Two or more machines can be combined so that the output from the first enters the second, making a new number. Teachers can prepare worksheets of simple or combined function machines to provide children with practice in basic skills. Given several inputs and their corresponding output values, children can work out the rule for one or more function machines. The problem can be made more challenging by leaving out the interim results.

Coordinate Graphs

A graphic display of functional relationships can be created using a coordinate system of graphing. *Ordinate* refers to a position on a number line. A *coordinate* refers to a pair of such position values on a two-dimensional surface. The *Cartesian coordinate plane* is formed by positioning two number lines perpendicular to each other so that they cross at zero (see Figure 9.15).

The horizontal number line is called the *x*-axis, and the vertical line, the *y*-axis. Associated values (coordinate pairs) in a two-column function table can be displayed, or graphed, by first counting on the *x*-axis the number of spaces indicated by the *x* value, followed by the number of spaces indicated by the *y* value in the direction parallel to the *y*-axis. For example, have children graph the coordinate pairs (1, 1), (2, 3), and so on, in the odd-number table on the coordinate graph as shown in Figure 9.16.

Note that the graph of this set of coordinate pairs forms a pattern of points on a straight line. This type of graph is called a *linear graph.* Extending the line makes it possible to predict terms further along in the sequence. The process of extending the graph of a functional relation to predict further (x,y) values is called *extrapolation* (see Figure 9.17). The graph of the square numbers (Figure 9.18) forms a curved line, called a *parabola.* The graph of the triangle numbers is also a curved line (see Figure 9.19).

Equations like $2x = y$, $2x - 1 = y$, and $5x = y$ generate linear graphs. For each of these functions, the *x* term has an exponent (power) equal to 1 (if there is no exponent shown, it

TABLE 9.15
Odd Numbers ($2x - 1 = y$)

X	Y
1	1
2	3
3	5
4	7
5	9
6	11
—	—
—	—
—	—

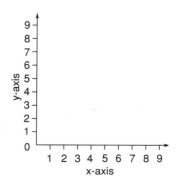

FIGURE 9.15
Cartesian Coordinate Plane

FIGURE 9.14
Function Machines

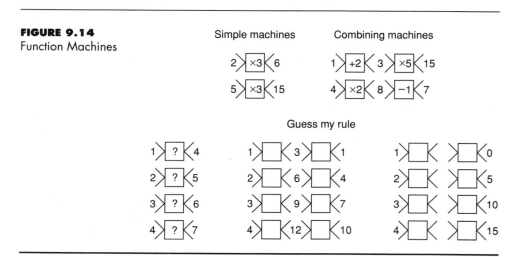

TABLE 9.16
Multiples of Five ($5x = y$)

x	y
1	5
2	10
3	15
4	20
5	25
6	30
—	—
—	—
—	—

TABLE 9.17
Square Numbers ($x^2 = y$)

x	y
1	1
2	4
3	9
4	16
5	25
6	36
—	—
—	—
—	—

TABLE 9.18
Triangle Numbers
($\frac{1}{2}x^2 + \frac{1}{2}x = y$)

x	y
1	1
2	3
3	6
4	10
5	15
6	21
—	—
—	—
—	—

TABLE 9.19
Tetrahedral Numbers ($\frac{1}{6}x^3$
$+ \frac{1}{2}x^2 + \frac{1}{3}x = y$)

x	y
1	1
2	4
3	10
4	20
5	35
6	56
—	—
—	—
—	—

FIGURE 9.16
Graphing Odd Numbers

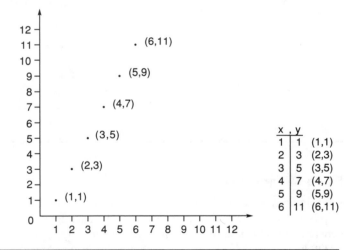

x	y	
1	1	(1,1)
2	3	(2,3)
3	5	(3,5)
4	7	(4,7)
5	9	(5,9)
6	11	(6,11)

9.14
✎ **FIGURE IT OUT**

Many functions have linear graphs. Verify that the even-number and multiples-of-5 sequences generate linear graphs. What characteristics of these functions generate a linear graph? Look at the function and graph of the square numbers in Figure 9.18 to help solve this problem.

is assumed to be 1). The equations $x^2 = y$ and $\frac{1}{2}x^2 + \frac{1}{2}x = y$, called *quadratic equations,* contain an x term with the largest exponent equal to 2. Both functions generate a curved, parabolic graph. Such functions also may contain an x term with an exponent equal to 1, but the largest power of x must be 2.

Graphs of functions with exponents larger than 2 generate curved line graphs as well. However, these curves are not parabolas. Graphing the third-degree tetrahedral numbers (the largest power of x is 3) gives a curved graph that looks similar to the graph of the square numbers. However, extending the coordinate plane to include *negative* values shows the graphs to be distinctly different (see Figure 9.20).

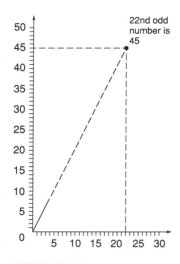

FIGURE 9.17
Extrapolation of Odd Numbers

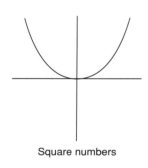

Square numbers

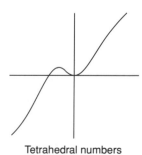

Tetrahedral numbers

FIGURE 9.20
Graphs of Number Sequences

TABLE 9.20
Function Table

	x	y
	0	1
	1	6
$5x + 1 = y \rightarrow$	2	11
	3	16
	4	21
	5	26
	—	—
	—	—
	—	—

FIGURE 9.18
Square-Number Graph

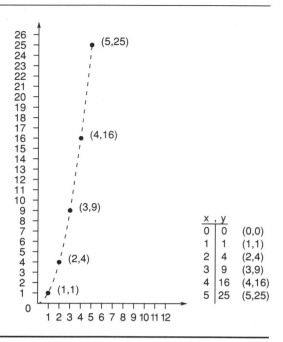

x	y	
0	0	(0,0)
1	1	(1,1)
2	4	(2,4)
3	9	(3,9)
4	16	(4,16)
5	25	(5,25)

FIGURE 9.19
Triangle-Number Graph

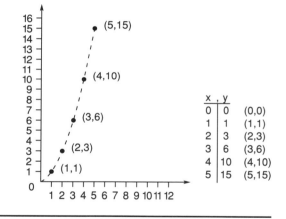

x	y	
0	0	(0,0)
1	1	(1,1)
2	3	(2,3)
3	6	(3,6)
4	10	(4,10)
5	15	(5,15)

Finite Differences

It is relatively easy for children to generate a table of (x,y) values if the functional relationship is already known. For example, given the equation $5x + 1 = y$, the Table 9.20 can be generated by substituting values for x and computing the corresponding y values.

Often, a table of (x,y) values is generated by an experiment. For example, in Figure 9.21, how many blocks will be needed for a building ten stories high? The task is to determine the function that relates the number of stories (x) with the number of blocks (y).

A procedure called *finite differences* offers a systematic way of finding a function from a table of (x,y) values. This procedure can assist more experienced students in grades 5 and up to write an equation for a function table. Linear functions can be uncovered quite readily with this procedure, while higher order functions are somewhat more complex.

As shown in Table 9.21, children first compute the difference between adjacent pairs of y values (notice this is the same function as shown in Table 9.20).

Notice the difference between adjacent y terms is always 5. Since we already know the function, let's see if this information gives a clue to the components of the function $5x + 1 = y$. The common difference 5 is equal to the coefficient (the number multiplied by a variable) of x. The results for $3x + 3 = y$, $4x + 3 = y$, and $5x + 3 = y$ are shown in Table 9.22.

FIGURE 9.21
How Many Blocks?

Stories	Blocks
0	1
1	6
2	11
3	16
4	21
5	26
6	?
7	?
8	?
9	?
10	?

1 Story

TABLE 9.21
Finite Differences

x	y	Δ
0	1	
		5
1	6	
		5
2	11	
		5
3	16	
		5
4	21	
		5
5	26	
—	—	
—	—	
—	—	

TABLE 9.22
Finite Differences

3x + 3 = y			4x + 3 = y			5x + 3 = y		
x	y	Δ	x	y	Δ	x	y	Δ
0	3		0	3		0	3	
		3			4			5
1	6		1	7		1	8	
		3			4			5
2	9		2	11		2	13	
		3			4			5
3	12		3	15		3	18	
		3			4			5
4	15		4	19		4	23	
		3			4			5
5	18		5	23		5	28	
—	—		—	—		—	—	
—	—		—	—		—	—	
—	—		—	—		—	—	

The common difference in each case corresponds to the coefficient of the x term. Also, the y value corresponding to the x value zero matches the constant number added to the x term in each function (1, 3, 3, and 3 for these four cases).

Functions involving x terms with powers of 2 (quadratic functions) also can be uncovered from tables of values using finite-difference methods. Notice that in Table 9.23, the square numbers require two differences before a constant difference arises.

The patterns for quadratic functions that emerge can be verified by working examples. Again, the y value corresponding to the x value zero gives the constant added to the x^2 term in the equation. The equation for the example in Table 9.23 can be written $x^2 + 0 = y$. In Table 9.24, because the y value corresponding to the x value zero equals 2, the equation is written $x^2 + 2 = y$.

The *coefficient* of the x^2 term can be found by observing the common *second* difference. Both of the preceding examples have a common difference of 2 and an x^2 coefficient of 1 (i.e., $1 \times x^2 = y$ and $1 \times x^2 + 2 = y$). Table 9.25 shows that, when the x^2 term has a coefficient of 2, the common difference is 4.

9.15
✎ **FIGURE IT OUT**

In 1955, a world-record pace for female marathon athletes was about 190 meters per minute and for men, about 300 meters per minute. In 1985, the pace for women had increased to 300 meters per minute and for men, to about 340 meters per minute. Draw a graph of the marathon pace for women and men over this period and extrapolate the graphs to predict the year the times will be the same. What will be the world-record pace that year? Looking at the graphs, what might you predict about marathon records for women and men in future years?

9.16
✎ **FIGURE IT OUT**

Make tables for $2x + 4 = y$ and $2x + 5 = y$ and verify that the finite-difference procedure can be used to find the coefficient and constant for each equation.

TABLE 9.23
Square numbers ($x^2 = y$)

x	y	FIRST Δ	SECOND Δ
0	0		
		1	
1	1		2
		3	
2	4		2
		5	
3	9		2
		7	
4	16		2
		9	
5	25		2
—	—		
—	—		
—	—		

TABLE 9.24
Finite Differences for Quadratic Function ($x^2 + 2 = y$)

x	y	FIRST Δ	SECOND Δ
0	2		
		1	
1	3		2
		3	
2	6		2
		5	
3	11		2
		7	
4	18		2
		9	
5	27		
—	—		
—	—		
—	—		

TABLE 9.25
Predicting Coefficients for Quadratic Functions ($2x^2 + 1 = y$)

x	y	FIRST Δ	SECOND Δ
0	1		
		2	
1	3		4
		6	
2	9		4
		10	
3	19		4
		14	
4	33		4
		18	
5	51		
—	—		
—	—		
—	—		

TABLE 9.26
Coefficient of x^2 Term

x	y	FIRST Δ	SECOND Δ
0	$\frac{1}{2}$		
		3	
1	$3\frac{1}{2}$		$6 \times \frac{1}{2}$
		9	
2	$12\frac{1}{2}$		6
		15	
3	$27\frac{1}{2}$		6 $3x^2 + \frac{1}{2} = y$
		21	
4	$48\frac{1}{2}$		6
		27	
5	$75\frac{1}{2}$		
—	—		
—	—		
—	—		

FIGURE 9.23
How Many Squares
in a Square?

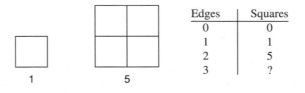

Edges	Squares
0	0
1	1
2	5
3	?

The following three rules will help children uncover the functions using two-column tables.

1. The number of finite differences required to arrive at a common value indicates the *largest* power for the x term (i.e., 2 differences means it is an x^2 function).
2. The y value corresponding to $x = 0$ indicates the constant added to the x term(s).
3. The common difference is related to the coefficient of the x term with the largest exponent. The common difference equals the coefficient for linear functions and is twice the coefficient for quadratic functions (other rules govern higher order functions).

D. CLASSROOM ACTIVITIES
Geometric Patterns and Functions

Geometry offers a rich source for the investigations of patterns and functions. For example, how many triangles pointing upward can you count in the diagram shown in Figure 9.22?

There are three small triangles and one large triangle. The pattern of triangles-in-a-triangle is summarized in Table 9.27, where x is the number of triangles on an edge and y is the total number of triangles pointing up. Notice that the sequence of y values is identical to that of the tetrahedral numbers.

Other geometric patterns are shown in Figures 9.23, 9.24, and 9.25.

These problems can be solved by looking for patterns and working out functional relationships. Many additional problem-solving situations can be found in the "Suggested Readings" listed at the end of this chapter.

Milk-Carton Computers

A convenient way for students to generate guess-my-rule number sequences to explore is with a simple milk-carton computer. The device is not really a computer but merely flips over previously prepared cards to give the illusion of an input/output operation. The x values are on the front, and the corresponding y values are on the back of each card (see Figure 9.26).

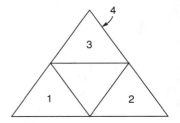

FIGURE 9.22
Triangles in a Triangle

TABLE 9.27
Triangles in a Triangle
$\left(\frac{1}{3}x^3 + \frac{1}{2}x^2 + \frac{1}{2}x = y\right)$

x	y
0	0
1	1
2	4
3	10
4	20
5	35
—	—
—	—
—	—

FIGURE 9.24
Chords in a Circle

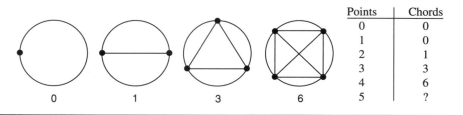

Points	Chords
0	0
1	0
2	1
3	3
4	6
5	?

FIGURE 9.25
Regions in a Circle

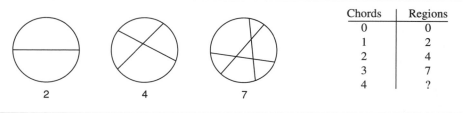

Chords	Regions
0	0
1	2
2	4
3	7
4	?

FIGURE 9.26
Milk-Carton Computer

Input

Front

2

Back

ᔭ

Output

Input	Output
0	0
1	2
2	4
3	6
4	8
5	10
6	12
7	14
8	16

The *x* values, say, 0 through 9, are written in red on one side of a 2-cm × 4-cm card. On the back of each card, corresponding *y* values are written in blue. Each card is inserted as *input* into the top of the computer with the *x* value showing. An internal channel turns the card over and presents it at the slot in the bottom of the computer as *output*. The input *x* and output *y* can then be organized into a table. Functional relationships can be worked out by carefully observing the patterns in the table or applying the finite-difference method.

Alphanumerics

An interesting activity for children in grades 4–9 involves looking for words that equal 1,000,000 (Bain, 1987). Each letter in the alphabet is assigned a number 1–26. The product

TABLE 9.28
Runner's Record ($6d = t$)

MILES d	MINUTES t	FIRST Δ
0	0	
		6
1	6	
		6
2	12	
		6
3	18	
		6
4	24	
		6
5	30	
		6
6	36	
—	—	
—	—	
—	—	

of the letters gives the value of the word (lumps → $12 \times 21 \times 13 \times 16 \times 19 = 995{,}904$). Use only English words and no proper nouns. Children can use a guess-and-test strategy or may use *prime* factors to identify special letters that are factors of 1 million (e.g., 2, 2, 2, 2, 2, 2, 5, 5, 5, 5, 5, 5 are the prime factors of 1 million). This is a good homework problem that can involve the entire family in finding a solution.

E. DEVELOPING FUNCTIONS TO SOLVE PROBLEMS

The finite-difference method can be used as a tool to uncover functions associated with problem situations. Once the general form of a function is known, an x value can be used to derive the corresponding y value.

For example, a good long-distance runner can run one mile every six minutes. Table 9.28 summarizes the distance d covered in time t.

As only one step is required to generate a common difference, the x-term exponent is 1. The coefficient equals the first difference 6, and the y value corresponding to the x value 0 gives the constant 0. Therefore, the function is $6x^1 + 0 = y$, or $6x = y$. Using this equation, we can quickly estimate the time required to run a marathon of 26.3 miles.

$$6 \times 26.3 = y$$
$$157.8 = y$$
$$= 2 \text{ hours } 37.8 \text{ minutes}$$

The result also can be displayed on a graph as shown in Figure 9.27.

Earlier, we discussed the extrapolation process for extending a graph beyond those values initially given in a table. This technique is useful for computing larger values of known functional relationships. Values also can be computed for points between existing solutions. For example, it is easy to plot the distance corresponding to a 15-minute run even though the time values are given in 6-minute intervals. This process, called *interpolation,* is shown in Figure 9.28.

F. COMPUTER APPLICATIONS
King's Rule

This program gives students practice discovering number patterns. A sequence of numbers is presented that represents an underlying mathematical pattern. Users try to guess the pattern and test hypotheses by entering sets of values. For example, Figure 9.30 shows the

FIGURE 9.27
Running Graph Extrapolation

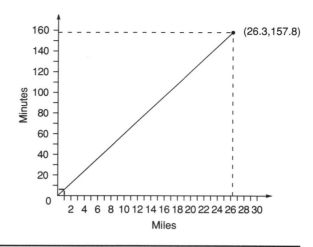

FIGURE 9.28
Running Graph Interpolation

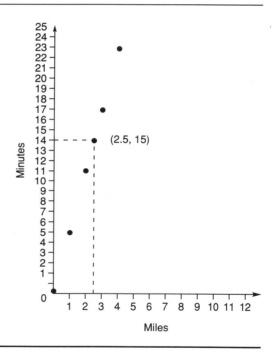

Table 9.29 shows the distance (*d*) an object falls in quarter-second time intervals (*t*). Find the function associated with this table and graph the results using Figure 9.29. Determine how far an object will fall in 10 seconds (40 quarter-seconds); in 1 minute; in 1 second.

TABLE 9.29
Falling Objects

t (1/4 sec)	*d* (ft)
0	0
1	1
2	4
3	9
4	16
5	25
6	36
—	—
—	—
—	—

sequence of trials entered by a student to discover the relationship represented by the sequence 8, 9, 73.

Once users think they know the rule, they can request a quiz. If the questions presented are answered correctly, a graphic reward is displayed. The program offers six levels of difficulty and requires only elementary arithmetic skills. *King's Rule* can be used effectively by individuals or groups of students to explore number patterns using *guess-and-test* and *make-a-table* problem-solving strategies.

G. ADAPTING INSTRUCTION FOR CHILDREN WITH SPECIAL NEEDS
Checking Factor Candidates

To help special-needs children be more systematic when computing the factors of numbers, have them write the number above a two-column table and list candidate factors (1, 2, . . . ,

FIGURE 9.29
How Fast Do Objects Fall?

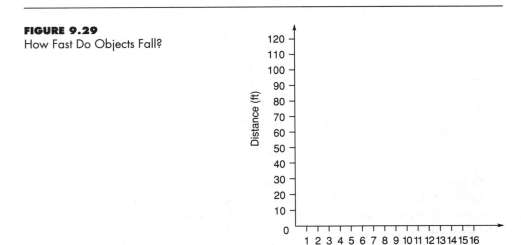

FIGURE 9.30
King's Rule
SOURCE: *King's Rule* [Computer program] by Sunburst Communications, 1985. Copyright 1985 by Sunburst Communications. Reprinted by permission.

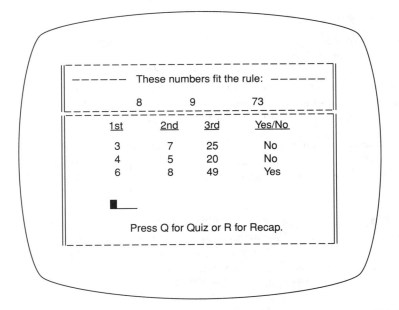

and so on) in the left column (Dearing & Holtan, 1987). Using a calculator, children divide each of the candidate factors into the number. If the decimal fraction part of the quotient has digits other than zeros, cross out the divisor as a factor candidate. Continue the process until all factor candidates have been tested. Initially, the teacher can prepare worksheets with factor candidates listed up to at least the square root of the number being tested. Due to the commutative property, factors larger than the square root will have been previously found. When completing factor trees, children need to find only one set of factors for any given number since they can repeat the process on each of the factors. The following is an example of checking factor candidates for the number 87.

```
                87
        ──────────────
         1   │   87
         2̶   │
         3   │   29
         4   │
         5̶   │
         6̶   │
         7̶   │
         8̶   │
         9̶   │
        1̶0̶   │
```

In practice, only the small prime divisors 2, 3, 5, and 7 need to be tested as factors for values less than 121 (i.e., 11 × 11). Once one pair of factors is found, the process is repeated on the nonprime factor (if any) until the prime-factor tree is completed. The number 66 can be factored in two steps using this method (the prime factors are circled).

To test values 121–169 for factors, include 11 in the list of factor candidates. By including the prime numbers 17, 19, and 23 in the candidate list, values to 841 (29 × 29) can be tested for factors.

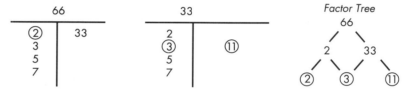

Patterns and Basic Skills

For children who find it particularly difficult to memorize sequences of symbols like the multiplication facts, it is often helpful to use number patterns as memory cues. The following activities provide experience working with patterns involving the addition table, multiplication table, and the hundred chart. Children should be encouraged to explain the underlying structure that causes the number patterns to appear. These pattern exploration activities also may generate useful memory cues for number facts.

Addition table patterns. An activity that many children find interesting involves completing a partially filled in table of addition facts by exploiting various number patterns. Notice the patterns of even numbers, whole numbers, and constant numbers (see Figure 9.31). Look for other patterns as well.

Multiplication table patterns. The table of multiplication facts also contains many number patterns. Children can find patterns in the completed multiplication table and color all the terms in a sequence with a marker. By using different colors, more than one pattern can be displayed on each table. Have children describe each pattern using a number sentence or written description below the table (see Figure 9.32).

FIGURE 9.31
Addition Table Pattern

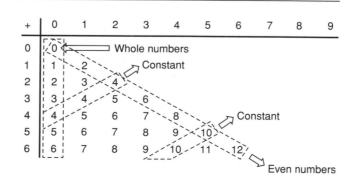

FIGURE 9.32
Multiplication Table Patterns

×	0	1	2	3	4	5	6	7	8	9
0	0	0	0	0	0	0	0	0	0	0
1	0	1	2	3	4	5	6	7	8	9
2	0	2	4	6	8	10	12	14	16	18
3	0	3	6	9	12	15	18	21	24	27
4	0	4	8	12	16	20	24	28	32	36
5	0	5	10	15	20	25	30	35	40	45
6	0	6	12	18	24	30	36	42	48	54
7	0	7	14	21	28	35	42	49	56	63
8	0	8	16	24	32	40	48	56	64	72
9	0	9	18	27	36	45	54	63	72	81

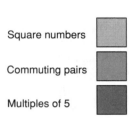

Square numbers

Commuting pairs

Multiples of 5

FIGURE 9.33
Can You Find
Hundred-Chart Patterns?

1	2	3	4	5	6	7	8	9	10
11	12	13	14	15	16	17	18	19	20
21	22	23	24	25	26	27	28	29	30
31	32	33	34	35	36	37	38	39	40
41	42	43	44	45	46	47	48	49	50
51	52	53	54	55	56	57	58	59	60
61	62	63	64	65	66	67	68	69	70
71	72	73	74	75	76	77	78	79	80
81	82	83	84	85	86	87	88	89	90
91	92	93	94	95	96	97	98	99	100

Hundred-chart patterns. Figure 9.33 shows number patterns on the hundred chart. Children can use crayons or felt pens to color the even and odd numbers, multiples of 5, multiples of 10, the prime numbers, and other patterns.

Gifted and talented children often benefit from extended explorations with patterns and functions. Such activities help children develop a mature understanding of functions and their applications to practical problems. Work with two-column tables and finite differences can motivate the need for integer arithmetic and lead to work with coordinate graphs, slopes, solving equations, and later, derivatives in calculus. A good source of classroom activities is *Finite Differences: A Problem Solving Technique* (Seymour & Shedd, 1973).

H. ASSESSMENT STRATEGY

Portfolios of student work are relatively new to mathematics teaching but have been used for many years with writing and fine arts instruction. It is difficult to assess the full range of problem-solving performance using written tests alone. Teachers at all levels are beginning to explore how portfolios can be used to expand the range of evidence available for grading student mathematical performance.

To establish a portfolio, students are asked to select examples of their work throughout the grading period and store them in a file folder maintained at a central location in the classroom. Selected homework, problem solutions, classroom warm-up exercises, reflective journal entries, exams, and projects are examples of items that may be included. Each item should contain the student's name and the date of the assignment. Near the end of a grading period, the teacher asks students to review their portfolios and reorganize them to best demonstrate their mathematical progress. Students in grades 4–9 are generally able to review their work and select appropriate examples for their portfolios.

It is helpful for children to include examples that are *not* their best work to show how they improved during the assessment period. Ask each student to write a reflective essay that includes specific examples of their work that describes what they have learned. Some teachers require every student to include specific items and allow additional materials to be included at the discretion of the child. Others feel it is best to allow students complete discretion to select the contents of their portfolio and how to best display what they know.

All mathematics portfolios should contain student reflective writing since the process of evaluating one's own work has been shown to be a powerful tool for learning. The teacher will need to model good reflective writing and provide opportunities for students to practice this skill before they develop their portfolios.

Students generally show a real sense of pride in their portfolios, and parents enjoy seeing their child's work. Teachers who have used portfolios report that grading is often easier than evaluating separate assignments since the students have to make a case for what they know and how much progress they have made. Parent conferencing is also facilitated when the portfolio is used as the basis of discussion.

I. PATTERN SAMPLE LESSON PLAN

An example of a lesson plan that introduces patterns and functions, written by Jasmine Lakdawala (UCSD, 1992), is presented here.

Patterns and Functions Lesson Plan

Grade Level: Grade 4   *Time Allotment:* 30 minutes

NCTM Standard: Recognize, describe, extend, and create a wide variety of patterns.

Essential Understanding: Patterns exist everywhere we look and often they can be described and extended to solve problems.

Goal: The learners will understand that by identifying a rule, then applying it, patterns can be created and extended indefinitely.

Objective: Given a geoboard sequence card, geobands, and a geoboard, the learners will copy a partial design onto their geoboards and extend it to complete the pattern in order to learn that patterns can be identified and extended indefinitely.

Motivation: A poster board tiled with one-inch squares with an initial pattern colored in its center will be placed in the middle of the table. Learners will be asked to describe the pattern they see. The learners will then work simultaneously to color in the squares

(Continued)

Patterns and Functions Lesson Plan

on the board by extending the pattern in all directions. While coloring, you will discuss what you believe the rules of the pattern are and how a pattern is continued.

Procedure: 1. Review standards of behavior. Materials are to be shared and explored. 2. Explain that you will be studying patterns today. Ask the learners if they can find any patterns in the clothes they are wearing. Give an example and then go around the group listening to several ideas and have them explain the pattern they found (e.g., goes in rows, uses different colors, stripes, diagonals, etc.). 3. Explain that patterns can be generated by identifying a rule. Discuss the rules you see on the poster board with regard to shape, color, size, distance, etc. Ask when and where this pattern stops, and why. Could the pattern extend to cover the entire surface of the table? The floor of the classroom? The entire school? The playground? What are you looking for when you are searching for patterns? 4. Show the geoboard sequence cards (triangles, squares, spiral, diagonal lines, etc.). Explain that these are the patterns the class will be working with and that all patterns can be extended indefinitely. 5. Work with one of the sequence cards. Begin the pattern on a geoboard, then ask the group where the next geoboard would be placed. Do the first card together as a group, giving the students a chance to work cooperatively to finish the pattern. 6. Give each of the learners a geoboard sequence card with a pattern to copy and extend on a geoboard. 7. As a challenge activity for early finishers, the patterns can be drawn onto geoboard worksheets using different colors to make the patterns more complex.

Closure: Learners will be asked to describe their pattern to the group. What is the rule that they have discovered? What colors were used to make the pattern different from the blackline master sequence card? How big can your pattern get? What is the smallest your pattern can be?

Assessment: Learners will make their own patterns on the geoboards and then share them with the group. Learners will identify the rule that creates each of their patterns and then draw their pattern on paper for review by the teacher.

Materials: Poster board with center pattern, crayons, geoboard sequence cards, geobands, geoboards handouts, and paper.

Extension: Have the learners make their own geoboard sequence cards and then exchange them with other students who will copy and extend them on geoboards. Once displayed on geoboards, patterns can be transferred to geoboard paper for display on the bulletin board.

SOURCE: Written by Jasmine Lakdawala, University of California, San Diego, 1992.

SUMMARY

- Patterns are systematic occurrences of a relationship within a set of objects or ideas.
- Number patterns and functions are important topics in mathematics. Pattern activities are an important component of early number and counting development.
- Older children work with number patterns occurring in arithmetic, geometry, algebra, and the other strands of mathematics.
- Common number patterns include the even, odd, square, triangle, and Fibonacci numbers. Patterns are also involved in finding prime factors, greatest common factors, and least common multiples.
- Some patterns express functional relationships that can be displayed in a two-column table and graphed on the coordinate plane.
- Whereas patterns allow the observer to predict the next element in a sequence, a function relates each x value (or position number) with a corresponding y value (or result), enabling the computation of any y value from a given x value.
- These functional relationships often can be written as number sentences, or equations. This powerful feature makes functions very useful in solving some types of problems.
- A systematic procedure called finite differences makes it possible to uncover linear, quadratic, and more complex functional relationships expressed in many problems that can be represented in two-column tables.

- Identifying patterns in the factor, addition, and multiplication tables can help special-needs children to memorize these basic facts. Exploring number patterns and functions can also provide engaging extension activities for gifted and talented children.

QUESTIONS AND ACTIVITIES FOR DISCUSSION

1. Write a lesson plan to introduce a number pattern to 4th-grade children. Use manipulative materials to display the pattern, and have the children predict the next value in the sequence. Use a two-column table to record the results. If possible, implement the lesson with a group of children and discuss with your peers the implications of including pattern work in mathematics instruction.

2. Think about how to introduce the notion of *function* to intermediate-grade students. What key features of this powerful concept would you include in your lesson? Make a list of examples that could be used to motivate these key features and help students understand the importance of uncovering functions when solving problems.

3. Look for patterns in Pascal's Triangle, shown in Table 9.30. Note that each value in the interior is the sum of the two adjacent numbers directly above. List and label as many familiar sequences as possible (e.g., the triangle numbers).

4. The period (one back-and-forth swing) of a pendulum remains constant regardless of the weight of the bob or length of the swing. Only the length of the pendulum itself governs the period (disregarding air friction). Using string and a washer, make a pendulum that has a period of 1 second. Measure its length and record it in Table 9.31. Next, construct a 2-second pendulum. Is it twice as long as the first? Record its length in the table. Construct a 3-second pendulum and record its length. From the table, can you predict the length of a 4-second pendulum? A 5-second pendulum? Graph the results of the pendulum experiment using Figure 9.34. What is the shape of its graph?

TABLE 9.30
Pascal's Triangle

```
              1
           1     1
        1     2     1  → Triangle Numbers
      1     3     3     1
    1     4     6     4     1
  1     5    10    10     5     1
1     6    15    20    15     6     1
1   7    21    35    35    21    7     1
1  8   28   56   70   56   28    8    1
```

TABLE 9.31
Pendulum Period

PERIOD DURATION (seconds)	PENDULUM LENGTH (cm)
1	—
2	—
3	—
4	—
5	—

FIGURE 9.34
How Fast Does a Pendulum Swing?

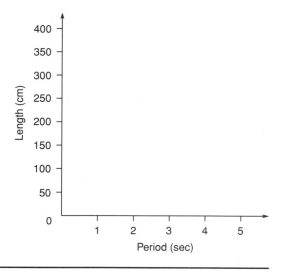

5. More than 200 years ago, the Russian mathematician Christian Goldbach discovered that all even numbers larger than two seemed equal to the sum of exactly two prime numbers ($12 = 7 + 5$; $4 = 2 + 2$; $48 = 31 + 17$). Using a calculator or computer, show that all the even numbers less than 100 are the sum of two prime numbers (if you don't have a computer, team up with classmates to solve this problem). Find pairs of primes whose sums are 1,000, 100,002, and 888,888. Try to find an even number that is not the sum of two primes. Does Goldbach's Conjecture seem to be true? To date, no one has proved whether it is always possible to subdivide all even numbers into exactly two primes. However, no counterexample has ever been found either.

6. Review the "Suggested Readings" at the end of this chapter and find several pattern and function lessons. Implement one or more activities with a small group of children, and discuss the experience with your peers.

7. Read one of the *Arithmetic Teacher* articles listed in the readings section. Write a brief report summarizing the main ideas of the article, and describe how the recommendations for instruction might apply to your own mathematics teaching.

INSTRUCTIONAL RESOURCES

CHILDREN'S BOOKS

Anno, M. *Anno's Math Games I*. Philomel Books. A delightful collection of illustrated mathematics problems and games for children of all ages.

Anno, M. *Anno's Math Games II*. Philomel Books. A delightful collection of illustrated mathematics problems and games for children of all ages.

Anno, M. *Anno's Math Games III*. Philomel Books. A delightful collection of illustrated mathematics problems and games for children of all ages.

Burns, M. *Math for smarty pants*. Little, Brown. A wonderful collection of thoughtful mathematics problems for children of all ages.

Mahy, M. *17 kings and 42 elephants*. Dial Books for Young Readers. Children help to figure out how many elephants belong to each king.

COMPUTER SOFTWARE

Bounce! WINGS for Learning/Sunburst. Students improve their pattern recognition skills by seeing, hearing, and physically demonstrating patterns.

Bumble Plot. Learning Company. Coordinate graphing activities in a game format.

Creative Play: Problem Solving Activities with the Computer. Math and Computer Education Project, Lawrence Hall of Science, Berkeley, CA. A collection of 25 programs that focus on interdisciplinary problem solving.

Graphing Equations. WINGS for Learning/Sunburst. Finding equations for given graphs and the interactive graphing game Green Globs.

Kings Rule. WINGS for Learning/Sunburst. Provides practice uncovering number patterns.

Pattern Poser. WINGS for Learning/Sunburst. Students create, explore, and extend patterns involving addition, subtraction, multiples, and factors.

Winker's World of Numbers. WINGS for Learning/Sunburst. Students practice using number patterns to predict missing values.

REFERENCES

Bain, D. (1987). The world of alphanumerics. *Arithmetic Teacher, 35*(1), 26.

Dearing, S., & Holtan, B. (1987). Factors and primes with a T square. *Arithmetic Teacher, 34*(8), 34.

National Council of Teachers of Mathematics. (1989). *Curriculum and evaluation standards for school mathematics*. Reston, VA: Author.

SUGGESTED READINGS

Beattie, I. (1986). Building understanding with blocks. *Arithmetic Teacher, 34*(2), 5–11.

Berman, B., & Friederwitzer, F. (1989). Algebra can be elementary . . . when it's concrete. *Arithmetic Teacher, 36*(8), 21–24.

Burns, M. (1977). *The good time math event book*. Palo Alto, CA: Creative Publications.

Burns, M. (1978). *The book of think*. New York: Little, Brown.

Burns, M. (1982). *Math for smarty pants*. New York: Little, Brown.

Burton, G. (1980). Definitions for prime numbers. *Arithmetic Teacher, 27*(6), 44–47.

Downie, D., Slesnick, T., & Stenmark, J. (1981). *Math for girls and other problem solvers*. Berkeley: University of California, Lawrence Hall of Science.

Duncan, D., & Litwiller, B. (1990). Number-lattice polygons and patterns: Sums and products. *Arithmetic Teacher, 37*(5), 14–15.

Edwards, F. (1987). Geometric figures make the LCM obvious. *Arithmetic Teacher, 34*(7), 17–18.

Gardella, F. (1984). Divisibility—another route. *Arithmetic Teacher, 31*(7), 55–56.

Geer, C. (1992). Exploring patterns, relations, and functions. *Arithmetic Teacher, 39*(9), 19–21.

Greenes, C., Spungin, R., & Dombrowski, J. (1977). *Problem-mathics: Mathematical challenge problems with solution strategies.* Palo Alto, CA: Creative Publications.

Greenes, C., Willcutt, R., & Spikell, M. (1972). *Problem solving in the mathematics laboratory: How to do it.* Boston: Prindle, Weber & Schmidt.

Huff, S. (1979). Odds and evens. *The Arithmetic Teacher, 27*(5), 48–52.

Immerzeel, G., & Ockenga, E. (1977). *Calculator activities for the classroom.* Palo Alto, CA: Creative Publications.

Lamb, C., & Hutcherson, L. (1984). Greatest common factor and least common multiple. *Arithmetic Teacher, 31*(8), 43–44.

Lappan, G., & Winter, M. (1980). Prime factorization. *Arithmetic Teacher, 27*(7), 24–27.

Litwiller, B., & Duncan, D. (1983). Areas of polygons on isometric dot paper: Pick's formula revised. *Arithmetic Teacher, 30*(8), 38–40.

Litwiller, B., & Duncan, D. (1985). Pentagonal patterns in the addition table. *Arithmetic Teacher, 32*(8), 36–38.

Loewen, A. (1991). Lima beans, paper cups, and algebra. *Arithmetic Teacher, 38*(8), 34–37.

Nibbelink, W. (1990). Teaching equations. *The Arithmetic Teacher, 38*(3), 48–51.

Norman, F. (1991). Figurate numbers in the classroom. *Arithmetic Teacher, 38*(4), 42–45.

Parkerson, E. (1978). Patterns in divisibility. *Arithmetic Teacher, 25*(4), 58.

Robold, A. (1982). Patterns in multiples. *Arithmetic Teacher, 29*(8), 21–23.

Schultz, J. (1991). Teaching informal algebra. *Arithmetic Teacher, 38*(9), 34–37.

Van de Walle, J., & Holbrook, H. (1987). Patterns, thinking, and problem solving. *Arithmetic Teacher, 34*(8), 6–12.

Vissa, J. (1987). Coordinate graphing: Shaping a sticky situation. *Arithmetic Teacher, 35*(3), 6–10.

Whitin, D. (1986). More patterns with square numbers. *Arithmetic Teacher, 33*(5), 40–42.

CHAPTER 10

Fraction Operations

his chapter focuses your attention on how to teach fraction operations. Specifically, it is designed to help you understand

1. The concept of fractional part.
2. Characteristics of rational and irrational numbers, and classroom activities used to introduce these numbers.
3. Procedures for renaming fractions in simplest terms, and classroom activities used to introduce this concept.
4. Development of alternative algorithms for adding, subtracting, multiplying, and dividing common fractions.
5. Techniques for incorporating technology into fraction operation lessons.
6. Alternative assessment techniques for mathematics instruction.
7. Techniques for accommodating special-needs students in fraction operation lessons.

NCTM Fraction Standards
K–4 level students will

- Develop concepts of fractions and mixed numbers
- Develop number sense for fractions
- Use models to find equivalent fractions
- Use models to explore operations on fractions
- Apply fractions to problem situations.

5–8 level students will

- Compute using fractions. (NCTM, 1989, pp. 57, 94)

Children begin using fractions the first time they have to share a cookie or a set of blocks with a friend. If both are satisfied with the distribution, they are building an understanding of the mathematical notion of one-half. These early, informal experiences provide the basis for the systematic development of concepts and operations associated with common fractions and decimals, or the *rational* numbers.

? *I WAS JUST THINKING* . . .

A farmer came to the market with a load of watermelons. He sold half of them plus one-half a melon, and had one whole melon left. How many melons did he take to the market?

Many educators predict that knowledge of operations involving common fractions is likely to decrease in importance over the next decade. The availability of calculators and personal computers, the use of metric units, and the nearly universal adoption of decimal-based money and numeration systems make operations using fractions less attractive in commerce and daily life. Fraction concepts are not likely to disappear, however, due to their use in the English vernacular and their applications in more advanced mathematics topics such as ratio, proportion, probability, and algebra. The stock market remains a notable exception to the conversion to a decimal representation of security values (a stock is often quoted as "up a half point," not "up 50 cents").

The prudent choice for teachers is to introduce fraction addition, subtraction, multiplication, and, to a lesser extent, division, while avoiding the use of unwieldy *junior-high fractions* (fractions like $\frac{9}{51}$, which you are unlikely to encounter anywhere except in junior high school!). Focusing attention on halves, thirds, fourths, fifths, eighths, tenths, and twelfths offers ample opportunity to introduce the basic fraction algorithms. Everyday problems involving fractions with less friendly denominators are likely to be solved using the decimal representation on a calculator or computer spreadsheet. The skill of renaming fractions as decimals, therefore, is likely to increase in importance.

A. INTRODUCING RATIONAL NUMBER OPERATIONS

Decimal notation is introduced in Chapter 11 following the presentation of common fraction operations in this chapter. It is possible, however, to introduce decimal concepts concurrent with, or even prior to, common fractions. Although there are several possible sequences that can be followed when introducing fraction and decimal concepts, some concepts depend on a prior understanding of others. For example, the ability to rename fractions in simplest terms, once referred to as reducing fractions, is facilitated by a knowledge of fraction multiplication.

Figure 10.1 shows one possible instructional hierarchy for introducing rational number concepts and operations. It is often helpful to refer to the steps shown in a hierarchy like this when first learning to organize activities into lesson sequences.

➡ *Answer to* **I WAS JUST THINKING** . . .

The farmer brought three melons to the market. Let x be the number of melons he brought to the market. Therefore:

$$x - \frac{x}{2} - \frac{1}{2} = 1$$

$$\frac{2x}{2} - \frac{x}{2} - \frac{1}{2} = 1$$

$$\frac{2x - x - 1}{2} = 1$$

$$\frac{x - 1}{2} = 1$$

$$x - 1 = 2$$

$$x = 3$$

FIGURE 10.1
Rational Number Operation Instructional Hierarchy

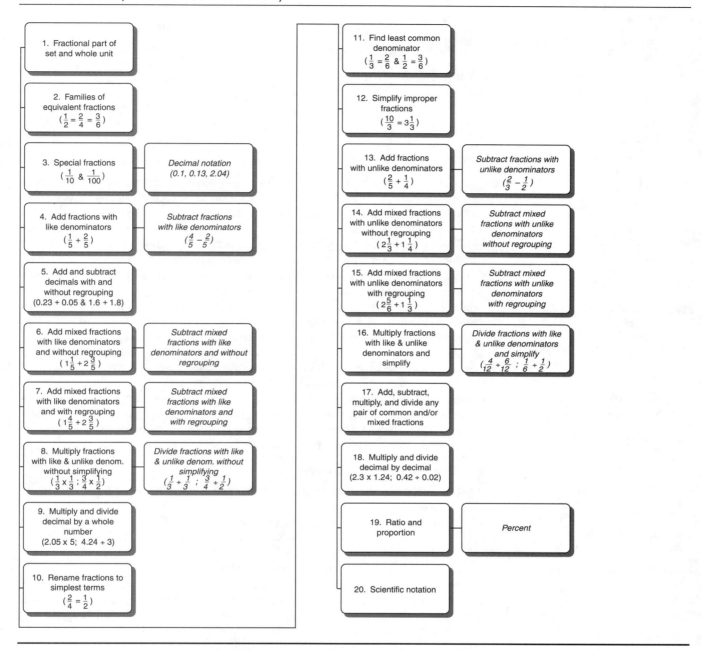

1. Fractional part of set and whole unit

2. Families of equivalent fractions ($\frac{1}{2} = \frac{2}{4} = \frac{3}{6}$)

3. Special fractions ($\frac{1}{10}$ & $\frac{1}{100}$)

   Decimal notation (0.1, 0.13, 2.04)

4. Add fractions with like denominators ($\frac{1}{5} + \frac{2}{5}$)

   Subtract fractions with like denominators ($\frac{4}{5} - \frac{2}{5}$)

5. Add and subtract decimals with and without regrouping (0.23 + 0.05 & 1.6 + 1.8)

6. Add mixed fractions with like denominators and without regrouping ($1\frac{1}{5} + 2\frac{3}{5}$)

   Subtract mixed fractions with like denominators and without regrouping

7. Add mixed fractions with like denominators and with regrouping ($1\frac{4}{5} + 2\frac{3}{5}$)

   Subtract mixed fractions with like denominators and with regrouping

8. Multiply fractions with like & unlike denom. without simplifying ($\frac{1}{3} \times \frac{1}{3}$; $\frac{3}{4} \times \frac{1}{2}$)

   Divide fractions with like & unlike denom. without simplifying ($\frac{1}{3} \div \frac{1}{3}$; $\frac{3}{4} \div \frac{1}{2}$)

9. Multiply and divide decimal by a whole number (2.05 x 5; 4.24 ÷ 3)

10. Rename fractions to simplest terms ($\frac{2}{4} = \frac{1}{2}$)

11. Find least common denominator ($\frac{1}{3} = \frac{2}{6}$ & $\frac{1}{2} = \frac{3}{6}$)

12. Simplify improper fractions ($\frac{10}{3} = 3\frac{1}{3}$)

13. Add fractions with unlike denominators ($\frac{2}{5} + \frac{1}{4}$)

    Subtract fractions with unlike denominators ($\frac{2}{3} - \frac{1}{2}$)

14. Add mixed fractions with unlike denominators without regrouping ($2\frac{1}{3} + 1\frac{1}{4}$)

    Subtract mixed fractions with unlike denominators without regrouping

15. Add mixed fractions with unlike denominators with regrouping ($2\frac{5}{6} + 1\frac{1}{3}$)

    Subtract mixed fractions with unlike denominators with regrouping

16. Multiply fractions with like & unlike denominators and simplify

    Divide fractions with like & unlike denominators and simplify ($\frac{4}{12} \div \frac{6}{12}$; $\frac{1}{6} \div \frac{1}{2}$)

17. Add, subtract, multiply, and divide any pair of common and/or mixed fractions

18. Multiply and divide decimal by decimal (2.3 x 1.24; 0.42 ÷ 0.02)

19. Ratio and proportion

    Percent

20. Scientific notation

Understanding Fractional Part

The concept of fractional part involves making equal-sized partitions of an area or set. For example, partition an area to specify three-fourths ($\frac{3}{4}$) of a square. First, the figure is partitioned into four equal-sized areas, then three of these fourths are selected. Initially, the equal-sized partitions should be congruent (i.e., same size and shape), as shown in the first drawing in Figure 10.2. Later, noncongruent equal-sized partitions can be introduced, as shown in the second drawing in Figure 10.2.

Similarly, two-fifth ($\frac{2}{5}$) of a set of peanuts can be shown by partitioning the set into five equal groups and selecting two of these groups (see Figure 10.3).

As Piaget observed, the meaningful use of the equal-partitioning fraction model is related to conservation. A thorough understanding of conservation of area, number, volume,

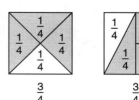

FIGURE 10.2
Squares with Three-Fourths Shaded

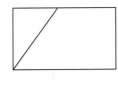

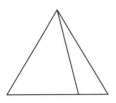

FIGURE 10.4
Two-Part Partitionings Not Representing One-Half

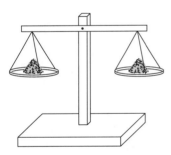

FIGURE 10.5
Balance with Two Equivalent Piles of Sand

Halves

Thirds

Fourths

FIGURE 10.6
Fractional Parts of a Whole

FIGURE 10.3
Two-Fifths Shaded

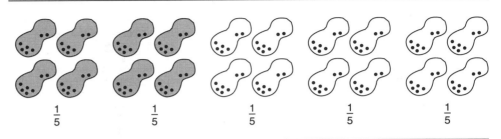

$$\frac{1}{5} \qquad \frac{1}{5} \qquad \frac{1}{5} \qquad \frac{1}{5} \qquad \frac{1}{5}$$

and mass can help children model the partitioning operation using concrete measurement experiences. Fortunately, by the time rational number operations are formally introduced in grade 4 or 5, most children have a good grasp of these conservation concepts. Teachers can therefore be reasonably assured that most children are capable of learning from different types of instructional materials when learning about rational-number concepts and skills.

Children often misinterpret the fractional whole-part relationship to include unequal partitionings as well as equal-sized divisions. Any of the partitionings shown in Figure 10.4 might be misinterpreted as one-half by some children.

When children are first introduced to the notion of fractional part, activities should offer physical evidence of equal partitions. For example, a balance can be used to verify that a container of sand has, indeed, been divided into two equivalent amounts (see Figure 10.5).

Symmetry also can be used to verify the equal partitioning of geometric figures. Cutting along the lines in Figure 10.6 gives identical subdivisions representing fractional parts of the whole. Partitions can be superimposed to show congruence.

Children can also construct *fractional parts of sets*. Peanuts, lima beans, blocks, or other uniform counters can be arranged in piles or arrays to show fractional parts of a set. To show halves, two equal stacks or rows must be formed from the given set of objects. To show thirds, three piles are constructed (see Figure 10.7).

Other Meanings of Fractions

Two other situations also can be recorded using fraction notation: (a) *division meaning of fractions* and (b) *ratios*.

The division operation can be interpreted as a fraction. For example, the exercise $2 \div 3 = ?$ can be interpreted to mean "divide two into three equal parts." The answer for this division exercise is $\frac{2}{3}$ (i.e., $2 = \frac{6}{3} = \frac{2}{3} + \frac{2}{3} + \frac{2}{3}$). The indicated-division meaning of fractions is used to rename fractions as decimals.

Problems in everyday life often require working out a *ratio* of one set of objects to another. For example, if two pencils cost nine cents, we could say a ratio of 2:9 (read "ratio of two to nine") exists between pencils and pennies. The yellow and green M&M candies appear in a ratio of about 3:5. Ratios do not indicate the total number of objects involved. Rather, a ratio specifies that for each occurrence of the first value (two pencils), one should expect the occurrence of the second (nine pennies). For example, suppose it is possible to purchase two bus tickets for 75 cents. The ratio of tickets to pennies would be 2:75. If four tickets were required, the cost would increase proportionally to $1.50, giving the ratio 4:150. Unlike fractions, however, ratios cannot be added, subtracted, multiplied, or divided ($2:1 + 4:1 \neq 6:1$).

Many elementary children have difficulty using proportional reasoning. By grades 5–6, however, most children can benefit from experiences involving ratio and proportion such as scale drawing, map reading, and percent. Further development of ratio and proportion is included in Chapter 11.

Fraction Notation

The symbol we use to represent fractional parts was invented by Hindu mathematicians and later adapted by the Arabic culture. The now-familiar convention $\frac{a}{b}$ was not common in Europe until the Middle Ages. In some cultures today, different fraction notations are used.

For example, in Japan fractions are written with the total number of partitions on top and the number of partitions being considered on the bottom, exactly opposite the convention used in the United States ($\frac{2}{1}$ = one-half in Japan).

A rational number is any value that can be written in the form $\frac{a}{b}$ where a, the numerator, is an integer (a positive or negative whole number), and b, the denominator, is a nonzero integer. The denominator indicates the total number of equal partitions and the numerator specifies the number of those partitions being considered (e.g., 3 out of 5 equal partitions = $\frac{3}{5}$).

Work at the elementary level is generally limited to fractions involving positive integers. Many familiar numbers are rational. For example, all the counting numbers can be written as fractions. The negative integers, money values, and the value zero are also rational numbers,

$$1 = \frac{1}{1} \qquad\qquad -3 = \frac{-3}{1} \qquad\qquad \$0.50 = \$\frac{50}{100}$$

$$2 = \frac{2}{1} \qquad\qquad 0 = \frac{0}{4} \qquad\qquad 98.6 = 98\frac{6}{10}$$

Families of Equivalent Fractions

The fractions $\frac{1}{2}$ and $\frac{2}{4}$ are equivalent since they represent the same total fractional part of a set or whole (see Figure 10.8). A *common unit* is required to compare fractional parts of objects. For example, $\frac{1}{2}$ of an orange is not equal to $\frac{2}{4}$ of an apple.

A convenient way to generate an entire family of equivalent fractions is to exploit the special property of multiplication by one, the *multiplicative identity*. Any number n multiplied by one gives the product n:

$$n \times 1 = n$$

To show students that the fraction $\frac{2}{2} = 1$, make two identical squares from tagboard and cut one in half. Demonstrate that, when the two halves are recombined, they are congruent to the whole square. Multiplying any number by $\frac{2}{2}$, therefore, is equivalent to multiplying it by one. Have the children cut geometric figures to show that $\frac{3}{3}$, $\frac{4}{4}$, and $\frac{5}{5}$ also equal one. Students must have an understanding of fraction multiplication in order to construct a family of equivalent fractions using this procedure. For example:

$$\frac{1}{2} \times 1 = \frac{1}{2}$$

$$\frac{1}{2} \times \frac{2}{2} = \frac{2}{4}$$

$$\frac{1}{2} \times \frac{3}{3} = \frac{3}{6}$$

$$\frac{1}{2} \times \frac{4}{4} = \frac{4}{8}$$

$$\frac{1}{2} \times \frac{5}{5} = \frac{5}{10}$$

Because each of these exercises involves multiplying the fraction $\frac{1}{2}$ by one (i.e., $\frac{2}{2}$, $\frac{3}{3}$, etc.), each result must remain equal to $\frac{1}{2}$. An infinite family of equivalent fractions exists for any rational number $\left(\text{e.g.}, \frac{1}{2}, \frac{2}{4}, \frac{3}{6}, \frac{4}{8}, \frac{5}{10}, \frac{6}{12}, \ldots\right)$.

B. ADDITION AND SUBTRACTION OF COMMON FRACTIONS
Adding and Subtracting Fractions with Like Denominators

In the previous section, fractions were implicitly added when counting the number of fourths equivalent to one-half. Adding fractions with the same, or *like*, denominators is a simple counting process like adding whole numbers. Whole-number operations involve counting whole units. For fraction operations, the units are always smaller than one whole (see Figure 10.9).

Fraction pies and *strips* are instructional materials based on an area model. These materials can be constructed by reproducing each shape in Figure 10.10 out of a different color of construction paper. The circles (or squares) are then cut into the fractional pieces 1, $\frac{1}{2}$, $\frac{1}{3}$,

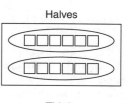

Halves

Thirds

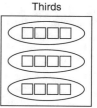

Fourths

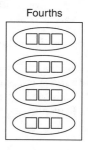

FIGURE 10.7
Fractional Parts of a Set

FIGURE 10.8
Equivalent Fractions $\frac{1}{2}$ and $\frac{2}{4}$ Using a Common Whole Unit

10.1
✎ **FIGURE IT OUT**

Compute five equivalent fractions for each of the following values.

1. $\frac{1}{2}$

2. $\frac{2}{3}$

3. $\frac{3}{4}$

4. $\frac{2}{5}$

5. $\frac{3}{10}$

FROM A DIFFERENT ANGLE

ST: I was thinking about how much time we spend learning about fractions in the upper grades. I wonder if it's a good use of everyone's time. I know the *Standards* recommend less emphasis on paper-and-pencil fraction calculations, but what happens to my kids in the meantime? Do you think teachers in the next grade are rethinking the role of fractions in their curriculum, too?

CT: Well, there are plenty of ways for things to go wrong as we reform mathematics education throughout the country. To find time for real problem solving and teaching for meaning, we'll have to decrease emphasis on some topics. I think paper-and-pencil fraction computation is a good candidate.

ST: But don't kids still need fractions?

CT: Sure, we still need to do lots of work on things like naming fractional parts, fraction notation, equivalent families of fractions, and the relationship between fractions and decimals. Students need to know these concepts for everyday life

and to help them with math topics like ratios, proportion, and probability. But with calculators so available, kids won't need so much practice working with complicated fractions like $\frac{8}{17} + \frac{3}{51}$.

ST: You know what this reminds me of? When I was in school in the '70s and the metric system was supposed to be coming in. We had lots of lessons on metric units, but 20 years later, we're still relying on customary units. What if some teachers go right on teaching "junior high" fractions? How will my kids compete?

CT: You're right—we can't just change our own teaching and expect the children to work out their problems in later grades. The only way to avoid problems like this is for the whole curriculum to adapt to the goals of the *Standards*. In our district, we have a curriculum committee to plan for this change over the next decade. The middle schools and high schools are doing the same. It won't be easy, but we think it'll be better for the students in the end. You should come to our meeting next week and see what we're doing.

FIGURE 10.9
Sum of Three-Fourths

FIGURE 10.10
Fractional Parts of a Whole

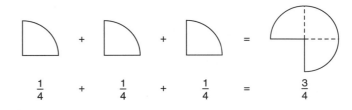

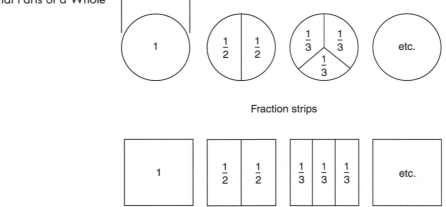

$\frac{1}{4}, \frac{1}{5}, \frac{1}{6}, \frac{1}{8}, \frac{1}{9}, \frac{1}{10}$, and $\frac{1}{12}$. Each piece is labeled with the symbol (e.g., $\frac{1}{3}$) on the front and the fraction word (one-third) on the back. Each student can construct a personal fraction set.

Addition and subtraction exercises can be represented using pies (or strips). To add two fractions with like denominators, have children count out the number of pieces needed to

FIGURE 10.11
Fraction Addition

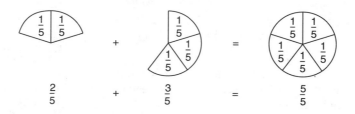

$$\frac{2}{5} \quad + \quad \frac{3}{5} \quad = \quad \frac{5}{5}$$

FIGURE 10.12
Fraction Addition
with Regrouping

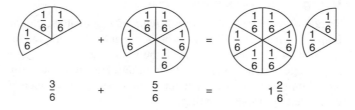

$$\frac{3}{6} \quad + \quad \frac{5}{6} \quad = \quad 1\frac{2}{6}$$

FIGURE 10.13
Fraction Subtraction

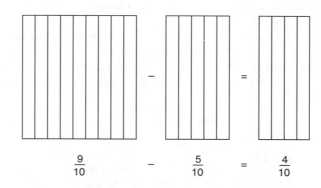

$$\frac{9}{10} \quad - \quad \frac{5}{10} \quad = \quad \frac{4}{10}$$

represent each value, put the two piles together, and count the total number of identical pieces (see Figure 10.11).

Notice the sum $\frac{5}{5}$ is equal to one whole. Sums larger than one whole also can be shown using strips and pies. Children can work in pairs to do mixed-number problems since they will need two or more sets of materials (see Figure 10.12).

As with whole numbers, to subtract fractions with like denominators it is necessary to remove from the minuend the number of identical fraction pieces indicated by the subtrahend. The *difference* is the number of remaining pieces (see Figure 10.13).

Comparing Fractions

To compare the relative size of $\frac{1}{2}$ and $\frac{1}{3}$, have children select the $\frac{1}{2}$ and $\frac{1}{3}$ strips (or pie sections) and place one over the other. Part of the $\frac{1}{2}$ strip sticks out beyond the $\frac{1}{3}$ strip, which shows that $\frac{1}{2} > \frac{1}{3}$.

Fraction families also can be used to compare the relative size of fractions. If two fractions have a common denominator, it is easy to compare their size by simply comparing their numerators. For example, to determine whether $\frac{3}{5}$ or $\frac{5}{7}$ is larger, first list the family of equivalent fractions for each value until a member with the same denominator is found in each list. The underlined values that follow are a common denominator for the $\frac{3}{5}$ and $\frac{5}{7}$ families. Children can now easily find the larger fraction by directly comparing the numerators $\left(\frac{21}{35} < \frac{25}{35}\right)$.

10.2
✎ **FIGURE IT OUT**

Using fraction pies or strips, carry out the necessary actions to compute the following sums and differences. Record the results using symbols.

1. $\frac{1}{2} + \frac{1}{2} = ?$
2. $\frac{2}{3} + \frac{1}{3} = ?$
3. $\frac{3}{10} + \frac{1}{10} = ?$
4. $\frac{3}{8} + \frac{1}{8} = ?$
5. $\frac{3}{5} + \frac{2}{5} = ?$
6. $\frac{3}{4} - \frac{1}{4} = ?$
7. $\frac{2}{2} - \frac{1}{2} = ?$
8. $\frac{5}{8} - \frac{2}{8} = ?$
9. $\frac{7}{10} - \frac{5}{10} = ?$
10. $\frac{5}{8} - \frac{3}{8} = ?$

Three-fifths family $\frac{3}{5}, \frac{6}{10}, \frac{9}{15}, \frac{12}{20}, \frac{15}{25}, \frac{18}{30}, \underline{\underline{\frac{21}{35}}}, \frac{24}{40}$

Five-sevenths family $\frac{5}{7}, \frac{10}{14}, \frac{15}{21}, \frac{20}{28}, \underline{\underline{\frac{25}{35}}}$

In this case, 35 is the *smallest* denominator that is common to both families ($\frac{42}{70}$ and $\frac{50}{70}$ are the next larger set of common denominators). The smallest common denominator is called the *least common denominator* (LCD). The LCD for fifths and sevenths is 35ths. The LCD also can be found using the same prime factor method used for calculating the least common multiple (LCM).

Using Common Denominators

To add or subtract fractions with *unlike* denominators, children must first rename one or both fractions so the denominators are identical. Using manipulatives, this means the denominators are constructed using the same sized fraction pies or strips. The process does not change the actual value of the fractions, but simply substitutes one member of an equivalent family for another. Once the denominators are identical, sums and differences can be calculated by simple counting.

Teachers can demonstrate how to find common denominators for two fractions using fraction pies or strips. For $\frac{1}{2}$ and $\frac{1}{3}$, have children cover the $\frac{1}{2}$ and the $\frac{1}{3}$ pieces exactly with several identical strips. In this case, three $\frac{1}{6}$ strips exactly cover the $\frac{1}{2}$ strip, and two $\frac{1}{6}$ strips exactly cover the $\frac{1}{3}$ strip. Therefore, as shown in Figure 10.14, sixths is a common denominator.

Children may use any of the following algorithms to find common denominators. The first technique does not require prior knowledge of fraction multiplication. The second and third techniques assume that children have already been introduced to the multiplication of fractions. The following examples show how to find a common denominator for $\frac{5}{6}$ and $\frac{3}{4}$.

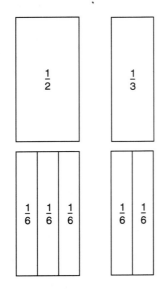

FIGURE 10.14
Common Denominator for $\frac{1}{2}$ and $\frac{1}{3}$

Algorithm 1:

$\frac{5}{6} = \frac{5+5}{6+6} = \frac{10}{12}$

$\frac{3}{4} = \frac{3+3+3}{4+4+4} = \frac{9}{12}$

a. Repeatedly add respective denominators to each series below the line until the sums are equal.
b. Then add the same number of respective numerators above each line.
c. Total the values in the numerator and denominator.

Algorithm 2:

$\frac{5}{6} \times \frac{2}{2} = \frac{10}{12}$

$\frac{3}{4} \times \frac{3}{3} = \frac{9}{12}$

a. Determine LCM of the denominators by computing the product of the maximum set of unique prime factors ($6 = 2 \times 3$; $4 = 2 \times 2$; LCM $= 3 \times 2 \times 2 = 12$).
b. Determine the unit multipliers ($\frac{2}{2}$ and $\frac{3}{3}$) needed to give a denominator equal to the LCM (12).
c. Multiply the numerator and denominator by the unit multiplier.

Algorithm 3:

$\frac{5}{6} \times \frac{4}{4} = \frac{20}{24}$

$\frac{3}{4} \times \frac{6}{6} = \frac{18}{24}$

a. Multiply the numerator and denominator of each fraction by the denominator of the other fraction ($\frac{4}{4}$ and $\frac{6}{6}$).

Algorithms 1 and 2 will always give results in terms of the least common denominator. Algorithm 3 always gives a common denominator but not necessarily the smallest possible. Although Algorithm 3 is easy to apply, the fractions that result may yield sums or differences that are not in simplest form.

10.3

✎ **FIGURE IT OUT**

Using the three techniques shown, write each of the following pairs as fractions with common denominators. Show each example using fraction strips or pies.

1. $\frac{1}{2}, \frac{3}{4}$
2. $\frac{2}{3}, \frac{1}{6}$
3. $\frac{3}{5}, \frac{1}{10}$
4. $\frac{1}{4}, \frac{2}{3}$
5. $\frac{5}{6}, \frac{5}{12}$

Adding and Subtracting Fractions with Unlike Denominators

To add $\frac{1}{2}$ to $\frac{1}{4}$, children must first find a common denominator. Using fraction strips, children can substitute $\frac{2}{4}$ for $\frac{1}{2}$ and solve the equivalent exercise:

$$\tfrac{1}{2} + \tfrac{1}{4} \rightarrow \tfrac{2}{4} + \tfrac{1}{4} = \tfrac{3}{4}$$

As shown in Figure 10.15, it is also possible to substitute $\frac{4}{8}$ for $\frac{1}{2}$ and $\frac{2}{8}$ for $\frac{1}{4}$, giving the equivalent exercise:

$$\tfrac{1}{2} + \tfrac{1}{4} \rightarrow \tfrac{4}{8} + \tfrac{2}{8} = \tfrac{6}{8}$$

Subtraction follows a similar process. For example, $\frac{3}{5} - \frac{1}{2}$ can be shown by first finding a common denominator using strips, then matching the appropriate number of minuend pieces to the subtrahend display. As shown in Figure 10.16, the pieces left over represent the difference.

Teachers must carefully select exercises to ensure that the required denominators can be represented by the pies or strips available. For example, to add thirds and fifths $\left(\text{e.g., } \frac{1}{3} + \frac{2}{5}\right)$, the required common denominator 15 is not represented in the fraction pies and strips. These manipulative materials can be used to calculate problems involving the pairs of denominators shown in Table 10.1.

Algorithms for Adding and Subtracting Fractions

After children demonstrate facility calculating exercises using fraction pies and strips, teachers can introduce symbolic algorithms. Note that children who have no prior knowledge of fraction multiplication can display addition and subtraction of appropriate fractions with like and unlike denominators using fraction pies or strips. Similarly, Algorithm 1 allows children with no prior knowledge of fraction multiplication to add fractions with *unlike* denominators. Algorithms 2 and 3 do require a prior understanding of fraction multiplication.

FIGURE 10.15
Addition with Unlike Denominators Using Fraction Strips

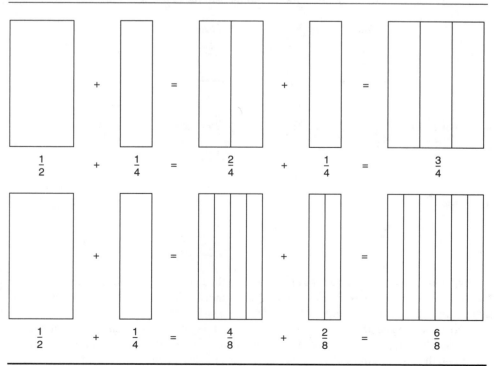

FIGURE 10.16
Fraction Subtraction with
Unlike Denominators

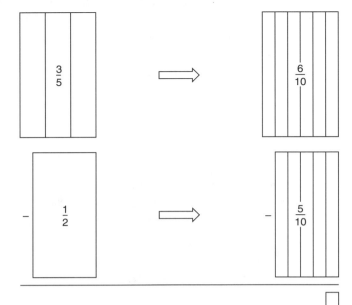

10.4
✎ FIGURE IT OUT

Using fraction pies or strips, show the actions required to compute the following exercises.

1. $\frac{1}{2} - \frac{1}{3} = ?$
2. $\frac{1}{3} + \frac{5}{12} = ?$
3. $\frac{1}{4} + \frac{1}{3} = ?$
4. $\frac{3}{10} - \frac{1}{5} = ?$
5. $\frac{2}{3} - \frac{3}{6} = ?$

10.5
✎ FIGURE IT OUT

Calculate each of the following exercises using the three alternative algorithms.

1. $\frac{1}{2} + \frac{3}{4} = ?$
2. $\frac{2}{3} - \frac{1}{6} = ?$
3. $\frac{3}{5} - \frac{1}{10} = ?$
4. $\frac{1}{4} + \frac{2}{3} = ?$
5. $\frac{5}{6} + \frac{5}{12} = ?$

These three algorithms may be used for adding and subtracting fractions and mixed numbers. Note that Algorithm 3 requires mixed numbers to be renamed as improper fractions.

	Addition	*Subtraction*
Algorithm 1:	$\frac{1}{2} + \frac{1+1}{2+2} = \frac{2}{4}$	$\frac{1}{2} + \frac{1+1}{2+2} = \frac{2}{4}$
	$+\frac{1}{4} = +\frac{1}{4} = +\frac{1}{4}$	$-\frac{1}{4} = -\frac{1}{4} = -\frac{1}{4}$
	$\frac{3}{4}$	$\frac{1}{4}$
Algorithm 2:	$\frac{1}{2} \times \frac{2}{2} = \frac{2}{4}$	$\frac{1}{2} \times \frac{2}{2} = \frac{2}{4}$
	$+\frac{1}{4} \times \frac{1}{1} = +\frac{1}{4}$	$-\frac{1}{4} \times \frac{1}{1} = -\frac{1}{4}$
	$\frac{3}{4}$	$\frac{1}{4}$
Algorithm 3:	$\frac{1}{2} \times \frac{4}{4} = \frac{4}{8}$	$\frac{1}{2} \times \frac{4}{4} = \frac{4}{8}$
	$+\frac{1}{4} \times \frac{2}{2} = +\frac{2}{8}$	$-\frac{1}{4} \times \frac{2}{2} = -\frac{2}{8}$
	$\frac{6}{8}$	$\frac{2}{8}$

Algorithm 1 uses repeated addition to calculate the common denominator for the pair of fractions. While often more time consuming than other methods, this algorithm does not require children to initially specify the unit multiplier.

Algorithm 2 is generally accepted as the standard procedure for adding and subtracting fractions. Although this procedure is efficient, many children find it difficult to accurately determine the unit multiplier $\left(\text{i.e., } \frac{2}{2}\right)$ that generates the least common denominator.

Algorithm 3 removes the guesswork of finding the least common denominator and appropriate unit multiplier since both denominators are automatically selected as the unit multiplier.

TABLE 10.1
Possible Fraction Pie and Strip Exercises

UNLIKE DENOMINATOR PAIRS	EXAMPLE
2, 3	$\frac{1}{2} - \frac{1}{3}$
2, 4	$\frac{1}{2} + \frac{3}{4}$
2, 5	$\frac{2}{5} + \frac{1}{2}$
2, 6	$\frac{5}{6} - \frac{1}{2}$
2, 8	$\frac{3}{2} + \frac{1}{8}$
2, 10	$\frac{2}{10} + \frac{1}{2}$
2, 12	$\frac{1}{2} + \frac{7}{12}$
3, 4	$\frac{1}{3} - \frac{1}{4}$
3, 6	$\frac{1}{3} + \frac{5}{6}$
3, 9	$\frac{5}{9} + \frac{1}{3}$
3, 12	$\frac{1}{3} - \frac{1}{12}$
4, 8	$\frac{3}{4} - \frac{1}{8}$
4, 12	$\frac{1}{4} + \frac{9}{12}$
5, 10	$\frac{3}{10} - \frac{1}{5}$
6, 12	$\frac{5}{6} + \frac{3}{12}$

FIGURE 10.17
Fraction Number Line

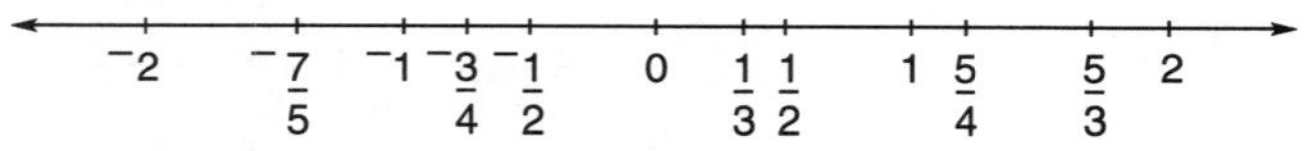

Note that although all three algorithms can give results that are not in simplest form $\left(\frac{8}{15} - \frac{1}{3} = \frac{8}{15} - \frac{5}{15} = \frac{3}{15}\right)$, techniques 1 and 2 minimize the amount of renaming required. Give children the opportunity to try each algorithm and practice using the one that suits them best.

Mixed Numbers

Although fractions often are thought of as numbers between zero and one, rational numbers can be larger than one and smaller than zero (see Figure 10.17).

Fractional numbers larger than 1 (or smaller than -1) are called *mixed numbers*. Mixed numbers are the sum of a whole number and a fraction. On the number line, the values $1\frac{3}{4}$, $5\frac{1}{2}$, and $152\frac{7}{8}$ are represented by the point three-fourths the distance from 1 to 2, one-half the distance from 5 to 6, and seven-eighths the distance from 152 to 153, respectively. Children in grades 4–9 can graph fractions on the number line as a way to compare the relative size of values (see Figure 10.18).

Mixed numbers are also rational numbers because they can be written in the form $\frac{a}{b}$. For example:

$$1\frac{3}{4} = \frac{4}{4} + \frac{3}{4} = \frac{7}{4}$$
$$5\frac{1}{2} = \frac{10}{2} + \frac{1}{2} = \frac{11}{2}$$
$$152\frac{7}{8} = \frac{1216}{8} + \frac{7}{8} = \frac{1223}{8}$$

Draw a number line and graph the following rational numbers in their proper positions.

1. $\frac{1}{3}$
2. $1\frac{1}{5}$
3. $4\frac{3}{4}$
4. $3\frac{2}{3}$
5. $6\frac{7}{8}$

Write each of the following mixed numbers as improper fractions. Then rename the result as a mixed number again.

1. $2\frac{1}{3}$
2. $3\frac{3}{5}$
3. $5\frac{3}{4}$
4. $2\frac{1}{7}$
5. $6\frac{3}{10}$

FIGURE 10.18
Graphing Fractions on the Number Line

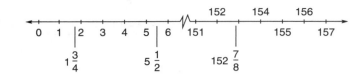

FIGURE 10.19
Mixed-Number Addition with Fraction Pies

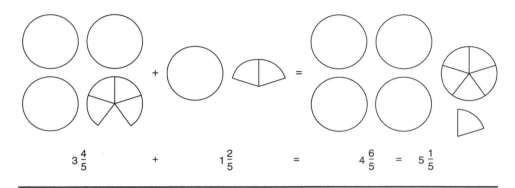

$$3\frac{4}{5} \quad + \quad 1\frac{2}{5} \quad = \quad 4\frac{6}{5} \quad = \quad 5\frac{1}{5}$$

When mixed numbers are written in $\frac{a}{b}$ form, the resulting fraction always has a numerator equal to or larger than the denominator. Such numbers are called *improper fractions.* Children can rename, or *simplify,* improper fractions as a mixed number by dividing the denominator into the numerator. The quotient is the number of whole units contained in the fraction, and the remainder indicates the number of fractional parts remaining. For example:

$$\frac{9}{2} \rightarrow 9 \div 2 = 4R1 \rightarrow 4\frac{1}{2}$$

This division procedure can be verified by reversing the process. Using the previous example, since $4 = \frac{8}{2}$, the number $4\frac{1}{2}$ can be written as $\frac{8}{2} + \frac{1}{2} = \frac{9}{2}$. An algorithm that converts between mixed and improper fraction form can be introduced once students understand the relationship between these representations. Multiplying the denominator in a mixed number by the whole number and adding the result to the numerator is an efficient way to calculate the new numerator for the equivalent improper fraction $\frac{a}{b}$. For example:

$$4\frac{1}{2} = \frac{(2 \times 4) + 1}{2} = \frac{9}{2}$$

Figure 10.19 shows how to solve the exercise $3\frac{4}{5} + 1\frac{2}{5} = ?$ using fraction pies. The two fraction parts are added, giving $\frac{6}{5} = 1\frac{1}{5}$, and then the whole units are combined $\left(3\frac{4}{5} + 1\frac{2}{5} = 4\frac{6}{5} = 4 + 1 + \frac{1}{5} = 5\frac{1}{5}\right)$.

Addition and subtraction of mixed numbers with unlike denominators is similar to operations with other fractions. First, children must find a common denominator using pies or strips. For addition, students combine the strips, or, for subtraction, students match those in the minuend with those in the subtrahend, and the remainder is the difference. Subtraction exercises like $3\frac{1}{4} - 1\frac{1}{2} = ?$ require regrouping one whole unit in the minuend in order to subtract the fraction part of the subtrahend. To regroup, substitute the correct number of strips for one whole unit in the minuend, for example $\frac{4}{4}$ for 1. As shown in Figure 10.20, this provides enough strips to match with the fraction part of the subtrahend, and the remaining strips are the difference. Note that substituting four-fourths for one whole does not change the overall value of the mixed number.

FIGURE 10.20
Subtraction with
Unlike Denominators

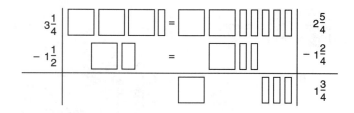

$3\frac{1}{4}$ $= $ $2\frac{5}{4}$

$-1\frac{1}{2}$ $=$ $-1\frac{2}{4}$

$1\frac{3}{4}$

C. MULTIPLICATION AND DIVISION OF FRACTIONS
Multiplying Fractions

Multiplying two fractions between zero and one always gives a product less than either of the two factors. Children may find this confusing when compared with the products of numbers greater than one.

Fraction strips can be used to demonstrate how these small numbers behave when multiplied. The area of the whole square is considered as one unit. To multiply $\frac{1}{2} \times \frac{1}{3}$, children select the half and third strips and position them on the *unit square*. The dark shaded area in Figure 10.21 indicates where the two strips overlap. The figure shows that the shaded region comprises $\frac{1}{6}$ of the total unit area. The process can be verbalized as, "One-half of one-third of the unit square equals one-sixth of the unit square."

Different combinations of fraction strips can be used to show multiplication exercises. The product of two fractions is represented by the overlapping region (see Figure 10.22).

After children successfully use fraction strips to solve multiplication exercises, teachers can introduce an algorithm for multiplying fractions. To multiply two fractions, calculate the products of the numerators and denominators as shown in the following examples.

$$\frac{1}{2} \times \frac{1}{3} = \frac{1 \times 1}{2 \times 3} = \frac{1}{6}$$

$$\frac{2}{3} \times \frac{3}{5} = \frac{2 \times 3}{3 \times 5} = \frac{6}{15}$$

$$\frac{1}{4} \times \frac{3}{8} = \frac{1 \times 3}{4 \times 8} = \frac{3}{32}$$

While mixed numbers can be multiplied using procedures similar to whole-number multiplication, it is generally more efficient to first rename each mixed number as an improper fraction, then use the standard fraction multiplication algorithm. For example:

Vertical Algorithm

$1\frac{2}{3}$

$\times 4\frac{1}{2}$

$\frac{2}{6} = \frac{1}{2} \times \frac{2}{3}$

$\frac{1}{2} = \frac{1}{2} \times 1$

$\frac{8}{3} = 4 \times \frac{2}{3}$

$+ 4 = 4 \times 1$

$7\frac{1}{2} = 4 + \frac{8}{3} + \frac{1}{2} + \frac{2}{6}$

Improper Fraction Algorithm

$1\frac{2}{3} \times 4\frac{1}{2} = \frac{5}{3} \times \frac{9}{2} = \frac{45}{6} = 7\frac{3}{6} = 7\frac{1}{2}$

Reciprocals

A special pair of fractions called *reciprocals* always has a product of one, the multiplicative identity. For example, $\frac{3}{4}$ and $\frac{4}{3}$ are reciprocals since their product equals one.

$$\frac{3}{4} \times \frac{4}{3} = \frac{12}{12} = 1$$

✎ **FIGURE IT OUT**

Use fraction strips to compute the following products.

1. $\frac{1}{2} \times \frac{1}{4} = ?$
2. $\frac{1}{2} \times \frac{1}{3} = ?$
3. $\frac{1}{2} \times \frac{3}{4} = ?$
4. $\frac{1}{3} \times \frac{1}{4} = ?$
5. $2\frac{2}{5} \times 3\frac{2}{3} = ?$

FIGURE 10.21
Fraction Multiplication
Using Strips

$$\frac{1}{2} \times \frac{1}{3} = \frac{1}{6}$$

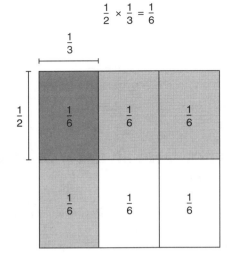

Shaded area is
one-half of one-third
of the unit square.

FIGURE 10.22
Fraction Multiplication

$$\frac{2}{3} \times \frac{3}{5} = \frac{6}{15}$$

$$\frac{1}{4} \times \frac{3}{8} = \frac{3}{32}$$

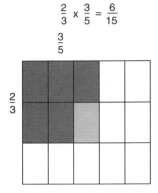 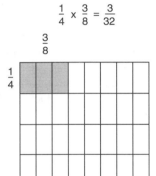

The reciprocal of a number is also called its *multiplicative inverse.* Several numbers and their multiplicative inverses (reciprocals) are listed in Table 10.2.

To introduce children to reciprocals, give them a set of missing-factor exercises such as the following.

$$\frac{2}{3} \times ? = \frac{6}{6}$$

$$\frac{4}{5} \times ? = \frac{20}{20}$$

$$\frac{7}{3} \times ? = \frac{21}{21}$$

$$5 \times ? = \frac{5}{5}$$

$$1\frac{3}{4} \times ? = \frac{28}{28}$$

TABLE 10.2
Reciprocals

NUMBER	RECIPROCAL
$\frac{3}{4}$	$\frac{4}{3}$
3	$\frac{1}{3}$
10	$\frac{1}{10}$
$2\frac{1}{2}$	$\frac{2}{5}$

Discuss what is special about all of the answers for this type of exercise (the missing factor is the reciprocal of the first factor). Have the children make up missing-factor and missing-product exercises involving reciprocals and various types of numbers.

$$\frac{2}{3} \times \frac{3}{2} = ?$$

$$? \times \frac{10}{12} = \frac{144}{144}$$

$$? \times \frac{10}{12} = 1$$

$$4 \times ? = 1$$

$$2\frac{1}{3} \times \frac{3}{7} = ?$$

Dividing Fractions

As the inverse of multiplication, division by a number between zero and one always gives a quotient *larger* than the dividend. This observation is often confusing for children. For example, $4 \div \frac{1}{2}$ can be thought of as, "How many halves are contained in four?"

$$4 \div \tfrac{1}{2} = 8$$

Children also may confuse "division by one-half" with dividing something "in half." For example, dividing four in half means you want to find one-half of four, or to *multiply* by one-half, not divide by one-half.

$$4 \times \tfrac{1}{2} = \tfrac{4}{2} = 2$$

Give oral examples of problems using very simple fractions to help children establish the difference between these English phrases. For example:

A recipe calls for four cups of flour. How much flour is needed if we cut the recipe in half?

$$\left(4 \times \tfrac{1}{2} = 2 \text{ cups of flour}\right)$$

Plans for a bookcase call for $\frac{1}{2}$-foot shelves. How many shelves can be cut from an 8-foot board?

$$\left(8 \div \tfrac{1}{2} = \tfrac{16}{2} \div \tfrac{1}{2} = 16 \text{ shelves}\right)$$

How many pieces of cheese will there be if we cut a $5\frac{1}{2}$-inch block into $\frac{1}{4}$-inch slices?

$$\left(5\tfrac{1}{2} \div \tfrac{1}{4} = \tfrac{11}{2} \div \tfrac{1}{4} = \tfrac{22}{4} \div \tfrac{1}{4} = 22 \text{ slices}\right)$$

Teachers can introduce fraction division by initially selecting exercises with whole-number dividends *and* quotients (e.g., $1 \div \frac{1}{2} = 2$). Using fraction strips, have children show $2 \div \frac{1}{2}$ as pictured in Figure 10.23. Children should solve several carefully selected exercises that have whole-number quotients ($3 \div \frac{1}{6} = ?$; $2 \div \frac{2}{5} = ?$; and so on) and record the solutions using symbols.

Common denominator algorithm. An intuitive algorithm for fraction division is the inverse of the multiplication algorithm. To find the quotient, divide the numerators and divide the denominators. The algorithm works fine for exercises that give whole-number quotients for both the numerator and the denominator of the answer. For example:

$$\tfrac{2}{8} \div \tfrac{1}{2} = \tfrac{2}{4} = \tfrac{1}{2}$$

$$\tfrac{10}{12} \div \tfrac{2}{3} = \tfrac{5}{4} = 1\tfrac{1}{4}$$

For fraction pairs that do not give whole-number quotients for the numerator and denominator, children can first rename one or both fractions so they have a common denominator. This procedure always generates a one in the denominator of the quotient so the final answer is simply the numerator. For example:

$$\tfrac{2}{1} \div \tfrac{1}{2} = \tfrac{4}{2} \div \tfrac{1}{2} = \frac{\frac{4}{1}}{\frac{2}{2}} = \tfrac{4}{1} = 4$$

$$\tfrac{2}{3} \div \tfrac{1}{2} = \tfrac{4}{6} \div \tfrac{3}{6} = \frac{\frac{4}{3}}{1} = \tfrac{4}{3} = 1\tfrac{1}{3}$$

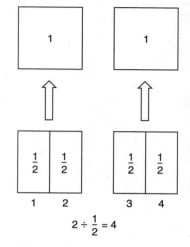

How many halves are contained in two wholes?

$$2 \div \tfrac{1}{2} = 4$$

FIGURE 10.23
Division Using Fraction Strips

Reciprocal algorithm. The standard fraction division algorithm, *invert the divisor and multiply,* uses a property of reciprocals that describes the inverse relationship between multiplication and division. Demonstrate to the class that dividing by any number gives the same answer as multiplying by its reciprocal. In other words, to divide one fraction by another, multiply the dividend by the *reciprocal* of the divisor. For example:

$$6 \div 2 = 6 \times \tfrac{1}{2} = 3$$

$$6 \div \tfrac{1}{3} = 6 \times 3 = 18$$

$$\tfrac{1}{6} \div \tfrac{2}{3} = \tfrac{1}{6} \times \tfrac{3}{2} = \tfrac{3}{12} = \tfrac{1}{4}$$

Children can practice dividing fractions using this procedure and check their results using the common denominator algorithm. For simple examples, have them show the results using fraction strips. Once students become proficient multiplying and dividing fractions, give them sets of mixed exercises to allow them to practice applying the appropriate algorithm.

Renaming Fractions in Simplest Form

One member of each family of equivalent fractions has the smallest denominator. For example, in the one-half family $\left(\tfrac{1}{2}, \tfrac{2}{4}, \tfrac{3}{6}, \text{ and so on}\right)$, $\tfrac{1}{2}$ has the smallest denominator. The process of finding the family member with the smallest denominator is called *simplifying*.

To rename a fraction in simplest form, we use the principle that dividing by one does not change the size of the original number. Therefore, a fraction divided by any unit fraction $\left(\tfrac{2}{2}, \tfrac{3}{3}, \tfrac{4}{4}\right)$ gives a quotient in the *same* fraction family. Children need to understand fraction division to use this technique to simplify fractions. For example:

$$\tfrac{2}{4} \div \tfrac{2}{2} = \tfrac{1}{2}$$

To rename a fraction in simplest form, children must first find a *common factor,* or divisor, for the numerator and denominator. For numerators and denominators to 120, children only need to check the prime divisors 2, 3, 5, and 7 (i.e., the prime factors less than or equal to the square root of the value). For example, to simplify $\tfrac{8}{12}$, check to see if 2 is a common factor for 8 and 12. Since both values are even, they are divisible by 2. Dividing $\tfrac{8}{12}$ by the unit $\tfrac{2}{2}$ gives $\tfrac{4}{6}$, which is a member of the same fraction family. The process is repeated until no common factor remains (except 1, of course).

$$\tfrac{8}{12} \div \tfrac{2}{2} \qquad = \qquad \tfrac{4}{6} \div \tfrac{2}{2} = \tfrac{2}{3} \qquad \rightarrow \textit{fully simplified}$$
First common   Second common
factor (2)   factor (2)

$$\tfrac{8}{12} \div \tfrac{4}{4} = \tfrac{2}{3} \rightarrow \textit{fully simplified}$$
Greatest common
factor (4)

Notice that when the greatest common factor (GCF) was selected for the unit divisor in the second preceding example, the resulting quotient was fully simplified in one step.

The term *simplified* (and especially the outdated term *reduced*) may give the mistaken impression that the value of the fraction has changed. It is very important to consistently remind children that the change in the numerator exactly compensates for the change in the denominator, so the value of the fraction remains the same.

This raises a question as to the value of teaching fraction simplification at all. While $\tfrac{1}{2}$ may appear to be a simpler description of the fraction concept of *halfness,* other representations of $\tfrac{1}{2}$ can be useful as well (e.g., $\tfrac{50}{100}$ to show cents when writing a check). As my grandfather, who was a boat builder, used to say, "I always leave my tools right where I used them last since it's just as likely I will need them again where I left them as on my tool bench." Perhaps the best advice is to simplify fractions only when necessary. For example, when adding $\tfrac{1}{3}$ and $\tfrac{8}{12}$, you could simplify the $\tfrac{8}{12}$ to $\tfrac{2}{3}$ and find the sum rather than renaming

$\frac{1}{3}$ as $\frac{4}{12}$ to get the answer. Otherwise, it may be just as useful to leave your fractions in the form you last used them.

When carefully used, concrete models, like fraction pies and strips, allow children to develop a meaningful understanding of fractional numbers and operations. As with whole numbers, the concrete displays can support learning during initial concept development. The use of concrete materials is reduced as students gain facility with the more flexible symbolic representations and algorithms.

Cancellation

An application of fraction simplification provides a shortcut procedure for multiplying some fractions. Often multiplication exercises can be simplified by dividing the numerator of one fraction and denominator of another by the same value. This process is commonly called *cross canceling*. For example, in $\frac{3}{8} \times \frac{12}{15}$, the 3 in the numerator of the first fraction and the 15 in the denominator of the second can be *canceled* by dividing each by 3. Similarly, the 8 and 12 can be canceled by dividing each by 4.

$$\frac{{}^{1}\cancel{3}}{{}_{2}\cancel{8}} \times \frac{{}^{3}\cancel{12}}{{}_{5}\cancel{15}} = \frac{1}{2} \times \frac{3}{5} = \frac{3}{10}$$

It is possible to use *lateral canceling* for fraction division. This involves dividing both numerators or both denominators of the two fractions by the same value.

$$\frac{{}^{1}\cancel{3}}{4\cancel{8}} \div \frac{{}^{3}\cancel{9}}{{}_{5}\cancel{10}} = \frac{1}{4} \div \frac{3}{5} = \frac{1}{4} \times \frac{5}{3} = \frac{5}{12}$$

Of course, you can also "cancel" the numerator and denominator of the *same* fraction when multiplying and dividing since this is just simplifying the fraction and does not change its value. With practice, canceling procedures can help students multiply and divide fractions mentally. Caution children not to attempt cross canceling or lateral canceling when adding and subtracting fractions since both procedures change the size of the values. Only simplification can be used with addition and subtraction (i.e., apply a unit multiplier or divisor to the numerator and denominator of the *same* fraction so the values remain the same).

D. CLASSROOM ACTIVITIES

Sharing Equally

Some children may be satisfied with unequal divisions when constructing fractional parts of a set or whole. For example, when asked to draw lines to partition a circle into thirds, a child might make the divisions shown in Figure 10.24.

Equivalent Fraction Chart

To help children visualize equivalent families of fractions, construct a bulletin board chart of the equivalent fraction families shown in Figure 10.25. Using nine different colors of construction paper, cut one 5-cm $\times$ 100-cm (2-in $\times$ 36-in) strip of each color. By measuring or folding, mark each strip to show one of the following fraction partitions: $\frac{1}{2}, \frac{1}{3}, \frac{1}{4}, \frac{1}{5}, \frac{1}{6}, \frac{1}{8}, \frac{1}{9}, \frac{1}{10}, \frac{1}{12}$. The final strip represents one whole. Children can position a stick vertically to show equivalent fraction families. The stick shown in Figure 10.25 crosses the strips to show the equivalent fraction family: $\frac{2}{3}, \frac{4}{6}, \frac{6}{9}$, and $\frac{8}{12}$.

Cuisenaire™ Rods

Cuisenaire™ Rods can be used to display fraction values and operations (see Figure 10.26). To show $\frac{1}{2}$, first select a rod to represent a whole unit. This rod must be selected such that two identical rods laid end to end exactly match its length. As shown in Figure 10.27, five rods can be chosen as a whole unit (red, purple, dark green, brown, or orange) that will allow an associated rod to show $\frac{1}{2}$ (white, red, light green, purple, or yellow). The light green, dark green, or blue rod could be selected as a whole unit that will allow white, red, or light green to show $\frac{1}{3}$ (Figure 10.28).

10.9

✎ **FIGURE IT OUT**

Explain why cancellation enables multiplication exercises to be simplified. Why is canceling different for fraction division? Work some examples to show why canceling does not work with addition, subtraction, and division exercises.

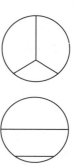

FIGURE 10.24
Unequal Thirds Partition

FIGURE 10.25
Equivalent Fraction Family

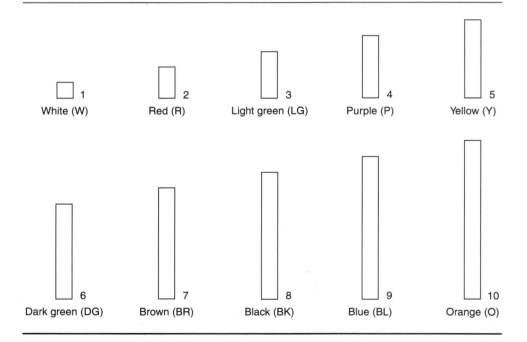

Meter stick
goes through
$\frac{2}{3}, \frac{4}{6}, \frac{6}{9},$ and $\frac{8}{12}$.

FIGURE 10.26
Cuisenaire™ Rods

1 White (W)	2 Red (R)	3 Light green (LG)	4 Purple (P)	5 Yellow (Y)
6 Dark green (DG)	7 Brown (BR)	8 Black (BK)	9 Blue (BL)	10 Orange (O)

To show the addition exercise $\frac{1}{2} + \frac{1}{3}$, have children select the unit rod that allows the representation of both halves and thirds. Selecting the correct unit rod (the dark green rod in this case) is equivalent to finding a common denominator since both halves and thirds can be represented using other rods (light green and red). As shown in Figure 10.29, the dark green rod also can be partitioned into sixths (white).

To show $\frac{1}{2} + \frac{1}{3}$, place the $\frac{1}{2}$ rod (light green) and $\frac{1}{3}$ rod (red) end to end. Since the blocks are not identical, their total length cannot be described by simply counting. As shown in Figure 10.30, after subdividing each fraction into sixths (white rods), the total can be found by counting the five white rods, each representing one sixth $\left(\frac{1}{6} + \frac{1}{6} + \frac{1}{6} + \frac{1}{6} + \frac{1}{6} = \frac{5}{6}\right)$.

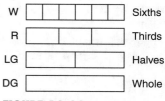

FIGURE 10.29
Fractional Parts of Dark
Green Rod

FIGURE 10.27
Representations of $\frac{1}{2}$
Using Cuisenaire™ Rods

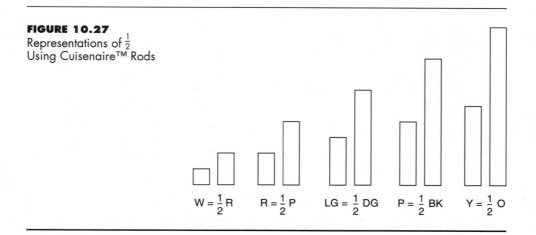

FIGURE 10.28
Three Representations of $\frac{1}{3}$

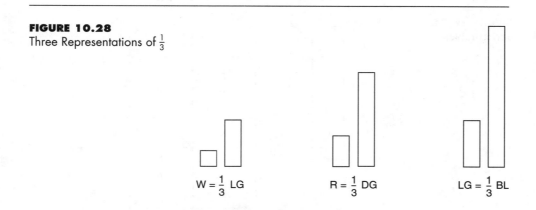

FIGURE 10.30
Cuisenaire™ Rod Fraction Addition $\left(\frac{1}{2} + \frac{1}{3} = \frac{5}{6}\right)$

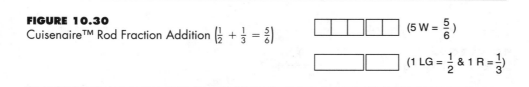

Sums and differences involving halves, thirds, fourths, fifths, sixths, eighths, ninths, and tenths can be readily displayed using Cuisenaire™ Rods.

E. PROBLEM SOLVING INVOLVING RATIONAL NUMBERS AND RATIOS

With a partner, try working several of the following problems. Keep a journal of your procedures and solutions to share with other members of your class.

Billiard Table Math

In which corner will the ball end up if it is shot from the lower left corner at a 45° angle? Figure 10.31 shows *interesting* paths traced by the ball on several rectangular tables of different dimensions. Figure 10.32 shows other tables that display *boring* paths in which some squares are not crossed by the ball.

Using centimeter-squared paper, carry out several billiard table experiments and make a list of interesting tables (where all the squares are crossed by the path of the ball) and boring tables (those that contain some squares not crossed by the path of the ball). Record the results as in Table 10.3. Look for a pattern based on the dimensions of the billiard table that will predict whether a table will generate an interesting or boring display.

TABLE 10.3
Billiard Table Math

INTERESTING TABLES	BORING TABLES
(2,3)	(2,4)
(3,4)	(4,6)
(1,5)	(2,6)
(3,8)	(4,8)
(7,10)	(4,12)

NOTE: The first coordinate represents the length along the horizontal axis, the second coordinate the length along the vertical axis.

FIGURE 10.31
Interesting Tables

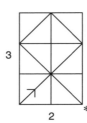
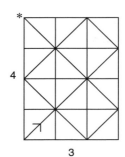
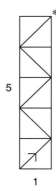

FIGURE 10.32
Boring Tables

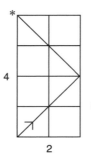
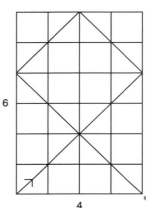
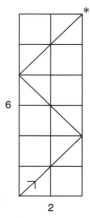

FIGURE 10.33
Similar Pool Table Paths

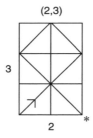
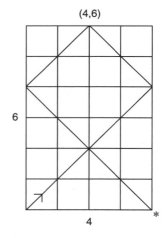

When the edge lengths of *interesting* tables are written as fractions $\left(\frac{2}{3}, \frac{3}{4}, \frac{1}{5}\right)$, notice that they are renamed in simplest terms. *Boring* tables are represented by fractions that can be further simplified $\left(\frac{2}{4}, \frac{4}{6}, \frac{2}{6}\right)$. In Figure 10.33, two billiard tables that represent fractions in the same family display similar paths. Will simplifying the fraction representing a boring table always give an interesting table that ends at the *same* corner?

TABLE 10.4
Billiard Table

PATH FINISHES IN CORNER		
UL	**UR**	**LR**
(3,4)	(3,5)	(2,3)
(5,8)	(1,1)	(4,9)
(7,10)	(7,9)	(6,11)

FIGURE 10.34
Fraction Bars
SOURCE: *Fraction Bars* [Computer program] by Scott Resources, 1984. Copyright 1984 by Scott Resources, Inc.
Reprinted by permission.

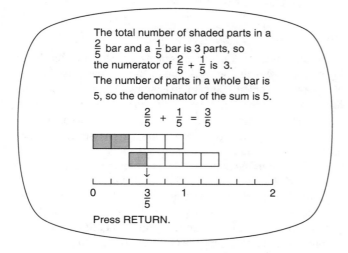

The ball can end in one of three corners: upper left (UL), upper right (UR), and lower right (LR). Using *only* interesting games, organize a table by the ending corner of the ball. Table 10.4 shows the ending corner for several interesting tables. Observe the dimensions of each table and try to find a pattern that accurately predicts the ending corner based on the table dimensions.

See the computer software *Problem-solving Strategies* (MECC) for a useful simulation of *Pooling Around* to help solve these problems.

F. COMPUTER APPLICATIONS
Fraction Bars

The *Fraction Bars Computer Program* (Scott Resources) is a series of programs that uses graphics of fraction bars, number lines, blocks, and dots to introduce the concepts of fractional part, fraction operations, and ratio. Fraction bars are identical strips of cardboard (approximately 1 in × 6 in) that are marked off in fractional parts. Common fractions are shown by shading the appropriate part of each bar. For example, two-thirds would be shown by shading two of the three equal segments on a bar. Each of the seven disks covers one of the following fraction topics: basic concepts, equality, inequality, addition, subtraction, multiplication, and division. Each topic begins with graphic representations of the concepts and moves to symbolic exercises (see Figure 10.34). By typing HELP, children receive step-by-step tutorial assistance on the current exercise. Word problems are included on each disk to provide practice using newly learned fraction concepts and operations. Additional practice is provided in a card game format for each topic. Each disk contains an achievement test to help children determine when to move on to the next topic and what concepts they need to review.

G. ADAPTING INSTRUCTION FOR CHILDREN WITH SPECIAL NEEDS

Operations with fractions are often difficult for special-needs children. Early work with concrete models and clear graphic representations of fraction concepts are critical for children with visual discrimination and figure-ground problems. The use of colored materials such as Cuisenaire™ Rods may aid such children in understanding fraction concepts. For example, have children use like-colored crayons to record the numeral for fractions represented by Cuisenaire™ Rods (one-half can be represented as a red rod over a purple rod and recorded by writing the value 1 in red and 2 in purple in the number $\frac{1}{2}$).

Finding Error Patterns

Observing error patterns can be helpful when children are learning to use the fraction algorithms. Recognizing such patterns early may make it easier for teachers to correct misconceptions before they become routinized. The errors described in Table 10.5 are common among elementary children.

Assigning Mixed Practice

Special-needs children often display more rigid thinking patterns than other students. Teachers may unnecessarily reinforce this tendency by assigning work that focuses on one subskill at a time. For example, after completing several problems containing examples of addition of fractions with like denominators, children may not recognize the need to find common denominators when faced with a set of mixed exercises. While focused skill practice seems to be particularly important for the special-needs learner, limiting practice to a *single* type of exercise may be misleading and cause unintended reinforcement of incorrect procedures.

To help students develop more flexible thinking patterns, you can prepare practice worksheets with mixed examples. Before children begin to calculate, have them determine which exercises require the procedure being practiced and systematically cross out those that do not. They then solve only those exercises not crossed out. For example, if a child needs to practice finding common denominators, mix unlike-denominator addition and subtraction exercises with like-denominator exercises. Have the child determine which require finding a common denominator and cross out the other exercises. They then work only the unlike-denominator exercises. This procedure gives children practice thinking about the underlying characteristics of the exercises to be solved before practicing the specific skill.

Invented Algorithms

Gifted and talented children can explore fraction concepts to extend their understanding of the algorithms and their problem-solving applications. Mathematically mature children should be encouraged to invent their own algorithms and explain why they work. As de-

TABLE 10.5
Common Errors among Elementary Children

	PROBLEM	ERROR
ADDITION:	$\frac{2}{3} + \frac{3}{4} = \frac{5}{7}$	Adding numerators and denominators
SUBTRACTION:	$\frac{4}{5} - \frac{2}{3} = \frac{2}{2}$	Finding difference between numerators and denominators
	$\frac{1}{2} - \frac{5}{8} = \frac{4}{6}$	
	$3\frac{3}{5} - 1\frac{2}{5} = \frac{1}{5}$	Ignoring whole numbers when subtracting mixed numbers.
MULTIPLICATION:	$\frac{3}{8} \times \frac{5}{8} = 1\frac{5}{8}$	Failure to multiply denominators when they are the same value.
	$\frac{2}{3} \times \frac{3}{5} = \frac{2}{3} \times \frac{5}{3} = \frac{10}{9}$	Inverting and multiplying
DIVISION:	$\frac{3}{4} \div \frac{1}{8} = \frac{3}{4} \times \frac{1}{8} = \frac{3}{32}$	Failure to invert before multiplying.

scribed previously, Algorithm 1 for adding and subtracting fractions with unlike denominators uses a skip-counting technique to locate a common denominator. Have children practice using this procedure. By comparing it with Algorithm 2, see if they can explain why it works. As a hint, have them think about how skip counting is related to multiplication. Similarly, children can explore the common denominator algorithm for dividing fractions.

H. ASSESSMENT STRATEGY

Student learning logs are increasingly used by teachers as a regular part of mathematics instruction. Students keep a separate mathematics journal and make daily entries reflecting on their successes, challenges, and frustrations while learning mathematics. The teacher should model good reflective writing and give students constructive feedback on their journals to help them develop their writing skills. Research on the writing process and problem solution has shown that active and repeated reflection on one's own learning fosters meaningful thinking, deeper understanding, and increased motivation for learning.

For students and parents to take learning logs seriously, teachers must systematically monitor student journals and include them as an important part of regular assessment procedures. Evaluation of the quality of writing is not necessary. For this writing activity to be effective, students should be required to make journal entries daily if possible, or at least every other day. Student-developed summaries of the logs may also be included in their assessment portfolios.

I. FRACTION SAMPLE LESSON PLAN

An example of a lesson plan, provided here, introduces addition of fractions with unlike denominators to students in grade 4. This lesson assumes that the class has already worked with fraction strips, can add like fractions, and can find common denominators.

Fraction Lesson Plan

Grade Level: Grade 4   *Time Allotment:* 45 minutes

NCTM Standard: Use models to explore operations on fractions.

Essential Understanding: Partitioning a unit square can be used to describe fractional part and fraction addition.

Goal: Students will understand why fractions must have common denominators to add them.

Objective: The learner will be able to add simple fractions with unlike denominators using fraction strips.

Motivation: Tell your class that a friend is having a party and you need to help him figure out how much food to cook. The recipe calls for one-quarter pound of hamburger for the spaghetti sauce and one-half pound for the meat balls. Can the class figure out how much meat he should buy from the butcher?

Procedure: Pair off the children. Give each pair a set of fraction strips. Review the unit square and each fractional part. Have one student come to the front with the $\frac{1}{4}$ strip and place it on the overhead projector. Have a second child bring the $\frac{1}{2}$ strip and place it next to the first strip. Tell the students that these two pieces can represent the two amounts of hamburger. Ask how the two pieces can be combined. Say that he could buy two packages, a half-pound package and a quarter-pound package, but the butcher might not like having to wrap two packages. Remind the class that to combine fractions, all the pieces must be the same size as when you added like fractions earlier. Ask if the big piece could be divided into smaller pieces the same size as the one quarter. Have a student come to the front and try it. Have all the pairs show that two quarters is the same size as one-half. Ask if we can count the pieces if we substitute the two quarters for the one-half. Have someone come to the front to count the pieces. On the

(Continued)

Fraction Lesson Plan   cont'd

---

overhead, write the symbols $\frac{1}{4} + \frac{1}{2} = \frac{1}{4} + \frac{2}{4} = \frac{3}{4}$ to record the results of the problem. Do several similar problems as a group, followed by work in pairs.

Closure: Have the students make up a problem for their partners and solve them in pairs.

Assessment: Have a few of the pairs report to the whole class using the overhead display. Also, circulate around the class during seat work, observe their work in pairs, and help where needed.

Materials: Set of fraction strips for each pair, overhead projector, and pen.

Extension: Have the children ask their parents when they use fractions around the house (cooking, gardening, carpentry, etc.). Have them bring in one realistic fraction problem to solve the next day.

SUMMARY

- While the fraction number concept is introduced as early as kindergarten and developed through grade 3, systematic work with common fraction operations is a major component of the mathematics curriculum in grades 5 and 6.
- Conservation of length, area, and quantity are associated with the meaningful understanding of the concept *fractional part* since models representing fractions are commonly based on these attributes.
- The concept of fractional part involves partitioning a whole unit, or set, into a given number of equal parts, or groups.
- Other meanings for common fractions include division of the numerator by the denominator and a representation of a ratio.
- Instructional materials like fraction pies, fraction strips, and Cuisenaire™ Rods can be used to introduce fraction concepts and operations.
- Fractions can be classified into families of equivalent fractions. The family member with the smallest denominator is said to be in simplest terms. Families of fractions can be used to find common denominators for two or more fractions.
- Adding and subtracting fractions with unlike denominators requires finding equivalent members of the respective families that have the same, or common, denominator.
- Several algorithms are available for adding and subtracting common fractions. The most efficient algorithm requires finding least common multiples and multiplying each fraction by an appropriate unit multiplier.
- Multiplication of common fractions can be shown using a rectangular area model like fraction strips. Division is introduced as the inverse of fraction multiplication.
- Special-needs children often exhibit rigid thinking patterns. Providing sets of mixed exercises may promote more flexible thinking in such children. Gifted and talented children benefit from experience inventing their own algorithms and should be encouraged to try to justify why common algorithms work.

QUESTIONS AND ACTIVITIES FOR DISCUSSION

1. Construct a complete set of fraction pies and strips. Practice showing representations of specific fractions, developing families of equivalent fractions, simplifying fractions, adding and subtracting like and unlike fractions and mixed numbers, and multiplying and dividing selected fractions and mixed numbers. Give a demonstration for your peers. If possible, write a lesson plan and try out at least one activity with a group of students in a classroom setting.

2. Using squared paper, draw sketches of rectangular billiard tables (corner pockets only) with sides of various whole-number lengths. Work out a rule, based on the length and width of the table, that predicts how many times the ball will bounce off the edge (see Figure 10.35). Always shoot the ball at 45° from the lower left corner. Make a table of results, look for patterns, and develop a function.

3. Read at least two articles listed in the "Suggested Readings" that discuss changes in the role of fractions in the mathematics curriculum. Include a report about the possible effects of increased

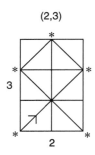

(2,3)

FIGURE 10.35
Billiard Table Paths

use of calculators, computers, and metric units. List ways standard fractions will continue to be used in work and everyday life, and discuss why their importance is likely to diminish.

4. Read one of the *Arithmetic Teacher* articles listed in the readings section. Write a brief report summarizing the main ideas of the article, and describe how the recommendations for instruction might apply to your own mathematics teaching.

INSTRUCTIONAL RESOURCES

CHILDREN'S BOOKS

Anno, M. *Anno's math games I.* Philomel Books. A delightful collection of illustrated mathematics problems and games for children of all ages.

Anno, M. *Anno's math games II.* Philomel Books. A delightful collection of illustrated mathematics problems and games for children of all ages.

Anno, M. *Anno's math games III.* Philomel Books. A delightful collection of illustrated mathematics problems and games for children of all ages.

COMPUTER SOFTWARE

Edu-Ware Fractions. Edu-Ware Services, Inc. Tutorial on fraction concepts and practice with operations.

Fraction Bars Computer Program: Basic Concepts, Equality, Inequality, Addition, Subtraction, Multiplication, Division. Scott Resources. A series of seven disks that use fraction bars as a model for introducing fraction concepts and operations.

Fractions—Basic Concepts. Sterling Swift Publishing. Practice with fraction number and operation skills.

Partial Fractions. Sunburst Communications, Inc. Students guess answers for fraction multiplication and division exercises to develop an understanding of the relative size of answers.

Problem Solving Strategies. Minnesota Educational Computer Consortium. Set of four problem-solving situations, including *Pooling Around,* that employ the solution strategies of making a table, looking for patterns, and guess-and-test.

REFERENCE

National Council of Teachers of Mathematics. (1989). *Curriculum and evaluation standards for school mathematics.* Reston, VA: Author.

SUGGESTED READINGS

Bennett, A., & Davidson, P. (1978). *Fraction bars.* Fort Collins, CO: Scott Resources.

Carpenter, T., Corbitt, M., Kepner, H., Lindquist, M., & Reys, R. (1981). Decimals: Results and implications from the national assessment. *Arithmetic Teacher, 28*(8), 34–37.

Cathcart, W. (1977). Metric Measurement: Important curricular considerations. *Arithmetic Teacher, 24*(2), 158–160.

Chiosi, L. (1984). Fractions revisited. *Arithmetic Teacher, 31*(8), 46–47.

Coxford, A., & Ellerbruch, L. (1975). Fractional numbers. In J. Payne (Ed.), *Mathematics learning in early childhood: 1975 yearbook* (pp. 192–203). Reston, VA: National Council of Teachers of Mathematics.

Cramer, K., & Bezuk, N. (1991). Multiplication of fractions: Teaching for understanding. *Arithmetic Teacher, 39*(3), 34–37.

Davidson, P. (1969). *Using the Cuisenaire Rods: A photo/text guide for teachers.* New Rochelle, NY: Cuisenaire Co. of America.

Davidson, P. (1977). *Idea book for Cuisenaire Rods at the primary level.* New Rochelle, NY: Cuisenaire Co. of America.

Edge, D. (1987). Fractions and panes. *Arithmetic Teacher, 34*(4), 6–7.

Esty, W. (1991). The least common denominator. *Arithmetic Teacher, 39*(7), 47–49.

Firl, D. (1977). Fractions, decimals and their futures. *Arithmetic Teacher, 24*(2), 238–240.

Kalman, D. (1985). Up fractions! Up *n/m. Arithmetic Teacher, 32*(8), 42–43.

Litwiller, B., & Duncan, D. (1985). Pentagonal patterns in the addition table. *Arithmetic Teacher, 32*(8), 36–38.

Ott, J. (1990). A unified approach to multiplying fractions. *Arithmetic Teacher, 37*(7), 47–49.

Ott, J., Snook, D., & Gibson, D. (1991). Understanding partitive division of fractions. *Arithmetic Teacher, 31*(2), 7–11.

Pothier, Y., & Sawada, D. (1990). Partitioning: An approach to fractions. *Arithmetic Teacher, 38*(4), 12–17.

Quintero, A. (1987). Helping children understand ratios. *Arithmetic Teacher, 34*(9), 17–21.

Steiner, E. (1987). Division of fractions: Developing conceptual sense with dollars and cents. *Arithmetic Teacher, 34*(9), 36–42.

Sweetland, R. (1984). Understanding multiplication of fractions. *Arithmetic Teacher, 32*(1), 48–52.

CHAPTER 11

Decimals, Proportions, and Integers

This chapter focuses your attention on how to teach the concepts of decimals, proportions, and integers. Specifically, it is designed to help you understand

1. The relationship between common and decimal fractions.
2. Manipulative materials used to introduce decimal operations.
3. Models for integer operations and their applications in scientific notation, measurement, algebra, and geometry.
4. Proportional reasoning and its importance for mathematical problem solving.
5. Methods for teaching percent.
6. Decimal operation problem-solving activities.
7. Techniques for incorporating technology into decimal operation lessons.

NCTM Decimal, Percent, Ratio, Proportion, and Integer Standards
K–4 level students will

- Develop concepts of decimals
- Develop number sense for decimals
- Use models to relate fractions to decimals
- Use models to explore operations on decimals
- Apply decimals to problem situations.

5–8 level students will

- Compute using decimals, integers, and rational numbers
- Use computation, estimation, and proportions to solve problems. (NCTM, 1989, pp. 57, 94)

The term *decimal* is based on the Latin word *deci*, meaning *ten*. Decimals are simply fractions that are written with powers of 10 as denominators $\left(\frac{1}{10}, \frac{1}{100}, \text{etc.}\right)$. Using the indicated-division meaning, any fraction can be written as a decimal with a finite number of decimal places $\left(\frac{1}{10} = 0.1 \text{ or } \frac{1}{2} = 0.5\right)$, or as a decimal with a pattern of digits that repeat indefinitely $\left(\frac{1}{3} = 0.333\ldots \text{ or } \frac{2}{11} = 0.1818\ldots\right)$.

> **?** *I WAS JUST THINKING . . .*
>
> The teachers' union is negotiating a salary increase over the next two years.
> Three options are being considered. Which option should the teachers choose?
> *Plan A:* 5% raise in year one and 8% raise in year two
> *Plan B:* 8% raise in year one and 5% raise in year two
> *Plan C:* 12% raise in year one and 0% raise in year two

A. INTRODUCING DECIMAL FRACTIONS
Decimals as Special Fractions

Because decimals are extensions of the base-10 place-value system, many concepts and procedures developed for whole numbers carry over to work with decimals. It is important, however, to introduce decimal fraction concepts using concrete models to give meaning to the decimal point and the decimal fraction place values (Hiebert, 1987). Most children do not recognize the relationship between common fractions and decimals (Bell, Swan, & Taylor, 1981; Hiebert & Wearne, 1986). Also, without meaningful instruction, the shortcut rules used to manipulate decimals are confusing to students. For many children, skill in working decimal algorithms does not improve with time (Carpenter, Corbitt, Kepner, Lindquist, & Reys, 1981; Grossman, 1983).

Manipulatives can be used to extend the base-10 relationship to numbers between 0 and 1. To accomplish this, the block previously associated with the hundreds place (100 block) is simply reassigned as the 1 unit. As shown in Figure 11.1, the 10-rod becomes one-tenth $\left(\frac{1}{10}\right)$, and the small cube becomes one-hundredth $\left(\frac{1}{100}\right)$.

Children learn about decimal fraction place values by first constructing concrete representations for digits in the tenths and hundredths place values. Initially, values composed of only one nonzero digit should be used. Numbers are recorded in place-value tables as shown in Figure 11.2.

Next, problems composed of digits in the ones place and either the tenths or hundredths place values are introduced (Figure 11.3).

Reading Decimal Values

After the teacher introduces the tenths and hundredths place values separately, the teacher can then introduce values composed of digits in the ones, tenths, *and* hundredths place values. Values such as 0.23 are not normally read as "two tenths and three hundredths" since the fraction part of the decimal is read as a single value rather than as separate fractions. Since two-tenths is equal to twenty-hundredths $\left(\frac{2}{10} = \frac{20}{100}\right)$, it is customary to state the sum of the two place values $\left(\frac{23}{100} \rightarrow \text{twenty-three hundredths}\right)$ when saying the number 0.23. Fortunately, the base-10 system offers a built-in shortcut to this process. In English, the decimal fraction is read as if it were a separate whole number, and the place value of the final digit is appended. Reversing the process allows students to construct decimal representations from values presented orally (see Figure 11.4).

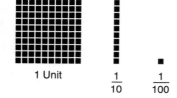

FIGURE 11.1
Base-10 Block Decimal
Representation

1 Unit $\frac{1}{10}$ $\frac{1}{100}$

> ➥ *Answer to* **I WAS JUST THINKING . . .**
>
> Plan C pays the most over the two years. This choice is not affected by the individual teacher's salary. Let a teacher's salary be x. Then, Plan A pays $1.05x$ the first year and $1.08(1.05x)$ the second year, for a total of $1.05x + 1.08(1.05x) = 2.184x$ for the two-year total. Plan B pays $1.08x$ the first year and $1.05(1.08x)$ the second year, for a total of $1.05x + 1.05(1.08x) = 2.214x$. Note that Plan A and Plan B pay the same amount in the second year, but Plan B pays more overall since the 8% raise is given first, and Plan A pays only 5% in the first year. Plan C pays $1.12x$ the first year and $1.00(1.12x)$ the second year (there is no increase the second year, but the teacher continues to receive the 12% increase from the first year). This gives a total of $1.12x + 1.00(1.12x) = 2.24x$ over the two years. For example, for each $1,000 in initial salary, Plan A would return $184, Plan B, $214, and Plan C, $240, over the two-year period.

FIGURE 11.2
Base-10 Blocks and
Place-Value Tables

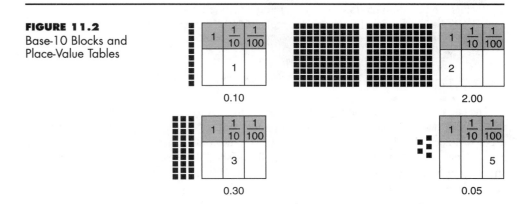

FIGURE 11.3
Decimals Representations

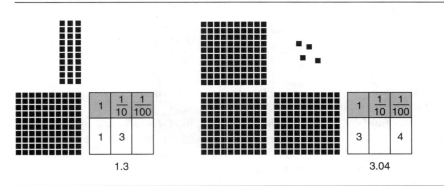

FIGURE 11.4
Verbal Representations

Because the denominators can be accurately specified based on the relative position of each digit, they are omitted from the decimal symbol. For example:

$$42 + \frac{2}{10} + \frac{3}{100} = 42.23$$

$$36 + \frac{6}{100} = 36.06$$

The convenience of not having to write the denominators (tenths, hundredths, and so on) when using decimals may be confusing for some students initially when the zero digit is used. If a zero placeholder is overlooked in a number like 2.001, a serious error will occur—just as with the whole number 2,001. Children should have considerable practice constructing numbers such as 0.04 and 1.03 using base-10 materials, recording them in place-value tables, and expressing each number orally.

The Decimal Point

It is customary to include at least one whole-number digit (it may be zero in the ones column) when writing a decimal fraction. The *decimal point* is simply a convention to separate the whole number from the fraction component of the decimal. We write *0.14* not *.14*.

Normally, any trailing zeros in the decimal fraction are dropped. Some specific applications, such as currency or rounded measures, require that extra zeros be retained:

0.2	not	0.20
$0.20	not	$0.2
$12.00	not	$12

And when rounding 2.58 m
to the nearest decimeter: 2.60 m   not   2.6 m

Note that whole numbers are also decimals. Decimal numbers are made up of a whole number component and a decimal fraction component (either of which may be zero), separated by a decimal point. When writing *only* the whole number component of a decimal number, it is customary to omit the decimal point.

234 not 234.

Money, Metrics, and Calculators

In addition to the base-10 system of numeration, money, metric measures, and calculators can be used to introduce decimal concepts and skills. Each offers a representation of decimal fraction place values (see Figure 11.5).

FIGURE 11.5
Decimal Place-Value Representations

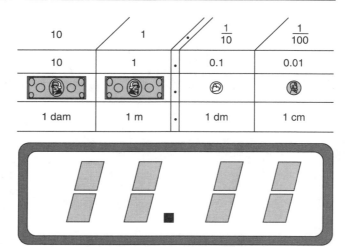

Children who can readily recognize pennies, dimes, and dollars can be introduced to decimal notation and operations through comparing, recording, and reading decimal values. Cash register tapes, price tags, menus, and price lists show how decimals are used in everyday life. It is important for children to understand the relationship between the use of the $ sign and the ¢ sign (e.g., $0.42 = 42¢).

A useful activity to help children see the two ways money is represented is to compare item pricing and cash register pricing. Keep the register tape the next time you go to a grocery store. As the items you buy are used at home, open the cans and boxes so the prices remain visible (cut the bottom out of the cans instead of the top). When the empty packages and cans are all available, take them to school and make an overhead transparency of the register tape. Show the class each priced item (a can of soup for 65¢) and have them identify its value printed on a register tape ($0.65). Using a place-value table on the overhead, record the price of each item in dollars, dimes, and pennies (use play money if desired) in the ones, tenths, and hundredths columns. The can of soup, for example, can be recorded as six dimes in the tenths column and five pennies in the hundredths column, which matches the decimal representation on the register tape (see Figure 11.6).

Collect menus and price lists from fast-food restaurants, auto parts stores, record shops, and newspaper ads to use in class. Plan activities in which students use play money to represent decimal amounts and record the values in place-value tables. For example:

1. Have each student plan a birthday party by listing the items needed, the cost of each, and the total.
2. Have small groups of students compute the cost of items needed for a backpacking trip.
3. Have each student design a private classroom study area and compute the cost of the required building materials.

One of the important advantages of metric units is that they are based on the decimal system. Working with metric measures can provide practice with reading, writing, and comparing decimals. For example, the meter is the basic unit of metric length. Its subunits include the decimeter (0.1 m) and centimeter (0.01 m). When measuring a length, the result is written in whole and decimal parts of a meter (see Figure 11.7).

Another way to introduce work with decimals is to use an accurate graduated cylinder to measure the volume of common containers in liter units (see Figure 11.8). Decimal calculations involving weight require accurate scales that weigh in grams.

Comparing Decimals

Calculators are useful tools for experimenting with decimals at all grade levels. As a beginning activity, have the class work in pairs, each with their own calculator. Have each child press the CLEAR key and the DECIMAL POINT key. Then, with eyes closed, one child enters a two- or three-digit decimal on the calculator. The second child does the same. Both values are recorded in a place-value table and compared. Any disagreement about which is larger can be resolved by constructing each number using base-10 materials or play money. If desired, each pair of children can keep track of who accumulates the highest number or larger (or smaller) decimal values in 10 rounds.

FIGURE 11.6
Price on Can, Tape, Till, and Place-Value Table

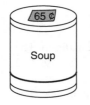
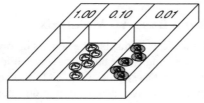

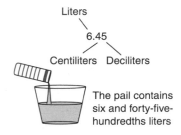

Liters

6.45

Centiliters   Deciliters

The pail contains six and forty-five-hundredths liters

FIGURE 11.8
Measuring Volume in the Metric System

FIGURE 11.7
Metric Measures

TABLE 11.1
Comparing Common Fraction and Decimal Addition

COMMON FRACTION NOTATION	DECIMAL FRACTION NOTATION
$42 + \frac{2}{10} + \frac{3}{100}$	42.23
$+36 \qquad \frac{6}{100}$ $\rightarrow$	$+36.06$
$78 + \frac{2}{10} + \frac{9}{100}$	78.29

B. DECIMAL OPERATIONS
Introducing Addition and Subtraction

Finding sums and differences of decimal fractions is easier than with common fractions since the corresponding digits (digits having the same place value) in decimal numbers always have common denominators. Finding sums and differences of decimal fractions, therefore, is similar to finding sums and differences of common fractions *with* like denominators. Since the denominators for each corresponding pair of digits are the same, the numerators can be added or subtracted just like when adding or subtracting whole numbers.

To accomplish this, children must carefully line up the columns so that the corresponding place values have common denominators. Table 11.1 compares addition of common and decimal fractions. Note that when the decimal points are lined up, the corresponding decimal fraction place values always have the same denominator. The zero placeholder in the number 36.06 makes it clear that the 6 digit is in the hundredths column.

Similarly, Table 11.2 compares subtraction using common fraction and decimal fraction notation.

Adding Decimals Using Base-10 Materials

Children can use base-10 materials to display the actions involved in decimal addition. The procedures parallel those for adding whole numbers. Have children display the exercise 3.42 + 1.89 on a decimal-addition mat as shown in Figure 11.9. The ones column is represented by the flat, the tenths column by the rod, and the hundredths column by the small cube. The hundredths column is combined first (Figure 11.9a). There are more than 9 hundredths in the sum, so 10 hundredths are regrouped into 1 tenth and placed in the tenths column, leaving 1

11.2
✎ **FIGURE IT OUT**

Calculate the following decimal sums using base-10 materials and record the results in place-value tables.

1. 2.47 + 1.72 = ?
2. 1.34 + 2.85 = ?
3. 2.06 + 1.64 = ?
4. 0.78 + 1.7 = ?
5. 2.81 + 1.09 = ?

TABLE 11.2
Comparing Common Fraction and Decimal Subtraction

COMMON FRACTION NOTATION	DECIMAL FRACTION NOTATION

$42 + \frac{2}{10} + \frac{3}{100} = 42 + \frac{1}{10} + \frac{13}{100}$ 42.23

$-36 \qquad + \frac{6}{100} = 36 + \qquad \frac{6}{100}$ -36.06

$\qquad\qquad\qquad 6 + \frac{1}{10} + \frac{7}{100}$ 6.17

FIGURE 11.9
Decimal Addition Using Base-10 Materials (3.42 + 1.89)

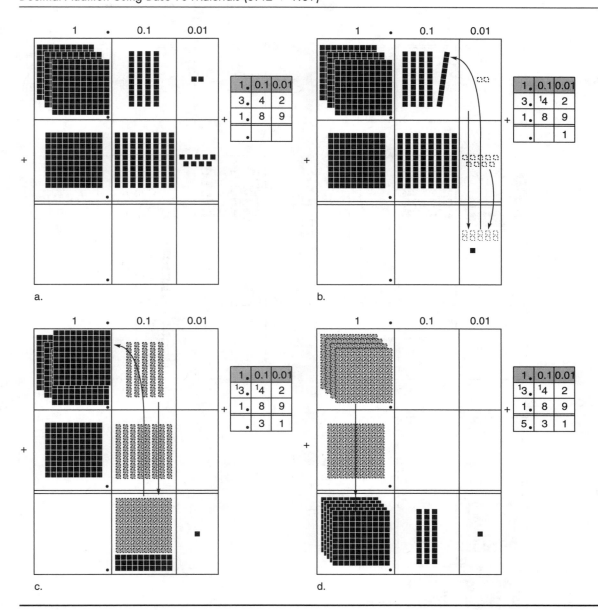

a.

b.

c.

d.

hundredth in the hundredths column. Children combine each column in turn and regroup as required and record each step using place-value tables or standard decimal notation.

Subtracting Decimals Using Base-10 Materials

The actions involved in decimal subtraction also parallel the whole-number algorithm. Figure 11.10 shows the steps for 4.13 − 1.26. Because there are not enough hundredths in the minuend to subtract 6 hundredths, 1 tenth is regrouped into 10 hundredths and placed

FIGURE 11.10
Decimal Subtraction (4.13 − 1.26)

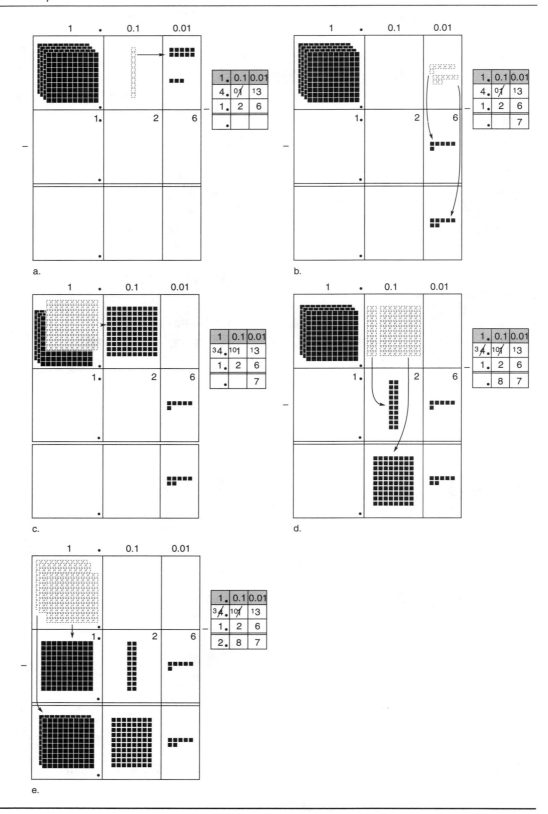

in the hundredths column. We can then subtract the 6 tenths (Figure 11.10b) and move the difference to the answer box. Since there are 0 tenths remaining in the minuend, 1 one must be regrouped into 10 tenths and placed in the tenths column (Figure 11.10c). We can then subtract 2 tenths from the 10 tenths and move the difference to the answer box. Finally, the ones column can be subtracted (Figure 11.10e).

Introducing Multiplication and Division

Unlike for common fractions, the multiplication and division of decimal fractions parallels the procedures for whole numbers since decimals are extensions of the base-10 system. However, unless you are selective in the exercises assigned, the number of objects often gets quite large, making the use of physical models unwieldy. Fortunately, by the time decimal fraction multiplication and division are introduced in grades 5–6, children are better able to extend the symbolic algorithms for work with decimals.

Multiplication of Decimals Using Fraction Strips

Fraction strips or base-10 materials can be used to introduce multiplication of decimal fractions. When using fraction strips, have children use only the whole square and $\frac{1}{10}$ strips. To show 0.3×0.4 using strips, have the children first represent $0.3 \left(\frac{3}{10}\right)$ and $0.4 \left(\frac{4}{10}\right)$ and position them on the whole square as shown in Figure 11.11 (dotted lines on the whole square show 100 small squares in ten rows and columns). As with common fraction multiplication, the area of the overlapped strips (12 hundredths) is the product: $0.3 \times 0.4 = 0.12$. Have the class do several exercises involving tenths $\times$ tenths.

The products of two decimals such as 2.3×1.2 also can be shown using base-10 materials. Let 1 be represented by the 100-flat, 0.1 by the 10-rod, and 0.01 by the small cube. Following the familiar whole-number procedures, children can display each factor and construct an array with 2.3 rows and 1.2 columns as shown in Figure 11.12. Each of the four subproducts is represented by a component of the array. Teachers can use several exercises of this type to show how decimal multiplication can be accomplished using the same algorithm as for whole-number products.

Decimal Multiplication Algorithm

After children are confident with the decimal actions using manipulatives, introduce more complex exercises. As students gain experience, there will be less need to keep track of the place value of each subproduct. Finally, as a shortcut, point out that by initially ignoring the decimal point, the values can be multiplied using the standard whole-number algorithm and the decimal point positioned in the answer. The number of places to the right of the decimal point can be determined by mentally calculating the decimal place value of the product.

For example, tenths $\times$ tenths = hundredths, so the decimal point in the first example should be placed so that the decimal fraction part of the product shows hundredths (i.e., so the decimal point has two place values to its right). Eventually, children should discover that the number of decimal places in the product is the sum of the numbers of decimal places in the two factors.

$$
\begin{array}{r}
0.5 \\
\times\ 0.6 \\
\hline
0.30
\end{array}
\quad
\begin{array}{l}
\textit{(1 decimal fraction place value)} \\
\textit{(1 decimal fraction place value)} \\
\textit{(2 decimal fraction place values)}
\end{array}
$$

$$
\begin{array}{r}
0.31 \\
\times\ 0.2 \\
\hline
0.062
\end{array}
\quad
\begin{array}{l}
\textit{(2 decimal fraction place values)} \\
\textit{(1 decimal fraction place values)} \\
\textit{(3 decimal fraction place values)}
\end{array}
$$

$$
\begin{array}{r}
2.43 \\
\times\ 0.17 \\
\hline
1701 \\
243 \\
\hline
0.4131
\end{array}
\quad
\begin{array}{l}
\textit{(2 decimal fraction place values)} \\
\textit{(2 decimal fraction place values)} \\
\\
\\
\textit{(4 decimal fraction place values)}
\end{array}
$$

11.3

✎ FIGURE IT OUT

Calculate the following decimal differences using base-10 materials and record the results in place-value tables.

1. $2.67 - 1.23 = ?$
2. $3.62 - 1.27 = ?$
3. $3.42 - 2.69 = ?$
4. $2.04 - 1.27 = ?$
5. $3.2 - 2.04 = ?$

11.4

✎ FIGURE IT OUT

Calculate the following decimal products using base-10 materials and record the results using place-value tables.

1. $2.1 \times 1.4 = ?$
2. $1.3 \times 1.6 = ?$
3. $2.4 \times 2.1 = ?$
4. $1.5 \times 2.5 = ?$
5. $2.4 \times 3.6 = ?$

FIGURE 11.11
Decimal Fraction Multiplication Using
Fraction Strips

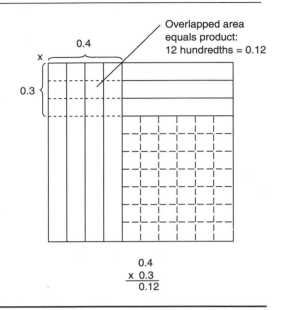

$$\begin{array}{r} 0.4 \\ \times\ 0.3 \\ \hline 0.12 \end{array}$$

FIGURE 11.12
Decimal Multiplication
Using Base-10 Materials

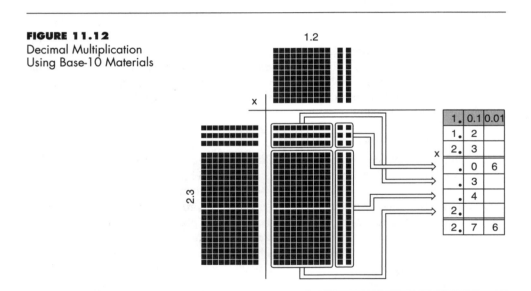

You can create a useful exercise for children by making a worksheet showing several possible answers for each decimal multiplication problem. The children estimate the decimal fraction place values and circle the correct answer. For example:

| 3.9 × 12.4 = 4836 | 483.6 | 48.36 | 4.836 | 0.4836 |
| 12.04 × 0.204 = 24561.6 | 2456.16 | 245.616 | 24.5616 | 2.45616 |

C. DECIMAL DIVISION

Since division is the inverse of multiplication, the base-10 array model for whole-number division also works for decimals. The array in Figure 11.12 also shows $2.76 \div 2.3 = 1.2$. See Chapter 8 for a detailed discussion of this model using whole numbers. Decimal division exactly parallels whole-number division.

Teachers also can use the number line to show division of a decimal fraction by a decimal fraction. For example, suppose a group of friends are planning to row a boat 2.5 miles

FIGURE 11.13
Decimal Division on the
Number Line

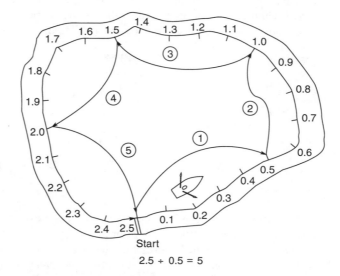

Start

$2.5 \div 0.5 = 5$

FIGURE 11.14
Division of Decimal
Fraction by Whole
Number Using Money

$0.24 \div 3 = 0.08$

around a lake and each person can row 0.5 miles. How many people are needed to complete the trip around the lake? This model uses the repeated subtraction model of division discussed in Chapter 8. Figure 11.13 shows how this division problem can be solved using the number line.

Work with money can likewise be used to show division of a decimal fraction by a whole number. For example, to show $0.24 \div 3$, have children start with two dimes ($20¢ = \$0.20$) and four pennies ($4¢ = \$0.04$). Partitioning these coins into 3 equal groups requires regrouping the dimes into 20 pennies as shown in Figure 11.14. Each group contains eight pennies, so $0.24 \div 3 = 0.08$. Have children do several examples using play money.

Decimal Division Algorithm

Division of a decimal fraction by a whole number uses the same algorithm as whole numbers. Just as with whole number division, the decimal point must be positioned above the decimal point in the dividend to keep the place values properly lined up (note that the decimal point is generally omitted when the quotient is an exact whole number).

$$\begin{array}{r} 0.58 \\ 4\overline{)2.32} \\ 2\,0 \\ \hline 32 \\ 32 \\ \hline 0 \end{array} \qquad \begin{array}{r} 3.18 \\ 8\overline{)25.44} \\ 24 \\ \hline 14 \\ 8 \\ \hline 64 \\ 64 \\ \hline 0 \end{array}$$

The remainder is not written as part of the quotient for decimal fraction division since it is typically not a whole number. Instead, when greater accuracy is required, additional zeros are appended to the dividend and the division is carried out to further decimal places.

11.5
✎ **FIGURE IT OUT**

Calculate the following decimal quotients on a number line or as money and record the results using standard symbols.

1. $0.36 \div 3 = ?$
2. $0.45 \div 5 = ?$
3. $2.2 \div 0.2 = ?$
4. $1.6 \div 0.4 = ?$
5. $8.4 \div 4 = ?$

For example, to compute 14.24 ÷ 6 to the nearest hundredth (rounded off to two decimal places), children append one zero to the dividend, carry out the division three decimal places (thousandths place value), and round off to the nearest hundredth.

$$
\begin{array}{r}
2.373 \approx 2.37 \\
6\overline{)14.240} \\
\underline{12} \\
22 \\
\underline{18} \\
44 \\
\underline{42} \\
20 \\
\underline{18} \\
2
\end{array}
$$

To position the decimal point correctly, division exercises involving decimal fraction divisors require an additional step prior to carrying out the standard algorithm. Because it is more difficult to divide by a fraction than by a whole number, have children first multiply the divisor by the power of 10 (10, 100, 1,000, and so on) that will convert it to a whole number. Then multiply the dividend by the same power of 10 to maintain an equivalent proportion between the divisor and the dividend. Dividing these two new values gives the same quotient as in the original exercise, because both are increased proportionally (i.e., 8 ÷ 4 = 80 ÷ 40 = 800 ÷ 400).

After children have completed several examples using this method, ask the class to figure out why moving the decimal point an equal number of positions in both the divisor and dividend has the same effect as multiplying each by the same power of 10. When applying this rule, insert a *caret* (∧) to stand for the new decimal point in the divisor that will make it a whole number. Place a caret in the dividend the same number of places to the right of its decimal point.

Solving the exercises marked with the caret in the following examples will give the same answer as in the original problem. Since each of the divisors is transformed into a whole number, the division algorithm is the same as for whole numbers. The decimal point, of course, must be placed in the quotient directly above its *new* position in the dividend, identified by the caret. Each of the exercises has a remainder, so the quotient is approximate. Students can check the results of their work using a calculator.

$$2.4\overline{)42.68} = 2.4_\wedge\overline{)42.6_\wedge8} \quad \overset{17.7}{}$$ *(position caret one place value to the right in divisor and dividend)*

$$.34\overline{)5.276} = .34_\wedge\overline{)5.27_\wedge6} \quad \overset{15.5}{}$$ *(position caret two place values to the right in divisor and dividend)*

$$.71\overline{)64.9} = .71_\wedge\overline{)64.90_\wedge} \quad \overset{91.}{}$$ *(position caret two place values to the right in the divisor and dividend by appending a 0)*

As with whole number operations, the meaningful use of manipulatives can help children develop decimal fraction concepts and skills. After students achieve meaningful understanding, systematically reduce the reliance on these perceptual supports to improve their ability to apply decimal skills to problem-solving situations.

D. RATES, RATIOS, AND PROPORTIONS

Real-world situations sometimes require the systematic comparison of measures or sets of objects. These comparisons are typically expressed as rates, ratios, or proportions.

Rates and Ratios

To describe how fast you ride a bicycle requires thinking about two measures—the elapsed time and the distance traveled. It might take two hours to ride 20 miles. More commonly, speed is reported as a standard *rate,* or the distance traveled in each unit of time. For example, suppose a triathlon racer can ride her bicycle at a steady rate of 30 miles per hour. This rate can be written as the ratio 30:1 (every 30 miles takes one hour). If the athlete is able to maintain this level of effort for several hours, a table of equivalent ratios, like families of fractions, can be constructed that will predict the distance traveled for any number of hours (see Table 11.3).

A *ratio* is a way of describing the relationship between two or more groups. For example, the normal ratio of people to shoes is one person for every two shoes, or one to two. This ratio is commonly written 1:2 or (1,2). The ratio 1:2 appears to give the same information as the fraction $\frac{1}{2}$. However, the ratio 1:2 establishes a more powerful relationship between people and shoes than the fraction $\frac{1}{2}$. The ratio 1:2 tells us that *every* person has two shoes. The fraction $\frac{1}{2}$ only suggests that there are half as many people as shoes. A fraction does not guarantee an even *distribution* of objects. For example, one person may wear two pairs at the same time (e.g., boots over shoes), while another may be barefoot. There are still half as many people as shoes but not in a ratio of 1:2. Figure 11.15 shows some possible arrangements for ratio and fraction distributions.

Children often misinterpret ratios, especially when a comparison is made between a set of objects and a subset. For example, suppose a pencil sharpener breaks the lead one time for every five times that it functions properly (i.e., a ratio of 1:5). Now suppose that all 30 children in the class sharpen their pencil. How many will break their lead? Children frequently answer incorrectly that there will likely be six broken pencil leads. As shown in Figure 11.16, this comparison involves class inclusion. There is one broken pencil lead for each six sharpenings. Therefore, there would be five broken leads in thirty sharpenings.

Ratios cannot be added, subtracted, multiplied, or divided like fractions. To combine two different ratios, we add the number of events in each category. For example, suppose another

TABLE 11.3
Equivalent Ratios
30:1
60:2
90:3
120:4

FIGURE 11.16
Ratio of Broken to
Sharpened Pencils

Ratio

1:5

5:25

The ratio of people to shoes is 1:2
(each person wearing 2 shoes)

$\frac{1}{2}$ as many people as shoes
(2 people with 4 shoes and
2 shoeless people)

FIGURE 11.15
Ratio and Fraction Distribution

FROM A DIFFERENT ANGLE

ST: Our class seems to be having a lot of trouble learning about ratios. How much more time do you think I should spend on this concept?

CT: Ratios are important because they lead to proportions. Do you remember how helpful proportional reasoning was when you studied physics and chemistry? If you understand the proportional relationships in mechanics and electronics, you don't need to memorize so many formulas. You can often reconstruct a formula if you know how the quantities are related.

ST: Sure, but why is it so hard for a lot of upper-grade students to work with ratios and proportions?

CT: Well, kids in the fifth and sixth grade are usually introduced to proportions when they solve percents. We may find it's useful to think about percents in terms of the proportional relationship between the rate, base, and percentage, but kids need more concrete examples of proportions first.

ST: Like similar triangles and other geometric figures?

CT: Right, or increasing the measures in a recipe to serve more people. There are lots of ratio and proportion problems that elementary and middle school children can understand.

ST: But why is it so hard for some children to understand ratios and proportions?

CT: Because proportional reasoning is probably one of the most difficult and most important concepts for elementary students. If you can give students a good understanding of equivalent fractions and teach them something about equations, they'll have an easier time with proportions. Try starting with some simple unit ratios, like 1:2 or 1:3 to help them deal with two ratios at a time. Dealing with simpler numbers puts less stress on their working memory, so they can focus on the process of making the ratios equivalent.

ST: Thanks, I'll give it a try tomorrow with the flagpole problem—you know, where we measure shadows and use similar triangles to measure the height of a flagpole?

CT: Good idea, but you may want to plan an alternative lesson just in case it rains!

class has a better sharpener, and their ratio of broken to sharpened pencils is 2:15. The combined performance of the two sharpeners is $(1 + 2):(5 + 15)$, or 3:20.

Proportional Reasoning

Two ratios are said to be proportional if their corresponding fractional representations are equivalent. For example, the ratios 1:2 and 2:4 are *proportional* because $\frac{1}{2} = \frac{2}{4}$.

Proportional ratios, however, do *not* infer an identical relationship. For example, a 1:2 ratio assumes a different *distribution* than a 2:4 relationship. Suppose a 1:2 ratio stipulates that each person receives two hamburgers and a 2:4 ratio stipulates that each two persons must receive four hamburgers. As shown in Figure 11.17, it is possible that with a ratio of 2:4, someone will have nothing to eat, which is not the case with the 1:2 ratio.

Proportions can be written using three different notations. The third notation is typically used for solving proportion problems since corresponding fraction operations can be used. The symbol :: means *is proportional to*.

1. 1:2::2:4
2. (1,2)::(2,4)
3. $\frac{1}{2}::\frac{2}{4}$

Exploring proportional relationships may help children solve a wide range of practical problems. We learned that the sides of similar triangles are proportional. Using this information, it is possible to calculate the height of a flagpole by comparing the length of its shadow to that of a meter stick. As these two shadows form similar triangles, the unknown height can be computed by solving the proportion:

$$\frac{\text{pole height (?)}}{\text{pole shadow length (known)}} = \frac{\text{meter stick height (1 m)}}{\text{meter shadow length (known)}}$$

For example, suppose the meter stick cast a shadow of 3 meters and the pole cast a shadow of 24 meters. The pole height P can be calculated from the proportion:

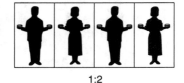

1:2

2:4   2:4

FIGURE 11.17
Ratio of Persons to Hamburgers

P:24::1:3

Since the meter stick and its shadow form a unit ratio, children can generally solve this proportion by inspection. For the two ratios to be equivalent, *P* must be one-third of 24, or 8 meters.

To solve more complex proportions, write the ratios as fractions and substitute an equal sign for the proportion symbol. Like a pan balance, we can add (or subtract) the same value to both sides of an equation or multiply (or divide) both sides by the same value without upsetting the balance. To solve this proportion, multiply both sides of the equation by the denominator (24) of the missing term *P* and simplify the equation to arrive at the solution: *P* = 8. Therefore, the flagpole is 8 meters high.

$$\frac{P}{24} = \frac{1}{3} \qquad \textit{Initial proportion}$$

$$24 \times \frac{P}{24} = 1 \times \frac{24}{3} \qquad \textit{Multiply both sides of equation by 24}$$

$$P = 8 \qquad \textit{Simplify}$$

When the missing term in a proportion is in the denominator, it is generally more convenient to invert both ratios before solving the equation $\left(\text{e.g.,} \frac{1}{n} = \frac{5}{8} \rightarrow \frac{n}{1} = \frac{8}{5}\right)$. Try to justify that the proportion of two ratios is equivalent to the proportion for the reciprocal ratios. Many children in grades 5–6 are able to solve simple proportions. Some will not be ready to work with equations, however, but can benefit from experiences with concrete or graphic representations.

E. USING PERCENTS

An important application of ratio and proportion is the concept of percent, or *rate*. The term *percent* (%) literally means *for each hundred*. For example, if 10 percent of the students in a school were absent with the flu, 10 out of each 100 students, on an average, were sick. If there are 400 students in the school, the number of sick students is a ratio of 10:100, or 40 students. The total number of objects considered (student population) is called the *base,* and the result (sick students) is called the *percentage.*

To introduce percents, give each child one base-10 flat and a supply of unit cubes (10 × 10 squares and single squares made from centimeter-squared paper can be substituted). Ask the class to put 10 unit-cubes on the flat and write a fraction that describes how much of the flat is covered by the cubes $\left(\text{e.g.,} \frac{10}{100}\right)$. Repeat the process with 6, 18, 25, 40, 70, and 85 cubes. Finally, have the students cover the flat with cubes and record the fractional part covered $\left(\frac{10}{100}\right)$. Have each child write each fraction as a decimal $\left(\frac{10}{100} = 0.10\right)$. Next, explain that we often write these special *hundredths* fractions another way and call them *percents*. Percent means per hundred, so we write $\frac{10}{100}$, or 0.10, as 10 percent, or 10%. Have the class write each decimal they recorded in the previous exercise as a percent. Have them make up other problems using the flat and cubes and record the results as a fraction, decimal, and percent (Figure 11.18).

Other fractions also can be written as percents if they can be renamed as hundredths. For example, $\frac{1}{2}$ can be renamed as $\frac{50}{100} = 50\%$. Have children use flats and cubes to find the percent equivalents of common fractions such as $\frac{1}{4}, \frac{3}{4}, \frac{2}{5}$, and $\frac{3}{10}$ (i.e., $\frac{1}{4} = \frac{25}{100} = 0.25 = 25\%$).

Fractions such as 1/3 cannot be exactly renamed as hundredths. However, using the division meaning of fractions, children can rewrite it as a decimal approximation and, therefore, a percent (i.e., $\frac{1}{3} \approx 0.33 = 33\%$). Students can use calculators to help them write fractions as approximate percent equivalents. Note that some fractions like $\frac{1}{8}$ can be written as exact percents if we allow for fractional parts of a percent (i.e., $\frac{1}{8} = 0.125 = 12.5\%$).

Finding the Percentage

Twenty-five percent is equivalent to $\frac{25}{100}$, or 0.25. To calculate $\frac{1}{2}$ of 6, we multiply $\frac{1}{2} \times 6$. Similarly, to find 25% of 60, multiply 0.25 × 60.

$$25\% \text{ of } 60 = 0.25 \times 60 = 15$$
$$50\% \text{ of } 150 = 0.50 \times 150 = 75$$
$$90\% \text{ of } 35 = 0.90 \times 35 = 31.5$$
$$100\% \text{ of } 85 = 1.00 \times 85 = 85$$

11.6

✎ **FIGURE IT OUT**

Solve the following proportions for *n*. Make up a word or picture problem to go with each example.

1. 4/20::n/80
2. 15/3::n/12
3. n/10::7/35
4. 12/7::36/n
5. 2/10::n/25

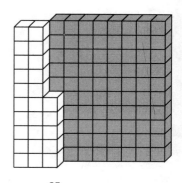

$$\frac{25}{100} = 0.25 = 25\%$$

FIGURE 11.18
Finding Percents

Stores often have sales that advertise discounts in terms of percents. The sale price is the original price minus a discount. If items are reduced 30%, the sale price is computed by multiplying the regular price by 0.30 and subtracting the resulting percentage from the original price. Have children cut out ads from the newspaper and make their own sale by marking everything down by 30%. Have them calculate the sale price for each item and record their results as shown in Table 11.4.

Sales tax can then be computed. Have children calculate a sales tax of 6% on each item and add it to the sale price (Table 11.5).

Finding the Rate

A bank loans money and charges the borrower a fee for its use. A $100 loan might require a repayment of $110 at the end of one year. The extra $10, called *interest,* is generally expressed as a percent of the amount borrowed. In this case, the percent, or *rate,* of interest is $10 per $100 per year, or 10 percent per year. Students can compute the interest rate by using a calculator to divide the yearly fee (percentage) by the total amount borrowed (base). The resulting decimal is renamed as a percent by dividing the percent by 100 $\left(0.25 = \frac{25}{100} = 25\%\right)$. Remind students that dividing a number by 100 has the effect of moving the decimal point in the dividend two places to the right (Table 11.6).

Students also can calculate the percent of return, or *profit margin,* for an investment. Suppose a storekeeper purchased an item wholesale for $1.92 and thought she could sell the item for $2.15. Her profit is $0.23, or about 12%. Make up a list of items with the purchase and sale prices and have children use a calculator to compute the rate of return, or percent return, by dividing the profit by the original price. Have them record the results as shown in Table 11.7.

Finding the Base

Some applications ask that the *base* amount be computed given the percentage and rate. For example, suppose someone was willing to spend $15 in interest on the purchase of a bicycle. If the current rate of interest is 10%, how expensive a bicycle can be purchased if

TABLE 11.4
Finding Percentage

ITEM	DISCOUNT	PERCENTAGE	SALE PRICE
$11.95	30%	$3.59	$ 8.36
$ 8.50	30%	$2.55	$ 5.95
$22.75	30%	$6.83	$15.92

TABLE 11.5
Calculating Sales Tax

SALE PRICE	SALES TAX	PERCENTAGE	TOTAL COST
$ 8.36	6%	$0.50	$ 8.86
$ 5.95	6%	$0.36	$ 6.31
$15.92	6%	$0.96	$16.88

TABLE 11.6
Calculating Interest

INTEREST FEE (PERCENTAGE)		AMOUNT BORROWED (BASE)		INTEREST RATE (RATE)
$42	÷	$500	=	0.084 = 8.4%
$12	÷	$ 95	=	0.126 = 12.6%
$25	÷	$295	=	0.085 = 8.5%

it is financed for one year? Since the percentage and rate are known, the base amount can be found by dividing the percentage by the rate:

$$\text{rate} \times \text{base} = \text{percentage}$$

$$\text{base} = \frac{\text{percentage}}{\text{rate}}$$

$$0.10 \times b = 15$$

$$b = 15 \div 0.10 = \$150.00$$

Students can use a calculator to compute the amount that could be borrowed for various interest rates and record the results as shown in Table 11.8. Discuss why the amount that can be borrowed increases as the interest rate decreases (i.e., as the divisors get smaller, the quotients get larger). How much money can be borrowed if the interest rate drops to 0% (i.e., as the rate gets closer to zero, the amount borrowed increases dramatically; at 0%, the amount is undefined since we cannot divide by zero)?

Proportion Method for Working Percents

A proportional algorithm can be used to solve all three types of percent problems. The three values, percentage (p), rate (r), and base (b), can be expressed as a proportion. A rate expressed as a percent must be divided by 100 to transform it to its decimal equivalent.

$$\frac{r}{100} = \frac{p}{b}$$

Given any two of the values r, p, or b, the third can be calculated by solving the proportion equation for the missing value. The following three examples show how to solve for each unknown.

1. *Type 1:* Find the percentage p given $b = 160$ and $r = 25\%$.

$$\frac{25}{100} = \frac{p}{160}$$

$$\frac{160 \times 25}{100} = p$$

$$40 = p$$

TABLE 11.7
Calculating Profit Margin

PROFIT (PERCENTAGE)		ORIGINAL PRICE (BASE)		PROFIT MARGIN (RATE)
$0.23	÷	$1.92	=	0.119 ≈ 12%
$0.40	÷	$2.34	=	0.171 ≈ 17%

TABLE 11.8
Computing the Base

PERCENTAGE (INTEREST)	RATE (PERCENT)	BASE (PRICE)
15	0.13	$115.39
15	0.10	$150.00
15	0.08	$187.50
15	0.06	$250.00
15	0.01	$1,500.00
15	0.00	—

11.7
✎ **FIGURE IT OUT**

Solve the following percent problems using the proportion method.

1. How much sales tax (6%) should be charged for the purchase of a $4,500 automobile?
2. What is the rate of return on a $1,000 investment that pays a return of $1,135 at the end of one year?
3. How much money could be borrowed for one year at a 10% interest rate by making a single interest payment of $25 at the end of the year?

TABLE 11.9
Decimal Place Values Written in Scientific Notation

100,000	10,000	1,000	100	10	1	.	0.1	0.01	0.001	0.0001	0.00001
1.0×10^5	1.0×10^4	1.0×10^3	1.0×10^2	1.0×10^1	1.0×10^0		1.0×10^{-1}	1.0×10^{-2}	1.0×10^{-3}	1.0×10^{-4}	1.0×10^{-5}
			2	0	0		$= 2 \times 10^2$				

TABLE 11.10
Representing Large Values

DECIMAL NOTATION	SCIENTIFIC NOTATION
a. 330 m/sec	$= 3.3 \times 10^2$ m/sec (approximate speed of sound)
b. 928,000,000 km	$= 9.28 \times 10^8$ km (length of earth orbit)
c. 299,800,000 m/sec	$= 2.998 \times 10^8$ m/sec (approximate speed of light)
d. 1,440,000,000,000,000,000	$= 1.44 \times 10^{18}$ metric tons (amount of water in oceans)

2. *Type 2:* Find the rate r given $b = 160$ and $p = 40$.

$$\frac{r}{100} = \frac{40}{160}$$
$$r = \frac{40 \times 100}{160}$$
$$r = 0.25 = 25\%$$

3. *Type 3:* Find the base b given $p = 40$ and $r = 25\%$.

$$\frac{25}{100} = \frac{40}{b}$$
$$\frac{100}{25} = \frac{b}{40}$$
$$\frac{40 \times 100}{25} = b$$
$$160 = b$$

F. SCIENTIFIC NOTATION

People often use very small and very large numbers without truly understanding the magnitude of the values involved. Have students try to imagine 1 millionth of a second (how far would light travel in this period?), or 1 billion dollars (how long would it take to count it?). Engineers and bankers work with these numbers every day, yet it is difficult indeed to visualize the magnitude of these measures.

Scientific notation is a way of representing very small and very large numbers by writing decimals as a product of two values. The first factor is a decimal value 1 through 9 and the second factor is a power of 10. For example, the number 200 is written 2×10^2 using scientific notation. The decimal place values are written in scientific notation as shown in Table 11.9.

Table 11.10 gives several examples of special decimal numbers written in scientific notation.

Numbers written in scientific notation that have the same power of 10 are said to be of the same *order of magnitude*. This is another way of saying they are about the same size relative to other very big numbers. For example, give children in grades 4–6 a list of the planets and their distances from the sun. Have them write each distance in scientific notation and classify the planets according to the magnitude of their orbits. Table 11.11 shows that the orbits of the nine planets can be classified into three orders of magnitude. Ask the students what information order of magnitude provides (i.e., any values of the same order of magnitude different by no more than a multiple of 10).

TABLE 11.11
Distance of Planets from Sun

PLANETS	ORDER OF MAGNITUDE
Mercury, Venus, Earth	7
Mars, Jupiter, Saturn	8
Uranus, Neptune, Pluto	9

TABLE 11.12
Representing Small Numbers

DECIMAL NOTATION	SCIENTIFIC NOTATION
0.0001 meter	$= 1.0 \times 10^{-4}$ meter (diameter of a hair)
0.000 000 000 000 000 000 000 001 67 gm	$= 1.67 \times 10^{-24}$ gm (mass of a hydrogen atom)
0.000 000 000 000 000 000 000 000 000 091 gm	$= 9.1 \times 10^{-28}$ gm (mass of one electron)

The results in Table 11.11 do not mean that Mercury, Venus, and Earth are in exactly the same orbit. In fact, the distance from the sun to Mercury is 3.6×10^7 miles; to Venus is 6.7×10^7; and to Earth is 9.3×10^7. Saying that the distances of these planets from the sun are of the same order of magnitude indicates that their orbits are similar when compared with the other planets.

As shown in the place-value table, decimal fractions also can be written using scientific notation. To show fractions, powers of 10 are written using negative powers. This notation is simply another way that mathematicians write fractions. For example:

$$10^{-1} = \frac{1}{10^1} = 0.1$$

$$10^{-2} = \frac{1}{10^2} = \frac{1}{100} = 0.01$$

$$10^{-3} = \frac{1}{10^3} = \frac{1}{1,000} = 0.001$$

Table 11.12 shows several very small numbers written in scientific notation.

G. INTEGER OPERATIONS
Graphing Integers on the Number Line

Negative whole numbers can be introduced as a way to record temperatures below zero. The set of whole numbers and their negative counterparts constitute the set of *integers*. Negative values used as *ordinal* labels on a scale such as temperature can be introduced in grade 4 or earlier. *Cardinal* applications involving integer operations such as balancing a checking account are generally introduced as a prealgebra topic in grade 6 or later. Scientific notation also requires a knowledge of integer operations.

Introduce the comparison of positive and negative values using a number line. As with whole numbers, for any two integers on the number line, the value farthest to the *left* is smaller. As a way to introduce the idea that $^-10 < {}^+5$, have students plot the values on a number line as shown in Figure 11.19 and select the value farther to the left. Real-world applications of positive and negative values can be used to practice work with integers. For example, receiving a check for $5.00 (positive integer) is more pleasant for the recipient than a bill for $10.00 (negative integer).

Other real-world uses of integers include measuring distances above and below sea level. For example, the lowest dry-land point on earth, the Dead Sea between Israel and Jordan, has an elevation of $^-1,312$ feet, and the highest point, Mt. Everest between China and Nepal,

FIGURE 11.19
Checks and Bills on the
Number Line

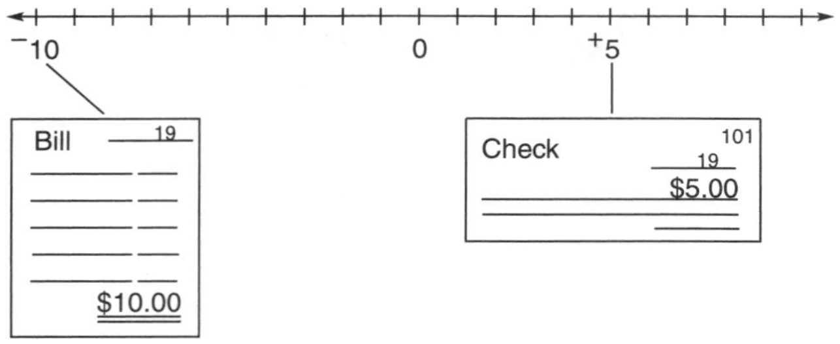

FIGURE 11.20
Cartesian Coordinate Plane

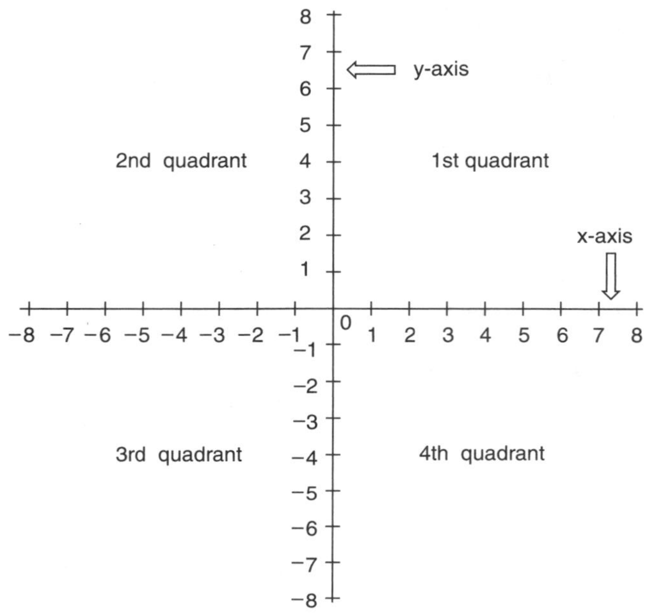

has an elevation of $^+$29,028 feet. This is a distance of nearly 6 miles. If we include the deepest point in the ocean, the Mariana Trench near Guam with an elevation of $^-$35,640 feet, the difference between highest and lowest point on earth is more than 12 miles.

Businesses use positive and negative values to indicate profit and loss. These figures are sometimes listed as percent of change from the previous quarter or year (i.e., change in profit for the second quarter was $^-$6%). The government keeps track of tax receipts and spending using integers as well.

Coordinate Geometry

Euclidean geometry does not allow the use of measurement as a tool in studying relationships among points, lines, and planes. Coordinate geometry, on the other hand, uses measurement to explore many of the same geometric concepts. This geometry depends on two fundamental ideas developed more than 300 years ago by the French mathematicians Descartes and Fermat. The first idea combined the concepts associated with the geometric plane with those of the number line into what is called the *Cartesian coordinate plane.* The second development was the invention of a symbolic notation called *coordinate pairs,* which made it convenient to identify individual points in the coordinate plane. Figure 11.20 shows the coordinate plane consisting of two perpendicular number lines drawn on a flat surface intersecting at zero. The number lines are divided into equal units labeled with integer values. The horizontal number line is called the *x-axis* and the vertical number line is the *y-axis.* Fractional values between the integer points also can be used. Often, it is convenient to work with only the positive values in the upper-right quarter of the plane, the *first quadrant.*

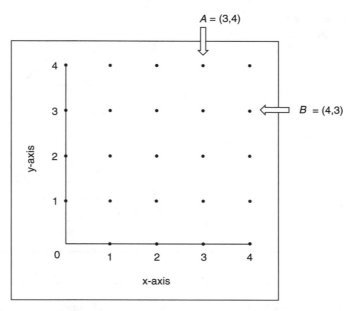

FIGURE 11.21
Graphing Ordered Pairs

As shown in Figure 11.21, a geoboard can be used as a model of a coordinate plane. Specific points on the coordinate plane can be named by first counting the number of spaces along the x-axis, followed by the number of spaces in the direction of the y-axis. For example, the position of point A in Figure 11.21 would be specified by counting three horizontal units along the x-axis followed by four vertical units in the direction parallel to the y-axis. The symbol for point A is the coordinate pair (3,4). Notice that the order of these two values is important because each position identifies both a direction (axis) and a distance. Reversing the coordinates to (4,3) names a different point on the coordinate plane. Graphing points in the other three quadrants involves the use of negative numbers (integers).

We can plot, or graph, a set of coordinate pairs by reversing the process. The first coordinate value x indicates the distance along the x-axis, and the second value y indicates the distance in the direction parallel to the y-axis.

Young children can be introduced to coordinate graphing by demonstrating its use on a transparent geoboard or a large-grid transparency on an overhead projector. Give each student a geoboard and a quantity of very small rubber bands (those that just fit over a finger). It may be helpful for some children to use chalk to draw an x-axis and y-axis along the bottom row and left column, respectively, of pegs on each geoboard. Select an ordered pair in the first quadrant [e.g., (2,3)] and ask a child to come forward to help you find its place on the geoboard. Have the child count the appropriate number of spaces along the x-axis and place a finger on the correct peg. Then have the child count the correct number of spaces in the direction of the y-axis and put a small rubber band over the peg representing the ordered pair. Have the rest of the children follow along on their own geoboards.

Once children know how to graph ordered pairs, they can get additional practice by creating pictures from previously prepared lists of coordinates. Figure 11.22 shows the picture created by graphing a list of coordinate pairs. This list was compiled by first drawing a simple picture on the coordinate plane and then identifying coordinate pairs for points that roughly corresponded to the outline of the sketch. Children also can create lists of coordinate pairs in this way and give them to their classmates to complete.

Older children can use the coordinate plane to graph many types of relations. For example, children can graph the division (and multiplication) table. Graph the dividend along the x-axis and the divisor along the y-axis. As shown in Figure 11.23, each resulting line on the graph represents one set of multiplication facts (in this case, quotients 2 and 5).

The Cartesian coordinate plane allows students to graph each point in the coordinate plane using ordered pairs. The first value in the ordered pair represents the distance in the direction of the horizontal axis and the second indicates the distance in the direction paral-

FIGURE 11.22
Coordinate Graph Art

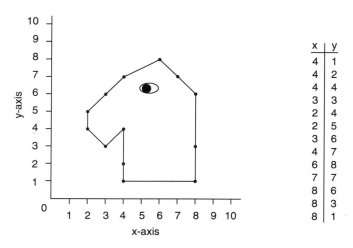

x	y
4	1
4	2
4	4
3	3
2	4
2	5
3	6
4	7
6	8
7	7
8	6
8	3
8	1

11.8

✎ **FIGURE IT OUT**

Complete the graph of the division table shown in Figure 11.23. Construct a line for division facts with quotients 1–9. How could this graph be used as a multiplication learning aid?

FIGURE 11.23
Graph of Division Table

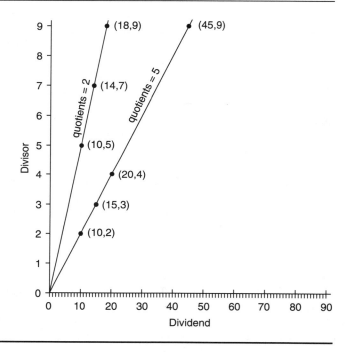

lel to the vertical axis. Point $(^+2,^+3)$ is located by moving two units to the right and then up three units. Similarly, students can use integer values to show points to the left and below the origin (0,0). For example, $(^-2,^-4)$ is graphed by moving two units to the left then four units down. To introduce graphing with integer coordinates, develop sets of ordered pairs that create a simple picture when connected (see Figure 11.24).

Integer Chips

An effective way to introduce integer operations is with red and green integer chips. Red chips represent negative integers and green chips represent positive integers. To add $^+5 +$ $^-3$, select three red chips and five green chips and put them in two rows as shown in Figure 11.25. Then place one red chip on top of a green chip until all the red chips have a pair, and remove the matched chips. The remaining chips are the answer, $^+5 + ^-3 = ^+2$.

Students can also use integer chips to show subtraction. For example, for the exercise $^+5 - ^-2$, select five green chips. To subtract two red chips, place two pairs of red and green

FIGURE 11.24
Cartesian Coordinate Plane

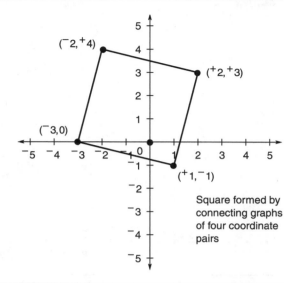

Square formed by connecting graphs of four coordinate pairs

$^+5 + {}^-3 = {}^+2$

FIGURE 11.25
Integer-Chip Addition

$^+5 - {}^-2 = {}^+7$

FIGURE 11.26
Integer-Chip Subtraction

FIGURE 11.27
Adding Integers

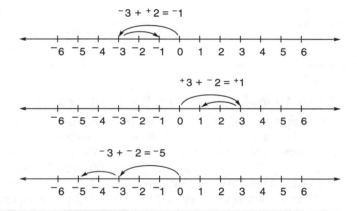

chips next to the five green chips. Since a red and green pair is zero, the total is still $^+5$. Now remove two red chips to represent subtracting $^-2$, leaving seven green chips as shown in Figure 11.26. Therefore, $^+5 - {}^-2 = {}^+7$.

Integer Addition Using the Number Line

The number line can be used for integer addition as well. When *adding,* a negative sign attached to a value indicates a move to the left and a positive sign indicates a move to the right. To compute $^-3 + {}^+2$, begin at 0 on the number line, move $^-3$ units to the left and then $^+2$ units to the right, giving the sum $^-1$. To solve $^+3 + {}^-2$ on the number line, begin at 0, move $^+3$ units to the right, then $^-2$ units to the left, ending at the point $^+1$. Similarly, for $^-3 + {}^-2$, begin at 0, move $^-3$ units to the left followed by $^-2$ more units to the left, giving the sum $^-5$ units to the left of 0 (see Figure 11.27).

Integer Subtraction Using the Number Line

Since subtraction can be written as a missing-addend exercise, it is convenient to rewrite all integer subtraction problems in this form before solving them on the number line. For example, to solve the integer subtraction problem $^+5 - {}^+2 = ?$, first rewrite the exercise as $^+2 + ? = {}^+5$. Then begin at 0, move $^+2$ units to the right, and count the number of units to the right needed to arrive at $^+5$ ($^+3$). Similarly, for $^+3 - {}^-7 = ?$, rewrite the exercise as $^-7 + ? = {}^+3$. Then begin at 0, move $^-7$ units to the left, and count the number of units to the right needed to arrive at $^+3$ ($^+10$) (see Figure 11.28).

11.9
✎ **FIGURE IT OUT**

Compute the following sums using a number line:

1. $^-4 + {}^-2 = ?$
2. $^+3 + {}^-4 = ?$
3. $^+5 + {}^+3 = ?$
4. $^-8 + {}^+9 = ?$
5. $^-5 + {}^+5 = ?$

11.10
✎ **FIGURE IT OUT**

Rewrite the following subtraction exercises as missing-addend examples and solve each using a number line.

1. $^+4 - {}^+6 = ?$
2. $^+5 - {}^-3 = ?$
3. $^-7 - {}^+5 = ?$
4. $^-6 - {}^-10 = ?$
5. $^-8 - {}^+12 = ?$

FIGURE 11.28
Subtracting Integers

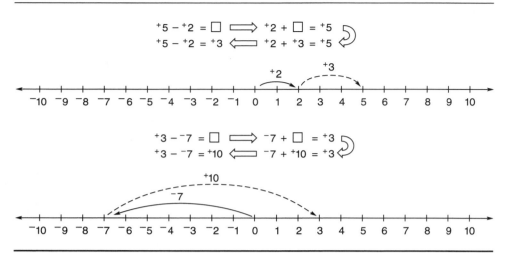

FIGURE 11.29
Multiplying Integers

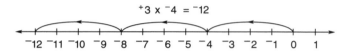

Integer Multiplication Using the Number Line

Some integer multiplication exercises can be shown on the number line by using repeated addition. For example, to show $^+3 \times {}^-4$, have children first write the exercise as an equivalent repeated addition example $^-4 + {}^-4 + {}^-4$ and show the sum $^-12$ on the number line as in Figure 11.29. Examples such as $^-5 \times {}^+4$ can be rewritten as $^+4 \times {}^-5$ using the commutative property. Then write the exercise as $^-5 + {}^-5 + {}^-5 + {}^-5$.

When both factors are negative like $^-3 \times {}^-4$, the solution cannot be directly displayed on the number line. The following algebraic example shows why a negative integer times a negative integer gives a positive product (any integer ^-n can be substituted for $^-3$).

$^-3 = {}^-3$	*Identity relation*
$^-3 \times ({}^+1 + {}^-1) = {}^-3 \times ({}^+1 + {}^-1)$	*Identity relation*
$({}^-3 \times {}^+1) + ({}^-3 \times {}^-1) = {}^-3 \times 0$	*Distributive property*
$^-3 + ({}^-3 \times {}^-1) = 0$	*Multiplication of a negative times a positive integer and multiplication by 0*
$({}^+3 + {}^-3) + ({}^-3 \times {}^-1) = {}^+3 + 0$	*Adding same value to both sides of an equation*
$({}^-3 \times {}^-1) = {}^+3$	*Therefore negative $\times$ negative = positive*

Integer Division Using the Number Line

When demonstrating integer division on the number line, show children that they can use the partitive meaning of division whenever the divisor is positive. For example, $^-15 \div {}^+3$ can be shown on the number line by first plotting the dividend $^-15$, then partitioning this length on the number line into three equal segments (the divisor). As shown in Figure 11.30, the quotient $^-5$ is the value of each equal segment.

FIGURE 11.30
Dividing Integers

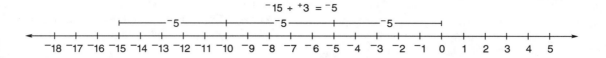

FIGURE 11.31
Integer Division Using Repeated Subtraction

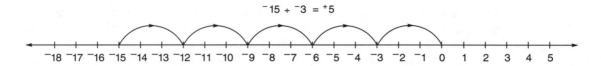

For exercises with negative dividends and divisors like $^-15 \div {}^-3$, the repeated subtraction meaning of division can be used. For example, Figure 11.31 shows how the value $^-3$ can be subtracted from $^-15$ five times. Therefore, $^-15 \div {}^-3 = {}^+5$.

Exercises that involve positive dividends and negative divisors like $^+12 \div {}^-4$ cannot be directly modeled on the number line since it is not possible to construct negative partitions, or to count the number of times $^-4$ can be subtracted from $^+12$. To solve this type of exercise, use the principle that division and multiplication are inverse operations. For example, $^+12 \div {}^-4 = ?$ is another way of writing $? \times {}^-4 = {}^+12$. Since $^-3 \times {}^-4 = {}^+12$, we know that $^+12 \div {}^-4 = {}^-3$.

Integer Operation Rules

Students may experience difficulty consistently carrying out integer operations, especially subtraction exercises involving negative minuends. After students have had initial integer-chip and number-line experiences with simple integer exercises, teachers can introduce students to rules for adding, subtracting, multiplying, and dividing integers. One useful simplification is to convert *all* subtraction exercises immediately into addition exercises by changing the *operation sign* and the *value sign* of the minuend. This rule reflects the fact that subtracting any value *n* from a number gives the same result as adding its inverse ^-n. For example:

$$^-4 - {}^+9 = {}^-4 + {}^-9 = {}^-13$$
$$^-4 - {}^-9 = {}^-4 + {}^+9 = {}^+5$$
$$^+4 - {}^+9 = {}^+4 + {}^-9 = {}^-5$$
$$^+4 - {}^-9 = {}^+4 + {}^+9 = {}^+13$$

A simple rule for integer multiplication and division is that when the value signs are *alike* (i.e., both negative or both positive), the answer is positive. When the value signs are different (i.e., one negative and the other positive), the answer is always negative.

H. CLASSROOM ACTIVITIES
Decimal Chip Trading

Decimal operations can be performed using place-value mats and colored chip-trading counters. The procedure is similar to whole-number operations. The counters, or *chips,* are used like money and are assigned an exchange rate of 10 to 1 for each of four colors (in order from left to right—red, green, blue, and yellow). Initially, let the green chips represent the one unit, or $1.00, then red = $10.00, blue = $0.10, and yellow = $0.01 (see Figure 11.32).

11.11

✎ **FIGURE IT OUT**

Convert the following subtraction examples into equivalent addition exercises and use a number line to verify that both forms give the same answers.

1. $^+14 - {}^-9 = ?$
2. $^-5 - {}^+20 = ?$
3. $^+7 - {}^-10 = ?$
4. $^-12 - {}^+9 = ?$
5. $^+6 - {}^-15 = ?$

Solve the following integer exercises using a number line.

6. $^-25 + {}^-9 = ?$
7. $^+14 - {}^-10 = ?$
8. $^-4 \times {}^-5 = ?$
9. $^-7 \times {}^+4 = ?$
10. $^+18 \div {}^-9 = ?$

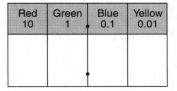

FIGURE 11.32
Chip-Trading Place-Value Mat

Children play the "banker's game" in groups of four. Each group needs a pair of dice, a blue die representing tenths, or dimes, and a yellow die representing hundredths, or cents (any two colors will work). Each child also needs a chip-trading mat and supply of chips. Players roll the dice in turn and add the appropriate number of yellow and blue chips to their mats, regrouping as necessary. The first player to get $10 wins the round. All players record their final amounts in place-value tables, remove their chips, and resume play. After five rounds, the player with the largest total wins.

Students can play the game in reverse by beginning with a $10.00 red chip on each mat. On each roll of the dice, the amount shown is removed from the mat by regrouping the $10 chip as necessary. When one player runs out of chips, the round ends. The player with the largest total at the end of five rounds wins the game, called the *Tax Game*.

Rounding Off to the Nearest 1, $\frac{1}{10}$, and $\frac{1}{100}$

Rounding off decimal fractions is a practical skill for work with money and measures. To give students practice rounding off, give them a list of meter measures with one digit circled or written in italics. Point out that when rounding off to the indicated place value, first look at the digit in the next smaller place value. If it is 5, 6, 7, 8, or 9, the italic digit is increased by one and the remaining digits to the right are dropped; if not, the italic digit stays the same and the remaining digits to the right are dropped. Note that if the digit 9 is rounded up to 10 as in example 2, the result must be regrouped into the next larger place value. A zero is left in the tenths column to indicate that the value was rounded to the nearest hundredth. Similar procedures are followed for rounding gram and liter measures.

11.12 ✎ FIGURE IT OUT

Round off $162.48 for each place value indicated below.

1. tenths (or dimes)
2. hundreds (or hundred dollars)
3. ones (or dollar)
4. tens (or ten dollars)
5. hundredths (or pennies)

Rounding Off

To the nearest cm (0.01):	1. 2.042 m = 2.04 m
	2. 35.799 m = 35.80 m
To the nearest dm (0.1):	3. 2.042 m = 2.0 m
	4. 35.799 m = 35.8 m
To the nearest m (1):	5. 2.0.42 m = 2 m
	6. 35.799 m = 36 m

Prices often are rounded to the nearest dollar to enable quick estimates of values and totals. In this case, rounding to the nearest *dollar* is the same as rounding a decimal fraction to the nearest 1 unit. Give students a copy of a cash register tape showing the cost of 10–15 items without the total. Have them mentally round each value to the nearest dollar and find the sum to see if a $20.00 bill would be enough money to buy the items. Similarly, students can use copies of actual menus and price lists to create an order or shopping list and round off to estimate the total bill.

Rounding Off to the Nearest Dollar
$12.95 ≈ $13.00
$5.39 ≈ $5.00
$124.50 ≈ $125.00

I. PROBLEM SOLVING INVOLVING DECIMALS, PROPORTIONS, AND INTEGERS
Foreign Travel

Most countries have their own type of money. When traveling, people from the United States exchange their dollars for the local currency. Suppose one U.S. dollar could be exchanged for $1.30 in Canadian dollars. Have children use a calculator to compute the amount of money in U.S. dollars that a family would have to take in order to pay for the travel expenses listed in Canadian dollars in Table 11.13 (i.e., 150 ÷ 1.30 = 115.39). Children should first predict if there are more or fewer U.S. dollars than Canadian dollars for each item.

Suppose the family decided to go to Mexico the following summer. One U.S. dollar can be exchanged for about 3,000 Mexican pesos. Have the class calculate the number of Mexican pesos the family would need if the family planned to spend the same amount of

TABLE 11.13
Travel Expenses

EXPENSE	COST IN CANADIAN $	COST IN U.S. $
Food	$150	$115.39
Gasoline	85	—
Motel rooms	225	—
Other	175	—
Total	$635	—

U.S. dollars for their expenses. Again, have children predict whether there will be more or fewer U.S. dollars than Mexican pesos.

As a follow-up activity, have each child select a country to visit from an exchange-rate table in the business section of the newspaper. Each should list the expenses his or her family will have during the visit and convert the amounts to the local currency using a calculator. Finally, have the children record the results in a table.

Using Proportions

Problems involving conversions between measures also can be solved using proportions. For example, suppose a family traveling in Canada bought gasoline that cost $1.50 in Canadian money per Imperial gallon (one Imperial gallon equals about 1.2 U.S. gallons). If gasoline at home costs $1.25 per U.S. gallon in U.S. money, was the gasoline more or less expensive in Canada?

One way to approach this problem is to develop an example. Let's assume that the family bought 10 Imperial gallons at a cost of $15 in Canadian money. How many U.S. gallons would they have bought? The ratio 1.2:1 describes the relationship between the Imperial and U.S. gallons. Solving the proportion 1.2:1 = □:10 gives the number of U.S. gallons equal to 10 Imperial gallons:

$$(10 \times 1.2) \div 1 = \square$$
$$10 \times 1.2 = \square$$
$$12 = \square$$

The ratio 1:1.3 describes the relationship between the U.S. and Canadian dollar. Solving the proportion 1:1.3 = □:15 gives the number of U.S. dollars equal to 15 Canadian dollars:

$$(1 \times 15) \div 1.3 = \square$$
$$15 \div 1.3 = \square$$
$$11.54 = \square$$

Ten Imperial gallons purchased for $15 in Canadian money is equivalent to 12 U.S. gallons purchased for $11.54 in U.S. money. Therefore, the price of Canadian gasoline per U.S. gallon in U.S. dollars is 11.54 ÷ 12 = $0.96 per gallon. Gasoline was less expensive in Canada since one U.S. gallon of gas costs $1.25 in U.S. money at home. Have students make up similar problems for Mexico, where gasoline is sold by the liter (1 liter ≈ 0.25 gallons and costs about 700 pesos).

Graphing Proportions

A family of equivalent ratios can be graphed on the coordinate plane. For example, suppose six arcade tokens to play electronic games cost 75 cents. This relationship can be written as the ratio 6:75. Twelve tokens would cost $1.50, giving the ratio 12:150. Table 11.14 lists the set of equivalent ratios for this example.

This table describes a proportional relationship that can be graphed on the coordinate plane. Each ratio is graphed as a coordinate pair (see Figure 11.33). The line connecting the points on the graph represents the cost of tokens if they could be purchased in quantities other than groups of six. The graph shows the functional relationship between the tokens (t) and the cost (c). The *finite difference* method can be used to verify that the equation is $12.5t = c$.

TABLE 11.14
Equivalent Ratio Table

TOKENS	COST (CENTS)
0	0
6	75
12	150
18	225
24	300
—	—
—	—
—	—

FIGURE 11.33
Cost of Game Tokens

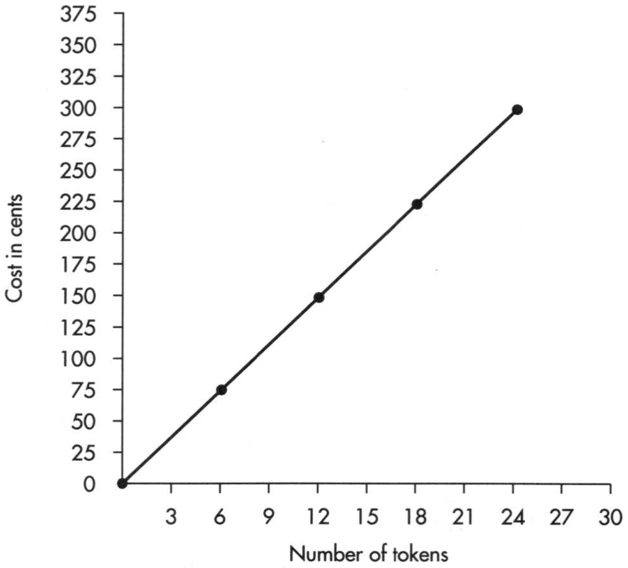

Checks and Bills

To practice adding and subtracting integers, children can use simulated checks and bills to represent positive and negative. Prepare sets of green and red file cards with various whole-dollar amounts ($1–$20). The green cards represent *checks* received for work done and the red cards are *bills* received for amounts owed. When you receive a check for $5, you record the transaction as adding a positive (i.e., + $^{+}$5); and when you give someone else a check, you record it as subtracting a positive (i.e., − $^{+}$5). When someone gives you a bill, you record it as adding a negative (i.e., + $^{-}$5), and when you give someone a bill, you record the transaction as subtracting a negative (i.e., − $^{-}$5). Children can use checks and bills to solve word problems such as those shown in Figures 11.34–11.36.

1. One day, Sharon earned $5 for mowing the lawn, and afterwards her sister sold her a book for $2. How much money did she have left at the end of the day?
2. Dana owed Danny $8 yesterday. Today he worked for his mother in the garden and made $5. How much money would Dana have if he paid Danny the $5 towards his debt?
3. Brandon had $3 and was paid back a loan for $10 he made to Jenny. How much money does Brandon have now?

Each of these problems can be solved using the checks and bills. Have students make up their own problem situations, and exchange and solve them. They also can invent multiplication and division problems involving integers that can be solved using checks and bills.

J. CALCULATOR AND COMPUTER APPLICATIONS
Exploring Repeating Decimals

Calculators can help students rename common fractions as decimals. Using the division meaning of fractions, fractions can be written in decimal form by dividing the denominator *into* the numerator. For example:

$$\tfrac{1}{2} = 1 \div 2 = 0.5$$

Remind students that $\tfrac{1}{2} = \tfrac{5}{10}$, which is just another way of writing 0.5. Verifying the decimal equivalent for other fractions is not as convenient. For example, $\tfrac{1}{3}$ can never be exactly renamed as a fraction with a power of 10 as a denominator since no number times

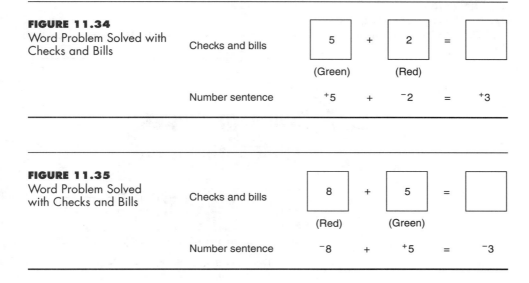

FIGURE 11.34
Word Problem Solved with Checks and Bills

Checks and bills

| 5 | + | 2 | = | |
| (Green) | | (Red) | | |

Number sentence $^+5$ + $^-2$ = $^+3$

FIGURE 11.35
Word Problem Solved with Checks and Bills

Checks and bills

| 8 | + | 5 | = | |
| (Red) | | (Green) | | |

Number sentence $^-8$ + $^+5$ = $^-3$

FIGURE 11.36
Word Problem Solved with Checks and Bills

Checks and bills

| 3 | – | 10 | = | 3 | + | 10 | = | |
| (Green) | | (Red) | | (Green) | | (Green) | | |

Number sentence $^+3$ – $^-10$ = $^+3$ + $^+10$ = $^+13$

three equals any power of 10 (i.e., the digital root of all powers of 10 is 1 and 1 is not evenly divisible by 3). However, a calculator gives a decimal approximation for such fractions $\left(\text{e.g., } \frac{1}{3} = 1 \div 3 = 0.33333333 \ldots\right)$.

Although the calculator is unable to continue dividing forever, three dots, called an *ellipsis,* are appended to the sequence of threes to indicate that the pattern continues indefinitely (the calculator does not show the ellipsis).

For most applications, decimal approximations are computed to the nearest hundredth or thousandth. Banks carry out their computations to five or more decimal places to maintain accurate interest calculations.

Decimal Estimation Games

Computer simulations can provide motivating practice for identifying and comparing decimal numbers. *Decimals: Practice* (Control Data Publishing Company), appropriate for students in grades 4–9, presents students with a dart game in which they try to pop balloons arranged at random along a number line by identifying the corresponding decimal locations. There are two sets of lessons, each containing multiple levels of difficulty. The first type uses integers as end points for the number line and the second has decimal end points. Students make an estimate of the decimal position on the number line and refine their choices on successive selections until they pop the balloon.

Decimal Squares Computer Games

This series of eight activities (Scott Resources, Inc.) offers children practice in recognizing and representing decimal values using base-10 displays. Children use their knowledge of decimal equality, inequality, place value, addition, and subtraction to win games like miniature golf, tug-of-war, and blackjack (see Figure 11.37). The programs offer several levels of difficulty to accommodate grades 4–6.

FIGURE 11.37
Decimal Squares Computer Game
SOURCE: *Decimal Squares* [Computer program] by Scott Resources, Inc., 1985. Copyright 1985 by Scott Resources, Inc. Reprinted by permission.

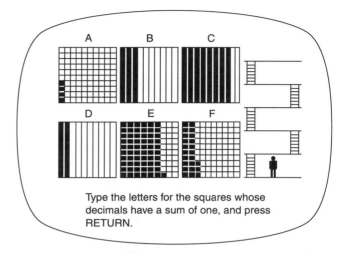

FIGURE 11.38
Coin Base-10 Materials

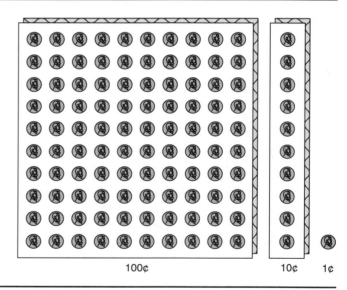

K. ADAPTING INSTRUCTION FOR CHILDREN WITH SPECIAL NEEDS
Using Money to Introduce Decimals

Learning to work with decimal numbers and operations is often difficult for special-needs students. Money can be an effective material for introducing decimal operations. After students have had extensive experience counting money and making change, teachers can introduce decimal operations using money as a model. Limiting decimal fractions to two decimal places (i.e., tenths—dimes; hundredths—pennies) simplifies the process of lining up the decimal point when adding and subtracting. Relating base-10 materials to pennies, dimes, and dollars helps children visualize the place-value relationship between the decimal fraction and whole-number component of numbers. Figure 11.38 shows a set of printed base-10 materials that uses coins to graphically show the place-value relationship. One set of these materials can be constructed from play money coins, photocopied, and glued to cardboard squares. They can then be used like base-10 materials by special-needs children when solving decimal addition and subtraction and percent exercises.

Exploring Decimal Patterns

Gifted and talented students can extend their understanding of decimal notation by exploring the patterns of digits in common fractions renamed as decimals. Some fractions, like $\frac{1}{2}$, repeat zeros after one or more nonzero digits. These are called *terminating decimals*. The fraction $\frac{1}{9}$ written as a decimal equals 0.1111 . . . repeats every digit. Some fractions repeat pairs of digits $\left(\frac{5}{11} = 0.454545 \ldots\right)$, some repeat in cycles of three digits $\left(\frac{1}{27} = 0.037037 \ldots\right)$, or longer cycles $\left(\frac{1}{13} = 0.076923076923 \ldots\right)$. Students can use calculators to rename fractions as decimals and classify them according to the number of digits in their repeating cycles. Some calculators round to the last digit and show $\frac{1}{6} = 0.166666667$. Tell children to ignore the last digit when using such calculators or to cover it with tape.

Rational Numbers Generate Repeating Decimals

$\frac{2}{3} = 2 \div 3 = 0.6666$ *Repeats every digit*

$\frac{1}{7} = 1 \div 7 = 0.142857142857$ *Repeats every sixth digit*

$\frac{1}{2} = 1 \div 2 = 0.5000$ *Repeats every digit after first*

To help children understand why fractions always generate repeating decimals, have them carry out the long-division exercise for $\frac{1}{7}$. Since we are dividing by 7, the only possible remainders are the values 0–6. Notice that once a remainder repeats, the cycle starts over again at that point in the division process. If the remainder is zero, the decimal terminates.

Have children find the prime factors of the denominator for all the fractions that generate *terminating* decimals (i.e., repeat zeros). If the fractions are renamed in lowest terms $\left(\text{i.e., } \frac{1}{2} \text{ not } \frac{3}{6}\right)$, students should discover that these denominators all have sets of prime factors that contain only 2s and 5s. Reduced fractions that contain other prime factors generate nonterminating repeating decimals (i.e., the set of prime factors must contain at least one prime factor that is not a 2 or 5). Why is this true? (Hint: what characteristics must a divisor have to get the remainder zero when dividing into any multiple of 10?)

Many numbers cannot be written as a fraction or a repeating decimal and, therefore, are not rational numbers. These values are called *irrational* numbers. Numbers that cannot be written as fractions include π, $\sqrt{2}$, and 0.10110111011110 . . . . No repeating pattern of digits can be found for these values regardless of the number of decimal places calculated. Although they are not frequently encountered in elementary mathematics, such irrational numbers are important for the study of algebra and geometry. Together, the set of rational (repeating decimals) and irrational (nonrepeating decimals) numbers constitute the set of *real numbers*.

L. ASSESSMENT STRATEGY

Student-constructed tests offer an excellent opportunity for students to reflect on what they have learned before taking a test. To use this technique, divide students into small groups and have them write test items that assess the concepts, procedures, and problems in the current unit of study. The teacher then selects items from each group (they may need to be edited somewhat) and includes additional items if critical topics are overlooked by the students.

This procedure motivates students to think about what they have learned. The test may also be less intimidating since the students were involved in writing it. When going over the results of the test, it is a good idea to ask students who wrote an item to explain its solution (Clarke et al., 1990).

M. PROPORTION SAMPLE LESSON PLAN

Presented here is an example of a lesson plan that introduces proportional reasoning and indirect measurement to students in grade 6.

11.13
✎ FIGURE IT OUT

Use a calculator to compute the decimal equivalent of each of the following fractions. Carry out the division to sufficient decimal places to verify a repeating pattern.

1. $\frac{1}{3}$
2. $\frac{1}{5}$
3. $\frac{1}{4}$
4. $\frac{2}{7}$
5. $\frac{1}{13}$

11.14
✎ FIGURE IT OUT

Write five rational and five irrational numbers. Make a sketch of a "real-number bulletin board" showing examples and key features of rational and irrational numbers.

Proportion Lesson Plan

Grade Level: Grade 6   *Time Allotment:* 45 minutes

NCTM Standard: Use computation, estimation, and proportions to solve problems.

Essential Understanding: Proportions are useful for solving many real-world problems.

Goal: Learners will understand that when two ratios are equivalent, they form a proportion.

Objective: Learners will use indirect measurement and the proportional relationship of similar triangles to find the height of a flagpole.

Motivation: Tell the class that the principal asked if your class could find out the amount of rope needed to replace the halyard that disappeared from the flagpole. She said that since the pole is not strong enough for someone to climb up, you will need to use your most powerful mathematics tools to accomplish her request.

Procedure: Take the class outside and have them form a circle around the teacher. Using two yardsticks, hold one vertical to the ground and have a student measure the length of its shadow. Next move to the corner of the building and measure the length of its shadow. Return to the classroom with the data. Show the two ratios of height: shadow length for the yardstick and building *(b)*. Early in the morning the ratios might be about 36:54 and *b*:144. Introduce the notion that the ratio between the yardstick and its shadow is the same as for any object and its shadow. Therefore, you say the two ratios are proportional. Show how to solve the proportion $\frac{36}{54} = \frac{b}{144}$ (answer $b = \frac{36 \times 144}{54} = 96$) and write the height of the building on the board. Give each student a yardstick and go outside again. Have pairs of students measure the length of a yardstick's shadow and the shadow of some other object (e.g., fence pole, backstop, classmate, and don't forget the flagpole). Return to the classroom with the data and have each pair use a calculator to solve the proportion for their object's height. Have each pair include their result in a list of object heights on the board. Circulate to assist with the solution of the proportions as necessary.

Closure: Review the list of heights on the board. If two teams measured the same object (e.g., fence post), compare the measures. Discuss why the answers might be slightly different (e.g., measurement error, perhaps the yardstick was not held exactly vertical) and how to improve the measure (e.g., take a protractor to improve the accuracy of the vertical angle). Discuss how much rope would be needed for the flagpole (twice the height).

Assessment: Circulate around the room and observe students working out proportions. Keep a record of students who have difficulty with the algebra.

Materials: Yardsticks, calculators, and a sunny day

Extension: At one time each day, the length of the shadow of a yardstick is exactly one yard long (mid-morning or mid-afternoon, when the sun is at a 45° angle above the horizon). If you knew the correct time, you could just run out and measure the shadow of the flag pole and would not have to calculate a proportion (the ratio is 1:1). Have the students take turns going outside every five minutes to find the time when the height and shadow are the same length. Measure the flagpole length and compare it to previous indirect measures.

SUMMARY

- Decimal fractions are another way to write common fractions having only powers of 10 for denominators.
- Each component of a decimal fraction is displayed in its own place value, separated from the whole-number place values by the decimal point.
- Operations with decimals never require finding common denominators, since all decimal denominators are powers of 10 that can be easily aligned.

- Concrete materials used to develop whole-number operations and algorithms can be adapted to introduce decimal operations.
- The equivalence of two ratios is called a proportion. An important application of proportional thinking is work with percents.
- Proportional thinking is an important problem-solving skill, particularly for geometry, measurement, science, and work with scales. Children in grades 4–9 can approach proportional situations using graphic and concrete representations, and many can be introduced to solving simple proportion equations.
- Scientific notation can be used to record and compare very large and small values.
- Addition and subtraction of integers is needed to use the features of scientific notation.
- Special-needs children may require additional work with concrete materials to extend whole-number operations to work with decimals. Decimals, percents, and proportions offer excellent extension opportunities for gifted and talented children.

QUESTIONS AND ACTIVITIES FOR DISCUSSION

1. Using base-10 or chip-trading materials, practice representing, adding, and subtracting decimal fractions involving tenths and hundredths. Give a presentation to your peers and, if possible, write a lesson plan and introduce decimal addition to a group of students in grades 4–9 in a classroom setting. Keep track of points students have difficulty understanding, and discuss possible teaching solutions with your peers.

2. Most calculators are unable to display more than 8–10 digits. Work out a way to use the calculator to carry out the divisions to more decimal places than can be displayed. Use this trick to help you find fractions that repeat in groups of 5, 6, or more digits. Make a list of fractions that repeat in groups of 1, 2, 3, 4, 5, 6, and 7 digits.

3. Using a calculator, find a fraction that can be renamed as a decimal with a single-digit repeating pattern; with a pattern consisting of 2 digits, 3 digits, and 4 digits. Rename the six fractions ($\frac{1}{7}$, $\frac{2}{7}$, $\frac{3}{7}$, $\frac{4}{7}$, $\frac{5}{7}$, and $\frac{6}{7}$) as decimals carried out to 12 decimal places. Look for patterns in the decimal representations. As an extension activity, do the same with other series of fractions (e.g., $\frac{1}{13}$, $\frac{2}{13}$, . . .) and look for repeating patterns. Discuss how this activity could be incorporated into a lesson on decimals in grades 4–9. Write a lesson plan that uses this activity.

4. Design a bulletin board idea to display the proportional relationship involved in percent. Try to arrange the display such that the viewer must engage in some activity. List ways bulletin boards can be integrated into learning experiences rather than being used primarily as decoration.

5. Include examples of decimal, percent, ratio, and proportion lessons in your idea file. Organize them according to appropriate grade levels.

6. Read the *Arithmetic Teacher* article by L. Chang listed in the "Suggested Readings" section. Write a brief report summarizing the main ideas of the article and describe the advantages of each instructional model for teaching integer operations.

INSTRUCTIONAL RESOURCES

CHILDREN'S BOOK

Burns, M. *The $1.00 word riddle book.* Cuisenaire Company of America. Children solve riddles and puzzles with answers that always add up to $1.00.

COMPUTER SOFTWARE

Base Ten on Basic Arithmetic. Minnesota Educational Computer Consortium. Practice working with multiples of 10 and decimal numbers.

Decimals: Practice. Control Data Publishing. Practice identifying decimals on a number line in order to pop balloons in a simulated dart game.

Decimal Skills & Mixed Number Skills. Milton Bradley. Tutorial on decimal and fraction operations.

Decimal Squares Computer Games. Scott Resources. Eight computer games that provide practice with decimal place value and operations with decimals using base-10 representations of decimal fractions.

Get to the Point. Sunburst Communications, Inc. Students practice ordering, estimating, and computing decimal numbers.

Integers. JHM Software. A set of five programs that provide tutorials and practice in integer operations using a number-line model.

Shark Estimation Games. InterLearn. Practice estimating the position of a shark fin on the coordinate plane using integer and decimal values.

REFERENCES

Bell, A., Swan, M., & Taylor, G. (1981). Choice of operation in verbal problems with decimal numbers. *Educational Studies in Mathematics, 12,* 399–420.

Carpenter, T., Corbitt, M., Kepner, H., Lindquist, M., & Reys, R. (1981). Decimals: Results and implications from national assessment. *Arithmetic Teacher, 28*(8), 34–37.

Clarke, D. J., Clarke, D. M., & Lovitt, C. (1990). Changes in mathematics teaching call for assessment alternatives. In T. Cooney & C. Hirsch (Eds.), *Teaching and learning mathematics in the 1990s: 1990 yearbook* (pp. 118–129). Reston, VA: National Council of Teachers of Mathematics.

Grossman, A. (1983). Decimal notation: An important research finding. *Arithmetic Teacher, 30*(9), 32–33.

Hiebert, J. (1987). Decimal fractions. *Arithmetic Teacher, 34*(7), 22–23.

Hiebert, J., & Wearne, D. (1986). Procedures over concepts: The acquisition of decimal number knowledge. In J. Hiebert (Ed.), *Conceptual and procedural knowledge: A case for mathematics* (pp. 199–223). Hillsdale, NJ: Lawrence Erlbaum.

National Council of Teachers of Mathematics. (1989). *Curriculum and evaluation standards for school mathematics.* Reston, VA: Author.

SUGGESTED READINGS

Battista, M. (1983). A complete model for operations on integers, *Arithmetic Teacher, 30*(9), 26–31.

Cathcart, W. (1977). Metric measurement: Important curricular considerations. *Arithmetic Teacher, 24*(2), 158–160.

Chang, L. (1985). Multiple methods of teaching the addition and subtraction of integers. *Arithmetic Teacher, 33*(4), 14–20.

Clason, R. (1986). How our decimal money began. *Arithmetic Teacher, 33*(5), 30–33.

Cole, B., & Weissenfluh, H. (1974). An analysis of teaching percentage. *Arithmetic Teacher, 21*(3), 226–228.

Dirks, M. (1984). The integer abacus. *Arithmetic Teacher, 31*(7), 50–54.

Klein, P. (1990). Remembering how to read decimals. *Arithmetic Teacher, 37*(9), 31.

Lichtenberg, B., & Lichtenberg, D. (1982). Decimals deserve distinction. In L. Silvey & J. Smart (Eds.), *Mathematics for the*

middle grades: 1982 yearbook (pp. 142–152). Reston, VA: National Council of Teachers of Mathematics.

Litwiller, B., & Duncan, D. (1991). Rhombus ratio activities. *Arithmetic Teacher, 38*(4), 39–41.

Payne, J., & Towsley, A. (1987). Ideas: Dollars and cents, tenths and hundredths, comparing and ordering decimals, estimating with decimals. *Arithmetic Teacher, 34*(7), 26–28.

Priester, S. (1984). SUM 9.9: A game for decimals. *Arithmetic Teacher, 31*(7), 46–47.

Stevenson, C. (1990). Teaching money with grids. *Arithmetic Teacher, 37*(8), 47–49.

Zawojewski, J. (1983). Initial decimal concepts: Are they really so easy? *Arithmetic Teacher, 30*(7), 52–56.

CHAPTER 12

Graphing, Statistics, and Probability

This chapter focuses your attention on how to teach graphing, statistics, and probability. Specifically, it is designed to help you with an understanding of

1. Types of graphs and classroom activities used to introduce them.
2. Measures of central tendency and classroom activities to introduce the concept.
3. Systematic counting procedures and classroom activities to introduce the concept.
4. Probability of an event and classroom activities to introduce this concept.
5. Characteristics of independent and dependent events, random samples, and theoretical and experimental probabilities, and classroom activities used to introduce these concepts.
6. Probability and statistics problem-solving activities.
7. Techniques for incorporating technology into probability and statistics lessons.

NCTM graphing, statistics, and probability standards
K–4 level students will

- Collect, analyze, and describe data
- Construct, read, and interpret displays of data
- Formulate and solve problems that involve collecting and analyzing data
- Explore concepts of chance.

5–8 level students will

- Systematically collect, organize, and describe data
- Construct, read, and interpret tables, charts, and graphs
- Make inferences and convincing arguments that are based on data analysis
- Evaluate arguments that are based on data analysis
- Develop an appreciation for statistical methods as a powerful means for decision making
- Model situations by devising and carrying out experiments or simulations to determine probabilities
- Model situations by constructing a sample space to determine probabilities
- Appreciate the power of using a probability model by comparing experimental results with mathematical expectations

? *I WAS JUST THINKING . . .*

Hidden behind one of three doors is a prize. You choose Door #1. Monty Hall tells you that the prize is *not* behind Door #3. He offers you a chance to switch your choice to Door #2. Should you? Explain your reasoning.

- Make predictions that are based on experimental or theoretical probabilities
- Develop an appreciation for the pervasive use of probability in the real world. (NCTM, 1989, pp. 54, 105, 109)

The study of statistics and probability arises from a need to make informed judgments about uncertain events. For example, to establish an appropriate inventory, the manager of a shoe store must decide which sizes and brands to restock. The weather bureau must issue reports that indicate the likelihood of rain, sunshine, hurricanes, tornadoes, and other conditions. Consumers are bombarded with often conflicting claims about product quality from which they must make informed purchasing decisions.

Learning to interpret statistical summaries, such as the *frequency* (number of occurrences of an event), the *mean* (average), and the *range* (difference between the smallest and largest values observed), is fundamental to making informed decisions at work and in the marketplace. These statistics often are presented as *graphs, charts,* and *tables*. The ability to interpret graphs is an increasingly important skill in our society. Television and print advertising rely heavily on the convincing arguments embodied in well-designed graphs.

Graphs can be misleading, however, if key information necessary for making an unbiased comparison is omitted from the display. For example, a recent advertisement compared two headache remedies claiming that Brand 1 was more effective because it has more pain relief medication. The two analgesics were graphically compared by pouring the powdered medicine into two clear tubes (see Figure 12.1). Sure enough, Brand 1 rose higher than Brand 2. The careful consumer might question whether both powders contained the same concentration of medications. Was the claimed effectiveness due to the *quantity* of medication, as shown in the graph; or was it a question of the *quality* of the ingredients, which could be verified only by clinical evaluation?

A. USING GRAPHS AND STATISTICS
Introducing Graphs

Many of the activities presented in this book include suggestions that children record the results of their experiments using individual or class graphs. The following section reviews the construction and application of several types of elementary graphs.

The study of elementary statistics initially involves organizing and summarizing data collected from experiments. Often data is displayed in tables, charts, and graphs so that relationships become clear. The amount of information presented can be reduced by using summary descriptions of data such as the *mean, median, mode,* and *range*.

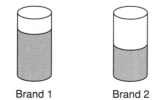

Brand 1   Brand 2

FIGURE 12.1
Which Medication Is More Effective?

➡ *Answer to* **I WAS JUST THINKING . . .**

Switch to Door #2. Throughout the game, the probability is   that the prize is behind Door #1,   that the prize is behind Door #2, and   that the prize is behind Door #3. Thus, there is a   probability that the prize is behind Door #2 or Door #3. When Monty tells you that the prize is not behind Door #3, the   probability that the prize is behind Door #2 or Door #3 now can be interpreted to mean that there is a   probability that the prize is behind Door #2. There is still a   probability that the prize is behind Door #1.

Empirical Graphs

Empirical graphing activities provide direct experience in constructing and interpreting graphs. For example, Figure 12.2 shows children standing in two lines that form an empirical graph of the number of lunch buyers and brown baggers. Empirical graphs enable teachers to introduce graphing concepts to young children. For example, the children must stand in straight lines, and the lines must start at the same *baseline,* if accurate comparisons are to be made. The same is true for representational graphs that students construct later.

In Figure 12.3, children line up to find out if there are more shoes with laces in the classroom than without.

Representational Graphs

A more *representational* attendance graph can be constructed using pictures of each student with their names written on the back. The children turn their pictures face-out when they arrive in the morning, making it easy to take attendance. The pictures can be displayed in two rows to show clearly the relationship between the number of students present and absent. Graphs can be displayed using either vertical or horizontal columns. All columns (or rows) must begin at a common baseline, and the elements in each must be uniformly separated. This allows direct comparison of the number of elements in each category (see Figure 12.4).

The next stage is to have children substitute uniform objects, such as blocks or colored squares on graph paper, to represent each item or event graphed. Because the objects are

FIGURE 12.2
Are There More Brown
Baggers or Buyers?

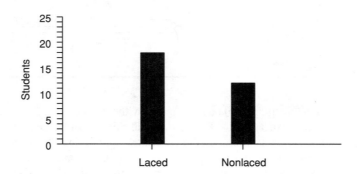

FIGURE 12.3
What Is the Most
Popular Shoe Type?

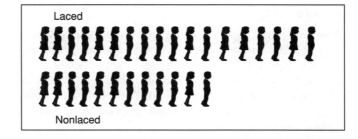

FIGURE 12.4
Representational Graph

Attendance chart

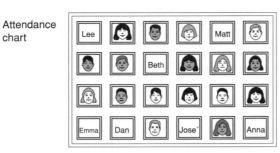

How many people are absent?

Present

Absent   Lee   Matt   Beth   Joe   Emma   Jose   Anna   Dan

FIGURE 12.5
Are There More
Brown or Blue Eyes?

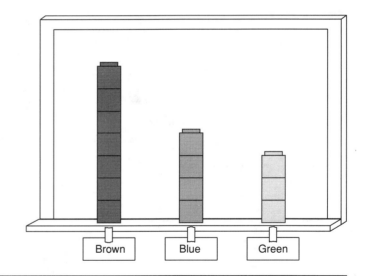

Brown   Blue   Green

discrete, the graph can be reorganized without a record of the change if students change their mind or make a mistake. For example, all children with blue eyes can select a blue Unifix Cube and construct a column on the chalk tray representing blue-eyed children. Those with brown and green eyes can construct columns using like-colored cubes (Figure 12.5). Representational graphs provide a useful intermediary step for children learning to construct graphs.

Picture Graphs

A picture graph, or *pictograph,* is constructed using sketches or pictures to represent objects or events. Initially, each element in a picture graph can represent *one* object. Later, to save space, each element might represent several objects or events. A scale, or *key,* must be included to show the ratio of real objects to those represented in a pictograph so that the graph can be accurately interpreted. The pictographs shown in Figure 12.6 indicate the number of calculators used in a classroom and the number of calculators sold by a department store over a 5-year period.

Have children graph the area of their hand using their own thumbprint. Suppose it takes 22 thumbprints for a child to cover a cutout of her hand. Have her stamp 22 new thumbprints

FIGURE 12.6
Calculator Graph

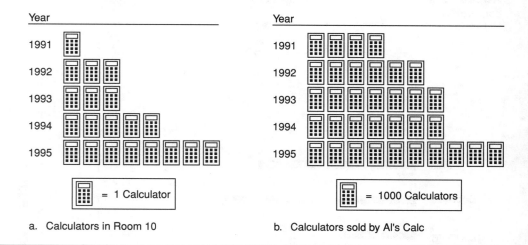

a. Calculators in Room 10   b. Calculators sold by Al's Calc

FIGURE 12.7
How Many Thumbprints
in a Handprint?

in a column above her name on a class graph to record the results. The whole class should record their own hand area on the graph. To reduce the number of thumbprints needed to show the handprint area, children can use one print on the graph to represent five actual thumbprints. A key showing the ratio should be included on the graph to ensure accurate interpretation, as shown in Figure 12.7.

Bar Graphs

Representational graphs and pictographs often are displayed in a simplified form called the *bar graph*. The bars, positioned horizontally or vertically, represent the number of items in each category. A scale is generally displayed along one axis and the categories are listed along the second. These scales and labels facilitate the interpretation of the graph. A scale must be selected to accommodate the smallest and largest values to be graphed. Graphs used in school are generally titled with a question to stimulate viewer involvement (Figure 12.8a, b).

Line Graphs

Connecting the midpoints of the ends of each bar on a graph gives a simplified graphic display called a line graph, or *frequency polygon*. For example, children can make a line graph showing their favorite pets. First, identify the categories of pets (dogs, cats, birds, fish).

FIGURE 12.8
Bar Graphs

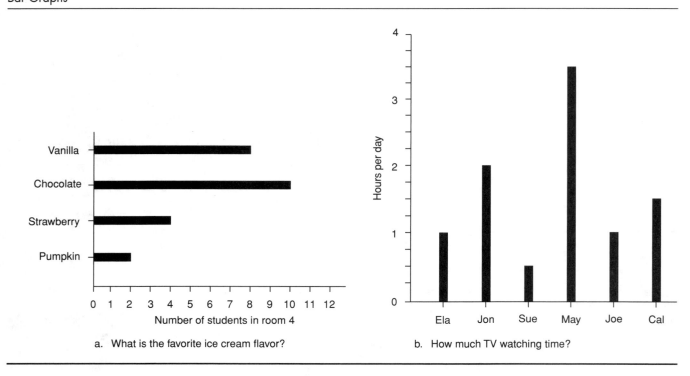

a. What is the favorite ice cream flavor?

b. How much TV watching time?

FIGURE 12.9
What Is Your Favorite Pet?

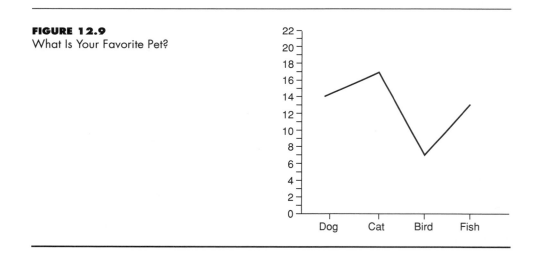

Then, call out the categories and have the children vote for their favorite. Graph the results as shown in Figure 12.9. How would the results change if each child could vote twice, or as often as he or she wished? Discuss different ways to collect the opinions and construct the graph (e.g., have everyone number the categories 1, 2, 3, and 4, indicating least to most favorite pet, and graph the average class results for each pet).

Line graphs often are used to show continuous data rather than discrete categories. For example, in situations where intermediate values exist, such as temperatures, speed, money, and length, a line graph generally gives a more accurate picture of the relationship than a bar graph. Figure 12.10 shows the relationship between the radius and area of several circles. Figure 12.11 shows the relationship between time and distance for a falling object. Both relationships have line graphs called *parabolas*.

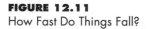
FIGURE 12.11
How Fast Do Things Fall?

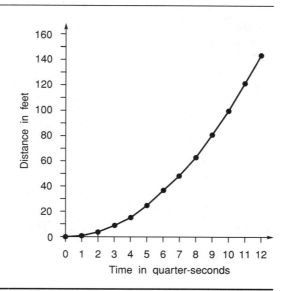

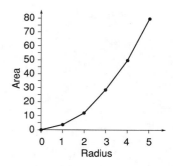

FIGURE 12.10
How Do Circles Grow?

Coordinate Graphs

Line graphs are used to show the *relationship* between two events. *Coordinate graphs,* which were introduced in Chapter 11, can also be used for this purpose. A coordinate graph has a horizontal and a vertical scale. Two related events can be graphed at the same time by plotting one event on the horizontal scale and the other on the vertical scale. For example:

The years 1980–1990 and the number of people living in Kansas

The ages 0–90 and the average height at each age

The grade levels K–12 and the number of students in a district

The heights 50–200 cm and the average shoe size for each height

The amount of money in children's pockets and their grade levels

The months in the year and the average number of colds each month.

Notice that the scales do not have to be represented by numbers. However, each element in the sequence must have an easily interpreted, fixed position relative to all other members (e.g., October must follow September and precede November).

Students might use a coordinate graph to investigate the relationship between grade level and the number of parents who attend Open House. The students first collect the Open House attendance data and organize the information as shown in Table 12.1. They then construct a coordinate graph by writing the grade levels along the horizontal axis and a scale to record the number of parents along the vertical axis (Figure 12.12).

The number of parents in attendance can be graphed by looking at each row in Table 12.1. Each row can be written as an ordered pair. For example, the fourth grade can be represented by the ordered pair (4,23). To graph this ordered pair, remind children to first move horizontally along the grade level scale to the point marked fourth grade (4). Then count up 23 spaces in the direction parallel to the vertical axis. Place a dot at the point (4,23). The remaining pairs can be graphed, or *plotted,* and the points connected in order with straight-line segments (Figure 12.13).

The graph shows that fewer parents from the upper grades than the lower grades attended Open House. There could be several reasons to account for this trend. Possibly, there were more lower-grade children than upper-grade children. Because parents of older children have, on the average, been married longer, there may have been fewer parents in the upper grades due to divorce. Reduced parental interest in older children's schooling might also account for the variation.

TABLE 12.1
Parent Attendance Data

GRADE LEVEL	NUMBER OF PARENTS
4	23
5	19
6	18
7	12
8	6
9	4

FIGURE 12.12
Did You Attend
Open House?

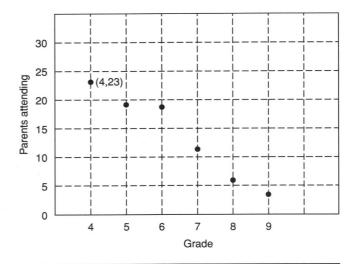

FIGURE 12.13
Open House Attendance
Line Graph

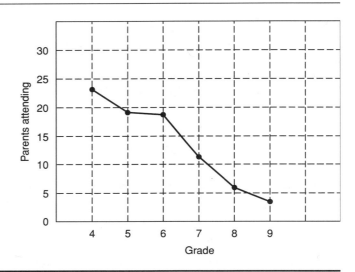

Graphs are an excellent way for students to organize information, to look for patterns to solve problems, and to make predictions and then collect additional data about these predictions. For example, from the data shown in Figure 12.13, students could predict the number of parents attending Open House for lower grades (K–3) and for upper grades (10–12) and then find out how accurate their predictions were.

Circle Graphs

Another popular graph format uses fractional parts of a circle to show the amount each component contributes to making up the whole. The way a child spends her or his allowance can be shown as pie-wedge shaped regions of a silver dollar (see Figure 12.14).

As an introduction to circle graphs, have children keep a diary of their activities for a complete day organized into five categories: studying, eating, playing, watching television, and sleeping. Have them make a table showing the total amount of time (to the nearest half hour) spent in each category. Using a compass, each child draws a circle with an 8-inch (or 16-centimeter) diameter (4-inch radius) and marks off 24 equal segments (approximately 1-inch or 2-centimeters arcs) around the edge. Each segment equals one hour. Children shade an appropriately sized wedge-shaped section for each category. Younger children may have difficulty constructing pie graphs because of the dexterity involved in using a compass and marking off units around the circumference. Prepared circles with the circumference marked off in appropriate units will assist such children in constructing circle graphs (Figure 12.15).

Box and Whisker Graphs

Specialized graphs can be used to show two or more types of information at the same time. Box and whisker graphs can be used to show the mean or median, the range and distribution of a set of data. For example, suppose your class investigated the change in height for each grade in the school. Arrange for pairs of students to go into a class at each grade level and record the height of each student. Take the list of measures for each class and order them from small to large. The range is the difference between the smallest and largest measure. The median is the middle height of all the students in a class (note that the median and mean will be quite similar for a class of 30 students).

Figure 12.16 shows the box and whisker graph of median height and range for seven classrooms. The end of the left whisker is the low end of the range and the end of the right whisker shows the high end. The length of each whisker represents 25 percent of the measures. The box indicates the middle 50 percent of the measures, 25 percent above the median and 25 percent below. Just looking at the graph gives a pictorial view of the entire data set for seven grade levels. Notice that the graph for each grade level overlaps with the previous and following grade, yet the median continues to increase 5–6 centimeters per year. Also, the range increases over the years from 16 centimeters in kindergarten to 26 centimeters in Grade 6. A box and whisker graph offers much more information to the viewer than a bar graph of median heights. Have your students measure their heights and correct and complete this graph for grades 7–9.

Measures of Central Tendency

To communicate with other people, we often need to describe a collection of information in a simple way. The children in a classroom are all different ages unless two were born at exactly the same moment. Yet a fourth-grade teacher, when asked what age children he or she teaches, might answer, 9-year-olds. A value that is used to stand for a collection of numbers or objects is called a *measure of central tendency*. Three common measures of central tendency are the *mean, median,* and *mode.* Each of these statistics gives a single value, or category, that can be used to represent an entire set of observations.

The average, or *mean,* is the sum of a set of values divided by the number of values. To introduce this idea to children, use three towers of Unifix Cubes (4 red, 7 black, 11 yellow) or similar materials positioned on the chalk tray or table. Tell the class to imagine that the towers represent the number of minutes three children took to ride their bicycles to school. Ask the class to estimate the average amount of time it took for the trip.

Figure 12.17 shows two ways to solve the problem using the cubes. First, children might move cubes from the tall tower to the shorter ones and adjust as necessary until all three towers are as near the same length as possible. Alternately, the towers could be dismantled and divided into three equal piles (with a possible remainder). Give several examples using three to five small values, and have each child compute the mean using Unifix towers. An important generalization is that dividing the total number of cubes into equal sets gives the same result as adding the values and dividing by the number of sets. It is important for children to possess the necessary computation skills or have access to a calculator before the teacher introduces the concept of mean.

Students can calculate the mean height of the grade 5 students at their school by dividing the sum of the heights by the total number of fifth graders. Ask the class if they would expect the mean height for grade 5 children to fall between those of grade 4 and grade 6. Why? Have them do the box and whisker graph investigation above to find out.

Sometimes the mean is not the best measure of central tendency. For example, a family moving to a new city may want to know the likely cost of a new home. If the real estate agent simply averaged the cost of all the homes sold in the past year, a small number of very expensive estates or very inexpensive homes might change the mean sufficiently to give a distorted impression of the cost of housing. Real estate values are generally reported in terms of the *median* price of homes sold in the past year. This statistic is found

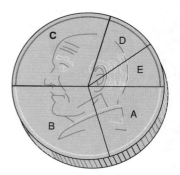

A	20%	Movies
B	30%	Sports
C	30%	Gifts
D	10%	Snacks
E	10%	Other

FIGURE 12.14
How Do You Spend Your Allowance?

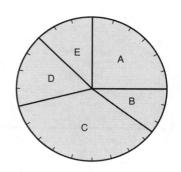

A	6 hr	Study
B	2.5 hr	Eat
C	8.5 hr	Sleep
D	4 hr	Play
E	3 hr	TV

FIGURE 12.15
What Do You Do All Day?

FIGURE 12.16
Box and Whisker Graph
of Student Height

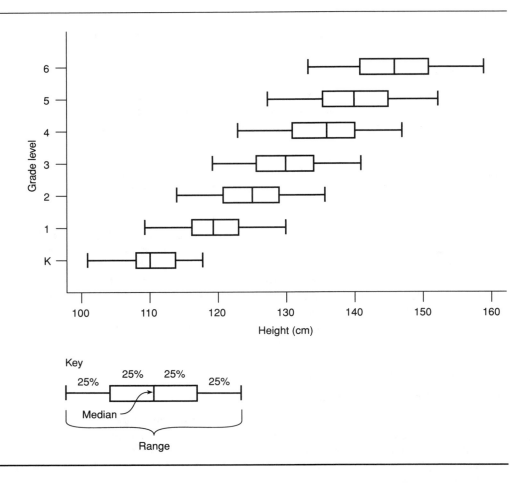

FIGURE 12.17
Finding the Mean

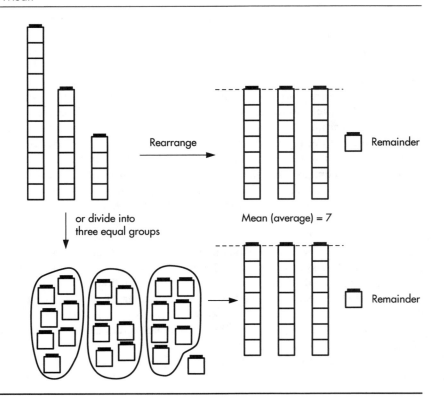

FIGURE 12.18

What Is the Average Number of Pencils Owned by Students?

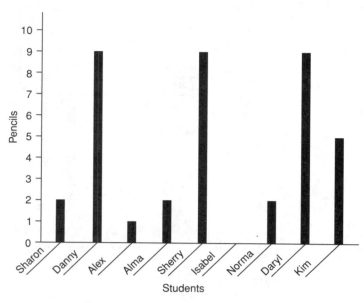

List: 0,1, 2, 2 ,②, 5, 9, 9, 9
Mean ≈ 4.4 pencils
Median (circled) = 2 pencils
Mode = 2 and 9 pencils

by seriating the cost of all homes sold and selecting the value in the middle. (If there is an even number of values, the median equals the mean of the two middle values.) Notice that this technique ignores the size of the values once they are placed in order. A box and whisker graph showing the median and range house prices would help consumers interpret the cost of housing.

For example, to introduce the idea of median, have children count the number of pencils they own. On a prepared graph like Figure 12.18, have students record the number of pencils above their name. To find the median, have each child list the pencil counts in order from small to large and circle the value in the middle (if there are an even number of children, average the two middle values). Write the median on the graph. Also, compute the mean for comparison with the median.

A third measure of the central tendency is the *mode,* the value or category that occurs most frequently. It would not make sense to find the mean or median of popular ice cream flavors since there is no natural order for flavors (i.e., ordering alphabetically and finding the median would not give useful information on the favor preferences). However, the fact that chocolate is the most frequently chosen flavor for a particular school would be a useful statistic for the cafeteria manager. The most popular category (chocolate ice cream) is called the *mode.*

If a graph has two modes (two categories with equal frequencies larger than all others), we say the graph is *bimodal.* For example, in the pencil graph shown in Figure 12.18, three children have two pencils and three have nine pencils. This graph is bimodal.

The *range* of a set of observations is simply the numerical difference between the smallest and largest values. Sometimes we use the term *range* for sets of values or categories that can be naturally sequenced according to size or time (i.e., range of dates from 1850 through 1950 or people with a last name initial that falls in the range M through Z). However, this use of the term *range* is different from its use in mathematics. You can introduce the mathematical concept of range by constructing a box and whisker graph. Subtract the shortest height from the tallest to compute the range (e.g., if the tallest child is 4-feet 6-inches and the shortest is 4-feet 1-inch, the range is 5 inches). Figure 12.19 shows the mean, median, mode, and range for a graph of the high temperature for each day in the month of June.

FIGURE 12.19
Daily High Temperature
in June

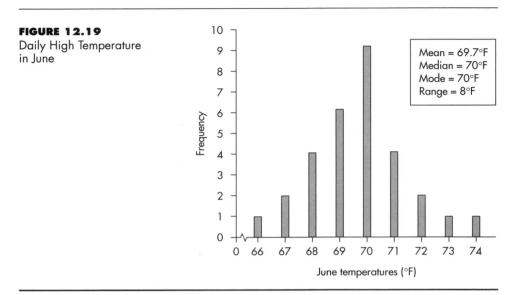

Mean = 69.7°F
Median = 70°F
Mode = 70°F
Range = 8°F

TABLE 12.2
Test Scores with Same Mean and Different Range
and Median

	TEST 1	TEST 2	TEST 3
	100	100	80
	100	100	80
	100	100	75
	100	80	75
	100	80	65
	100	80	65
	100	40	65
	0	40	65
	0	40	65
	0	40	65
Total	700	700	700
Mean	70	70	70
Median	100	80	65
Mode	100	40	65
Range	100	60	15

In general, if the range is relatively small, the mean is likely to be the best indicator of central tendency. As the range increases, the median or mode often gives a better indication of central tendency. For example, for the three sets of test scores listed in Table 12.2, the mean stays the same while the range and median change. Which measure seems to give the best indication of central tendency in each case? Notice that when the range is large, the mean does not represent the data as well as the median or mode. Have students work examples like these to help them develop an understanding of each statistic and its limitation.

Slope

Coordinate graphs show how rapidly one variable changes in relation to a second variable. For example, to compare the effect of different interest rates on the value of a $100 bank deposit, construct a table showing the account balance at the end of each year. For simplicity, ignore any interest paid on previous years' earnings (i.e., no compounded interest). Table 12.3 shows the balance of the account at the end of each year for three different rates of interest: 5 percent, 10 percent, and 15 percent.

Plotting the three columns of account balances at the end of each year on the same graph shows the different rates of growth. Notice in Figure 12.20 that the vertical axis (balance)

12.2
✎ FIGURE IT OUT

Construct a graph showing the following golf-putting distances. Determine the mean, median, mode, and range for the set of measures. Which measure of central tendency best describes this set of data? (2 m, 1 m, 3 m, 3 m, 5 m, 6 m, 1 m, 5 m, 12 m, 1 m, 3 m, 1 m, 7 m, 1 m, 10 m)

TABLE 12.3
Growth of Funds

| END OF YEAR | BALANCE IN ACCOUNT AT: | | |
	5%	10%	15%
0	$100	$100	$100
1	105	110	115
2	110	120	130
3	115	130	145
4	120	140	160
5	125	150	175
6	130	160	190

FIGURE 12.20
Growth of Funds

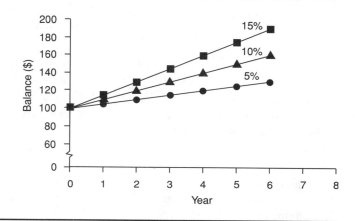

is interrupted with a broken line. This convention is used to indicate that a segment of the axis has been omitted to allow the graph to fit on the page. It is important to remind children to check both axes of a graph to make sure they begin at zero. Sometimes graphs are purposely distorted by configuring the scales of the axes to exaggerate the magnitude of the relationship displayed.

The steepness, or *slope*, of the lines in Figure 12.20 indicate that a 15-percent rate of return generates the largest increases in balance. The slope is the amount of rise on the vertical axis for each unit of length on the horizontal axis. For example, the 5-percent line rises 5 units for each year on the horizontal axis. We say the 5-percent line has a slope of 5. The 10-percent line, therefore, has a slope of 10, and the 15-percent line, a slope of 15. (Note: Banks frequently *compound* interest payments by including previous years' earnings in their computations. The slope of the graph increases more rapidly for each subsequent year when interest is compounded.)

B. EXPLORING PROBABILITY

Elementary probability concepts can be introduced in grades 4–6. Children in grade 4 can make graphs of experiments with coins, dice, and spinners and use this information to informally predict the likelihood of specific events occurring in the future. Ask children to predict the likelihood of an event on a scale of 1 to 10 (1 = impossible, 10 = certain). Possible events to evaluate might include whether the entire class will attend school the next day, the sun will rise tomorrow, more than one-half the class will buy lunch today, or everyone will wear the same-color socks tomorrow.

Children in grades 5–6 can be introduced to counting using combinations and permutations, can explore more complex probability experiments, and can compare experimental and theoretical probabilities. Decimal probabilities between zero (impossible) and one (certain) are also introduced.

12.3
 **FIGURE IT OUT**

What would be the slope for 20 percent, 50 percent, and 100 percent interest? Could the slope line ever be vertical? What percent return would be required? What would a zero percent graph look like? Could the line ever descend (taxes!)?

CT: I heard the term *discrete math* the other day and I had no idea what it meant. Have you heard of it?

ST: Yes, I took a course last year that dealt with a number of discrete math topics.

CT: What kind of things did you study? What exactly is discrete math?

ST: Well, discrete math is a general term for areas of math that deal with discrete—or noncontinuous—numbers rather than topics that depend on the continuity of numbers. The real numbers are continuous, but integers are discrete. Algebra, trigonometry, and calculus all depend on continuous numbers.

CT: So counting is discrete, but what other topics are included?

ST: Familiar topics like combinations, permutations, and probability. Network theory and other topological concepts like the four-color map problem and the Möbius

Strip are discrete, too. Some professors even include matrix algebra as a discrete topic.

CT: The NCTM *Standards* recommend more emphasis on discrete topics. Why do you think there's more interest in these topics?

ST: Apparently because there are lots of applications of discrete math in industry and everyday life.

CT: Such as?

ST: Well, things like scheduling tournaments, for instance, or determining the minimum flight routes between cities, or figuring out the number of different license plates that can be manufactured using a certain number of characters.

CT: It sounds like a lot of these applications would relate to our students, too. I'd like to see some ideas for our class. Can you bring some in tomorrow?

ST: Sure. Maybe I can plan a lesson on counting using combinations before we start talking about probability.

The probability that an event will occur is simply the ratio between the number of desired outcomes and the total number of possible outcomes. For example, the probability of a head showing when flipping a normal coin is 1:2, or $\frac{1}{2}$, because there is one desired outcome (a head) and two possible outcomes (head and tail).

To apply the concept of probability, children need to have an understanding of fractions, ratios, and proportions. Children need proportional reasoning, for example, to understand that there is an equal likelihood of a red marble being drawn from each of the bags pictured in Figure 12.21.

Teachers can introduce children to probability with carefully chosen experiments using familiar objects such as coins, dice, cards, spinners, marbles, and counters. Children compare the results of these experiments with the computed probability of each situation. These experiences help children see how probability allows us to predict the likelihood of some random event. In fact, it was just such an interest that prompted wealthy gamblers in the 16th and 17th centuries to support the research of prominent mathematicians to improve their understanding of games of chance.

Probability of an Event

To calculate the probability of an event, you require two values:

1. *The number of ways a desired event can occur:* Favorable events (F)
2. *The total number of possible events:* Total events (T)

To be subject to the laws of probability, each event, or *outcome,* must have the same likelihood of occurring for each trial in an experiment. For example, to determine how likely it is that an ace will be drawn from a deck of cards, it is necessary to know the following:

- the number of aces in the deck (desired events)
- the number of cards in the deck (total events)
- whether the deck has been thoroughly shuffled (randomness of events).

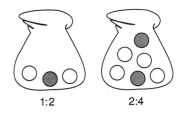

FIGURE 12.21
Ratio of Red Marbles to White Marbles

When cards are selected one at a time from a standard deck, returned to the pack, and thoroughly shuffled after each draw, an average of 4 out of 52 cards drawn will be aces. Although it is highly unlikely, it is possible that the *same* ace will be drawn each time an ace appears.

The probability of an event is defined as:

$$\frac{\text{Favorable events}}{\text{Total events}} = \frac{F}{T}$$

$P_{(3)} = \frac{1}{4}$
The central angle of section 3 is 90°, or $\frac{1}{4}$ of the circle.

FIGURE 12.22
Spinner

A *certain* event has a probability of one, because the number of possible events equals the number of desired events (the probability of selecting a peanut from a jar containing n peanuts: $P = \frac{n}{n} = 1$). An *impossible* event has probability zero, because there are zero desired events (the probability of catching a shark in a freshwater stream containing n fish):

$$P_{certain} = \frac{n}{n} = 1$$

$$P_{impossible} = \frac{0}{n} = 0$$

The probability of a head showing when one coin is flipped is an example of two equally likely events:

$$P_{head} = \frac{\text{Ways to show a head}}{\text{Possible events}} = \frac{1}{2}$$

Drawing an ace from a well-shuffled deck has the following probability:

$$P_{ace} = \frac{F}{T} = \frac{4}{52}$$

The probability of an even number showing on the roll of a standard die is as follows:

$$P_{even} = \frac{3}{6}$$

The probability of getting the number 3 on the spinner in Figure 12.22 is found by determining the fractional part of the circle covered by the 3 section. As this section is one-fourth of the circle, the arrow should land on three, on the average, about one-fourth of the time.

Probability Experiments

Probability is introduced using experiments involving random samples. To determine the likeliness of a specific event, all events must arise fairly. For a sample to be *random,* each event must have the same probability of being chosen for each selection, or *trial.* Flipping coins, rolling dice, using spinners, drawing thoroughly shuffled cards, and selecting similar marbles of different colors from a bag all generate random samples.

To be predictive, the laws of probability require that several random samples be taken. Sampling a single event gives little information about the likelihood of similar events occurring in the future. Suppose a card that is drawn from a pack is a jack. This result indicates that a jack is possible but does not indicate what is likely to occur on future draws. Normally, children conduct a random sample of 30 to 100 trials to establish a reliable pattern of outcomes.

To test whether the calculated, or *theoretical,* probability adequately predicts a pattern of outcomes, children should conduct experiments and compute *experimental* probabilities. An experimental probability is simply the ratio of the number of trials showing favorable events F and the total number of events T:

$$P_{experimental} = \frac{\text{Trials showing favorable events}}{\text{Total trials}} = \frac{F}{T}$$

As the number of trials gets large (30 to 100 or more), the experimental probability should approximate the calculated probability. Students can carry out probability experiments such as flipping coins, drawing cards, tossing tacks, drawing marbles from a bag, and rolling dice and keep systematic records of their results. Table 12.4 shows the results of flipping two coins 50 times.

12.4
✎ **FIGURE IT OUT**

Compute the probability of selecting a white marble from the bag pictured in Figure 12.23. Do an experiment to verify your result.

FIGURE 12.23
Probability of Drawing a White Marble

12.5
✎ FIGURE IT OUT

Flip two coins 100 times and record the results in a table. Compute the experimental probability that at least one head will show. Is the experimental probability result close to the theoretical probability? What is the experimental probability for at least one tail showing? What is the calculated probability? How do the results compare with the experimental probability for exactly one head showing?

TABLE 12.4
Flipping Two Coins

HH	HT	TH	TT
///// ///// //	///// ///// /	///// ///// ////	///// ///// ///
12	11	14	13

TABLE 12.5
Fundamental Counting Principle

	COIN 1	COIN 2			
Event 1	H	H			
Event 2	H	T	Coin 1	Coin 2	Coin 1 and 2
Event 3	T	H	Events	Events	Events
Event 4	T	T	2 ×	2 =	4

The experimental and calculated probability for *at least* one head showing can be written in decimal form to ease comparison:

$$P_{experimental} = \frac{12 + 11 + 14}{50} = 0.74$$

$$P_{calculated} = \frac{3}{4} = 0.75$$

12.6
✎ FIGURE IT OUT

Using the FCP, compute the number of possible events for each of the following experiments. Make a table showing the results.

1. Three coins flipped together.
2. Two dice rolled at the same time.
3. Three cards selected from a deck without replacing any cards as they are drawn.

Fundamental Counting Principle

To calculate a probability, it is necessary to count the total number of possible outcomes. Several counting techniques are available to assist with this task. In a full deck of cards there are 52 possible events. Flipping one coin represents two possible events. There are six possible events associated with rolling a standard die.

When more than one object is involved, as when flipping two coins at the same time, counting the total number of possible events is more complex. A procedure called the *fundamental counting principle (FCP)* is an efficient procedure for calculating the total number of possible outcomes for experiments that involve the combination of two or more *independent* events, or when the outcome of one experiment is not influenced by the outcome of another. The FCP states that, for two or more independent experiments, the total number of possible events for the combined experiment is the product of the number of events for each experiment.

For example, when tossing two coins at the same time, each coin independently has two possible events. The FCP tells us that there are $2 \times 2 = 4$ possible outcomes. Table 12.5 shows the four possible outcomes when tossing two coins. Students can verify the FCP by listing the *sample space,* the set of all possible outcomes, for rolling two dice ($6 \times 6 = 36$ outcomes; [1,1], [1,2], [2,1], [1,3], [3,1], . . . [5,6], [6,5], [6,6]).

Some situations are not composed of independent events. For example, the number of ways to deal two cards from a deck are *dependent* events. There are 52 possible first draws, or events. After the first draw, there are 51 cards left from which to select the second card. The first event affects the probability of the second event. We can still apply the FCP to calculate the total number of ways two cards can be dealt from a deck. For nonindependent events, multiply the number of possibilities for the first event times the number of possibilities for the second event, or $52 \times 51 = 2,652$ events.

Permutations

A second counting principle involves arrangements where *order matters*. Such arrangements are called *permutations*. Serious ice cream eaters know that the order of scoops on a cone makes a great deal of difference. A double scoop with Jamoca Almond Fudge on top and German Chocolate Cake on the bottom is an entirely different Epicurean experience

FIGURE 12.24
Ice Cream Cone
Permutations

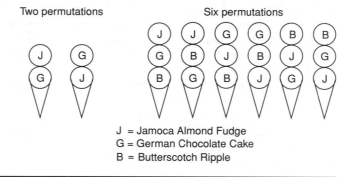

Two permutations   Six permutations

J = Jamoca Almond Fudge
G = German Chocolate Cake
B = Butterscotch Ripple

than when the order is reversed. As shown in Figure 12.24, two-scoopers can be constructed in two ways, or two permutations. For three-scoopers, there are three choices when selecting the first scoop, leaving two choices for the second and one choice for the third. Applying the FCP gives $3 \times 2 \times 1 = 6$ possible events. There are six permutations for three-scoop cones. (Note: For these permutation problems, each scoop must be a different flavor. The "special-needs" ice cream eater wouldn't have it any other way!)

Four types of ice cream can be stacked $4 \times 3 \times 2 \times 1 = 24$ permutations. Note that because order matters, each arrangement of a permutation is *unique* (the same flavors can occur, but the different arrangements make each cone unique).

Finding permutations involves calculating the product of a sequence of counting numbers $(1, 2, 3, \ldots n)$. This calculation is called a *factorial*. The previous ice cream examples can be written using the largest factor and the exclamation point (!) to indicate a factorial calculation:

$$3! = 3 \times 2 \times 1 = 6$$
$$4! = 4 \times 3 \times 2 \times 1 = 24$$

Combinations

A third counting principle calculates the number of arrangements of two or more objects *without regard to order.* Such arrangements are called *combinations.* For example, suppose a chef has 10 cookbooks but has room for only 2 at a time in a stovetop book rack. To determine the number of combinations, the FCP is first used to compute the total number of possible pairings. This result is divided by the number of ways each pair can be arranged, because the order in which the books are displayed does not matter to the chef.

Choosing two books from the same library are not *independent* events, as selecting the first book reduces the number of choices remaining for the second. In the chef's case, there are 10 possible first choices and 9 possible second choices. Applying the FCP gives $10 \times 9 = 90$ possible outcomes. There are two possible arrangements (the first book chosen can be placed on the left and the second on the right, or vice versa). Since the chef is not concerned about their order, there are $90 \div 2 = 45$ possible *combinations* of 10 books chosen two at a time.

Notice that for combinations and permutations, the same object is never used twice in a single arrangement (e.g., a book cannot be placed in the rack with itself; you do not shake hands with yourself; only amateurs eat two scoops of the same type of ice cream). The fundamental counting principle makes no such distinction (heads or tails can appear on both coins when flipping two coins). Selecting among these three counting methods depends on the application. Children must carefully consider the types of events and conditions of the experiment when selecting a counting method to help them work probability problems.

C. CLASSROOM ACTIVITIES
Opening Exercises

Daily graphing experiences arise naturally when updating daily attendance, lunch count, calendar, and weather information. A well-designed bulletin board display can turn the often tedious opening exercises into a valuable classroom learning experience for grade 4. In September, make a graph of everyone's birthday and leave it posted throughout the year as a reminder. Make attendance reports a graphing activity by having children, as they arrive in the morning, turn their picture cards from the side showing their name to the side showing their picture. The children whose names are showing after class begins are absent. Record daily lunch and milk counts on a prepared monthly bar graph. Daily temperature, cloud cover, and precipitation conditions also can be displayed graphically. A monthly calendar and a time line showing the cumulative record of days from the beginning of school can be used to introduce the decade numbers, place value, and large numbers. The dates and time line initially can be recorded using base-10 materials cut from squared paper. The time line also can be used to post a memorable occasion for each day. A missing tooth, a new brother or sister, or a holiday can be noted on the daily time line as a concrete record of historical events and can be reviewed at the end of the year. It is fun to have a celebration on the 100th day of school. Have everyone bring 100 of something (small) from home that day. Children also enjoy graphing their height and weight at the beginning of the year to compare with an end-of-year graph.

Surveys and Polls

An interesting probability activity for students in grades 4–6 involves making a survey of people's opinions. Analyzing the results can help children see how to make more objective decisions.

The public opinion poll has become an important tool in marketing and politics. For the results of a poll to be reliable, the persons surveyed must constitute a representative, random sample of the target population. Today, a national survey of about 1,000 systematically selected individuals can predict, with considerable accuracy, the outcome of an election, the most popular television programming, or the color preferences for new cars. These experiments generally produce results close to actual outcomes involving a population of hundreds of millions of people.

Surveys differ from probability experiments involving coins and dice in that the individual's personal preferences are not likely to be random, but instead are guided by some underlying value or belief. Carrying out a reliable survey involves selecting representative individuals whose responses are likely to agree with characteristic segments of the total population. If the population is small, one might simply poll everyone. However, for large populations ($n > 100$), it is more efficient to survey a random sample within identifiable segments of the population.

Students can conduct a survey of food preferences by randomly selecting a sample of, say, three students from each grade level at a school and asking them to sequence the items on the school lunch menu in their order of preferences. Such a sample is said to be *stratified*, because subjects are selected from naturally occurring subcategories (in this case, grade levels) in the population. The results of this opinion poll can then be compared with the actual cafeteria lunch counts. A discussion of this experiment might include student opinions on the randomness of the sample, whether cafeteria sales really reflect student preference, and how these results might compare with the opinions of a second sample of students.

Charting the Market

Students may enjoy trying their hand at investing in the stock market (Kelly, 1986). Detailed listings of stock prices are published in most daily newspapers. Give each student an investment fund of $1,000. Have students select a portfolio of 5 to 10 stocks and record their purchases with their broker/teacher. Once a week, supply a current report of stock prices from the newspaper and have the children compute the total current value of their portfolio. A line graph showing the performance of the portfolio should be maintained by each investor (see Figure 12.25). Have students also write a quarterly financial report describing their investment performance and what they plan to buy and sell for their portfolio for the next quarter.

Letter Frequency

Which letter appears most frequently in written English? Children can investigate this problem by selecting one paragraph from a textbook and making a bar graph of the frequency

FIGURE 12.25
How Is My Portfolio Doing?

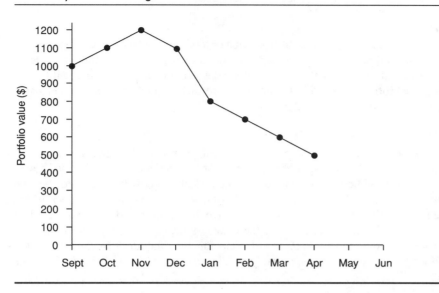

FIGURE 12.26
Which Are Popular Letters?

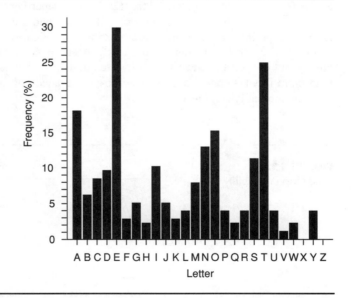

of each letter. Students can compare their results to see if their experimental probabilities are similar (Figure 12.26).

The following is the list of letters in the order of frequency in written English:

E T A O N R I S H D L F C M U G Y P W B V K X J Q Z

The five most popular letters (E, T, A, O, and N) constitute more than 35 percent of all letters used in English writing. The first nine letters in the frequency list constitute 70 percent of all the letters used in English words (Zim, 1975). The vowels make up about 40 percent of all English words. Have children look at a commercial set of rub-on letters and see if the letters appear in proportions that agree with the class results. Compile the individual results in a class bar graph. A class-size sample should produce a reliable experimental probability.

Additional questions to explore: How does the letter frequency of written English compare with that of other languages, such as Spanish? Does letter frequency vary among mathematics, basal, science, and social studies books? Students can construct a class graph to explore these questions. Have each student in the class make up additional language-based probability experiments using dictionaries and almanacs.

Tube Caps

Collect a class set of similar plastic caps from glue or toothpaste tubes. Have students compute the experimental probabilities of a cap landing on its big end, small end, and side by carrying out 100 trials. Compare the results among the students in the class to see if the experimental probabilities are similar. Compare the results to the same experiment using thumb tacks and coins (see Figure 12.27).

Matching π

Children can approximate the number π (≈ 3.14) using a probability experiment. Trim 10 matchsticks or toothpicks to a length of two inches (or 5 cm). On a piece of unlined paper, draw a series of parallel lines two inches apart. Have each child lay the prepared sheet on a table and carefully drop 10 sticks from a height of about one foot onto the paper, trying to keep the sticks within the edges of the paper. Have the children make a table recording the number of sticks touching a line (*T*) and the number lying completely between the lines (*B*) for 30 trials. Dividing the total number of sticks touching the line *T* by the number between the lines *B* gives a result approximately equal to π (Figure 12.28). Why do you think this is true?

Spinners and Quiet Dice

Spinners can be easily constructed from tag board, paper fasteners, small washers, and paper clips. Constructed with various colored or numbered divisions, spinners can offer a range of experimental probability combinations (see Figures 12.29 and 12.30).

Quiet dice can be fashioned from thick sheets of foam rubber. Cut out cubes (equal edges) and use felt-tipped markers to write numbers or letters on the six faces. *Fair* dice with more faces (tetrahedrons, octahedrons, dodecahedrons, and icosahedrons) are available commercially (Figure 12.31).

FIGURE 12.27
Tube Cap Probability

	Small end	Big end	Side
	I I I I	⊥⊥⊦⊤	⊥⊦⊤
		⊥⊦⊤	⊥⊦⊤
			⊥⊦⊤
			I I

FIGURE 12.28
Calculating π

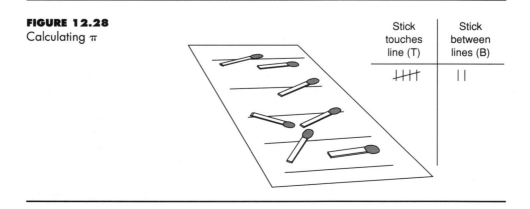

Stick touches line (T)	Stick between lines (B)
⊥⊦⊤	I I

D. USING STATISTICS AND PROBABILITY TO SOLVE PROBLEMS
Popular Television Programs

To investigate the popularity of television programming, have each child list his or her favorite television program. Construct a class bar graph showing the frequency of each program reported. Which is the most popular program (the mode)? Which programs are reported by only one student? To compute the experimental probability of the most popular program, divide the number of times the program was reported by the total number of students sampled. For the example shown in Figure 12.32, 8 out of 31 students reported program C. The experimental probability that a student in the class would select program C is as follows:

$$P_{exp} = \tfrac{8}{31} = 0.26$$

Have the class survey another class at the same grade level and compute the experimental probabilities for each program selected. How do the results compare with the previous example? If the experimental probabilities are similar, we say the results are *stable* across groups. Students can survey other grade levels to see if they get similar results. Is it

FIGURE 12.29
Plans for Constructing
a Spinner

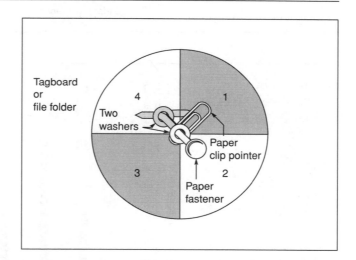

FIGURE 12.30
A Probability Quiz Using a Spinner

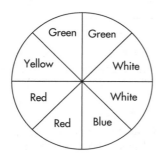

What is the probability of the spinner landing on:
  1. a yellow section? _____
  2. a blue section? _____
  3. a green or blue section? _____
  4. not a green section? _____
  5. not white or blue? _____
  6. green, white, or red? _____
  7. not red? _____
  8. a white section? _____

FIGURE 12.31
Alternate Dice

Quiet dice

Foam rubber

Other dice

Tetrahedron
(4 triangular faces)

Dodecahedron
(12 pentagonal faces)

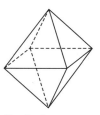

Octahedron
(8 triangular faces)

Icosahedron
(20 triangular faces)

FIGURE 12.32
Popular Television Programs

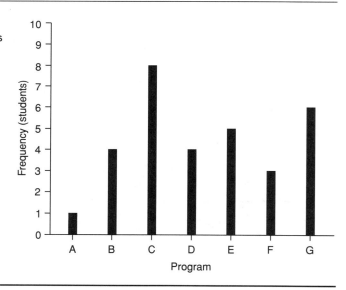

likely that children of different ages will express different preferences? This experience points out the need to understand the population surveyed before generalizing results to other groups.

How Many Handshakes?

We can use a table to find out how many handshakes there would be in a party of ten persons, as shown in Figure 12.33. Two people require one handshake, three people require three handshakes, and four people require six handshakes.

For five people, there are five choices for the first person in the handshake couplet, leaving four choices for the second member. Using the fundamental counting principle, there are $5 \times 4 = 20$ possible pairings. Since there are two equivalent ways for each pair to be arranged (first choice on the left and second choice on the right, or vice versa), the number

FIGURE 12.33
Handshake Problem

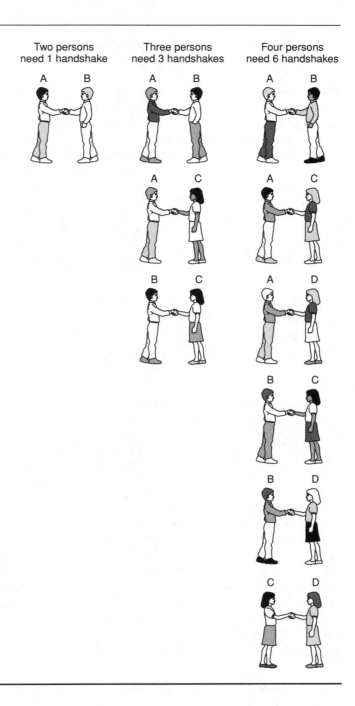

Two persons
need 1 handshake

Three persons
need 3 handshakes

Four persons
need 6 handshakes

of combinations (handshakes) is $20 \div 2 = 10$. Using the rule for counting combinations, a formula can be written relating the number of people *P* and handshakes *H:*

$$\frac{P(P - 1)}{2} = H$$

Therefore, ten people require $(10 \times 9) \div 2 = 45$ handshakes.

Suppose, in some other culture, three people are required for a proper handshake. For a party of ten, how many handshakes would be required for all possible groups of three to shake hands exactly once? Children can use the procedure for counting combinations. There are ten choices for the first member of the triplet, nine for the second, and eight for the third, giving $10 \times 9 \times 8 = 720$ groupings. As there are six equivalent ways to arrange

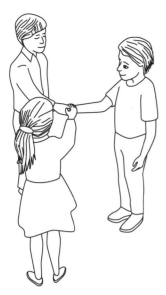

FIGURE 12.34
How Many Three-Person Handshakes Would There Be for a Party of Ten People?

TABLE 12.6
How Many Fish in the Lake?

TAGGED FISH	UNMARKED FISH
5	115

12.9

✎ **FIGURE IT OUT**

The "Counting Fish" estimation technique is used in medicine to determine the number of cancerous cells in patients by marking certain cells with small amounts of radioactivity. Wildlife biologists also use this technique to estimate populations of birds, rodents, insects, and other animals living in specific regions. List additional practical applications for this indirect counting technique.

three persons (permutations of left, right, and middle positions), the number of handshakes required would be 720 ÷ 6 = 120 (see Figure 12.34). Students can try extending this reasoning to *four-way* handshakes.

Counting Fish

Wildlife biologists use probability to estimate the number of fish in a lake. First they net 30 or so fish, *tag* them with special paint, and return them to the lake. The next day they net a large number of fish and record the number of tagged and nontagged fish. A proportion can be written that relates the ratio of tagged fish netted to the number originally tagged with the ratio of netted *unmarked* fish to the total population of fish in the lake. Solving this proportion gives an estimate of the original number of fish in the lake.

For example, suppose 30 tagged fish were returned to the lake containing an unknown number of fish. The next day, 120 fish were netted, and 5 of them were tagged (see Table 12.6).

The following proportion can be written relating the ratio of tagged fish netted to the total number of tagged fish and the total number of fish netted to the total number of fish in the lake (*F*). Solving for *F* gives the estimated number of fish in the lake.

$$\frac{5}{30} = \frac{120}{F}$$

$$\frac{30}{5} = \frac{F}{120}$$

$$\frac{30 \times 120}{5} = 720 = F$$

Children can explore this procedure using goldfish crackers (Vissa, 1987). Put a box of goldfish crackers in a bowl and use a spoon to net several fish for tagging (dye them with green food coloring). Have the class estimate the fractional part of the total number of fish represented by the tagged fish. Return the tagged fish to the bowl, mix them thoroughly, and net a sample with a large spoon. Have the children record the results in a table and compute the proportion using a calculator. The process can be repeated several times and the results compared. Are the results always the same? Why not? Average the results of several trials to get a more stable estimate. Why do the fish have to be thoroughly mixed between trials? Why do the biologists wait a day after releasing the tagged fish before taking a sample?

An alternate activity to introduce population sampling involves estimating the total number of raisins in a loaf of bread by projecting from the number in an individual slice. Divide the class into groups of three students and give each child one slice of raisin bread and, together, count the number of slices of raisin bread in a loaf. Have the group count the number of raisins in each slice and record its data. Each group calculates the average number of raisins in a slice of bread and predicts the total number in the loaf. Graph the predictions of all the groups. Discuss why the predictions may vary and how this procedure can be used to solve real-world problems.

E. CALCULATOR AND COMPUTER APPLICATIONS
Calculators

The development of statistics and probability concepts will be enhanced if students have access to calculators. The tedious calculations involved in computing means, decimal equivalents, probabilities, and proportions can divert attention from important concept development and problem-solving tasks. Ready access to a calculator allows children to focus more of their attention on the organization and interpretation of data when working on probability experiments.

Probability Simulations and Tools

Computer simulations that model probability experiments can be helpful when extending concepts explored earlier using manipulatives. Although it is possible to run an experiment of 1,000 trials by dividing the task among the children in the class, a computer can simu-

FIGURE 12.35

A Chance Look

SOURCE: *A Chance Look* [Computer program] by Sunburst. Copyright by Sunburst Communications, Inc. Reprinted by permission.

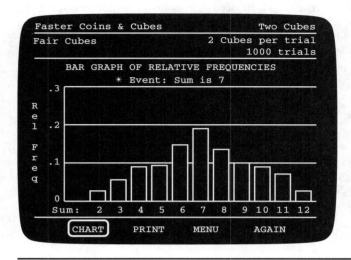

FIGURE 12.36

How Many Computers in Schools?

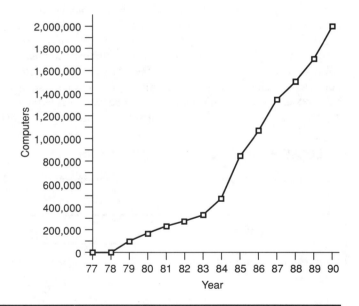

late the experiment in a few seconds. Software like *Probability* (MECC) and *A Chance Look* (Sunburst) allows students to flip simulated coins and roll simulated dice, predict outcomes, organize data, and compute experimental probabilities (Figure 12.35). By doing the same experiment several times using different numbers of trials, students gain an understanding of the importance of how sample size can affect the accuracy of predictions. Students can make and test conjectures more efficiently using computer simulations.

Another software application useful for studying statistics and probability is a *graphing tool.* Examples of easy-to-use graphing tools are *Exploring Tables and Graphs* (Weekly Reader Family Software) and *MECC Graph* (MECC). These tools allow students to enter their own data to produce bar, line, and pie graphs (see Figure 12.36). For any given data set, several different graphic representations can be selected to ensure the graph communicates the desired information.

F. ADAPTING INSTRUCTION FOR CHILDREN WITH SPECIAL NEEDS

The graphing and probability concepts introduced in this chapter are important learning objectives for *all* children. At a minimum, students need to be able to construct and interpret simple bar graphs and find averages.

To help children with learning problems, prepare the axes for graphs on one-inch squared paper ahead of time. Supply one-inch colored cubes and like-colored felt pens to facilitate the construction of bar graphs. Students first construct the graph on the prepared template with blocks using a different color for each bar (e.g., color of hair for students in the class). Each bar is then reproduced using a like-colored felt pen.

Probability and statistics are particularly appropriate enrichment topics for gifted and talented students. Comparing measures of central tendency, interpreting slopes of graphs, calculating probabilities, and solving proportions are powerful mathematical ideas that have wide application in solving practical problems. The study of permutations and combinations offers an interesting introduction to number theory for mathematically mature children in grades 4 and up. Problems that can only be solved by using the laws of probability extend students' ability to apply proportional thinking. Many of the readings listed at the end of this chapter include enrichment activities appropriate for gifted and talented children.

G. ASSESSMENT STRATEGY

Oral/audiovisual presentations offer an alternative to written tests. Some students may prefer to develop an oral or audiovisual report to demonstrate their knowledge. Individuals or pairs can present to the entire class or to small groups. Grading criteria should be established before the students begin to design their presentations. It is helpful to allow the audience to rate the presentation for clarity, accuracy, and creativity.

Encourage students to design visuals, write rap songs, use readers theater (chorale and individual readings of dramatic narrative or poetry), or use a videotape or other media in their presentations. The presenters should be responsible for making an audiotape or some other record of the presentations so it can be included in their assessment portfolio.

H. GRAPHING SAMPLE LESSON PLAN

Presented here is an example of a lesson plan that introduces graphing to students in grade 4.

Graphing Lesson Plan

Grade Level: Grade 4   *Time Allotment:* 30 minutes

NCTM Standard: Construct, read, and interpret displays of data.

Essential Understanding: Information can be displayed graphically to communicate ideas.

Goal: To understand how bar graphs are constructed and interpreted

Objective: The learners will construct a graph by placing columns of blocks on a common baseline and using the vertical axis to determine the number for each category.

Motivation: Have each student take off one shoe. Place a meter stick on the floor in front of the room as a baseline with labels "laces" and "no laces" on each end. Have the class predict whether there are more shoes with laces or without. Next, have each student in turn place his or her shoe in the correct row across the front of the classroom. Ask which row is longer and the difference between the two. Tell the class this is a graph of your shoes. Ask how you could make a record of your graph since they will need their shoes before they go home.

(Continued)

Graphing Lesson Plan   cont'd

Procedure: Have the class work in pairs and hand out a supply of colored blocks, like-colored crayons, and one-inch-square paper. With the shoes still on the floor, ask if they could be graphed in another way (e.g., by color, number of lacing holes, Velcro closes or not, or shoe height). Do another empirical graph using one of these criteria. Then have each pair make a copy of the empirical graph on the squared paper using the blocks. Ask why the bars need to start at the same baseline (point out the meter stick on the floor). Have several pairs describe their graphs. Make special note of those graphs that use the same color for the entire bar and different colors for each (it makes the graph easier to read). Have each student-pair color in the bars with crayons for each row. Have each pair label and title their graph to help tell the graph's story.

Closure: Select one graph for the class to review. Have the student pair explain their graph. Check for different colored bars and a common baseline. Ask them to point at the longest and shortest bar. Ask if it would help if they numbered the second axis (0, 1, 2, . . .). How would this help when counting the number of shoes in each category?

Assessment: Collect the graphs and comment on the story each tells so students can finalize them for display on the bulletin board.

Materials: One-inch-squared paper, crayons, colored inch cubes, meter stick, and floor graph labels.

Extension: Have the students write a story, to be displayed with their graphs on the bulletin board, about how they made their graphs.

SUMMARY

- Graphing, statistics, and probability are important topics in the grade 4–9 mathematics curriculum.
- Designing and interpreting graphs can be integrated into all strands of mathematics.
- Objects can be arranged in lines starting with a common baseline to create an empirical graph.
- Representational bar graphs, pie graphs, line graphs, and box and whisker graphs are used to display information graphically and help to solve problems.
- Coordinate graphs can display the relationship between two variables.
- The slope of a line graphed on the coordinate plane is a measure of how rapidly one variable changes relative to the other. Calculating the slope of a graph can be useful when solving some types of problems.
- The mean, median, and mode are measures of central tendency that are used to summarize large amounts of information. The mean is appropriate for evenly distributed data. The median is used when a small number of very large or small values is included in a set of data. The mode is useful for describing unordered categories of data like favorite flavors of ice cream.
- The calculated probability of an event is the ratio of desired events to the total number of possible events.
- The experimental probability of an event is calculated from the ratio of the number of times a desired event occurs to the total number of events.
- Independent events do not affect each other's chances of occurring, while a dependent event changes the chances of another event occurring.
- The fundamental counting principle states that, for two or more independent events, the total number of possible outcomes is the product of the number of outcomes for each separate event.
- Special applications of this principle make it possible to count the number of combinations (groupings where order does not matter) and permutations (groupings where order matters). These counting techniques are useful for computing theoretical probabilities.

- If the samples are random and sufficient trials are recorded (more than 30 or so), the experimental probability will approximate the calculated probability.
- Probability can be used to solve many nonroutine problems.
- Special-needs children should, at a minimum, learn how to interpret graphs and compute means. Statistics and probability are appropriate topics for extended work by gifted and talented children.

QUESTIONS AND ACTIVITIES FOR DISCUSSION

1. Make a list of 20 objects and events that could be used for empirical graphing experiences. Try a class graphing activity with a group of children or peers.

2. Figure 12.37 shows a graph of the probability of two persons in various sized groups having the same birthday (date only, not year). In a class of 30 students, how likely is it that 2 will have the same birthday? How large a group is needed to have a 50 percent chance that two birthdays will coincide? How many people would have to be present to be certain ($P = 1$) that two birthdays would coincide? Try this experiment with your peers and, if possible, with a class of children.

3. Pascal's Triangle is a useful tool for computing probabilities of situations such as flipping coins. The first row in Table 12.7 represents the two events associated with flipping one coin (H,T). The second shows the four possible events from flipping two coins (HH, HT, TH, TT).

   Using Pascal's Triangle, compute the probabilities of getting *at least* one head when flipping one coin, two coins, three coins, four coins, five coins, and six coins. To calculate the numerator of each probability, note how many arrangements contain at least one head and look for a pattern in Pascal's Triangle. Enter the results in Table 12.8.

4. The sums of all possible values showing on two dice range from 2 to 12. Conduct an experiment of 50 trials using two dice and construct the bar graph of the sums as shown in Figure 12.38. Compute the experimental probabilities for each sum, 2 through 12. Which sum is most likely to occur? Which is least likely to occur? Try the same activity with commercially available 8-, 12-, or 20-sided dice, or two spinners with appropriate divisions.

5. Invent a board game for children that requires an understanding of simple probability to win. Implement the game with a group of peers and, if possible, students in an actual classroom setting. Evaluate the effectiveness of the game as a teaching aid. Swap game ideas with your peers.

FIGURE 12.37
Chances of Having the
Same Birthday

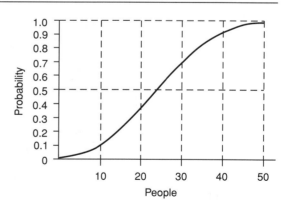

TABLE 12.7
Pascal's Triangle

```
           1 + 1 = 2 events  →  1   1  ← one coin
         1 + 2 + 1 = 4 events  →  1   2   1  ← two coins
       1 + 3 + 3 + 1 = 8 events  →  1   3   3   1  ← three coins
   1 + 4 + 6 + 4 + 1 = 16 events  →  1   4   6   4   1  ← four coins
              32 events  →  1   5   10   10   5   1  ← five coins
              64 events  →  1   6   15   20   15   6   1  → six coins
```

TABLE 12.8
Probability of at Least One Head

COINS	PROBABILITY
1	$P_{head} = 1/(1+1) = 1/2$
2	$P_{head} = (1+2)/(1+2+1) = 3/4$
3	$P_{head} =$
4	$P_{head} =$
5	$P_{head} =$
6	$P_{head} =$

FIGURE 12.38
How Do Dice Add Up?

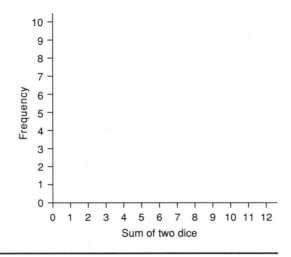

6. Include examples of statistics and probability activities in your idea file.

7. Read one of the *Arithmetic Teacher* articles listed in the "Suggested Readings" section. Write a brief report summarizing the main ideas of the article and describe how the recommendations for instruction might apply to your own mathematics teaching.

INSTRUCTIONAL RESOURCES

CHILDREN'S BOOK

Anno, M. *Anno's magic hat tricks.* Philomel Books. Children learn to think like a scientist while they learn about binary logic and mathematical problem solving.

COMPUTER SOFTWARE

A Chance Look. Sunburst. A probability simulation that shows graphs of experiments with coins, cubes, and spinners.

Exploring Tables and Graphs: Levels 1 and 2. Weekly Reader Family Software. Two programs that teach children how to construct and interpret tables and graphs.

The Graphics Department. Sensible Software, Inc. Makes it easy to generate bar, line, and pie graphs from student-entered data.

MECC Graph. MECC. Easy-to-use graphing tool.

MECC Graphing Primer. MECC. Tutorial that provides instruction in analyzing bar, line, and pie graphs.

REFERENCES

Kelly, M. (1986). Elementary school activity: Graphing the stock market. *Arithmetic Teacher, 33*(7), 17–20.

National Council of Teachers of Mathematics. (1989). *Curriculum and evaluation standards for school mathematics.* Reston, VA: Author.

Vissa, J. (1987). Sampling treats from a school of fish. *Arithmetic Teacher, 34*(7), 36–37.

Zim, H. (1975). *Codes & secret writing.* New York: Scholastic.

SUGGESTED READINGS

Bright, G. (1989). Teaching mathematics with technology: Probability simulations. *Arithmetic Teacher, 36*(9), 16–18.

Bruni, J., & Silverman, H. (1986). Developing concepts in probability and statistics—and much more. *Arithmetic Teacher, 33*(6), 34–37.

Burns, M. (1983). Put some probability in your classroom. *Arithmetic Teacher, 30* (7), 21–22.

Christopher, L. (1982). Graphs can jazz up the mathematics curriculum. *Arithmetic Teacher, 30*(1), 28–30.

Glicksberg, J. (1990). Taste that graph. *Arithmetic Teacher, 38*(4), 53.

Goldman, P. (1990). Teaching arithmetic averaging: An activity approach. *Arithmetic Teacher, 37*(7), 38–43.

Hoffer, A. (1978). *Statistics and information organization.* Palo Alto, CA: Creative Publications.

Horak, V., & Horak, W. (1983). Take a chance. *Arithmetic Teacher, 30*(9), 8–15.

Jacobs, H. (1970). *Mathematics: A human endeavor.* San Francisco, CA: Freeman.

Johnson, E. (1981). Bar graphs for first graders. *Arithmetic Teacher, 29*(4), 30–31.

Nibbelink, W. (1982). Graphing for any grade. *Arithmetic Teacher, 30*(3), 28–31.

O'Neil, D., & Jensen, R. (1982). Looking at facts. *Arithmetic Teacher, 29*(8), 12–15.

Paull, S. (1990). Not just an average unit. *Arithmetic Teacher, 38*(4), 54–58.

Shaw, J. (1984). Dealing with data. *Arithmetic Teacher, 31*(9), 9–15.

Shulte, A. (1979). A case for statistics. *Arithmetic Teacher, 26*(6), 24.

Shulte, A. (Ed.). (1981). *Teaching statistics and probability: 1981 yearbook.* Reston, VA; National Council of Teachers of Mathematics.

Shulte, A., & Choate, S. (1977). *What are my chances? Books A & B.* Palo Alto, CA: Creative Publications.

Silvey, L. (1978). *Polyhedra dice games for grades 5 to 10.* Palo Alto, CA: Creative Publications.

Slaughter, J. (1983). The graph examined. *Arithmetic Teacher, 30*(7), 41–45.

Souviney, R. (1976). Probability and statistics. *Learning Magazine, 5*(4), 51–52.

Souviney, R. (1977). Quantifying chance. *Arithmetic Teacher, 25*(3) 24–26.

Souviney, R. (1986). Problem solving tips for teachers: Conducting experiments. *Arithmetic Teacher, 33*(6), 56–57.

Vissa, J. (1988). Probability and combinations for third graders. *Arithmetic Teacher, 36*(4), 33–37.

Woodward, E. (1983). A second-grade probability and graphing lesson. *Arithmetic Teacher, 30*(7), 23–24.

Zawojewski, J. (1988). Teaching statistics: Mean, median, and mode. *Arithmetic Teacher, 35*(7), 25–26.

PART

III

Methods and Activities for Science

As an esteemed subject of the curriculum, science has had a roller-coaster ride in the twentieth century. This final decade of the century has seen a rejuvenation of national and local emphasis on the importance of children having early, continued, and meaningfully connected experiences in science. Science is at last recognized as a basic discipline. As stated in *Educating Americans for the 21st Century,* "The basics of the twenty-first century are not only reading, writing and arithmetic . . . [but also] include communication and higher problem-solving skills, and scientific and technological literacy" (National Science Board Commission on Precollege Education in Mathematics, Science and Technology, 1983, p. v.). And, from a 1990 publication of the American Association for the Advancement of Science, "Human survival and the quality of life depend on liberally educated citizens who are able to make informed assessments of the opportunities and risks inherent in the scientific enterprise. . . . Science must be taught as one of the liberal arts, which it unquestionably is" (p. xi).

As you have learned, for higher levels of thinking and for learning that is connected and most meaningful, research supports the use of an integrated curriculum and instructional techniques for social interaction. As a classroom teacher, your instructional task is twofold: (1) to plan for and provide developmentally appropriate hands-on experiences, with useful materials and the supportive environment necessary for children's meaningful exploration and discovery; and (2) to know how to facilitate the most meaningful and longest lasting learning possible once the child's mind has been activated by the hands-on experience. To help you complete those tasks, Chapters 13–17 present instructional techniques that reflect the current best thinking about science teaching.

While preparing national standards for K–12 science education, the National Committee on Science Education Standards and Assessment has articulated a commitment to the following principles (July 1993, p. 1):

1. All students should have the opportunity to learn science.
2. With appropriate opportunities, all students can learn science.
3. Students should learn science in ways that reflect the modes of inquiry that scientists use to understand the natural world.
4. Learning is an active process that occurs best when students act as individuals who are members of a community of learners.
5. The quantity of factual science knowledge that all students are expected to learn needs to be reduced so that students can develop a deeper understanding of science.
6. Science content, teaching, and assessment need to be considered in context and in relationship to each other.

Guided by the work that led to the *Curriculum and Evaluation Standards for School Mathematics* (NCTM, 1989), standards being developed for K–12 science education will center around four general content categories: science as inquiry;

CHAPTER 13
The Science Curriculum
This chapter is adapted from Leslie W. Trowbridge and Rodger W. Bybee, Becoming a Secondary School Science Teacher, *5th ed. (New York: Merrill/Macmillan, 1990), pp. 273–285. By permission of Leslie W. Trowbridge and Rodger W. Bybee and the Macmillan Publishing Company.*

CHAPTER 14
Science-Technology-Society (STS): A Conceptual Framework for Science Curriculum Design
This chapter is adapted from Leslie W. Trowbridge and Rodger W. Bybee, Becoming a Secondary School Science Teacher, *5th ed. (New York: Merrill/Macmillan, 1990), pp. 417–436. By permission of Leslie W. Trowbridge and Rodger W. Bybee and the Macmillan Publishing Company.*

CHAPTER 15
Science Projects, Science Fairs, and Field Experiences
This chapter is adapted from Alfred T. Collette and Eugene L. Chiappetta, Science Instruction in the Middle and Secondary Schools, *3rd ed. (New York: Merrill/ Macmillan, 1994), pp. 259–285. By permission of Alfred T. Collette and Eugene L. Chiappetta and the Macmillan Publishing Company.*

science subject matter; scientific connections; and science and human affairs (National Committee on Science Education Standards and Assessment, July 1993, p. 3).

Chapter 13 of this book focuses on the science curriculum. Chapter 14 narrows in on Science-Technology-Society (STS) as the primary theme for an integrated curriculum design for grades 4–9. STS is one of the most promising aspects of the trend to integrate student learning, an approach that engages students in the active exploration of problems and issues that they have identified and encountered, helping them to make the important connections between science and human affairs.

Student-centered instruction and project-centered methodology are especially emphasized in Chapter 15, which is about projects, science fairs, and field experiences. Because they tend to be direct experiences that employ all sensory input modalities and because they tend to connect student learning in meaningful ways, field trips, science fairs, and project-based instruction are among the most powerful instructional tools available to the classroom teacher. A discussion of the use of demonstrations and student-centered investigations follows in Chapter 16. Building on the topic of aids and resources that was first introduced in Chapter 6, Chapter 17 focuses on the use of modern electronic technology. ■

REFERENCES

American Association for the Advancement of Science. (1990). *The liberal art of science: An agenda for action.* Washington, DC: Author.

National Committee on Science Education Standards and Assessment. (1993, July). *National science education standards: July '93 progress report.* Washington, DC: National Research Council.

National Science Board Commission on Precollege Education in Mathematics, Science and Technology. (1983, September 12). *Educating Americans for the 21st century.* Washington, DC: Author.

CHAPTER 13

The Science Curriculum

This chapter is designed to assist your understanding of the science curriculum relevant to grades 4–9. Specifically, it provides

1. A review of the history of the junior high school and the emergence of the middle school
2. A brief history of the reform of middle school science programs
3. An understanding of the nature of science courses in middle and junior high schools
4. A description of an ideal middle school and its science program
5. A description of newly developed middle school science programs
6. A listing of recently developed science programs for grades 4–9.

By now, you probably recognize that curriculum is really more than content. Your curriculum includes science content, manipulative skills, attitudes you wish to achieve, the context or environment of the classroom, and the means you use to assess student progress. There will be a difference between the science curriculum represented in your school district syllabus, what your textbook presents, what you emphasize, and what your students learn. Discussing the curriculum is more complex than it may seem. Rather than resolve all the issues surrounding the curriculum, we direct most attention here to instructional materials representing different courses of study you may encounter.

Before discussing the curriculum, it is important to provide some background and context for later discussions. We begin with a brief overview of curriculum reform.

A. THE NEED FOR CURRICULAR CHANGE

A major reform in American science education began in the late 1950s.

The date most often referred to as marking the beginning of this reevaluation of our science programs is October 4, 1957, the launching date of *Sputnik I,* the first man-made satellite to orbit the earth. Russian scientists beat our own scientists by a mere four months, but the reverberations set off in education by the rumblings of the first Russian satellite booster were felt for many years.

The curriculum development projects in the United States sparked by this event went on for more than 15 years. A host of new and exciting curricula came into being at all levels, from elementary grades through college. Although the "Golden Age" of curriculum development has now run its course, its impact on curriculum change will continue to be felt well into the future.

The late 1980s and early 1990s is another period of curriculum reform. The issue is not a race to space; instead, it is a need for a strong defense, a sound economy, and a stable environment that is shaping the new curriculum (Champagne & Hornig, 1987). Why do reforms such as these occur? What happens to the science curriculum?

From time to time science programs, or aspects of them, become outdated. Though reasons for curricular obsolescence vary, they are relatively few. Briefly put, changes in society, new understandings about students and learning, and advances in science and technology result in the need for curricular reform. Let us look at the reform movement of the 1960s with these themes in mind.

Before *Sputnik I* spurred reform, science teaching had traditionally been concerned mainly with knowledge—the product of science. Textbooks in subjects such as physics, chemistry, biology, physical science, and general science were written predominantly by high school teachers, whose primary concern was accurately communicating scientific knowledge to the student. As teachers, they were rarely involved in actual scientific research; consequently, the methods of scientific research were given lip service, but students were not given experience using these methods.

As scientific knowledge compounded in the first half of the twentieth century, textbooks became larger, so that they might include the scientific advances and their technological applications. The science disciplines became, for the student, a compendium of knowledge to be memorized. Little attention was paid to the logic of thought development and to the basic cohesiveness of the scientific disciplines.

Recognition of the burgeoning knowledge in each of the sciences led curriculum planners to try new arrangements. However, the real problems caused by excessive attention to applications of scientific knowledge and an encyclopedic approach to the subject were not solved.

The advent of *Sputnik I* was another powerful force for educational reform. When a rival nation launched a satellite before the United States, our society demanded the educational system be severely overhauled and the science curricula received attention first. A new group of individuals took charge of the curriculum—scientists, not teachers, directed most of the major curriculum projects. Their emphasis was vastly different from that of traditional textbooks. The new emphasis was on the structure of knowledge that formed the scientific disciplines and the modes of inquiry used by scientists. The programs of the 1960s and 1970s were quite different from those of the 1940s and 1950s.

The new authors emphasized "big ideas" or conceptual schemes instead of information, and they made extensive use of the laboratory instead of lectures and demonstrations. The curriculum program of the 1960s also incorporated the most recent understanding of how students learn and develop. The works of theorists such as B. F. Skinner, Jean Piaget, and Jerome Brunner were central to the new programs.

To review, science courses remain relatively stable over the years. New courses enter the curriculum from time to time, but only after the character of the student population changes, new scientific and technologic advances are made, or national emergencies make their existence necessary. Courses that come into being often find permanent status. Changes in the science curriculum are gradual and reflect changing conditions such as industrial advancements, compulsory school laws, or national defense needs.

From the mid 1970s through the 1980s, there was a gradual shift in textbooks away from the models of the "Golden Age" of reform. Science textbooks became larger as more and more information was included; they reduced the emphasis on the laboratory and teachers and returned to an emphasis on lecture, discussion, and demonstrations (Brunkhorst & Padilla, 1987). For the reasons just cited, the late 1980s and 1990s are a new period of reform for middle/junior high and high school science programs.

B. JUNIOR HIGH AND MIDDLE SCHOOLS

As you learned in Chapter 1, adolescence is a period of significant physical, intellectual, social, and emotional development. The fact that adolescence generally spans the years of secondary education makes understanding this period generally important, but of particular importance is the period of junior high or middle school. Education during the middle school years, generally from ages 10 to 14, must extend the experiences of elementary school; the goals, curriculum, and instruction for science should be conceptualized and implemented as unique and congruent with the particular needs of the developing adolescent. In recent years, educators have increasingly realized the crucial and singular role of education during adolescence. In the next section, we review the history of junior high and middle schools, then return to science programs for this level of secondary education.

History of the Junior High Science Curriculum

Describing science education during early adolescent years is somewhat confused by the fact that there are apparently two different school systems for this age group; one is termed middle school, the other junior high school. This situation is clarified by a brief history.

In the latter part of the nineteenth century, most elementary schools included grades 1 through 8 while high schools included grades 9 through 12. By 1920, about 80 percent of students graduating from high school had experienced eight years of elementary and four years of high school. While the schools were actually structured in this eight-four plan, leading educators continually debated school organization for over three decades beginning in the 1890s. Junior high schools, or school systems with six years elementary, three years junior high, and three years of high school, had emerged in the early 1900s. Not until the 1918 Commission on the Reorganization of Secondary Education (CRSE) did the junior high become firmly established in the American education system. The 1918 CRSE report, *Cardinal Principles of Secondary Education,* stated

> We, therefore, recommend a reorganization of the school system whereby the first six years shall be devoted to elementary education designed to meet the needs of pupils approximately 6 to 12 years of age, and the second six years to secondary education designed to meet the needs of pupils approximately 12 to 18 years of age. The six years to be devoted to secondary education may well be divided into two periods which may be designated as the junior and senior periods (pp. 12–13).

The concept of junior high schools was established, and their numbers grew. In 1920 there were an estimated 800 junior high schools in the United States. And by 1930 there were 1,787 separate junior high schools. While the numbers of junior high schools were increasing, so were criticisms of these schools. The reasons for the rapid increase of junior high schools were shortages of facilities and economic restraints placed on schools between World War I and World War II. Justifications for junior high programs cited the needs of adolescents, the transition to high school, the elimination of dropouts, and vocational preparation. By 1940 prominent educators had developed a rationale for the junior high school. Gruhn and Douglas summarize the essential functions of junior high schools as

- *Integration.* Basic skills, attitudes, and understanding learned previously should be coordinated into effective behaviors.
- *Exploration.* Individuals should explore special interests, aptitudes, and abilities for educational opportunities, vocational decisions, and recreational choices.
- *Guidance.* Assistance should be provided for students making decisions regarding education, careers, and social adjustment.
- *Differentiation.* Educational opportunities and facilities should provide for varying backgrounds, interests, and needs of the students.
- *Socialization.* Education should prepare early adolescents for participation in a complex democratic society.
- *Articulation.* Orientation of the program should provide a gradual transition from preadolescent (elementary) education to a program suited to the needs of adolescents (1977, p. 133).

The reality of the time, however, was that most teachers were trained for the high school and had little desire to teach at the junior high level. A junior high school teaching job was perceived as a stepping stone to a high school position. The important goals of education for early adolescents were forgotten or ignored, and education in grades 7, 8, and 9 became scaled-down versions of that in grades 10, 11, and 12. Criticisms of junior high schools continued into the 1960s. Some of the criticisms were

- a shortage of qualified professionals,
- lack of agreement on purpose,
- high dropout rates,
- programs (athletics, music, and social) that were inappropriate for early adolescents,
- ineffective discipline, and
- teachers who did not understand early adolescents.

Emergence of Middle Schools

During the 1960s, several factors contributed to the emergence of the middle school as an alternative to junior high schools. Some of the factors included general criticisms of the schools and a need to increase the quality of education; an emphasis on curriculum improvement in science, mathematics, and foreign language; renewed interest in preparation for college; recognition of Jean Piaget's work in developmental psychology; the need to eliminate de facto racial segregation; restructuring of schools due to overcrowding; and a general desire to improve education. These and other factors contributed to an increase from 100 middle schools in 1960 to over 5,000 in 1980. In 1988, there were 12,000 separate middle schools with an estimated enrollment of 8,000,000 students.

We think the middle school is an important conceptual and physical change in the education system. Some of the important characteristics of the middle school were described in a 1981 report, *The Status of Middle School and Junior High School Science* (Hurd, Robinson, McConnell, & Ross):

- A program specifically designed for pre- and early adolescents
- A program that encourages exploration and personal development
- A positive and active learning environment
- A schedule that is flexible with respect to time and grouping
- A staff that recognizes students' needs, motivation, fears, and goals
- An instructional approach that is varied
- An emphasis on acquiring essential knowledge, skills, and attitudes in a sequential and individual manner
- An emphasis on developing decision-making and problem-solving skills
- Interdisciplinary learning and team teaching.

Middle schools, in structure and function, have many advantages; several thought important follow.

- The middle school has a unique status; the school and program are not "junior" to another program.
- Specific subjects, like science and mathematics, can be introduced at lower grades by specialists.
- Developing new middle schools provides the impetus for redesigning goals, curriculum, and instruction for the early adolescent learner.
- Development of middle schools can facilitate changes in teacher certification standards and, subsequently, teacher education programs.
- Some discipline problems can be eliminated through different groupings of students, primarily the inclusion of younger students.
- Middle schools can be designed to provide greater guidance and counseling at the time it is needed.

Time will answer questions about the role of middle schools in American education. We believe their time has come, and they will be recorded as an important educational advance. The present period of reform should contribute substantially to their implementation, but in the interim we have both middle and junior high schools. Science programs and science teachers must be prepared for either, since student characteristics are not changed by the grade-level designation of the school.

C. REFORM OF JUNIOR HIGH SCHOOL SCIENCE PROGRAMS

Science in the junior high school has been faced with perplexing problems since its inception. General science was the course offered in the ninth grade of 84 schools when the first junior high schools came into existence. Begun in the decade 1910–1920, the course was designed to satisfy the needs and interests of students in early adolescence. The first course was established through research and was designed to fill a perceived need.

Several difficulties were encountered in junior high school science. There was a shortage of well-trained general science teachers. Many teachers at this level were physics, chemistry, and biology teachers whose primary interest was not the problems of junior high school science. Also, teachers in other disciplines such as English, mathematics, and physical education were recruited to teach science. For these reasons, the general science texts for these grades were written in an effort to relieve this problem, but the variations in school organization such as six-three-three, eight-two-two, and eight-four necessitated much repetition of science topics to produce universally salable textbooks.

There were deficiencies in equipment and facilities for teaching science. Many science classes were taught in ordinary classrooms without water or gas outlets and without adequate facilities for demonstrations and experiments.

There was no clear knowledge of what junior high school science should actually accomplish. Objectives ranged from "preparation for the rigorous science courses in the senior high school" to "general education for good citizenship." Much thought was given to development of attitudes and interests. Some felt that general science should be exploratory in nature. Courses designed on this premise became rapid surveys of chemistry, physics, astronomy, meteorology, biology, and geology. Others believed that students should study the applications of science in the world around them. Courses of this kind dwelt on home appliances, transportation, communication, health problems, and natural resources.

Enrollments in general science grew to about 65 percent of the ninth-grade classes by 1956, then declined as new courses began to permeate the ninth grade and as the seventh and eighth grades took over more of the general science offerings (Brown & Obourn, 1961).

Revision of junior high school science courses through national curriculum studies of the 1960s was delayed, while attention was centered on the senior high school courses. With time, attention turned to the junior high science curriculum.

Middle and junior high school science is usually organized in one of three patterns: (1) a one-, two-, or three-year program called general science; (2) a three-year program in which life, physical, and earth sciences are taught individually for a year each; (3) a one-, two-, or three-year program of integrated or thematically organized science. One of the first two patterns is found in the majority of schools (Hurd et al., 1981, p. 15). Before reviewing some programs developed during the "Golden Age" of science education, we will note that the reform movement of the 1960s and 1970s made no effort to improve general science. In fact, the hope was that by implementing new life, earth, and physical science programs, the traditional general science would eventually be replaced. As we shall see later, this has not occurred. Following is a review of some life, earth, and physical science programs for the middle and junior high school.

Science Courses in the Junior High School

Earth science. Early in 1963, the American Geological Institute was given a grant to support a curriculum development, called the Early Science Curriculum Project (ESCP) for the ninth grade. This course was interdisciplinary, involving geology, meteorology, astronomy, and oceanography. Its emphasis was on laboratory and field study, in which students actively participate in the process of scientific inquiry.

Materials of the ESCP included a textbook, *Investigating the Earth;* the laboratory was augmented by the text, teacher's guide, films, laboratory equipment and maps, and a pamphlet series. After three years of testing and preparation of materials, the course was published commercially.

The Table of Contents from the first edition (1967) included the following chapters:

1. The Changing Earth
2. Earth Materials
3. Earth Measurement
4. Earth Motions
5. Fields and Forces
6. Energy Flow
7. Energy and Air Motions
8. Water in the Air
9. Waters of the Land
10. Water in the Sea
11. Energy, Moisture, and Climate
12. The Land Wears Away
13. Sediments in the Sea
14. Mountains from the Sea
15. Rocks within Mountains
16. Interior of the Earth
17. Time and Its Measurement
18. The Record in Rocks
19. Life—Present and Past
20. Development of a Continent
21. Evolution of Landscapes
22. The Moon: A Natural Satellite
23. The Solar System
24. Stars as Other Suns
25. Stellar Evolution and Galaxies
26. The Universe and Its Origin

The project continued its programs until 1969, when two offshoots, Environmental Studies (ES) and Earth Science Teacher Preparation Project (ESTPP), were initiated to deal specifically with the environmental problems and issues of teacher preparation in the earth sciences.

A serious problem faced by the ESCP was the preparation of persons qualified to teach the course, because of the increasing demand for earth science teachers. Recent efforts in teacher preparation have narrowed the gap between supply and demand. Many earth science teachers have been recruited from other disciplines. Still, there is a problem concerning preparation of qualified earth science teachers. The advances made in the design and implementation of *Investigating the Earth* were commendable. The text design, integration of concepts from life and physical sciences, and careful presentation of knowledge, process, and skills were unprecedented. Subsequent revisions of the text have replaced many traditional topics and realigned the book with other standard earth science texts.

Physical science. Another program developed for the junior high school was the Introductory Physical Science Program of Educational Services, Incorporated. This project was supported by the National Science Foundation. Its purpose was to develop a one-year course in physical science for use in junior high schools. Laboratory work is emphasized, and equipment has been designed in such a way that students can perform the experiments in ordinary classrooms. The Table of Contents of the IPS course includes the following chapters:

1. Introduction
2. Quantity of Matter: Mass
3. Characteristic Properties
4. Solubility and Solvents
5. The Separation of Substances
6. Compounds and Elements
7. Radioactivity

8. The Atomic Model of Matter
9. Sizes and Masses of Atoms and Molecules
10. Molecular Motion
11. Heat

The Introductory Physical Science (IPS) course was tested in several centers throughout the United States and the materials, which included textbooks, teachers' guides, laboratory notebooks, and comprehensive apparatus kits, were eventually made available through commercial sources.

The attractiveness of the IPS course to better-than-average junior high school students was made clear in the results of a test survey of representative IPS students in the 1965–1966 school year. "In that year, 1,005 ninth-grade IPS students and 400 eighth-grade IPS students took the School and College Abilities Test (SCAT) Survey Form, a test of verbal and mathematical ability. The results made it clear that the IPS students were more scholastically able on the average than typical junior high school students in the nation" (*Introductory Physical Science—Physical Science II: A Progress Report,* 1968, p. 16).

As the success of a new course depends on well-qualified teachers, the National Science Foundation supported a program to locate qualified science teachers and to prepare them to instruct other teachers in the use of IPS. The program was quite successful; in IPS workshops, teachers were trained by their peers in the local environment.

Integrated science. Several other junior high school courses have appeared on the scene in recent years. Among them are the Intermediate Science Curriculum Study (ISCS), financed by the U.S. Office of Education and National Science Foundation and developed at Florida State University. Three levels were prepared, corresponding to the junior high school grades seven, eight, and nine. Level I for seventh grade was tightly structured. Its title, *Energy, Its Forms and Characteristics,* permitted students to delve into physical-science principles by dealing with things of science in their environment. Level II puts the student more and more on her own in designing experiments and recording and interpreting her data. This level deals with *Matter and its Composition and Model Building.* Level III for the ninth grade deals with biological concepts and is designed to use laboratory blocks six to eight weeks long as its basic plan of operation. The student is expected to use the concepts and investigative skills acquired in the seventh and eighth grades. All of the class activity in the ISCS course is planned for individualized work. The teacher's main duty is assisting students to work on their own. No formal lectures or information-dispensing sessions are planned for the course, unless needed on a short-term basis by a small group of students.

An innovative feature of the ISCS course is the production of a complete course on Computer-Assisted Instruction (CAI). Using behavioral objectives and a system of computer feedback, it was possible to obtain detailed information on the progress and problems encountered by each student working in the system. This information was used to modify and revise the trial versions of the course.

There are other smaller-scale projects for revising junior high school science. Among them are the Interaction Science Curriculum Project (ISCP), Ideas and Investigations in Science (IIS), and a BSCS program titled *Patterns and Processes in Science.* Each has been extensively field-tested, and certain elements of success have been claimed. It is safe to say that the field of science teaching in the junior high school has received an impetus similar to that enjoyed by senior high school teaching a few years earlier. Since the basic philosophy in the two areas was the same, it is likely that pupils fortunate enough to participate in these courses at both the junior and senior high school levels will be prepared in science more effectively than before.

The Junior High and Middle School Science Curriculum of the 1970s

A report by Iris Weiss provides some valuable insights concerning the science curriculum in middle and junior high schools, classes offered, and enrollments (Weiss, 1977). General science was offered in 70 percent of all schools with only grades 7–9. This far surpasses the percentage of schools offering life science (21 percent), earth science (20 percent), and physical science (13 percent). The most commonly offered science course in grades 7–9 was general science; 30 percent of all science classes were general. Twenty-five percent of all classes in grades 7–9 were earth science, 16 percent life science, and 15 percent physical science (Weiss, 1987). In 1978, the largest science enrollment in junior high and middle schools was in general science, with approximately 5 million students. Another 2 million students in schools with grades 7–12 or 9–12 were also enrolled in general science. In all, approximately 7 million students were enrolled in general science in 1978. In comparison, life, earth, and physical enrollments for comparable schools had about 1.25 million students per discipline area. The total enrollment in discipline-oriented science did not exceed that in general science. Enrollment in life, earth, and physical science courses was just over half (about 4 million) of the total number of students in general science in 1978. In 1986, life science, earth science, and physical science were the most commonly offered science courses in grades 7–9. This is a shift away from general science courses.

The Junior High and Middle School Science Curriculum of the 1980s

Curriculum programs at the middle/junior high school level take one of three forms: (1) a factually oriented textbook based on the premise that students must develop a background of information before concepts and inquiry can be used; (2) a "middle-of-the-road" textbook that has encyclopedic facts and vocabulary, a separate laboratory guide, and a separate guide for the "inquiry" teacher to use; and (3) a program that presents science as active involvement by the student. Ninety percent of curriculum programs are represented by textbooks of types (1) and (2). The next paragraphs summarize programs of types (1) and (2), the present status for about 90 percent of the middle/junior high school science curriculum.

The goals are typically (1) to present the fundamental concepts representative of biological, physical, and earth science disciplines; (2) to acquaint students with scientific inquiry (the scientific method) such as by making observations, recording information, and reporting findings; (3) to acquire "scientific attitudes," such as curiosity, respect for valid and reliable information, critical thinking, willingness to be wrong, and appreciation of the cultural contributions of science; and (4) to acquire skills associated with inquiry development, such as recording observations in suitable ways (e.g., as tables, charts, and graphs) and doing experiments or designing investigations.

The goal dominating all of the textbooks is scientific knowledge. The major emphasis is upon acquiring information about the physical and biological world. Scientific knowledge is presented as knowing facts. In some textbooks an effort is made to have students organize their learning into concepts, for example, "living things are related to their environment," or "matter is neither created nor destroyed."

Scientific inquiry as represented in laboratory activities is usually distributed throughout textbooks. These activities require students to actually do something in the laboratory. In contrast to this type of "activity" there are occasional experiments or situations in which students have to answer questions or solve problems by gathering and interpreting information in an organized way. In experiments students are required to measure, count, or describe observations in some quantitative way. Only a few textbooks make a special effort to use laboratory activities as an integral part of the curriculum program.

What about the goals of social issues and personal needs? Social issues such as population growth, air quality, health and disease, land use, water resources, energy shortages, and environmental pollution are typically presented in a single chapter in the textbook. Science-related social issues are identified but are not explored or investigated in terms of the complexities of problems; the short- and long-term effects of the problems; appropriate, reasonable, and prudent actions that might be taken; or the role of personal, governmental, or industrial responsibilities. The goal of personal needs is really only recognized in life science programs. Topics such as health, nutrition, disease, and drugs are examples of this goal in middle and junior high school science programs.

Little effort is made in middle/junior high school programs to develop career awareness. There are occasional photographs of famous scientists, engineers, or individuals working in health professions. The variety of career options within the sciences and engineering is usually not presented. However, the extent to which science teachers actually direct attention toward this goal is not known. Greater recognition should be given to this goal since adolescence is a time when attitudes about career options are formulated.

What about the NSF curriculum programs developed in the 1960s? In 1976–1977, at least one federally funded science program was being used in 39 percent of the school districts. The programs being used in school districts and the percentage of districts using the materials were Earth Science Curriculum Project (ESCP)—12 percent, Intermediate Science Curriculum Study (ISCS)—11 percent, Introductory Physical Science (IPS)—8.6 percent, and Outdoor Biology Instructional Strategies (OBIS)—3 percent. In the 1986 National Survey only one program, Introductory Physical Science (IPS), was used by more than 2 percent of teachers. Dominating the middle/junior high school market are commercial programs that were certainly influenced by, but not developed during, the "Golden Age" of reform.

In most ways, the middle and junior high school science curriculum is once again a reflection of high school programs. It is a "junior" version of senior high school science. Reading level is lower, vocabulary is defined more frequently, and there is some recognition of the needs and interests of early adolescents. We think there is a vital need to redesign middle and junior high school science programs. Adolescence is a unique period of human development and the education program should reflect this uniqueness.

Table 13.1 shows selected science curricula. Some of the NSF programs developed during the "Golden Age" are presented, as well as some of the most frequently used programs.

The need for curricular change was evident. In the first years of the 1980s there were numerous committees, commissions, reports, and books proclaiming the need for reform in American education. These reports return to themes mentioned in an earlier section. Changes in society, new understandings about students, and advances in science and technology all underscore the need for change in the curriculum.

TABLE 13.1
The Grade 4–9 Science Curriculum: Selected Programs

	HIGHLY STRUCTURED	MODERATELY STRUCTURED	LOOSELY STRUCTURED
4TH & 5TH GRADES	SCIENCE—A PROCESS APPROACH (S—APA) Text Series e.g. *Accent on Science* (Merrill) *Concepts in Science* (Harcourt) *Health Science Series* (Heath)	SCIENCE CURRICULUM IMPROVEMENT STUDY (SCIS) LIFE-PHYSICAL SCIENCE SEQUENCE	ELEMENTARY SCIENCE STUDY (ESS) UNITS • Pond Water • Microgardening • Changes
6TH GRADE	S—APA Text Series e.g. *Accent on Science* (Merrill) *Concepts in Science* (Harcourt)	SCIS— • Life Science • Physical Science	ESS UNITS • Small Things • Streamtables
7TH GRADE	*Energy—Its Form and Characteristics* (ISCS) *Interaction of Man and Biosphere* (Rand) *Focus on Life Science* (Merrill) *Life Science* (Scott, Foresman)	*Modular Activities in Science* (Houghton-Mifflin) *You and the Environment* (Houghton-Mifflin)	ESS UNITS • Rocks & Charts • Mapping
8TH GRADE	*Introductory Physical Science* (IPS) *Interaction of Matter and Energy* (Rand) *Principles of Science* (Merrill) *Focus on Physical Science* (Merrill)	*Matter and Its Composition and Model Buildings* (ISCS) *Ideas and Investigations in Science—Physical Science* (Prentice-Hall)	ESS UNITS • Kitchen Physics • Pendulums • Batteries and Bulbs II
9TH GRADE	*Focus on Earth Science* (Merrill) *Investigating the Earth* (ESCP) *Physical Science II* (Prentice-Hall) *Modern Biology* (Holt) *Introductory Physical Science* (Prentice-Hall)	*Ideas and Investigations in Science—Earth Science* (Prentice-Hall)	*Probing the Natural World*—Biology (ISCS)

NOTE: These programs were selected on the basis of frequency of use, NSF development, and different organizational structure. Curriculum project or publisher is given in parentheses.

The 1980s was a period of transition and reform for middle/junior high school programs. In 1986, the National Science Teachers Association (NSTA) published a position statement entitled "Science Education for Middle and Junior High Students."

This position statement described the goals and orientation for curriculum and instruction:

> The primary function of science education at the middle and junior high level is to provide students with the opportunity to explore science in their lives and to become comfortable and personally involved with it. Certainly science curriculum at this level should reflect society's goals and scientific and technological literacy and emphasize the role of science for personal, social, and career use, as well as prepare students academically (Brunkhorst & Padilla, 1987, p. 62).

This position statement continued with a specific discussion indicating that the science curriculum should fulfill the needs of the early adolescent and address both the personal needs of students and issues of a global society. Experience at this level should be concrete, manipulative, and physical. The position statement recommended the curricula should focus on the relationship of science to

- content from life, physical, earth sciences, and ecology, with frequent interdisciplinary references;
- process skills, such as experimenting, observing, measuring, and inferring;
- personal use in everyday applications and in practical problem solving that allows open-ended exploration;
- social issues that involve individual responsibilities and call for decision making;
- all careers;
- limitations of science and the necessity of respecting differing, well-considered points of view;
- developing written and oral communication skills; and
- positive attitudes and personal success (p. 62).

The NSTA position statement is important for two reasons. First, the clear emphasis on the student differentiates this curriculum from high school programs. And second, there is a definite trend toward the middle school and away from the junior high school. Table 13.2 displays some characteristics of science curricula for middle schools and aligns those characteristics with middle school programs.

The Middle School Science Curriculum of the 1990s

In 1988, the National Science Foundation (NSF) issued a request for proposals to develop programs for middle school science. The NSF solicitation contained descriptions of the orientation for middle school programs, emphasizing that students in middle school years should develop a disciplined approach to inquiry and experimentation, that they should improve their skills in organizing and articulating knowledge, and that they should develop their skills at approaching problems systematically (National Science Foundation, 1988).

Included in the solicitation were some characteristics of middle school materials. Those characteristics included the following:

- integration of science with other subjects,
- hands-on experiences,
- establish a coherent pattern of science topics,
- capitalize on the interests of students,
- use of recent research on teaching and learning, and
- identification of standards of student achievement.

In the 1990s, the programs developed with these NSF grants will be available. You should be familiar with the orientation of the programs. What follows is a brief description of the programs developed in this reform of science education at the middle school.

Science and technology: investigating human dimensions (Rodger W. Bybee, Biological Sciences Curriculum Study). This Biological Sciences Curriculum Study (BSCS) project is a three-year, activity-based, middle school science and technology program for grades 5–9 with the following characteristics:

TABLE 13.2

Ideal Middle Schools and Science Programs

CHARACTERISTICS OF AN IDEAL MIDDLE SCHOOL	CHARACTERISTICS AND/OR NEEDS OF A NEW SCIENCE PROGRAM
• Teachers knowledgeable about and committed to the education of early adolescents	• Teacher education programs and staff development specifically for middle school science
• A balanced curriculum of academic goals and developmental needs of adolescents	• A balance of knowledge, inquiry, personal needs, social issues, and career awareness goals
• Different organizational arrangements for instruction, e.g., individual, small group, large group	• A mixture of instructional groupings, e.g., individual projects, group activities, and large group presentations
• A variety of instructional methods	• Use of traditional and new methods such as simulations, role modeling, debate, and use of computers
• An active learning environment	• Use of problem-solving, laboratory investigations, field studies, and other activities
• Flexible scheduling	• Schedules designed for class presentations, field trips, individual projects, etc.
• Continuous progress	• A coordinated science program across the middle school years to provide a smooth transition from elementary to high school
• Students master skills of decision making and problem solving	• Emphasis on scientific processes, information processing, and decision making
• Cooperative planning and coordinated teaching	• Science, mathematics, and social studies teachers plan the STS program and teach units in parallel or as a team
• Exploratory and enrichment studies	• Opportunities to meet and interact with a variety of individuals in the community whose careers are in science, technology, and mathematics
• Interdisciplinary learning	• An integrated approach to science
• Emphasis on all three domains	• Science programs that emphasize knowledge, attitudes, and skills related to science and technology integrated with personal needs and social issues

SOURCE: The characteristics of an ideal middle school are based on several sources including *The Exemplary Middle School* by William Alexander and Paul George (1981), *The Essential Middle School* by G. Wiles and H. Bondi (1981), *This We Believe* by the National Middle School Association (1982), *The Middle School We Need* by Thomas Gatewood and Charles Dilg (1975), and a 1973 article entitled, "Do You Have a Middle School?" by Nicholas Georgiady and Louis Romano.

- a focus on the development of the early adolescent,
- strategies to encourage the participation of female, minority, and handicapped students,
- an emphasis on reasoning and critical thinking skills,
- cooperative learning as a key instructional strategy,
- an instructional model that enhances student learning,
- a conceptual approach to science and technology,
- an introduction to careers in science and technology fields,
- a continuation of the BSCS K–6 program,
- inclusion of science-technology-society (STS) themes, and
- a plan to enhance the implementation of the program.

Science and Technology: Investigating Human Dimensions will be a unique program for the middle school. Because the program is unique, both evaluation and implementation will be an integral aspect of the program.

The BSCS program will be published by Kendall/Hunt Publishing Company and the materials supplied by Science Kit & Boreal Laboratories.

Improving urban middle school science (Judith Opert Sandler, Educational Development Center). Educational Development Center's proposed project is a multidisciplinary science program for the seventh and eighth grade that is targeted to the needs of early adolescents in urban environments. Modules integrate scientific concepts and understandings from the physical, human and health, life, and earth sciences within the context of science, society, and technology problems. This project will build on the conceptual framework and pedagogical strategies, school district partnerships, teacher training design, and assessment and publishing partnerships established through the NSF-funded Improving Urban Elementary Science Project currently under development at EDC and Sunburst Communications.

School districts and teachers in Boston, Cleveland, Los Angeles, San Francisco, Baltimore, and Montgomery County, Maryland, will collaborate fully in the development effort and field-testing. Operation SMART, a research and development project of the Girls Clubs of America, will consult on informal science education strategies which are particularly responsive to urban youth and which will complement the curriculum. The materials will be reviewed for scientific accuracy and pedagogical soundness by a distinguished advisory panel, while field-testing and evaluation will be conducted by the Boston College Center for the Study of Testing, Evaluation, and Educational Policy (CSTEEP). Sunburst Communications, Inc., will publish the final product and field-test materials, contribute to a Teacher Development Fund, and provide technical assistance throughout the project to ensure marketability of the proposed modules.

Explorations in middle school science (Ruth Von Blum, Education Systems Corporation).

To address the special needs of our middle schools and junior high schools, Education Systems Corporation promises a computer-based program that will be developed by a highly qualified team of content experts, science educators, instructional designers, and marketers. Participants will include practicing scientists; teachers and other representatives from such professional organizations as the National Science Teachers Association and the National Association of Biology Teachers; seven major school districts; the California State Department of Education; Apple, Tandy, and IBM; and Education Systems Corporation, a successful developer and marketer of computer software for schools. And the University of California, Irvine, will be responsible for the evaluation and teacher-training portions of the project.

Explorations in Middle School Science will provide a set of 90 computer lessons in life, earth, and physical science for grades 6–9. At the heart of each lesson will be a computer-simulated laboratory to involve students in "doing" science and improving (1) understanding of science concepts by applying critical thinking to solve problems; (2) skills in scientific processes and communication; and (3) attitudes about science.

These lessons will reflect specific science education objectives in state guidelines from across the country and realize the full power of computer technology to reach these objectives. Students will use a number of online tools (notebook, data base manager, calculator) to help them perform the simulated laboratory experiments, most of which would be too difficult, dangerous, or time consuming to be done in a "live" laboratory. Suggested extension investigations will lead the students to experience nature firsthand, away from the computer. Explorations in Middle School Science will be modular, flexible, and well documented. The lessons will be strongly curriculum based and run on a networked, managed system of microcomputers with 16 colors, sound, mouse input, and excellent graphics.

Interactive Middle Grades Science (George Dawson, Florida State University, science education program).

The Interactive Middle Grades Science (IMS) Project will apply many of the latest recommendations for change in science education to the critical middle grades. Florida State University at Tallahassee and Houghton Mifflin Company will develop a science program for grades six through eight that will meet the diverse needs of today's teachers and students. IMS will integrate teachers, textbook, and laboratory with applications of the microcomputer and the laser videodisc, producing a commercially marketable system for science instruction, classroom management, and student evaluation. Science content, processes, and skills focusing on appropriate problems of science, technology, and society will be integral parts of the program. This joint effort will involve professional societies and distinguished science educators and will be consistent with guidelines offered by the National Science Teachers Association and National Association of Secondary School Principals.

Florida State University has built a reputation in curriculum development through the principal investigator in this project and other well-known staff members who will be available to assist in the development of the IMS program. The partners in this project, the School and Educational Software Divisions (ESD) of Houghton Mifflin Company, have designed and marketed high-quality computer software for the elementary and secondary school market since 1966. The publisher will invest in excess of $14 million in this project during the three-year development phase and will contribute substantially to its continuance and teacher training.

Additional Programs for Teaching Science, Grades 4–9

Other programs for teaching science in grades 4–9, most of which reflect in some way the principles discussed at the introduction to Part III, are as follows.

For grades k–6:

Britannica Science System and the *Full Option Science System* (Encyclopaedia Britannica Educational Corporation). A middle school component is under preparation (Lowery, 1994).

Discover Science (1993, Scott, Foresman).

Elementary Science Study (ESS) (Delta Education, Inc.).

Explorations in Science and *Addison-Wesley Science* (Addison-Wesley).

Exploring Science (Macro Press).

HBJ Science, Nova Edition and *Holt Science,* and *Concepts in Science* (Harcourt Brace School Publishers).

Science Curriculum Improvement Study (SCIS3) (Delta Education, Inc.).

Science—A Process Approach (SAPA) (Delta Education, Inc.).

Science and Technology for Children (Carolina Biological Supply Company).

Silver Burdett & Ginn Science (1989) and *Science Horizons* (1990) (Silver Burdett & Ginn).

For grades k–8:

Macmillan/McGraw-Hill Science (1989).

For grades 6–8:

Merrill Science (1993–1994, Glencoe).

Middle School Science & Technology (Kendall/Hunt).

Prentice-Hall Science Learning System (1994).

For grades 6–9:

Challenge of Discovery science program (D. C. Heath).

Foundational Approaches in Science Teaching (University of Hawaii).

Macmillan science program (1989, Macmillan/McGraw Hill).

Prentice-Hall Science Integrated Learning System (1994) and *Prentice-Hall* earth science, physical science, and life science programs (1993).

Science Insights (1994–1995, Addison-Wesley).

For grade 7:

Science 2000 (Decision Development Corporation).

For grades 7–8:

Spaceship Earth program (Houghton Mifflin).

For grades 7–9:

Holt Science program (Holt, Rinehart, and Winston).

Science Plus, Technology and Society (Holt, Rinehart, and Winston).

SUMMARY

Adolescence is a unique period of life. Over our educational history, we have seen changes in the science curriculum for this age group. The junior high school was created in the late 1800s. Then in the late 1900s, there emerged the middle school. Junior high schools were "junior" versions of high school programs. The middle school curriculum is uniquely designed for the early adolescent.

Although textbooks were significantly changed during the 1960s and 1970s, the 1980s and 1990s have witnessed a return to models similar to those prior to the 1960s. Contemporary reform will have an impact on middle/junior high school programs to come. Several new NSF programs serve as models for science education at the middle school level.

QUESTIONS AND ACTIVITIES FOR DISCUSSION

1. Based on the statistics cited in this chapter, what conclusion do you reach about (a) science curriculum changes in middle and junior high school, (b) the role of the government in curriculum development, and (c) the role of science teachers in curriculum reform?

2. If you were going to reform the science curriculum in one middle school, how would you approach the task?

3. At some time in your career, you will select a new textbook. This activity introduces you to that process. The form you will complete is adapted from the American Association for the Advancement of Science publication *Science Books & Films.* (See also Chapter 4.)

Select three textbooks from the discipline and grade level you intend to teach. Review the textbooks and complete the following chart. List the textbooks you compare by author(s), title, publisher, and copyright date.

Textbooks

1.

2.

3.

GENERAL EVALUATION	N/C	POOR	FAIR	ADEQUATE	GOOD	EXCELLENT
Text						
Content accuracy						
Content currency						
Content scope						
Structure and methods of science						
Organization and coherence						
Comprehensibility						
Labs: in text/ supplementals						
Comprehensibility						
Practicality of required apparatus						
Summary: text supplementals						
Teach the nature of scientific enterprise						
Encourage students to reason to testable conclusions						
Stimulate awareness of science, technology, and society						

1. Were the textbooks for middle school or junior high school?
2. How were the textbooks similar? Different?
3. Describe an outstanding feature of each textbook.
4. Describe the weakest feature of each textbook.
5. Which textbook would you select to use? Why?

REFERENCES

Brown & Obourn (1961). *Offerings and enrollments.* Washington, DC: U.S. Government Printing Office.

Brunkhorst, B., & Padilla, M. (1987). Science education for middle and junior high school students: An NSTA position statement. *Science and Children, 24* (3), 62–63.

Champagne, A. B., & Hornig, L. E. (Eds.). (1987). *This year in school science: The science curriculum.* Washington, DC: American Association for the Advancement of Science.

Commission on the Reorganization of Secondary Education. (1918). *Cardinal principles of secondary education,* Bulletin 1918 (35). Washington, DC: U.S. Bureau of Education, 12–13.

Gruhn, W. T., & Douglas, N. R. (1977). *The modern junior high school* (3rd ed.). New York: The Ronald Press.

Hurd, P. D., Robinson, J. T., McConnell, M., & Ross, N. (1981). *The status of middle school and junior high school science.* Colorado Springs, CO: Center for Educational Research and Evaluation. The Biological Sciences Curriculum Study, The Colorado College.

Introductory physical science—Physical science II: A progress report. (1968). Newton, MA: IPS Group, Educational Development Center.

Lowery, L. F. (1994). Inquiry: The emphasis of a bold, new science curriculum. *T.H.E. Journal, 21* (8), 50, 52.

National Science Foundation. (1988). *Program solicitation: Programs for middle school science instruction.* Washington, DC: National Science Foundation.

Weiss, I. (1977, March). *Report of the 1977 national survey of science, mathematics, and social studies education.* Washington, DC: U.S. Government Printing Office.

Weiss, I. (1987). *Report of the 1985–86 national survey of science and mathematics education.* Research Triangle Park, NC: Research Triangle Institute.

SUGGESTED READINGS

Andersen, H. O. (1994). Teaching toward 2000. *The Science Teacher 61*(6),49–53.

Selby, C. C. (1993). Technology: From myths to realities. *Phi Delta Kappan 74*(9), 684–689.

Science-Technology-Society (STS): A Conceptual Framework for Science Curriculum Design

This chapter is designed to further your understanding of the significance of science-technology-society to science curriculum and instruction. Specifically, it is designed to help you understand the

1. Contributions of science and technology to society.
2. Significance of science-related social changes that have occurred in society.
3. Contemporary challenges of science and technology in society.
4. Importance of science-technology-society connections in the science curriculum and the themes associated with STS interaction.
5. Importance of integrating science and mathematics.
6. Importance of a curriculum that is organized around problem-solving skills, real-life issues, and personal and community decision making.
7. Meaning of scientific and technologic literacy.
8. Conceptual framework for knowledge, skills, and values of scientific and technologic literacy.
9. Unifying concepts for science-technology-society.
10. Inquiry skills based on science and technology.

As we approach the year 2000, most people living in industrial societies are enjoying a quality of life unprecedented in history. Children survive traumas and diseases of premature birth and early childhood that would have been fatal a few decades ago. The elderly live longer and enjoy the benefits of health and well-being. Personal living is more convenient and pleasant, and our natural and human environments enrich our lives. Science and technology are largely responsible for these and many other benefits that enhance life and living.

The year 2000 is also growing near for the three-quarters of the world's population not living in industrialized societies. These people still await the benefits of science and technology that promise to ease their pain, feed their hungry, and reduce their burdens of labor. Science and technology could also contribute to improving their quality of life. But as yet the promises have not come to fruition.

Until recently, one could not have written these paragraphs about the benefits and promises of science and technology. The degree to which science and technology influence our lives and transform societies is only now being realized. For two centuries science and technology have increasingly shaped the character of American society. Throughout most of history the interaction and significance among science, technology, and society went unrecognized. During this time, however, the interaction continually changed. Citizens became aware of the promises of science and technology. Government became involved in the support of research and development. Science evolved from "little" to "big." Technology also became larger and more sophisticated. With little fanfare, science and technology slowly moved to center stage in society.

A paradox has also recently emerged. Scientific advances and technological innovation have contributed to *both* social progress and cultural problems. And, many of the same citizens who became aware of the scientific and technological promises also became aware of the problems. While science and technology moved to center stage, the stage was also being set for a conflict between science, technology, and democratic participation. How is the conflict to be resolved? Enter here the increasing role of public policy debates.

Many critical decisions related to the role of science and technology have to be made by the nation. The decisions will be made relative to many local and regional issues—land use, acid rain, atmospheric conditions, carbon dioxide, toxic waste dumps, energy shortages, preservation of endangered species, and water resources to name only a few examples. Decisions will also be made concerning budgets for research and development and the role of public and private institutions' support of science and technology. Who should make decisions about problems, research, development, or applications? The federal government? Scientists? Citizens? On what basis should these decisions be made? Economic? Moral? Contributions to the public health and social welfare of the nation? Increasing knowledge for knowledge's sake? Fulfilling the needs of humanity? General recognition of these questions has brought about problems concerning the public's ability to participate in decision making and policy development within American society.

Several factors underlie the general problems of public participation in science- and technology-related issues. Democratic participation is more widespread, *but* the groups often have a single-issue orientation. Public interest in participation has increased, *but* the public often lacks the ways and means to influence decisions. There has been greater reliance on experts to explain complex issues related to science and technology, *but* the experts often do not agree and, in addition, many have ventured beyond facts into the domain of ethics and values. The media have increased public awareness of science- and technology-related issues, *but* public understanding of the concepts, values, and processes involved in contemporary issues is lacking.

These and other factors converge on the need to identify appropriate means of directing science and technology while simultaneously maintaining the independence of scientists and engineers to pursue their research and development and the freedom of the public to participate in decisions and policies affecting their lives. With time, this fundamental tension between scientific independence and social control will only increase. A careful balance must be reached in the coming years. Achieving a balance between the values of science and society suggests the need for citizens to be well informed concerning social issues and the facts and values related to the costs, benefits, and consequences of decisions about science, technology, and society (STS). There is need for a new scientific and technologic literacy. Recognizing and responding to this need means there will be a fundamental reform of science education.

This is a general introduction to more specific themes and discussions of this chapter. First, there is a science education context for later discussion. A second section is on the historical contributions of science and technology to society. Next is a section describing some significant science-related social changes that have occurred since the *Sputnik*-inspired curriculum reform era. Finally there is a section outlining the contemporary challenges of science and technology in society.

A. A SCIENCE EDUCATION PERSPECTIVE

The date October 4, 1957, was historic in science education. The Soviet Union launched *Sputnik I* on that day, and a curriculum reform movement that was already in progress was propelled forward with both spiritual and fiscal support. Twenty-five years later, October 1982, was an occasion to ask about the condition of science education. Upon examination, the public found that science education was in a state of crisis.

Questions about the curriculum reform movement were pointed. Did the reform movement of the 1960s and 1970s fail? If the new science programs were a success, then why is there a crisis? What was wrong with the new science programs? All of these are legitimate questions and should be answered.

First of all, it can be said that the initial goals were achieved. Thousands of scientists and engineers were brought into the work force. A national goal and appropriate technology landed men on the moon and returned them safely to Earth. In the process, science and mathematics programs and teachers' backgrounds were updated.

Second, why is there a crisis? The answer can be stated directly—the goals for past social challenges are not adequate for present social challenges. The "golden age" of science education has passed. Many of the "new" science programs are twenty-five-years-old or older! Now is the time to develop a perspective suitable for the 1990s and beyond.

Third, at least one mistake was made in the 1960s that is related to the present situation in science education. An implicit question to the reform movement was—"What does a student need to know and do in order to be a scientist or engineer?" The answer—the student should understand the structure of science disciplines and processes of scientific investigation. With these answers, science educators developed programs that appealed primarily to students bound for colleges and universities and eventually for careers in research and development. The mistake was to purge programs of any emphasis on a citizen's use or understanding of science and technology. Teachers continued to claim they were "preparing students for life," but failed to characterize it as the life of a scientist or engineer. This is not an argument about what was done, or what should have been done, if the goal was preparation for careers in science and engineering. This goal was, and continues to be, inappropriate for the majority of our students and inconsistent with the historical goals of public education. The new STS thrust in science education is toward what was *not* done in the 1960s and 1970s, and what must be done in the 1990s. We should provide an education appropriate to needs and concerns of students as future citizens which will enable them to live, work, and participate in a society which is increasingly scientific and technological. There is a need to reinstate personal and societal goals that were eliminated in the 1950s and 1960s. Additionally, we need to update science education to include changes in STS that have occurred in the past decades.

This discussion and brief analysis of science and technology in part serves as a context for the following discussions of STS. It also establishes the position that this chapter is also a rationale and justification for the STS theme.

B. CONTRIBUTIONS OF SCIENCE AND TECHNOLOGY TO SOCIETY

Bertrand Russell's 1952 book, *The Impact of Science on Society,* stands as a particularly cogent early analysis of the interactions among science, technology, and society. Russell suggests that the effects of science have taken several different forms. Science has had *intellectual effects,* for example, a greater stress on empirical observations and the scientific method; *technological effects,* for example, in industry and war, work is more efficient and nations are more powerful; *social organizational effects,* for example, control is more centralized and experts can gain more power; and *philosophical effects,* for example, a new pragmatic philosophy has developed based on utility rather than on truth which ultimately could have disastrous consequences for society. The next paragraphs describe some of the details relative to these contributions.

The first influence science had on society was *intellectual.* Stress on empirical observations and use of scientific methods have served to dispel such things as belief in witchcraft and demons. The result has been a mechanistic world view with the following ingredients:

1. *Observation versus authority.* The resolution of matters concerning the natural world can be ascertained through observation and not through appeal to authorities.
2. *The physical world conforms to natural laws.* There is no need to invoke external forces, such as deities, to explain the movement of objects. The causes for certain effects in the

natural world are found in the natural world itself. We have Galileo and Newton to thank for this world view.

3. *Dethronement of "purpose."* While there is human purpose, there is not room for purpose in scientific explanation. Darwin's theory of evolution through natural selection is a good example of the scientific dethronement of purpose as an explanation.

4. *Human place in the world.* There are two aspects to this intellectual influence. One was the humbling of human perceptions about our place in the universe. Kepler and Copernicus contributed to this changed world view. On the other hand, humans gained a degree of power to cause changes. Prior to the scientific world view, prayer and humility were thought to influence change. This view was replaced with one that encouraged acquiring knowledge and understanding natural laws. The power of the latter was found to be greater and more reliable.

Technology has a long history of important contributions to society. Russell describes two discoveries of the late Middle Ages—gunpowder and the mariner's compass—as critical in the interaction between technology and society. Gunpowder gave military power to governments. The long development and escalation of weapons of war have continued to this day. The compass opened the age of discovery. After these important technologies there was a long period with relatively few applications of knowledge to more efficient ways of doing things. Most people are familiar with other major technological contributions such as the cotton gin, electricity, and the internal combustion engine.

Invention of the telegraph influenced social organizations. Messages could travel faster than people; subsequently, governments had more power to enforce law and order. Power could be located in a central position in governmental and private organizations. This observation is true of many technologies. Power is centralized in a few, and the power is greater than it had been historically.

A very important point about the contributions of technology to society is that technology increases the interactions and interdependence among social systems. In a word, societies become "organic." Witness the more "organic" nature of society as new techniques for information dissemination have developed.

There is an additional point worth noting. Since 1952, when Russell published his essays, the society has extended to a global community that is interdependent in large measure due to technology. The size and power of social organizations have grown not only to international, but global, dimensions.

In a later chapter on "Democracy and Scientific Technique," Russell returns to this "organic" theme and makes a point related to public participation that is common to discussions of STS themes in science education. The message to educators is clear. The means to preserving personal initiative is through educating people about the ways and means of participating in the democratic process. This seems especially applicable in the context of science- and technology-related social issues. This point is even more relevant today than in the 1950s when Russell wrote his essays.

Russell's fourth contribution about philosophy argued strongly that John Dewey's pragmatism ultimately would not be beneficial. Russell maintained that substituting the value of utility for truth was inappropriate.

Additionally, the pragmatic philosophy shifts the balance of science and technology toward technology, due to the emphasis on application and utility. No effort will be made to resolve the philosophical point here. Suffice it to note that different philosophies do prevail and do influence the public's perceptions about science and technology in society.

In his book, Russell identified many contemporary issues that are discussed in the next two sections. In a chapter entitled "Can a Scientific Society be Stable?", he concludes with a set of conditions that a scientific society must fulfill if it is to be stable. These are mentioned here because they are ideal precursors to discussions in the next section on "Contemporary Challenges of Science and Technology in Society." Conditions put forth by Russell included not using soil and raw materials faster than scientific and technological progress can replace the loss. Population growth must be controlled at levels lower than the rate of food production. Finally, he suggested the need for a general diffusion of prosperity, a single world government, provisions for individual initiative in work and play, and a diffusion of power compatible with the maintenance of political and economic frameworks.

All through this discussion of the contributions of science and technology to society, a tension exists between the potential goods and possible evils. From gunpowder to atomic weapons, there is simultaneously security and insecurity. In the centralization of power and authority, there is efficiency and loss of personal freedom. These issues are not unlike those we confront today as a society. One point is different from the Middle Ages, or even the 1950s, when Russell wrote. Science and technology are much more influential. They are powerful forces for social transformation and the need for public understanding—scientific and technological literacy—is even more urgent.

C. SCIENCE AND TECHNOLOGY: A SOCIAL PERSPECTIVE

Significant social changes have occurred since Bertrand Russell wrote *The Impact of Science on Society* and *Sputnik* was launched. Examples particularly important to science and technology education will be used to highlight some of the fundamental social changes that have occurred in the past two and a half decades.

Silent Spring was published by Rachel Carson in 1962. This powerful book directed the world's attention to the detrimental effect of chemicals. Carson warned that the indiscriminate use of chemicals could "linger in the soil," "slow the leaping of fish," and "still the song of the birds." If society continued contaminating the environment, then one day society would experience a silent spring. Carson did go beyond the available evidence and was criticized for the book's alarming message. But, the book became a symbolic figure, and the environmental movement was born. Carson's basic conviction was stated in a Congressional hearing when she urged that this generation must come to terms with nature. For the remaining years of the decade, society began coming to terms with its effect on the environment. We witnessed the establishment of many public policies: In 1965, Congress passed the Clean Air Act and the Solid Waste Disposal Act. In 1966, the Species Conservation Act was passed, and in 1969, the National Environmental Policy Act was passed.

In 1969 the world witnessed the achievement of the greatest technological challenge in human history. Men landed on the moon and returned safely to Earth. Clearly, this was a decade that closed with scientific success. But other societal issues had occurred during this period. Protests began against the war in Vietnam. And in the United States, urban problems generated social concerns. Comparisons of money spent on space programs versus poverty-related problems were reported and debated. Technological advances were identified both with space exploration and the power of destruction in war. The advantages of industrial growth were weighed against the disadvantages of pollution. By the end of the 1960s, some of the science-related issues that were so important at the beginning of the decade were achieved, resolved, or forgotten, and entirely new problems had emerged. But the reader should note that many themes identified in Russell's analysis of science and society were clearly evident.

In the 1970s, past ideas and values about growth were questioned. High technology was challenged in the specific form of the supersonic transport (SST). After a long Congressional battle, support for the SST was terminated. In 1972 the public heard that we needed to recognize *The Limits to Growth* (Meadows & Meadows) and we had *Only One Earth* (Ward & Dubos). In the event that people had missed the messages of these books, the Organization of Petroleum Exporting Countries (OPEC) made it explicitly clear through the oil embargo of 1973–1974. The embargo brought the issue of energy to the public's attention, and it has been there ever since.

During the decade 1970–1980, Congress passed a number of bills related to the environment, including the Water Pollution Control Act (1972), the Endangered Species Act (1973), the Toxic Substances Control Act (1976), and the Clean Air and Clean Water Acts (1977). But, as the decade drew to a close, the Three Mile Island incident further underscored the impact of technology on society and brought the themes of science, technology, and society to the public consciousness. This incident symbolizes the ambivalence between society and science that had developed for two decades. There was, simultaneously, the hope for cheap energy and the disillusionment with technology; the need for energy and the questioning of nuclear power; the possibility of unlimited energy and profound vulnerability based on science and technology.

Many themes of the 1960s and 1970s were substantiated in the 1980s and extended from local or national levels to global concerns. The *Global 2000 Report to the President: Entering the Twenty-First Century* (Barney, 1980) stands as an example.

In the nearly 40 years since *Sputnik* and more than 40 years since Russell's book, there has developed an environmental movement, a growing concern about the role of science and technology in society, a recognition that the rate and direction of social growth must change, and a realization of the global dimensions of problems and the interdependence of human beings with each other and their environment.

D. CONTEMPORARY CHALLENGES OF SCIENCE AND TECHNOLOGY IN SOCIETY

Economic growth results from the combination of labor, capital, and land (natural resources) for the production of social goods and services. Science and technology contribute to economic growth in several different ways. There is the creation of new products and services with the resulting expansion of consumer choice. Science and technology also contribute to more efficient (less expensive) production of goods and services. And, finally, the resources used for economic growth are extended through better extraction and processing and through development of synthetic substitutes that can replace natural resources which are too expensive and/or not available. In the example of economic growth, one can see the symbiotic relationship that has been established within science, technology, and society. Support for research and development contributes to economic progress which, in turn, provides more support for scientific investigation and technological innovation.

While this makes sense, many people know that all is not well in industrialized societies. There are many characteristics of industrial societies such as advanced technology, complex social organizations, and rapid social transformation. However, it is worth directing our attention to the characteristic mentioned above, namely a commitment to continued economic growth. In *Problems of an Industrial Society* (1981), William Faunce suggests that we are witnessing problems *of* an industrial society as opposed to problems *in* an industrial society. That is, there are problems unique to and inherent in the social structure and function of industrial societies. There are some problems common to all societies—crime and poverty, for example. But there are some problems only found in contemporary industrial societies. What are these problems? And, more importantly, how are they related to science and technology? Here is William Faunce's list of problems: resource depletion, environmental degradation, individual alienation, and threats to personal freedom. Two of these problems, resource depletion and environmental degradation, are very closely related to science and technology. Alienation and loss of freedom are indirectly related through large bureaucratic organization, mechanization, and lack of participation in public policy. Science educators are more concerned about resources and the environment because they pose a more fundamental threat to long-term social stability. Recommendations for an STS emphasis in education programs include public participation which, at least partially, recognizes the problems of alienation and loss of freedom.

The Industrial Revolution was based on the use of fossil fuels to run machines. Very importantly, these fossil fuel resources (such as various metals) were also basic to the industrialization of society. Along with the perception of unlimited resources, there was an apparently unlimited environment for waste disposal. With these perceptions, and the advances of science and technology, the economy prospered. But now we realize that resources and environments are finite. These are the related challenges for science and technology.

Science and Technology: Promises and Dangers in the Eighties (Watts, 1980) outlines four challenges to future expectations for science and technology. The first two are external to society. The primary challenge is *limited resources*—physical, social, and economic restraints on growth. The second external challenge is from a *changing world order*—emergence of Third World powers and interdependence of nations. There are two challenges from within society. One is *public participation* in science policy making—institutional forms and legislation. And, second, an *understanding of the increasing complexity of the science and society relationship*—scientific and technologic literacy.

Limited resources are seen by many as the most critical challenge because resources essential to traditional economic growth are diminishing. As resources continue to decrease, prices of goods and services will increase, and science and technology will strain to extend the limited resources through new discoveries. But there are inevitably going to be diminishing returns. And, as noted earlier, the symbiotic relationship between science, technology, and society could be broken due to decreased financial support on the one hand, and fewer innovations to spur economic growth on the other.

Other social concerns such as the national debt and the rising cost of government are outside the scientific and technologic enterprise, but do affect it. There are, however, constraints directly related to science and technology. The cost of doing research has increased enormously in recent decades. And, when you consider that physics and chemistry are no longer the only major research areas (there are also the life, earth, and social sciences), then it is fairly easy to see that fewer dollars are being spread further, to cover increased costs. And, all of this is done with higher expectations for economic returns from investments in research and development.

The paradox in this situation is that investments in science and technology are critical if society is to move beyond the present situation. Vital resources are found within the community of scientists and engineers that can help with natural resource problems, policy options, and economic and political choices.

Without much notice, we have become a global community. This constitutes the second challenge. After World War II, the United States was a world leader in science and technology. In the decades since the war, Western Europe and Japan have also become world leaders. In addition to this, Third World countries have emerged with coalitions of power that influence the economies of other, more developed, countries. The 1973 OPEC oil embargo serves as a good example of this challenge (and the one of limited resources).

After World War II, there were increased numbers of countries with the basic skills for labor. They possessed equal abilities to manufacture products at less cost. The result has been a shift of production of goods and services to other countries. The balance of foreign trade shifted as the United States bought more from and sold less to other countries. To this scenario add the development of multinational corporations and the fact that they use natural and human resources from other countries, often Third World, and one can easily see the significance of the new world order.

How does this relate to science and technology? Several examples may make this relationship clear. Most scientists and engineers reside in developed countries and pursue the research and development priorities of their countries. These priorities are seldom aligned with the real human needs of the developing world, and there is a problem with the transfer of technologies to the Third World. When technologies are transferred, they are often either inappropriate or maintained for an elite group. Other examples include development and sale of armaments and use of resources.

The complexity of science and technology and its powerful influence in society, combined with greater citizen participation in decisions and policy, forms the third challenge. Many decisions concerning science and technology—and issues related to science and technology—will have to be made in the 1990s and in future decades. Who should make the decisions? On what basis should decisions be made? And, how should the decisions be made in a democratic society?

There is increased public participation in various forms which is significantly related to science and technology. Debates over the siting of nuclear power plants and recombinant DNA technology serve as two examples. The use of computers, issues of privacy, and problems involving risk and uncertainty have also brought public attention.

Tension is growing between the necessary freedom of scientific enterprise and the requirement of public participation in a democratic society. This is related to the fourth challenge, scientific literacy. There is a strand of logic that connects this challenge to all of the others. An imperative in today's world is for individuals to understand the impact of the science and technologic enterprise on their *personal* lives in relation to important *social issues*. That is, they need to know about the history, philosophy, and social role of science and technology as well as the concepts, processes, and skills of science. Finally, there is a need to introduce students to the ways and means of democratic participation in the context of science- and technology-related social issues (Bybee, 1984a, 1985a). The interaction and significance of science and technology in society is clear. That science and technology education is related to, but not reflective of, the needs of individuals and of society is cause for concern and the basis for a contemporary reform of science education.

E. THE CONTEMPORARY REFORM OF SCIENCE EDUCATION

It is difficult to identify the exact time when the need for curricular reform became recognized as important. When the Department of Education's report *A Nation At Risk* was published in 1983, the debate became widespread. Other books and reports on general education followed—*Action for Excellence* (Task Force on Education for Economic Growth, 1983), *Making the Grade* (Twentieth Century Fund, 1983), *The Paideia Proposal* (Adler, 1982), *High School* (Boyer, 1983), and *A Place Called School* (Goodlad, 1984). Science education was a prominent theme in the literature on the need for educational reform.

One of the first indicators of a need for change in science education came in a 1980 report jointly prepared by the National Science Foundation and the Department of Education—*Science and Engineering Education for the 1980s and Beyond*. There were concerns about student achievement, lack of participation in science and mathematics courses, low standards, and inadequate requirements. There was also concern about science curricula and programs, namely, that the science curricula gave little attention to students who were not intent on careers in science and engineering, and that this was the majority of students.

> . . . There is a great mismatch between the content of secondary school science and mathematics courses and the needs and interests of students for whom these courses will contribute their entire formal scientific education. With few exceptions, these courses are not directed toward personal or societal problems involving science and technology; nor do they offer any insight into what engineers and scientists do; nor do they have vocational relevance except for the chosen few (National Science Foundation and Department of Education, 1980, p. 5).

The report recommends that curriculum materials be developed that will motivate students to take science beyond tenth grade, and that will emphasize the special needs of minorities, women, and the disabled. The recommendation also included a focus on the scientific and technologic basis of national problems such as energy, natural resources, and health.

Other reports followed. In 1981, the recommendations of Project Synthesis were published (Harms & Yager). Project Synthesis was a major effort to bring together the best information available on the present state and future direction of science and technology education. The curricular recommendation was congruent with that discussed so far—there is a need for science programs for *all* students, ones that include an emphasis on personal, social, and career goals.

In 1982, the National Science Teachers Association issued a position statement entitled "Science-Technology-Society: Science Education for the 1980s." Again, the theme was that of the title—science and technology education should focus on literacy for all students. Recommendations for the curriculum included

- Development of scientific and technological process and inquiry skills
- Provision of scientific and technologic knowledge
- Use of skills and knowledge of science and technology as they apply to personal and social decisions
- Enhancement of attitudes, values, and appreciation of science and technology

- Study of interactions among science-technology-society in context of science-related societal issues.

A prestigious National Science Board report, *Educating Americans for the 21st Century* (1983) furthered the reform. In particular, one aspect of the report outlined new goals under the provocative title "A Revised and Intensified Science and Technology Curriculum Grades K–12 Urgently Needed For Our Future." There were recommendations for a proposed curriculum. Though some recommendations are for lower grades, we think it appropriate to give the entire list.

- Science and technology education should be taught daily in every precollege year
- Emphasis in grades K–6 on phenomena in the natural environment, collecting and processing data, and a balanced physical and biological sciences program
- Emphasis in grades 7–8 on biological, chemical, and physical aspects related to the personal needs of adolescents and to development of quantitative analysis skills
- Emphasis in grades 9–11 on the application of science and technology to improvement of the community, local and national
- Options in grades 11–12 for discipline-oriented career preparation courses, preferably with several disciplines taken each year rather than one science subject each year
- Grades K–11 program be an integration of science and technology and practical mathematics
- Introduction of concepts of technology, such as feedback, along with concepts of science
- Curriculum be organized around problem-solving skills, real-life issues, and personal and community decision making
- Research in teaching and learning be applied to identify desirable characteristics of curricular materials and teaching methods
- Coverage of what is basic in contemporary science and engineering concepts and methods
- Provision for interaction with the community and with informal education centers
- Implementation of the previous curriculum in stages as new material and qualified teachers become available.

The National Science Teachers Association (NSTA) Yearbooks also expressed the need for curricular reform. The 1983 Yearbook, *Science Teaching: A Profession Speaks* (Brown & Butts) conveyed the practical, program, and policy concerns of the science education profession. The 1984 Yearbook, *Redesigning Science and Technology Education* (Bybee, Carlson, & McCormack, p. 246) expressed the fact that we are in the process of change. The first section of this yearbook reviewed several of the contemporary reports mentioned at the beginning of this section. Other chapters addressed the essential components of science and technology education—requirements and standards, curriculum, instruction, teacher education, and research and leadership. The last section outlined an agenda for action based on the yearbook chapters. According to this agenda, science and technology education's curriculum should include the following:

- integrate science-technology-society themes, problems, and issues;
- present a multidisciplinary analysis of science- and technology-related problems;
- provide opportunities for informal learning;
- demonstrate relevance to the student's world; and
- include computer literacy in the context of science knowledge, skills, and values.

The science-technology-society theme has been prominent in the recent literature on reform in science education (Bybee, 1985b). The guest editorial by Paul DeHart Hurd and Table 14.1 provide overviews of changes in science education and the STS theme. In the next sections of this chapter, we discuss scientific and technologic literacy and the STS theme.

GUEST EDITORIAL

Science Teaching in a New Key

■ **Paul DeHart Hurd**
Professor Emeritus, Stanford University,
Palo Alto, California

Educators, scientists, and people at large increasingly sense that science must be taught in a new key to bridge the gap between the search for knowledge and its utilization. Science and technology have a significant capacity to shape nearly every aspect of human experience, including the social structure and personal and cultural values. The educational issue we face is a reconstruction of science teaching for making wise use of knowledge to improve the quality of life and living.

In the history of science teaching, every age has its own preoccupations. New advances in theory influence what should be taught. At the turn of this century, for example, the works of Mendel, Einstein, and Mendeleev had this effect. As industrialism grew in the United States, topics on farm machinery, the internal combustion engine, and steel-making were added to science textbooks. The rapid growth of "big science" and technology at midcentury threatened America with a possible shortage of scientists and highly trained engineers and technicians. Thus it became important to develop science courses that stressed the basic theories and principles of a discipline which, if properly taught, might attract students to careers in science or technical fields. Today, because science and technology have become central to our social, political, and economic process, science teaching takes on a new perspective that binds science, technology, and values to human welfare—a new key for the teaching of science.

Throughout history, intellectual, social, and cultural events have, at times, accumulated to produce a major turning point in human affairs. The introduction of agriculture, the Industrial Revolution, and the development of modern science mark such times. Again we find human beings challenged with a plethora of circumstances, events, and innovations in sociotechnical systems that assure us that our future will not be like our past, no matter how we deal with them. Thus the 1990s represent a critical juncture for all humankind. The intellectual context and substance for science teaching are equally critical.

The major educational issue that we face has developed from our extraordinary ability to generate new knowledge. In the 400 years of modern research in science, the amount of new knowledge introduced into human experience has been astronomical. It continues to grow exponentially. No longer can we legitimately conceive of a science course, at any level of schooling, as sampling the total knowledge of a discipline or even its underlying principles and theories. For most disciplines, this would require a lifetime of learning. Researchers in science first sought to resolve this situation by specializing and then by using an integrated team attack on problems. But the complexity of modern problems in science, technology, and society is rapidly exceeding human capacities for dealing with it. There is too much to know. Technologies have had to be developed to serve as multipliers of the mind, technologies such as computer-based information-storing systems and systems for synthesizing and interpreting knowledge, popularly known as "artificial intelligence." The impact of the growing knowledge base of science portends the need for new goals for science teaching.

The magnitude of the knowledge transformation in our time will influence the cultural and social arrangements of people throughout the world. Primarily, the difference between a developed and an undeveloped country is a capacity to produce and use knowledge, particularly that which is a product of science. These conditions also influence people as individuals. In the United States we are rapidly dividing into two groups of people: the knowledge-poor and the knowledge-rich. The knowledge-poor are those who are unable to tap, manage, and use the continuous flow of new knowledge that might enrich their lives. In recent years a major goal of science teaching has been the discovery or creation of new knowledge in science. The information revolution of the 1980s represents pressures to extend the sphere of science-derived knowledge into areas of personal utilization and social problem solving. Science teaching under these conditions seeks to develop the insights and skills that link the creation, diffusion, and utilization of knowledge for the common good.

The goal of science teaching for this new age of information is to discover how we can best use what knowledge we now have as a means to learn more. The learning task is one of knowing how to obtain and decipher information that already exists to further improve our knowledge base and our ability for making informed decisions. Much of what we need to know in life cannot be perceived during the years of schooling. What can be learned, however, are the skills for tapping knowledge sources at any time in life.

The complexity of science-based personal and social problems is so great that we cannot comprehend all knowledge. Science teaching must focus on knowing what to do with what is known and must cultivate the ability to translate knowledge into wise action.

F. WHAT SHOULD THE SCIENTIFICALLY AND TECHNOLOGICALLY LITERATE PERSON KNOW, VALUE, AND DO—AS A CITIZEN?

Answering this question sets the task for the following sections. Science educators have developed admirable, and in many ways adequate, answers to the question that heads this section. For example, Paul DeHart Hurd has long argued that personal and social goals are essential to scientific literacy (1970, 1972, 1984). Other science educators and organizations

TABLE 14.1
Science Education: Past, Present, and Future

PAST TO 1950s	1960s TO PRESENT	1990s TO . . .
1. Personal/social goals were somewhat recognized.	1. Personal/social goals were largely unrecognized.	1. Relationships among science, technology, and society will be the organizational core of curriculum.
2. Scientific knowledge was presented in a logical progression.	2. Scientific knowledge is presented as the "structure of the discipline."	2. Scientific knowledge will be presented in the context of science-technology related social issues.
3. Scientific method was presented as a specific procedure—"the scientific method."	3. Scientific methods are presented as inquiry and discovery processes designed to involve students in "pure" science.	3. Scientific methods will be presented as inquiry into personal, environmental, and social problems to acquire information for decision making.
4. Laboratory work was to demonstrate, visualize, or confirm knowledge.	4. Laboratory exercises are to develop inquiry skills and to "discover" knowledge (mostly reductive analysis).	4. Laboratory exercises will provide opportunities to solve technologic problems, to learn scientific inquiry (both reductive and holistic), and to develop decision-making skills.
5. Science programs were determined primarily by textbooks and authors.	5. Science programs are determined by curriculum developers and scientists.	5. Science programs will be determined by teachers, curriculum developers, supervisors, national organizations, and textbooks.
6. The textbook was the curriculum.	6. The textbook and laboratory are the curriculum.	6. Textbook, laboratory, simulation games, community experiences, electronic media, and other informal educational resources will be the curriculum.
7. Science related to technology much of the time.	7. Science-technology relationship is largely neglected for "pure" science.	7. Interdependence of science, technology, and society will be stressed.
8. Science was presented as established knowledge.	8. Science is presented as an ever-changing body of knowledge that is updated through inquiry processes.	8. Science will be presented as an ever-changing body of knowledge having important influences on society. Updating and using the knowledge for democratic participation will be underscored.
9. Disciplinary and multidisciplinary (within scientific disciplines, e.g., general science) approach was used.	9. Disciplinary approach is used.	9. Interdisciplinary approach (extending beyond natural sciences and including social sciences, humanities, philosophy, and history) will be used.
10. Careers were represented by stereotyped male scientists in the laboratory.	10. Career information in science is largely ignored; the programs were primarily directed toward science and engineering.	10. Career information will be directed to multiple scientific and technological occupations for all citizens.

SOURCE: Adapted from R. Bybee, "Citizenship and Science Education," *The American Biology Teacher, 44,* no. 6 (September 1982), p. 344. Reprinted with permission of the National Association of Biology Teachers, Reston, VA.

have made various contributions to the theme of scientific and technologic literacy. See, for example, Agin (1974); Anderson (1983); Berkheimer and Lott (1984); Champagne and Klopfer (1982); Chen and Novik (1984); Gallagher (1971); Miller (1984); National Science Teachers Association (1971, 1982); Pella (1976); "Scientific Literacy" (1983); and Zeidler (1984). Several things ought to be made explicit about the perspective presented in this chapter.

The last phrase of the heading—"as a citizen"—is a controlling statement concerning the reformulation of goals. The aim is to assure that science teaching contributes to the student's personal development and to his or her realization as a citizen; that is, a person with civic duties, rights, and obligations. Included also in this formulation of goals is the important aim of all public education—informed and rational participation in the democratic process. This includes the development of individual sensibilities about science, technology, and society. The word *sensibilities* incorporates intellectual, ethical, and emotional responses to conditions and events. Our perspective for scientific and technologic literacy is concerned with citizens' receptivity and responsiveness to science and technology as an important cultural enterprise with influences ranging from the individual to global dimensions (Bybee, 1982). How can we help citizens respond sensibly to the personal, environmental and public policy issues involving science and technology? Obviously, there is need for students to understand something about the nature of science and technology. And, they should understand the limits and possibilities of science and technology as a force for social change.

The question "What should the scientifically and technologically literate person know, value, and do—as a citizen?" implies that all knowledge, attitudes, and skills concerning science and technology are not essential. Science teachers are being called on to ask and answer for the 1990s a contemporary and expanded version of Herbert Spencer's 1859 question—"What knowledge is of most worth?" Spencer's answer was science. But, then, what science is of most worth to the citizen? Considering the social, scientific, and technologic situation in the 1990s, it seems reasonable to suggest that some essential topics might include population growth, air quality and atmosphere, water resources, land use, world hunger and food resources, hazardous substances, human health and disease, and war technology (Bybee, 1984a, 1984b; Bybee & Bonnstetter, 1985). In addition to this list, other vital topics are quality of life, transportation, space exploration, microelectronics, and biotechnology.

All of this is to say that one must answer the question in a contemporary context. If it were the 1890s, when the United States was in the process of transformation from an agricultural to an industrial society, the question would be the same, but the answer would be quite different. Likewise, in A.D. 2010 the question would be the same, but the answer will undoubtedly vary.

The question considers *both* science and technology. Recently, science has been the primary concern of most education programs. Yet, citizens actually experience more technology than science. To be sure, science is basic to technology, but technology is a part of each citizen's direct and daily experience, and generally, science is not. However, technology is not a part of education programs. It seems reasonable to recommend that acquiring knowledge about technology be included in educational goals.

There is an attitudinal dimension of scientific and technologic literacy. Public attitudes affect social policies as much as knowledge and skills. And, when asked, the public demonstrates attitudes toward basic and applied science—be they informed or ill-informed, accurate or inaccurate perceptions (Bybee, Harms, Ward, & Yager, 1980; Miller, 1983; National Assessment of Educational Progress, 1979; National Science Board, 1976). Citizens are called on to understand and evaluate the uses and consequences of science and technology in society. They must decide to support or reject programs having to do with basic and applied research, and to help establish public policies that enhance or protect the quality of life. Concluding the need for recognition and enlarged understanding of attitudes as a part of science and technology educations seems, at this time, obvious.

G. A FRAMEWORK FOR SCIENTIFIC AND TECHNOLOGIC LITERACY

While developing a conceptual framework for scientific and technologic literacy, we came upon an excellent 1975 essay by Benjamin S. P. Shen, "Science Literacy: The Public Need." In this paper, Shen writes about three distinct, but related, forms of scientific literacy: practical, civic, and cultural. Practical literacy is having the scientific and technical knowledge that can be put to immediate use to solve basic human needs for a healthy survival. The aim of civic science literacy is to increase citizens' awareness of science and technology as they relate to social problems so that they and their representatives can bring common sense to bear on the issues. Cultural science literacy is directed toward the citizen's understanding of science and technology as major human achievements. Practical problems and civic issues are not necessarily solved by cultural literacy, but it helps bridge the gap between "the two cultures" (Shen, 1975).

Table 14.2 is a conceptual framework for scientific and technologic literacy. The framework is based on the main categories of the question that heads this section—knowledge,

TABLE 14.2
A Conceptual Framework for Knowledge, Skills, and Values of Scientific and Technologic Literacy

ACQUISITION OF KNOWLEDGE	UTILIZATION OF LEARNING SKILLS	DEVELOPMENT OF VALUES AND IDEAS
Related to	*Based on*	*About*
Science and technology	Scientific and technologic inquiry	Science and technology in society
through study of	*by means of active participation in*	*through investigation of*
Personal matters	Information gathering	Local issues
Civic concerns	Problem solving	Public policies
Cultural perspectives	Decision making	Global problems

skills, and values. Secondly, the framework identifies three essential themes, science and technology *concepts;* the process of *inquiry;* and *science-technology-society* interactions. Under each of the three main categories we suggest general areas of emphasis, participation, and study. Each column does fulfill several important criteria for the translation of the concepts, processes, and attitudes to curriculum programs.

Note that any program based on this framework would progress from personal to cultural, information gathering to decision making, and local issues to global problems. In general, the framework goes from simple to complex, concrete to abstract, immediate to past and future perspectives. Tables 14.3, 14.4, and 14.5 further elaborate some concepts, skills, and ideas for the conceptual framework.

The acquisition of knowledge related to science and technology continues to be a central purpose of science teaching. Ten sets of general concepts are presented in Table 14.3. The concepts are consistent with the personal, social, and world view essential to contemporary life and living. One of the main criteria for including these, as opposed to other, concepts is that they unify the apparently disparate content areas of science, technology, and society. That is, the concepts are integrative. Undoubtedly there are other important concepts. This set should provide an initial overview of the knowledge component of scientific and technologic literacy.

Inquiry skills based on science and technology are described in Table 14.4. Initial curiosity and questioning by students about the natural world around them is the basis for these skills. Questioning and searching for information, combined with observing and organizing information, are processes of informal inquiry emphasized in elementary science education that set the stage for formal inquiry during secondary science education. Measuring, classifying, comparing, conserving, analyzing, and synthesizing skills are also included. Problem solving includes the identification and description of problems, hypothesizing and predicting outcomes of experiments, situations, and events. Separation and control of variables is central to the design of scientific experiments, development of technologies, and analysis of policy issues. Finally, inquiry skills are extended to the realm of decision making—the exploration and evaluation of decisions to be made and actually making and acting on the choice.

Themes important to the development of ideas and values about science and technology in society are outlined in Table 14.5. Simple definitions of science, technology, and society are presented first. From this point various combinations of interactions are described, e.g., science, technology, science and society, society and technology, and so on.

This section outlines a general framework for scientific and technologic literacy. In doing so, our purpose is to answer the question, "What should the scientifically and technologically literate person know, value, and do—as a citizen?", and to provide concrete examples of some knowledge, skills, and values appropriate for science education. This is a framework, not the final structure. The complete structure will have to be developed by science teachers, science supervisors, and curriculum developers as they answer the central question in the context of their students, schools, and communities. Some discussion of goals based on the categories of emphasis, participation, and study is described in the next sections.

TABLE 14.3
Unifying Concepts for Science-Technology-Society

SYSTEMS AND SUBSYSTEMS

Systems are groups of related objects that form a whole. A system is also a collection of materials isolated for the purpose of study. Subsystems are systems entirely within another system. Elements of a system, and systems, often interact. There is usually evidence for the interaction. Evidence of interactions provides opportunities for identification and analysis of causal relationships.

ORGANIZATION AND IDENTITY

Systems have characteristics that give them identifiable properties. There are boundaries, components, flow of resources, feedback, and open and closed aspects of systems organization. Changes in systems may alter some properties but maintain the system's identity. Some changes of systems result in different identities.

HIERARCHY AND DIVERSITY

Matter, whether nonliving or living, natural or manmade, is organized in hierarchical patterns and systems. There are hierarchical levels of organization from subatomic to the cosmologic levels. There is also increasing complexity in physical, biological, and human systems. Diversity can result in stability of systems.

INTERACTION AND CHANGE

Components within systems, and systems, interact. There is usually evidence of the interaction. All things change over time. The course of change may be influenced in such a way to modify the properties, organization, and identity of systems.

GROWTH AND CYCLES

Growth is an increase in size, number, complexity, or value. Linear growth changes by a constant amount over a time interval. Exponential growth occurs by an increasing rate at a constant percentage for identifiable periods of time. Some systems change in regular sequences, or in cycles, in time and/or space. There are biogeochemical cycles essential to life and living.

PATTERNS AND PROCESSES

Interactions, change, growth, and cycles often occur in observable patterns and as a result of identifiable processes.

PROBABILITY AND PREDICTION

Some changes are more predictable than others. Statistical calculations allow some degree of accuracy—a probability—in the prediction of future events.

CONSERVATION AND DEGRADATION

Matter and energy are neither created nor destroyed. Both may be changed to different forms. This is the first law of thermodynamics. Considered as a whole, any system and its surroundings will tend toward increasing disorder or randomness. This is the second law of thermodynamics.

ADAPTATION AND LIMITATION

All systems—nonliving, living, and social—exhibit a range of capabilities in responding to environmental or cultural challenges. There are limits to environmental, organismic, and social changes. Adaptations may be biological, physical, technological, social, political, economic, or human.

EQUILIBRIUM AND SUSTAINABILITY

Components of a system act with one another in ways that maintain a balance. Due to adaptation, growth, and change, all systems exist on a continuum of balanced to unbalanced. The extent of the equilibrium or disequilibrium observed at any point is a function of the system's capacity to carry the load created by factors operating in and on the system. Sustainability describes a human system that has adapted its economic and social systems so that natural resources and the environment are maintained within the limits of adaptation.

TABLE 14.4
Inquiry Skills Based on Science and Technology

QUESTIONING AND SEARCHING

Curiosity and questions about the world are basic to inquiry skills. Thus locating or discovering information based on questions is essential. Informal inquiry—questioning and searching—are first steps toward scientific and technologic problem solving and personal and social decision making.

OBSERVING AND ORGANIZING

One or more senses are used to gather information about objects, events, or ideas. Once observed and gathered, there is need to group information in relation to space, time, and causal relationships.

MEASURING AND CLASSIFYING

Counting objects or events, establishing one-to-one correspondence, and organizing objects according to numerical properties. Quantifying descriptions (e.g. length, width, duration) of objects, systems, and events in space and time. Forming meaningful groupings. Putting objects or events in order by using a pattern or property to construct a series (seriation). Classifying includes defining similarities and identifying subsystems based on a property and arranging subsystems and systems in a hierarchy.

COMPARING AND CONSERVING

Identifying similarities, differences, and changes in objects and systems in space (local to global) and time (past, present, future). Understanding that quantitative relationships between materials and systems remain the same even though they have undergone perceptual alterations.

ANALYZING AND SYNTHESIZING

Reducing information to simpler elements for better understanding of the organization and dynamics of objects, systems, events, and ideas. Analysis includes describing components, clarifying relationships among systems or subsystems, and identifying organizational principles of systems. Where analysis stresses reduction and parts, synthesis stresses construction and the whole. Bringing together information to form unique organizations, patterns, or systems. Understanding the whole is greater than the sum of parts.

IDENTIFYING AND DESCRIBING

These skills extend those of gathering information to problem solving. Problem identification and description are first steps in formal inquiry. Included are identification of personal and/or social problems, gathering information, and describing what is known and unknown about a problem.

HYPOTHESIZING AND PREDICTING

When confronting a problem, making reasonable guesses, or estimates based on information. Making statements of conditionality—"If . . . then . . . " concerning a problem. Predicting possible conclusions. Inductive (specific to general) and deductive (general to specific) thinking as well as propositional thinking are included.

SEPARATING AND CONTROLLING

Applying logical patterns of reasoning, whether to the design of formal experiments, analysis of data, solution of problems, or evaluation of policies, is based on the skill of separating and controlling variables. Making clear how a condition or event is similar to or different from other conditions or events. Identifying factors and all possible combinations of factors relative to the problem. Use hierarchical thinking such as building classification keys.

EXPLORING AND EVALUATING

Describing decisions to be made, using skills developed earlier to identify and gather information, converting information to alternatives, and examining the consequences of different decisions are all part of the exploration of a decision. Evaluating consists of making value judgments based on the internal consistency of information and clearly defined external criteria such as costs, risks, and benefits of alternatives.

DECIDING AND ACTING

Selecting from among alternatives, making an intelligent and responsible choice. Using available information and justifying the decision. Also, identifying ways and means of taking responsible action to reduce or eliminate problems.

TABLE 14.5
Themes of Science-Technology-Society Interaction

SCIENCE

A systematic, objective search for understanding of the natural and human world. A body of knowledge, formed through continuous inquiry, having significant interactions with technology and society. Science is characterized by use of an empirical approach, statements of generality (e.g. laws, principles, theories) and testing to confirm, refute, or modify knowledge about natural and human phenomena.

TECHNOLOGY

The application of knowledge to solve practical problems to achieve human goals. Body of knowledge available to a culture that can be used to control the environment, extract resources, produce goods and services, and improve the quality of life.

SOCIETY

The collective interactions and relationships among human beings at local, regional, national, and global levels. Human groups that are differentiated from other human groups by mutual interests, distinctive relationships, shared institutions, and common culture. The human setting in which the scientific and technologic enterprise operates.

SCIENCE AND TECHNOLOGY

Knowledge generated by the scientific enterprise contributes to new technologies.

SCIENCE AND SOCIETY

Scientific knowledge has a practical influence on the quality of life and on the collective perceptions and actions of those in society. The knowledge produced by science and the processes used by scientists influence our world views—the way we think about ourselves, others, and the natural environment. There may be functional and dysfunctional social consequences of scientific knowledge. The impact of science on society is never entirely beneficial nor uniformly detrimental. The impact varies with persons, populations, places, and times. Science and society controversies usually center on issues of research priorities and proprietorship of knowledge.

TECHNOLOGY AND SCIENCE

New technologies influence the scientific enterprise, often determining research problems and the means employed to solve research problems. Technological developments can lead to improved methods and instruments for scientific research.

TECHNOLOGY AND SOCIETY

Technology influences the personal quality of life and how people act and interact locally, nationally, and globally. Technological change is accompanied by social, political, and economic changes that may be beneficial or detrimental for society. The impact of new technology is never entirely beneficial nor uniformly detrimental. The impact varies with persons, populations, places, and times. Technology and society controversies usually center on issues of efficiency, equitability, benefit, risk, and regulation.

SOCIETY AND SCIENCE

Society is often the source of ideas and problems for scientific research. Research priorities are influenced by requests for proposals, grants, and funding through public and private sources. The social context (dominant social paradigms) affects the reception of new ideas, and social factors within the science community (dominant scientific paradigms) influence the research undertaken and the acceptance of new findings. Social control over science is seen in public demands for the assessment of research priorities.

SOCIETY AND TECHNOLOGY

Social needs, attitudes, and values influence the direction of technological development. Technologies often arise as expressions of cultural values and serve the needs of dominant social groups. Social control over technology is seen in increased demands for the assessment of new technologies.

SCIENCE AND TECHNOLOGY IN SOCIETY

Personal and social systems are subject to complex interactions among science, technology, and society. There is a history and future of science and technology in social development from the local to global levels.

Science and Technology in Personal Matters

One of the most fundamental aspects of education for scientific and technologic literacy is the practical use of knowledge, skills, and understandings that will help citizens in personal matters. Examples are plentiful in which some basic information could help improve the quality of life. For example, the United States could reduce its infant mortality rate by providing basic health and nutrition information through education. Knowledge of basic developmental needs of children would result in better parenting, thus reducing the possibility of problems such as abuse and neglect.

Some examples of topics that will help translate the goal to practice concerning the application of science and technology in personal matters: appropriate personal diets; adequate health practices; increasing energy efficiency in a house; conservation; short- and long-term effects of inappropriate food, air, and water on personal health and welfare; evaluation of practical problems of living.

Science and Technology in Civic Concerns

Citizens need to comprehend environmental and resource problems. Before citizens can participate in the democratic process there must be some minimal level of comprehension of civic concerns. An estimated half of legislative bills are related in some way to science and technology. Unfortunately, many citizens think that science is beyond their grasp. Science- and technology-related civil concerns can be presented in clear and precise ways. From this point, the common sense, rational judgments, and practical awareness of decisions and consequences can be considered. Environmental and resource issues are too important to be left to bureaucrats and technocrats. Sample topics of this goal might include renewable and nonrenewable resources; short-, middle- and long-range proposed solutions to the energy problem; the limits of population growth and the consequences of exceeding the limits to growth; environmental quality for home, school, community, and globe; and the role technology has had in increasing and decreasing resources.

Science and Technology in Cultural Perspectives

Understanding science and technology as a human endeavor and appreciating the limits and possibilities of science and technology are also important for citizens. This type of literacy is directed toward knowledge and attitudes *about* science and technology in society. There are some essentials for citizens concerning science and technology: the relationship between research and development and social progress; the connection between technological innovation and employment; problems within and outside the realm of science and technology. Topics such as these and others related to historical-philosophical and social-political perspectives of science and technology are important. Other topics might include interrelationships among science, technology, and society; the connection between science, technology, and social change; basic research and applied research; the social role of science and technology in matters such as energy, armaments, and mining; and the role of science and technology in developing countries.

Scientific and Technologic Inquiry for Information Gathering

We live in an information society. A goal of obtaining and using information is not something new or unusual for science education. It has been a long-standing aim of science. For contemporary purposes the goal includes not only gathering information from observations of nature, but also gathering information from various sources that exist in society. Traditional topics include questioning, observing, organizing, measuring, and classifying. New goals might include knowing various sources of information, gaining access to information, and using different information about retrieval systems.

Scientific and Technologic Inquiry for Problem Solving

Problem solving in a personal-social context is a goal that has been unrecognized for over two decades of science teaching. Replacing a once-important goal requires only building on the essential structure of problem solving. Identifying problems, hypothesizing, predicting, and separating and controlling variables are commonly recognized goals of science

Superconductivity: A Revolution in Physics

■ **Paul Chu, Ph.D.,**
Program Director
Solid State Physics Program

To illustrate the excitement of working on the frontiers of science, I would like to share some of my experiences in the recent discovery of "high-temperature" superconductors.

Unlike ordinary electrical conductors, in which some of the useful electrical energy is always lost as heat, superconducting materials can carry a current with no loss, and so if a current were set up in a loop of superconducting wire, the current would go around and around forever.

Kamerlingh Onnes discovered superconductivity in 1911. While exploring the properties of matter at very low temperatures, Onnes found that wires of frozen mercury became superconducting at about −275° C. By the start of 1986, the highest superconducting temperature known was only about −251° C. Because such a temperature is difficult to produce and maintain, these superconductors were useful only when the alternatives were even more difficult and expensive.

Late in 1986 all this began to change. Georg Bednorz and Alex Mueller, who both work at the IBM research lab in Zurich, Switzerland, found that a compound of barium, lanthanum, copper, and oxygen superconducts at about −240° C. I first learned of their discovery in November, 1986, when I saw an article they had published. I became excited, because I too had worked with metal oxides of this type, and my experience told me that it should be possible to make similar compounds and perhaps raise the temperature for superconductivity even higher. The goal was

−196° C because it is relatively easy to cool to that temperature using liquid nitrogen. We knew that if we would make a −196° C superconductor, it would have many revolutionary uses. Of course, other scientists had also read the article by Bednorz and Mueller. I now know that a group in Tokyo was on the same track I was. My group quickly managed to find superconductivity at −223° C. When the reports of our work and of similar work by the group in Tokyo were given in December at a meeting in Boston, even more scientists became interested. By this time everyone knew that to be first would require hard work, good intuition, and a bit of luck. We were in a race with the best. On January 29, 1987, our group observed superconductivity above −184° C in an yttrium–barium–copper oxide sample with a structure different from the compound studied by Bednorz and Mueller. We immediately knew that we had opened the door to widespread applications of superconductivity.

Every year in March the American Physical Society holds a meeting devoted to solid state physics. The new discoveries in superconductivity had occurred too late to be included in the scheduled program, but we nevertheless presented our discoveries at a special session, dubbed the "Woodstock of Physics," that started at 7 P.M. and lasted until 3 A.M. The excitement and enthusiasm evident at that special session have continued, with everyone working hard to achieve still higher temperatures than before and to get a theoretical understanding of the new superconductors. Much remains to be done to make practical use of these materials. They are, as yet, difficult to form into useful films and wires, but with luck we will soon see superconducting computers, loss-free electricity transmission, and trains that "float" in a magnetic field.

teaching. But which problems are worth solving? Those of personal and social concern to citizens. Addition of the personal-social theme is clearly recognizable in the framework presented throughout this essay.

Scientific and Technologic Inquiry for Decision Making

The goal is new to science teaching. It is, however, a logical extension of problem solving in a personal and social context. Once one has information and attempts to resolve problems, decision making cannot be avoided. This is true for problems related to science and technology; it is equally true for life and living. Some practical objectives are describing a decision to be made; utilizing various information gathering skills; clarifying alternatives; assessing costs, risks, and benefits of various alternatives; and choosing the best alternatives.

Developing Ideas and Values about Science-Technology-Society Interactions in Local Issues

This goal combines with the other goals of science and technology in personal matters and the skills of information gathering. The exact nature of personal matters and local issues will vary with science teachers' locations. Likewise the magnitude and seriousness of the topics will vary. Emphasizing local issues for the clarification and development of STS themes seems an appropriate starting point. Topics will certainly relate to larger concerns, but from a developmental perspective they are much better introduced at the personal and local levels. Examples of topics include pollution, energy resources, waste disposal, erosion, recycling, ground water, and food production.

Developing Ideas and Values about Science-Technology-Society Interactions in Public Policies

The interactions among science, technology, and society can be illustrated through education about public policies. Issues of public policy also provide opportunities for teaching basic science concepts and a forum for introducing the theme of civic participation. Where earlier study was directed toward local issues, the study of public policies can include that level, but extends the study to state, regional, and national levels. Topics such as conservation and utilization of the environment, resources, and population could be included.

Developing Ideas and Values about Science-Technology-Society Interactions in Global Problems

Because many problems related to science and technology have global dimensions, there is a need for students to develop a global perspective. Recent surveys I have completed (Bybee, 1984a, 1984b) identify important global problems and suggest the need for education concerning these issues. I might also note that the theme of citizenship is equally applicable at this level (Bybee, 1982). Topics of study include world hunger and food resources, population growth, air quality and atmosphere, water resources, war technology, and human health and disease.

SUMMARY

Educators at all levels, preschool to graduate school, are keenly aware of the scientific advances and social problems as we progress toward the twenty-first century. And, more than most, we recognize the disparity between the needs of society and appropriateness of our programs. At the same time, education is beset with budget cuts, staff reductions, disruptive students, and numerous new requirements. Other unsettling issues render the daily task of teaching difficult at best and impossible at worst. Reluctance to reform programs is understandable, but so are the reasons and responsibilities to change. We have a choice. We can give in to the forces acting on us, or we can continue our educational mission. Science and technology education awaits our new initiative. We cannot have a failure of will and professional obligation at this crucial period in history. Citizens have a genuine need to understand science and technology in our society. Educators have a responsibility to meet this public need. And so, again, we question—what should the scientifically and technologically literate person know, value, and do—as a citizen?

QUESTIONS AND ACTIVITIES FOR DISCUSSION

1. Many public policy problems confront citizens. And, many of these public policy problems have a significant scientific or technologic component. As a science teacher who has to design new curriculum programs, it may be of interest to you to see how you would rank some of the common science/technology/society-related policy issues. The easiest way to rank the 12 issues is to first rank those items you think are *most* important (i.e., 1, 2, 3, 4). Then rank the *least* important items (i.e., 12, 11, 10, 9). Finally, rank the *middle* options from most to least important (i.e., 5, 6, 7, 8).

   _____ **Air quality and atmosphere** (acid rain, CO_2, depletion of ozone, global warming)

   _____ **Energy shortages** (synthetic fuels, solar power, fossil fuels, conservation, oil production)

   _____ **Extinction of plants and animals** (reducing genetic diversity)

   _____ **Hazardous substances** (waste dumps, toxic chemicals, lead paints)

   _____ **Human health and disease** (infectious and noninfectious diseases, stress, diet and nutrition, exercise, mental health)

   _____ **Land use** (soil erosion, reclamation, urban development, wildlife habitat loss, deforestation, desertification)

_____ **Mineral resources** (nonfuel minerals, metallic and nonmetallic minerals, mining, technology, low-grade deposits, recycling, reuse)

_____ **Nuclear reactors** (nuclear waste management, breeder reactors, cost of construction, safety)

_____ **Population growth** (world population, immigration, carrying capacity, foresight capability)

_____ **War technology** (nerve gas, nuclear development, nuclear arms threat)

_____ **Water resources** (waste disposal, estuaries, supply, distribution, groundwater contamination, fertilizer contamination)

_____ **World hunger and food resources** (food production, agriculture, cropland conservation)

2. Now that you have ranked these items, it may be of interest to discuss some of the following questions with other students or colleagues.

- How much do you know about each of the 12 science-related social issues? Quite a lot? Some? Very little? Nothing?
- How important is it to study these issues as a part of science courses in middle, junior high, or high school? Very important? Fairly important? Not too important? Not important at all?
- How do you think each of the science-related problems will change by the year 2000? Will the individual problems be much better? Better? About the same? Worse? Much worse?
- What does your response to these questions mean for you as a citizen?
- What are the implications of your responses for the science curriculum you will teach?

REFERENCES

Adler, M. (1982). *The Paideia Proposal: An education manifesto.* New York: MacMillan Publishing.

Agin, M. (1974). Education for scientific literacy: A conceptual frame of reference and some applications. *Science Education, 58* (3).

Anderson, R. (1983). Are yesterday's goals adequate for tomorrow? *Science Education, 67* (2).

Barney, G. (1980). *The global 2000 report to the president: Entering the twenty-first century.* Washington, DC: U.S. Government Printing Office.

Berkheimer, G., & Lott, G. (1984). Science educators' and graduate students' perceptions of science education objectives for the 1980's. *Science Education, 68* (2).

Boyer, E. (1983). *High school.* New York: Harper and Row.

Brown, F. K., & Butts, D. (Eds.). (1983). *Science teaching: A profession speaks, 1983 NSTA yearbook.* Washington, DC: National Science Teachers Association.

Bybee, R. W. (1982). Citizenship and science education. *The American Biology Teacher, 44* (6).

Bybee, R. W. (1984a). Global problems and science education policy. In R. W. Bybee, J. Carlson, & A. McCormack (Eds.), *Redesigning science and technology education,* 1984 Yearbook of the National Science Teachers Association. Washington, DC: NSTA.

Bybee, R. W. (1984b). *Human ecology: A perspective for biology education.* Reston, VA: National Association of Biology Teachers.

Bybee, R. W. (1985a). The restoration of confidence in science and technology education. *School Science and Mathematics, 85,* (2), 95–108.

Bybee, R. W. (Ed.). (1985b). *Science-Technology-Society.* In the 1985 NSTA Yearbook. Washington, DC: National Science Teachers Association.

Bybee, R. W., & Bonnstetter, R. (1985). Science, technology, and society: A survey of science teachers. In R. W. Bybee (Ed.), *Science-Technology-Society.* 1985 Yearbook of the National Science Teachers Association. Washington, DC: NSTA.

Bybee, R. W., Carlson, J., & McCormack, A. (1984). Redesigning science and technology education: An agenda for action. In the 1984 NSTA Yearbook, *Redesigning science and technology education.* Washington, DC: National Science Teachers Association.

Bybee, R. W., Harms, N., Ward, B., & Yager, R. (1980). Science, society, and science education. *Science Education, 64* (3).

Carson, R. (1962). *Silent spring.* Boston: Houghton Mifflin.

Champagne, A., & Klopfer, L. (1982). Actions in a time of crisis. *Science Education, 66* (4).

Chen, D., & Novik, R. (1984). Scientific and technological education in an information society. *Science Education, 68* (4).

Committee on NSTA Position Statement. (1982). Science-Technology-Society: Science education for the 1980's. Washington, DC: National Science Teachers Association.

Faunce, W. (1981). *Problems of an industrial society.* New York: McGraw Hill.

Gallagher, J. J. (1971). A broader base for science teaching. *Science Education, 55* (3).

Goodlad, J. (1984). *A place called school.* New York: McGraw Hill.

Harms, N., & Yager, R. (1981). *What research says to the science teacher, vol. III.* Washington, DC: National Science Teachers Association.

Hurd, P. D. (1970). Scientific enlightenment for an age of science. *The Science Teacher, 37* (3).

Hurd, P. D. (1972). Emerging perspectives in science teaching for the 1970's. *School Science and Mathematics, 72* (3).

Hurd, P. D. (1984). *Reforming science education: The search for a new vision.* Washington, DC: Council for Basic Education.

Meadows, D. H., & Meadows, D. L. (1972). *The limits to growth.* Washington, DC: Potomac Associates.

Miller, J. (1983). *The American people and science policy.* New York: Pergamon Press.

Miller, R. (1984). Science teaching for the citizen of the future. *Science Education, 68* (4).

National Assessment of Educational Progress. (1979). *Attitudes toward science.* Denver, CO: Education Commission of the States.

National Science Board. (1976). *Sciences at the bicentennial: A report from the research community.* Washington, DC: U.S. Government Printing Office.

National Science Board Commission on Pre-College Education in Mathematics, Science, and Technology. (1983). *Educating Americans for the 21st century: Source materials.* Washington, DC: National Science Foundation.

National Science Foundation and the Department of Education. (1980). *Science and engineering education for the 1980's and beyond.* Washington, DC: U.S. Government Printing Office.

National Science Teachers Association. (1971). School science education for the 1970's. *The Science Teacher, 38* (3).

National Science Teachers Association. (1982). Science-Technology-Society: Science education for the 1980's. An NSTA Position Statement. Washington, DC: National Science Teachers Association.

Pella, M. (1976). The place and function of science for a literate citizenry. *Science Education, 60* (1).

Russell, B. (1952). *The impact of science on society.* London: Unwin Books.

Scientific Literacy. (1983). *Daedalus, 112* (2).

Shen, B. (1975). Science literacy: The public need. *The Sciences, 27* (6).

Task Force on Education for Economic Growth. (1983). *Action for excellence.* Denver, CO: Education Commission of the States.

Twentieth Century Fund. (1983). *Making the grade.* New York: Twentieth Century Fund, Inc.

Ward, B., & Dubos, R. (1972). *Only one earth.* New York: W.W. Norton.

Watts, G. (1980). *Science and technology: Promises and dangers in the eighties.* Englewood Cliffs, NJ: Prentice-Hall.

Zeidler, D. (1984). Moral issues and social policy in science education: Closing the literacy gap. *Science Education, 68* (4).

SUGGESTED READINGS

Hamm, M. (1992). Achieving scientific literacy through a curriculum connected with mathematics and technology. *School Science and Mathematics, 92*(1),6–9.

Lux, D. G. (Ed.). (1992). Science, technology, society: Opportunities. *Theory Into Practice, 31*(1),88.

Selby, C. C. (1993). Technology: From myths to realities. *Phi Delta Kappan, 74* (9).

Stahl, N. N., & Stahl, R. J. (1995). *Decision-Making Episodes for Exploring Society, Science, and Technology.* Arlington, VA: National Science Teachers Association.

Yager, R. E. *The Science, Technology, Society Movement.* (1993). What Research Says to the Science Teacher, Volume 7. Arlington, VA: National Science Teachers Association.

Science Projects, Science Fairs, and Field Experiences

S cience instruction should not be limited to routine activities conducted in the classroom. Science instruction can also take place outside of the classroom and even after school hours. Projects, science fairs, and fieldwork have a definite place in the science curriculum, since they can provide students with experiences and understandings they would not normally obtain through routine classroom instruction. Planned and unplanned projects, science fair programs, and certain types of fieldwork activities will not only enrich the science background of students but at the same time reinforce the goals of science teaching.

Because they tend to be direct experiences (see the Learning Experiences Ladder, Chapter 6) engaging all sensory input modalities and because they tend to connect student learning in motivating and meaningful ways, field trips, science fairs, and project-based instruction, when well planned and carried out, are among the most powerful instructional tools available to the classroom teacher.

This chapter is designed to help you understand:

1. The role and importance of science project work.
2. How science fair programs encourage students to pursue activities they would not normally carry out during regular class time.
3. The functions and benefits of field experiences in the science curriculum.

The following scenario is not uncommon in science instruction. The approach presents a view of science that is void of enrichment activities which can make science more meaningful and interesting to students.

❖ Mrs. Hampton teaches ninth-grade biology in a small, rural high school. She planned the following instructional activities for one school week in early September.

Monday. Mrs. Hampton presented a lecture on the annelids. During her lecture, she compared and contrasted the structure and physiology of annelids with those of previously discussed platyhelminths and nematodes.

Tuesday. Mrs. Hampton completed her lecture on annelids and then gave specific instructions to prepare students for a laboratory exercise on the dissection of the earthworm to be conducted the next day.

Wednesday. Students dissected the earthworm. Mrs. Hampton handed out a prepared laboratory exercise to students that specified the directions to be followed. Students were required to label diagrams of earthworm anatomy and provide information to answer a series of questions listed on the laboratory exercise form. Some of the students expressed their dislike for having to learn about worms.

Thursday. Mrs. Hampton reviewed various points regarding earthworm anatomy that the students should have learned during the dissection. Then she conducted a short review for the test on worms to be given the next day.

Friday. Test on worms. ✚

The instructional activities just described have their place in science teaching because they can provide factual information upon which students can build their knowledge for subsequent learning situations. Unfortunately, many science teachers consistently use this instructional approach, resulting in a distorted view of the investigative nature of science.

Science should be taught so that students can view it as a dynamic activity rather than a static, uninteresting enterprise. Science instruction should not be limited to common, routine instructional activities—lecture, cookbook laboratory exercises, and testing. It should involve inquiry activities that go beyond classroom walls to give students a broader view of science and make science more meaningful and exciting.

Mrs. Hampton's plans for the week could have included activities that present science as a dynamic enterprise that involves discovery and inquiry. The following plan for the week illustrates an alternative instructional approach that gives students some firsthand experiences.

✚ **Monday.** Mrs. Hampton presented a lecture that compared and contrasted the structure and physiology of platyhelminths and nematodes.

Tuesday. Mrs. Hampton took her class on a field trip to a nearby stream where students collected samples of nematodes and platyhelminths. In addition, students gathered annelid specimens from soil samples taken from the grassy field adjacent to the school building.

Wednesday. The students compared the behavior and external anatomy of earthworms with nematodes and platyhelminths, using the live specimens they collected the previous day. The students also dissected preserved specimens of earthworms to investigate the internal structure. Students were required to label diagrams and answer questions that compared the internal structure and physiology of earthworms with those of round and flatworms.

Thursday. Mrs. Hampton reviewed the laboratory exercise and discussed the anatomy and physiology of annelids. She conducted a short review for the next day's examination on the three main worm phyla. During the discussion of annelids, one student wondered why earthworms often come to the surface of the soil when it rains. Mrs. Hampton helped this student design a project to investigate the reactions of earthworms to varying levels of moisture and light. The student was asked to prepare a report to present to the class after the project was completed.

Friday. Test on worms. ✚

This scenario of Mrs. Hampton's instructional approach to teaching differs from the previous one in that she enriched her biology course by including a number of stimulating experiences. The field trip to the nearby stream gave students a first-hand experience in collecting specimens to study in the laboratory. This activity no doubt generated a great deal of student excitement and enthusiasm. The students studied the behavior of worm specimens that they collected during the field trip, and they compared the external anatomy of live specimens with preserved specimens. The interest of one student concerning the behavior of earthworms during heavy rain resulted in a student project on the reactions of earthworms to moisture and light. This activity helped to develop the student's inquiry skills and led to a project that was entered in the school's annual science fair. This approach to teaching science takes advantage of the beneficial outcomes of field experiences, which in turn may pave the way to involve students in science fair projects.

A. SCIENCE PROJECTS

Science projects are larger in scope than laboratory exercises, which are usually one or two periods in length. Projects usually require many hours of student involvement, spanning several days to several months. Projects may be conducted during or outside of class time, be unplanned or planned, and involve one student or the whole class. The examples that follow illustrate the nature of science projects and how they can be initiated.

> ❖ Mr. Gibson teaches in a rural school district in the Midwest. He was summarizing an ecology unit by discussing air pollution. When the subject of acid content in the atmosphere was brought up, Doug indicated that he heard that the new factory built just outside town was polluting the air. He asked Mr. Gibson if it was true that the factory was responsible for acid emission in the air. ❖

How should Mr. Gibson respond to the student's questions? Should the teacher tell the student that he will find out the answer to the question or, if he knows the answer, should he give it to the student? If Mr. Gibson selected either of these options, he might stifle inquiry into the problem. However, if he responds by saying, "How can we find out if the factory is contributing to acid emission in the air?" he can invite the student to answer his own question. This is a ready-made opportunity to allow the student to apply knowledge and skills gained in the classroom to a real-world situation. Mr. Gibson could design a class laboratory exercise in which the whole class pursues the answer to Doug's question. However, Mr. Gibson had not budgeted time for such an exercise, which would take at least a week to do properly. Also, Doug's question is quite specific and may be of interest to him alone. Surely Mr. Gibson does not want to plan his class activities around the specific interest of just one student. On the other hand, Mr. Gibson would like to provide Doug with the opportunity to investigate the answer to his question. The obvious solution to this situation is the science project. With inexpensive materials (sodium bicarbonate, methyl orange, glycerin, hydrochloric acid, paper towels, rubber band, thistle tube, bicycle pump), Doug is shown how to perform a fairly accurate atmospheric test. Mr. Gibson assists Doug in the design and use of the apparatus for this investigation at convenient times outside of the regular period (e.g., before and after class, before and after school, during free periods). Mr. Gibson does, however, plan a specific class time during which Doug can present his findings to the class.

Let us now summarize what has transpired:

1. Mr. Gibson's class is allowed to proceed uninterrupted to the next unit.
2. Mr. Gibson has been able to provide a learning experience directly related to a student's individual interest.
3. The student is given an opportunity to apply what he has learned in class to a relevant, real-world situation.
4. The student's quest for knowledge has not been cut short by classroom or time restrictions.
5. The student becomes highly motivated, and gains in the cognitive and affective domains are facilitated. Doug is pursuing a question of individual interest, and his feeling of achievement and self-worth can be enhanced by his responsibility for imparting his findings to the class.

Science teachers like Mr. Gibson may be reluctant to interrupt their classes for unplanned learning experiences. However, these experiences are important and can be addressed through projects. It is not necessary that teachers forge through the planned curriculum and that they pass up ideal opportunities in class to involve students in inquiry activities. Science teachers should constantly take advantage of unplanned learning experiences. Very often, "side trips" or tangential inquiries produce the greatest cognitive gains because they tend to be more relevant to students' daily lives. This is why science projects are so valuable; they allow for pursuit of those highly motivating areas of interest but do not reduce the teacher's highly valuable class time.

In the previous example, the science project was assigned to an individual student. However, keep in mind that such projects can be performed by groups of students as well. Indeed, a group project may be preferred because it adds to the comprehensiveness and diversity of an investigation through assignment of tasks, cooperation, and interaction among individuals.

Planned Science Projects

There are alternative ways to reap the benefits of science projects than those just described. The science project is a valuable teaching tool, and the teacher should not limit or discard its use in response to the problems that may arise from unplanned assignments. Very often, students simply need more structure and direction. In short, the curriculum can be structured so that students' participation in a science project is ensured because they do not have the option of simply refraining from using this approach. Let us return to Mr. Gibson's ecology unit to illustrate this alternative classroom approach.

At the beginning of the unit, or even halfway into it, Mr. Gibson divides the class into groups. Each group is required to plan and complete an ecology-related project. Mr. Gibson may do any of the following:

1. Assign a specific problem to each group.
2. Allow the groups to pick a problem from a list of suggested problems.
3. Allow the groups to develop their own problem to investigate.

Through one of these approaches, all students will gain exposure to a science project and its inherent educational rewards. How much flexibility the teacher allows with regard to the project topic depends on the teacher's preference and the particular class. For example, certain classes might be quite capable of developing relevant areas of inquiry. In these situations, the teacher would do well to allow groups of students to develop their own projects. This freedom would further ensure that the students would investigate a topic of interest. Other classes may need more direction and assigned problems to investigate; this may be the case in grades 4–9.

Many teachers prefer in-class science projects. Although such activities require more of the teacher's time and effort, the increased teacher supervision helps minimize "wasted" and undirected student behavior. The in-class project gives the teacher more supervisory flexibility than do those that are conducted outside of school. The teacher is able to decide freely on the level of independence to give to students; in the out-of-school projects, the students are completely autonomous during the major portion of the project. Experienced teachers fully recognize that students vary in their ability and the amount of autonomy they can efficiently handle. Thus, the in-class science project is the most convenient way to allow students' pursuit of individual interests without sacrificing the teacher's opportunity to monitor students' work.

The student or group of students who pursue in-class science projects should be given the opportunity to present the results to the whole class. The motivational aspects of such an opportunity have already been discussed. In addition, criteria for the grading of such projects should be clearly stated. The classroom presentation, as well as a final written product, should be included in the total evaluation.

Class Projects

Class projects that employ large groups of students such as those described next are becoming more common in science instruction. This type of cooperative learning requires that all students in the class work together toward a common objective. The participation of all students in a class toward a common goal may prescribe that students work in pairs, work in groups of three or more students, or work in groups composed of boys and girls or solely of boys or girls. There may also be assignments where a student may work alone for a period of time. Grouping during project work, when properly conducted, can produce a number of beneficial outcomes, such as the following:

1. Permits close matching of assignments to abilities of students
2. Takes advantage of adolescents' and preadolescents' desire to work together
3. Encourages students to explore their leadership potential and qualities
4. Helps teachers become better acquainted with student personalities, strengths, and abilities
5. Provides tasks for shy and retiring students
6. Provides for a wide range of interests and talents
7. Gives direct experience with materials
8. Provides tasks to take care of special interests and skills of male or female students
9. Allows students to work cooperatively on a single task or on several tasks
10. Encourages verbal communication among students within a group or team
11. Exposes students to the democratic process
12. Encourages all students to actively participate in scientific inquiry.

The next three examples show how students can work cooperatively on a class project for an extended period of time. (The teacher has the option of assigning the students to work in pairs, groups of three or four or more, all boys, all girls, or a mix.) In the first example, the science teacher suggested a class project in which the students might have an interest because they were studying a unit on the weather and the atmosphere. The teacher had given considerable thought to the project before suggesting it. It was not a spontaneous decision. The teacher was prepared to offer suggestions during the planning session, but because the students were interested in the topic, they came up with the idea of using an outside expert to help them design a weather station. The students also took the initiative to contact the weather forecaster and invited her to give them guidance over an extended period of time. During the project they also assumed many responsibilities that were assigned by the student project director or mandated by the group assignments.

❖   Mr. Geral teaches physical science to a group of ninth graders in a small suburban high school. During the study of a unit on weather and the atmosphere Mr. Geral suggested that the students set up a weather station on the school grounds as a class project. The students became excited about the project and agreed that it would be a good learning experience for the whole class. To start the project, one student indicated that they should invite a local weather forecaster to help them plan the weather station. Another student said that the weather forecaster seen on local television often announced her willingness to visit schools to instruct classes on the weather. The students thought that it would be an excellent idea to invite the weather forecaster to their class to discuss the project. Several students volunteered to make an appointment with her at the TV station in order to explain the project and invite her to visit their class. Ms. Mahar, the weather forecaster, accepted the invitation and visited the class. She indicated that she would help them with the project provided that all the students in the class participated in the activities and that they took their assignments seriously.

After an introduction to weather observing and forecasting, Ms. Mahar told the students that some weather equipment was needed to establish the weather station and that some pieces could be constructed using cheap and simple materials. She recommended that for a class project it would be a good idea for them to make some of the equipment rather than to purchase it from a supply house. Ms. Mahar said that she would break the class up into small groups and give each group instructions for making one piece of equipment. She provided the instructions for making a rain gauge, a hygrometer, a psychrometer, and a wind velocity instrument. She said that other items needed, such as barometers and thermometers, were probably available in the science equipment inventory, but if they were not, she could provide them. She also said that she would provide the class with other specialized equipment needed for the station for an extended period of time. Ms. Mahar also gave a group of students the specifications for building a weather shelter in a specified area on the school grounds. With the help of the industrial arts teacher, they built the shelter and placed it in an area designated by Ms. Mahar.

After two weeks the weather station was set up and operating. Two students were assigned each day to collect and record data. They recorded the temperature and dew point, relative humidity, barometer readings, type of clouds, height of clouds, rain gauge measurements, wind direction and velocity, and other pertinent data.

The data were given to Ms. Mahar during her weekly visits. She showed them how the data were used in producing a weather map for forecasting the weather. She visited the class for four consecutive weeks and exposed the students to some of the principles of weather observing and weather forecasting. The students prepared their own weather maps from data Ms. Mahar collected from other weather stations all over the country. With Ms. Mahar's help, the students attempted to forecast the weather using the weather maps they had plotted. The students collected and recorded the weather data on a daily basis for the remainder of the term and found that their data compared well with data collected by professional weather observers. ✤

The second example illustrates a situation in which the students came up with the idea of a class project on contour maps. The science teacher had not suggested the activity but was alert enough to realize the importance of capitalizing on the interests and motivation of his students. The students were academically above average and in the past had demonstrated that they were capable of working cooperatively on assigned tasks and handling problems in depth. The students carried out the project with some direction from the science teacher and a civil engineer, but many of the tasks were designed and assigned by the students themselves.

✤ Mr. Elm is an earth science teacher in a rural school. He allows students with good academic records to substitute earth science for the usual general science course available to ninth-grade students.

Early in the course, Mr. Elm provided the class with contour maps of various areas in the United States and spent a great amount of time teaching the students how to read and use them. When the class became proficient in reading and using the maps, one student suggested that the class actually make a contour map and a model of the area surrounding the community as a class project. Mr. Elm thought the project was feasible and asked the class to plan the strategy to carry out the project. The students elected a very capable student as project director. As project director, she appointed a committee of students to discuss the project and propose a plan of attack. Since a contour map of the local area was not available, initial discussion centered around the need for a careful survey of the area in order to produce the map. One committee member indicated that they needed the advice of a civil engineer in order to proceed with the project. Another student on the committee said that his father was a civil engineer who might be willing to visit the class to explain the nature of a survey. The engineer accepted the invitation and then proceeded to conduct a demonstration on the school grounds to show how he generated the data to make a survey using special instruments he brought to class. He allowed a number of students to use the instruments during the demonstration and they became very excited when they learned that the readings they took were accurate as confirmed by the engineer. At the end of the demonstration they asked the engineer if he would be willing to help them throughout the project. He accepted, and since the students exhibited such enthusiasm and a sense of responsibility, he loaned them a set of instruments to use during the project.

The survey required several class periods, and many of the students also provided additional time after school to collect data. After the survey was completed, the students made a contour map of the area with the help of the engineer and the science teacher. The map was then used to construct a model of the surrounding area.

The students had to determine the material that could be used to make a model. For this phase of the project, they sought advice from the art teacher. She suggested papier mâché and plaster of paris since the materials were readily available and easy to work with. The girls in the class were very interested in this phase and worked diligently, experimenting with the media.

After they determined procedures for building up the contours, they started to make the model. Each class member was busy performing one or more tasks. Some made molds, others mixed plaster, while others prepared trees from rubber sponges. They constructed small houses from balsa wood and other materials.

As work progressed, the accuracy of the model was constantly checked against the data they had collected. The model measured about 6 by 9 ft. and was made in three sections so that it could be moved easily.

The model was well executed and attractive with its miniature trees, woods, buildings, streams, and bridges. It was also very informative because of its wealth of detail.

Many of the students in the school were aware of the model that had been produced and asked if they could see it when they had a free period. The demand was so great that the principal decided to place it in the school lobby for about one week so it could be viewed by all interested students in the school. The project received much publicity in the local newspaper when the students were invited to place the model in a public area in the city hall. Several students who participated in the project were selected by the class to deliver a series of talks about the project before town officials and other community leaders. ✤

The third example illustrates a situation in which the teacher utilizes Gardner's theory of multiple intelligences. You may recall from Chapter 1 that Howard Gardner has introduced seven learning styles that individuals exhibit in differing ways: verbal-linguistic, logical-mathematical, intrapersonal, visual-spatial, musical-rhythmic, body-kinesthetic, and interpersonal (Blythe & Gardner, 1990; Gardner, 1987; Gardner & Hatch, 1989). Many educators believe that students who are at risk of not completing school are those whose dominant cognitive learning style is not in synch with traditional teaching methods. Traditional methods are largely of an analytic style, where information is presented in a logical, linear, sequential fashion, and of the first three Gardner types: verbal-linguistic, logical-mathematical, and intrapersonal (Armstrong, 1988). Consequently, to better synchronize methods of instruction with learning styles, some teachers and schools have restructured the curriculum and instruction around Gardner's seven ways of knowing (see, for example, Ellison, 1992; Hoerr, 1992).

✤   This is the case at the inner-city school where Ms. Downing teaches fourth grade. For example, during their study of a thematic unit on weather, for one afternoon her children are concentrating on learning about the water cycle. She has divided her class of children into several groups of three or four children. While working simultaneously to learn about the water cycle, several children are conducting and repeating an experiment to find out how many drops of water can be held on one side of a new one-cent coin versus how many can be held on the side of a worn one-cent coin. Another group of children is preparing graphs to illustrate the results of those experiments. A third group of children is creating and composing the words and music of a song about the water cycle. A fourth group is creating a colorful bulletin board about it. A fifth group is reading about the water cycle in books obtained from the library. Finally, a sixth group is creating a puppet show about the water cycle. When each group has finished its project, it will share it with the others in the class. ✤

In summary, a class project should be considered in science instruction since it may add to the comprehensiveness and diversity of an investigation through student cooperation and interaction over an extended period of time.

B. SCIENCE FAIRS

During the spring semester of each school year thousands of science fairs are conducted in the elementary, middle, and secondary schools throughout the nation. These are big events for science teachers, students, parents, and other members of the community. Science fairs stimulate enormous interest in science. They provide students with the incentive to study problems in depth and to communicate their findings. Science fair programs give students a chance to pursue investigations that they would not ordinarily be able to carry out during regular science class periods because of limitations on equipment, space, and time. In addition to identifying the gifted science students, these events encourage all students to get involved in "sciencing." Science fairs not only display the talents and interests of students but also reveal the orientation of a school's science program and the type of science teaching that is taking place in the classrooms.

How does a science fair reflect a school's science program and what the teachers actually emphasize in their teaching? This question can be answered by categorizing the type of projects that students enter in the science fair. One scientist (Smith, 1980, pp. 22–23) who has been a judge at many fairs has observed that science fair projects can be placed in the following categories:

1. Model building (e.g., the solar system, volcanoes, clay models, and frog organs)
2. Hobby or pet show-and-tell (e.g., arrowheads, slot cars, dogs, and baby chicks)
3. Laboratory demonstrations right out of the textbook or laboratory manual (e.g., distillation, electrolysis, and seed germination)
4. Report-and-poster projects from literature research (e.g., fossils, birds, bees, astronauts, and the car)
5. Investigative projects that involve the students in critical thinking and science processes, such as measuring, consolidating data, and drawing conclusions (e.g., tests of reaction time, data on the effectiveness of various detergents, and comparisons of performances of vacuum bottles and insulated jugs).

With such variety in project types, judges are often bewildered as to how to compare and evaluate them. How can one objectively compare a model with an investigative project when each has different amounts of student involvement? Each of these categories is so different that it presents a serious problem for those who judge science fairs. It is difficult for individuals to judge students fairly when they are not instructed to evaluate projects on a comparative basis by category. Projects in a science fair are often evaluated haphazardly when judges compare investigative projects with models, models with charts, laboratory demonstrations with investigative projects, and so on. A fair should be organized in a way that permits judges to make awards within particular categories. However, this does not solve one of the major problems concerning science fairs: that is, what types of projects should be included in a science fair to make it an outstanding event in the community and one that emphasizes the scientific enterprise?

The emphasis of science teaching should be one of inquiry and investigation. This suggests that fair entries should be the types of projects mentioned in category 5 of Smith's list of science fair categories. Investigative projects require students to use many of the other activities (categories 1 to 4), but these projects require much more. They involve students in planning and thinking scientifically and not stopping short by reproducing a model from a textbook or simply copying information from an encyclopedia. Investigative projects require students to ask questions, plan procedures, collect data, and make conclusions based on information. These types of activities require students to think critically and to solve problems and minimize the conveying of science as a fixed body of knowledge, which should be deemphasized as a primary goal of science teaching.

It is recommended that teachers discourage students from preparing projects in the first four categories (models, posters, show-and-tell, and laboratory demonstrations) for a science fair program. Although they may stimulate student interest in science, these projects make science fairs uninteresting and monotonous and present a false image of what science really involves.

Students who enter projects in the first four categories described in the list are often placed at a disadvantage when judges attempt to evaluate them. In many instances, judges who have good credentials—engineers, scientists from universities and industries, and science teachers—will immediately discount the worth of these projects and spend little time evaluating them or talking to the students who prepared them.

Projects that students enter into a fair need not involve elaborate equipment or complex problems to be science fair winners. At first glance, projects involving expensive and elaborate equipment such as computers are impressive. The terminology students use to present demonstrations involving the computer is impressive. Nevertheless, the problems the students investigate and the conclusions they present often lack clarity and depth because the students become enamored and preoccupied with a complex piece of equipment and are less concerned with the investigation. They often become confused and muddle the investigation. This also happens when students are involved with sophisticated equipment such as oscilloscopes, scintillators, and amplifiers. Investigations that ask simple questions and use simple and clearly stated procedures often make the best fair projects.

Judging Projects

The procedures and criteria for judging science fairs vary, but there are common elements that can be considered. Generally, a common set of categories is used to judge science fair projects. The following categories and their respective point breakdowns are often used:

1. Creativity (20)
2. Investigative procedures (30)
3. Understanding of the topic (20)
4. Quality of the display (15)
5. Oral presentation (15)

The first category, *creativity,* asks the question, How unique is the project? Is the project significant and somewhat unusual for the age of the student? To answer these questions, a judge must take into consideration the student's grade level and science background, as well as the type of science course the student is currently taking. A judge must also determine how the student arrived at the project—was it conceived by the student or suggested by a parent, a teacher, another adult, or another student? The judge will take the responses to these questions into consideration when assessing the creativity of the project.

The *investigative procedure* is the second category that is used when judging a project. The aspects of an investigation that a judge considers include the conciseness of the problem statement, the appropriateness and thoroughness of the procedures, the completeness of the information collected, and the accuracy of the conclusions. Often, students go through an elaborate set of procedures during their investigations and then either fail to answer the original question or provide an answer that is not substantiated by the data presented.

Understanding of the topic is another category that should be considered when judging a project. Did the student bother to learn about the topic? Did he or she go to the literature to investigate it? Can the student answer questions about the topic? Did he or she provide a list of references and bibliography used in connection with the investigation?

Quality of the display is a category that is generally used in judging projects. How well does the student present the project? Are the problem, procedures, data, and conclusions presented clearly? Is the display organized and understandable? Is it visually appealing? A judge must also determine how much help a student received in presenting the project. Students generally get help from others in making their displays, but they should acknowledge the work of others in writing and give credit to those who helped them. Teachers should make certain that students are given awards for what they have done rather than for what someone else has done for them.

Another category judges use to evaluate projects is the *clarity of the presentation,* in which they determine how well students can orally present their investigation. Can the student clearly communicate the nature of the problem, how he or she solved the problem, and how he or she arrived at the conclusion? Judges should give students the opportunity to answer questions and articulate what they have accomplished.

To direct the judges' attention to the various points discussed in these categories, an evaluation form that contains the following list of elements may be useful during the judging procedure.

- The problem was stated clearly.
- Background reading was appropriate.

- The hypothesis was clearly stated and reflected the background readings.
- The experimental design demonstrated understanding of the scientific method.
- Apparatus and equipment were appropriately designed and used.
- Observations were clearly summarized.
- Interpretations of data conformed with the observations.
- Tables, graphs, and illustrations were used effectively in interpreting data.
- Conclusions and summary remarks were justified on the basis of experimental data.
- The logbook was used to record experimental data, ideas, interpretations, and conclusions.
- The bibliography contained a significant number of relevant and timely references.
- Limits of accuracy of measurements were stated.
- Work on the project suggested new problems.
- Oral presentation was made in the time allocated with all phases of the project discussed.
- The research covered all questions effectively and accurately.
- The oral presentation made good use of visual aids.
- The display board was effective in presenting the project (Goodman, 1985).

The elements in the preceding list can be rated by judges using a suitable scale, for example:

0—cannot make judgment

1—poor

2—fair

3—satisfactory

4—good

5—excellent

Goodman (1985) suggests a rating scale with a maximum of 100 points and that the awards be given based on the following scores:

60–69 Honorable mention

70–79 Third prize

80–89 Second prize

90–100 First prize

Select several judges to evaluate a given number of projects. Have the judges interview and assess the projects individually, rather than as a group, to prevent them from influencing each other. Ask the judges to provide supportive comments to students on the projects and also to recommend to students what they might do to improve their investigations. Students can use this information to better understand what they are attempting to accomplish through their procedures and their investigations.

Science fair judges should have good credentials. Selection of judges should be based on their scientific proficiency, their understanding of the scientific enterprise, and their familiarity with the cognitive abilities of the students being judged. Engineers, scientists from universities and industry, and qualified science teachers make excellent judges. However, the criteria by which projects are to be judged should be made clear to the judges before they begin to make their evaluations. It is good practice to provide them with a list of the criteria they are to use as well as some examples of questions they might ask to make judgments regarding each criterion. Encourage judges to talk to students and write comments and suggestions about each project on an evaluation form. Allow students to review the comments and suggestions so that they can further profit from the experience.

Taking Care of Inequities when Judging

In order to take care of inequities when judging science fairs, Levin and Levin (1991) suggest that entries be divided into categories or subject areas such as astronomy, bacteriology, ecology, physics, and so forth. This permits the number of projects to be judged per subject area to be small and the number of judges assigned to each area also to be small. Small groups of judges are assigned to each category, headed by one person who is so designated by the fair officials. At least two judges are assigned to interview each contestant in the category. The judges use a checklist provided by the fair officials to evaluate the projects that they are assigned to judge. The checklist is a guide that contains the criteria that should be used to evaluate the entries. Numerical scores are sometimes used in the checklist to help judges rank and compare projects that they judge. When all the projects in a category are evaluated, the judges in the area meet to discuss their findings. Their rankings are presented to the group's head judge, indicating the projects which have been ranked the highest. The highest ranking projects are then visited by those judges who had not evaluated them in the first place. If time does not allow these judges to have a full judging session with the students involved in the projects, they must at least have a short discussion with them in order to become familiar with the projects that have been ranked the highest. The group of judges then discusses all of the entries that have been ranked the highest in order to share any details that may be of interest to the whole group. During this session the judges reach a consensus and present a list of winners, including honorable mentions, to the head judge of the category.

According to Levin and Levin (1991), the consensus process eliminates a number of problems that often arise when judges merely average numerical scores to make decisions. The consensus method allows the judges to become immersed in the judging process and thus to judge each project carefully. Group discussions permit the judges to compare the strengths and weaknesses of each project. In this way, judges with little or no experience will realize their shortcomings when they overestimate or underestimate the worth of a project. This procedure and exposure will also permit inexperienced judges to be more competent when they judge projects in future fairs.

According to Levin and Levin (1991), the consensus method produces results that are more reliable and fairer as indicated by individuals who have had experience in judging other fairs using different systems. The procedures involved in other systems make it difficult to compare projects that are very similar or identical. The consensus method takes care of this problem.

The Competitive Aspect

A word of caution should be extended here to both experienced and inexperienced teachers. There is often too much emphasis on the competitive aspect of science fairs. Often, some of the less able students have done their best work and have invested a great amount of effort in their projects. These students take real pride in their projects and receive many benefits through their involvement. The science fair should offer less able students the chance to obtain recognition for what they accomplish outside of the regular science class—recognition that they cannot receive through normal class activity.

In some instances the competition gets so fierce that parents get overly involved in the science fair projects of the students. In such cases the projects actually reflect the thinking of the parents rather than the students. Children whose parents are affluent or professionals in medicine, engineering, and scientific fields have a distinct advantage and usually win science fair competitions. This is certainly unfair to less affluent students. Policies should be stated and enforced so that the students plan their own projects and carry out their own investigations with little or no outside help.

Fierce competition can be reduced when fairs are restricted to classrooms and schools as opposed to district-wide competitions. Grades or awards can be granted to a student based on a contract that the student has made with the teacher. This approach reduces competition among students and makes the science fair a more academically oriented activity.

Committees

The success of a science fair is determined by the types and strengths of the committees that are involved in its organization. The planning of a fair involves many facets—judging, publicity, advertising, awards, soliciting funds, program, and so on. The success of a fair is also contingent on obtaining responsible individuals to head as well as participate in the committee work. Selected parents, teachers, students, and members of the community can be placed on committees, depending on their interests and qualifications. Table 15.1 is a sample timetable for organizing a science fair. The following are some suggested committees:

TABLE 15.1
Sample Timetable for Organizing a Science Fair

MONTH	ACTIVITY
September	Set a date. Identify a place. Determine a budget. Place on school calendar. Inform administrators, teachers, and students when it will take place.
October	Organize fair into divisions and categories. Prepare procedures for entry, guidelines, and rules. Identify criteria for judging. Communicate this information to teachers and students.
November	Verify the reservation for the facilities. Order medals, ribbons, and trophies. Design certificates of participation.
December	Identify judges and prepare letters of request.
January	Solicit judges. Distribute entry blanks. Contact news media.
February	Receive entry forms. Map out the facility on paper noting the following: space, table, and electrical needs. Assign numbers to projects and assign them a space and location. Construct a map of the facilities, spaces, and locations. Arrange for tables, electricity, etc. Notify students of their project number and location. Confirm judges' participation. Get the awards and certificates.
March	Conduct fair. Provide refreshments. Present awards. Send thank-you notes to judges and others who helped organize the fair and activities during the fair.

1. *Planning.* Concerned with general organization of the fair; coordinates the work of other committees.
2. *Judging.* Responsible for selecting judges and orienting them regarding the evaluation of entries. A running list of judges should be kept, and evaluation of the individuals should be available for future use. Letters of appreciation for their help should be sent after the fair is over.
3. *Publicity.* Notifies news media regarding dates and activities of the fair. Prepares news releases.
4. *Awards.* Responsible for designating and ordering types of awards by category. Identifies appropriate individuals to make award presentations.
5. *Printed matter.* Prepares printed matter for the science fair including programs, floor plans, checklists for judges, and rules and regulations regarding students' conduct during the fair.
6. *Financing.* Solicits funds, contacting individuals and industry for contributions. Orients possible contributors by giving slide presentations and/or talks indicating categories of possible costs. Prepares a list of contributors for the publicity committee so they can be recognized in the news media.
7. *Set-up and take-down.* Prepares layout for the fair, obtains furniture, and arranges electrical wiring. Monitors safety during the fair.
8. *Refreshments.* Organizes groups to provide refreshments while judging is taking place. Organizes luncheons for judges and participants.
9. *Special programs for participants.* Plans activities for student participants while judges are conducting their evaluations. Activities include special tours, films, games, music, and athletic events.
10. *Applications and entry.* Sends out applications, receives entries, and contacts all possible participants about irregularities concerning their applications. Assigns numbers to projects. Checks projects in and out. Takes care of all correspondence and paperwork regarding entry into the fair.

C. THE SCIENCE OLYMPIAD

The Science Olympiad has become popular in many areas of the United States. The Science Olympiad is a nonprofit organization that is dedicated to "improving the quality of science education, increasing student interest in science, and providing recognition for outstanding achievement in science education by both students and teachers" (Science Olympiad, 1992a, 1992b). Science Olympiads are organized around interscholastic academic competitions called tournaments that consist of a rigorous series of individual and team events for

TABLE 15.2

Titles of Selected Events Included in Division B (Grades 6–9) and Division C (Grades 9–12), Science Olympiad 1992

Science concepts and knowledge
Rocks and fossils
Anatomy
Balancing equations
Chemistry lab
Designer genes

Science processes and thinking skills
Metric estimation
Water quality
Measurements
Qualitative analysis
Map reading
Physics lab

Science applications and technology
Heat transfer
Computer programming
Aerodynamics
Egg drop contest
Meteorology
Bridge building

which students prepare during the academic year. The preparation for the National Olympiad is accomplished through classroom activities, research, training workshops, and regional and state tournaments having the olympiad format. Television game shows, olympic games, and popular board games are used as the format for competitions. The Olympiad programs also include open house activities such as demonstrations in science and mathematics and career counseling sessions that are provided by professors and scientists at the host institution (Science Olympiad, 1992a, 1992b).

State, regional, and national olympiads are organized into two divisions: Division B (grades 6–9) and Division C (grades 9–12). There are no state or national tournaments for the elementary division, Division A (grades 3–6), but schools have organized local, school district, or regional competitions for this division. Some schools conduct their own mini-olympiads for Divisions B and C, during which tournaments are held to select students to compete in regional and state tournaments. Students in the entire school are invited to compete for a place on the team going to the regional or state competitions.

National, state, and regional competitions involve approximately 32 events in various science areas—biology, chemistry, earth science, physics, and computers and technology. Each year the Science Olympiad Executive Board selects the events to be scheduled for the tournaments. These events are evenly distributed among three broad goal areas of science education: science concepts and knowledge, science processes and thinking skills, and science applications and technology. (See Table 15.2.) The events are designed to use a variety of intellectual and practical skills. Some events require the recall of facts, others require concept development, a process skill, or the application of a concept. Some require the use of a specific skill, and others require a student to design and build a piece of apparatus (Science Olympiad, 1992a and 1992b).

Awards for first, second, and third place for each event at state, regional, and national competitions consist of olympic-style medals. Championship trophies are awarded to school teams in Division B and C that have the greatest number of total points during the national Olympiad. Scholarships are also awarded for selected gold medal winners at the national tournament in Division B and C.

State and regional tournaments are held mainly at colleges and universities throughout the country. The funding for the competitions has come from many sources. National tournaments have been subsidized by Army Research Office, U.S. Army R.O.T.C., IBM, Ford Motor Co., Dow Chemical, Du Pont, and other organizations. For further information concerning the Science Olympiad write to: Science Olympiad, 5955 Little Pine Lane, Rochester, Michigan 48306.

D. FIELD TRIPS AND FIELD EXPERIENCES

I remember vividly the first science field trip that I conducted. . . . How well I recall surrendering to my students' insistence that "the weather is so nice, we should go on a field trip." I certainly agreed with their opinion of the weather for it was ideal and our science program had been indoors for eight months. My hesitancy to enter the outdoor classroom with my students stemmed from my lack of acquaintance with local biota and my inexperience in designing and conducting meaningful field trip experiences. However, I have found over the years, that my preparation in this important aspect of teaching was no more inadequate than that of most science teachers who have recently graduated from our colleges and universities. This lack of preparation keeps many teachers of science indoors with their classes, aliens to the real world of science in the outdoors (Keown, 1984, p. 43).

Field trips require a great deal of preparation and planning to be effective. Consequently, many teachers avoid using this strategy because they lack the know-how for conducting successful field trips. Science teachers should learn how to conduct effective field trips so as not to deprive their students of the benefits of such experiences. Teachers who are hesitant about conducting field trips should consult with teachers who have had successful results with the approach. Keown (1984) indicates that it is important for science teachers to share their knowledge about successful field experiences, especially the "how to" and the "where to."

Because field trips and field experiences are generally much more closely related to the experiences of teenagers than most science classroom activities, they tend to be much more meaningful. They usually take place in areas that are familiar to the students, such as hospitals, fields, streams, and parks. Instructional activities in these settings make students aware of organisms, phenomena, and activities that they did not realize existed and link science with the "real world." For example, a trip to a nearby field with a teacher experienced in botany and field plants can awaken students to a whole new world of flowers that they never noticed before, resulting in a new interest on the part of many students to undertake excursions on their own to locate plants and wildflowers.

The natural setting is appropriate for reasons other than stimulating student interest. Most living things react differently when removed from their natural habitat. Native plants are adversely affected by artificial light and indoor humidity. Animals are usually deprived of the proper diet, exercise, and seclusion that they require.

Field studies permit the firsthand study of many things, both natural and man-made, that cannot be brought into the classroom because of size or inconvenience. It is only in the field that students can study trees, power shovels, or rock formations. It is only on field trips that students can observe the behavior of birds in their natural habitat. And it is only outside of the classroom that they can investigate the operation of a factory assembly line.

Using familiar settings outside of the school allows students to engage in activities that are too noisy or violent to be used in the classroom. A soda acid fire extinguisher must be operated outdoors. A model airplane gasoline engine creates a loud sound that would be very disturbing to many classrooms if operated indoors.

Short Field Experiences

Some field experiences need only a few minutes for completion and can be accomplished within the limits of a class period. They can be conducted on the school grounds or in the areas adjacent to the school grounds. Let us now consider a few situations in which a field study is appropriate and preferable to the traditional in-class laboratory.

❖ Returning to Mr. Gibson's ecology unit, we find that he is now discussing the various organisms that inhabit the different levels of soil in a typical grassy field. Mr. Gibson shows his class a film on the topic and then further reinforces the content of the film by using a cross-sectional chart of soil that indicates the various organisms and their habitats. Mr. Gibson realizes the importance of multiple presentations of important content, and thus he has his students view slides and specimens of the various organisms that inhabit the soil. ❖

The preceding lesson is typical of most life science classes. However, there is an alternative approach that may be more motivating to students. Why not study soil in its natural environment? There is nothing wrong with films, models, and slides, but why not use these materials to reinforce and supplement what the students experience in the real world? Time is not an issue; the students could quickly collect a 1-by-1 foot soil sample within a class period. Transportation is not a problem; most schools have large grassy areas within short walking distance if not actually on the school grounds. Furthermore, the expense of specimens and supplies purchased through biological supply companies can be avoided or reduced when a class gathers its own samples. Finally, students gain expertise in soil sampling and other data-gathering techniques when they perform these activities themselves. If Mr. Gibson were to use this type of field study, his students would benefit more from actually working with the soil and organisms. The objects are concrete and more relevant than pictures and models. Furthermore, if real soil samples are used, the class could perform further analyses of the samples, such as determining population densities.

✤ Mr. Gibson is finishing up a unit on genetics and is explaining the applications of genetic principles to agriculture (e.g., corn hybridization). He has just purchased some charts illustrating corn hybridization. The charts illustrate the various reproductive organs of the corn plant in great detail. In addition, the life cycle of a corn plant is presented from seed to sexual maturity. Mr. Gibson uses these charts to conclude the instruction on the unit about genetics. ✤

Here the opportunity for a field experience has been ignored. Note that Mr. Gibson teaches in a rural midwestern school district. The farms of the surrounding area have many cornfields, and there are hybrid seed corn farms as well. Many fields are within walking distance of the school. Certainly Mr. Gibson could have taken his class on a short trip to such a field. Even the most insensitive observer would quickly note the unusual format of a hybrid seed corn field. Such an unusual arrangement would evoke numerous inquiries from the students, such as: Why are there alternating groups of short and tall stalks? Why is there a gap every four rows? Why are the stalks along the field edges all the same size? Why are only stalks with silk left standing? The answers to these questions and other factors would give Mr. Gibson's class a concrete illustration of how such a field applies the genetic principles that they have studied in class. The advantages of using materials in the environment, as opposed to classroom models, charts, and diagrams, are obvious. Consider, for example, the following: Will students learn more by inspecting actual tassels and silks or by studying diagrams? Will the format of the seed corn field illustrate forced cross-pollination more efficiently than a theoretical explanation? Will a theoretical explanation of the rationale for planting rows of corn at systematic time intervals serve as well as simply observing a detasseling machine in operation? Such questions seem foolish because no doubt exists as to the pedagogical superiority of the use of real objects as opposed to mere representations.

Planning Field Experiences

One must plan ahead in order to be successful with field trips and experiences. First, determine how and when these activities will fit into the curriculum. Second, survey the resources that are available for field experiences and, finally, carefully review the policy on fieldwork.

Curriculum adaptation. Conventional planning procedures usually begin with the identification of instructional objectives, followed by selection of the most suitable activities for attaining these objectives. With conventional planning, however, many opportunities for fieldwork are neglected because their contributions seem insignificant. One teacher, Miss Rogers, describes an urban field study as follows:

✤ Many students have never seen a clover plant growing in a natural environment, although the plants are commonly found in vacant lots and fields. I take my students to a nearby lot and direct them to measure off one square foot and then count the number of plants in that area to determine how many four-leafed clovers they can find. They are also asked to compare the sizes and shapes of the leaves and to dig up several plants to see the root nodules. ✦

If Miss Rogers were teaching a conventional unit on reproduction, she might feel little enthusiasm for walking her students down three flights of stairs merely to see clover plants spreading by means of trailing stems. She might prefer to dig up clover plants herself and take them into the classroom to explain how the plants reproduce. However, Miss Rogers can get more instructional mileage by taking her students on a field trip to study clover plants in their natural environment. Here she can bring in many aspects of biology other than reproduction, such as nutrition and symbiosis, which will be taken up in the course at a later time. Thus, the fieldwork will offer experiences that can be used to introduce new topics, providing advance organizers for future instruction.

Surveying resources. Study indoors the things that are best studied indoors; study outdoors the things that are best studied outdoors. This is a rule that one might use to govern fieldwork.

Within and around each school, whether urban or rural, are hundreds of things worthy of study—resources far more valuable than those available in the most expensively equipped laboratories. Common things are often best to study; one does not need a volcano, a blast furnace, or a botanical garden for effective fieldwork.

To make a survey of resources, it is best to begin within the school building and on the school grounds because there are comparatively few problems when trips are taken within school boundaries. One may then explore the immediate neighborhood. Table 15.3 lists some possible field study situations.

Administrative policy. Field experiences within the confines of the school property present few administrative problems. Most school systems permit teachers to take their students anywhere within these limits without special permission. Sometimes, however, a principal may want a written notification of intent to leave the classroom.

Excursions off school property, on the other hand, involve the problem of liability for accidents. Policies governing such trips have usually been established by the school officials. Most principals justifiably insist on a written notice, which includes the names of the students and the destination of the trip. Some systems require written permission from parents before students can be taken from the school grounds. This last requirement is a serious handicap in the case of short trips, and teachers should try to obtain blanket permission from parents for trips within the immediate vicinity of the school.

Conducting Field Experiences

An observer of a well-planned field study would be surprised at some teachers' apparent calmness during this activity. The observer might wonder how the teacher can be so composed with students moving about in all directions. If questioned about this, the teacher may respond with an oversimplified answer such as "I expect them to behave properly and they do." In reality, much practice and preparation precede the successful field experience.

It is true that the teacher expects students to control themselves during fieldwork, but students are given a great deal of practice in self-control before such work. In addition, the planning before fieldwork must be extensive to ensure that each student is sufficiently occupied and has little opportunity to get into mischief. The following example of a field study should serve to illustrate the logistics of such an endeavor:

✦ Miss Hunter took her seventh-grade class to study the plants and animals that live in and around a small pond a short distance from the school grounds. She made preparations well in advance. She organized the students into several groups: one group looked for submerged aquatic plants; another looked for aquatic plants on the surface of the water; a third group looked for aquatic birds; a fourth group looked for amphibians and reptiles; a fifth group looked for aquatic insects; and a sixth group looked for aquatic mammals or signs of their presence.

TABLE 15.3
Examples of Field Study Situations

School building
  Heating plant: transfer of heat
  Wood shop: electric motor ratings
  Metal shop: gear ratios in machinery
  Art department: temperatures in pottery kiln
  Cafeteria: diet choices of pupils
  Kitchen: bacterial counts from dishes and food
  Corridors: emergency exit patterns
  Music department: sound
  Medical office: blood pressure measurement
  Auditorium: acoustics

School grounds
  Lawns: habitats of plants and animals
  Shrubs: effects of light and shade
  Trees: seasonal changes
  Flagpole: shadow studies
  Concrete walk: friction studies
  Macadam pavement: absorption of heat
  Soil around building: spatter erosion
  Teeter-totters: level action
  Swings: centers of gravity
  Snow bank: insulation effect of snow
  Bicycles: gear ratios

Streets
  Automobiles: analysis of exhaust
  Bicycles: Doppler effect
  Pedestrians: pedestrian safety habits
  Driver-training car: stopping distances
  Intersections: traffic patterns
  Traffic lights: control mechanisms
  Fire box: method of signaling
  Electric lines: pole transformers

Residential dwellings
  Gardens: topsoil and subsoil
  Flower beds: phototropisms of flowers
  Porch boxes: slips for regeneration
  Lawns: earthworm castings
  Lawn sprinklers: rainbows
  Outdoor fireplaces: convection around fire

Community services
  Water system: chlorination of water
  Fire station: fire extinguishers
  Police station: radar transmission equipment
  Hospital: sterilization procedures
  Church: pipe organs

Rural areas
  Woodlands: analysis of soil
  Ponds: temperature distribution
  Streams: transportation of sediments
  Fields: collection of insects
  Roadsides: seed distribution
  Ploughed soil: animals in the soil
  Hillsides: erosion effects
  Cliffs: rock structures
  Beaches: wave action

Small businesses
  Service stations: hydraulic lift
  Garages: differential pulleys
  Music store: electronic organs
  Radio shop: oscilloscopes
  Plumbing store: water softeners
  Building supplies: insulation materials
  Appliance store: refrigerators
  Lumberyard: kinds of lumber
  Transformer station: circuit breakers
  Coal yard: types of fuel
  Junkyard: electromagnetic cranes
  Gravel pit: sedimentary deposits
  Quarry: rock specimens

Hobbies
  Astronomers: telescopes
  Fish fanciers: aeration of water
  Radio hams: antenna characteristics
  Hi-fi enthusiasts: speaker characteristics
  Beekeepers: life history of bees
  Gardeners: fertilizers
  Photographers: darkroom techniques
  Rabbit raisers: inheritance

Construction projects
  Excavations: soil-moving equipment
  Foundations: concrete making
  Bridges: derricks
  Small homes: electric wiring
  Office buildings: air conditioning systems
  Schools: plumbing

Small manufacturing plants
  Bakeries: action of yeast
  Sawmills: structure of tree trunks
  Dairies: pasteurization
  Ice plants: use of ammonia gas
  Greenhouses: photoperiodism, transpiration, plant growth
  Foundries: metal casting

Within each group there was a division of responsibility. One student carried the special equipment, such as dip nets and field glasses; another student carried containers for specimens that might be collected; a third carried a field guide. One student took notes and another drew sketches for the display on aquatic life that had been planned.

Before making this trip, the students examined maps of the area to be studied, and they established limits within which they were to stay during the trip. Furthermore, all procedures to be followed were outlined before the field experience. ✣

In short, all conceivable situations and problems should be taken into account before any field experience. Initially, the planning might appear to be time consuming. Indeed, many teachers will forgo fieldwork because they feel the effort is not worth the outcomes. This view, however, is more a reflection of the teacher's apathy than anything else. In truth, the planning and conducting of field experiences is tedious, but the experienced teacher and students find it well worth the effort. As must be expected, the necessary planning becomes easier and more efficient with time as teachers and students become experienced in fieldwork. But a word of caution is necessary. Teachers who superficially plan fieldwork are inviting trouble, because a disorganized field experience is self-defeating. The purpose of the field experience is to achieve certain learning outcomes, and it should be treated as seriously as any classroom teaching strategy—it is not merely a day in the sun.

Psychology of fieldwork. The boys and girls whom teachers take on supervised field studies are the same boys and girls they have in the classroom; only the surroundings are different. It is the impact of these new surroundings that causes the students to react differently.

The four walls and the patterns of behavior in restricted environments that were established during four or more school years no longer exist during fieldwork. The reflective surfaces that throw back the students' own noise and make them conscious of their actions are also gone, as are the reverberations that give strength and authority to the voice of the teacher.

Lectures in the field are difficult unless the teacher has a megaphone, a public address system, or an unusually loud voice. Discussions generally fail because students cannot hear each other and because there are so many distractions. Reading is difficult in bright sunlight. Writing is usually awkward. And students are too exhilarated to sit passively.

However, many constructive things can be done in the field. Students can explore, collect, take measurements, experiment, or do anything that demands physical activity. Therefore, when considering problems for fieldwork, it is generally wise to select those that permit students to work with their hands in some way. Assume that if no provision for this type of activity is made, some of the students will probably find things to do with their hands that teachers would rather they not do. During a five-minute walk on the way to a park, students in a seventh-grade class were observed doing the following, which were unrelated to the purpose of the trip:

1. Two girls walked along, their arms about each other.
2. Four girls picked up colored leaves.
3. Five boys picked up black walnuts and threw them.
4. Two boys tripped the girls ahead of them.
5. One girl chased the boy who tripped her.
6. One boy punched the boy ahead of him, was punched in return, and grappled with the boy momentarily.
7. Two boys continually pushed each other as they walked along side by side.
8. One boy broke twigs from bushes and a low branch and threw them at others.
9. One boy jumped up and pulled some leaves from a low-hanging branch, then wadded up the leaves and threw them at students ahead of him.
10. One boy pretended to put a caterpillar on one of the girls ahead of him.
11. Three girls ducked and squealed at the caterpillar. A fourth girl slapped the boy's face.
12. One boy snatched the cap from another boy's head but was forced to return it by the teacher.

These are the normal reactions of preadolescents and early adolescents. The experienced teacher is familiar with such behaviors and is able to control them by providing rules and actions that will reduce their occurrence.

Teachers should remember that the attention span of young people is no greater in the field than in the classroom. In fact, it is considerably shortened by the many more distracting influences confronted outside the classroom. Therefore, students should not be held to one type of activity for long intervals; a variety of activities is desirable.

Finally, consider the overall time element of a field study. In general, several short experiences are usually more effective than one long one. Preparation and follow-up for short field studies should center on small problems rather than extensive ones. The factor of fatigue is also eliminated during short field experiences.

The teacher's role. Teachers should serve as consultants for students during fieldwork. They should avoid lecturing or interrupting the work of students with comments of last-minute directions. Good planning easily prevents such common pitfalls.

Personal enthusiasm for fieldwork is a great asset to science teachers. If they react to field activities with interest and excitement, the prospects are good that their students will do the same. Teachers must work along with the students, always displaying their own inquisitiveness and interest.

Generally, a teacher should not interrupt the work of students or become the focus of attention. Occasionally, however, something unusual arises and justifies an interruption. Teachers should remember at all times why they are conducting the field experience. They should try not to turn the outdoors into a confining space by adding undue structure and constraints. The students should be allowed to interact with their environment.

Extended Field Experiences

Thus far two types of approaches that use field experiences have been discussed—projects and field studies. There is a third instructional approach as well. Extended field trips have aspects in common with field studies and projects, but they also may present a number of problems. Properly conducted, however, they can be among the most rewarding educational experiences for those involved.

Time constraints. The classification of a field experience as an extended field trip is largely based on the criterion of time. That is, the time required to conduct such a field trip exceeds the normally allotted time for a class period. There are two reasons for this extended time requirement. First, many field experiences involve locations that are not within short walking or driving distance from the school. Thus, much of the class time is used up just getting to and from the site. Naturally, it is assumed that the destination is worth reaching. Second, the fieldwork to be conducted (nature walk, museum tour, etc.) must require a few hours to complete, which would also preclude this endeavor from taking place during a single class period.

The extended field trip does, however, differ from a project in that the teacher wants all students to have the same experiences in the same learning environment. For example, the teacher would want all students to view certain exhibits in the museum. Therefore, such a trip must be directly supervised. Conversely, projects are normally individual or group pursuits. Finally, such extended field trips always involve locations off school grounds, usually long distances away, so that the issue of liability makes class supervision necessary. Projects performed out of school, on the other hand, are not legally considered formal school-sanctioned activities.

The extended field trip can be as short as a few hours or sometimes extend overnight. Overnight field trips such as camping are less common but are occurring with greater frequency in some school districts. The following discussion is limited to one-day excursions.

Transportation. Extended field trips are most commonly taken to such places as nature trails, zoos, museums, planetariums, botanical gardens, hospitals, and factories. Most schools do not have such resources within short distances, and if they do (e.g., a hospital) the guided tours usually take longer than an hour. The choice of transportation will depend on the distance to be traveled. If the destination is close enough for the students to leave after the school day begins and return to school before the end of the school day, there is the possibility of using school buses. Some schools commonly provide buses for field trips without question of limitation. Others allow a certain number of miles to each teacher, giving the teacher the option of using the mileage for a few longer trips or several short ones. Still other school systems permit the use of buses on an hourly basis. Some systems restrict the use of buses if the destination is so far away that departure is scheduled before school begins or return occurs after school ends.

There are many charter bus companies that can transport students on field trips. Occasionally, a school system budgets money for hiring buses, but in many cases students are asked to share the cost of transportation. The individual cost imposed on the student is usually nominal and normally does not create a financial burden on the student or family. However, the teacher should be prepared to make appropriations for students who have special financial problems. One way to offset costs is to find individuals, perhaps parents, who are willing to transport students in their personal automobiles. The use of private cars for field trips must be cleared by the administration for reasons of liability. Some school districts will not normally allow the use of private automobiles. Another point to consider is efficiency: if large groups of students are involved, the use of private automobiles becomes rather cumbersome and inefficient.

Administrative policies. The school policy for extended field trips is usually much more definitive and restrictive than it is for short field studies. Quite often, the teacher will have to submit a proposal to the school board or principal for approval. Overnight trips are either very rarely approved or are strictly forbidden. The teacher should be prepared to defend, in detail, the purpose of the trip and the outcomes she expects. This may be perceived as extra tedium for the teacher, but if the trip actually has instructional value the teacher should have already outlined expected outcomes.

Most school systems require written permission from each parent before students can be taken from the school grounds. It is advisable for the teacher to require such permission regardless of whether the school requires it.

When a teacher is planning an extended field trip, she finds that specific rules for supervision are often stipulated. Such rules usually require an adult chaperone for every group of ten students. If more than one bus is being used for the trip, it is a good idea to have a teacher on each bus. Obviously, if other teachers are to be used as chaperones, they will need permission from the principal, because their absence from school will necessitate having substitute teachers for their classes.

A final point is necessary concerning student permission to participate in such a trip. Usually the school simply requires parental and administrative approval, but keep in mind that the students will be missing other classes while attending the field trip. Whether or not it is required, approval should be obtained from each student's teachers for the student to miss class that day. Some teacher might feel that a particular student cannot afford to miss class. Such a concern is usually valid and should not be challenged.

Legal aspects. In most states, if not all, a signed permission form from a parent does not release the teacher from liability for accidents on field trips. The standard of reasonable and prudent care applies on field trips just as it does in the classroom. The teacher must show that necessary precautions have been taken and adequate and appropriate supervision has been provided. There must also be evidence of sufficient planning and warning of possible dangers.

A permission slip is merely a way of informing parents that a field trip is to take place—not a release of responsibility. It does provide evidence that the parent had knowledge of the trip and that the student had the parents' permission to attend.

A field trip planning form such as the one in Figure 15.1 is evidence that the trip has been well planned and that possible problems have been identified. This also shows that proper supervision was provided on the trip.

Preparation and management. The preparation of students for an extended field trip does not differ significantly from the preparation provided for any field study. Students should be told that they are expected to behave properly. If the trip is to a museum, zoo, botanical gardens, or similar institution, the facility will gladly send maps and information before the visit. This information should be given to students and reviewed in class in advance of the trip. For example, if the trip is to a museum, students can plan in advance what they wish to see. Although most extended field trips do not involve experimenting and manipulating, students can be given instructional materials to work on. Experienced teachers find that worksheets with questions referring to various exhibits throughout a museum direct student attention and ensure achievement of the intended outcomes. Such a technique can work equally well for planetariums, aquariums, nature

FIGURE 15.1
Extended Field Trip Planning Checklist

	PLANNED	CONFIRMED
1. Objectives of field trip	_____	_____
2. Date of field trip	_____	_____
3. Time of departure	_____	_____
4. Anticipated date of return	_____	_____
5. Anticipated time of return	_____	_____
6. Destination	_____	_____
7. Type of transportation: bus, car	_____	_____
8. Anticipated costs	_____	_____
9. Teacher supervisors	_____	_____
10. Parent chaperones	_____	_____
11. Teacher plans	_____	_____
a. Permission from school administrators	_____	_____
b. Permission letters to parents sent		
c. Reservations made for tour	_____	_____
d. Reservations made with appropriate individuals to use the site	_____	_____
e. Rules of conduct for students	_____	_____
f. Permission letters from parents returned	_____	_____
g. List of special supplies needed for the trip	_____	_____
h. Dress requirements for students for trip	_____	_____
i. First aid kit	_____	_____
j. Lunches	_____	_____
k. Follow-up activities	_____	_____
l. References	_____	_____
m. Materials students need to bring for the trip		
n. Evaluation of field trip		

walks, and so on. The key element here is that the teacher must be very familiar with the place being visited. If the teacher is not, it is hard to conceive of how she decided that such a trip was of educational value. Remember that long trips are advisable only when the learning opportunities justify the additional time and effort needed.

The best way to illustrate the "nuts and bolts" of the extended field trip is to describe two different types of such trips: a half-day trip to a local hospital and a full-day trip to the Museum of Science and Industry in Chicago. The planning and procedural steps are presented in sequential form, which can be used as a checklist of responsibilities.

✤ Mr. Dansert teaches in rural Illinois. He has decided to take all his classes on a full-day field trip to the Museum of Science and Industry in Chicago. Because the trip takes three hours each way, his classes must leave before the school day begins and return after it ends. The sequence of events essential to the successful completion of such a trip follows:

1. Mr. Dansert takes an informal poll in all his classes to assess student interest.
2. A proposal is submitted to the school board and/or principal.
3. After approval has been granted, Mr. Dansert takes another poll among his students to assess how many buses are required, the cost per student, and how many chaperones are needed.
4. Three buses are needed for the 125 students who will be attending the trip; those not attending will have a study hall during the biology time period that day.
5. Three buses are reserved at least one month before departure.
6. Students are asked to get permission slips signed by teachers and parents.
7. Money is collected for the trip.
8. Eight chaperones are selected from parent volunteers to go along with three teachers (one per bus), making a total of eleven chaperones.
9. Mr. Dansert meets with the chaperones to discuss the format of the trip.
   - Each of the eleven chaperones will be assigned approximately ten students.
   - A schedule is worked out so that chaperones know the sequence of locations within the museum to take their students.

- It is suggested that each chaperone allow his or her students one hour in each section. Students should have freedom to move around individually in each section.
- Parent chaperones should be advised of their jurisdiction regarding what responsibilities they should assume. They should be informed of the types of behaviors they should expect the students to exhibit and what the students are expected to accomplish. They should be made aware of the procedures involved in case of emergency or unexpected problems and informed of liability involved. The teacher should not assume that parents know how to serve as adult exemplars or that they know how to manage groups of students.

10. Students sign up for specific chaperones. Depending on the students, they may be allowed to choose a chaperone or chaperones are assigned.
11. Necessary class periods are spent preparing for field trip procedures.
12. Museum worksheets are given to students to structure their experience and ensure that the proper learning outcomes are considered.
13. Buses leave at 7:00 A.M. and arrive at the museum at 10:00 A.M. The museum has already opened at 9:30 A.M.
14. 10:00 A.M. to 1:00 P.M.: Students view museum with their chaperones.
15. 1:00 to 2:00 P.M.: Students and chaperones eat lunch in designated lunch area.
16. 2:00 to 4:30 P.M.: Students continue to view exhibits with chaperones.
17. 5:00 P.M.: Buses leave Chicago and arrive at school at approximately 8:00 P.M.
18. On the next school day Mr. Dansert begins review of the museum experience. ❖

❖ Mr. Donahue wishes to take his students on a tour of a local hospital. Only 20 students are involved but, because of time constraints, they will be gone from school for four class periods. Since students can leave the school grounds after the school day has started and will return before the end of the school day, school buses can be used.

Because of the number of students involved, and because the hospital will conduct a guided tour, Mr. Donahue does not require chaperones. Once again, permission is obtained from the school board and principal. The students obtain permission from their teachers and parents. Mr. Donahue reserves the school bus two weeks before the trip. Since Mr. Donahue is not taking all his students along, he designs an assignment for those classes that he will miss that day. The principal will either hire a substitute or place Mr. Donahue's students in study hall.

The following events occur on the field trip day:

1. Bus leaves school grounds at 10:00 A.M. and arrives at hospital at 10:45 A.M.
2. Hospital tour starts at 11:00 A.M. and continues until 1:30 P.M. with a 20-minute break for lunch in the cafeteria.
3. Bus returns to school grounds at 2:15 P.M. ❖

Selection of students. The selection of students for a field trip may cause difficulties for some teachers. Such decisions often depend on the science teacher's philosophy and attitude and the policies of the school administration. If the trip is viewed as a reward of some sort, then teachers may bar students from participating who are known troublemakers and potential discipline problems. They may also bar students from participating who are uninterested, lazy, lack initiative, and do not perform to the teacher's expectations. These may include students who do not do their classroom and homework assignments or do a mediocre job even though they are capable of performing at a higher level. On the other hand, if the field trip is viewed as a unique and innovative activity and an important part of the course, then no students should be omitted. Indeed, slow learners and unmotivated students probably need the trip more than those of high ability, and some students, particularly slow learners, are not necessarily stimulated through traditional classroom procedures.

Teachers who instruct mainstreamed classes will be confronted with special problems when planning a field trip. First of all, they cannot and should not prevent students with disabilities from participating unless the students impose a danger to themselves or others. Depending on the field experience, teachers may have to make special arrangements for students with certain types of disabilities in order for them to participate. Certainly the school administration should be consulted regarding policy that has been established for students with disabilities.

Purposes. Whether the field experience is included in a project, field study, or extended field trip, the teacher must not forget that it is merely an alternative to the classroom approach. The goals are the same; the field experience is not just a vacation from classroom tedium.

The teacher must carefully plan all field experiences. Students should know where they are going, why they are going, what they are going to do, and what skills and materials they are to master. Field experiences can and should be structured to ensure achievement of stated goals. This is most often accomplished through a particular task assignment, as is done with field studies and projects, or a worksheet, which is common to extended field trips.

The sample planning checklist such as the one in Figure 15.1 may be helpful to make certain that all the necessary details of the trip have been attended to. The items are checked off as they are handled. The checklist helps the teacher remember what has been done and what needs to be done during the course of planning.

It is extremely important that the field experience "fit" properly into the instructional sequence. Students should be quite clear on how the field experience relates to what has been discussed in the classroom. Additionally, classroom activities after the field trip should refer back to the lessons and perceptions gained during the field experience. Field experiences have as wide a range of functions as any other instructional method. They can easily be used to set problems, perform experiments, reinforce classroom instruction, and review content already covered. The list is endless.

If field experiences are not planned properly or treated as serious instructional approaches, they will result in failure. However, a well-planned field experience can be the most powerful educational tool a teacher has. High-ability students are stimulated to explore areas that they had not even imagined, whereas low-ability or uninterested students can suddenly "see the light" that many years of classroom teaching have failed to impart.

SUMMARY

Hands-on, minds-on learning, supported today by recent cognitive research (as addressed in Chapter 1) has a long history of trials (similar to the NSF-funded curriculum projects of the 1960s) and research-based support, with its inception going back to John Dewey. Project-based instruction and field-based learning are examples of learning by doing, where the focus is on students investigating authentic problems.

When properly carried out, science fairs can stimulate enormous interest in science and valuable opportunities for students to study problems in depth, communicate their findings to a larger audience, and acquire a real sense of accomplishment and self-worth.

Because they tend to be direct experiences engaging all sensory input modalities and tend to connect student learning in meaningful ways, field trips, science fairs, and project-based instruction, when well planned and carried out, are among the most powerful instructional tools available to the classroom teacher.

QUESTIONS AND ACTIVITIES FOR DISCUSSION

1. Plan a project-centered unit in which the students work individually or in small groups on an investigation. The students may want to suggest their own investigation, or you can suggest one that you feel the students would enjoy and be able to conduct.

2. Prepare a project unit for a seventh-grade science class on a topic of your choice that requires that students work alone on individual projects. Make a list of the possible projects in connection with the unit. Discuss the topic and the list of possible projects with other members of your science methods class.

3. Plan a field trip to a gravel pit or another geological site and have the members of your science methods class perform certain assigned activities at the site you select. Plan and discuss the activities before the trip so that the students understand what is to take place at the site.

4. Plan a short field trip for members of your science methods class to identify ten trees on your college or university campus. Prepare an identification key for the trees you want to have identified, and instruct the members of your science methods class on how to use the key before taking them

on the trip. On the trip, assign each student at least five trees to identify using the key. Ask the students to compare their results. Some students may have difficulty using the key while they are on the trip. Students who are having problems can be instructed by those who have mastered the use of the key. When the students return to the classroom, ask them to suggest ways to conduct the trip more effectively.

5. With other members of your science methods class, visit two local science fairs, one devoted to projects prepared by high school students and the other devoted to projects prepared by middle school students. Independently evaluate a selected group of projects in each situation using evaluation forms you and your classmates prepare beforehand. Compare your evaluations with those of other members of your class.

6. Volunteer to be a judge at a local or regional science fair where the participants are middle school students. Prepare a checklist you would use to evaluate the projects, and evaluate them using your checklist. Compare your evaluations with those of other judges who participated.

7. Visit a regional or state Science Olympiad. Compare a Science Olympiad with a local or regional science fair. What are the benefits that students derive from participating in a Science Olympiad? Which activity better meets the goals of science education, the Science Olympiad or the science fair? Why?

REFERENCES

Armstrong, T. (1988). Learning differences—Not disabilities. *Principal, 68* (1), 34–36.

Blythe, T., & Gardner, H. (1990). A school for all intelligences. *Educational Leadership, 47*(7), 33–37.

Ellison, L. (1992). Using multiple intelligences to set goals. *Educational Leadership, 50* (2), 69–72.

Gardner, H. (1987). The theory of multiple intelligences. *Annals of Dyslexia, 37,* 19–35.

Gardner, H., & Hatch, T. (1989). Multiple intelligences go to school: Educational implications of the theory of multiple intelligences. *Educational Researcher, 18* (8), 4–9.

Goodman, H. 1985. At the science fair. In *Science fairs and projects.* Washington, DC: National Science Teachers Association.

Hoerr, T. R. (1992). How our school applied multiple intelligences theory. *Educational Leadership, 50* (2), 67–68.

Keown, D. 1984. Let's justify the field trip. *The American Biology Teacher, 46* (1), 43.

Levin, K. N., & Levin, R. E. 1991. How to judge a science fair: Use the consensus method. *The Science Teacher, 58* (2), 43.

Science Olympiad. 1992a. *Coaches' manual and rules, Division B (Gr: 6–9).* Rochester, MI: Science Olympiad, Inc.

Science Olympiad. 1992b. *Coaches' manual and rules, Division C (Gr: 9–12).* Rochester, MI: Science Olympiad, Inc.

Smith, N. F. 1980. Why science fairs don't exhibit the goals of science teaching. *The Science Teacher, 47* (1), 22.

SUGGESTED READINGS

American Association for the Advancement of Science. 1989. *Science for all Americans: Project 2061.* Washington, DC: Author.

Baca, B. J. 1982. Teaching biology field courses in the wake of environmental disasters. *The American Biology Teacher, 44* (1), 21.

Benson, B. W., & Kirby, J. A. 1982. Science fairs: Do your students measure up? *The Science Teacher, 49* (1), 49.

Bicak, L. J. 1982. Schoolyard science. *The American Biology Teacher, 44* (3), 153.

Biggs, A. L. 1982. An interdisciplinary course in Big Bend National Park, Texas. *The American Biology Teacher, 44* (4), 27.

Blumenfeld, P., et al. (1991). Motivating project-based learning. *Educational Psychologist, 26* (3 and 4), 369–398.

Calinger, B., Champagne, A., & Lovitts, B. 1990. *Assessment in the service of instruction.* Washington, DC: American Association for the Advancement of Science.

Carlisle, R. W., & Deeter, B. C. (1989). A research study of science fairs. *Science and Children, 26* (4), 24–27.

Cramer, N. 1981. Preparing for the fair: Fifteen suggestions. *Science and Children, 19* (3), 18.

Fay, G. M., Jr. 1991. The project plan. *The Science Teacher, 58* (2), 40.

Fitzsimmons, C. P. 1983. Field trips within easy reach. *The Science Teacher, 50* (1), 18.

Giese, R. N. 1989. An open letter to science fair judges—focus on projects and presenters. *Science Scope, 12* (2), 38.

Hamrick, L., & Hart, H. 1983. Science fairs: A primer for parents. *Science and Children, 20* (5), 23.

Harley, David W., Jr. 1990. Track and field work. *The Science Teacher, 57* (6), 58.

Johnson, J. R. 1989. *Technology report of Project 2061 Phase 1 Technology Panel.* Washington, DC: American Association for the Advancement of Science.

King, D. T., & Abbott-King, J. P. 1985. Field lab on the rocks. *The Science Teacher, 52* (4), 53.

Lagueux, B. J., & Amols, H. I. 1986. Make your science fair fairer. *The Science Teacher, 53* (2), 24.

National Science Teachers Association. 1985. *Science fairs and projects.* Washington, DC: Author.

Powell, R. 1987. Research projects in high school biology. *The American Biology Teacher, 49* (4), 218.

Quint, W. C. 1980. Science activities for school trips. *The Physics Teacher, 18* (8), 584.

Rivard, L. 1989. A teacher's guide to science fairing. *School Science and Mathematics, 89* (3), 201.

Russell, H. R. *Ten-Minute Field Trips.* (1991). Arlington, VA: National Science Teachers Association.

Schellenberger, B. 1981. Take your class outdoors. *Science and Children, 19* (2), 28.

Science Fairs and Projects, Grades K-8. (1988) Arlington, VA National Science Teachers Association.

Science Fairs and Projects, Grades 7-12. (1988) Arlington, VA National Science Teachers Association.

Stronck, D. R. 1983. The comparative effects of different museum tours on children's attitudes and learning. *Journal of Research in Science Teaching, 20* (4), 283.

Teachworth, M. D. 1987. Surviving a science project. *The Science Teacher, 54* (1), 34.

Troy, T., & Schwaab, H. E. 1981. Field trips and the law. *School Science and Mathematics, 81* (8), 689.

Weisgerber, R. A. 1990. Encouraging scientific talent. *The Science Teacher, 57* (8), 38.

Weld, J. D. 1990. Making science. *The Science Teacher, 57* (8), 34.

Williams, R., & Sherwood, E. 1982. Activities in mathematics and science for young children using the school yard. *School Science and Mathematics, 82* (1), 76.

Winicur, S. (1989). Variations on a (science fair) theme. *Science and Children, 26* (4), 27.

Yager, R. E., & Penick, J. E. 1985. (Eds). *Focus on excellence: Science in non-school settings* (vol. 2, no. 3). Washington, DC: National Science Teachers Association.

CHAPTER 16

Demonstration and Laboratory Work

T his chapter is designed to help you understand the use of demonstrations and laboratory work for science instruction. Specifically, it is designed to help you with an understanding of

1. The laboratory as the key instrument in effective science teaching
2. The value of inductive investigatory activities
3. When and how to plan and perform a demonstration
4. The laboratory's role in learning
5. Skills that can be developed through laboratory investigations
6. How to organize for laboratory activities
7. Safety precautions in the classroom laboratory.

In the first-period general-science class, Mr. O'Brien took a candle out of a box and placed it on the demonstration desk. He told the class he would show them the difference between a physical and chemical change. He struck a match and placed the candle over the flame until the wick burned. Soon, some of the wax was melting, dripping, and then solidifying. He said, "This is an example of a physical change. The candle is partially burning and the wax is changed in the process of burning to carbon dioxide and water. This is a chemical change." The students watched the demonstration and some wrote notes in their notebooks.

Across the hall, Mr. Jackson was teaching the same unit. He also wanted to have students learn about physical and chemical changes. Mr. Jackson was not certain how he was going to do this. He asked Mr. O'Brien if he knew a good demonstration to show these changes. Mr. O'Brien suggested he burn a candle. Mr. Jackson, however, taught these concepts differently. After the bell rang and the students were seated, he took a candle and a matchbox out of his demonstration desk, placed them on top of the desk, and asked, "What am I going to do with the candle and match?"

Art answered, "You are going to light it."

Mr. Jackson replied, "That's right, but what will happen to the match and candle when I light them? How will they vary? What will happen to the candle when it burns? Will it drip?"

Several students raised their hands and suggested answers to his questions. He lit the candle and it started to drip. He asked, "Why does the candle drip? What will happen if we try to burn the dripped material? Where did the dripped material come from and how did it change while the candle was burning?"

George explained that the material merely melted and then solidified. Mr. Jackson asked the rest of the class what they thought of George's explanation: "What evidence was there for his suggestion?"

Several members of the class discussed the matter and agreed that this material had only changed form in the process of melting and resolidifying.

Mr. Jackson asked, "What is this type of change called?"

Two students raised their hands and suggested that it might be a physical change.

Mr. Jackson then asked what was happening to the candle as it burned. What caused it to get shorter and why would it eventually have to be replaced? The class discussed this matter and eventually discovered that the candle was also changing chemically.

A. INQUIRY THROUGH DEMONSTRATION

Which of these teaching methods do you think would be the more effective way to demonstrate physical and chemical changes and why? What did students learn from Mr. Jackson's approach that they might not have learned from Mr. O'Brien's? Which of the methods stressed the inquiry approach and why? Which method do you think took instructors more time to prepare? Which would be more inductive in its approach? Why do you think teachers have traditionally emphasized the deductive method in giving demonstrations? If you were going to teach this lesson, how would you do it better?

A demonstration has been defined as the process of showing something to another person or group. Clearly, there are several ways in which things can be shown. You can hold up an object such as a piece of sulfur and say, "This is sulfur," or you can state, "Sulfur burns; light some sulfur, and show that it burns." Showing in this way mainly involves observation or verification. Mr. O'Brien's use of demonstration was of this type.

A demonstration can also be given inductively by the instructor asking several questions but seldom giving answers. An inductive demonstration has the advantage of stressing inquiry, which encourages students to analyze and make hypotheses based on their knowledge. Their motivation is high because they like riddles, and in an inductive demonstration they are constantly confronted with riddles. The strength of this motivation becomes apparent if you consider the popularity of puzzles. Inviting students to inquire why something occurs taxes their minds and requires them to think. Thinking is an active mental process. The only way in which students learn to think is by having opportunities to do so. An inductive demonstration provides this opportunity because students' answers to the instructor's questions act as "feedback." The teacher has a better understanding of the students' comprehension of the demonstration. The feedback acts as a guide for further questioning until the students discover the concepts and principles involved in the demonstration and the teacher is sure that they know its meaning and purpose.

Demonstrations, in addition to serving as simple observations of material and verification of a process, may also be experimental in nature. A demonstration can become an experiment if it involves a problem for which the solution is not immediately apparent to the class. Students particularly like experimental demonstrations because they usually have more action. Students enjoy action, not words! They love to watch something happening before their eyes.

Demonstration versus Individual Experimentation

Educators have stressed the importance of self-instruction and less reliance on large-group or class instruction. Education should be preparation for life, and part of that preparation must be to ensure that the individual continues to learn long after formal education ends. It is important that the school reinforce habits and patterns of learning which will prepare individuals to continue their education many years after leaving organized instruction. Laboratory work, because it involves the individual directly in the learning process, as well as imparting working skills, is thought to be superior to teaching by demonstration. A person working on a laboratory problem has learned far more than just the answer to the problem. He or she may learn to be efficient, self-reliant, and analytical; to observe, manipulate, measure, and reason; to use apparatus; and, most importantly, to learn independently. Individual laboratory experimentation helps to attain these goals better than demonstrations do. For this reason demonstrations should play a lesser role in science instruction, with individual student investigation receiving top priority.

Demonstrations can be justified for the following reasons:

1. *Lower cost.* Less equipment and fewer materials are needed by an instructor doing a demonstration. It is, therefore, cheaper than having an entire class conduct experiments. However, cheaper education is not necessarily better education.
2. *Availability of equipment.* Certain demonstrations require equipment not available in sufficient numbers for all students to use. For example, not every student in a physics class needs to have an oscilloscope to study sound waves.
3. *Economy of time.* Often the time required to set up equipment for a laboratory exercise cannot be justified by the educational value received. A teacher can set up the demonstration and use the rest of the time for other instruction.
4. *Less hazard from dangerous materials.* A teacher may more safely handle dangerous chemicals or apparatus requiring sophisticated skills.
5. *Direction of the thinking process.* In a demonstration, a teacher has a better indication of the students' thinking processes and can do much to stimulate the students to be more analytical and synthetic in their reasoning.
6. *Need to show the use of equipment.* An instructor may want to show the students how to use and prevent damage to a microscope, balance, oscilloscope, etc.

Planning a Demonstration

To plan an efficient and effective demonstration requires extensive organization and consideration of the following points:

1. The first step is to identify the concept and principles you wish to teach. Direct the design of the entire demonstration to their attainment.
2. If the principle you wish to teach is complex, break it down into concepts and give several examples for each concept. For example, photosynthesis involves understanding concepts of radiant energy, chlorophyll, carbon dioxide, glucose, water, temperature, a chemical change, and gases. A student's memorizing that green plants can make sugar in light with water results in little understanding if he or she does not know the meaning of these concepts.
3. Choose an activity that will show the concepts you wish to teach. Consult the sources at the end of this chapter for possible suggestions for activities.
4. Design the activity so that each student becomes as involved as possible.
5. Gather and assemble the necessary equipment.
6. Go through the demonstration at least once before class begins.
7. Outline the questions you will ask during the demonstration. This procedure is especially important in doing an inquiry-oriented demonstration.
8. Consider how you will use visual aids, especially the overhead projector, to supplement the demonstration.
9. Decide on the evaluation technique to use.

   Written techniques
   a. *Essay.* Have students take notes and record data during the demonstration, and then have them write a summary of the demonstration.
   b. *Quiz.* Have students write answers to questions or prepare diagrams to see if they really understood the demonstration. Stress application of principles.

   Verbal techniques
   a. Ask students to summarize the purpose of the demonstration.
   b. Give them problems in which they will have to apply these principles they have learned.
10. Consider the time a demonstration will take. Try to move it rapidly enough to keep students attentive. Prolonged or complicated demonstrations are generally undesirable because they don't hold the students' attention.
11. When you plan a demonstration, do it well, with the intention that you will probably use it for several years. It will then take less time to prepare in the future. Evaluate a demonstration immediately after giving it to determine its weaknesses and strengths.

Add any questions which will contribute to the inquiry presentation when you use the demonstration again.

Giving a Demonstration

When giving a demonstration, keep the following guidelines in mind.

1. Make it easily visible. If you are working with small things, can you use an overhead projector to make them more visible?
2. Speak loudly enough to be heard in the back of the room. Do you speak loudly enough and modulate the tone and volume of your voice to avoid monotonous delivery? When a student responds, do you ask him or her to speak up so other students can hear? Do you repeat students' questions and answers for emphasis and audibility?
3. Do you display excitement in giving the demonstration? Do you make it come alive? A good demonstrator is somewhat of a "ham." She or he uses dramatic techniques to excite and involve students. The way in which a teacher makes a demonstration come alive is as much an art as is reading Shakespeare well to an enraptured audience.
4. How do you stage the demonstration? How do you start it to involve everyone immediately? One suggestion is to place unique objects on a demonstration desk. For example, a transfusion container or a Van de Graff generator placed on a desk immediately motivates students' inquisitive minds. Before you even begin, you have the students with you, wondering what you are going to do.
   a. Teach inductively. Start your demonstration with a question. If you have interesting equipment, ask your students what they think you are going to do with it. Spend some time just questioning about the apparatus. In the construction of a transfusion container, for example, there are several scientific principles involved, such as partial vacuum, air pressure, sterile conditions, nutrient for the cells placed in the bottle, and anticoagulants to prevent clotting of the blood.
   b. Ask questions constantly about what you are going to do, what's happening, why they think it is happening, and what the demonstration is proving or illustrating.
   c. Know the purpose of what you are demonstrating. Use your questions as a guide only. The questions you have anticipated may be excellent, but also be ready to pick up suggestions from the questions students ask while they are observing the demonstration.
   d. Give positive reinforcement. Always recognize a reply: "Say, I think you have something there." "Good, you're thinking." "What do the rest of you think of John's remarks?" When a student gives a good explanation, compliment him or her. Seldom react negatively to a student's answer. Don't say, "That's wrong." Rather say, "It's good you're thinking, but your answer is not quite right."
5. Allow at least three seconds for students to reply to your questions. This wait time is important so that the students may think and reason about the demonstration.
6. Use the blackboard to describe the purpose of the demonstration. Verbal explanations are seldom enough. Any picture or diagram you make on the board immediately attracts the students' attention. Remember that your students have lived in a TV-centered environment; as soon as they see a visual representation on the board, they are drawn to it. A beginning teacher often fails to realize or ever consider how the blackboard can complement the learning activity.
7. At the conclusion of the demonstration, have a student summarize what has occurred and its purpose. This summation helps to fix the purpose of the demonstration in the minds of the students.
8. Evaluate your lesson—orally or in a written summary.

Ways to Present a Demonstration

Of the several ways in which a demonstration can be given, a teacher-centered demonstration is seldom the best way because it does not provide enough student involvement. When students participate actively in giving a demonstration, they are more interested and, consequently, learn more. Here are five ways in which a demonstration can be presented.

1. *Teacher demonstration.* The teacher prepares and gives the demonstration herself or himself. This approach usually has the advantage of better organization and more sophisticated presentation.
2. *Teacher-student demonstration.* This is a team approach in which the student assists the teacher. This type of demonstration gives recognition to the student. The class may be more attentive because they like to watch one of their peers perform.
3. *Student-group demonstration.* This method can be used on occasion; it has the advantage that it more actively involves students in the presentation. The group approach can be used to advantage if students are allowed to select the members of their group. The teacher should evaluate the group as a whole and assign the group a grade which is the same for each of its members. The groups will form at first among friends. However, if some of the members are not productive, they will be rejected the next time groups are selected. The peer pressure to produce and become actively involved replaces the necessity for a teacher to encourage students to work. This group arrangement may also be effective in organizing laboratory work. The only problem is that the teacher must be patient until group pressure is brought to bear on the nonproductive students in the class.
4. *Individual student demonstration.* This method can produce very effective demonstrations, especially if the student has status among his or her peers. An effective way to have individual student demonstrations is to have students from advanced science classes demonstrate to those in lower-level classes. A ninth-grade general-science class may become enthralled when a physics or chemistry senior comes into the class to give a demonstration. The senior, excited about giving a demonstration, helps to convey that excitement to the students.
5. *Guest demonstration.* Guest demonstrators can do much to relieve a boring pattern of routine class activities. Other science teachers in the school may be called in to present a demonstration or activity in which they have some special competence. Professional scientists are often willing to give special demonstrations.

Silent Demonstration

Some authors stress the importance and desirability of a silent demonstration. See, for example, Obourn, 1961. The silent demonstration, since it cannot be supplemented or strengthened by explanation, requires more careful planning than does the teacher-talking demonstration. (See Table 16.1.) In preparing the silent demonstration, the teacher may find this general procedure a good one.

TABLE 16.1
Comparison of Teacher-Talking and Silent Demonstration

TEACHER-TALKING DEMONSTRATION	SILENT DEMONSTRATION
Teacher states purposes of the demonstration.	Student must discover purpose as the demonstration progresses.
Teacher names pieces of apparatus and describes arrangement.	Teacher uses apparatus. Students observe equipment and arrangement.
Teacher is manipulator and technician, tells what is being done, points out and usually explains results.	Teacher performs experiment. Students observe what is being done and then describe results.
Teacher often points out the things which should have happened and accounts for unexpected results.	Students record results as observed. Teacher checks for accuracy and honesty in reporting. Teacher repeats the experiment if necessary.
Teacher summarizes the results and states the conclusion to be drawn. Students usually copy the conclusions as stated.	Students summarize data and draw their own conclusions based on what they observed. Teacher checks conclusions and repeats experiment if necessary.
Teacher explains the importance of the experiment and tells how it is applied in everyday life.	Students attempt to answer application questions related to the demonstration.

1. Fix clearly in mind the object of the demonstration.
2. Select the apparatus and materials best suited for the demonstration.
3. Determine the beginning point of the demonstration. The beginning is based on what the teacher assumes that the students know.
4. Consider difficulties as learning steps. Perform the parts of the demonstration to explain these difficulties.
5. Perform the techniques so that they may be observed in all parts of the room. The steps should follow some order in relation to the learning steps.
6. Give students an outline of the steps to be used. Outlines may be mimeographed or put on the chalkboard.

Silent demonstrations should not be used frequently because there is no way for the teacher to determine if the students are achieving the objectives while the demonstration is being given. Silent demonstrations can, however, provide a welcome change in the routine activity of the class. They can be used effectively if an instructor accentuates his or her movements in the demonstration so that the students can see and have some hints about what is relevant. In a silent demonstration, *visibility* is extremely important and must be ensured; otherwise, the students will quickly become frustrated, and eventually discipline problems will ensue.

Storage of Demonstration Equipment

Equipment made by you or your students can lend an added fascination to a science demonstration because students are often more impressed by homemade equipment. Parents, industrial companies, and students will often construct or provide apparatus for the school without cost. Having students build equipment involves them in improving the science instruction of the school. This personal investment helps to build student morale and to show the community that the science department is an active and dynamic part of their school.

Much thought should be given to storing equipment after use so that it may be found easily in the future and set up again with little effort. One way to do so is to establish a list of headings under which to store materials. For example, in physics, storage areas might be labeled "electricity," "magnetism," "heat," "light," "sound," "atomic structure," etc. In biology, storage categories might be "glassware," "chemicals," "slides," "preserved plant and animal specimens," etc. The next time you wish to find the equipment, it can be easily located under the proper storage title. Such a system also makes it easy for students to assist you in storing or obtaining equipment for use in demonstrations.

An efficient way to store small demonstration materials for future use is to obtain several shoe boxes. (See Figure 16.1.) Place all of the materials you need for a demonstration in the box and label the end. For example, a box might be labeled "electrostatic demonstration materials." You might also include in the box a sheet of paper describing the demonstration. This procedure helps lessen future preparation time for the same demonstration. A student laboratory assistant can get the box down, read the included sheet describing the demonstration, check to see if all of the equipment needed is present, and replenish needed supplies. The box then will be ready for use and you will require practically no preparation time. This storage procedure works particularly well with general-science and simple physical materials. A drawback is that when many materials and articles of

FIGURE 16.1
Storage Box for Demonstration Equipment

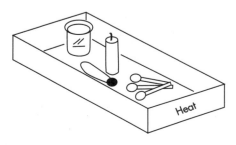

equipment are stored in the boxes they are not then easily available for other demonstration work during the year.

Special Equipment

Free sources of equipment. Science courses often require special science equipment. Some of this specialized equipment may be available to the teacher without cost through the proper channels. In some areas of the country, companies will donate materials to the schools when they receive a written request from the teacher. Consult with experienced teachers or professional scientists in your community to determine what is available.

Overhead projector. Every science class should have an overhead projector with suitable transparency supplies. Such a projector can become a valuable teaching aid during a demonstration or discussion. For example, in biology a teacher may want to show how to make a wet-mount slide. This procedure cannot be demonstrated easily except by using an overhead projector. Many of the properties of magnetism can be demonstrated by the use of such a projector.

Microprojector, videotape recorder, and amplifier. Another special piece of equipment of particular value to biology classes is the microprojector to project slide material. The advantage of this projector is that the teacher and the student view the material simultaneously. These microprojectors cost over $2,000 and are beyond the reach of most schools. An alternative to the use of the microprojector is a closed-circuit television camera adapted for use over a microscope; the students view the material on a television console. Amplifiers can be used to good advantage to study heartbeats of various animals and to let the class hear them. Some teachers have a small tape library which may contain information that can be used as an actual part of a demonstration. In the study of sound in general science or physics, tape recorders can be put to good use.

Stressing the Higher Levels of Learning

A demonstration should contribute to the objectives of the course and school. It should be used to stimulate critical thinking and offer opportunities for creativity. A demonstration may further be used to develop understanding of the philosophical basis of science. For example, the instructor may ask

- How certain are we of our data?
- What evidence is there of certainty in science?
- How do scientists fractionate knowledge to find answers to bigger problems?
- How are the fractional bits of knowledge related to the whole?
- I have just produced a pollutant. What are the social implications of this act?
- How can a scientist be moral, immoral, or amoral?

Questions of this type can be used discriminately throughout a series of demonstrations to build a philosophical awareness of the foundations of modern science. The responsibility to build knowledge of this sort offers great challenge to the teacher in formulating lessons.

B. INQUIRY THROUGH LABORATORY WORK

It has often been said that science is not really science unless it is accompanied by experimentation and laboratory work. There continues to be interest in the laboratory as the focal point for the study of science. It is worth noting that this is not the first time in the history of science education in the United States that the laboratory has come into prominence. The late 1800s saw the construction of laboratories in secondary schools and colleges, with a corresponding change in emphasis on the methods of instruction in the sciences. The recitation method and the catechetical approach for learning science principles were gradually replaced by "experiments" in laboratories with the expressed purpose of verifying the laws of physics and chemistry. It was believed that students would learn science best by repeating, in an abbreviated fashion, the classical experiments of Newton, Galileo, Hooke, Priestley, Boyle, and many others. Students would see principles of natural science at work, enabling them to understand the underlying science concepts. Laboratories and apparatus were designed to duplicate as nearly as possible the materials and equipment used in the original experiments, with "modern" refinements to ensure reasonable accuracy in the hands of science students.

The Inquiry Approach

Beginning in the late 1950s, there was a definite shift in emphasis in school science. The laboratory became the center of attention at all levels, including the junior high school. Without exception, the science programs emphasized and provided for inquiry methods, in which students themselves were the investigators, allowing many opportunities for creativity.

The inquiry method in the science laboratory can be promoted by several fairly simple but important changes. Paul Brandwein and Joseph Schwab, in describing the "inquiry curriculum," had this to say about inquiry methods:

> In general, conversion of the laboratory from the dogmatic to the inquiring mode is achieved by making two changes. First, a substantial part of the laboratory work is made to lead rather than lag the classroom phase of science teaching . . . Second, the merely demonstrative function of the laboratory (which serves the purpose of the dogmatic curriculum) is subordinated to two other functions.
>
> One of these functions consists in a new service to the classroom phase of instruction. With classroom materials converted from a rhetoric of conclusions to an exhibition of the course of inquiry, conclusions alone will no longer be the major component. Instead, we will deal with units which consist of the statement of a scientific problem, a view of the data needed for its solution, an account of the interpretation of these data, and a statement of the conclusions forged by the interpretation. Such units as these will convey the wanted meta-lesson about the nature of inquiry. But they will appear exceedingly easy and simple, conveying little of the real flavor of scientific inquiries, unless the verbal statement of the problem situation and of the difficulties involved in the acquisition of data is given meaning by an exhibition of their real physical referents. . . .
>
> The second function of the inquiring laboratory is to provide occasions for an invitation to the conduct of miniature but exemplary programs of inquiry. The manual for such a laboratory ceases to be a volume which tells the students what to do and what to expect. (Brandwein & Schwab, 1962, pp. 52–53)

The inquiry mode of teaching, in addition to requiring a different philosophical approach by the teacher and students, also demands higher levels of proficiency in the use of the tools of inquiry. These tools consist of the skills needed to inquire into natural events and conditions. For example, one could not learn very much about how forces cause masses to accelerate unless he or she could make careful measurements of distance, time, force, and mass. To learn the interrelationships between all of these factors requires that the student refine his or her measurement skills. It is necessary to know how to use a meter stick or measuring tape, to read the units correctly, to read a stopwatch, to operate a beam balance correctly, and to measure force with a spring scale or some other method. In the classroom, the student must have opportunities to practice the skills required for a particular inquiry situation; otherwise, the experience will probably be frustrating and the learning minimal.

Research on the Laboratory's Role in Science Teaching

Science educators over the years have examined the influence of the laboratory on achievement and other variables such as reasoning, critical thinking, understanding science, process skills, manipulative skills, interests, retention, and ability to do independent work, among others. Much of this research gave inconclusive results, but science teachers in general feel that the laboratory is a vital part of science teaching.

Some positive findings can be cited. Three studies done between 1969 and 1979 found that laboratory instruction increased student problem-solving abilities. Other researchers reported positive results when working with disadvantaged students in the laboratory to encourage cognitive development, introduce scientific ideas, give concrete examples, and learn how to manipulate materials (Blosser, 1983).

Data from a national survey in 1978 show that laboratory work and hands-on science activities are not used optimally in science teaching. Many teachers say students are apathetic about laboratory work and that labs are difficult to stock, maintain, and control. However, it is not likely students will experience much of the nature, methods, and spirit of science without this important component of science teaching.

Skill Development in the Laboratory

The complaint has frequently been lodged against science teaching that students and teachers alike have difficulty in expressing exactly what the goals of science teaching should be.

In taking up this challenge, we will identify the types of skills which science students ought to be able to do better after having taken the courses in science in the junior and senior high schools. We have listed five categories of skills: acquisitive, organizational, creative, manipulative, and communicative. No attempt is made to rank these categories in order of importance, or even to imply that any one category may be more important than any other. Within each of the categories, however, specific skills are listed in order of increasing difficulty. In general, those skills that require only the use of one's own unaided senses are simpler than those that require use of instruments or higher orders of manual and mental dexterity.

Categories of skills

A. Acquisitive skills
   1. Listening—being attentive, alert, questioning
   2. Observing—being accurate, alert, systematic
   3. Searching—locating sources, using several sources, being self-reliant, acquiring library skills
   4. Inquiring—asking, interviewing, corresponding
   5. Investigating—reading background information, formulating problems
   6. Gathering data—tabulating, organizing, classifying, recording
   7. Research—locating a problem, learning background, setting up experiments, analyzing data, drawing conclusions

B. Organizational skills
   1. Recording—tabulating, charting, working systematically, working regularly, recording completely
   2. Comparing—noticing how things are alike, looking for similarities, noticing identical features
   3. Contrasting—noticing how things differ, looking for dissimilarities, noticing unlike features
   4. Classifying—putting things into groups and subgroups, identifying categories, deciding between alternatives
   5. Organizing—putting items in order, establishing a system, filing, labeling, arranging
   6. Outlining—employing major headings and subheadings, using sequential, logical organization
   7. Reviewing—picking out important items, memorizing, associating
   8. Evaluating—recognizing good and poor features, knowing how to improve grades
   9. Analyzing—seeing implications and relationships, picking out causes and effects, locating new problems

C. Creative skills
   1. Planning ahead—seeing possible results and probable modes of attack, setting up hypotheses
   2. Designing a new problem, a new approach, a new device or system
   3. Inventing—creating a method, device, or technique
   4. Synthesizing—putting familiar things together in a new arrangement, hybridizing, drawing together

D. Manipulative skills
   1. Using an instrument—knowing the instrument's parts, how it works, how to adjust it, its proper use for a given task, its limitations

   2. Caring for an instrument—knowing how to store it, using proper settings, keeping it clean, handling it properly, knowing its rate capacity, transporting it safely
   3. Demonstration—setting up apparatus, making it work, describing parts and functions, illustrating scientific principles
   4. Experimentation—recognizing a problem, planning a procedure, collecting data, recording data, analyzing data, drawing conclusions
   5. Repair—repairing and maintaining equipment, instruments, etc.
   6. Construction—making simple equipment for demonstration and experimentation
   7. Calibration—learning the basic information about calibration, calibrating a thermometer, balance, timer, or other instrument
E. Communicative skills
   1. Asking questions—learning to formulate good questions, to be selective in asking, to resort to own devices for finding answers whenever possible
   2. Discussion—learning to contribute own ideas, listening to ideas of others, keeping on the topic, sharing available time equitably, arriving at conclusions
   3. Explanation—describing to someone else clearly, clarifying major points, exhibiting patience, being willing to repeat
   4. Reporting—orally reporting to a class or teacher in capsule form the significant material on a science topic
   5. Writing—writing a report of an experiment or demonstration, not just filling in a blank but starting with a blank sheet of paper, describing the problem, the method of attack, the data collected, the methods of analysis, the conclusions drawn, and the implications for further work
   6. Criticism—constructively criticizing or evaluating a piece of work, a scientific procedure or conclusion
   7. Graphing—putting in graphical form the results of a study or experiment, being able to interpret the graph for someone else
   8. Teaching—after becoming familiar with a topic or semiexpert in it, teaching the material to one's classmates in such a manner that it will not have to be retaught by the teacher

Is there a need for science skill development? Courses in elementary and secondary schools emphasize the processes of science as much as the concepts and generalizations. Understanding a process involves skill competencies. Learning "how to learn" requires adequate learning tools. In addition, students need confidence in their ability to perform the tasks needed in self-learning. Skill competency strengthens self-reliance.

Can skill development be guided through a graded sequence of difficulty— from simple to complex? This progression is possible because of certain characteristics of skills themselves, such as level of difficulty and complexity. For example, skills requiring the use of unaided senses are simpler than those requiring the use of instruments. It is easier for students to use their unaided eyes to compare the colors of minerals than to operate a petrographic microscope to do the same thing at a higher level of sophistication. Also, groups of simple skills may be included in more difficult complex skills. Graphing, for example, requires competency in the simpler skills of counting, measuring, and using a ruler (instrument). In the same way, higher levels of learning, such as analysis, synthesis, and evaluation, require higher levels of skill proficiency.

Does skill development enhance or preclude concept development? Growth in conceptual understanding is enhanced by expertise in skill usage. In teaching skills, concepts form the vehicle by which the skills are learned. One cannot learn a skill in a void— there must be substantive information on which to operate. The skill of comparing, for example, is useless unless there are things to compare. In the same context, a hierarchy of skills forms a framework to which concepts can be attached. As one learns increasingly sophisticated skills, the subject matter (concepts) can be adapted and changed as required.

Can achievement of skill competencies be tested? There is ample evidence that skill achievements can be structured in behavioral terms. Performance can be observed and evaluated. Various performance levels of individual skills can be graded on a continuum from minimum to maximum success. Not only is it possible for teachers to create testing situations using performance objectives, but it is equally possible to provide self-evaluation opportunities for students to gain knowledge of their own progress and levels of performance.

What are the implications of the skill-development approach in the science classroom? Conditions necessary for success when emphasizing the skill or process goals are

1. Time must be provided for practice and experience in the skills being developed. One does not become proficient without practice and drill.
2. Teachers must clearly understand the skill objective. Planning must revolve around these objectives rather than traditional content goals alone.
3. Ample materials must be available. There must be a "responsive environment" permitting students to operate with the "things of science."
4. A variety of conceptual materials may be selected to facilitate skill development. Most conceptual themes or topics provide ample opportunities for teaching varied skills. In planning for teaching, however, it is important to concentrate on a few skills in any particular lesson.
5. Evaluation emphasis must be placed on performance or behavioral terms, not mere factual memorization or recitation. The superficial coverage of content must be de-emphasized, and performance and depth of understanding brought to the foreground.

Mere identification of skills to be taught is, of course, only a first step in the realization of a science objective. To aid in skill development and ultimate mastery of the desired skills, the teacher must devise suitable teaching plans and student activities. In this type of learning, "learning by doing" is an important maxim. Students must be given opportunities for activities which give repeated practice in the desired skills. The laboratory becomes an important facility at this point because most of the skills involve procedures which, to a greater or lesser extent, require materials and apparatus.

Organizing Laboratory Work

Effectiveness of the laboratory experience is directly related to the amount of individual participation by students. *Individual participation* here means active involvement in the experiment with definite responsibilities for its progress and success. In theory, the ideal arrangement would be to have each student wholly responsible for conducting the experiment from start to finish. In this way, the preliminary planning, gathering materials, preparation of apparatus, designing the method, collecting data, analyzing results, and drawing conclusions are unmistakably the work of the individual student, and the accompanying learning is at a maximum.

In reality, the maximum learning may be achieved, for certain students, by working in pairs or very small groups. With good cooperation and sharing of duties, the stimulation of pair or small-group activity may be beneficial. In group work, a shy student may be stimulated into action and thought processes which he may be entirely incapable of by himself. An extroverted student may assume directive and leadership qualities not developed in individual work. The science teacher must be aware of these possibilities and plan the methodology of laboratory work accordingly. There should be opportunities in the laboratory to provide experiences using both arrangements. Avoiding stereotyped and inflexible arrangements should be of concern to the teacher of laboratory sciences.

Experiments will vary greatly in complexity. In a typical laboratory, "experiments" may be no more than carrying out a preplanned exercise of observation and data gathering, or they may be as extensive and demanding as research on a problem whose solution is totally unknown. Arrangements for laboratory work must accommodate these extremes. A student of general science in the junior high school may need more of the "exercise" type of experiment to gain the skills needed for complex experiments. However, he or she should also be given opportunities to work on true experiments to sense the joy of discovery in the same way as a practicing scientist.

Handbook for Laboratory Assistants

Philosophy

Each laboratory assistant should constantly be working to make the Science Department more successful. There are definite responsibilities, duties, and dangers involved in the program for assistants. The department of science depends on you to a great extent. It is expected that each assistant is to be trusted and relied upon to perform his or her duties properly without the necessity of close supervision.

Responsibilities and Duties

It is the purpose of the Laboratory Assistants Program to aid science teachers, help maintain and organize the equipment and supplies of the department, and improve the science program.

Specifically, this includes

1. The care and organization of the stockroom.
2. The preparation of laboratory exercises and demonstrations for teachers.
3. The preparation of papers, information sheets, class lists, and other clerical work for the teachers.
4. The inventorying of supplies.
5. The correction of papers for teachers.
6. The preparation of charts, posters, signs, and labeling of shelves, etc.

Required Individual Project

In all classes you will have tests and homework, but in the Laboratory Assistants Program an individual project is required instead. One project is required each semester, or a partially completed project will be accepted the first semester if the project is extremely complex and permission has been given in advance.

Project Proposal (plan). At the end of the first quarter, a proposal should be submitted. If accepted by the science department, the student will then take data in the experiment.

The Project: The project should include a substantial report discussing the project, theories, procedure, data, etc. The report is due the last day of the semester.

Special Short Courses

Classes on special skills will be conducted at the weekly meetings to improve your abilities.

1. Handling glassware I (cleaning)
2. Handling glassware II (cutting, bending, and assembling)
3. Preparation of solutions (molarity, normality)
4. Safety in the laboratory
5. Analytical weighing
6. Setting up a biology lab
7. Setting up a chemistry lab

Grading

Grades will be determined and recorded objectively. A conscientious student should receive an A or B in science. However, it is possible to receive a lower grade for unsatisfactory performance. Grades will be based on the following items:

Required Projects: Each laboratory assistant will be required to complete one project each semester. This project may be in any area of science.

The Use of Laboratory Assistants

Preparations for laboratory work require exorbitant amounts of time on the part of the conscientious science teacher. Ordering materials, providing for their storage, inventorying, repairing equipment, and preparing for laboratory experiments daily add up to a tremendous

---

Handbook for Laboratory Assistants   cont'd

Special Projects: Each laboratory assistant should be constantly working to make the Science Department better. Any ideas that you may have for improving the department will be considered a special project when organized and completed by the student. Projects of a student's own initiative must be cleared through a faculty member before starting.

Demonstrations: Teachers will assign demonstrations to the laboratory assistants, whose responsibility it will be to find the equipment, set up the demonstration, and run it at least twice to make certain it works properly.

Laboratory Experiments: Teachers will assign experiments to be set up and tried by the laboratory assistants. Students are required to clean up the laboratory after the experiments.

Sections: Each laboratory assistant will have an assigned section in the preparation room and will be responsible for organizing it, inventorying, and seeing to the cleanliness of the section. The section assignments will be rotated on a regular basis.

Attendance at Meetings: Failure to come to a meeting may drop your grade.

Daily Grades: Teachers will be evaluating the laboratory assistants at all times for cooperation, fulfillment of responsibilities, and adherence to rules and regulations.

Logbook: Keep a notebook to include daily accomplishments and notes of meetings and special classes, to be turned in at the end of each quarter.

Point System	*Maximum Points*
Section grade =	100 points/week
Preparation of laboratory experiments =	100 points/experiment prepared
Special projects =	200 points/special project
Demonstrations =	100 points/demonstration (if performed for a class)

Semester Grade: Determined from the average of the two quarter grades and the semester special science project.

Meetings

All laboratory assistants are required to attend all meetings since this is a credit course.

Meeting Schedule:
Noon meetings every other week on Monday. All students must be present at 12:00 noon. Bring your lunch.
Seventh-period meetings on the week when there are no noon meetings (Tuesday, 7th period at 2:10 to 3:05). These meetings are for organizing sections, working on special projects, classes, and individual projects.

Procedure for preparing a chemistry experiment
  I. Obtain experiment number and approximate date it is to be ready.
 II. Preparation
     a. Read experiment in laboratory manual.
     b. Read directions in teacher's manual.
        1. Equipment needed
        2. Precautions
        3. Laboratory hints
III. Setup
     a. Check all chemicals, etc.
        (Report anything not available in proper quantities.)

(Continued)

---

drain on the science teacher's time and energy. Some teachers have developed systems where student laboratory assistants are used to perform many of the tasks needed to carry on successful laboratory programs. One teacher has prepared a handbook for laboratory assistants included here to illustrate the organization of such a program (Hofwolt, 1968). Students are given credit for participation.

Handbook for Laboratory Assistants   cont'd

    b. Check to see if solutions are old.

    c. Make all necessary solutions in proper quantities.

    d. Make one set of chemicals per table (8). Label solutions with formula and concentration. Use the correct size bottles.

    e. If experiment has unknown, prepare a key to unknowns to be turned in.

  IV. Perform experiment

    a. Make certain experiment is completely set up.

    b. Check to see if proper results were obtained.

    c. Record data.

  V. Experiment report ready

  VI. Clean up all glassware and put away all materials after experiment is completed.

Procedure for preparation of demonstrations

  I. Find a demonstration to prepare.

    a. Use any source you can find.

    b. Consult with a science teacher.

    c. Use special demonstration books in science department.

  II. Read demonstration carefully.

  III. Organize, collect all material necessary.

  IV. Try demonstration, *perfect it;* be certain that it works.

  V. Find out when teachers could utilize demonstration.

  VI. Store chemicals in a proper place for safekeeping, and clean up work area.

  VII. Perform demonstration.

    a. Give demonstration for proper class, or

    b. Bring in all the material for demonstration (on a cart) for the teacher at the *proper* time.

    c. Don't leave demonstration or experiment lying around if you don't complete it in one period—always put material in proper place even if overnight.

Orienting Students for Laboratory Work

In general, students of the sciences look forward to a laboratory class with pleasant anticipation. Being pragmatic by nature, they sense that this is "truly science" and that an exciting experience awaits them. This attitude, most prevalent in middle school children, must be carefully nurtured and guided as students progress to more rigorous disciplines. If laboratory work becomes a bore because of excessively rigid formality, unexciting exercises, "cookbook" techniques, or for whatever reason, the student will probably have been lost as a potential science participant. An atmosphere of excitement, curiosity, interest, and enthusiasm for science should be encouraged in the laboratory, tempered by care and restraint in use of apparatus and diligence in the tasks assigned. Obviously a hands-off policy regarding equipment cannot be adopted nor can a complete laissez-faire attitude be condoned. Respect for the problem, the materials, and the probable results of experimentation must be developed. The laboratory experience is but one vehicle by which the objectives of science teaching are developed. Suitably carried out, it can be one of the most effective methods of teaching and learning.

Orientation for laboratory work may involve creating a suitable frame of mind for investigating a problem. The problem must appear real to students and worthy of study. They must have some knowledge of possible methods of attack. They should know what equipment or apparatus is needed and be familiar with its use. They must have time to work on the problem. In a given situation, the science teacher may need to give attention to one or more of these factors to begin students on their laboratory investigations.

GUEST EDITORIAL[1]

The Laboratory in Science Teaching: Main Course or Dessert?

■ **Robert Yager**

Director—Science Education Center
The University of Iowa
Iowa City, Iowa

For many years the laboratory was thought to be an extra in science teaching in the secondary school, even though science educators have expounded on the values of laboratory teaching for many years. Seemingly, the laboratory was established as central to secondary science teaching with the advent of the national curriculum efforts of the 1960s. Before 1970, few would have thought that anyone would conceive of school science without students active in laboratory settings.

The 1980s brought disillusionment—with Vietnam, national goals, the promises of science, the polluted environment, and other societal problems. The decline in school enrollments, fragile economic conditions for schools, and the loss of "a place of honor" for science in school programs have brought clear questions of the importance of the laboratory for science instruction for the 1980s.

That the place of the laboratory in school science could be questioned is amazing. Apparently the centrality of the laboratory to the programs for the past two decades was not verified in practice, either for teachers or students. Again the laboratory appears to be the "dessert" for science teaching rather than the "main course." How could this be? Could it be related to disagreement as to the features and functions of an ideal laboratory in science instruction?

A general classroom may be a place for students to learn *about* science, but a laboratory is a place where students *do* science. Can a meaningful experience with science exist only in the "about" realm with no experience "with" science?

Science is a human enterprise where persons ask questions of nature in an effort to understand it better. To ask questions is an important first step, but to seek answers to such questions is basic to science. The laboratory is the typical place where the seeking occurs. It does not have to be the traditional room with laboratory tables, test tubes, special electrical outlets, and the rest. However, to assume that science can be learned and/or experienced without a place to seek answers to questions about nature is much like assuming that one can learn auto mechanics without a shop, or music without instruments, or art without specific media, or physical education without a place to practice physical skills.

The problem with laboratories in a traditional sense is the fact that they are not treated as "laboratories" in the sense that science is done in such places. Too many so-called laboratories are merely places for checking out what the teacher or the textbook says, or places where one goes to manipulate with approaches, or places where one goes to follow the directions in a manual or a so-called laboratory sheet. Such inappropriate labeling of a laboratory (or such inappropriate use of the laboratory) should not be used as a reason for abandoning real laboratories or the central role that laboratories must have for meaningful science learning.

Laboratories help correct the erroneous idea that scientific information exists only to be learned. Scientific information is valuable only if it is learned *and* used. A laboratory is a place where knowledge can be used; hence knowledge is exemplified as a means for action, not as an end in itself. Science laboratories should enable students to use information, to develop a general concept, to determine a new problem, to explain an observation or nonconformity in nature, or to make a decision. Laboratories are active places where the unknown is confronted. When laboratories are so defined and viewed, they do exemplify the essence of science. As such, they are indispensable.

If the laboratory is viewed as "dessert," it probably does not meet the criteria for a science laboratory. Classifying the laboratory as "dessert" probably means that it is being used to test knowledge and/or it is being used as an interesting digression from the more important mastery of information which occurs in the regular classroom setting. When laboratories are viewed as "dessert," they do not meet the basic criteria for laboratories and hence are misnamed. Laboratories when properly defined must be the "main course" in science programs. They become the place where science is experienced!

There are several features of an effective laboratory for school science. Such laboratories are places of action where something is done to satisfy curiosity. They are not necessarily special rooms in schools. They are often interdisciplinary in nature, often open ended; they are places where questions are raised, procedures defined, and tentative decisions reached. Actions in the laboratory often become the basis for discussion, for use of iteration, for practice with logic, for the formulation of new questions, for explaining observations. Laboratories in good science instruction cannot be "extra"; they cannot be the dessert after a meal. Laboratories should be the "meal"—the main course of student experiences with science.

SOURCE: R. Yager, Director General, NSF and DEA research and training project.

The Place of Discussion in Laboratory Work

In recent years, there has been a trend toward placing laboratory work at the very beginning of a new unit of study. The laboratory guidebook or manual is designed to identify problems requiring observation and solution. The student performs the assigned tasks or devises procedures of his or her own to arrive at a solution to the problem. While doing so, students discover the need for further information to explain their observations. They are motivated to read a textbook, search for information in a sourcebook or handbook, read supplementary material, or consult a teacher.

Laboratory work is followed by class discussion, short lectures, or question periods. During these activities, student questions are answered, observed phenomena are clarified, and certain misconceptions may be discussed. Other activities such as problem assignments, projects, extra reading, reports, tests, and demonstrations may follow in their proper context as part of the teaching and learning process.

In this method, it is likely that more than half of the total class time is spent in laboratory activities. The follow-up sessions become extremely important. The teacher usually must ascertain the accuracy of the learned concepts, correct misconceptions, and promote maximum learning more than in a conventional course. At the same time, the student is more directly involved in the task and may be more highly motivated than otherwise.

Laboratory Work in the Middle School

Extension of laboratory practices to the middle school and junior high school is occurring with greater frequency. Facilities for effective laboratory work are being built into modern schools, and youth of this age level are beginning to experience laboratory work on a regular, planned basis.

Middle-level school students are enthusiastic participants in the laboratory method of teaching. Curiosity and a buoyant approach to learning make this group responsive to the laboratory approach, and proper guidance by the teacher can make this method a fruitful one for these students. Because middle-level school science leads to more rigorous and laboratory-oriented sciences in the senior high school, it is worthwhile to consider its contributions to more effective learning when the student reaches biology, chemistry, or physics. It is reasonable to assume that certain attitudes, knowledge, and skills learned in the middle school years contribute to better and perhaps more rapid learning in the senior high school.

Following is a suggested list of basic knowledge and skills which might be developed in fourth- through ninth-grade science and which are considered desirable prerequisites for senior high science:

1. To understand the purposes of the laboratory in the study of science
2. To understand and be familiar with the simple tools of the laboratory
3. To understand and use the metric system in simple measurement and computation
4. To attain the understanding necessary to properly report observations of an experiment
5. To keep neat and accurate records of laboratory experiments
6. To understand the operation of simple ratios and proportions
7. To understand the construction and reading of simple graphs
8. To understand and use the simpler forms of exponential notation
9. To understand the proper use and operation of the Bunsen burner
10. To use the calculator for simple operations
11. To understand and demonstrate the use of a trip balance
12. To work with glass tubing in performing laboratory experiments
13. To keep glassware and equipment clean
14. To put together simple equipment in performing laboratory experiments
15. To measure accurately in linear, cubic, and weight units.

Laboratory work in the middle school can be broadened to include such features as out-of-doors observations, excursions, and certain types of project activities, as well as conventional experimentation in laboratory surroundings. Systematic nighttime observations of planets, constellations, meteors, the moon, and other astronomical objects may properly be considered laboratory work. Similarly, meteorological observations and experiments involving record keeping and correlations of data are included under this heading. Excursions for collecting purposes, observations of topographical features, studies of pond life, and ecological investigations are true laboratory work. The narrow connotation of *laboratory work* as something which takes place only in a specially designed room called a laboratory must be avoided in the middle school sciences.

The range and variety of activities performed by students in the laboratory make it necessary to use many evaluation methods.

A teacher of science must be aware of these prerequisites and alert to new possibilities as well. Increasing emphasis on laboratory methods is almost certain to broaden, rather than narrow, the range of individual differences among students. Suitable means must be devised for evaluating the progress and achievement of these students in their laboratory experiences.

C. SAFETY PRECAUTIONS IN THE LABORATORY

An inevitable result of greater student participation in laboratory work is increased exposure to potentially dangerous apparatus and materials. Instead of viewing this fact as a deterrent to the laboratory method of teaching, the alert and dedicated science teacher will approach the problem realistically and will take the proper precautions to avoid accidents among students in the laboratory.

Accidents and injuries often occur because students lack knowledge of the proper techniques and procedures. These techniques can be taught in advance if the teacher plans properly. Certain minimum standards of acceptable procedures may be demanded of students before they are allowed to work in the laboratory. The motivation to engage in laboratory work is usually strong enough to overcome students' reluctance to develop the requisite skills, particularly if they are convinced of the inherent dangers and the need for proper safety techniques.

According to the National Safety Council, about 32,000 school-related accidents occur each school year; about 5,000 of these are science related. Grades 7–9 experience the highest frequency of accidents, while elementary grades report the lowest accident frequency. Another source estimates one major accident per 40 students per year in laboratory settings throughout the country (O'Neill, 1975).

The prevention of accidents can be accomplished through a positive science safety educational program which places emphasis on teacher and student awareness of the potential dangers in science-related activities. "SAFETY FIRST" should be the basic motto for the school science program. However, safety considerations should seldom rule out a science lesson. Effective planning can sometimes be used to capitalize on safety problems. Developing and maintaining positive attitudes toward safety requires continual efforts in safety education. Hopefully, safety training in the science program will instill in the student the importance of safety in all areas of work and play (*Safety First in Science Teaching*, 1977).

Some general laboratory skills which will prepare the student to work safely are these:

1. Ability to handle glass tubing—cutting, bending, fire-polishing, drawing tubing into capillaries, inserting tubing into rubber stoppers, and removing tubing from rubber stoppers
2. Ability to heat test tubes of chemicals—knowledge of proper rate of heating, direction, use of test tube racks, etc.
3. Ability to handle acids—pouring, proper use of stopper to avoid contamination, dilution in water, return of acid bottles to designated shelves, etc.
4. Ability to test for presence of noxious gases safely
5. Ability to treat acid spillage or burns from caustic solutions
6. Ability to operate fire extinguishers
7. Ability to set up gas generators properly
8. Ability to use standard carpenter's tools
9. Ability to use dissecting equipment, scalpels, etc.

D. SAFETY AND LAW

The principal is responsible for the overall supervision of the safety program in the school. Likewise, the science teacher is responsible for the supervision of safety in the science class.

Individual teachers can be held liable for negligent acts resulting in personal injury to students. Some school boards have liability coverage which might support teachers if legal action is brought against them. Teachers should inquire about the nature of local board coverage and/or their own personal liability coverage.

~ *From the Teacher* ~

Suggestions for a Safe Science Project

■ **National Science Teachers Association Subcommittee on Safety**

To avoid accidents and injuries in the science classroom, both teachers and students should heed the following safety suggestions.

The teachers should be aware that:

1. It is the initial responsibility of teachers to prevent accidents and assure that the laboratory is as safe as possible.
2. Laboratory safety should be taught continuously. Safety rules should be posted in a conspicuous place in the laboratory.
3. Teachers should demonstrate where possible and instruct students on necessary safety procedures immediately before beginning laboratory work.
4. Teachers are responsible for following prescribed accident procedures if an injury or accident occurs.
5. In case of an emergency, the prompt and calm handling of an emergency situation is imperative if panic is to be avoided.
6. Teachers should receive certification from the American National Red Cross in First Aid.
7. Teachers should notify those in authority of the existence or development of any hazard that comes to their attention.
8. When using flammable volatile liquids, such as alcohol, in a demonstration experiment, care must be taken that all ignition sources are removed from the classroom.
9. Demonstrations involving explosive mixtures must be so arranged as to shield both students and teachers from the results of the explosion. Even when there is no likelihood of an explosion, students should be asked to evacuate seats directly in front of the demonstration table whenever there is any possibility of injury to them by the spattering of a chemical, an overturned burner, inhalation of fumes, etc.
10. Class conditions for lighting, ventilation, heating, and orderliness should be controlled by the teacher.
11. Readily accessible spill packages for cleaning spills and metal containers for the disposal of broken glass should be available.
12. The floor should be kept free of equipment, refuse, and spilled materials. Good housekeeping is essential to proper safety.
13. Reagent shelves should be equipped with a ledge or restraining wire to prevent slipping or sliding of bottles or glassware.
14. Teachers should know the location of and how to shut off utilities. Label and/or color code all master shutoffs clearly.
15. Ventilation hood escape outlets and fans should be checked periodically to assure proper operation.
16. All poisons and dangerous reactants should be locked when not being used.
17. Teachers should know the location and proper operation of fire extinguishers.
18. Sand, fire blanket, vermiculite, bicarbonate of soda, etc., should be kept on hand for fires and absorption of spilled reactants.
19. Safety shower and eye and face shower should be checked daily.
20. A well-supplied First Aid kit should be provided. A chart showing proper treatment for specific injuries should be prominently posted.
21. Teachers should dispose of dangerous waste chemicals and materials as prescribed by appropriate standards and the laws for your community. Provide separate waste receptacles for broken glass and waste paper.
22. Laboratories and storage facilities should be locked at all times when not under direct supervision of a responsible person.
23. You should have a thorough understanding of the potential hazards of all the materials, processes, and equipment that will be in the school laboratory.
24. Students should not have indiscriminate access to the laboratory stockroom and should never be permitted to study, work, or experiment without competent supervision in the laboratory.
25. All reagent bottles should be prominently and accurately labeled with labeling materials not affected by the reagent.
26. Teachers set an example for their students. Follow all safety regulations and constantly remind students of hazards.
27. Teachers should guard against poisoning by:
    a. Providing adequate ventilation for students working with volatile substances.
    b. Instructing about the avoidance of the ingestion of chemicals.
    c. Identifying plants and animals that may cause poisoning by contact or by a bite.
    d. Setting up safeguards against exposure to radioactive substances.

SUMMARY

A demonstration has been defined as showing something to a person or group. The techniques of planning a demonstration involve determining the concepts and principles to be taught, deciding on activities, gathering the materials, practicing the demonstration, outlining the questions to be asked, and deciding on the evaluation methods to be used.

Plan a demonstration with the intention of using it again. A teacher, in giving a demonstration, should be aware of visibility, audibility, and all the aspects of good staging. He or she should have zest, present the demonstration inductively, ask inquiry-oriented questions, give positive techniques, summarize, and

~ *F r o m   t h e   T e a c h e r — c o n t ' d* ~

28. Make complete accident reports promptly and accurately.

The student should be aware that:

1. All accidents should be reported to the teacher immediately, no matter how minor.
2. Only those laboratory activities where instructions and permission have been given by the teacher should be performed.
3. Only materials and equipment authorized by your instructor should be used.
4. Written and verbal instructions should be followed carefully.
5. Chemical goggles should be used when working with dangerous chemicals, hot liquids or solids, radioactive materials, and other potential sources of splashes, spills, or spattering.
6. Students should prepare for each laboratory activity by reading all instructions before they come to class. Follow all directions implicitly and intelligently. Make note of any deviations announced by your instructor.
7. Labels and equipment instructions should be read three times before using. Be sure that you are using the correct items and that you know how to use them.
8. No food, beverage, or smoking is permitted in any science laboratory.
9. Never taste or touch chemicals with the hands unless specifically instructed to do so.
10. While in the laboratory using solutions, specimens, equipment, or materials, hands should be kept away from the face, eyes, and body. Gloves should be worn when handling some reagents. Hands should be washed thoroughly with soap at the conclusion of each laboratory period.
11. Students should note the location of the emergency shower, eye and face wash fountain, fire blanket, and fire extinguishers and know how to use them.
12. Students should know the proper fire drill procedure.
13. Long sleeves should be rolled up above the wrist. Ties, coats, and sweaters should be removed. Long hair should be tied back during laboratory activity, especially when an open flame is nearby. (Use hairnets, if necessary.)
14. Student apparel should be appropriate for laboratory work. Long hanging necklaces, bulky jewelry, and excessive and bulky clothing should not be worn in the laboratory.
15. Work areas should be kept clean and tidy.

16. Students should always clean, and wipe dry, all desks, tables, or laboratory work areas at the conclusion of each laboratory activity.
17. Broken glass should be removed from work area or floor as soon as possible. Never handle broken glass with your bare hands. Use counter brush and dustpan and/or wet cotton wads held with forceps, and dispose in proper containers.
18. All solid waste should be thrown in separate wastebaskets, jars, or other designated receptacles. Do not discard any solids in the laboratory sinks, especially glass items such as tubing or cover glasses.
19. Matches should not be thrown into waste paper baskets. A metal container with sand should be provided for them.
20. Litmus paper, wooden splints, toothpicks, etc. should be disposed of in the same manner as matches.
21. Gas burners should be lighted only with a sparker in accordance with your teacher's instructions.
22. Extreme caution should be exercised when using a burner. Keep your head and clothing away from the flame and turn off when not in use.
23. Do not bring any substance into contact with a flame, unless specifically instructed to do so.
24. Only lab manuals and lab notebooks are permitted in the working area. Other books, purses, and such items should be placed in your desk or storage area.
25. Students are not permitted in laboratory storage rooms or teacher workrooms, unless directly instructed to do so.
26. Upon first entering the laboratory, students are not permitted to touch laboratory equipment until directed to do so.
27. Any science project or experiment that requires the use of dangerous drugs or chemicals that are caustic or poisonous must be approved by the teacher in accordance with school policies.
28. Always twist, never push, glass tubing into stopper holes. Lubricate stopper hole and glass tubing with water or glycerin to insert easily. Always use glass tubing with fire-polished ends.
29. Students should be alert and proceed with caution at all times in the science laboratory. Take care not to bump another student, and remain in your lab station while performing an experiment. An unattended experiment can produce an accident.

SOURCE: Reprinted with permission from NSTA Publications, Copyright National Science Teachers Association Subcommittee on Safety, 1840 Wilson Blvd., Arlington, VA 22201-3000.

evaluate the demonstration. A demonstration may be conducted by the teacher, by the teacher and students together, by a group of students, by an individual student, or by a guest. More attention should be given to demonstrations presented by someone other than the teacher, with accompanying comments. Silent demonstrations offer a different approach and emphasize observational techniques.

Equipment should be stored so that it is easily located for future demonstrations. Special equipment can often be secured from local industries without cost. The overhead projector and microprojector are excellent teaching aids for demonstrations.

Individual experimentation is usually a more desirable teaching technique than are demonstrations, but demonstrations have the advantage of economy of time and money, allow for greater direction by the teacher, and provide certain safety precautions. Demonstrations should contribute to the higher levels of learning—those requiring critical thinking and creativity.

Laboratory work in the middle, junior, and senior high school is constantly changing. From the emphasis on "verification" experiments in the traditional mode, the student is now invited to "inquire into" or "investigate" a problem. Laboratory experience becomes the initial experience with a new topic of subject matter, followed by discussion, reading, and further experimentation. The experiment may lead to new problems that warrant investigation.

The middle and junior high school is becoming increasingly oriented toward a laboratory approach. Not only does this approach give students an early start in learning the methods of science, but certain skills are introduced and practiced that will have value in later sciences taken in the senior high school.

With more of the responsibility for learning in the laboratory being allocated to the student, the matter of safety becomes even more important. The science teacher must carefully train students in the use of laboratory apparatus and materials. This training may precede actual work in the laboratory or be an intrinsic part of the laboratory work early in the students' experience.

The promise of science for the future continues. A breakthrough has been achieved in which students at last have become participants in the search for knowledge, not mere recipients of facts and generalizations dispensed by authoritative teachers and textbooks. The laboratory is the key instrument in science teaching.

QUESTIONS AND ACTIVITIES FOR DISCUSSION

1. Suppose that you wanted to teach the molecular theory of matter. How would you start your unit? What demonstrations would you do and why?

2. What does the word *demonstration* mean?

3. How does an experimental demonstration differ from a scientific verification?

4. What are the advantages and disadvantages of giving a demonstration?

5. How is the staging of a theatrical production similar to the staging of a demonstration? What considerations must be made in preparation for both?

6. What can you do to determine if you are moving through a demonstration at the right rate?

7. What advantages are there to a student demonstration?

8. How would you give a silent demonstration?

9. What are the advantages and disadvantages of demonstrations compared to student laboratory work?

10. Explain how you would give a demonstration to ensure that higher levels of learning would be required.

11. How would you store demonstration equipment so that you would be able to use it with greater efficiency?

12. Two science teachers were talking. One said, "I never answer questions." How could the teacher do this and still be a good teacher?

13. Do you now feel more competent to give a demonstration than before reading this chapter? Why?

14. Design an experiment that students can do in the classroom or laboratory and which gives practice in the skills of science. Choose a particular grade level, and select suitable apparatus and materials to achieve the "skill-development" objectives.

REFERENCES

Blosser, P. (1983). The role of the laboratory in science teaching. *School Science and Mathematics, 83* (2).

Brandwein, P. F., & Schwab, J. J. (1962). *The teaching of science as enquiry.* Cambridge: Harvard University Press.

Hofwolt, C. (1968). *Laboratory science course handbook for laboratory assistants.* Mimeographed. University of Northern Colorado, Greeley: Department of Science Education.

Obourn, E. S. (1961). *Aids for teaching science observation—Basis for effective science learning.* Office of Education Publication No. 29024. Washington, DC: U.S. Government Printing Office.

O'Neill, G. J. (1975). *Safety in the science laboratory* [Television series program #1. Sponsored by the N. E. Tennessee Section of the American Chemical Society in cooperation with WSJK, Knoxville, TN].

SUGGESTED READING

Dean, R. A., Dean, M. M., Gerlovich, J. A., & Spiglanin, V. (1993). *Safety in the elementary science classroom.* Arlington, VA: National Science Teachers Association.

CHAPTER 17

Computers and Electronic Technology for Science Teachers

With a reformation in science education under way, newly available methods, materials, and instructional delivery systems must be considered. Teachers can become overwhelmed by their daily tasks. Many teachers instruct from 100 to 150 students per day. They have tests to construct and grade, daily attendance to keep, and makeup work to prepare, in addition to their normal instructional activities and laboratory work. All of these normal duties require an enormous amount of record keeping. Consequently, electronic technology can be adopted to lessen these burdensome tasks as well as to provide excellent instructional programs to enhance learning.

Expanding on the more general aspects of related content in Chapter 6, this chapter is designed to help you understand the use of computers and electronic technology to further enhance your instruction in science and to lessen the burdensome aspects of the job of teaching. Specifically, it:

1. Describes several general computer and technological systems for instructional purposes, such as interactive microcomputer programs, interactive multimedia systems, telecommunication networks, and virtual reality technology.
2. Provides detailed examples of microcomputer programs that can be used to enhance science teaching, including programs that focus on microcomputer-based laboratories, simulations, tutorials, drill and practice, and problem solving.
3. Describes how computers can be used for record keeping, testing, and preparing instruction.
4. Highlights aspects of microcomputer software that should be examined before adoption.

A. USEFULNESS OF MODERN TECHNOLOGY FOR TEACHERS AND STUDENTS

The conventional group-paced approach to science instruction is too limited to fulfill today's educational requirements. The lecture, laboratory, textbook, and worksheet delivery systems cannot possibly address the range of abilities and learning styles of all students. The American society is heterogeneous. Students' cultural and academic backgrounds vary greatly. Many large school districts report that more than 50 different languages are spoken in their students' homes. Many students lack the most basic skills such as reading, writing, and speaking proper English. Absenteeism, students enrolling in schools at various times during the academic year, neglect, and abuse are just some of the problems that science teachers face when students enter their classrooms. Unfortunately, most of the resources in school districts go for administrative services and salaries, not for the support of instruction. Science teachers need all of the help that modern technology can give them in order to provide an effective science education for their youths.

Computers and electronic technology have great potential for aiding science teachers to improve the scientific literacy of more students. This technology can help science teachers perform their jobs more efficiently and instruct students in a variety of ways. Computers and electronic technology can engage students in many forms of learning that will help them process information and develop cognitive skills in a more individualized manner than conventional instruction. Microcomputers, videodisc players, and videotape players can bring visuals of events to the classroom that ordinarily would not be experienced in daily life by most students. These devices present spectacular images of natural phenomena, from the far regions of the universe to the depths of the atom. They can simulate or show actual events that would be too expensive or impossible to present firsthand in the classroom. They can be used to develop and retrieve data bases with useful information that can aid in inquiry and problem solving. Computers can accomplish many useful tasks with lightning speed and accuracy.

For the student, computers and related technology can be used along with other forms of instruction to improve learning. These devices help individuals visualize concepts and principles. Interactive microcomputer programs, for example, can be used to help students restructure and modify their conceptions by presenting a more correct illustration of scientific ideas than what they hold in their minds. Videodisc presentations can provide advance organizers for subsequent instruction through lecture/discussion and laboratory work, or they can be used to illustrate natural phenomena previously discussed in class.

One advantage of computers is that they can provide immediate feedback to students who are trying to master a given concept. These electronic devices are "patient" and can provide an endless amount of instruction or drill and practice. Individuals or small groups of students can receive quality instruction from a well-designed computer program without the direct supervision of the teacher, who may be attending to other students and tasks. Students who are ill and confined at home can be provided with programs that address material they normally would receive in the science classroom. With the quality and quantity of software that is available for science teaching, microcomputer programs can assist in daily instructional tasks as well as eliminate some of the drudgery involved in basic teaching functions such as designing instruction, record keeping, and grading.

An important use for computers is to help teachers and students learn about special topics. Certainly, it is everyone's responsibility to take care of our planet so that succeeding generations will have natural resources to enjoy. As a result of this concern, science educators can use the environment as a major theme in science education. In fact, the 1990s has been designated as the decade to study the environment. How can middle and senior high school teachers instruct students on environmental issues and problems, especially if they are not well versed on these matters?

Computer programs devoted to the environment can educate science teachers and students about the environment. Many programs for microcomputer systems address this important topic. For greater effectiveness, Eiser (1991) advises teachers to begin instruction by studying local problems before addressing those on a more global scale. Fortunately, software exists that pertains to such urban problems as land pollution, waste management, water quality, recycling, air pollution, traffic problems, and energy consumption. Some of these programs do more than present information; they engage users in problem solving whereby they can make decisions based on data and values. After students experience local environmental problems, they are in a better position to interact with situations that address global issues such as the depletion of the ozone layer, warming of the planet, and large-scale deforestation.

Computer usage in science teaching is on the rise. Consequently, this chapter describes many uses for computers and related technology that can help science teachers cope with the task of educating students to live and work in a technologically oriented world in the twenty-first century.

B. USES FOR COMPUTERS AND ELECTRONIC TECHNOLOGY IN SCIENCE INSTRUCTION

Interactive Microcomputer Programs

Microcomputer programs can help students develop abstract concepts and principles. The power of these instructional resources lies in their interactive capabilities whereby students can manipulate what takes place on a video screen. Students seem to gain greater understanding of a science law, for example, when they can alter variables or parameters and then observe the effects. This type of instruction permits students to predict what they believe is going to take place as a result of their intervention, and then observe what actually happens. These programs can help students develop correct notions of science concepts and principles through the use of science process reasoning. They also hold great promise for improving students' abilities to manipulate variables, understand graphs, and reason about events.

✤   Consider an introductory physical science course in which motion is a topic in the curriculum. An interactive program on velocity can be used to assist students to better understand this principle. On the monitor (Figure 17.1), the student can view an object moving from left to right at a constant velocity along the x-axis. As motion is observed on the screen, the velocity (in meters per second) of the moving object is shown in the upper left corner of the monitor and a graph of this motion is shown in the upper right corner of the monitor. After studying a given event, the learner can speed up or slow down the motion of the object. This will change the rate of motion and produce a different graph of the distance per unit of time, which will appear in the upper right corner of the screen. Another benefit of this exercise is derived when the student must construct a graph representing a given velocity, and then can verify the numerical relationships by running the program to observe the motion and the resulting graph. This type of computer program is ideal for representing uniform motion, often difficult to produce in many laboratory settings. ✤

Here is another example of an interactive microcomputer program. However, this one is used for teaching biology.

✤   Genetics is one of the most abstract and complex areas of biology. Concepts such as the gene and the chromosome cannot be directly observed. Phenotypes and genotypes are often confused by students. The molecular composition of DNA is complex even when simplified. Most students enrolled in biology courses require a great deal of in-

FIGURE 17.1
A View of the Monitor for an Interactive Computer Program on Velocity

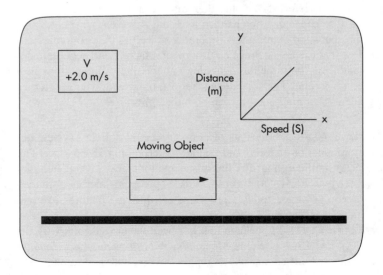

structional time to master these fundamental concepts and principles of genetics, especially when very little laboratory work and few firsthand experiences are provided.

An interactive microcomputer program, for example, can instruct students on the effects of radiation on *Drosophila* (fruit fly). On the monitor, students are given opportunities to select the trait to be altered, the sex of the fly, and the amount of radiation to be given. After each trial, the results appear on the monitor. The learner can conduct repeated trials to select the appropriate level of radiation so that the organism is not rendered infertile or killed outright. From the program, students get a sense of what research biologists think about when they perform their work. As students work through the program, they can produce a variety of phenotypes; for example, wingless, short body, and curly wing, all of which can be observed on the monitor. The students who use this type of program, along with classroom discussion and textbook reading, will likely gain greater understanding of sex chromosomes, sex linkage, somatic mutation, germ mutations, and other concepts than they would without this instruction. ✤

Interactive Multimedia Systems

Computer and video technology have been combined to provide some of the most powerful curriculum resources that science teachers can have at their fingertips. With a videodisc, images can be viewed in full color on a large TV monitor. The videodisc can store thousands of images that can be accessed by videodisc players. Science teachers or students can select still pictures and view them as they would colored slides. They can also view pictures that show movement. Some of these multimedia systems have been referenced to many commercial textbook series so that teachers can access the system with a bar-code device.

There is a movement at the middle school level to promote multidisciplinary science programs. These programs also include themes that are useful for organizing science concepts and principles. Middle school science teachers need a variety of resources to instruct students in these programs. Consider for example a unit of study concerning ecosystems and the environment. Most likely the assigned textbook provides only definitions and explanations of common ideas related to this area such as niches, adaptation, competition, food webs, and biomes. Laboratory exercises would probably accompany the textbook, with additional hands-on activities from the teacher's resource files. However, an interactive multimedia system, such as the one described next, would enhance this unit of study.

> ✤ A videodisc program on ecology and the environment can take students to different parts of the world to illustrate simple and complex relationships among organisms. A video of the logging industry in British Columbia and the northwest United States can show that cutting down large trees affects certain bird populations. Furthermore, students can view the size of this deforestation and then discuss how it appears to be affecting other animal life. The scene can be changed to South America, where students can view the relationships between plants and vertebrates as well as the economic conditions of people who live in these areas. Since environmental factors and economic development are interrelated, this multimedia technology shows these interactions in a very powerful instructional format. The science teacher can team with a social studies teacher to reinforce students' learning outcomes in both disciplines. ✤

As introduced in Chapter 6, CD/ROM systems offer a very useful delivery system because they can store large amounts of pictorial and textual material on a 12-cm disk. The amount of information this system can house is literally encyclopedic—several hundred thousand pages of typewritten text. Early versions of CD/ROM programs merely produced printed material on the screen. However, today's programs can provide pictures in vivid color and action along with textual material.

An example of a spectacular CD/ROM package that has been developed jointly by the National Geographic Society and IBM is called *Mammals: A Multimedia Encyclopedia* (Salpeter, 1990). The program contains sound, photographic images, text, and moving pictures. The user can select and view hundreds of different species of animals. For each animal, the program provides information about its habitat, diet, survival status, life span, and reproductive patterns. This teaching resource supplies the user with the quality of animal study that has characterized the National Geographic Society's long tradition of excellence.

Multimedia presentations can benefit a large number of students at a given time, if they can see what is taking place. Several devices are available for classroom presentations that permit large groups to view multimedia presentations. For example, large-screen monitors ranging in size from 26 to 35 inches provide excellent color images for student audiences. Video projectors can be used in large meeting rooms or auditoriums because they can project images directly onto large screens. Flat-panel LCD displays can provide images produced from computers and lasers, which can be projected on a screen by a device similar to an overhead transparency machine. This device can be transported easily from classroom to classroom and used for large group instruction.

Telecommunication Networks

Electronic technology has made it possible for communications to take place between classrooms across the globe. Some schools are connected to telecommunication networks via satellite through computer and modem. This electronic system permits students, teachers, and administrators to communicate and share information with others living in different locations. Now it is possible for schools, planetariums, museums, educational centers, and other facilities to share programs and exchange ideas through this network.

✤ Middle school students studying earth science can communicate with other students around their state to gather on-the-spot data concerning the weather. They can construct regional weather maps by contacting students in other schools that are 50, 100, 200, or more miles away to determine weather conditions in those locations. Students can provide information about the temperature, cloud formations, wind direction, and wind speed that exist in their locations. The students can attempt to forecast the weather. They can provide students in the rest of the school with daily weather reports over the announcement system. Furthermore, the students can attempt to predict the next day's weather from the information they gather and can determine which factors seem to provide the most useful information for this purpose. ✤

Telecommunications has made possible "distance learning" for many years, and some people living in remote places use it regularly. Distance learning is the application of electronic technology to help students receive instruction that originates from a distant location. The quality of these programs varies greatly. At one end of the continuum are programs where students merely view an instructional presentation. On the other end are programs that are interactive and where the learner must prepare assignments and react to the instruction. The National Science Teachers Association (Harkness, 1991) has produced a position statement on criteria for high-quality distance learning in science education. A summary of this position follows:

1. *Interaction* should occur between the instructor and students so that critical thinking and feedback take place.
2. *Flexibility* should exist in the program so that it can be adjusted to a given group of learners and locality.
3. *Manipulative experiences* should accompany instruction so that it is hands-on as well as minds-on.
4. *Competent instructors* conducting the instruction must be able to interact with the intended audience.
5. *A variety of appropriate resources* must accompany the program to supplement it and reinforce learning.
6. *Appropriate technology* should be used that provides the best instructional delivery system for the material to be learned, and not to use technology just for the sake of using technology.
7. *Evaluation* of the program and student learning must be part of the instructional package, and it should occur at several points during the instruction.

Obviously, a long-distance learning situation must go beyond individuals sitting passively and watching a video, regardless of how spectacular it is. Harkness (1991) cites the NSTA-sponsored JASON Project as a telecommunications program that merits science teachers' attention. To participate in the JASON Project, students and teachers meet at a museum on a designated day to accompany Robert Ballard on an undersea exploration. The students are expected to prepare beforehand for this experience using materials developed by NSTA. Other telecommunications programs to consider are National Geographic Society's Kids Network and NASA's Spacelink, in which teachers and students can collaborate with scientists.

Virtual Reality Technology

Perhaps the most powerful instructional resource for science education is what is termed "virtual reality" or "virtual environments" or "virtual worlds." A virtual reality environment is created to be like a real environment but is not the real thing. Virtual reality technology goes beyond the common visual and auditory experiences from computer and video monitors; it includes perceptual and tactile interactions as well. By wearing a special helmet (or headgear) and gloves, the learner can experience a new world, a virtual world, different from anything experienced before. During the past decade, military and space programs have used this technology to train individuals in flying and space travel. The hardware for this technology exists at certain government-supported science and technology centers such as the Johnson Space Center and private corporations that develop and support high-tech industries. Today, software is in the design stage for science educational purposes. However, this technology is still very expensive, and this must change before it appears in classrooms.

C. SPECIFIC TYPES OF MICROCOMPUTER PROGRAMS
Microcomputer-Based Laboratories

Microcomputer-based laboratories (MBLs) involve laboratory and firsthand experiences using the microcomputer to gather and display data. These laboratories may be used to quantify a variety of phenomena such as temperature, speed, length, force, heart rate, light intensity, and brain waves, force, heart rate, light intensity, and brain waves. MBLs offer science teachers a powerful technology to enhance laboratory work, often making it more exciting and meaningful to students. Students can explore science phenomena in more accurate and precise ways than are possible by traditional laboratory methods—at least for certain experiences. As a laboratory tool, this technology permits students to be engaged actively in their laboratory work and to focus on the data almost immediately. "The students are not automated out of the experimental process but given powerful tools which may help them gain a 'feel' for the data: data become almost palpable as their links to sensory experience are clarified" (Lam, 1984–1985, p. 1).

Unlike a simulated lab in which the computer is not employed to make actual measurements, MBLs require students to manipulate equipment and to observe data measured by a sensor and then displayed on the screen. Consider, for example, a laboratory exercise to measure temperature. With a simulation, a student might see several objects on the screen, each having a different temperature. The temperatures are displayed, along with questions about the causes of these differences. However, with MBL programs students are required to take temperature measurements from real objects. They gather these data with a temperature-sensitive device called a thermistor. Thermistors that are properly interfaced to a computer are accurate instruments that can measure temperatures to within less than $\frac{1}{10}$ of a degree Celsius. The student immediately observes the temperature readings and changes on the screen.

Many laboratory exercises can be carried out with the microcomputer. Some of these labs are already prepackaged and sold by software companies, while others have been developed by science teachers. Any science teacher can learn to use this technology.

In order to use the computer for measuring and recording, one must obtain a device called a transducer or sensor to pick up the data from the environment. The transducer converts physical or chemical changes into electrical signals. Sensors are available to detect changes in pressure, sound, light, temperature, pH, etc. However, one must convert the electrical signal produced by the transducer from an analog signal to a digital signal.

Analog signals are smooth, continuous electrical signals, similar to what one observes when drawing a line or a curve. Computers mainly use digital impulses to process information. A digital signal is discrete, or broken into small pulses. Analog signals entering the microcomputer from sensors are converted into digital signals before they are processed by the computer. The joystick that is connected to the game paddle port of the computer, which many youngsters use when they play computer games, facilitates the digitizing process. Since the joystick moves back and forth, this type of motion creates an analog signal that is fed into the computer at the game port connection, digitized inside the computer. Once the signal from the sensor is digitized, the data can be analyzed and displayed on the screen and calculations can be performed. In addition, the computer can transform data into graphs to help students see trends and anomalies.

The potential uses of MBLs in science instruction cannot be overemphasized. Not only is the microcomputer an excellent measuring instrument, but students are fascinated by it. The computer, and the graphics that it generates, gets students' attention and motivates them to participate in science laboratory work (Bross, 1986).

A science teacher might wonder how to conduct an MBL if many microcomputers are not available. If one computer is available, pairs or small groups of students can use it on a rotating basis to conduct laboratory measurements while the other members of the class are engaging in other types of work. With three microcomputers, one can accommodate 24 students. For example, consider an MBL that uses the thermistor to study heating and cooling. Organize the students into six groups of four students each. Two groups of students can connect their thermistors to an adaptor box which in turn is connected to one computer. Each of these two groups can independently input the thermistor data into the one computer and observe it separately. If two groups of students can use one computer, then six groups of students can use three computers. Nevertheless, it would be easier to have six computers, one for each lab group. Many science teachers borrow five or six microcomputers from other rooms or from the school's microcomputer lab so that they will have enough for a special MBL they wish to conduct. Planning ahead can facilitate all of these arrangements.

The IBM *Personal Science Laboratory (PSL)* is a microcomputer-based laboratory designed for science instruction from middle school through college (IBM Educational Systems). This program provides its users with two options when electronic technology is employed to conduct laboratory work. Individuals can select experiments that are already designed, or they can create an experiment. The former is ready to go and comes with preset parameters. The latter allows the user to set the parameters for an experiment. Probes are available for collecting data on distance, temperature, light, pH, and time.

For the Apple Macintosh systems, Vernier Software has developed the *Universal Interface*. This is a flexible MBL program that is user friendly (Sneider & Barber, 1990). The software consists of simple pull-down menus. The data can be displayed in one, two, or four graphs. The probes that are available for investigating phenomena are as follows: photogates, voltage sensors, thermocouples, temperature probes, and radiation monitors. Users can also build a magnetic field sensor and pressure strain gauge to extend the capabilities of the program.

Simulations

Computer simulations permit science teachers to bring rich learning experiences into the classroom. Simulations illustrate real-life or hypothetical situations that help the learner to visualize, in black and white or color, concepts and principles in "action" that would not be possible through lecture, laboratory experiences, demonstrations, or pictures. They often permit learners to manipulate variables or parameters and then to observe the consequences of their choices. Simulations can bring into the classroom aspects of the world or universe that are too expensive, too dangerous, too difficult, or too slow or too fast in occurrence to be experienced firsthand (Tamir, 1985–1986). Objects in space, molecular motion, radioactive material, electrical current, predator/prey relationships, and breeding are just some of the topics around which science simulations have been developed.

For example, a simulation of the heart can show the path of blood flow, highlighting the function of the chambers and valves. With the use of color graphics, oxygenated and deoxygenated blood is traced as it flows through the chambers and vessels of the heart. Other simulations can be used to illustrate the parts of the human circulatory system—its major arteries and veins, along with capillaries. Also available for science instruction are simulations of heart abnormalities, which are presented along with EKGs and their interpretations. Students can realize how technology is used to study the function and diseases of the heart—all of which makes this area of study more relevant and interesting.

Simulations of weather fronts are also available for science instruction. These simulations show the movement of cold and warm fronts across regions and continents. They help the viewers locate where various types of weather patterns originate and how they produce rain and snow. These simulations make the study of meteorology more real and concrete for middle and junior high school students.

Simulations with various amounts of detail have been developed to illustrate the growth of plants. These programs show how plants develop from fertilization to seed germination, to the young plant, and to the mature plant. These simulations detail seed development, show tropisms, and illustrate how environmental factors affect plant growth.

Tutorial Programs

Tutorial programs go beyond drill and practice. They are used to teach concepts, skills, and new information. These programs, being highly interactive, require active participation from the learner. They often involve reading, solving problems, analyzing graphics, simulating laboratory experiments, and completing word problems. Although they are sometimes expensive, they can be very useful because they provide valuable learning experiences. Every science course has certain concepts and principles that many students fail to learn. For example, some students have trouble understanding density, genetic crosses, Ohm's law, balancing chemical equations, solving mole problems, and determining acceleration. Even after science teachers have invested considerable class time in attempting to teach these ideas to students, many students still fail to understand the concepts and principles.

The science teacher can provide tutorial programs for situations when students are not learning important concepts and principles. These programs will carefully guide the learner through the steps necessary to develop the subconcepts that underlie the major learning outcomes. For example, a good tutorial program on balancing chemical equations might begin with writing chemical formulas, proceed to discussing chemical equations, continue with writing chemical equations, and end with balancing chemical equations.

Authors of good tutorial programs analyze the learning tasks involved in performing a given learning outcome. They break the learning into steps to increase the probability of the student performing the terminal task. These authors also include much practice after each step to promote understanding and retention. Branching is an important aspect of good tutorial programs because it provides appropriate remediation based on the student's incorrect answers.

Tutorial programs can be given to students to use during the school day or after school. They can be used in instruction if there is a microcomputer available. A display device can be placed on an overhead projector that permits many students to view the computer output on an AV screen or wall. An entire class can use tutorial programs in the microcomputer lab when many computers are available. Tutorial programs can be taken home by students who have computers in their home. They can also be used by homebound students.

Drill and Practice

The microcomputer can help students improve their performance in the science classroom. Many students who do not study or complete their homework and other assignments often do poorly on tests. These students fail to learn new vocabulary words and concepts that are found in their science textbooks or that are presented during a unit of study. They need to practice identifying, defining, writing key words, and solving word problems. Many students need repetition to achieve retention of the subject matter. Drill and practice microcomputer programs provide valuable practice for these students.

Drill and practice programs provide the learner with exercises that review subject matter. The list of commercial and teacher-prepared programs for this purpose is long.

Problem Solving

Computer-assisted problem-solving experiences hold great promise for maximizing the potential of the computer as an instructional tool. Problem-solving programs for the microcomputer go beyond computing numerical answers or producing verbal responses similar to those found in drill and practice, simulation, and tutorial programs. Good problem-solving programs center on real situations that may have significant meaning to students. These learning experiences require considerable involvement and interaction before solutions are proposed and results are determined with the aid of the computer.

The Voyage of the Mimi, for example, is a program that involves students in a great deal of study and analysis. It was developed by the Bank Street College Project in Science and Mathematics (1985). This technological-age instructional program combines television video, microcomputer software, and printed material to engage students in the study of whales during a sea voyage. The study of whales provides students a real context in which they can study nature and be involved in learning about the human aspect of science. The program also shows students how mathematics and technology are applied to study and solve problems in daily life.

The instructional package just described consists of thirteen episodes of an adventure story on video, each lasting 15 minutes and paired with a 15-minute documentary. The students use printed guides and interactive software to explore selected concepts in depth. They also engage in LOGO activities (a special type of graphics program) and microcomputer-based laboratory simulations. Printed material and software that accompany the TV series stimulate problem solving by encouraging students to experiment with the elements of the natural world as observed through this instructional package.

Most problem-solving programs are not as extensive as The Voyage of the Mimi, which has been a program series on PBS. Nevertheless, there are many worthwhile problem-solving programs for science teachers to preview for use in their teaching. One excellent microcomputer-based problem-solving program can generate a great deal of student excitement in a science class.

D. USING COMPUTERS FOR RECORD KEEPING, TESTING, AND PLANNING

Record Keeping

A microcomputer can offer great assistance to a teacher who must keep daily records for many students. Entering and averaging grades, maintaining daily attendance records, and recording information about students can consume a great deal of time and be very tedious. Fortunately, many computer programs can be used to simplify these tasks and to save considerable time.

Most computer-assisted grading programs permit the teacher to list alphabetically the students in a given class along a left-hand column of the page, and allow the entry of grades across the top of the page, as in a grade book. These programs also permit the teacher to weight the grades and to find numerical averages. For example, some science teachers count laboratory work one-third, daily work one-third, and tests and quizzes one-third. Others may have lab work count twice as much as daily grades. Whichever way teachers desire to weight the grades, the program will compute the averages. Some science teachers have written their own programs so that they can produce a letter grade (see Figure 17.2).

Teachers do not necessarily have to use a predeveloped software grading package. Spreadsheet programs can also be useful. Spreadsheets are commonly used in business for record keeping. They produce rows and columns, neatly displaying many data. Not only do spreadsheets permit freedom and flexibility, but they also save time. Fortunately, many individuals in local communities and schools can help a teacher get started in using the microcomputer for record keeping.

In addition to grading, the computer can generate seating charts to keep attendance. The seating chart is a matrix with squares that represent seats or desks in the classroom. When teachers place students' names in the appropriate spaces, they can take attendance easily while learning students' names.

Constructing Tests

Constructing science tests is a time-consuming task that can be facilitated with the microcomputer. One option is to use the machine's word-processing capability to construct the

FIGURE 17.2

An Example of a Gradebook for Recording and Averaging Grades Generated by a Microcomputer Program

Science Pd. 3

STUDENT	LOCKER	TS0828	LB0902	LB0909	LB0911	TS0917	LB0924	TS0929	DG1005	TS1009	AVE	GRADE
1 AVOGADRO, AMEDEO	77	90	100	95	100	100	100	98	98	99	98	A
2 BECQUEREL, ANTOINE	23	80	89	90	90	82	92	87	52	70	82	C
3 CURIE, MARIE	93	88	84	90	95	93	97	83	100	99	91	B
4 DALTON, JOHN	59	90	100	95	90	71	92	78	76	77	85	C
5 EINSTEIN, ALBERT	59	92	91	100	95	84	95	93	90	74	90	B
6 FARADAY, MICHAEL	85	96	100	95	90	92	90	83	90	88	91	B
7 GAY-LUSSAC, JOSEPH	29	90	100	95	95	86	90	89	96	84	91	B
8 HEISENBERG, WERNER	69	94	100	90	95	74	97	69	90	0	75	D
9 JOULE, JAMES	29	84	100	100	100	73	97	59	64	70	82	C
10 LEWIS, GILBERT	69	84	89	95	100	56	98	61	64	64	77	D
11 MENDELEEV, DIMITRI	93	88	82	85	85	78	97	89	68	76	84	C
12 MITCHELL, MARIA	53	90	98	100	100	97	95	89	100	92	95	A
13 PASTEUR, LOUIS	85	80	100	50	50	69	95	78	90	68	75	D
14 RICHARDS, ELLEN	53	86	98	90	100	75	100	89	76	89	89	B
15 TERESHKOUA, VALENTINA	77	92	98	100	100	67	100	100	100	100	94	A

CLASS AVERAGE = 87

test. Since the test is stored as a file, teachers can easily modify a test before administering it, if they so desire. They can easily make two versions of a multiple-choice test by taking the first version, modifying some of the stems and choices, and then saving it as a second version of the test. This procedure can be repeated several times to produce many versions of a given test.

Software and textbook companies have developed test generators for many science courses. These test packages are versatile and easy to use. They can produce many types of test items such as multiple choice, matching, true/false, and short answer. The programs also randomize test items, construct several test versions, and produce an answer key for each version of the test. Test generators that are designed for specific textbooks are keyed to the objectives for each chapter, and the user can select the objectives for the test items desired.

Preparation of Instruction

One of the most satisfying uses of the personal computer is for the preparation of instruction. Science teachers can use the computer's word-processing and graphic capabilities to construct lesson plans, unit plans, paper-and-pencil exercises, lecture notes, laboratory exercises, assignments, word puzzles, and so forth in much less time than it would take to prepare these instructional materials with pencil or using a conventional typewriter since modifications of these written materials can be made in minutes. Corrections can be made without retyping the entire text. Since textual materials are stored in files, they can be saved and recalled for use at a future time. This saves a great deal of time retyping and modifying an exercise or a lesson plan.

Many school districts require teachers to prepare daily lesson plans and to submit plans to the principal or department head. This requirement provides both the administration and teachers with a record of what is expected of the students and the activities that will be used to help students achieve the objectives. These lesson plans always call for a list of instructional objectives, which can be prepared quickly with the computer because it permits the teachers to make changes and modifications on the screen. Some school districts require the objectives to be given to students on a handout so that students and their parents can study the learning outcomes for a given unit plan.

The Biological Sciences Study Committee (BSCS) has produced a staff development program to help science teachers use microcomputers in their curriculum. The program is called ENLIST Micros and its main objectives are to improve teachers' knowledge, attitude, and self-efficacy regarding the use of computers in instruction (Ellis, 1992). The ENLIST Micros workshop package is distributed by EME and covers the following topics: (a) the anatomy and use of microcomputer systems, peripheral devices, and trouble shooting; (b) science courseware such as tutorial, drill and practice, game, simulation, and data base; (c) the assessment of software and where to find it; (d) software utilities such as data bases, spreadsheets, graphing, data analysis, word processing, record keeping, test construction, and telecommunications; (e) the use of optical equipment; and (f) the linking of lab instruments to computers to build simple sensor interfaces.

E. SELECTING GOOD SOFTWARE

The quality of the instructional computer software is a major factor in determining the benefits students derive from it. The quality must be high and the program easy to use and instructive—otherwise the computer will make little contribution to science education. Many educational programs are available, but not all of them are effective for instruction. A number of programs appear to be useful when first examined, but a closer look will lead science teachers to conclude that they have little educational value. It is easy for commercial courseware developers to make colorful, flashy-looking programs that appear useful; however, in the final analysis these teaching aids have little instructional significance. Careful review and analysis of a microcomputer program is essential before it is used in science instruction.

Perhaps the first thing that science teachers should do before selecting a program is to reflect on the course they are teaching or will be teaching. They must identify key concepts, principles, laws, and science process skills they wish students to master or what aspects of the nature of science and technology they want students to explore. This process will give purpose to their search for quality software and will help them to incorporate computers into the curriculum as opposed to using them because "it seems to be the thing to do."

To examine a program, science teachers should read the author's description of the purpose. What is the program trying to teach? Some programs, for example, attempt to teach scientific laws. Chemistry programs instruct students on Boyle's and Charles's laws, which address gas pressure and temperature. Life science programs instruct students on plant growth and human anatomy. Other programs emphasize problem solving and the scientific method. Next, science teachers must decide on the type of instructional program they want to use, such as drill and practice, tutorial, simulation, or microcomputer-based labs. Then, from the program description, determine for whom the courseware is intended. Usually the grade level is given for the program, but often this information is too general. In addition to determining the merits of various important aspects of the software, a teacher should also take into consideration the cost of the courseware.

A teacher reviewing software should take into consideration the following factors (also refer to section H of Chapter 6):

- Ease of use
- Ease of learning
- Error handling
- Flexibility
- Documentation
- Accuracy of subject matter content
- Appropriateness of instructional approach to material
- Appropriateness of material for audience
- Adequacy of screen displays/prompts/instructions and so on
- Interest appeal
- Absence of features that restrict the utility of the program (Smith, 1985, p. 50).

Make sure a program is easy to use before purchasing it. Are the instructions easy to follow, or does one have to spend a great deal of time figuring out what to do? Good programs must be user friendly or students will become frustrated and avoid using them.

Science teachers need to be concerned about content accuracy of microcomputer programs. They should become mindful of programs that contain factual errors and outdated information. They should also seek programs that use appropriate statistics and accurate graphs. Graphs are an important consideration because graphing is one of the process skills stressed in science education. Often computer programs use graphs that are attractive, yet difficult to read. Remember that not all microcomputer programs intended for science instruction have been developed or carefully reviewed by classroom teachers before they have been placed on the market. Individuals with programming background, who often take the major part in software development, may not know the type of graphing skills, for example, taught at a particular grade level. Also, these people are often not subject matter specialists.

Sethna (1985) suggests that an easy way to evaluate courseware is to develop a form to rate its important aspects. He recommends that users rate software in at least the following five areas: (a) ease of use, (b) documentation, (c) graphics, (d) content, and (e) instruction. Each area can be rated on a scale from 1 (low) to 10 (high).

Sethna points out that perhaps the best people to assess the merits of science instructional software are the students. He suggests that students be given the program to work through. Some of the statements that Sethna (1985, Appendix A) has given to students to evaluate science simulations are

- The program was easy to use without help from the teacher.
- The program helped me learn what I was supposed to learn.
- The program was related to other work on the same topic.
- The meaning of special symbols used in the program could be displayed on the screen when needed.
- The program told me when I had control over waiting time.
- Helpful shortcuts were given when I was expected to run the program many times.

SUMMARY

With a reformation in science education under way, new methods, materials, and instructional delivery systems must be considered. A microcomputer and the right software can assist you in enhancing your instructional program. Nevertheless, you must be keenly aware of the technical and instructional quality of the courseware you wish to adopt. Technically, the courseware must be easy to use, and the screen display and graphics must be easy to view. Instructionally, the content of the program must be accurate and appropriate for your students. Good software can be selected only through systematic inquiry into what is available and careful evaluation of its appropriateness for a given group of students.

New instructional delivery systems made possible by microcomputers and multimedia workstations will likely fundamentally alter the role of the classroom teacher. You should remain alert to developing technologies for your teaching. Laser videodiscs and CD-ROMs interfaced with computers and telecommunications offer exciting technologies for science instruction. New instructional technologies are advancing at an increasingly rapid rate. You and your colleagues must maintain vigilance over new developments, constantly looking for those that will not only help make student learning meaningful and interesting and your teaching effective and efficient, but be cost effective as well.

QUESTIONS AND ACTIVITIES FOR DISCUSSION

1. Compile a list of individuals who can help you use the microcomputer and identify software for your personal and instructional use. Science teachers experienced in this area are a valuable resource. Some high school and college students are knowledgeable about microcomputers and software. Neighbors who work with computers can be of assistance.

2. Visit with science teachers who use the computer as a tool for record keeping and for instruction. List the many uses that these professionals have for the computer and the frequencies that they report for each purpose.

3. If you do not own a microcomputer, ask teachers who own them for their recommendations on which computer is most suitable for your needs.

4. Obtain catalogs and periodicals that review software. Identify programs that you might use in your instruction. Refer to the list of suggested resources at the end of this chapter.

5. Analyze microcomputer software that you might use in a science course. You may wish to use the rating scales discussed in this chapter.

6. If you have not used a microcomputer, arrange time to become familiar with one. Microcomputer labs are open to students on college and university campuses, and many public libraries have computer rooms for general use.

SUGGESTED RESOURCES FOR MICROCOMPUTER USERS

BSCS. ENLIST Micros, 830 North Tejon, Suite 405, Colorado Springs, CO 80903. Information on teacher and leadership training for using microcomputers in science teaching.

COMPress, A Division of Wadsworth, Inc. P.O. Box 102, Wentworth, NH 03282. A source for science course software.

CONDUIT. The University of Iowa, Oakdale Campus, Iowa City, Iowa 52242. See its catalog of educational software.

Electronic Learning. Scholastic, Inc., 730 Broadway, New York, NY 10003-9538. This magazine is published eight times a year and has many software reviews and useful information.

EME. Old Mill Pond Rd., P.O. Box 2805, Danbury, CT 06813-2805. See its catalog of science software and materials for ENLIST Micros training package produced by BSCS.

IBM Educational Systems. P.O. Box 2150, Atlanta, GA 30055. See its Personal Science Laboratory.

Journal of Computers in Mathematics and Science Teaching. The Association for the Advancement of Computing in Education, P.O. Box 2966, Charlottesville, VA 22902. A periodical devoted to the use of computer technology in mathematics and science teaching.

Optical Data Corporation. 30 Technology Dr., Warren, NJ 07059. See its catalog for science programs, especially Windows on Science.

Preview! Cambridge Development Laboratory, Inc., Newton Lower Falls, MA 02162. A catalog of science courseware.

Project SERAPHIM. NSF Science Education, Department of Chemistry, Eastern Michigan University, Ypsilanti, MI 48197. See its catalog for descriptions of hundreds of inexpensive chemistry programs on floppy disk.

Sunburst Communications. 101 Castleton St., Pleasantville, NY 10570.

The Computer Teacher. University of Oregon, 1787 Agate St., Eugene, OR 97403-1923.

The Science Teacher. National Science Teachers Association, 1840 Wilson Boulevard, Arlington, VA 22201-3000. Refer to the "Idea Bank" and "Reviews" sections for information and ideas on science courseware.

Vernier Software. 2920 S. W. 89th Ave., Portland, OR 97225. Get its catalog, *Science Software for the Classroom and Lab.*

REFERENCES

Bank Street College Project in Science and Mathematics. 1985. *The voyage of the Mimi: A teacher's guide.* New York: Holt, Rinehart, & Winston.

Bross, T. 1986. The microcomputer-based science laboratory. *Journal of Computers in Mathematics and Science Teaching, 5*(3), 16–18.

Eiser, L. 1991, March. Learning to save the environment. *Technology and Learning,* 18–26.

Ellis, J. D. 1992. Teacher development in advanced educational technology. *Journal of Science Education and Technology, 1*(1), 49–65.

Harkness, J. L. 1991, February/March. NSTA issues new position statement on distance learning criteria defined for high quality instruction in science education. *NSTA Reports,* 3–5.

Lam, T. 1984–1985, Winter. Probing microcomputer-based laboratories. *Hands On! Microcomputers in Education—*

Innovations and Issues. Cambridge, MA: Technical Education Research Centers.

Salpeter, J. 1990, Oct. Multimedia spreads its wings: New applications for the Amiga and PS/2. *Technology & Learning,* 40–44.

Sethna, G. H. 1985. *Development of an instrument for evaluation of microcomputer-based simulation courseware for the high school physics classroom: Appendix A.* Unpublished doctoral dissertation, University of Houston.

Smith, R. L. 1985, Spring. JCMST Guidelines for evaluation of software. *Journal of Computers in Mathematics and Science Teaching,* 50.

Sneider, C., & Barber, J. 1990. The new probeware: Science labs in a box. *Technology & Learning,* 32–39.

Tamir, P. 1985–1986, Winter. Current and potential uses of microcomputers in science education. *Journal of Computers in Mathematics and Science Teaching,* 18–28.

SUGGESTED READING

Ellis, J. D. (Ed.). 1989. *1988 AETS yearbook: Information technology and science education.* ERIC Clearinghouse for Science, Mathematics, and Environmental Education. Columbus, OH: Ohio State University.

Ganiel, U., & Idar, J. 1985, Spring. Student misconceptions in science—How can computers help? *Journal of Computers in Mathematics and Science Teaching,* 14–18.

Hirschfelt, J. M. 1987. A spread sheet for your gradebook. *The Science Teacher, 54*(6), 72.

McGreevey, M. W. 1991, March. Virtual reality and planetary exploration. In *Proceedings of the 29th AAS Gooddard Memorial Symposium.* Washington, DC.

Sherwood, R. D. 1985, Summer. Computers in science education: An AETS position paper. *Journal of Computers in Mathematics and Science Teaching,* 17–20.

Stevens, D. J., Zech, L., & Katkanant, C. 1987, Spring. The classroom applications of an interactive videodisc high school science lesson. *Journal of Computing in Mathematics and Science Teaching,* 20–26.

Vockell, E. L., & van Deusen, R. M. 1989. *The computer and higher order thinking skills.* Watsonville, CA: Mitchell Publishing.

Woerner, J. J., Rivers, R. H., & Vockell, E. L. 1991. *The computer in the science curriculum.* Watsonville, CA: Mitchell Publishing.

Selected Activities for Integrated Mathematics and Science

As has been discussed throughout this book, for higher levels of thinking and for learning that is most meaningful and longest lasting for children, it is absolutely necessary to use instructional techniques that encourage interaction and cooperation among all students, that depend upon collaborative learning between the students and the teachers, and that integrate the disciplines.

Further, as we have emphasized throughout, as a classroom teacher and as a member of a community of learners, your instructional task is to (1) plan for and provide developmentally appropriate hands-on experiences and to (2) facilitate the most meaningful and longest lasting learning possible once the children's minds have been activated by those experiences. Part IV presents activities designed to help you do just that in your teaching.

The activities presented in this final part and chapter are designed to encourage interaction and cooperation among students, to encourage collaborative learning between students and their teachers, and to integrate in interesting and meaningful ways the disciplines of mathematics and science, and sometimes other disciplines as well. Where the use of each falls on the spectrum of integrated learning is up to you. When selecting activities that integrate children's active learning, you should ask yourself:

- Does the activity involve more than one subject area?
- Does the activity involve the children in exploring a topic in depth and over an extended period of time?
- Does the activity provide interesting, meaningful, and accurate learning that relates to children's daily lives?
- Does the activity provide opportunity for the children to work collaboratively and cooperatively while making and recording observations, gathering and defending their own evidence, and to express their results in a variety of ways?
- Does the activity accomplish the objective(s) for which it is intended?
- Is the activity within the ability and developmental level of the students?
- Is the activity worth the time and cost needed to do it?
- Within reasonable limits, is the activity safe for children to do?

The activities selected for Chapter 18 are likely to meet these guidelines for you and your children. ∎

CHAPTER 18
Activities for Integrated Mathematics and Science
Activity 18 is from Edward Victor and Richard D. Kellough, Science for the Elementary School, *7th ed. (New York: Macmillan, 1993). Activities 3, 4, 6, and 13 are from Arthur A. Carin,* Science Teaching Through Discovery, *7th ed. (New York: Macmillan, 1993). All others are from Leslie W. Trowbridge and Rodger W. Bybee,* Becoming a Secondary School Science Teacher, *5th ed. (New York: Merrill/Macmillan, 1990). By permission of Arthur Carin, Edward Victor, Richard D. Kellough, Leslie W. Trowbridge, Rodger W. Bybee, and the Macmillan Publishing Company.*

OPENING THE OCEAN AN INTERDISCIPLINARY THEMATIC UNIT (GRADE 5)
This unit is contributed by Chris Harrigan, Deanne Sacchi, Erika Yee, and Shannon Zudel.

Activities for Integrated Mathematics and Science

In this final chapter, we present a collection of activities that encourage interaction and cooperation among students, that depend upon collaborative learning between the students and the teachers, and that in interesting ways integrate the disciplines of mathematics and science and—in some instances—other disciplines as well.

Each integrated activity is presented in a way that should make it immediately usable to you. Some take more class time to do than do others. All activities are appropriate for any grade 4–9. The interdisciplinary thematic unit, which follows this chapter, is designed for use with fifth graders. You are advised to study each one in order to select those best for your own use with your own distinctive group of students.

The titles of the activities and their order of presentation are as follows.

Activity 1   **An Introduction to Scientific Inquiry**

AIMS

To develop a fundamental understanding of, and ability to use, the methods of scientific investigation

OBJECTIVES

At the completion of this lesson the student should be able to:

1. Identify and state a simple problem
2. Collect data relative to a simple problem
3. Draw conclusions relative to data
4. Form hypotheses based on observations and data
5. Design a simple experiment to confirm/refute a hypothesis.

MATERIALS

1. Dice (or small cubes with numbers 1–6 on different sides), one die for each pair of students.
2. "Mystery Boxes" (small closed boxes with objects inside. Each box may contain a different object), one box for groups of 3–4 students.

PROCEDURES

Anticipatory set
1. Ask students to review what they think scientists do (investigate, solve problems, inquire).
2. Which goal of science is important? Why? How does the process of inquiry apply to them?

Objective and purpose
1. Today's lesson is an introduction to scientific inquiry.

Instructional input
1. *Introductory Exploration*
   Prior to your discussion, place a die on each desk. Give very clear directions that they are *not* to touch the die.
   - A problem exists relative to the die. What is it? (Let them give their ideas.)
   - Direct discussion to the identification of a problem. (What is on the bottom?)
   - Focus discussion on assumptions, data, inference, etc.
2. *Explanation of Inquiry*
   - Systematic approach to problems
   - Collection of data (not assumptions)
   - Form hypothesis based on data
   - Confirm or refute hypothesis
   - Design of experiments
   - Present the information supporting your conclusion, i.e., by writing a scientific paper.
   - Have students summarize the process of inquiry in terms of their observations of the die. How would they best support the case for their hypothesis of what is on the bottom, e.g., adding sides of the die, sequence of numbers, the missing number, and so on. Ask them to show how they could systematically approach the problem, collect data, form hypotheses, confirm or refute hypotheses, and design an experiment to support their hypothesis. Have the students write a short paper based on this activity. They should use the scientific protocol for the paper's organization.

3. *Extension of Ideas to a New Problem*
   ● Present mystery box
   ● Allow students to state problem, collect data, form hypothesis, design experiment, and present final conclusions.

Evaluation of objectives
1. Present a new problem that you have designed.
2. Have the students collect information, etc., and write a "scientific paper."
3. Evaluate the "scientific paper" and provide feedback relative to the students' understanding of the inquiry process.

Inquiry Skills   ACTIVITY 2

OBJECTIVES

To gain practice in the skills of (1) measurement, (2) record keeping, (3) graphing

SUBJECT

Forces produced by springs

PROBLEM

How does the length of spring depend on the force exerted on it?

PROCEDURE

Work in pairs, or do as a student demonstration with all students recording the data and drawing the graph. Set up the spring and weights as shown in Figure 1. Add weights one at a time and check the readings each time.

Record the results as shown in Table 1. Graph the results as shown in the graph in Figure 2.

FIGURE 1
Demonstration Setup

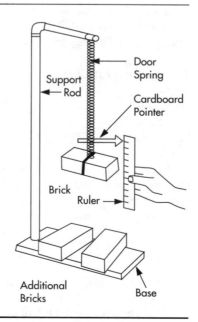

Table 1

Weight (Bricks)	Stretch (cm)
1	1.5
2	3.0
3	4.5
4	6.0

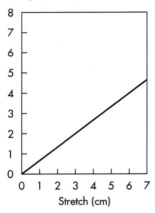

FIGURE 2
Results Recorded in Table
and Graph Form

MATERIALS

Door springs   Ruler
Several bricks   String

CONCLUSION

The change in length of a spring is directly proportional to the change in the force exerted on it—if the spring is not stretched beyond its elastic limit.

PROBABLE SKILLS DEVELOPED

1. Setup and adjustment of apparatus (manipulative)
2. Observation of initial conditions and changes due to experimental factors (acquisitive)
3. Recording of data (organizational)
4. Graphing and analysis of data (organizational and communicative)
5. Drawing conclusions (organizational)

EVALUATION

Can the student

1. Set up the apparatus for use?
2. Devise a plan of procedure?
3. Read a scale to the limits of its accuracy?
4. Record data in a tabular form?
5. Plot a graph?
6. Interpret a graph?
7. Draw conclusions from the experiment?
8. Recognize sources of error?
9. Report results lucidly?

ACTIVITY 3	**Investigating Thermal Energy**

What Do I Want Students to Discover?

When an object is heated, its molecules move faster or vibrate more.
When an object is cooled, its molecules move more slowly.
Heat is the total energy an object has because of the motion of its molecules.

What Will I Need?

Baby-food jar with screw top   Tea bags
Sand   Pencils
Thick towel   Sugar cubes
Thermometer   2 Pyrex™ or tin pans
12 baby-food jars or clear plastic tumblers   Colored cinnamon candies

What Concepts Might Students Discover or Construct?

Motion (shaking, stirring, rubbing, etc.) can be a source of heat.
The molecules in liquids are in continuous motion. This is called Brownian motion.
Scientists use controlled experiments to test their ideas.
Solids break into smaller pieces (dissolve) faster in hot water than in cold water.

PROCESSES

What Will Students Do?

PART I

What do you think will happen to the sand in a baby-food jar if we shake it many times?

Hypothesizing

1. Fill a baby-food jar 3/4 full of sand, screw the top on the jar, and then wrap it with a thick towel.

2. Each person should take a turn doing the following:
   a. Shake the sand vigorously for 5 minutes.
   b. Measure the temperature of the sand.
   c. Write your findings on this chart.

Collecting Data

Measuring
Recording

Number of Shakes	Temperature in °F or °C

   d. Pass the jar to the next person.

   e. When everyone has had a turn, compare the temperature of the sand from the first to the last reading.
      How were they different? (The temperature rose higher after shaking.)
   f. Set up a graph like the one shown, then graph the data from the record sheets.

Comparing

Analyzing
Communicating Results

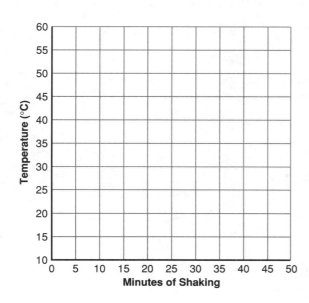

PART II

Hypothesizing
Designing an Investigation

What caused the molecules to move?
How could we set up an experiment to test the effect of heat on molecule movement in a liquid?

1. Fill three baby-food jars or plastic tumblers with water to within 1/2 in (1 cm) of the top and let them stand until the water is room temperature.
2. Slowly lower a sugar cube into one jar, a handful of cinnamon candies into the second jar, and a tea bag into the third jar or tumbler. (See diagram.)

CONTROL: Substances dissolving without stirring

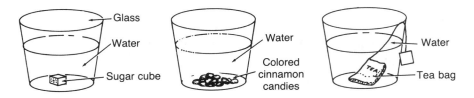

Make certain that the jars are in a spot where they will not be moved or jostled.

3. Set up three more jars and materials the same as in step 2, but this time stir the water in the jars until the materials dissolve, as shown in the diagram.

EXPERIMENT: Substances dissolving with stirring

Hypothesizing

The way this experiment was set up is called a controlled experiment in science. *Why do you think it is called this?*

4. Taking observations every 1/2 hour, record how long it takes for the control jars to look like the experimental jars.

Hypothesizing
Inferring
Designing an Investigation

Which materials do you think will dissolve first? Why?
Would the results be different if hot water were used? If cold water were used? Why?
How could we test this?

PART III

1. Set up two more sets of jars with sugar, cinnamon candies, and tea bags.
2. Place one set of jars in ice-cold water in a pan and the other set in a pan of very hot water.

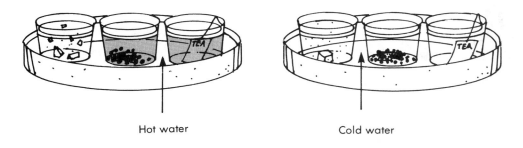

Hot water   Cold water

In which jars—in pans of hot or cold water—will the materials dissolve first?
What does the hot water in the pan do to the molecules in the baby-food jars?

This is a review of Brownian motion, the continuous movement of particles suspended in a liquid. This activity also introduces several new concepts. Students will be helped to see that increasing the motion of molecules generates considerable heat. Therefore, matter that displays greater heat has greater movement of its molecules. In addition, the concept of a control is used as a standard against which scientists check their experimental work. If you think your students are ready, you can introduce the concept of variables. For instance, in Part III, the variable being tested is heat and its effect upon dissolving.

1. *Why do you rub a match against the side of a matchbox?*
2. *Why do matches not catch fire while sitting in a matchbox?*
3. *When you bend a wire back and forth several times, why does it get warm?*
4. *When you put two pencils together and rub them back and forth several times, what happens to your hands?*
5. *A person tried to strike a match against a piece of glass to light it. The match would not light. Why?*
6. *If you feel the tires of your car before you take a trip and then just after you get out of the car, they will not feel the same. How do you think they will differ? How would you explain the difference?*
7. *A person was chopping wood with an axe. After chopping very hard for about 10 minutes, she felt the axe. How do you think the axe felt and why?*

HOW IS HEAT TRANSMITTED BY CONDUCTION AND RADIATION?

The sun or light bulbs give off radiant heat.
Heat can be transmitted from one body to another by conduction and radiation.
Light objects reflect radiant energy more than do dark objects.
Dark objects absorb more radiant energy than do light objects.
Some objects conduct heat better than others.

3 tin cans of same size	Lamp with 150 to 300 watts
Small can of shiny white paint	Small can of dull black paint
Candle	Silver or steel knife
4 × 4-in square of aluminum foil	9 thumbtacks
Styrofoam covers for cans	Tripod stand
4-in length of copper	3 thermometers
	2 small paintbrushes

These activities may be done in groups. For immature or unruly children, the teacher should demonstrate these activities.

PART I RADIATION

What do you think will happen to the three thermometers in the three different cans after being in the sun or near light bulbs for a while? (See diagram.)

1. Obtain three identically sized cans and remove all labels. Paint one can dull black and another can shiny white; leave the third can unpainted, shiny metal.
2. Fill each can with regular tap water.
3. Put a styrofoam cover on each can and insert a thermometer through each cover.
4. Set the cans in direct sunlight or at equal distances from a 150- to 300-watt light bulb.
5. Prepare a table for data collection and record the temperature of the water in each can at one-minute intervals.

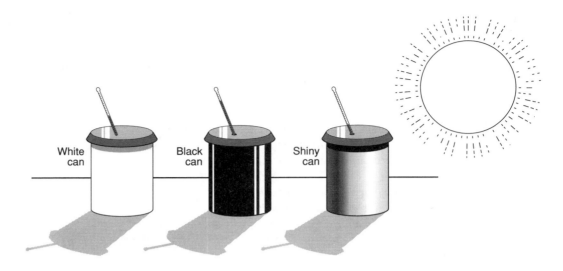

Hypothesizing

What do you think will happen to the water temperature in the different cans?
If there are different temperatures, how would you explain that?

Inferring

How would you relate the result of the unequal absorption of heat in the tin cans to different land and water surfaces of the earth?

Inferring

Knowing what you do about how radiant (light) energy reacts on different surfaces, how would you explain the differences in the three thermometers?

Hypothesizing

How might this be related to the microclimates of certain geographic areas?

What Must I Know?/Where Do I Find It?

The shiny aluminum of the unpainted can and the shiny white paint of the second can reflect radiant energy, whereas the dull black paint absorbs most of the radiant energy. Dark patches of ground absorb more radiant energy faster than do shiny water surfaces or lighter colored land surfaces.

PART II CONDUCTION

Hypothesizing

What do you think will happen to tacks that have been attached with wax to a strip of aluminum foil, to a silver or steel knife, and to a copper tube when the tips of these metals are heated?

1. Obtain a 4 × 4-in square of aluminum foil, a candle, a match, and nine tacks.
2. Roll the aluminum foil tightly.
3. Light the candle. Drip some wax onto three tacks and the aluminum foil rod so the tacks stick to the foil.
4. Obtain a tripod stand, silver knife, and a 4-in length of copper tubing.
5. Stick three tacks each to the knife and to the copper tubing as you did with the foil.
6. Place the foil, knife, and copper tubing on a tripod stand as shown in the diagram. Heat the tips of each of these with a candle flame.

Observing
Inferring
Inferring

Observe and record what happens.
Why did the tacks not all fall at the same time?
From observing this activity, how do you think the heat affected the three metals?

How Will Students Use or Apply What They Discover?

1. *When you stand in front of a fireplace and the front of you only is warmed by the fire, how is the heat transferred?*
2. *How does heat or thermal energy come from the sun?*
3. *What colors are more likely to absorb heat?*
4. *Why do people generally wear lighter colored clothes in the summer?*
5. *In the can experiment, what kind of energy did the black surface absorb?*
6. *How was the heat transferred from the black surface to the thermometer?*
7. *Why is it desirable to have a copper-bottomed tea kettle?*

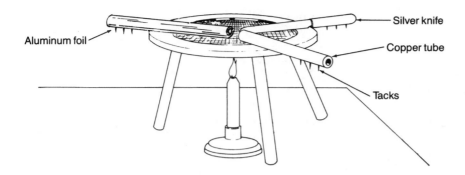

8. *Why would you not want a copper handle on a frying pan?*
9. *What metals conduct heat well?*
10. *What advantage would there be in having a car with a white top rather than a black top?*
11. *Why do many people in warmer climates paint their houses white?*
12. *Why would you prefer to put a hot dog on a stick rather than on a wire to cook the hot dog over a camp fire?*
13. *Why do astronauts wear shiny space suits?*

PART III CONVECTION

Where do you think the warmest and coolest spots are in your classroom? Try this activity to see if you can find the answer.

Hypothesizing

1. As far away as possible from the room's source of heat, tape three thermometers to a wall at these places: near the ceiling, halfway up the wall, and near the floor.
2. Make a chart of the thermometer readings once an hour for one day.

What Will Students Do?

Observation

Using the data collected, graph the results.
From your data and graph, answer these questions:
Which thermometer had the highest temperature? The middle temperature? The lowest temperature?
Why do you think the temperatures were different?

Communicating
Analyzing

Inferring

Convection is the transfer of heat by either a gas (air) or a liquid (water). When the air in the room is heated, it expands and becomes lighter per given volume. It then rises because it is lighter. This rising and falling is called a convection current.

What Must I Know?

When you see "wiggly lines" rising from the blacktop of a parking lot on a sunny day, how is this the same as the convection current in our classroom?
Why does a "cloud" fall down from a freezer that is above a refrigerator when you open the freezer door?
Why does smoke usually rise up a chimney? Under what conditions would smoke come into the house through the fireplace opening?
Why would a pinwheel start to spin if put over a lit light bulb?

How Will Students Use or
  Apply What They Discover?

Investigating Simple Machines

ACTIVITY 4

WHAT IS THE JACK AND HOW IS IT USED?

A screw is an inclined plane wrapped around a rod.
As with an inclined plane, force is gained at the expense of distance.
A large weight can be moved by a small force if the smaller force is applied over a greater distance.

What Concepts Might
Students Discover or
Construct?

What Will We Need?

Triangular pieces of paper   Model of a hill
Pencil   Board
Ring clamp   Nail
Hammer   Several screws
Screwdriver   Colored pencil or crayon
Tape measure

What Will We Discuss?

Show the class several examples of screws and ask the following questions:
What are these called?
What purpose do they serve?
Where are they in the classroom?
What advantage do they have over nails?
What type of machine studied thus far resembles a screw?

What Must I Know?
PROCESSES
What Will Students Do?

A screw is a circular, inclined plane.

1. Obtain a small piece of paper and cut it in the shape of a triangle as shown in the diagram. Color the edge of the paper so you can see it, then wind the paper around the pencil.

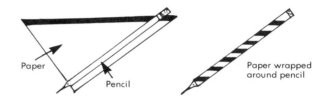

Paper

Pencil

Paper wrapped around pencil

Observing
Observing
Comparing

What kind of machine did the paper represent before you rolled it around the pencil?
What kind of machine did the paper represent after you rolled it around the pencil?
How are the screw and the inclined plane related?

2. Obtain a C-clamp and insert a pencil as shown in the diagram.

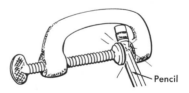

Pencil

Hypothesizing
Hypothesizing

What do you think will happen to the pencil when you move the screw inward?
How much effort will have to be applied to break the pencil?

3. Look at the diagram of the jack.

Jack

Communicating

Describe how the jack works.

How is the jack similar to a screw?

What is the purpose of using a jack on a car?

How is it possible for a person who weighs 150 pounds to lift a car weighing 3,000 pounds by using a jack?

Comparing

Inferring

Inferring

1. *When were jacks used in old barber shops?*
2. *Where else are jacks used?*
3. *How many seconds would a person have to exert a force to raise a car a small distance?*
4. *What machine is involved in a spiral notebook?*
5. *If you were asked to push a heavy rock to the top of a hill, how would you move it up the hill?*

How Will Students Use or Apply What They Discover?

WHAT IS A MOVABLE PULLEY AND HOW CAN YOU USE IT?

Pulleys that move with the resistance are called movable pulleys.

Movable pulley systems have a mechanical advantage greater than one.

The mechanical advantage of a movable pulley system is equal to the number of stands holding up the resistance.

What Concepts Might Students Discover or Construct?

Ring stand for attaching pulleys

Pull-type scale

50-g weight

String or nylon fishing line

2 single pulleys

100-g weight

Yardstick or meter stick

What Will We Need?

1. Obtain a ring stand and a clamp for attaching a pulley, a single pulley, a pull-type scale, and a 100-gram weight. Assemble your equipment as shown in the diagram.

PROCESSES
What Will Students Do?

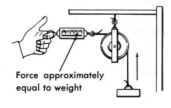

Force approximately
equal to weight

How much do you think you will have to pull on the scale to raise the 100-gram weight?

2. Pull on the scale and raise the weight.

How is the scale affected when you raise the weight?

3. Repeat this activity several times and record each measurement.

What do you think will happen when you use two pulleys to raise the 100-gram weight?

4. In addition to the equipment you have, obtain a single fixed pulley and a 50-gram weight. Assemble your equipment as shown in the diagram.

Hypothesizing

Observing
Measuring
Hypothesizing

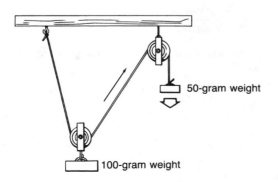

50-gram weight

100-gram weight

Observing

5. Pull the 50-gram weight and record your observations.
6. Remove the 50-gram weight and attach the scale.

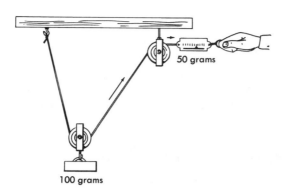

50 grams

100 grams

Hypothesizing

How will the scale be affected when you raise the 100-gram weight?
7. Raise the weight by pulling on the scale.

Observing
Measuring

What happens to the scale when you raise the weight?
8. Repeat the activity several times and record each measurement.
Why is there an advantage in using this type of pulley system?
9. Remove the scale and once again attach the 50-gram weight.

Hypothesizing
Hypothesizing

How far do you think the 50-gram weight will move when it raises the 100-gram weight?
How far do you think the 100-gram weight will move when it is raised by the 50-gram weight?
10. Obtain a yardstick or meter stick.

Observing
Measuring
Summarizing

11. Move the 50-gram weight and measure how far both the weights move.
12. Repeat this part of the activity several times and record your measurements.
What can you say about pulleys from the measurements you just recorded?
13. Look at the measurements you recorded when one pulley was used and those you recorded when two pulleys were used.
What does the information tell you about pulleys?

How Will Students Use or
  Apply What They Discover?

What kind of pulley system would be needed to raise a piano weighing 300 pounds?
Draw a sketch of that pulley system.

WHAT IS A LEVER AND HOW CAN YOU USE IT?

What Concepts Might
Students Discover or
Construct?

A lever is a simple machine.
A lever cannot work alone.
A lever consists of a bar that is free to turn on a pivot called the fulcrum.
By using a first-class lever, it is possible to increase a person's ability to lift heavier objects. This is called the mechanical advantage. The mechanical advantage of a lever is determined by the formula

$$\text{Mechanical advantage} = \frac{\text{Effort arm}}{\text{Resistance arm}}$$

The weight times the distance on one side of the fulcrum must equal the weight times the distance on the other side if the lever is balanced.
A first-class lever has the fulcrum between the resistance and the effort.

What Will We Need?

Meter stick or yardstick
100-g weight
20-g weight
Roll of heavy string or nylon fishing line
Assorted weights of various sizes
Platform with an arm for suspending objects

Define resistance, force, and fulcrum before beginning the activity.

1. Using some heavy string, a yardstick, a 100-gram weight, a 20-gram weight, a ring stand, and a ring clamp, assemble the apparatus as shown in the diagram.

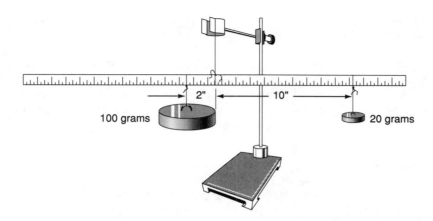

Where do you think you should attach the 100-gram weight and the 20-gram weight so the yardstick will balance?

2. Attach the weights so the yardstick is balanced.
   How far is the 100-gram weight from the end of the yardstick?
   How far is the 20-gram weight from the end of the yardstick?

3. Look at these three things: the string, which is suspending the yardstick, the 20-gram weight, and the 100-gram weight.
   What is the relationship between the weight and distance on each side of the fulcrum?
   What are the advantages of using a first-class lever of this type?

4. Use the following formula to calculate the mechanical advantage (M.A.) of the lever.

$$\text{M.A.} = \frac{\text{Effort arm}}{\text{Resistance arm}}$$

At the completion of the activity, explain to the class that a first-class lever consists of a bar that is free to turn on a pivot point called the fulcrum. The weight moved is called the resistance. The force exerted on the other end of the lever is called the effort. Draw the diagram on the board to illustrate this point. State that in a first-class lever, the fulcrum is always between the resistance and the effort. Have students do some different problems using the formula given in Step 4. Use metric measurements, if possible.

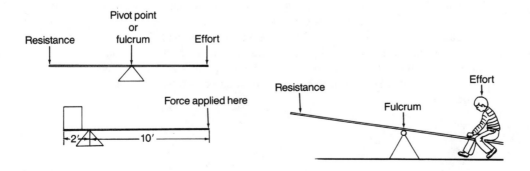

1. *How is the M.A. affected when different weights are used?*
2. *What does an M.A. of 4 mean?*
3. *Where are first-class levers used?*

REFERENCE BOOKS—SIMPLE MACHINES

Teacher: Harvey Weiss, *Machines and How They Work* (New York: Harper and Row, 1983).

Students: Rose Wyler, *Science Fun With Toy Cars and Trucks* (Englewood Cliffs, NJ: Messner, 1988).

ACTIVITY 5   ## Stimulating Mathematics Usage in Science Classes

The laboratory provides the opportunity for many data-gathering problems. The student may practice measuring, keeping records, and graphing. Analysis of experiments gives additional practice in using mathematics. For example, the data given in Table 1 show a record of the time required to empty a can of water through a hole punched in the bottom.

TABLE 1
Amount of Time to Empty (in seconds)

d (IN CM)	h (IN CM)			
	30	10	4	1
1.5	73.0	43.5	26.7	13.5
2.0	41.2	23.7	15.0	7.2
3.0	18.4	10.5	6.8	3.7
5.0	6.8	3.9	2.2	1.5

Students are told to plot graphs of the data to analyze the relationships between emptying times and two other variables, diameter of the hole (d) and height of water in the can (h). Types of graphs suggested are one showing time versus diameter for a constant height and one showing time versus square of diameter. Graphs for different heights are also suggested. Typical questions asked in this exercise are

1. From your curve, how accurately can you predict the time it would take to empty the same container if the diameter of the opening was 4 cm? 8 cm?
2. Can you write down the algebraic relation between t and d for the particular height of water used?
3. Can you find the general expression for time of flow as a function of both h and d?

This exercise illustrates clearly how using mathematics gives a student practice in analyzing the results of an experiment and demonstrates the integral nature of mathematics in science.

Students should learn the limitations of measurement, the sources of quantitative errors, and standards of accuracy. How accurate is a meter stick? To how many significant figures can a measurement be made? Of what value are estimated units? How accurate is a volume computation made from linear measurements which have estimated units? What are possible sources of error in an experiment? To what degree of precision are certain measurements made? How does one express the degree of precision when recording data in centimeters?

Investigating Electricity and Magnetism

ACTIVITY 6

WHAT IS STATIC ELECTRICITY?

All bodies are capable of producing electrical charges.
Conductors allow electrons to move, but insulators do not allow electrons to move easily.
Like charges repel; unlike charges attract.

What Concepts Might Students Discover or Construct?

Lucite or resin rod or a hard rubber comb	Large piece of paper
Wool cloth	Balloon
Glass rod	Tap water
Small pieces of paper	Piece of silk about the size of a
Flour	small handkerchief

What Will We Need?

What can you state about how poles of magnets react toward one another?
What is the energy that we use to produce light and to operate many machines and household appliances?
What things can produce electricity?
How can you find out if all charges of electricity are the same?

What Will We Discuss?

PART I

PROCESSES

What Will Students Do?

1. Obtain the following materials: a lucite or resin rod or a hard rubber comb, wool, flour, a glass rod, small pieces of paper, a large piece of paper, a balloon, tap water, and a piece of silk.
2. Take the resin rod (or hard rubber comb) and rub it with the wool cloth.

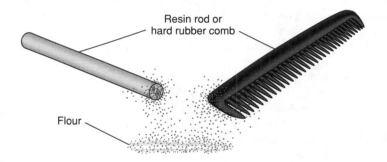

Resin rod or
hard rubber comb

Flour

What do you think will happen when the rod is touched to the flour?

Hypothesizing

3. Touch the rod to some flour.
   What happens to the flour?
   Why do you think the flour is affected by the rod?
4. Clean the rod, rub it again, and touch it to the small pieces of paper.
   What does the rod do to the paper?

Observing
Hypothesizing

Observing

PART II

5. Rub the rod briskly with the wool cloth.
6. Turn on a water tap so a very slow stream of water comes out.
   What do you think will happen to the stream of water when the rod is moved close to it?

Hypothesizing

7. Move the rod close to the stream.

Observing

What happens as the rod comes near?

Inferring

Why does the water react as it does?

Inferring

Why do you think it reacts as it does without being touched?

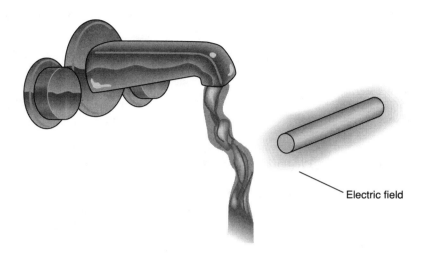

Electric field

What Must I Know?

The students should note how close they have to bring the rod before it affects the stream of water. Develop the concept that there is an invisible field of electrical force around the rod that either pushes or attracts the water. This force cannot be seen, but it must be there because it affects the stream of water. Define force as a push or pull. In this case, the water is pushed or pulled, without being touched, by moving the rod toward and away from the water.

Designing an Investigation

How can you find out if rubbing the cloth on the rod causes the electrical force?

8. Rub the rod again with the cloth.
9. Now rub your hand over the rod.

Hypothesizing

What do you think will happen to the stream of water?

10. Repeat the procedure by approaching the slow stream of water with the rod.

Observing

What effect does the rod have on the water this time?

Inferring

Why does the rod not have the same effect?

Inferring

What happened to the charge that the wool cloth induced in the rod?

Inferring

Why do you think the charge failed to last?

What Must I Know?

When the resin rod is rubbed with wool or fur, electrons are rubbed off these materials onto the rod. The rod, however, is an insulator, so the electron movement is slight. The rod becomes negatively charged since each electron produces a small amount of negative charge. When a hand is rubbed over the rod, the rod becomes discharged because the electrons leave the rod and enter the hand. The rod is then neutral. Explain the difference between a conductor and an insulator.

PART III

Summarizing

1. *After your discussion concerning conductors and insulators, would you say the rod is a conductor or an insulator?*
   Why do you think so?

Inferring

2. Obtain two balloons.
3. Inflate the balloons.
4. Tie a string to each balloon and suspend them from a bar or a coat hanger as shown in the diagram.

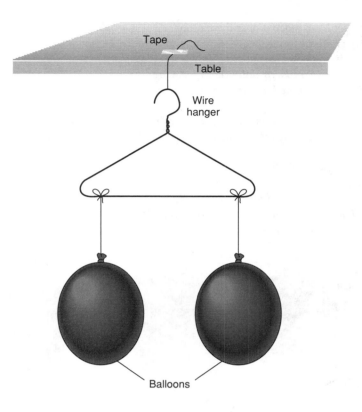

5. Rub each balloon with the wool cloth.
   What do the balloons do?
   Why do they repel each other?
   Do you think the balloons are conductors or insulators?
   What do you think will happen if a charged resin rod is brought near the balloons?

Observing
Inferring
Summarizing
Hypothesizing

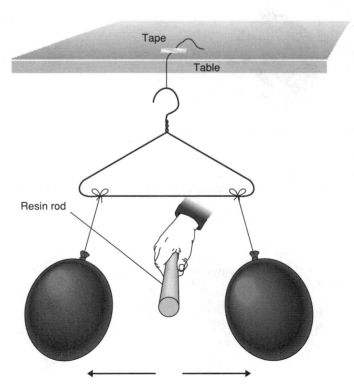

6. Rub the resin rod with wool and place it near the balloons.

Observing   *In which direction do the balloons move?*
Inferring   *Why do you think they were repelled by the rod?*
Assuming   *Do you think the balloons have a like or unlike charge? Why?*
Hypothesizing   *What do you think will happen to the balloons if you touch them with a glass rod?*

What Must I Know?   These balloons were charged in the same way; therefore, each must have the same charge. When they do have the same charge, they repel each other because like charges repel.

7. Rub the glass rod with the piece of silk.
8. Place it near the balloons.

Observing   *What happens as it comes near the balloons?*
Comparing   *How does the glass rod affect the balloons in comparison to the resin rod?*
Comparing   *What can you say about the charge on the resin rod compared to the glass rod?*

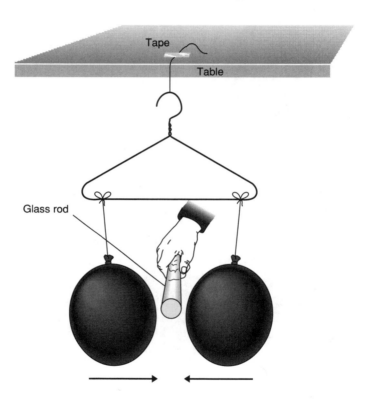

What Must I Know?   The glass rod will have a positive charge since electrons were rubbed off the rod onto the silk. It will attract the balloons because they were negatively charged by the resin rod, and unlike charges attract.

PART IV

1. Vigorously rub one of the inflated balloons against the piece of wool.
2. Place the balloon on a wall. (See diagram.)

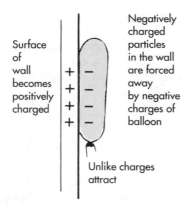

Surface of wall becomes positively charged

Negatively charged particles in the wall are forced away by negative charges of balloon

Unlike charges attract

What do you think will happen to the balloon?

Why does the balloon not fall?

Is the force that pulls the balloon to the wall greater or less than the gravitational force pulling the balloon down to earth?

What happened to the negatively charged particles in the wall when the balloon came near?

After following the previous steps, what can you say about charging matter?

What is a conductor?

What is an insulator?

Hypothesizing

Inferring

Inferring

Inferring

Summarizing

Summarizing

Summarizing

When you rub the balloon with wool, it becomes negatively charged, because it got an excess of electrons from the wool. When the balloon is placed next to the wall, the balloon's negative charge forces the electrons in the wall away from the surface, leaving the surface positively charged. The balloon sticks because the unlike charges attract. The balloon is negative and the wall surface is positive, as is indicated in the diagram.

What Must I Know?

1. *What is electricity?*
2. *How can you use a magnet to make electricity?*
3. *Why might you get a shock after walking across a wool carpet and then touching a metal doorknob?*
4. *Why does your hair get attracted to your comb? Why is this most noticeable on very dry days?*
5. *Why do clothes stick together after being dried in a clothes dryer?*

How Will Students Use or Apply What They Discover?

HOW CAN YOU MAKE ELECTRICITY BY USING MAGNETISM?

Around a magnet there are magnetic lines of force.

If you break the magnetic lines of force, you can make electricity.

A force is defined as a push or a pull.

What Concepts Might Students Discover or Construct?

Copper wire (about 3 yards)

Magnetic compass

Bar magnet

What Will We Need?

How is electricity used?

How does electricity get to your home for you to use?

What is the area of force around a magnet called?

What is a force?

How can you use a magnet to produce electricity?

What Will We Discuss?

PROCESSES
What Will Students Do?

1. With a partner, obtain a length of wire (about 3 yards), a bar magnet, and a magnetic compass.
2. Take the wire and wrap it 20 to 30 times around the magnetic compass as indicated in the diagram.
3. Loop the other end of the wire into a coil as shown in the diagram.

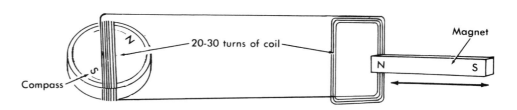

Inferring
Inferring
Inferring
Designing an Investigation
Observing

Observing
Inferring
Applying
Hypothesizing
Hypothesizing
Inferring or Interpreting

Inferring or Interpreting
Summarizing
Summarizing
Summarizing
Summarizing

What happens when electricity goes through a wire?
What do you think the area around the wire could be called?
What has the electricity produced?
How do you think magnetism could be used to produce electricity?

4. Take the bar magnet and plunge it back and forth through the coil of wire. Instruct your partner to watch what happens to the compass.
What happens to the compass?
Why do you think the compass needle does what it does?
What attracts the compass needle?
What do you think causes the needle to be deflected?
Where do you think the magnetism was produced to cause the compass needle to move?
If there is magnetism produced in the wire around the compass, what do you think the plunging of the magnet through the coil of wire has to do with it?
When is electricity produced in the wire?
What is the force of a magnet called?
What does a magnet do to a magnetizable object?
What does a magnet do to a nonmagnetizable object?
Explain how magnetism can be used to produce an electrical current.

What Must I Know?

Around every magnet there is an area that can push or pull susceptible objects such as iron filings. This area is thought to consist of lines of force. When these lines of force are broken by plunging the magnet back and forth through a coil of wire, electricity is made in the wire. Electricity is defined as a flow of electrons along the wire, producing an electrical current. Whenever there is an electrical current produced, there will be a magnetic field around the wire. This magnetic field causes the magnet (compass needle) in this activity to move. Using magnets to produce electricity is the principle involved in making electricity in a dynamo. Make certain that the compass is far enough away from the magnet to avoid direct magnetic influence.

How Will Students Use or
Apply What They Discover?

How can you use electricity to make a magnet?

HOW CAN YOU MAKE A TEMPORARY (ELECTRO) MAGNET?

What Concepts Might
Students Discover or
Construct?

When electricity passes along a wire, it produces a magnetic field around the wire that acts like a magnet.
A magnetic field can make iron temporarily magnetic.
The more electric current flows through a wire in a unit of time, the more magnetism is generated around the wire.
If a circuit is broken, electricity will not flow.

What Will We Need?

Insulated copper wire
Iron nail
Dry cell battery

Teaspoon of iron filings
Paper clips

How is magnetism made by electricity?
By using a wire that is carrying a current, how could you make a large magnetic field?
If you wanted to magnetize a nail, how would you do it?

The supplies listed under "What Will We Need?" are for two to four students.

1. Obtain a dry cell battery, an iron nail, a piece of insulated copper wire, some iron filings, and a paper clip.
2. Wrap the wire around the nail several times as shown in the diagram.
3. Scrape the insulation off two ends of the wire. Connect only *one* end of the wire to one terminal of the dry cell. When you do the activity, touch the other end of the wire to the other terminal of the dry cell for only a few seconds. *Caution:* Do not let the other wire and terminal remain in contact for more than a few seconds as intense heat builds up, and you could get a burn through the insulation.

What Will We Discuss?

What Must I Know?
PROCESSES
What Will Students Do?

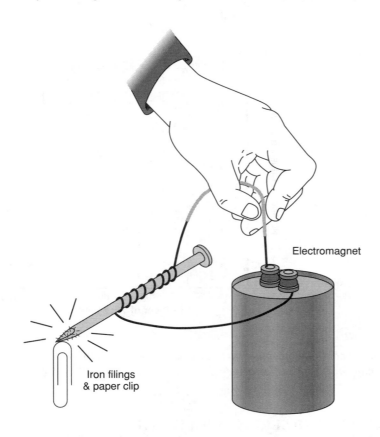

Electromagnet

Iron filings
& paper clip

CAUTION: DO NOT HOLD WIRE TO TERMINAL FOR MORE THAN 3 SECONDS!

What do you think will happen to some iron filings if you place them near the nail and then touch the loose end of the wire to the terminal? Do this carefully, and release one end of wire from the terminal after a few seconds.

4. Place a paper clip on the nail and repeat.
What happens to the filings and paper clip while the loose end of the wire is touching the terminal?
Why do the iron filings temporarily stay on the nail?
What is temporarily produced around the wire when both ends of the wire are touching both terminals?
What did the nail temporarily become?
What happened to the iron filings and nail when you removed the loose wire so that it no longer touched the terminal?

Hypothesizing

Observing

Inferring
Inferring

Inferring
Observing

Inferring	*Why do they fall when you disconnect the wire?*
Applying	*What must you do with the circuit to produce electricity?*
Summarizing	*What can you say about the production of magnetism around a wire when electricity goes through it?*
Summarizing	*What would you call the temporary magnet you made by passing electricity through a conductor?* (electromagnet)
Designing an Investigation	*How do you think you could increase the strength of the magnetism in the nail?*
Hypothesizing	*What do you think would happen if you wrapped more wire around the nail?*
Hypothesizing	*Will the magnetism increase or decrease? Why?*
Assuming	*Is the magnet you produced a temporary or a permanent magnet? Why?*
Inferring	*How do you know?*

How Will Students Use or Apply What They Discover?

1. Try an experiment where you test whether more turns of wire affect how many paper clips your electromagnet picks up.
2. Collect data and set up a graph like the one shown.

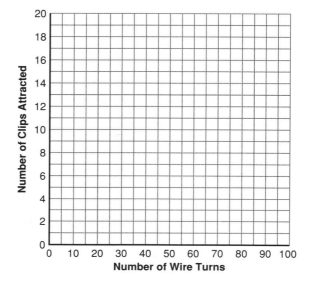

3. *By what other means could the magnetic field around the nail be increased? What do you think might happen if you used a bigger dry cell or more dry cells connected together?*

HOW ARE PARALLEL AND SERIES CIRCUITS THE SAME AND DIFFERENT?

What Concepts Might Students Discover?

For the electrons to move in a circuit, there must be a path that is unbroken to and from the source of electrical energy.

If one lamp burns out in a series circuit, the circuit is broken.

In a parallel circuit, one lamp can burn out, but the rest of the circuit will still function.

What Will We Need?

2 dry cells   Connecting wires
4 small lamps   2 switches
4 sockets

What Will We Discuss?

In what different ways can you use a dry cell and wire to make a circuit?
How could you make a parallel or series circuit?
What would happen if one light on a string of Christmas tree lights were unscrewed?
What would you do to find out?
Why is it that string of Christmas tree lights do not all behave the same?

1. Connect a dry cell, two small lamps, a switch, two sockets, and connecting wires so the light works.
   What do you need to do to make the lights work?

PROCESSES
What Will Students Do?
Hypothesizing

What Must I Know?

The diagram of the series circuit is for your information. It should not be shown to the students until they have completed the activity.

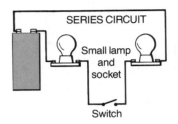

What purpose does the switch serve?
What do you think will happen when you unscrew one of the lights?
2. Unscrew one of the lights.
   Why did the other light go out?
   What can you do to make the lights go on again?
3. Using the same equipment, rearrange the circuit so that if one light goes out, the other will still burn.

Hypothesizing
Hypothesizing

Inferring
Hypothesizing

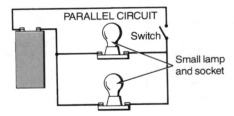

The diagram of a parallel circuit is available for your information. It should not be shown to the students until after they finish this activity.

What Must We Know?

4. Unscrew one of the lights. If you wired it differently than the first time, one of the lights should still burn even though you unscrewed the other.
   Why?
   What is the difference between the two types of circuits you have constructed?

Inferring
Comparing

In a parallel circuit, there may be more than two paths for the current to take to complete its circuit. If one of the circuits is broken, the current can still use the other circuit, as indicated in the preceding diagram.

What Must I Know?/Where
    Do I Find It?

1. *What kind of circuits do you have in your home?*
2. *How could you find out what kind of circuit a string of Christmas tree lights is?*
3. Examine a flashlight. *What kind of a circuit does it have?*

How Will Students Use or
    Apply What They Discover?

REFERENCE BOOKS—MAGNETIC AND ELECTRICAL ENERGIES AND INTERACTIONS

Teacher: Martin J. Gutnik, *Electricity from Faraday to Solar Generators* (New York: Watts, 1986).
Gerardo Torres Orozco, Pilar Segarra Alberú, & Elaine Reynoso Haynes. (1994, March). The electromagnetic swing. *Science and Children, 31* (6), 20–21.
Students: Melvin Berger, *Switch On, Switch Off* (New York: Crowell, 1989).

ACTIVITY 7   **Geologic Time**

ACTIVITY OVERVIEW

Students complete a scale model of geologic time. The primary goal of the activity is to give them a concept of the immensity of geologic time. Secondary to this, they are introduced to geologic periods and the record of life as recorded in rocks. The activity should last for two class periods.

SCIENCE BACKGROUND

There are two primary methods of determining the age of materials and thus establishing a time scale. The first is an ordering of events, simply determining what happened first, second, third, and so on. In this method the dating is *relative*. The second method establishes a specific time of an organism, event, or rock stratum. This is an *absolute* method of dating materials. Geologists have used the relative method of dating materials for years. It is represented classically in the time scale constructed in this activity.

William Smith, working in the nineteenth century, is credited with formally establishing the practice of ordering geologic events. He observed that rocks revealed an orderly succession of life; that is, older species were represented in older rocks (bottom layers) and as these species disappeared from the rock record, fossils of new species appeared. This is called *faunal succession*—groups of fossils succeed each other in sedimentary rock layers in such a way that the sequences of rocks are predictable. It should be noted that Smith did not develop the idea of evolution—the biological implication of his observations. He was only concerned with the fossils as chronological indicators. The method used by Smith also allowed him to correlate groups of rocks that were some distance apart. The assumption here is that similar fossils in rocks at two different locations means the rocks were deposited in the same period.

Nineteenth century geologists succeeded in ordering many formations of the world's rocks. The order was based on relative dates, since absolute dating methods had not been developed. Though there are inconsistencies and problems with this method of dating rocks, it does represent a good introduction to geologic time and the record of past life and events in the rocks.

Understanding the immensity of geologic time gives students some perspective relative to our time and influence on earth. Compared to other organisms, our time has been short and our impact can be viewed with mixed reactions; we probably represent the highest, most complex form of life and we have done the most to endanger our own existence and the existence of other species. It is well for students to understand the perspective of geologic time for these reasons as well as the knowledge contained about the earth's history in the rock record.

MAJOR CONCEPTS

- Environments can change and conserve their identities.
- Environments change because living and nonliving matter interact.
- The earth is very old; geologic time is immense.
- Interpretation of rocks and fossils provides a record of the earth's history.
- Geologic time is subdivided on the basis of natural events in the evolution of life.

OBJECTIVES

At the completion of this activity the student should be able to:

- Describe the immensity of geologic time
- Relate the relative ages of some geologic events
- Identify his/her location in the scale of geologic time.

MATERIALS

- Meter stick
- Colored pencils
- Adding machine tape (6 meter strips for each group of two)

VOCABULARY

Geologic time (you may wish to include the names of geologic eras)

PROCEDURES

1. Divide the students into groups of two.
2. Each group should have a piece of adding machine tape 6 meters long, a meter stick, and a pencil.
3. Mark off a line about 5 centimeters from one end of the tape. Label this line NOW (today's date).
4. Using the meter stick and the ages given in Table 1, plot the different times on the adding machine tape. Indicate that the students should start by using the scale 1 meter = 1 billion years. (NOTE: As the activity progresses the students will have difficulty with the scale of 1 meter = 1 billion years. They will have to change the scale in order to include recent events on their tape. The frustration of this change and the realization of the difference between 1 year, 100 years, 1,000 years, 1 million years, and 1 billion years is as much a part of the lesson as the geologic periods. Let them struggle with the new scale.

TABLE 1
Approximate Age in the Earth's History

1. Earth's beginning	4.5 billion years ago
2. Oldest rocks	3.3 billion years ago
3. First plants (algae)	2.0 billion years ago
4. First animal (jellyfish)	1.2 billion years ago
5. Cambrian Period (abundant fossils)	600 million years ago
6. Ordovician Period	500 million years ago
7. Silusian Period	440 million years ago
8. Devonian Period	400 million years ago
9. Mississippian Period	350 million years ago
10. Pennsylvanian Period	305 million years ago
11. First reptiles	290 million years ago
12. Permian Period	270 million years ago
13. Triassic	225 million years ago
14. First mammals	200 million years ago
15. Jurassic	180 million years ago
16. First birds	160 million years ago
17. Cretaceous Period	135 million years ago
18. Paleocene	70 million years ago
19. Eocene	60 million years ago
20. Oligocene	40 million years ago
21. Miocene	25 million years ago
22. Pliocene	11 million years ago
23. First humanlike mammals	2 million years ago
24. Pleistocene	1 million years ago
25. Humans make tools	.5 million years ago
26. Last Ice Age	10,000 years ago
27. Calendars used in Egypt	4234 B.C.
28. Pythagoras proposes theory of mountain origin	580 B.C.
29. Eratosthenes measures Earth circumference	200 B.C.
30. Mount Vesuvius eruption at Pompeii	79 A.D.
31. First U.S. satellite	1958 A.D.
32. Mount St. Helens eruption	1980 A.D.

It may help to point out that 1 millimeter equals a million years on a scale where 1 meter equals a billion. Or, one billion = 1,000 million.)

5. After the activity, discuss the problem of scale and how the students resolved it. Usually they decide to change the scale for the last meter and make 1 meter equal 1 million. Still, recent events are very hard to plot. Again, this is part of the realization of the immensity of geologic time.

EVALUATION TASKS

The students can use their tapes to explain some of the earth's history. Ask the students to explain *why* they had trouble plotting recent events. How did they overcome the problem?

EXTENDING THE ACTIVITY

The students can do a report on one geologic period.

ACTIVITY 8   ## Using Hardness to Identify Minerals

1. Obtain the following materials: steel file, copper penny, table knife, piece of glass, collection of minerals.
2. Discussion:
   a. What will scratch glass? Wood? A penny?
   b. How can hardness be used to identify minerals?
   c. A substance's resistance to scratching is called its *hardness*. If calcite scratches gypsum, which is harder? If calcite scratches both talc and gypsum, which is harder, talc or gypsum? How could you find out?
3. Investigation:
   a. Obtain a collection of minerals from a geology department. Make a list of minerals a fingernail will scratch, a file will scratch, a knife will scratch, and a copper penny will scratch. Which minerals are hardest?
   b. Find out about Moh's Hardness Scale. What is the hardness of a knife blade on Moh's Scale? A penny? A steel file? A fingernail?
   c. Using the hardness number of the knife blade, penny, file, and fingernail, determine the Moh number for each mineral in your collection. Record your results. Obtain a mineral from your classmate without finding out its name. Using your new knowledge, can you identify the mineral from its hardness?
4. Teacher's Information:

Moh's hardness scale

1. Talc	1. Fingernail scratches it easily
2. Gypsum	2. Fingernail scratches it
3. Calcite	3. Penny scratches it
4. Fluorite	4. Knife scratches it
5. Apatite	5. Knife scratches it
6. Feldspar	6. It scratches glass
7. Quartz	7. It scratches glass
8. Topaz	8. It scratches most minerals
9. Corundum	9. It scratches topaz and most all minerals
10. Diamond	10. It scratches all other minerals

ACTIVITY 9   ## Using Specific Gravity to Identify Minerals

1. Obtain the following materials: spring balance, string, can or jar of water, small iron object, small aluminum object, piece of glass, collection of minerals.

2. Discussion:
    a. State the following: "Mary had a rock that weighed different amounts at different times. The rock has not changed in any way."
    b. What ideas do you have about how this may happen?
    c. Have you ever picked up a large rock under water and then carried it out of the water? Was it heavier in water or out of water?
    d. How could we make sure of our answer?
3. Suspend a rock on a spring balance with a length of string. Record its weight. Immerse the rock in water. Record its weight under water. How much more or less does it weigh now?
4. Specific gravity is a way to help identify minerals. Specific gravity is found by comparing the weight of a mineral in air to the amount of weight the mineral loses in water. Specific gravity may be found as illustrated in the following example:

Weight of rock in air	35 grams
Weight of rock in water	15 grams (subtract)
Loss of weight in water	20 grams

TEACHER INFORMATION

The following table lists average specific gravities for common minerals.

Material	*Average Specific Gravity*
Pyrite	5.0
Halite	2.2 (dissolves in water)
Fluorite	3.2
Quartz	2.7
Calcite	2.7
Graphite	2.3
Galena	7.5
Hematite	5.3
Magnetite	5.2
Limonite	4.3
Talc	2.7
Mica	2.8
Gypsum	2.3
Glass	2.13–2.99
Feldspar (orthoclase)	2.6
Feldspar (plagioclase)	2.7

$$\text{Loss of weight in water} \overline{\left.\right|\; \dfrac{\text{Specific gravity}}{\text{Weight of rock in air}}}$$

$$
\begin{array}{r}
1.75 \\
20 \overline{\smash{\big)}\ 35} \\
\underline{20} \\
150 \\
\underline{140} \\
100 \\
\underline{100} \\
\end{array}
$$

The specific gravity of the rock is 1.75.
How can specific gravity be used to identify minerals?
5. What is the specific gravity of the rock you weighed in and out of water? Record your answer and show how you obtained it.
6. Obtain a piece of iron, aluminum, glass, and other objects. Using the method above, find their specific gravity. Compare your results with those of your classmates.

7. Make a list of the minerals in your collection and find the specific gravity of each. Record the specific gravity of each in a column beside the name of the mineral.

ACTIVITY 10   ## Using Simple Materials to Find the Earth's Magnetic Field

1. Obtain the necessary materials and set up the apparatus as shown in the diagram.

MATERIALS

1. Dry cell
2. Resistance box
3. Milliammeter (0–1 am. range)
4. Cardboard cylinder
5. Small sewing needle
6. Ten feet of no. 24 insulated copper wire
7. Protractor
8. Connecting wire
9. Knife switch
10. Terminal posts
11. Cellophane tape
12. Wood base

Construction as shown in Figure.

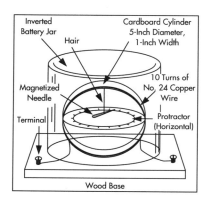
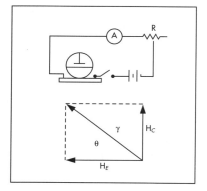

Calculations:

To find H_C, use $H_C = \dfrac{2\pi NI}{10\,r}$ where N = number of coils
I = current in amperes
r = radius of coil in cm
H_C = magnetic field strength of coil in oersteds
H_E = magnetic field strength of earth in oersteds (to be found)

To find H_E, use $H_E = H_C \tan \gamma \;\square$ where $\gamma = 90° - \theta$

EXPERIMENT (SEE FIGURE)

Align the magnetometer so that the needle which is pointing north-south will be parallel to the baseline of the protractor. Make the connections as shown and throw the knife switch. If the needle makes a full 90-degree turn, R must be increased so that the magnetic field H_c of the magnetometer is less strong. Adjust R so that the needle comes to rest somewhere between 0 and 90 degrees. Read the milliammeter and the angular deflection of the needle (θ). Take several trials.

Your result should be in the neighborhood of 0.2 oersted for H_E at 40 degrees latitude. The values of H_E in the United States range from 0.13 oersted at Gull Island in Lake Superior to 0.28 oersted near Brownsville, Texas. The higher values are at lower latitudes because it is the *horizontal* component which is being measured.

2. Where is mathematics needed in this experiment?
3. What could you learn about the magnetic field of the earth without the use of mathematics?
4. How much more can you learn using mathematics?

Astronomic Distances   ACTIVITY 11

ACTIVITY OVERVIEW

In this activity the students complete a scale model of astronomic distances. The goal is to have the students conceptualize the vastness of space. This activity should take two class periods.

SCIENCE BACKGROUND

A light year is an astronomic measure of distance. The words "light year" as said quickly may not capture the immensity of the distance involved. Try completing the following exercise so you will have an understanding of the astronomic distance. You can have the students do the same activity. Light travels about 298,000 kilometers per second (186,000 miles per second).

$$
\begin{array}{r}
298{,}000 \text{ kilometers per second} \\
\underline{\times\ 60\ } \quad\text{km per minute} \\
\underline{\times\ 60\ } \quad\text{km per hour} \\
\underline{\times\ 24\ } \quad\text{km per day} \\
\underline{\times 365\ } \quad\text{km per year}
\end{array}
$$

There are some terms and symbols in the activity (see Table 1) about which students may ask. Some of these are defined for you:

Cluster—a group of stars or galaxies often identified by the constellation in which they are located

Galaxy—a group of stars

M—this stands for Messier number, a way astronomers catalog stars

Milky Way—the galaxy in which our solar system is located

Nebula—a cloud of dust and gas

This activity should give students a new perspective relative to the earth in time and space. Our earth is small and insignificant in the scale of astronomic time and distance. Yet, our earth is the most important astronomic object as far as our existence is concerned.

MAJOR CONCEPTS

The average distance between stars in space is incredibly large. Stars are made of hot gases, but they differ in temperature, mass, size, luminosity, and density.

OBJECTIVES

At the completion of this lesson the student should be able to:

Describe the immensity of astronomic distance

Indicate that stars have different distances from earth

Identify his/her location in the scale of stellar space

Define a light year as the distance light travels in a year.

TABLE 1

Distances to Selected Objects in the Celestial Sphere

CELESTIAL OBJECT	DISTANCE IN LIGHT YEARS
Quasar—3c 295	4.5 billion
Hydra Cluster of Galaxies	3.9 billion
Quasar—3c 273	1.5 billion
Gemini Cluster of Galaxies	980 million
Ursa Major I Cluster of Galaxies	720 million
Cygenus A—radio source	500 million
Pegasus II Cluster of Galaxies	470 million
Hercules Cluster of Galaxies	340 million
Coma Cluster of Galaxies	190 million
Perseus Cluster of Galaxies	173 million
Pegasus I Cluster of Galaxies	124 million
Fornox A—radio source	60 million
Virgo Cluster of Galaxies	38 million
M49 in Virgo	11.4 million
M81	4.8 million
M31 in Andromeda	2 million
Leo II Galaxy	710 thousand
Fornox Galaxy	390 thousand
Megellanic Clouds	170 thousand
Center of Milky Way	30 thousand
Owl Nebula	12 thousand
Ring Nebula	4.5 thousand
Deneb—star	1.6 thousand
Regil—star	900 light years
Polaris—star	680 light years
Vega—star	26.5 light years
Sirius—star	8.7 light years
Alpha Centauri—star	4.3 light years
Sol—our sun	8 light minutes

MATERIALS

Meter stick
Colored pencils
Adding machine tape (6 meter strips for each group of two)

VOCABULARY

Astronomic	Quasar
Stellar	Star
Distance	Nebula
Galaxy	

PROCEDURES

1. Divide the students into groups of two or three.
2. Each group should have a piece of adding machine tape 6 meters long, a meter stick, and pencils.
3. Mark off a line about 5 centimeters from one end of the tape. Label this line EARTH.
4. Using the meter stick and the distances given in Table 1, plot the distances to the various stellar objects on the adding machine tape. Tell the students they should start by using the scale 1 meter = 1 billion light years. (Note: When the students start plotting distances closer to the earth: i.e., within millions of miles, they will find it impossible to use the scale of 1 meter = 1 billion light years. Frustration will be evident as they try to figure out how far a million is on their scale and finally how to get so many stellar objects located in such a small distance. This is the realization that is essential to the lesson. They will have to change the scale to 1 meter = 1 million light years and then they will still have difficulty with the last few distances.)

5. Discuss the problems students had with the scale 1 meter = 1 billion light years. Ask them "How did you resolve the problem?" "How does this distance make you feel in the scale of the universe?"

EVALUATION TASKS

The students can use their tapes to explain the immensity of space.

EXTENDING THE ACTIVITY

The students can report on some of the stellar objects named in Table 1.

Weather: Air Masses and Fronts   ACTIVITY 12

ACTIVITY OVERVIEW

Students observe weather reports on television over a period of a week. The concepts of air masses and fronts are then presented in a lecture-discussion format by the teacher. Weather maps are studied for the final section of the activity. Students watch weather reports on the evening news for one week. Spend one class period on lecture-discussion.

SCIENCE BACKGROUND

The movement of large air masses and the influence of more localized fronts determine the majority of daily weather. An air mass is a large body of air that originates in a particular location and then moves across the earth's surface. The important characteristic of air masses is that they acquire the properties (temperature and humidity) of the region in which they originate. Air masses are either tropical or polar and either continental or maritime. The major air masses and their origins are shown in Figure 1.

Continental polar air masses are cold and dry. Maritime tropical air masses are warm and moist. Continental tropical air masses are warm and dry. Maritime polar air masses are cold and moist. The different characteristics of the air masses greatly influence local weather.

A cold front is the phrase applied to the leading edge of a cold dense air mass. Since the air is cold and dense, it wedges under lighter, warmer air and forces some air up into the atmosphere. As the warm air is lifted it cools and has a reduced capacity to hold moisture. As this occurs, clouds form and precipitation falls. Cold fronts are often identified by a line of storm clouds (see Figure 2).

FIGURE 1
Air Masses Influencing the Continental United States

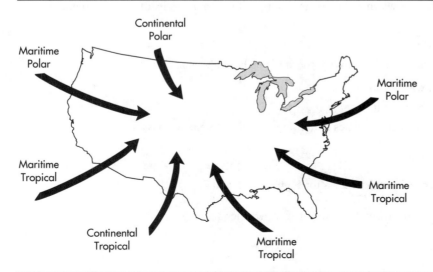

FIGURE 2
Cold Front

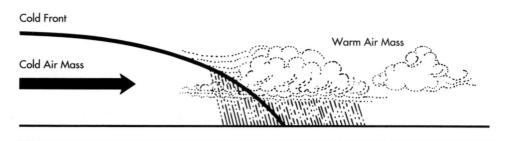

Cold Front

Warm Air Mass

Cold Air Mass

FIGURE 3
Warm Front

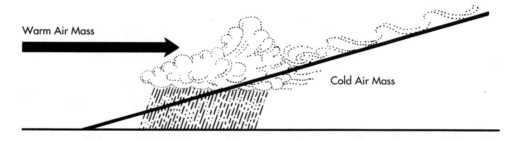

Warm Front

Warm Air Mass

Cold Air Mass

A warm front results when warmer, lighter air pushes behind colder, denser air. The result is that warmer air moves up over the colder air, producing a long area of precipitation as the warm air rises and cools. High cirrus clouds can precede the front by several days (see Figure 3).

We are influenced daily by the weather. Yet, many know little about the dynamics of this daily phenomenon. The implications of weather range from moisture for agriculture to severe weather that threatens human life.

MAJOR CONCEPTS

Atmospheric motion occurs on many scales.
Air masses have characteristics of the places of origin.
The interaction of warm and cold air results in different patterns of weather called *fronts*.

OBJECTIVES

At the completion of this activity, the student should be able to:

Identify a warm front

Identify a cold front

Describe the characteristics and influences of different air masses.

MATERIALS

Prepare overhead transparencies for Figures 1, 2, and 3.
Chalkboard
Old weather maps (from the newspaper or weather station)

VOCABULARY

Cold front   Air masses
Warm front   Weather

PROCEDURES

1. Present the concepts of air masses and fronts in a formal manner (15–20 minutes).
2. Have the students apply their observations to the presentation during a discussion period.
3. In the final section of the activity, have the students look at weather maps and see if they can discover the concepts of air masses and fronts as they have actually been recorded.

EVALUATION TASKS

Use Figures 1, 2, and 3 *without* labels and have the students identify air masses and fronts. Tell the students to observe weather forecasts for the next week and summarize their observations in terms of air masses and fronts.

EXTENDING THE ACTIVITY

Have the students look up occluded fronts and report on their characteristics.
Have a meteorologist (a local TV weatherperson) visit class and tell about predicting the weather.
The students can study the instruments used in recording atmospheric conditions.

Measuring Humidity   ACTIVITY 13

HOW CAN YOU MEASURE HUMIDITY CHANGES?/
WHAT IS A HYGROMETER?

Air contains moisture.
Pressure and temperature affect the amount of moisture air can hold at any given time.
Relative humidity is the amount of water vapor actually contained in the atmosphere divided by the amount that could be contained in the same atmosphere.
Relative humidity can be measured.

What Concepts Might Students Discover?

2 thermometers   Wide cotton shoelace
Small bottle or dish of water   Empty milk carton
Thread

What Will We Need?

What instrument in used to measure the amount of water or humidity in the atmosphere? How can this instrument be made and how does it work?

What Will We Discuss?

PROCESSES
What Will Students Do?

1. Obtain an empty milk container, two identical thermometers, a cotton shoelace, and some thread.
2. Cut a four-inch section from the cotton shoelace and slip the section over the bulb of one of the thermometers. Tie the shoelace section with thread above and below the bulb to hold the shoelace in place. Allow the other end of the four-inch section to rest in a small bottle or dish of water inside the milk carton.
3. Attach both thermometers to the milk carton as shown in the diagram.

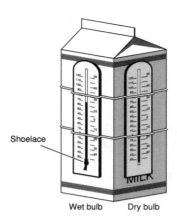

Shoelace

Wet bulb   Dry bulb

You now have a hygrometer—an instrument that measures the relative humidity in the atmosphere. *Caution:* The two thermometers should register the same temperature before the shoelace is placed over one of them; otherwise, the difference in readings must be considered a constant that is part of all computations.

4. When the shoelace is wet, fan it with a piece of cardboard for one minute.

Hypothesizing

What do you think might happen to the thermometer with the wet shoelace? Why do you think so?

Observing

5. Check the temperature readings of the two thermometers.

Hypothesizing

How do you account for the difference in readings between the thermometer with the shoelace (called the "wet-bulb") and the one without the shoelace (called the "dry-bulb")?

What Must I Know?

When the shoelace is wet, the evaporation of the water results in a cooling of the wet-bulb thermometer, while the dry-bulb thermometer will continue to read the temperature of the air around it.

6. Compute the relative humidity by recording the temperature of the dry-bulb thermometer and the difference between the readings of the two thermometers, and applying these to the relative humidity table.

7. Take readings on your hygrometer every day for two weeks and record your findings. Also try readings in different places.

Inferring

What reasons can you give for different readings?

Applying

Using your hygrometer, can you predict which days are better for drying clothes outside?

How Will Students Use or Apply What They Discover?

1. *What other instruments can you find that will indicate or measure relative humidity?*
2. *How is relative humidity used by weather forecasters to predict weather?*
3. *Why were you asked to fan the wet-bulb thermometer?*
4. *How does relative humidity explain why you feel more uncomfortable on a humid 90-degree day than on a dry 90-degree day?*
5. *Why might you feel more comfortable in winter in a room that is 70 degrees with 65 percent relative humidity, than in a room that is 70 degrees but with only 30 percent relative humidity?*

ACTIVITY 14   Evaluating Food Choices

ACTIVITY OVERVIEW

Students keep a record of the food they eat for one day. By means of a graph, the students evaluate their food choices.

Finding Relative Humidity in Percent
(Difference in Degrees between Wet-Bulb and Dry-Bulb Thermometers)

Air Temperature (Reading of Dry-Bulb Thermometer) in Degrees Fahrenheit

	1	2	3	4	5	6	7	8	9	10	11	12	13	14	15	16	17	18	19	20	21	22	23	24	25	26	27	28	29	30
30°	89	78	68	57	47	37	27	17	8																					
32°	90	79	69	60	50	41	31	22	13	4																				
34°	90	81	72	62	53	44	35	27	18	9	1																			
36°	91	82	73	65	56	48	39	31	23	14	6																			
38°	91	83	75	67	59	51	43	35	27	19	12	4																		
40°	92	84	76	68	61	53	46	38	31	23	16	9	2																	
42°	92	85	77	70	62	55	48	41	34	28	21	14	7																	
44°	93	85	78	71	64	57	51	44	37	31	24	18	12	5																
46°	93	86	79	72	65	59	53	46	40	34	28	22	16	10	4															
48°	93	87	80	73	67	60	54	48	42	36	31	25	19	14	8	3														
50°	93	87	81	74	68	62	56	50	44	39	33	28	22	17	12	7	2													
52°	94	88	81	75	69	63	58	52	46	41	36	30	25	20	15	10	6													
54°	94	88	82	76	70	65	59	54	48	43	38	33	28	23	18	14	9	5												
56°	94	88	82	77	71	66	61	55	50	45	40	35	31	26	21	17	12	8	4											
58°	94	89	83	77	72	67	62	57	52	47	42	38	33	28	24	20	15	11	7	3										
60°	94	89	84	78	73	68	63	58	53	49	44	40	35	31	27	22	18	14	10	6	2									
62°	94	89	84	79	74	69	64	60	55	50	46	41	37	33	29	25	21	17	13	9	6	2								
64°	95	90	85	79	75	70	66	61	56	52	48	43	39	35	31	27	23	20	16	12	9	5	2							
66°	95	90	85	80	76	71	66	62	58	53	49	45	41	37	33	29	26	22	18	15	11	8	5	1						
68°	95	90	85	81	76	72	67	63	59	55	51	47	43	39	35	31	28	24	21	17	14	11	8	4	1					
70°	95	90	86	81	77	72	68	64	60	56	52	48	44	40	37	33	30	26	23	20	17	13	10	7	4	1				
72°	95	91	86	82	78	73	69	65	61	57	53	49	46	42	39	35	32	28	25	22	19	16	13	10	7	4	1			
74°	95	91	86	82	78	74	70	66	62	58	54	51	47	44	40	37	34	30	27	24	21	18	15	12	9	7	4	1		
76°	96	91	87	83	78	74	70	67	63	59	55	52	48	45	42	38	35	32	29	26	23	20	17	14	12	9	6	4	1	
78°	96	91	87	83	79	75	71	67	64	60	57	53	50	46	43	40	37	34	31	28	25	22	19	16	14	11	9	6	4	1
80°	96	91	87	83	79	76	72	68	64	61	57	54	51	47	44	41	38	35	32	29	27	24	21	18	16	13	11	8	6	4
82°	96	91	87	83	79	76	72	69	65	62	58	55	52	49	46	43	40	37	34	31	28	25	23	20	18	15	13	10	8	6
84°	96	92	88	84	80	77	73	70	66	63	59	56	53	50	47	44	41	38	35	32	30	27	25	22	20	17	15	12	10	8
86°	96	92	88	84	80	77	73	70	66	63	60	57	54	51	48	45	42	39	37	34	31	29	26	24	21	19	17	14	12	10
88°	96	92	88	85	81	78	74	71	67	64	61	58	55	52	49	46	43	41	38	35	33	30	28	25	23	21	18	16	14	12
90°	96	92	88	85	81	78	74	71	68	64	61	58	56	53	50	47	44	42	39	37	34	32	29	27	24	22	20	18	16	14

Example:
Temperature of dry-bulb thermometer 76°. Temperature of wet-bulb thermometer 68°. The difference is 8°. Find 76° in the dry-bulb column and 8° in the difference column. Where these two columns meet, you read the relative humidity. In this case, it is **67 percent.**

SCIENCE BACKGROUND

Nutrients can be defined as the different substances in foods that function specifically to keep the body healthy, active, and growing. Some of the major nutrients needed by the body include protein, fats, carbohydrates, vitamins, and minerals.

Protein is the body's building material. It contains nitrogen, which is necessary for all tissue building. Protein is essential for maintaining body structure, for providing substances that act as body regulators, and for producing compounds necessary for normal body functions. Milk products, meat, fish, poultry, eggs, legumes, and nuts are good sources of protein.

While protein can also provide energy for the body, *fats* and *carbohydrates* are the major food substances that provide the body with calories for heat and energy. If the body lacks sufficient amounts of fats and carbohydrates, or if there is an excess of protein in the diet, the body will use protein for heat and energy. Fats are normally consumed from margarine, butter, mayonnaise, salad dressings, and meat. Carbohydrates are found in grain products, fruit, and sugar-sweetened foods.

Although vitamins and minerals are needed in smaller quantities than are protein, fats, and carbohydrates, they remain essential to normal body functioning. Our discussion is limited to those often lacking in the diets of adolescents.

Vitamin A is important for vision. Night blindness, an inability of the eye to adjust to dim light, can result from a lack of vitamin A in the diet. Yellow, orange, and dark green vegetables and fruits contain vitamin A (sweet potatoes, carrots, squash, spinach, broccoli, melon, apricots, and peaches).

Vitamin C contributes to the formation of a substance called *collagen,* which holds body tissue together and encourages healing. Vitamin C also strengthens blood vessel walls and helps the body utilize calcium in making bones and teeth. Scurvy, a disease characterized by swelling and tenderness of joints and gums, loosening of teeth, hemorrhaging, and puffiness, can result from severe lack of vitamin C. Citrus fruits, broccoli, spinach, greens, potatoes, tomatoes, melon, cabbage, and strawberries contain this vitamin.

Iron is a mineral that is essential to *hemoglobin,* the substance of the blood that carries oxygen. Oxygen is necessary for all cells. A diet that fails to supply a sufficient amount of iron may lead to anemia. This condition is characterized by a tired and listless feeling due to a lack of energy. Although liver is a major source of iron, greens, beans, beef, pork, prunes, and raisins are also good sources.

Calcium is the bone- and tooth-building mineral. It forms the structure of teeth and bones and helps keep them strong. Milk products are good sources for calcium.

MAJOR CONCEPT

Individuals should develop eating patterns that contribute to wellness.

OBJECTIVES

By the end of this activity, the students should be able to:

Analyze and evaluate food choices in terms of the Recommended Daily Allowance (RDA) of protein, energy, and selected vitamins and minerals

MATERIALS

"Comprehensive List of Foods" booklet with nutritive values and percent of U.S. RDA for 139 foods, available from the National Dairy Council. Contact the office serving your area or write National Dairy Council, 630 North River Road, Rosemont, Illinois 60018.

VOCABULARY

anemia	minerals	Recommended Daily
calories	night blindness	Allowance (RDA)
carbohydrates	nutrient	scurvy
fats	proteins	vitamins

PROCEDURES

1. Have the students keep a complete record of all foods eaten for one day.
2. Using the "Comprehensive List of Foods," the students should then determine the nutritive values and graph the percent of RDA that chosen foods contained. (See sample graph.)
3. Upon completion of the bar graphs, invite the students to answer the following questions:

    Is the percentage of calories (energy) in your daily diet too low, about right, or too high? Nutrients I need more of are _____.

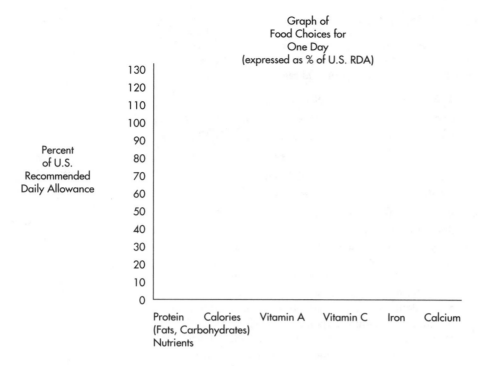

Graph of
Food Choices for
One Day
(expressed as % of U.S. RDA)

Percent
of U.S.
Recommended
Daily Allowance

130
120
110
100
90
80
70
60
50
40
30
20
10
0

Protein   Calories   Vitamin A   Vitamin C   Iron   Calcium
(Fats, Carbohydrates)
Nutrients

Which foods could provide these nutrients?

Foods I ate that had a lot of calories (energy) but not many other nutrients are

_____.

How can I improve my diet?

An Introduction to Population, Resources, and Environment   ACTIVITY 15

AIMS

To develop a general understanding of the technology, economics, environmental effects, and social issues related to finding and extracting resources

OBJECTIVES

At the completion of this lesson the participant should be able to:

- Describe the relationship between population growth and resource use
- Define resource
- Describe the difference between reserves and resources
- Describe the role of technology, economics, and environmental effects on the extraction and use of resources
- Describe the difficulties in making decisions about the distribution of limited resources.

MATERIALS

Pennies (300)	Other items commonly available in classrooms
Tweezers	Riddle of lily pond
Toothpicks	Handout of worksheets

INSTRUCTIONAL PLAN

A. Exploration
 1. Use riddle to focus attention and introduce relationship between population and resources.

    There is a lily pond that has a single leaf.

    Each day the number of leaves doubles.

    On the second day there are two leaves.

    On the third day there are four leaves.

    On the fourth day there are eight leaves.

    On the thirtieth day the pond is full.

    When was the pond half full?   *Set*
 2. Show film *World Population.*
 3. Purpose statement and transition to activity   *Purpose*
 4. Explain the activity.
    - The activity simulates the exploration and extraction of earth materials needed by individuals and society.
    - Students first *explore* the room to assess the availability of resources (pennies).
    - Report on resources that were observed and introduce definitions. Summarize data on overhead.
    - Have the students actually "mine" the resources. Students must record the number of pennies found each minute.
    - Students must use objects to extract pennies.
    - Students will have 10–15 minutes to obtain pennies.
    - Complete a graph of the pennies found each minute.
 5. Do the first exploration. Have the students spend 3 minutes looking around the room to determine how many pennies there are. (Review rules: they cannot touch, turn over, change furniture, and they cannot collect any pennies.)   *Active Participation*
 6. Return to groups. Have the groups report on their findings. Record observations on overhead.

B. Explanation
 7. Define reserves, resources, and technology.   *Information Input*
 8. Have the students actually "mine" the resources.   *Active Participation*
 9. Provide time to complete graphs.
 10. Summarize and discuss resource activity.
    - What happened as their extraction of resources continued?
    - Did they find all the resources?
    - How close were the estimates of the resources?   *Reinforcement*
    - What problems did they experience with time? Extraction? Location?
    - How is this activity like the actual extraction of resources?   *Transfer*
    - What is the relationship of technology to your activity? Of economics? Of population? Of environment?   *Assessment*

C. Extension
 11. Introduce the simulation game involving the distribution of resources.
 12. Have participants complete the individual and group decisions.

13. Discuss the distribution simulation.
    - What was the basis for your individual and group decision?   } *Transfer*
    - What other information would you have requested?

    - Would you change your decisions if more units of resources were available?   } *Decision Making*
    - How could more resources be obtained?   } *Values*
    - What lifestyle changes, price increases, environmental effects, etc., would you be willing to tolerate in order to have more resources?   } *Personal Meaning*

D. Evaluation
14. Conclude with a discussion of the interrelationship of population, resources, and environment.   } *Closure*

DEFINITIONS

Reserves:
The amount of a particular resource in known locations that can be extracted at a profit with present technology and prices.
Resources:
The total amount of a particular material that exists on earth.
Technology:

A. The application of science, especially to industrial or commercial objectives
B. The entire body of methods and materials used to achieve industrial or commercial objectives
C. The body of knowledge available to a civilization that is of use in fashioning implements, practicing manual arts and skills, and extracting or collecting resources

Groups	1	2	3	4	5	6	7
Reserves							
Estimates of Resources							
Actual Resources							

DATA SHEET FOR DISTRIBUTING RESOURCES

Your problem is to decide how to distribute resources among three groups who have requested your help. For this activity we are using the term *resources* to include many different things such as food, minerals, fuels, and other items needed by people. Here is the only information you have to make your decisions:

You have 300 units of resources

You presently use 200 units of resources

You can survive on 100 units of resources

Three groups want some of your resources. Here are their situations:

Group 1—needs 250 units of resources to survive
      —wants 250 units of resources

Group 2—needs 100 units of resources to survive
      —wants 200 units for survival *and* improvement

Group 3—needs 50 units for survival
—wants 100 units for improvement

Group 4—needs no units for survival
—wants 200 units for improvement

Your problem is to decide how you will distribute the resources. Complete the accompanying chart.

Individual Decisions				
Distribution of Resources	Group 1	Group 2	Group 3	Group 4
Reasons for Decision				

Group Decisions				
Distribution of Resources	Group 1	Group 2	Group 3	Group 4
Reasons for Decision				

ACTIVITY 16   A Place in Space

Overview:

Without technology, the exploration of space would be impossible. As we increase the possibility that humans will one day live and work in space, we also increase the need for more sophisticated technology. In this activity, the students identify the basic needs of living things, examine a variety of self-contained biospheres designed to support life, and construct a simple model of a space station. Through these experiences, the students will realize some of the challenges that scientists and engineers face when exploring the frontier of space.

Scientific Principles:

- The basic needs of living things include oxygen, carbon dioxide, water, light, food, and protection from extreme heat and cold.
- Artificial biospheres rely on technology to provide the basic needs of resident organisms.
- Engineers use scale models to help them in the design of complex systems.
- A closed system is an isolated system; neither energy nor material can pass through its boundaries.

Student Outcomes:

Upon completion of this activity, students will be able to

- Identify the basic needs of a living organism.
- Construct a biosphere for a simple organism such as a plant.
- Recognize different models of complex biospheres.
- Use scale models to design larger objects.

Skills:

Analyzing, discussing, constructing models

Related Disciplines:

Life science, Earth science, Physical science, Mathematics

Time Frame:

Life under Glass	45 minutes
A Human Terrarium?	45 minutes
Little Plans for Big Ideas	45 minutes

Materials and Advance Preparation

LIFE UNDER GLASS

Materials:

- Large potted plant
- 2-liter soft-drink bottles
- 1 small plant, no more than 8″ tall, for the demonstration terrarium
- Large scissors, 1 pair per lab group
- Potting soil, 10-pound bag
- Newspaper, enough to cover desks
- Seeds, 5 per student (suggested seeds: radish, marigold, alfalfa)
- 500 ml beaker of water, 1 per lab group
- Duct or electrical tape, 15 cm per lab group
- Masking tape, 30 cm per lab group

Before Class:

- A week in advance, ask the students to bring in empty, rinsed, clear 2-liter soft-drink bottles. You will need one per student.
- Organize materials for lab groups.
- Make a soft-drink bottle terrarium using a small plant instead of seeds. This will serve as the demonstration terrarium. (See Life under Glass, step 3.)

A HUMAN TERRARIUM?

Materials:

- Terrarium with small plant (from Life under Glass)
- Overhead projector

Before Class:

- Make transparencies of the Biosphere II and the EMU figures.

LITTLE PLANS FOR BIG IDEAS

Materials:

- Meter stick or metric tape measure
- Graph paper with metric divisions, 1 sheet per student
- Scissors, 1 per lab group
- Metric rulers, 1 per student
- Masking tape

Before Class:

- Write the dimensions of the space module on the chalkboard. (See Little Plans for Big Ideas, step 2.)

LIFE UNDER GLASS

1. Display a large plant and ask the students to explain what this organism needs to stay alive. List the students' responses on the chalkboard, and assist them in identifying needs that are basic to the plant's survival: minerals, water, air, and light.
2. Display the demonstration terrarium containing a small plant. Review the students' lists of basic needs. Will this plant stay alive? Why or why not? Have the class explain how each basic need of the plant is being met.
3. Divide the students into lab groups and distribute materials so students can construct terraria by doing the following:
   a. Use the large scissors to cut off the top of each plastic bottle.
   b. Separate the colored base from the rest of the bottle by tugging on it vigorously.
   c. Use the duct or electrical tape to seal the holes in the base from the inside. Do this carefully to make the base watertight.
   d. Fill the base with soil.
   e. Add 50 ml of water to moisten the soil. *Do not overwater.* Stir the soil.
   f. Use a pencil to poke five holes in the soil, and then plant a seed in each hole. Gently cover each seed with soil.
   g. Invert the clear plastic part of the bottle to create a dome to cover the base. Use masking tape to seal the base and dome. Record names on the tape.
4. Keep the students' terraria in a warm place until the seeds germinate (two to three days), and then place the terraria in sunlight. After the majority of the seedlings are well sprouted, ask the students to evaluate the varying success of individual terraria. Have the students discuss how the basic needs of the plants are, or are not, being met. Your students may want to design and conduct experiments to test the relative importance of different factors on plant life in a terrarium.

A HUMAN TERRARIUM?

1. Instruct the students to reexamine the terrarium containing the small plant. Ask the students if they think humans could live in a terrarium. Discuss the needs of humans, and list these needs on the chalkboard. Ask the students to decide which of the items listed are biological needs that are basic to the survival of humans (oxygen, light, water, food, protection from heat and cold) and which are psychological needs (companionship, entertainment, recreation). Have the class discuss how the biological needs could be met in a closed system like a terrarium.
2. Define a closed system for your students. In a closed system, the total amount of water and air remains constant. In addition, no new food or nutrients can enter the system, so food and nutrients must cycle through the system for plants and animals to use them again. The earth is a closed system; energy is the only resource that reaches the system from the outside. Sunlight is necessary to heat air and supply energy for various cycles.
3. In the Arizona desert, scientists built an artificial, closed biosphere—or a human terrarium—called Biosphere II. Modeled after the biosphere of the earth (Biosphere I), Biosphere II is a self-supporting ecosystem containing five biomes: a savanna, a marsh, a desert, a tropical rain forest, and an ocean 35 feet deep. A group of eight men and women inhabited the two-acre structure. The $30 million project could serve as a prototype for orbiting space stations or planetary outposts, and as a model for improved resource management.

   Use a transparency of the figure to present the Biosphere II project in Arizona, and discuss the project, asking the students to consider the following:
   a. What are the objectives of the project? (According to the planners, there are two: to develop technology for settlements on the moon and Mars, and to improve human stewardship of earth by learning how to manage such things as human wastes.)
   b. What problems require solutions if Biosphere II is to become self-sustaining? (Some suggestions are how to seal the glass roof so that no air can escape or enter;

Biosphere II

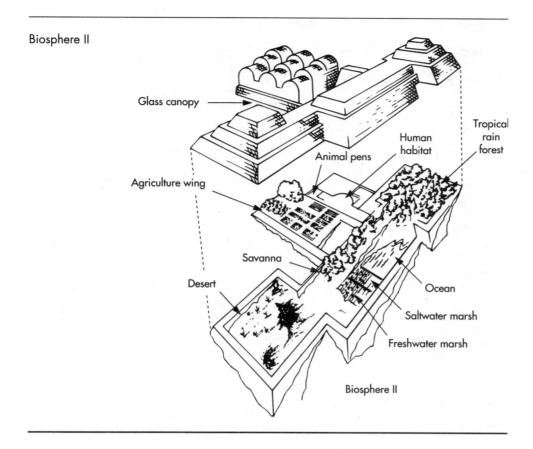

Glass canopy

Tropical rain forest

Human habitat

Animal pens

Agriculture wing

Savanna

Desert

Ocean

Saltwater marsh

Freshwater marsh

Biosphere II

how to cool the air temperatures, which could peak at 156°F, without using conventional methods that draw air from the outside; how to handle water purification and air quality; how to make sure there is adequate vegetation to sustain all life forms; and how to make sure that none of the selected life forms will be a hazard to the ecosystem.)

c. What would it be like to live in Biosphere II? What kind of people would be appropriate to include in the group of eight Biosphereans? What skills should they have?

d. What were the likely social dynamics of the Biosphereans? What strains do you imagine the Biosphereans encountered during their two-year stay in Biosphere II? Would the students like living for two years with seven other people in a closed system?

4. Another life-supporting biosphere model is the extravehicular mobility unit (EMU) used by astronauts in space. NASA developed the EMU to enable astronauts to work in space without the support of a spacecraft. An attachable manned maneuvering unit (MMU) allows astronauts to work untethered in space and return safely to the spacecraft. By providing the atmospheric pressure and oxygen necessary for human life as well as insulation from the sun's heat, the EMU protects the astronaut from the hostile environment of space. The technology involved in the EMU is complex; astronauts preparing to work in space must carry all of their life-support systems with them. Use a transparency of the figure to illustrate an EMU. Have the students identify the basic needs of an astronaut and describe how the EMU meets those needs.

LITTLE PLANS FOR BIG IDEAS

As we push back the frontiers of space, we must create self-supporting biospheres. Most people call these artificial biospheres *space stations*. In 1984, President Ronald Reagan directed NASA to develop a permanently occupied space station. Scientists once envisioned

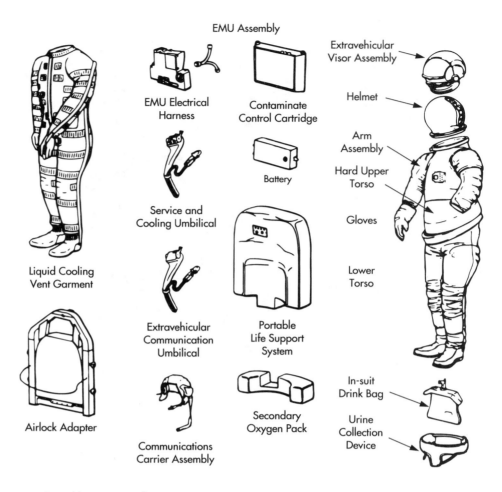

EMU Assembly

EMU Electrical Harness

Contaminate Control Cartridge

Extravehicular Visor Assembly

Helmet

Service and Cooling Umbilical

Battery

Arm Assembly

Hard Upper Torso

Liquid Cooling Vent Garment

Gloves

Lower Torso

Extravehicular Communication Umbilical

Portable Life Support System

Airlock Adapter

In-suit Drink Bag

Secondary Oxygen Pack

Urine Collection Device

Communications Carrier Assembly

Assembly instructions for EMU:
1. Put on urine collection device, cooling and ventilation garment, in-suit drink bag, communications carrier assembly, biomedical instrumentation subsystem, boot inserts.

2. Don space suit: hard upper torso, lower torso, gloves, helmet, extravehicular visor assembly.

a collection of modules that would form huge, spoked wheels that would spin through space. Current U.S. plans for the station, however, describe a structure that includes four pressurized, cylindrical modules, in the center of a huge supportive structure. Two of these modules will provide living space, and the other two will provide a working area. The space station will house a crew of six, with replacement crews arriving every 90 days.

1. If space is available, have the students measure the dimensions of one module on the classroom floor. Instruct six people to stand within the boundaries of the module, and ask the students to imagine living in that space for 90 days at a time. Remind the students that they would have only two modules available for sleeping, eating, recreation, and relaxation.

2. Currently, plans for the space station are only on paper. Because something as large as a space station is difficult to design, engineers use scale models. Scale models are small two- or three-dimensional renderings of a large object. With the advent of sophisticated computers, computer modeling has replaced paper-and-pencil drafting in the design of complex objects. In a scale model, the relative sizes of the parts of the model are the same as those of the larger object; all the proportions are identical. Introduce the students to the concept of a scale model. Use familiar examples, such as airplane models and architectural plans. Ask the students to make a three-dimensional scale model of one of the cylindrical modules:

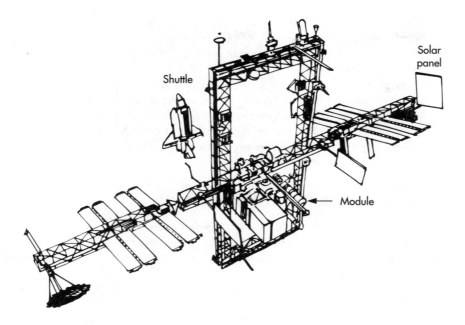

a. Review the dimensions with students:
   Diameter of module = 4.2 meters
   Length of module = 12.1 meters
   OPTIONAL: The module is cylindrical. In order to draw the module two-dimensionally and then roll it into a correctly scaled cylinder, ask the students to calculate the circumference of the module. Review with the students the formula for calculating the circumference of a circle from its diameter: circumference = $\pi\, d$. If students are not familiar with the formula for calculating the circumference, include the circumference (13.2 meters) in the dimensions.

b. Ask the students to convert the measurements of the module from meters to centimeters, using the scale of 1 cm = 1 m. In this way, one centimeter on paper will be equivalent to one meter on the module.

c. Supply each student with one sheet of graph paper with metric divisions. Ask the students to draw on the graph paper the scaled dimension they had calculated (length × circumference). The finished drawing will be a rectangle.

d. Instruct students to cut out the rectangle with scissors and tape the two short sides together to form a cylinder. This cylinder is proportionally accurate and resembles the proposed module. Each dimension is 1/100 of the size of the real module, making the scale model, with its three dimensions, 1/1,000,000 of the size of the real module.

e. The students can use a metric ruler to check their model by measuring the diameter of the cylinder. Being careful to maintain the cylindrical form, the students should measure the diameter as approximately 4.2 cm.

GOING FURTHER

- Have the students write a letter from space, describing where they live, what they do, and how they feel about living on a space station.
- Ask the students to search their school or local libraries for science fiction that includes predictions of how humans will live in space.
- Have the students conduct research on plans for the industrialization of space. Ask the students to find out the results of various projects on shuttle flights and what industrial applications may be suited for a space station.
- Have the students draw a scale model of one room of their house. Ask them to measure the room's size and the furniture, and to draw a two-dimensional plan with all parts of the room in relative proportion.

- Have the students investigate the numerous spin-offs produced by the space program, such as teflon, velcro, and temperfoam. Information on the products is available in the library or from the U.S. Government Printing Office (address listed under "Resources for the Classroom").
- Encourage the students to study the history of space exploration. What happened when? How did the explorations benefit life on earth? When did the first animal, man, or woman orbit the earth, walk on another planet, or travel past the moon?
- Let the students explore the accomplishments of the U.S. and U.S.S.R. in space. Why is there so much competition between these nations? When have they cooperated? What other nations have active space programs?

RESOURCES FOR THE CLASSROOM

Freundlich, N.J. (1986). Biosphere. *Popular Science, 229* (6), 54–56.

Maranto, G. (1987). Earth's first visitors to Mars. *Discover, 8* (5), 28–43.

NASA. (undated). NASA facts: Waste management. JSC-09696 (rev. ed.). Washington, DC: U.S.G.P.O.

NASA. (1984). NASA facts: A wardrobe for space. JSC-09378 (rev. ed.). Washington, DC: U.S.G.P.O.

Scobee, J. & Scobee, D. (1986). An astronaut speaks. *Science and Children, 23* (6), reprint.

Taylor, P. (1982). *The kid's whole future catalog.* NY: Random House.

Government documents can be ordered from the Superintendent of Documents, U.S. Government Printing Office, Washington, D.C. 20402. Many fliers are free, even in bulk quantities.

A teacher's companion to the space station: A multi-disciplinary resource, as well as other materials, is available at the NASA Teacher Resource Centers listed below:

Alabama Space and Rocket Center, Huntsville, AL 35807. Serves Alabama.

NASA Ames Research Center, Moffett Field, CA 94035. Serves Alaska, Arizona, California, Hawaii, Idaho, Montana, Nevada, Oregon, Utah, Washington, and Wyoming.

NASA Goddard Space Flight Center, Greenbelt, MD 20711. Serves Connecticut, Delaware, District of Columbia, Maine, Maryland, Massachusetts, New Hampshire, New Jersey, New York, Pennsylvania, Rhode Island, and Vermont.

NASA Jet Propulsion Laboratory, 4800 Oak Grove Drive, Pasadena, CA 91109. Serves inquiries related to space exploration and other JPL activities.

NASA Johnson Space Center, Houston, TX 77058. Serves Colorado, Kansas, Nebraska, New Mexico, North Dakota, Oklahoma, South Dakota, and Texas.

NASA Kennedy Space Center, Kennedy Space Center, FL 32899. Serves Florida, Georgia, Puerto Rico, and the Virgin Islands.

NASA Langley Research Center, Hampton, VA 23665. Serves Kentucky, North Carolina, South Carolina, Virginia, and West Virginia.

NASA Lewis Research Center, Cleveland, OH 44135. Serves Illinois, Indiana, Michigan, Minnesota, Ohio, and Wisconsin.

NASA Marshall Space Flight Center, Tranquillity Base, Huntsville, AL 35812. Serves Alabama, Arkansas, Iowa, Louisiana, Missouri, and Tennessee.

National Space Technology Laboratories, NSTL, MS 39529. Serves Mississippi.

The United States Space Foundation, 1522 Vapor Trail Drive, Colorado Springs, CO 80916, also has many teacher and student resource materials.

BACKGROUND FOR THE TEACHER

Space stations orbiting earth, space travellers living in artificial, enclosed biospheres, and shuttles transporting people between Earth and Mars—are these just science fiction images, or is the space program bringing us to the reality of settlements beyond Earth?

NASA has been working toward the settlement of space for many years. With President Ronald Reagan's directive in 1984 to "develop a permanently manned space station—and do it within a decade," (Anderson, undated, p. ii.) NASA has been able to put form to its concepts and deadlines to its timetable. An occupied space station requires a self-supporting biosphere—a closed, complex system in which organisms support and maintain themselves. Because human survival in space requires oxygen, water, food, light, protection from temperature extremes, and a shield from cosmic and solar radiation, scientists and technologists have several complex problems to solve.

The *Challenger* disaster in January 1986 changed NASA's schedule for launching a space station. Originally, NASA planned to build a station in space over the course of 18 months, taking up materials with 12 shuttle flights (National Commission on Space, 1986, p. 120). Because of the problems with *Challenger,* NASA decided to reduce each shuttle's cargo capacity from 65,000 pounds per launch to 40,000 pounds, thus changing the timetable for building the station. Current plans call for construction of a modest station, which NASA can enlarge later. Shuttle flights will ferry the modules for living and working, and, after 11 flights, a crew of four will occupy the station. The station originally scheduled for completion in 1996 will have required a total of 32 flights (Biddle, 1987).

For centuries, humans have been curious about the worlds beyond our planet. Why do we want to explore beyond the confines of Earth? Why do we need to? What do we hope to accomplish?

Research in space will help answer numerous scientific questions. Aboard the space station, specialists will conduct astronomical studies, such as mapping Venus with the Magellan probe, which has high-resolution radar equipment. There is widespread interest in manufacturing in space, because the micro-gravity environment eliminates heat convection, hydrostatic pressure, sedimentation, and buoyancy, and enables the fusion of mixed particles into homogeneous composites that are impossible to make on earth (The Futurist, 1987). Private industries hope to use the space station to purify pharmaceutical and biological products, such as erythropoietin, a kidney hormone that controls the production of red blood cells. Other products include nearly flawless glasslike linings for artificial hearts that would prevent clotting, and membranes coated with antibodies that could filter the blood of an AIDS patient (Biddle, p. 45). The computer industry hopes to improve high-speed computers by growing high-quality gallium arsenide crystals in space. Researchers also would like to develop new polymers and catalysts, to process improved fiber optics, and to create new metal alloys not produced on Earth.

The scientific purpose of space travel is the pursuit of new knowledge. Scientists, however, are not the only people interested in space travel. Others also see space as an avenue to pursue their goals. The National Commission on Space has said, in its rationale for exploring and settling the solar system, that exploring the universe is a goal that will encourage increased world cooperation and will be a peaceful mission with respect for the integrity of planetary bodies and alien life forms (1986, p. 4). The ratio of funding for space projects, however, is tipped heavily in favor of the armed services. The defense budget helps to build technological infrastructures and underwrites expensive high-tech science (Biddle, p. 45). The existence of the Strategic Defense Initiative (SDI) as an impetus for space research underscores that there may not be unity of purpose in space exploration. Space is a large frontier; how and why the United States ventures into it will determine the benefits derived from its exploration.

Consultant
Victoria Duca
Director of Special Projects
U.S. Space Foundation
Colorado Springs, CO

REFERENCES

Anderson, D. A. (undated). Space station. EP-211. Washington, DC: U.S.G.P.O.

Biddle, W. (1987). NASA: What's needed to put it on its feet? *Discover, 8* (1), 31–49.

National Commission on Space. (1986). *Pioneering the space frontier.* NY: Bantam Books, Inc.

Space Industries. (1987). Manufacturing facilities in space cited in *The Futurist, 21* (3), 33.

ACTIVITY 17   **Dirty Water: Who Needs It?**

Overview:

Life as we know it is not possible without water. Despite its importance, water has become improperly managed, seriously depleted, and contaminated by toxic materials. In this activity, students examine the distribution of water, investigate pollutants and treatment methods, and consider their roles in the water problem, thereby recognizing that we face a frontier in maintaining this valuable resource.

Scientific Principles:

- The world's supply of water remains constant, but the supply is neither readily available for human use nor distributed uniformly.
- Specialized treatments can remove impurities and pollutants from water, but those impurities and pollutants are not removed from the Earth's closed system. There is no such place as *away*.

Student Outcomes:

Upon completion of this activity, students will be able to

- State the percentage of water resources readily available for human use.
- Describe the steps used in water treatment and explain the results.
- Identify ways they contribute to the water pollution problem.

Skills:

Observing, Investigating, Measuring, Comparing, Discussing, Evaluating

Related Disciplines:

Environmental science, Life science, Mathematics, Chemistry

Time Frame:

Water, Water Everywhere	15 minutes	Where Is Away?	15 minutes
Pollution Solution?	45 minutes	Who, Me?	30 minutes

Materials and Advance Preparation

WATER, WATER EVERYWHERE

Materials:

- 7 *clear* containers—2 one-liter containers; 5 smaller containers, one of which is plastic
- 1 plate
- Overhead projector
- Masking tape
- Marking pen
- 1 liter of water
- Salt—34 grams
- Sand—approximately 250 ml
- Blue food coloring
- 1000-ml graduated cylinder
- One eyedropper

Before Class:

- Gather all materials.
- Fill one small container with sand.
- Fill a 1-liter container with water, add four drops of blue food coloring, and stir.

- Label the other five containers as follows:
  —a 1-liter container *oceans*
  —a small plastic container *polar ice*
  —a small container *other* (saltwater lakes, soil and atmospheric moisture, glaciers)
  —a small container *deep groundwater*
  —a small container *fresh water*.
- Make a transparency of the figure, "Distribution of the World's Water Supply."
- Measure and set aside 34 grams of salt.

POLLUTION SOLUTION?

Materials:

- Gravel, approximately 250 ml
- Sand, approximately 250 ml
- Soil, approximately 250 ml
- Salt, approximately 250 ml
- 1000-ml beaker, 1 per lab group
- 250-ml beaker, 1 per lab group
- 500-ml beaker, 1 per lab group
- Glass stirring rod, 1 per lab group
- Granulated alum ($KAl[SO_4]^2 \cdot 12H_2O$), approximately .05 g per lab group
- Coffee filter, 1 per lab group
- Rubber bands
- Masking tape
- Household bleach (sodium hypochlorite, $NaOCl$), 10 ml
- Eyedropper, 1 per lab group
- Balance, 1 per lab group
- Tray for evaporation, 1 for the class
- Distillation setup, 1 for the class (optional)

Before Class:

- Divide the students into lab groups.
- Prepare 1 liter of "polluted" water for each lab group by putting approximately 25 ml each of gravel, sand, soil, and salt into 1 liter of tap water.
- Write the directions for water treatment on the chalkboard or on a transparency.

WHERE IS AWAY?

Materials

- All Pollution Solution? materials (from completed previous activity)
- Salt residue from evaporation experiment

Before Class:

- Complete Pollution Solution? activity. Keep water and treatment materials.
- Complete evaporation experiment.

WHO, ME?

Materials:

- Overhead projector

Before Class:

- Make a transparency of the diagram entitled, "One Example of the Water Treatment Process."

SUBSTANCE	MCL[a]
Arsenic	0.05 mg/l
Lead	0.05 mg/l
Mercury	0.05 mg/l
Silver	0.05 mg/l
Fluoride	2.4 mg/l
Sodium	20 mg/l

[a]Maximum Contaminate Level.

Distribution of the World's
Water Supply

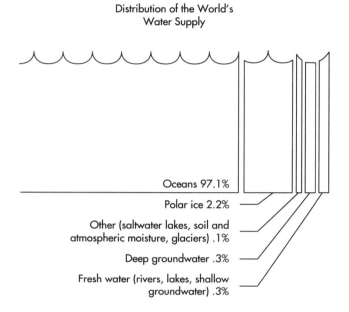

Oceans 97.1%

Polar ice 2.2%

Other (saltwater lakes, soil and
atmospheric moisture, glaciers) .1%

Deep groundwater .3%

Fresh water (rivers, lakes, shallow
groundwater) .3%

WATER, WATER EVERYWHERE

The world's supply of water covers more than 70 percent of the Earth's surface. Although the supply of water remains constant, it is not distributed evenly. Nearly 98 percent of the water is in the Earth's oceans, where salinity makes it unavailable for many human uses. The remaining 2 percent of the Earth's water is underground or in polar ice, lakes, rivers, and the atmosphere.

Perform the following class demonstration to help students visualize the distribution of the Earth's water resources:

A. Display the seven containers prepared for this activity (see "Materials and Advance Preparation").

B. Display a transparency of the figure, "Distribution of the World's Water Supply." Use a graduated cylinder to distribute the 1 liter of water into the five empty containers according to the percentages indicated in the figure. (For example, 97.1 percent of the water on the Earth is found in the oceans. Because 1 liter contains 1000 milliliters, 97.1 percent of 1 liter is 971 milliliters. Therefore, pour 971 milliliters into the container marked *oceans.*)

   NOTE: The percentages in the figure are rounded off to facilitate this demonstration. Take care to measure accurately so you have 3 milliliters of water left over. Also, these percentages will vary from source to source depending on the method of calculation and the divisions used. It may be an interesting project for students to examine a variety of sources that contain data about the distribution of water.

C. After you have filled the empty containers with the appropriate amounts of water, continue with the demonstration, as follows:

- Add 34 grams of salt to the *ocean* container; this will match the salinity of the water sample with the salinity of the Earth's oceans (3.5 percent).
- Place the plastic *polar ice* container in a freezer.
- Set the *other* container aside. We do not have access to this water.
- Pour the *deep groundwater* into the container of sand.
- Ask the students which of the containers represents fresh water that is readily available for human use. (They should easily see that only the jar marked *fresh water* has the readily available supply.) Initiate a discussion on the limits of freshwater supplies, the problems of population distribution, and the contamination of existing supplies (refer to "Background for the Teacher"). Only a small part of this fresh water (.003 percent of the Earth's total water supply) is accessible. The rest is too remote (found in Amazonian or Siberian rivers) to locate, too expensive to retrieve, or too polluted to use. Hold a plate in front of the class and dramatically drop the usable portion of fresh water onto it. (Represent this portion as one drop of water from an eyedropper.)

POLLUTION SOLUTION?

Faced with dwindling water resources, people have concentrated on two methods of alleviating the shortage problem. One is conservation, which includes management of toxic waste. The second method is treatment of already contaminated water. The technology exists to purify polluted water, but economics often determines whether we use the technology. To complicate matters, the pollutants removed from the water in the purification process still exist, and handling the toxic materials creates another pollution problem.

Ask the students to work in terms of two or three and to clean a prepared sample of contaminated water as follows:

A. Fill a 1-liter glass container with a well-stirred contaminated water sample (see "Materials and Advance Preparation"). Observe and record the water's color, clarity, and particulate pollution. Stir the sample and immediately pour 250 ml of the sample into a beaker. Determine and record the density of the 250-ml sample by measuring its mass and dividing mass by volume: density = grams of material/volume of material. Set this sample aside as a control.
B. Add approximately 0.5 g of alum to the water sample. Stir with a glass stirring rod for three to five minutes. Aluminum hydroxide particles (floc) will develop.
C. Allow the water to settle for 10 to 15 minutes. Observe and record the water's color, clarity, and particulate pollution.
D. Place a coffee filter over a 500-ml beaker and secure it with a rubber band or masking tape. Allow room for 250 ml of water between the bottom of the filter and the bottom of the beaker.
E. Carefully pour approximately 250 ml of the water through the filter, leaving the particles behind in the 1-liter container. (Be careful not to stir up the settled particles as you pour.) Observe and record the filtered water's appearance. Determine and record the density of the 250 ml of filtered water and compare it to the density of the 250-ml control set aside in step A.
F. Add one drop of household bleach to the filtered sample and stir the solution.
G. Observe the final sample and compare its appearance to the 250-ml control set aside in step A.
H. Keep all water and treatment materials for reference in the next activity, Where Is Away?

Help the students identify the four steps of water treatment used in this activity: flocculation, sedimentation, filtration, and sterilization. See the figure illustrating the water treatment process. Different treatment plants use different processes. One important process that students did not encounter in Pollution Solution? is biological treatment, during which microorganisms digest certain impurities. Encourage students to find out about the water treatment processes used in their community.

Identify the "pollutants" you used to prepare the water sample: gravel, sand, dirt, and salt. These materials are actually impurities, not pollutants. In this activity these impurities represent pollutants like sewage, dissolved minerals, and toxic chemicals. Ask the students if they think the treatment methods they used removed all the pollutants. They may suggest that the salt still remains in the water, and may ask to taste the water; but they should follow the universal laboratory rule: Don't taste. Instead, ask your students how they might test for salinity without tasting. Focus their suggestions on procedures they are capable of conducting. Measuring the mass of the polluted water and comparing its density to a sample of clean water of the same volume is one option; or, using a distillation process may also be a viable method.

Before dismissing the students for the day, have them set up the procedure they intend to use for testing for the presence of salt, and also have them pour a small amount of the treated water into a shallow tray so that complete evaporation will have taken place before the next class meeting.

WHERE IS AWAY?

Ask students to observe the results of the evaporation of the water sample from the previous day. What do they think is there? (The residue at the bottom of the tray does contain salt.)

Display the water and treatment materials saved from the previous activity, Pollution Solution? Ask the students to focus on each step of the water treatment process. Did they notice that although the water became cleaner with each step, the amount of waste material (flocculent debris, waste filter paper, salt residue) increased? Ask the students if they think we can depend on our current technology to remove pollutants and impurities completely from contaminated water. Can technology completely remove pollutants from the Earth?

Introduce the concept of *away.* Ask students where they think *away* is. When they throw something *away,* where does it go? When a pollutant is washed *away,* where does it go? After a treatment plant has treated the water, have the impurities gone *away?* Is there really a place called *away?* If students are ready, raise the issue of groundwater pollution. What happens to the groundwater when pollutants are thrown *away?*

WHO, ME?

With an understanding that pollution can never go *away,* your students should see that the most powerful solution to the problem of contaminated water supplies is to prevent contamination in the first place. Ask your students who they think contributes to the contamination of water supplies. Frequent answers will involve industry and agriculture. Students

One Example of the Water Treatment Process

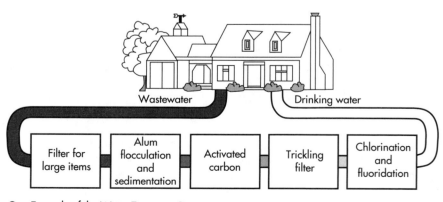

One Example of the Water Treatment Process

should be aware that, although industry and agriculture do contribute substantially to the contamination of water, individuals who use hazardous products in the home also contribute to pollution. Ask students what happens to household products that are dumped down the toilet or sink. Where is *away* in this case?

Materials are hazardous if they are toxic to living things, flammable, explosive, or corrosive. Display the "Toxic Household Products" table on an overhead projector covering up the third column, and ask the students to identify which hazardous products they have in their homes. Where are these products found?

Uncover the third column and discuss with the students the substitutes available for hazardous materials in the home. Ask students if they see any problem with using the substitutes instead of the hazardous products. Why don't more people use these safer substitutes? What are the trade-offs of using these alternatives? How would our life-styles change if we used "elbow grease" to clean ovens and no strong chemicals? When is the trade-off worth the consequence? Can action on the household hazardous waste front make a difference in the war against contamination of water? Why or why not?

Have students write a summary of their lessons on water. Ask them to identify the current "water crisis," some of its causes, how pollution of water is measured and then treated, and how the water crisis is closer to home than they might have expected.

RESOURCES FOR THE CLASSROOM

League of Women Voters. *A Hazardous Waste Primer.* Pub. No. 402. Washington, D.C. Available from: League of Women Voters, 1730 M. Street, NW, Washington, DC, 20036. (A short, unbiased survey of the issue of hazardous waste.)
Concern, Inc. *Groundwater: A Community Action Guide.* Washington, DC: Concern, Inc.
Consultant
Stephen W. Almond
Division Chemist
Halliburton Services
Oxnard, CA

BACKGROUND FOR THE TEACHER

Water is a vital resource. Human beings can live almost a month without food, but cannot survive more than two or three days without water. There are five properties that make water so essential: (1) high boiling point, (2) high heat of vaporization, (3) high heat capacity, (4) lower density as a solid than as a liquid, and (5) its solvency (Miller, 1979, p. 337).

Water is the universal solvent. It holds and transports, in solution, nutrients that nourish plant and animal systems. Water's powerful solvency also makes it an excellent cleanser, because it dissolves and dilutes so many substances. Unfortunately, this capacity for dissolving a wide variety of substances makes water easy to pollute.

Many different things pollute water: wastes that demand oxygen (sewage, manure); disease-causing agents (bacteria, viruses); inorganic chemicals (acids, salts, metals); organic chemicals (pesticides, plastics, detergents); fertilizers (nitrates, phosphates); sediments from land erosion; radioactive substances; and heat (Miller, pp. 357, 359). Most of these pollutants result from human activities. Water pollution is a serious problem because the supply of usable water is small, the distribution is uneven, the demand for use is high, and the rate of water's replenishment is low.

Although water covers more than 70 percent of the Earth, less than 1 percent is considered fresh water (Purdom & Anderson, 1983, p. 214). Because much of this fresh water is either too expensive to retrieve, too remote to reach, or too polluted to use, it turns out that only .003 percent of the Earth's total water supply is available for human use (Miller, p. 339). This small amount of fresh water comes from both surface waters and groundwater. In the United States, we draw about 75 percent of our water from lakes and rivers and 25 percent from groundwater (Chiras, 1985, p. 280). There are exceptions, however, to these average figures. For instance, the Greater New York area obtains 2 percent of its water from subsurface sources and 98 percent from surface sources (Brown et al., 1987, p. 51); yet

Toxic Household Products

PRODUCT	COMMENTS	ALTERNATIVES
CLEANERS		
Drain cleaner	Contains caustic poisons	Plunger, boiling water, plumber's snake
Oven cleaner	Contains caustic poisons; some are carcinogenic	Salt, self-cleaning oven, "elbow grease"
Toilet cleaner	Contains strong acid	Mild detergent, mix of Borax and lemon juice
Window cleaner	Contains toxic chemical compounds, sometimes carcinogenic; may cause birth defects	Vinegar and water
Spot remover	Contains poisonous solvents; some are carcinogenic	Wash fabric immediately with cold water and detergent
AEROSOL SPRAYS		
Most aerosol sprays	Contain highly toxic poisonous	Nonaerosol products
Hair spray	petroleum distillates, some are	Setting lotion/Gel
Shaving cream	carcinogenic. Most are flammable	Brush and shaving soap
Air fresheners	and toxic when inhaled.	Ventiliation, open bowl of fragrant spice
Furniture polish	Contains poisonous solvents, some are carcinogenic	Paste waxes, carnauba wax in mineral oil
PAINT PRODUCTS		
Paint (oil or alkyd)	Contains poisonous solvents; some are carcinogenic	Latex paint
Spray paint	Contains toxic solvents and propellants	Nonaerosol paint, mineral oil
Wood finishes	Most contain harmful solvents	
Paint strippers	Contain poisonous solvents; some are carcinogenic	Heat gun with ventilation, hand or electric sander, and wear respirator
OTHERS		
Mothballs	Contain poisonous chemical compounds; may be carcinogenic	Cedar closet, store woolens in plastic
Insect repellent	Can be lethal if ingested	Protective clothing
Disinfectants	Many extremely toxic	Soap, detergent, hydrogen peroxide

Tucson, Arizona, and San Antonio, Texas, are completely dependent on groundwater supplies (Schmitz, 1987, p. D-3).

Traditionally, water policies have been left to the states, and until recently, the federal government has been reluctant to become involved in this issue. Nevertheless, groundwater issues became serious enough for the Reagan Administration to acknowledge the need for limited federal action, and Environmental Protection Agency director Lee Thomas urged the creation of a combined state and federal groundwater program (Schmitz, p. 10).

In the United States, industry, agriculture, and our personal life-styles depend on huge quantities of water. Per capita use is now up to 200 gallons per day. This is the amount of water it takes per day to produce all the goods, grow all the food, and meet all the personal needs of each individual in the country. In contrast, countries with comparable levels of social and economic development use far less water; for example, per capita use in Germany is 37 gallons per day; in Sweden, 54 gallons per day; and in the United Kingdom, 53 gallons per day (Rogers, 1983).

This high level of use in combination with the unequal distribution of resources and the pollution of water sources has made the continued availability of clean water one of the prominent environmental issues in the world. As a result, we must advance the scientific and technological frontiers that deal with water issues. In addition, people must seriously consider their roles in conserving clean water. What can we find out about water, its sources, how it cycles, and how it becomes polluted? What technological advances produce pollution? What technologies can we develop to clean up the dirty water? What is each person doing to contribute to water problems and water clean-up? How can we adjust our lifestyles to preserve our most valuable resource?

REFERENCES

Brown, L. R., et al. (1987). *State of the world 1987*. NY: W. W. Norton & Co.

Chiras, D. D. (1985). *Environmental science*. Menlo Park, CA: Benjamin/Cummings Publishing Co.

Miller, G. T. (1979). *Living in the environment* (2nd ed.). Belmont, CA: Wadsworth Publishing Co.

Purdom, P. W. & Anderson, S. H. (1983). *Environmental science* (2nd ed.). Columbus, OH: Merrill Publishing Co.

Rogers, P. (1983). The future of water. *The Atlantic Monthly, 252* (1), 80–92. (This article discusses water issues and possible solutions.)

Schmitz, G. (1987, August 9). Poisons simmer in nation's aquifers. *The Denver Post.*

Investigating Seed Germination   ACTIVITY 18

1. *Test seeds for food used during germination.* Soak lima beans, peas, and kernels of corn in water overnight, remove the seed coats, and mash the seeds thoroughly. If you like, you may grind the dried seeds, and then add a little water to the flour and stir to form a paste.

   Add a few drops of tincture of iodine to some of the ground seeds. The seeds will turn a deep purple, showing the presence of starch.

   Put some of the mashed seeds in a test tube. Add a small amount of nitric acid, boil for a few seconds, and then add enough ammonia to neutralize the nitric acid. If protein is present, the nitric acid will turn the solution a bright yellow, and the ammonia will change the yellow color to orange.

   Rub a piece of walnut meat vigorously on a piece of white or brown paper. Warm the paper over a hot plate, but do not set the paper on fire. Then hold the paper up to the light and note the grease spot, showing the presence of fat.

   When seeds sprout, the starch is changed to sugar. Mash some sprouting seeds, add a small amount of water, stir, and transfer to a test tube. From the drugstore obtain Tes-Tape or Clinitest Tablets, which are used to test for presence of sugar. Follow the instructions carefully, and note the change in color, which shows the presence of sugar.

2. *Observe seeds germinating.* Obtain lima beans and kernels of corn from the seed store. Do not use grocery store seeds because they may be immature or heat-treated, and so may not germinate. Line a water tumbler with a rectangular piece of dark-colored blotter, and stuff absorbent cotton or peat moss into the tumbler to keep the blotter tight against the sides of the tumbler (Figure 1). Soak the lima beans and corn kernels overnight, and slip a few of each between the blotter and the sides of the tumbler. Moisten the cotton and keep it moist throughout the experiment to make sure the blotter is always moist. Place the tumbler in a warm place away from direct sunlight. Observe the tumbler each day and note the way the seeds germinate. Continue the germination until the seeds are well sprouted.

3. *Investigate conditions necessary for germination.* Prepare eight tumbler germinators described in step 2. Put one tumbler in the dark and one in the light (but not in direct sun-

---

FIGURE 1
A Tumbler Seed Germinator

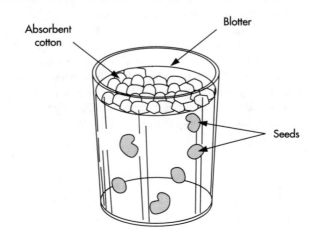

light). The seeds will germinate just as well in the dark as in the light. Point out that light is not necessary for germination and, in some cases, may even be harmful. However, once the plant has germinated and forms leaves, it needs light to grow.

Keep one tumbler watered regularly, and refrain from giving the other tumbler any water at all. The seeds in the dry tumbler will not germinate.

Cover one tumbler tightly with plastic wrap, or Saran Wrap, and keep the other tumbler continually exposed to the air. The seeds in the covered tumbler will not sprout because they need air to germinate.

Place one tumbler in the refrigerator and keep the other tumbler at room temperature. The seeds in the cold tumbler will not germinate because they need warmth to germinate.

Obtain three flower pots of the same size. Fill one pot with sand, the second with clay, and the third with rich soil containing humus. Soak some lima beans or radish seeds overnight, and then plant two or three seeds in each pot. Keep all three pots at the same temperature and give all of them the same amount of water. Although the seeds in all three pots may germinate, the plants in the pot containing the rich soil will eventually be taller and sturdier.

4. *Test seeds for percentage of germination.* Get radish seeds from the seed store. Soak 50 of them overnight, and obtain a piece of cotton flannel 30 centimeters (12 in) square. Moisten the flannel cloth and place the radish seeds on the flannel. Roll the flannel into a loose roll and place it in a shallow pan. Keep the flannel moist and warm for a week, and then unroll the flannel carefully and count the number of seeds that have germinated. The number of germinated seeds divided by the total number of seeds (50), multiplied by 100, will give you the percentage of germination. Repeat the experiment using bean, corn, and tomato seeds.

5. *Discover that germinating seeds give off carbon dioxide gas.* Obtain 20 to 30 lima beans from the seed store and soak them overnight. Put the seeds in a flask or jar and add enough water to cover about half the seeds. Fit the flask with a two-hole rubber stopper. In one hole insert a thistle tube and let the tube extend to just above the bottom of the flask. In the other hole insert a glass tube that leads to a water tumbler (Figure 2). Allow the beans to stay in the flask for a day or two. Then pour fresh limewater, which can be obtained from the drugstore, into the tumbler. Pour water slowly into the thistle tube until the flask is half-filled. The water will force the carbon dioxide, which is now above the seeds, through the glass tubing and into the limewater, making the limewater turn milky. You can first show that carbon dioxide turns limewater milky by bubbling air from your lungs into limewater through a soda straw.

6. *Measure the rate of seed growth.* Obtain some radish seeds from a seed store, soak them overnight, and then plant them in a flower pot filled with soil. Water the pot regularly and wait until the tiny plants begin to appear above the soil. Obtain two pieces of glass about 30 centimeters (12 in) square, and insert a wet piece of dark-colored blotter between them. Each day, for 10 to 14 days, carefully remove one entire radish plant from the soil and place it on the moist blotter. You can keep the panes of glass together with string or rubber bands. Keep the blotter moist at all times. At the end of 2 weeks you will have a clear-cut record of the daily growth of the radish seeds.

7. *Investigate how seeds travel.* Collect seeds (or pictures, if seeds are unavailable) that will show some ways that seeds travel. Discuss methods of seed travel, and list on the chalkboard all the possible ways that seeds travel.

8. *Classify seeds by use.* Make a display of seeds that are used by humans, using pictures when actual seeds are not available. Classify the seeds according to their uses, and label each seed, describing the purpose for which it is used.

FIGURE 2
When Seeds Germinate, the Carbon Dioxide Gas They Give Off Causes Limewater
to Become Milky

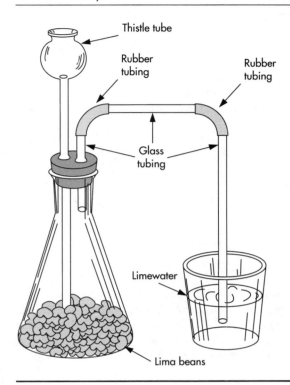

Thistle tube

Rubber tubing

Rubber tubing

Glass tubing

Limewater

Lima beans

Effect of Acid Rain on Seed Germination   ACTIVITY 19

ACTIVITY OVERVIEW

Students investigate the effects of acid rain on seed germination by conducting an experiment with bean seeds, or locally available seed, under varying pH conditions. The estimated time for this activity is one class period to organize groups and set up the experiment. Then, take a few minutes at the start of every other class for approximately two weeks to water and measure seed growth, and to record data on individual and class groups.

MAJOR CONCEPTS

- Seed germination is dependent upon proper conditions of pH.
- Increases of acidity due to acid rain may inhibit seed germination and plant growth.

STUDENT OBJECTIVES

After the activity students should be able to:

- Measure the growth of bean seed.
- Record data on an individual graph and on a class graph.

- Draw the bean seed before seed germination and each day that growth measurements are taken.
- Make a summary graph of individual graphs.
- Compare data to establish the optimum pH for the germination of a bean seed.

MATERIALS

- Petri dish
- 4 bean seeds (preferably seeds grown locally: alfalfa, pea, bean, etc.)
- Water solutions ranging in pH from 2–7 (boiling will be necessary to drive off CO_2 and raise pH to 7)
- Rainwater (optional)
- Absorbent paper towels
- Transparent metric ruler
- Graph paper
- Colored chalk or magic markers

PROCEDURES

Preparation of bean seed:

1. Assign each student a pH solution to "water" his or her bean seeds. A couple of students should be assigned distilled water or rainwater for a control. The class as a whole should represent increments on a pH scale ranging from 2–7.
2. Cut four paper discs the size of a petri dish from the absorbent paper towel.
3. Dampen the paper discs with appropriate pH or rainwater solution.
4. Place two discs at the bottom of the petri dish.
5. Measure the seeds and average them.
6. Arrange seeds in the petri dish and cover with the two remaining paper discs.
7. Replace lid on petri dish and label with student name.
8. Each student should hypothesize what will be the ideal pH on a piece of paper.

PREPARATION OF GRAPH

1. Obtain a piece of 8 × 11 graph paper.
2. Set up graph as follows: Horizontal axis, age of seed in days; Vertical axis, length of seed in mm.

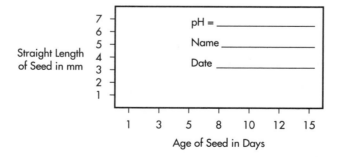

PROCEDURES FOR ALTERNATE DAYS

The students will be taking measurements of seed growth and recording data on individual and class graphs.

- Take measurements and plot data on individual graphs.
- Remove lid from petri dish.

- Sketch the shapes of the four seeds. Note the color of the seeds.
- Use transparent ruler to measure the straight length of seeds.
- Take the average straight-line length increase and plot it on your graph. (It is important to plot the increase of seed growth because seeds are different lengths before germination takes place.)
- Make sure paper towel is still moist. If not, add more pH solution (be sure pH solutions are not mixed).
- Replace lid on petri dish.
- Construct class graph on chalkboard or large piece of white construction paper on visible wall or board, to be saved throughout experiment. The graph should use same layout as individual graphs.
- Assign each pH a particular color (chalk or magic marker).
- More than one student may be experimenting with the same pH solution. These students should average their results of seed length.
- Have one student representing each pH record data on the board using the code color that represents pH used. (Example: a pH of 3 is represented by the color green: a pH of 7 is represented by the color purple.)
- After a few recordings have been plotted, students should draw a line connecting points of same pH.

DISCUSSION QUESTIONS

- What appears to be the first optimal pH solution for successful seed germination and growth? The least ideal?
- How does the local rainwater used compare to the other pH solutions used?
- From the data expressed on the class graph, what pH do you think the rainwater has?

EVALUATION

Each student should prepare a report that includes

- Brief description and purpose of experiment
- Data collected, individual graphs, and seed drawings
- Analysis of individual class results:
  1. Ideal pH
  2. Least ideal pH
  3. Comparison of rainwater to other pH solutions
- Discussion questions: What impact on local crops might an increased acidity have? Do you think there is a reason for concern?
- A concrete example of how acid rain and its effect on seed germination could affect food crops grown in the nearest agricultural area.

SUGGESTED READINGS

Fort, D. C. (1993). Science shy, science savvy, science smart. *Phi Delta Kappan 74* (9), 674–683.

Kulas, L. L. (1995). I wonder . . . *Science and Children 32* (4), 16–18.

Rossman, A. D. (1993). Managing hands-on inquiry. *Science and Children 31* (1), 35–37.

Stenley, L. (1995). A river runs through science learning. *Science and Children 32* (4), 13–15.

Welch, E. J., Jr. (1994). Animal behavior: An interdisciplinary unit. *Science and Children, 32* (3), 24–26.

Opening the Ocean: An Interdisciplinary Thematic Unit (Grade 5)

Opening the Ocean is a five-day unit designed for a fifth-grade classroom. For each day, we have focused on one aspect of the ocean: Water and Sound, Marine Life, People and the Ocean, and The Sandy Beach. For a culminating activity, we have suggested a field trip to the ocean. We have also included an anticipatory set for the unit—designing a class mural.

To help you out, we have included an additional reference list to provide more activities and to individualize the unit for your class. Good luck and enjoy "Opening the Ocean" with your starved-for-knowledge students!

OPENING THE OCEAN: CLASS MURAL

1. Have class brainstorm things that are needed for an ocean mural. Record the class suggestions on the overhead.
2. Hopefully your class will suggest sand, seaweed, boat, treasure chest, octopus, coral, fish, etc. If not, try to ask questions to stimulate the discussion towards these ideas.
3. Have students pick which items they would like to make. (You need to make sure you have at least two or three of each.)
4. Staple a 6′ × 5′ piece of dark blue butcher paper to the wall.
5. Have students by groups place their item on the wall. Because there were no specific instructions for where items should be placed, the mural will be very creative. (If you would rather have instructed areas, designate a "building engineer" to direct the placement of student work on the mural.)

SET 1: WATER AND SOUND

The Ocean: What Does It Say? — LESSON 1

This section of the unit combines water and sound, two vital influences in the ocean. Each day attempts to relate sound in some way to the study of the water of the ocean. Four lessons are represented in this section of the interdisciplinary unit. Specific materials as well as adjustments for needs of special and multicultural students are included in each lesson. This section can be taught as an entire day, as there are lessons involving language arts, science, math, and social studies. It may, however, be divided into separate days if desired, as the lessons do not directly depend on one another.

- Lesson 1: Language Arts. The Ocean: What Does It Say?
- Lesson 2: Math. Water and Sound: A Group Activity to Determine the Speed of Sound
- Lesson 3: Social Studies. The Ocean: A Newfound Planet
- Lesson 4: Science. Why Is the Ocean Salty? Myth and Fact

OBJECTIVE:

Having read the children's book *Fish Eyes,* a counting book, students will hopefully be inspired by the brilliant colors of the fish to be curious about the wonders and creatures of the ocean. Students will create an artistic representation of a sea creature. Students may research the means by which this animal communicates or create how they think the fish or mammal sounds. Students will then write on the back of their creation how this animal contributes to the sounds of the ocean.

MATERIALS:

Fish Eyes by Lois Ehlert, or any book that displays the brilliance and variety of sea life. Construction paper of various colors, colored pens, pencils, white lined paper for the backs of the creatures, a set of encyclopedias for researchers, a list of ocean dwellers as possible art projects, and a tape of whale or ocean sounds. *Interludes* is a great CD of ocean sounds and can be ordered through Great American Audio, 33 Portman Rd., New Rochelle, NY 10801.

ANTICIPATORY SET:

As you can hear, there is music of the ocean playing in the background. Close your eyes for a minute and listen to the sounds of the ocean. As we have been studying marine life, you now know about the many types of creatures that inhabit the ocean. What do you know about how they sound and communicate? Imagine that you are a fish swimming through the waters of the ocean. What do you hear? You see the sea horses. What are they saying? How do they communicate with one another? I am going to show you the pictures in this book, *Fish Eyes.* Look at them and notice their colors. We are now going to pick an inhabitant of the ocean. You are each responsible for creating a sea dweller. We will then write about how you think the animal communicates, and this will be attached to your creation. You may be creative or you may use the encyclopedia or books from the library These creations will be hanging in our classroom for everyone to enjoy and admire.

PROCEDURES:

1. Allow the students sufficient time to brainstorm and share ideas as well as ask questions. This assignment asks a lot of their creative juices.
2. Model both the creative choice as well as the factual.
3. Encourage the students to enjoy the art project and spend time designing their sea creature. The writing will mean more to the students if they have a personal attachment to the creations.
4. Limit the time for creation and encourage writing.
5. Do one yourself to model procedure.

CLOSURE:

Ask the students to share their writings or their creations or both. Have the students talk about whether they think that the ocean is quiet or loud. Collect the creatures and hang them from the ceiling or utilize them as part of a bulletin board.

EVALUATION:

To determine the level of the children's thinking, study the outcomes. Also compare the number of students who selected the creative option and those who selected the research option. Does this tell you anything about the individuals or your class?

Special-needs-students may need individual attention with this assignment. Match these students with a buddy in the class.

ASSESSMENT:

Ask the children what they learned and how they learned it. Use as a quick writing assignment in a journal.

Water and Sound: A Group Activity to Determine the Speed of Sound

LESSON 2

OBJECTIVE:

Students will create mathematical problems using the equations for the speed of sound in water. This is a group activity in which the groups work together to create and solve math problems involving water and sound.

MATERIALS:

Paper, pencils, at least one calculator per group, a chart with the equations and steps, and a map with mileage measurements

ANTICIPATORY SET:

Do you think sound travels faster in water or in air? Did you know that, if you were a sound wave, you could travel five times faster in water than in air? That means if you were whispering to your friend in class and all our classes were underwater, your friend would hear you five times faster than he/she would as you sit where you are right now. We are going to get into groups and create our own math problems using these equations. You may use any distance in the world that you wish as long as the distance is provided in your problem.

PROCEDURES:

1. Teach the math lesson that explains that the speed of sound is 5,000 ft per second in the water. One mile is equal to 5,280 ft. Thus, to compute the amount of time it would take for sound to travel from Sacramento to Davis underwater, assuming the distance is 30 miles, one would use the following procedure: 30 miles(the distance) times 5,280 ft (one mile) = the distance in feet, which is 158,400 ft. You know that sound travels 5,000 ft each second; thus, divide the 158,400 ft by 5,000 to reach the time in seconds. Answer: 31.68, or 32, seconds.
2. You will need a step-by-step chart for the students.
3. Have the students work in groups (incorporate strong math students).
4. Each student picks a distance for which they want to measure the speed of sound underwater (in this case, from Sacramento to Davis).
5. Each group writes its problem as a word problem on one paper and puts the solution on the other.
6. The teacher then collects the groups' problems and passes out the problems for another group to solve.
7. Groups check their answers with the original group.
8. If a discrepancy exists, the class may work together, facilitated by the teacher, to solve the problem.
9. Each problem must include the distance from Sacramento to the desired destination.

CONCLUSION:

Have students go over procedures for solving the problem with the teacher. Talk about problem solving and group work.

EVALUATION:

Collect problems and work to see how solutions were attempted and found.

ASSESSMENT:

Have the children write the steps needed to solve this equation, to be handed in to the teacher. Include why each step is necessary. (Because this activity is group oriented, special-needs students should be able to participate without any problem.)

LESSON 3   ## The Ocean: A Newfound Planet

OBJECTIVE:

After discussing the combined size of the oceans, students will realize the vastness of the ocean and question, Why not call this Planet Ocean since 75 percent of our Earth is covered by water? Students will create posters displaying the new Planet Ocean.

MATERIALS:

Poster board or construction paper, pens, glue, and magazines if you wish

ANTICIPATORY SET:

We all know what planet we live on. What is the name of it? Earth. Why do we call it Earth when 75 percent of it is covered with water? You have just been assigned to the committee to change the name of Earth to Planet Ocean. Your assignment is to create a poster, with a partner, which encourages us to change the name to Planet Ocean. The posters will be judged and given various prizes.

PROCEDURE:

1. Explain how the Earth is 75 percent water.
2. Have students work in pairs to create their poster.
3. Have other teachers and the principal select the most creative and influential poster (tell students the judging criteria beforehand).
4. Award all posters a prize if you wish!

CLOSURE:

Allow students to share posters and explain them to the class. Put them up in the classroom.

EVALUATION:

Check for understanding of surface area covered by water by evaluating posters. (Multicultural and special-needs students should have no problem with this activity if explained thoroughly.)

LESSON 4   ## Why Is the Ocean Salty? Myth and Fact

OBJECTIVE:

Students will discover why the ocean is salty by first creating their own myth in groups to explain the salt in the ocean. Second, students will research and present the facts about the salt in the ocean.

MATERIALS:

Paper, pencils, encyclopedia or science book that includes information on the ocean. A myth such as that of Johnny Appleseed.

ANTICIPATORY SET:

I am going to tell you why the ocean is salty today, class. In 1332 a gigantic ship was traveling from a faraway land carrying salt to sell to another nation. The ship hit a glacier and all the salt spilled into the ocean. The ship was so big that it made all the oceans in the world salty. Is that a fact or a myth? What do you think? Today you will be in groups to create your own myth about why the ocean is salty. We will then work together as a class to find out the facts about why the ocean is salty.

PROCEDURE:

1. Read a myth to the students so that they are clear on what one is. Johnny Appleseed is a popular myth.
2. Place students in groups, and ask them to brainstorm and create a reason or myth about why the ocean is salty.
3. Give the students ample time to work, and let them know their myths will be read aloud.
4. Have the students read their myths to the class.
5. Work together under teacher instruction to find the real answer. (Do you know? Work with your class to find out!)

CLOSURE:

Ask the students what they learned about myths as well as about the ocean and its salt. Place myths on the wall in your classroom.

EVALUATE:

Read students' work. Determine if they mastered the concept of a myth. Again, as this is a group activity, all students should be able to participate.

ASSESSMENT:

Ask children the following day to define *myth* and explain the facts about why the ocean is salty.

BOOKS

LANGUAGE ARTS

Fish Eyes by Lois Ehlert. Tein Wah Press, 1992.

MATH

Equations for sound from *Whales in the Classroom, Vol I: Oceanography* by Lary Wade, illustrated by Stephen Bolles. Singing Rock Press, 1992.

SOCIAL STUDIES

M.A.R.E.: A teacher's guide to the ocean. (These are ideas for the study of the ocean published by the University of California at Berkeley.)

SCIENCE

Johnny Appleseed, author unknown.

All lesson plans original; the term *Planet Ocean* was borrowed from the MARE program.

The lessons surround the kings of the ocean—whales. The disciplines covered are art, language arts (writing), science, physical education, and mathematics. Each lesson's time will vary from class to class, but here are some estimations:

- Lesson 1: The Art of Scrimshaw (art and social science) 90 minutes. This activity requires drying time for artwork. It may be beneficial to time this during a recess or natural scheduling break.
- Lesson 2: A Whale Story (language arts) 60 minutes. This activity needs to follow The Art of Scrimshaw lesson because one transitions into the other.
- Lesson 3: Blubber Is Beautiful (science) 45–75 minutes. Hands-on science! This activity may require a few minutes' setup by the instructor.
- Lesson 4: Migration Graph (math and physical education) 90 minutes. Time to exercise and think. Always a great wakening activity on distance and to spruce up a slow afternoon.

Have a whale of a time!

LESSON 1   **The Art of Scrimshaw**

OBJECTIVE:

After gathering information about scrimshaw art (history, examples), students will create their own artwork and distinguish its history.

MATERIALS:

Large, smooth white seashells	Linseed oil
Polish (light, clear cover-spray or paint)	Nails
Superfine sandpaper	Ink or watercolor

ANTICIPATORY SET:

Show students scrimshaw art. Can they figure out what materials it would take to create such beauty? What do they figure the art means to the artist? Provide students with prompts. Could the artist be a recycler? Could this be the work of a princess of Wales?

PROCEDURE:

Share with students the history of the art of scrimshaw.
Provide students with the materials and necessary steps for their artwork: Sand and polish the shell to be inscribed. Scratch, with a nail, a marine-oriented scene, using a nautical theme (for example, a whaler scene, harpooners, a battle scene, mermaids, or pirates). Cover the shell with ink and wipe with linseed oil. The inscribed design will be filled with ink.

CLOSURE:

Explain to students that this art activity is going to transition into their language arts later in the day. During language arts they will be writing or dictating their art's history. Be thinking about it! Discuss as a whole class their thoughts about scrimshaw.

EVALUATION:

What was scrimshaw art used for? (trade)
Why don't we see much scrimshaw anymore? (Few whales and even fewer whales' teeth are available)

A Whale Story   LESSON 2

OBJECTIVE:

Students will analyze and support their Art of Scrimshaw work through writing its history in the American whalers' setting.

MATERIALS:

Completed student scrimshaw work   Paper cut in whale shapes
Writing instruments   Historical vocabulary journals
Sand, seashells, other materials   Glue

ANTICIPATORY SET:

Read students a teacher-written history of your scrimshaw work. Be creative here—depending on your comfort level, try turning your history piece into a reader's theater or other dramatic presentation. Teacher models!

PROCEDURE:

Remind students of the historical and cultural importance of scrimshaw art. Provide students with whale-shaped paper and materials for authentic writings. Have students write their short historical fiction (extensions for able students: dictate history into a tape recorder, do buddy work, write poetry, provide historical vocabulary journals). After writing, provide students with marine materials (sand, shells) for writing decoration.

CLOSURE:

In groups, have students share their historical fiction along with their scrimshaw artwork. Ask each group to choose one piece they thought was historically accurate, interesting, funny, exciting, and/or had a strong correspondence with the artwork. The chosen piece will then be shared with the entire class—provide positive feedback!

EVALUATION:

After students have displayed their writing and artwork, evaluate their work based upon their ability to connect the art and history. Did the students place their writing in American history as asked to do?

Blubber Is Beautiful   LESSON 3

OBJECTIVE:

Students will investigate the beauty of whale blubber and compare and contrast blubber versus plain body heat.

MATERIALS:

plastic gloves (2 pairs for every two students)   water
crushed ice/ice cubes   shortening
laboratory thermometers (1 for every two students)   clock with second hand
buckets (1 for every two students)   recording sheet

ANTICIPATORY SET:

BLUBBER. "Blubber Is Beautiful"—today on (your name) talk show. Many in the United States are lean and slick. Few in the world are blubbers and beautiful. It is a personal choice for some but a genetic makeup for others. Join us today on (your name) talk show to hear from and examine the truth—blubber or not?

PROCEDURE:

Students are now the scientists testing the two opinions of blubber. In groups of two:

1. Fill a bucket with ice water. Measure and record the water temperature.
2. One student will put on a pair of gloves. The other student will spread a thick layer of shortening over student 1's right hand. Then put the second pair of gloves over the first.
3. Have the student put both hands in the ice water, being sure hands are not deeply immersed so no water enters from top of gloves.
4. Students will keep hands immersed, sharing feelings with student 2 (recorder).
5. Student will remove each hand as soon as it becomes uncomfortable. Record how long he or she was able to keep each hand in the water.
6. Repeat the activity, changing roles of students. (Be sure to measure water temperature to be sure it is the same each time.)
7. Each student-scientist pair will then answer the discussion questions on recording sheet and report findings to class chart.

CLOSURE:

Class discussion—review class chart findings. Ask following questions of (your name) talk show guests: Explain the scientific experiment to our audience. Which hand stayed in the water longer? Why? Discus why shortening insulated their hands. How does shortening compare to blubber? Why do marine animals need blubber to keep warm? Close as host of talk show: "As I promised, we have an answer to the Is Blubber Beautiful? debate. For the lean, slick fish, blubber is not so important. Yet for the survival of whales in our world's ocean, BLUBBER IS BEAUTIFUL!

RELATED ACTIVITIES:

To demonstrate how blubber helps prevent the loss of body heat, have students take their palm temperatures under the gloves directly before putting their hands in the water. For best results, use laboratory thermometers. After one minute, have them remove their hands from the ice water and immediately take their palm temperatures again. Subtract the end temperature from the start temperature. Repeat with other students. Compare temperature loss between the "blubber" and "plain" hands, and analyze the results. What was the average heat loss for each hand?

Is Blubber Beautiful?   Names: _____

_____

	#1	#2
Water Temperature:		
Which hand was removed first?		
How long were you able to keep hands in the bucket?	R | L	R | L

On a separate piece of paper, answer the following:
Which hand stayed in the bucket longer?
Why?
Did the shortening make a difference?
Share your findings and conclusions.

Migration Graph   LESSON 4

OBJECTIVE:

Students will develop an appreciation and understanding of the distance of the gray whales' migration (problem solving, graphing, physical education).

MATERIALS:

Example graphs
Materials for graph making
Exercise area for runner, swimmers, wheelchairs

ANTICIPATORY SET:

Challenge students to make predictions on how many days it would take for them to finish the 5,000-mile migration of the gray whale. Show students the teacher prediction graph. Display various types of graphs.

PROCEDURE:

Students will make their own prediction for the amount of time it would take for them to complete a 5,000-mile migration. Then students will create their own unique graph to illustrate their prediction and amount of distance per day using an equation; for example, 20 miles a day times days = migration distance.

Students will walk, run, or wheelchair a mile to determine the distance. Then they will return to their graphs to reestimate the distance and days. (Students will realize the distance and most likely adjust their prediction for days.) Redo estimated graphs and equations for distance.

CLOSURE:

Hold a class discussion sharing original estimations of distance and migration time with those post-mile thoughts. Graph student time estimates.

EVALUATION:

Did the students finish the activity with a stronger sense of distance? Were the equations generated acceptable for finding solutions? Have the students write their final estimation of time needed to complete the distance.

RESOURCES FOR MARINE LIFE

The following resources provided ideas, guidelines, and information for these lessons.

The Art of Scrimshaw

The art of scrimshaw has been considered a very important indigenous folk art of the Indians and, later, early Americans. It involved the carving and decorating of whales' teeth, walrus tusks, or bone (usually whales' teeth). Whalers had a considerable amount of time on their hands and with scant tools etched the teeth of the whale to pass the time. A trophy of a whale hunt—a large tooth—was the measure of the whaler's success, and the carefully etched pictures expressed great individuality.

Elk, C. Kiorpes. *Teacher's Guide to the Whales of the Gulf of Maine.*

Insulation Investigation. Sea World Materials, Inc., 1987.

Los Marineros Curriculum Guide. NOAA and Santa Barbara Superintendent of Schools.

M.A.R.E. Teacher Guide. UC–Berkeley, California.

Wet and Wild. USC Sea Grant Program, Institute for Marine and Coastal Studies, University of Southern California, 1983.

SET 3:
PEOPLE AND THE OCEAN

On this day, we will be discussing how people use the oceans and how people affect them. For a culminating activity, we will be cooking seafood recipes from different countries, utilizing at least one of our senses—taste.

The day is divided by the different disciplines: math, language arts, social studies, and science. An approximate time line for each discipline and a day's schedule follow, for your use in completing all activities in one day.

Time line
- Lesson 1: Gone Fishing (Sharing of Common Resources) (math)
  45 minutes
- Lesson 2: Mini-Paper (language arts)
  1 hour
- Lesson 3: Globetrotters (social studies)
  45 minutes
- Lesson 4: Plastic in the Sea (science)
  1 hour
- Lesson 5: Cooking
  1 hour, 20 minutes

Sample day's schedule
  8:00–8:45 Lesson 1
  8:50–9:50 Lesson 2
  10:05–10:50 Lesson 3
  11:10–11:40 Lesson 5
  11:45–12:45 Lesson 4
  12:50–1:40 Eating

Most of my activities contain cooperative group work, so you might want to pre-assign the groups to have some variety.

ANSWERS TO THE FACT SHEET (CHART A NEW COURSE)

1000: Greenland
1492: Bahamas
1513: Panama
1773: Antarctic Circle
1786: Gulf of Mexico
1831: Andes
1840: Antarctica
1866: Newfoundland
1872: Italy
1892: France
1905: California
1925: Germany
1930: Massachusetts
1934: Bermuda
1943: Mediterranean
1960: Guam
1969: Morocco
1970: Caribbean
1974: Atlantic
1975: North Carolina
1977: Galapagos
1979: Hawaiian
1985: Atlantic
1985: Florida

Approximate Routes of *Magellan* and *Challenger*

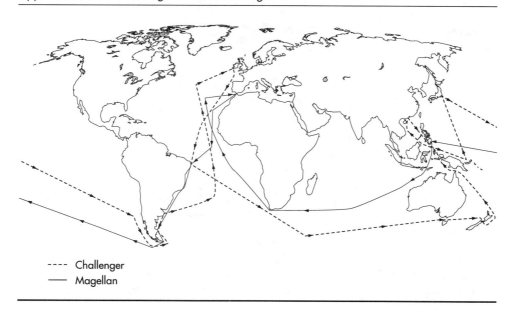

---- Challenger
—— Magellan

MAGELLAN'S ROUTE	**ROUTE OF THE *CHALLENGER***
start: 37°N, 6°W	start: 51°N, 1°W
1: 5°N, 15°W	1: 5°S, 35°W
2: 8°S, 35°W	2: 35°S, 20°E
3: 52°S, 68°W	3: 65°S, 80°E
4: 40°S, 80°W	4: 40°S, 174°E
5: 24°S, 100°W	5: 20°N, 112°E
6: 2°N, 170°W	6: 3°S, 145°E
7: 10°N, 124°E	7: 35°N, 140°E
8: 3°S, 126°E	8: 20°N, 155°W
9: 30°S, 90°E	9: 35°S, 75°W
10: 35°S, 20°E	10: 52°S, 68°W
11: 40°N, 30°W	11: 35°S, 57°W
end: 37°N, 6°W	end: 51°N, 1°W

Enlarge and place near large world map.

Gone Fishing   LESSON 1

OBJECTIVE:

After simulation, students will be able to discuss the different scenarios that could occur with a large group of people fishing in the same waters, as per teacher satisfaction.

MATERIALS:

600 paper clips, poster board, 50 square meters of area, and marking pens

PROCEDURES:

1. Randomly scatter paper clips within the 50 square meters.
2. Make this chart on the poster board.

★ = Number of fish harvested

✳ = $$ profit

	1	2	3	4	5
Country 1	★ ✳				
Country 2					
Country 3					
Country 4					

3. Divide the class into four groups, and have each group choose a name for its country.
4. Explain to students that they will be fishing in common waters, and each country depends on fishing for survival.
5. Each group is allowed one boat (one person) and 1 year (1 minute) to fish.
6. Each country sends out one boat, and he/she fishes for 1 year. After 1 minute is up, have each group divide its fish into piles of ten.
7. Each group must have at least ten fish a year to survive. Any extra fish can be used for profit.
8. Every ten fish after the first ten are worth $2. Groups can use the profit to purchase more boats for $20 each.
9. Have countries record their catch on poster board.
10. Have groups do their buying at this time. Each group also needs to choose another person to be the boat.
11. After a round, have students figure out how many fish are left from the original 600.
    - If 400 or more remain, you can collect all the fish that were caught and replenish the ocean.
    - If 300–399 remain, only 150 may be returned.
    - If less than 299 remain, then the ocean is left as is.
12. Continue the same steps for the four countries for five rounds, or until the fish are gone.

CLOSURE:

Ask the class to consider the following questions:

- Which country was most profitable in its fishing excursions?
- What happened to the number of paper clips students collected as fishing continued?
- If the goal was not to make money, but to sustain themselves on Earth for the longest time, did anyone win?
- What could the students have done to sustain the fish population?

EVALUATION:

Listen to discussion of closure questions to check for understanding of topic: the positive and negative effects of sharing an area of water for fishing.

LESSON 2   **Mini-Papers**✳

OBJECTIVE:

After discussion about how the ocean provides different uses for people, students will be able to research and write mini-papers about the uses in cooperative groups, as per teacher satisfaction.

✳Source: Diving into Oceans," *Ranger Rick's Nature Scope*, volume 4, no. 2.

MATERIALS:

Encyclopedia set, library access, poster board, construction paper, and markers

ANTICIPATORY SET:

Activate prior knowledge by brainstorming what uses we have for the ocean. Record the ideas on the overhead, chalkboard, or a large piece of butcher paper. I suggest the latter because it's mobile. (Students will likely describe uses very close to the ones that they will have to write their papers on.)

PROCEDURES:

1. Have class divide into six groups and choose which cooperative group jobs they want (i.e., recorder, speaker, editor, reader, illustrator, and runner).
2. Have runners come to the front of the class and draw their topic out of a hat or container.
3. Following is the list of topics students need to cover.
   - Mariculture (ocean agriculture): history of; uses and practices of; used in future, how?; and drawbacks and consequences of
   - Desalinization (getting fresh water from the sea): how can fresh water be obtained from the sea?; how could people benefit?; why isn't this a big industry?; how can this be more effective?; and possible environmental consequences
   - Ocean Fishing: foods we get from the sea; name several countries where ocean fishing is a major industry; describe methods for catching ocean fish; negative effects of ocean fishing
   - Mining at Sea: which minerals (if any) do we get from the sea?; what kind of minerals could we get?; problems with ocean mining
   - Ocean Energy: discuss ocean tides; ocean waves; thermal energy in the ocean
   - Ocean Pollution: name different kinds of ocean pollution; how this pollution affects the sea, animals, and plants; what's being done to help; what people can do to help
4. You need to explain that there are only 45 minutes to research and write about their topic, so they need to have a plan that utilizes all group members to complete the assignment.
5. Runner will also go to library to get books for the group. Make sure you have this time slot reserved, so that the runners will have access during the 45 minutes.

CLOSURE:

Have speaker from each group share a brief summary of its topic.

EVALUATION:

Read mini-papers and make sure every area that needed to be covered was completed.

Globetrotters*   LESSON 3

OBJECTIVE:

After playing a team game, students will know facts about important historical ocean explorations and will be able to read the longitude and latitude lines on a map, as per teacher satisfaction.

MATERIALS:

Fact sheet, "Chart a New Course" (included), *Magellan* and *Challenger* ships (included), straight pins, class set of small world maps, large world map (all maps need longitude and latitude lines), container for fact sheet, overhead projector, overhead pens, and transparency of each handout

---

*Source: "Diving into Oceans," *Ranger Rick's Nature Scope*, volume 4, no. 2.

CHART A NEW COURSE

Exploration Clues

1000: Many people believe the Vikings discovered America long before Columbus did. We know that Eric the Red got as far as what large island? (70°N, 40°W)

1492: Christopher Columbus reached the New World—now called the Americas—by sailing west across the Atlantic Ocean in search of a new route to Asia. The first island he landed on is in what island chain? (24°N, 74°W)

1513: The first European to see the Pacific Ocean was Vasco de Balboa. What country did he cross to see it? (8°N, 80°W)

1773: Captain James Cook sailed in search of a "southern continent." He never saw it, but while searching, he became the first person to cross what major latitude line? (66°S)

1786: Ben Franklin published the first map of the Gulf Stream to help sailors cross the ocean. The Gulf Stream originates in what body of water? (25°N, 90°W)

1831: Starting from England, naturalist Charles Darwin went on a worldwide research voyage aboard the HMS *Beagle*. He discovered fossil seashells 12,000 feet high in what mountain range? (33°S, 72°W)

1840: Charles Wilkes of the U.S. Navy proved the existence of a seventh continent by leading an expedition there. What is the seventh continent? (70°S, 135°E)

1866: The first successful transatlantic cable was laid across the ocean floor. Depth charts developed by Matthew Maury helped people know where to lay the cable. It stretched from Ireland to what Canadian province? (48°N, 56°W)

1872: Anton Dohm founded the first marine biological station. This research laboratory is in what country? (42°N, 14°E)

1892: Louis Boutan took the first underwater photographs. What country was Boutan from? (45°N, 4°E)

1905: Scripps Institution of Oceanography was founded. Many ocean research scientists work here. What state is Scripps in? (35°N, 120°W)

1925: A research ship named the *Meteor* crisscrossed the South Atlantic Ocean to survey it with echo sounding. What country did the *Meteor* belong to? (50°N, 10°E)

1930: Woods Hole Oceanographic Institute was founded. Many ocean research scientists work here. What state is Woods Hole in? (43°N, 71°W)

1934: William Beebe descended a half-mile into the ocean depths in a steel ball called a *bathysphere*. This deep-sea dive took place near what island? (32°N, 65°W)

1943: Jacques Cousteau developed the *aqualung*. The aqualung enables divers to carry their own air supply underwater. In what sea was this new invention tested? (40°N, 5°E)

1960: Jacques Piccard descended to the deepest known spot in the ocean in a submarinelike ship called the *Trieste*. This spot is nearly seven miles below the surface in the Mariana Trench. It's located at the bottom of the ocean near what island? (14°N, 145°E)

1969: Thor Heyerdahl sailed across the Atlantic Ocean in a reed raft called *Ra II* to show that sailors from ancient

Magellan

Challenger

Africa also could have done so. What African country did he sail from? (33°N, 7°W)

1970: Sylvia Earle led the first all-woman team of U.S. aquanauts. (Aquanauts are divers who live in an undersea laboratory and study the ocean while scientists on the surface study the divers' ability to live and work underwater.) Earle's team spent two weeks in the underwater station called *Tektite II* near a group of islands in what sea? (15°N, 65°W)

1974: Robert Ballard explored a volcanic mid-ocean ridge in a small submersible called *Alvin*. He saw lava oozing from an area where two plates of the Earth's crust are spreading apart. In which ocean was this discovery made? (38°N, 32°W)

1975: The United States established the first National Marine Sanctuary to protect the wreck of a Civil War ship that sank in an 1862 storm. The ship, called the *Monitor,* was discovered off the barrier islands of what state? (36°N, 76°W)

1977: Robert Ballard explored a mid-ocean ridge in a small submersible called *Alvin* and discovered an unusual community in the dark ocean depths. This community lives where heat from the Earth's core is released through vents. Giant tube worms and other strange creatures are part of this community. Near what group of islands was the community first discovered? (1°S, 91°W)

1979: Sylvia Earle dove to the ocean floor inside an armored suit called a Jim suit. The Jim suit is like a one-person submersible. Earle went to a depth of 1,250 feet—the deepest any person has ever been without being connected to a boat with a line. Near what islands did she make this historic dive? (20°N, 155°W)

1985: An undersea robot called *Argo* located the wreck of the *Titanic* at the bottom of the ocean. (The *Titanic* was a luxury ocean liner that hit an iceberg and sank in 1912.) In what ocean was the wreck found? (42°N, 50°W)

1985: A treasure hunter located millions of dollars' worth of silver, gold, and gems from the wreck of a Spanish galleon. The ship sank in a 1622 storm off the coast of what state? (25°;N, 82°W)

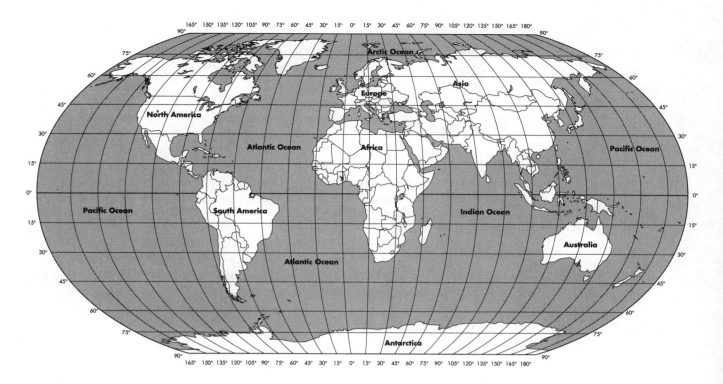

PROCEDURE:

Before students arrive

- place large map on a wall where straight pins can be used
- cut up fact sheet and place the facts in a container
- color the two ships.

1. Instruct the class on how to use longitude and latitude lines.
2. Divide the class into two groups.
3. Have a student volunteer or you plot the starting point for each ship (routes included). Use a transparency of the small map each individual student has to demonstrate the plotting on the overhead.
4. Explain the rules of the game:
   - Have two members from the *Magellan* group come up to the map. Have one student draw a fact from the fact can, and the other student read the fact.
   - Have the two members answer the question by finding the location on the map from the longitude and latitude clues (30-second time limit).
   - If their answer is *correct,* they attach the fact at the point, then move their ship to the next stop on their route. If their answer is *incorrect,* they put the fact back into the can and leave their ship where it is.
   - Now it is the *Challenger* team's turn.
   - Continue taking turns until one team completes its round-the-world voyage. (Answers to the fact sheet questions and map with approximate routes plotted are included.)

CLOSURE:

Ask students to recall what longitude and latitude are and some of the places both ships explored.

EVALUATION:

Make sure every student understands what longitude and latitude are. To check this, you can collect the small maps that each individual student worked on and make sure the exact points were marked.

LESSON 4   ## Plastic in the Sea*

OBJECTIVE

After discussion about plastic dumping in the ocean, students will be able to complete a graph-reading worksheet, explain how harmful dumping is to wildlife, and graph their own plastic use, as per teacher satisfaction.

MATERIALS:

Graph paper, Plastic in the Sea fact sheet, graphs, and "Graphing Activity" questions (included), overhead projector, overhead pens, and transparencies for all handouts

ANTICIPATORY SET:

Have students work in groups to answer the following questions:

- What types of trash have you seen wash up on beaches?
- How do you think the trash got there?
- How do you think this could harm wildlife?

PROCEDURE:

1. Show class statistics of what was collected on the Texas coast in 1986.
2. Have students graph these results on graph paper using a bar graph.
3. Have students read the fact sheet as a class.
4. You can include the following facts in addition to the fact sheet:
   - Trash is disposed of in the following ways: burned in an incinerator, put into landfills, or dumped into the oceans.
   - Plastic, metal, chemicals, paper, food, and other materials are dumped into the ocean.
   - Ocean dumping is harmful to wildlife. Poison in toxic chemicals kills fish, shellfish, and other creatures. Plastic cuts, tangles, poisons, and strangles turtles, seabirds, and sea mammals.
5. Have students complete the graphing activity (included) and graph their use of plastic, in groups.

CLOSURE:

Discuss ways that they themselves can help with the plastic problem.

EVALUATION:

Students should be able to complete the activities with at least 90 percent accuracy because they were done in groups.

---

*Source: "Diving into Oceans," *Ranger Rick's Nature Scope,* volume 4, no. 2.

Increase in U.S. Plastic Production

GRAPH 1

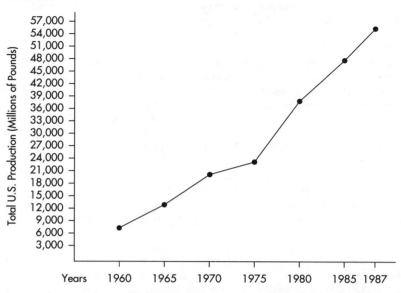

GRAPH 2

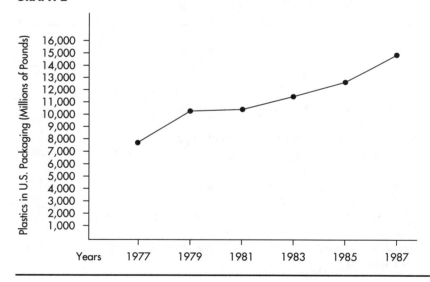

Graphing Activity

1. During which five-year period did the greatest increase in plastic production occur?
2. Compare the plastic production in 1987 and 1960. How much higher or lower was it in 1987?
3. How much did plastic production increase from 1975 to 1987?
4. Compare graph 1 and 2. Between the years of 1977 and 1987, which graph shows a greater increase? Can you explain why the rate of increase is different between the two graphs?
5. How many millions of pounds of plastic were used to make nonpackaging plastic in 1987? Name some other types of plastic products.
6. Given the trends you see in graphs 1 and 2, predict what each graph will look like ten years from now. What are some factors that might affect plastic production and packaging?

Fact Sheet: Plastic in the Sea

- Young seals often play with plastic six-pack rings and get the bands caught around their necks. These bands can strangle them as they grow.
- Over 14 billion pounds of trash are dumped into the ocean every year. A large percentage of this trash is plastic.
- Small pellets, beads, cylinders, and other types of raw plastic are dumped or spilled into the ocean. Seabirds often mistake this plastic for fish eggs, fish eyes, or plankton and sometimes die from eating it.
- Some states have banned nonbiodegradable plastic six-pack rings.
- Some plastics contain PCBs—chemicals that cause some birds to lay thin-shelled eggs that break easily.
- Every year, millions of pounds of plastic fishing nets, buoys, lines, and other gear are lost at sea.
- Sea turtles often feed on plastic bags, mistaking them for jellyfish. Many of these turtles eventually starve to death because the plastic clogs their digestive system.
- Over 30,000 northern fur seals die each year after becoming entangled in plastic nets and plastic six-pack rings. They die of strangulation, starvation, drowning, or exhaustion.
- Most plastic is not biodegradable. That means it takes many years for the plastic to break down, or disintegrate.
- Scientists have developed some biodegradable plastics. However, not enough research has been done to know if these biodegradable plastics break down into safe substances.
- In late 1988, an international treaty took effect that restricts plastic ocean dumping by the nations that ratified it—including the United States.

LESSON 5   ## Cooking

1. Start cooking after you have finished three of your lessons.
2. Recipes have been included.
3. *Caution:* Seafood can be lethal if not stored or cooked properly.
4. Students can help by cutting the vegetables and putting together all the ingredients that are needed.
5. If you can obtain a crockpot and skillet, you can cook inside your classroom, and believe me, the aroma will be mouth watering.
6. If timed properly, the food will be ready to eat after you finish your last lesson.

Note: You will need at least two parent volunteers to watch the food while it cooks and to help serve when it's finished.

BIBLIOGRAPHY

Carter, K. (1958). *The true book of oceans.* Chicago: Childrens Press.

Diving into oceans. (1988). *Ranger Rick's Nature Scope, 4,* (2).

Investigations in oceanography. (1976). Bellevue, WA: Bellevue Public Schools.

Lambert, D., & McConnell, A. (1985). *Seas and oceans.* New York: Facts on File Publications.

Sund, R., & Adams, D. (1985). *Accent on science.* Ohio: Bell and Howell Company.

Water wisdom. (1990). Oakland, CA: Alameda County Office of Education.

Recipes

Portugal
Fisherman's Stew

3 onions, peeled and sliced
2 cloves garlic, peeled and mashed
3 green bell peppers, seeded and diced
2 bay leaves
1/4 cup olive oil
1 pound tomatoes, peeled and diced
1/3 cup tomato paste
1 T. salt
1/2 tsp. white pepper
1/8 tsp. dried basil
1/8 tsp. dried thyme
6 pounds of varied fish slices—preferably snapper, cod, bass, perch, and flounder

Have fish prepared ahead of time. Students can prepare the vegetables and add them to the crockpot. Add 1 cup of water to the crockpot. Bring the vegetables and spices to a boil. After all vegetables are soft, add the fish, and stir until cooked (approximately 30 minutes).

Brazil
Broiled Salmon with Bearnaise Sauce

Salmon steaks
$1\frac{1}{2}$ tsp. salt
$\frac{1}{2}$ tsp. pepper
$\frac{1}{2}$ cup melted butter

Have salmon steaks prepared. All the students will need to do is baste the steaks. Have parent fry them in a skillet (10 minutes).

Shrimp Cocktail

Baby shrimp
Cocktail sauce

Fill dixie cups with baby shrimp and top with cocktail sauce. Students can do this right before the class is about to eat because this shrimp is already cooked when you purchase it at the store.

You can also buy dried cuttlefish at any Asian supermarket. This is usually eaten for dessert.

SET 4:
THE SANDY BEACH

This unit introduces the sandy beach. It contains activities and information on sand and other related aspects of the beach. Each lesson, along with its incorporated discipline, follows. The time required for each lesson is specified.

- Lesson 1: The Facts about Sand (social studies)
  Time needed: Approximately 1 to 1 1/2 hours
- Lesson 2: Sand Weight (math)
  Time needed: 45–60 minutes

- Lesson 3: Strange Beginnings—A Creative Writing Activity (language arts)
  Time needed: 40 minutes
- Lesson 4: What Is a Food Chain? (science)
  Time needed: Approximately 1 hour

LESSON 1   ## The Facts about Sand

KEY CONCEPT:

Sand grains can be made of many things and come in many different shapes, sizes, and colors. These differences can be clues about the material makeup and origin of sand.

OBJECTIVE:

Students, using magnifiers and working in small groups, compare the color, size, and shape of several sand samples to try to determine their material makeup and origin.

MATERIALS:

Magnifiers, zip-lock bags each containing a different type of sand, question worksheet, world map

BACKGROUND INFORMATION:

Nearly all solid materials in the world, both living and nonliving, will eventually be eroded into sand. Rocks, shells, corals, bones, metals, and glass are all worn over time by wind, waves, rivers, earthquakes, and other forces into smaller and smaller particles. For this reason, sand is often said to be the Earth in miniature.

The sand of every beach has its own unique history. Detailed observations combined with some good detective work, however, can often allow us to make some reasonable hypotheses about the material makeup and origin of the sand. Sand from the remains of plants or animals is referred to as "biogenic," while sand from nonliving sources is called "abiogenic." A closer look at sand through a hand lens or microscope also reveals a lot about the sand's individual grains.

Some sand is produced right at the shore, where waves crash on rocks, headlands, and reefs. For example, black or red sand beaches in Hawaii and the Galapagos are found directly next to or on top of lava flows of the same color. White sand beaches in Florida and in the Caribbean are primarily made of eroded coral reefs. Parrot fish, which eat coral polyps, grind up the corals with their sharp teeth and can excrete up to 100 pounds of coral sand per year. Pink sand might be full of coralline algae fragments. Other sand comes from far inland. Mountains are weathered by freezing, wind, rain, and streams, and their fragments are carried down streams and rivers to the seashore. Quartz, a glasslike mineral, is often the most common component of these transported sands. Quartz is the most common mineral on Earth, and it is nearly insoluble in water. Most light-colored sand beaches contain large amounts of quartz.

ANTICIPATORY SET:

Today we will be working as geologists. We are going to try to figure out what sand is made up of and where it came from. We will be doing some very interesting investigating!

PROCEDURE:

1. Divide students into groups of four. Each group will have two bags of sand and a magnifier.
2. Each group selects a recorder to record the answers to the questions on the worksheet.
3. Each group will be given five minutes to inspect its two sand bags and record its observations. When time is called, groups will switch sand bags until all sand bags have been rotated around the room.

4. When all types of sand have been observed by each group, allow about ten minutes for completion of the worksheet.

Worksheet questions
- **What material do you think your sand is made of?**
  (Small rocks? Shells? Wood? Glass? Plant material?)
- **What do you think the source of your sand is?**
  (A coral reef? A mountain? A lava flow? Clams or snail shells?)
- **Do you think the material makeup of sand or its color can tell us anything about where it was produced? If yes, how?**

5. Discuss worksheets. Encourage students to share their answers. Reveal answers.
6. Tell students that sand's makeup/color does give clues as to where it came from. For example, black or red sandy beaches in Hawaii and the Galapagos are found directly next to or on top of lava flows of the same color. White sand beaches in Florida and in the Caribbean are primarily made up of eroded coral reefs.
7. Prepare an index card for each location mentioned in the previous question number 6. Draw the color of sand likely to be found there on each card.
8. Call on volunteers to locate each place on the map. Tape the index card on its proper location.
9. Collect all worksheets.

CLOSURE:

Review knowledge covered. Inform students that this was only one of many interesting facts to be learned about sand.

EVALUATION:

Teacher will review worksheets. Students' work should demonstrate understanding of the task assigned.

Sand Weight   LESSON 2

FRAMEWORK:

Measurement, patterns, functions, statistics, and probability

OBJECTIVE:

After being introduced to sand and weight, students will work cooperatively in centers to estimate the weight of sand. Their results will be recorded and mapped out on a graph.

MATERIALS:

Scale, teaspoon, weights, small cup, 1 cup of sand, data sheet for each student, graph

DEMONSTRATION:

1. Show students $\frac{1}{2}$ teaspoon of sand.
2. Students estimate weight in grams.
3. Place $\frac{1}{2}$ teaspoon of sand in small cup. Place on scale.
4. Place smallest gram amount on opposite side of scale. Increase weight until the scale is even.
5. Then tell students that they will be weighing sand in a center in the same manner.

PROCEDURE:

Tell each student which sand center he or she will be working at. List the following steps at each center.

1. Estimate what 1 teaspoon of sand will weigh, and record your estimate on your chart.
2. Put 1 teaspoon of sand in the cup and place it on the scale.
3. Put the smallest weight on the scale. Increase the weights until you discover the actual weight of the sand.
4. Record on sheet.
5. Estimate what 2 teaspoons of sand will weigh.
6. Weigh and record the weight of 2 teaspoons of sand.
7. Repeat for 3 teaspoons and 4 teaspoons.
8. Look for a pattern. Then estimate the weight of 10 teaspoons of sand.
9. Fill out graph.

CLOSURE:

Review findings on chart, asking students to share their results. Ask if they had accurate estimations of how much the sand would weigh.

EVALUATION:

Collect graphs. Check each graph for accuracy. The results of the graphs will determine the success or understanding of the lesson.

LESSON 3   ## Strange Beginnings—A Creative Writing Activity

OBJECTIVE:

After becoming familiar with animals from the beach and ocean, students will practice creative writing skills by selecting one of the following questions and answering it as they choose.

MATERIALS:

Paper, questions (included), pencil, drawing paper, and markers/crayons

ANTICIPATORY SET:

Today we will be having some fun with creative writing. I want everyone to get in a creative mood. On the board, I have written three questions. It is your job to choose the one you would like best to write on and go with it. Remember, creativity makes the most interesting reading.

Questions
- How did the octopus get its tentacles?
- How did the sea urchin get its spines?
- How did the eel get its electricity?

PROCEDURE:

1. Have students select a question to write about.
2. Inform them of the amount of time they'll have to answer their question.
3. Set expectations (at least one page).
4. Inform students when it is time to start wrapping up their writing.
5. Give students the opportunity to share their stories if they choose to.
6. (Optional.) Have students draw a picture that corresponds with their story.
7. Collect stories and drawings.
8. Display works on a bulletin board if they turn out well.

CLOSURE:

Creative writing can be a lot of fun. How did you like this assignment? (Hopefully, the class will respond positively.) In the future, we will be doing a lot more of this type of writing.

EVALUATION:

Teacher will collect writings/drawings then determine by the outcome whether or not the assignment was a success.

OTHER OPTIONS:

1. Class can vote on the best creative writing/drawing. The winner's work can be displayed in a special place.
2. Rather than do this lesson on one given day, it can be spread out over a period of a week. This can be done by assigning one question a day.

　　For example, writing journals can be used. Time could be set aside (1/2 hour each day after lunch) for each question. Students would come in from lunch, and the day's question would be on the board. They would be given time to complete the question. Journals could be collected at the end of the week.

What Is a Food Chain?　　LESSON 4

OBJECTIVE:

After reading *Life in the Oceans,* students should understand what a food chain is. To demonstrate their understanding of a food chain, each student will complete a handout and construct her or his own food chain.

MATERIALS:

Worksheet (not included), *Life in the Oceans* by Lucy Baker, and a pencil

ANTICIPATORY SET:

Today we will be learning about food chains. First, you will hear some important information about food chains, and then you will design your own food chain.

PROCEDURE:

1. Read *Life in the Oceans.*
2. Discuss book and encourage students to ask questions.
3. Hand out worksheet and provide an example of a food chain.
4. Allow time needed for students to complete their food chain.
5. Encourage students to share their work.
6. Point out the importance of knowing how a food chain works.
7. Collect work.

CLOSURE:

Today we have learned that living things depend on each other for food and energy. We will learn more about food chains and their importance as we progress through this unit.

EVALUATION:

Teacher will collect and assess students' work. Their food chains will reflect whether or not they grasped the concept.

BIBLIOGRAPHY

Baker, Lucy. (1990). *Life in the oceans.* New York: Watts.

Lambert, D. (1984). *The oceans.* New York: The Bookwright Press.

Parker, S. (1989). *Seashore.* New York: Alfred A. Knopf.

Wood, J. M. (1985). *Nature hide and seek oceans.* New York: Alfred A. Knopf.

OPENING THE OCEAN: CULMINATING ACTIVITY: FIELD TRIP

For a culminating activity, we chose a hands-on experience: a trip to the ocean. Your students will enjoy this activity. They can relate and apply everything they have acquired during the week to the real thing.

All you need to do is contact your local Department of Parks and Recreation or the tourist information bureau for an oceanside city near you. If an ocean is not available, an aquarium would also be a worthwhile experience.

We hope you enjoy exploring the ocean with your class!

Opening the Ocean: Informal Student Assessment

How did you like the activities you did this week? Mark an X where it is appropriate and explain.

Loved Them   Thought They Were OK   Hated Them

Explain: _____

_____

_____

What would you have included in or deleted from your Opening the Ocean unit? Please take your time and share your expertise and knowledge.

Formal Student Assessment

Write about five things that made the greatest impact on you today. Be sure to explain your statements thoroughly.

1. _____

_____

2. _____

_____

3. _____

_____

4. _____

_____

5. _____

_____

ANSWER KEY

Informal Student Assessment: There are no right or wrong answers. This is just to see how your students felt about the day's lessons. The last question allows you to assess your plans. Your students may have great suggestions that you can incorporate in your plans the next time you teach these lessons.

Formal Student Assessment: These answers should have some depth. Try to get your students to achieve a higher level of thinking. Explain your expectations before you assess your class. Give a personal example of what impacted you that day.